THE RIDERS
COME OUT
AT NIGHT

THE RIDERS COME OUT AT NIGHT

BRUTALITY, CORRUPTION, AND **COVER-UP** IN **OAKLAND**

ALI WINSTON AND DARWIN BONDGRAHAM

ATRIA BOOKS

NEW YORK   LONDON   TORONTO   SYDNEY   NEW DELHI

An Imprint of Simon & Schuster, Inc.
1230 Avenue of the Americas
New York, NY 10020

First Atria Books hardcover edition January 2023

ATRIA BOOKS and colophon are trademarks of Simon & Schuster, Inc.

For information about special discounts for bulk purchases, please contact Simon &
Schuster Special Sales at 1-866-506-1949 or business@simonandschuster.com.

The Simon & Schuster Speakers Bureau can bring authors to your live event. For
more information or to book an event, contact the Simon & Schuster Speakers
Bureau at 1-866-248-3049 or visit our website at www.simonspeakers.com.

Interior design by Jill Putorti

Manufactured in the United States of America

1 3 5 7 9 10 8 6 4 2

Library of Congress Cataloging-in-Publication Data

Names: Winston, Ali, author. | BondGraham, Darwin, author.
Title: The riders come out at night : brutality, corruption, and cover up
in Oakland / Ali Winston and Darwin BondGraham.
Description: First Atria Books hardcover edition. | New York : Atria Books,
2023. | Includes bibliographical references and index.
Identifiers: LCCN 2022016023 (print) | LCCN 2022016024 (ebook) | ISBN
9781982168599 (hardcover) | ISBN 9781982168605 (paperback) | ISBN
9781982168612 (ebook)
Subjects: LCSH: Police brutality—California—Oakland. | Police corruption—
California—Oakland. | Police misconduct—California—
Oakland. | Criminal justice, Administration of—California—Oakland.
Classification: LCC HV7936.P725 W56 2023 (print) | LCC HV7936.P725
(ebook) | DDC 363.2/30979466—dc23/eng/20220706
LC record available at https://lccn.loc.gov/2022016023
LC ebook record available at https://lccn.loc.gov/2022016024

ISBN 978-1-9821-6859-9
ISBN 978-1-9821-6861-2 (ebook)

To our parents

CONTENTS

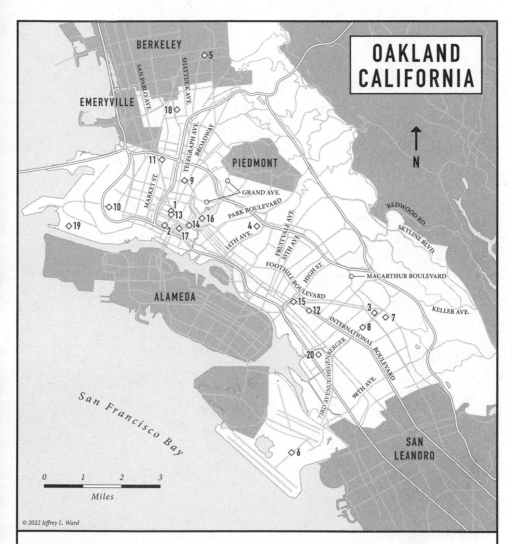

OAKLAND CALIFORNIA

BERKELEY

◇5

EMERYVILLE

SAN PABLO AVE.

SHATTUCK AVE.

18 ◇

TELEGRAPH AVE.

BROADWAY

PIEDMONT

11 ◇

MARKET ST.

◇9

GRAND AVE.

◇10

1 ◇
13 ◇
◇14 ◇16

PARK BOULEVARD

◇4

REDWOOD RD.

SKYLINE BLVD.

◇19

◇2
17

14TH AVE.

FRUITVALE AVE.

35TH AVE.

FOOTHILL BOULEVARD

HIGH ST.

MACARTHUR BOULEVARD

ALAMEDA

◇15 ◇12

INTERNATIONAL BOULEVARD

3 ◇ ◇7

◇8

KELLER AVE.

N

20 ◇

73RD AVENUE/HEGENBERGER

98TH AVE.

San Francisco Bay

◇6

SAN LEANDRO

0   1   2   3
Miles

© 2022 Jeffrey L. Ward

1– Oakland City Hall

2– Oakland Police Department Police Administration Building

3– Oakland Police Department Eastmont Substation

4– Highland Hospital

5– People's Park (slightly North in Berkeley)

6– Oakland Airport

7– Site of the Lovelle Mixon shootout

8– Site of Jerry Amaro's assault by OPD officers

9– The Light Cave

10– Site where OPD Officer John Frey was killed and Huey Newton wounded on October 28, 1967

11– Site where The Riders stopped, arrested Delphine Allen on June 26, 2000

12– San Antonio Village, base of Felix Mitchell's 69 Mob drug gang

13– Frank Ogawa Plaza, also known as "Oscar Grant Plaza"

14– René C. Davidson Courthouse

15– Fruitvale BART Station

16– Lake Merritt

17– Chinatown

18– Old Merritt College campus where the Black Panther Party was founded

19– Port of Oakland

20– Oakland Coliseum

THE RIDERS
COME OUT
AT NIGHT

PROLOGUE

American law enforcement is broken. Local and state governments spend more than $100 billion annually to operate eighteen thousand police and sheriff's departments, yet crime remains an intractable problem. Millions of people are arrested each year, filling the world's largest network of prisons and jails, but meaningful rehabilitation has never been achieved. Even when this system operates optimally—when police abide by the letter and spirit of constitutional law—it still produces disturbingly unequal outcomes. Black communities, in particular, have been harmed by policing since the dawn of the institution.

Corruption, brutality, secrecy, and racism have always shaped policing. Because of the inordinate power bestowed on law enforcement, these abuses cause immense damage to society.

This is why tens of millions of Americans, and people around the world, marched in the streets in the summer of 2020—amidst a global pandemic—to call for an end to police killings of Black people, and a reimagining of public safety. The street demonstrations following the murder of George Floyd, a forty-six-year-old Black man whose neck was knelt on by a Minneapolis police officer for over eight minutes because he was suspected of buying cigarettes with a counterfeit twenty-dollar bill, were estimated to be the largest in the nation's history.

Without a doubt, Americans want fundamental change. But can policing be fixed?

Since the mid-1990s, the primary tool to reform law enforcement has been the consent decree: a court-enforced agreement requiring a police department to overhaul itself under the supervision of external "monitors." This legalistic mechanism, authorized by Congress in the wake of the outrage over Rodney King's beating by Los Angeles cops in 1991 and the devastating riots following their acquittal a year later, focuses on reducing uses of force, police shootings, racial profiling, choke holds, and more. The results have been distinctly mixed.

Some of the first consent decrees in cities such as Pittsburgh (1997), Washington, DC (2001), and Cincinnati (2001) showed promise by changing long-held police practices and reducing police shootings. More recent interventions in cities like Portland, Oregon (2015), Albuquerque (2015), Ferguson, Missouri (2016), Baltimore (2017), and Chicago (2019) came on the heels of controversial police killings and verified the lived experiences of overpoliced communities by revealing the multitude of ways that law enforcement systematically abuses the poor.

But ask residents of these cities if they would consider their police forces "fixed," and many will tell you that real change remains to be seen.

These cities and others have struggled with violent, bigoted, unaccountable police whose behavior is often sheltered, protected, and even condoned by police brass, local politicians, prosecutors, and judges. When reforms do happen, they are rarely incorporated into an agency's culture, which is often driven by a reactionary ethos passed down through generations of rank-and-file cops. Most of the dozens of consent decrees pursued by the US Department of Justice ran their course in just a few years. Policies were rewritten, officers retrained, and the monitors packed up and left. Resistance to change imposed from outsiders, especially civilians, is baked into police culture in the United States. Backsliding is commonplace. New abuses constantly surface.

Outside the halls of government, policing has been challenged by protest movements against law enforcement corruption and brutality. Led by those most impacted, including Black, Latino, and LGBTQ communities, most major cities have seen sustained campaigns demanding change. At times, these have taken the form of riots—"the language of the unheard," as per Dr. Martin Luther King Jr. The Los Angeles neighborhood of Watts exploded in 1965. Detroit in 1967. San Francisco in 1979. Miami burned in 1980. Los Angeles in 1992. Cincinnati erupted in 2001. The more recent flare-ups in Ferguson and Minneapolis are only two of the latest examples of the thousands of rebellions against police abuses in small towns and big cities since the mid-1960s.[1]

More often, community resistance to police violence is less explosive, involving grueling campaigns by grassroots activists advancing demands such as the prosecution of violent officers, stripping departments of militarized weapons, and the establishment of strong civilian oversight boards.

Still, the police remain unreformed. Each year, new scandals erupt in cities large and small, exposing more than just a few bad apples. A rotten system continues to degrade the US Constitution by brutalizing and abusing marginalized communities. The stakes are incredibly high. Although many Americans still believe the police are necessary to defend life and property and to apprehend violators of the law, confidence in law enforcement dropped to a record low of 48 percent in 2020.[2] The crisis of policing is a crisis of governmental legitimacy. And the results of this crisis are the ruined lives of victims of police brutality and corruption, and the intractable public safety problems that police can never solve on their own.

———————

The city of Oakland is *the* edge case in American law enforcement, its police department having been placed under court oversight in 2003. More has been done to try to reform the Oakland Police Department than any other police force in the United States.

The saga of Oakland and its scandal-plagued police department illustrates the still-unfulfilled promise of reforming law enforcement. The OPD is by no means the only corrupt or brutal law enforcement agency in the country, but because of unflinching efforts by local activists, attorneys, the courts, and a few brave whistleblowers, more of the Oakland Police Department's secrets, failures, and scandals have finally been exposed.

This is the story of one police department and one city, but it's also a history of American policing and a look at where it's headed. The collective experiences of these Oaklanders—from a wide-eyed rookie cop realizing the depth of his superiors' sadistic behavior, to two attorneys hell-bent on seeing reform implemented despite obstacles thrown their way by a rotating cast of obstinate police chiefs and politicians, to the countless innocent victims of police brutality—hold parallels for other communities that have struggled to rein in the coercive arm of the state.

1

DOGWATCH, GHOST TOWN

Nobody really knows how Ghost Town got its name, but the moniker fits. Walled off from most of Oakland by freeways on its northern and eastern borders and warehouses to the west, Ghost Town—known formally as the Hoover-Foster neighborhood—has been haunted since the mid-twentieth century by the combined forces of racism, deindustrialization, and chronic unemployment. It was always a working-class community, but for most of its existence, Ghost Town residents could find decent-paying jobs on the East Bay's burgeoning industrial waterfront. That changed starting in the 1950s as factories closed, and Oakland's economy descended into a multi-decade decline.

White residents left the neighborhood, and much of the rest of Oakland, for the prosperity of expanding suburbs such as Pleasanton and Walnut Creek. Downtown Oakland's once bustling commercial corridors on both Broadway and Telegraph Avenue began emptying out in the 1970s, with the closures of major department stores. At one point, a high proportion of houses and storefronts in Ghost Town were vacant and boarded up. Huey Newton, cofounder of the Black Panther Party (BPP), referred to West Oakland in his autobiography as a "ghost town but with actual inhabitants." Newton's sour comment stuck in the minds of locals, who started using the epithet themselves. If there was any doubt about whether the area should be called a ghost town, it was settled by the 1980s.

The federal "War on Drugs," launched the previous decade by President Richard Nixon, transformed Ghost Town into a battlefield between rival dealers, and between dealers and cops. For the Oakland police, Ghost Town was hostile territory—a place to drive through cautiously while on patrol, meandering back and forth between West Street and San Pablo Avenue on long, numbered streets crowded with parked, semi-operable cars. In the 1990s Ghost Town truly felt abandoned. Darkness enveloped entire blocks of dilapidated bungalows, run-down apartment buildings, and weathered Victorians illuminated only by the neon glow of corner liquor stores. The sounds of gunfire and sirens were common. Murders were frequent. By this point, the social movements of the 1960s and 1970s were spent, no longer a counterforce offering hope and some measure of order to the mostly Black residents of Oakland's flatlands. The social decay of racism and poverty could not be held at bay.

—————

This was where Keith Batt found himself after having graduated from Oakland's 146th police academy on June 2, 2000. Just twenty-three years old, Batt hailed from the small, liberal, mostly white Northern California city of Sebastopol—about as far away from the mean realities of West Oakland as could be. But he'd wanted to be a cop in a place unlike his hometown. He'd heard good things about the Oakland Police Department. It was a professional, hardworking agency in a challenging environment. It was also the first police department that offered him a position.

Boyish, clean-cut, and straitlaced, Batt majored in criminal justice at Sacramento State University. He was a top student in OPD's academy and earned a reputation as one of the few trainees who would raise his hand to answer questions and volunteer for exercises. He was smart, confident, and energetic.

Batt got into policing for idealistic reasons and felt he could make a difference in a place like Ghost Town. What was obvious to him and other rookies was the scourge of gun violence, fueled by Oakland's drug trade. The solution, accepted by most of society at the time, was to throw police at these complex social problems. Arrest the bad guys, lock up the dealers, and make the streets safe for the average person. Batt believed in this mission, and he felt certain that it could be accomplished with integrity and compassion for the community.

The recently appointed chief of police, Richard Word, had told the eager rookie that he was among the best of the best. For this reason, he and other fresh-faced cops equipped with the latest training from OPD experts would work shifts under the tutelage of veteran officers in one of America's urban archetypes of segregation, poverty, and violence.

Batt's field training officer, Clarence Mabanag, was an entirely different breed. "Chuck," as he was known to other officers, sported a military-style buzz cut. Short, wiry, tough-talking, he had a reputation for arresting drug dealers by the dozens, often after foot chases that ended in scuffles. Although he was just a patrol officer, Mabanag was admired widely by other street cops and looked up to as a leader. However, many also felt intimidated by him. In the locker room, Chuck led boisterous, foulmouthed shit-talking sessions that created an atmosphere similar to a high school football team's inner sanctum. Police generally cultivate a sense of fraternity through ritual, language, and intense shared experiences. Mabanag, and OPD officers like him, created an in-group within this in-group. Their crew projected an overabundance of masculine confidence, and a sense among a few acolytes that they belonged to something special.

By any standards, Mabanag was also a problem officer, with the paper trail to prove it. Since he joined the department in 1988, dozens of citizens had filed complaints against Mabanag, including nineteen allegations of excessive force, several complaints over false arrests and false reports, and a 1998 accusation that he used a racial slur. Those arrested by the live-wire patrolman called him quick-tempered, violent, and insensitive.[1] Whereas most officers catch less than a handful of misconduct complaints in their entire careers, Mabanag collected them like baseball cards.

One man, Antonio Wagner, filed a complaint with the city's Citizens' Police Review Board (CPRB) claiming that Mabanag punched him in the mouth and handcuffed him during an arrest. Then Chuck lifted Wagner off the ground and dangled him like a yo-yo by the cuffs. Mabanag had also been sued three times in federal court over accusations of brutality. He was also a killer. In 1992 he fatally shot a twenty-six-year-old man who allegedly pointed a gun at other officers (the shooting was ruled in policy by OPD). By 1999, so many people had filed complaints and sued the OPD over Mabanag's misconduct that his superiors removed him from the field training program after six years.

But in September 1999 Chief Word reinstated Mabanag to the FTO program aft he'd participated in the department's early intervention program, a series of training courses intended to straighten out the behavior of "high-risk" officers.

Word wasn't particularly distinguished as an officer. In fact, virtually no one outside the agency had heard of him when Mayor Jerry Brown appointed him to lead the OPD in 1999. Even so, the new chief—at thirty-seven, the youngest in department history—was liked by many old-timers. He had his own reputation as a leathery cop's cop, and, like Mabanag, Word had worked in the Special Duty Unit (SDU), an antinarcotics program that, at the time, formed the core of the Oakland Police Department. SDU was one of the force's hardest-charging units during the chaotic 1980s and 1990s. Its members were known for busting down the doors of cocaine and heroin dealers, and SDU squads racked up thousands of felony arrests over the span of a few decades. At one point in the 1990s, these specialized units overwhelmed the Alameda County District Attorney's Office with so many felony drug and weapons possession cases that it simply couldn't charge them all. Word's rise to chief signaled a return to a more aggressive brand of policing, one that had waned slightly in the late 1990s under the previous chief, Joseph Samuels, and the previous mayor, Elihu Harris. And Mabanag's reappointment to the FTO program further cemented this shift in attitude.

In a speech before Batt's graduating class, Word described Mabanag and his peer group of FTOs as the "cream of the crop." What the chief meant was that Batt was privileged to have the opportunity to train with one of the OPD's elite patrol officers. Mabanag and his crew epitomized the department's style of law enforcement and would turn soft rookies into hardened, streetwise officers capable of surviving "Croakland,"[2] as some police referred to it cynically. During the academy, a few senior OPD officers working as trainers gave Batt a sense of what kind of trainer Mabanag was. One officer told him not to worry if Mabanag teased him ruthlessly and cruelly. "If he's making fun of you, it means he likes you," the cop explained. "If he doesn't talk to you, that means he doesn't like you." In the locker room one day, several of the other trainees told Batt that Mabanag had asked about him, remarking disdainfully that "he better not be some kind of pussy."

Mabanag and many other senior officers weren't just physically aggressive. They were openly contemptuous of the idea of constitutional rights for suspects. As soon as they started patrolling together, usually with Mabanag driving and Batt seated shotgun, Mabanag told the rookie to forget what he'd been taught in the academy. Real police work was different. Real police work wasn't pretty. It was physical, ugly, and dangerous.

True to his reputation, Mabanag bullied Batt incessantly. It began the day they met, with Mabanag dismissively calling his charge "Ike"—short for "I know everything." It was his way of shutting down the rookie's concerns about following department policy and abiding by the letter of the law. Mabanag wanted Batt to know that only a few methods worked on Oakland's streets. He wanted to humble the newcomer, who had performed well in the police academy but was genuinely naïve about Oakland's dangers. Batt, Mabanag also said, needed to show that he was a "soldier."[3]

This wasn't just Mabanag's view but a message that field training officers throughout the department were getting from the top. New cops needed to be seasoned properly. Criminals in West Oakland were heavily armed and contemptuous of law enforcement. Cops had to be even more dangerous than the bad guys. Another message was that it was time to take back West Oakland from drug dealers. Some local residents who led several of the city's politically influential neighborhood crime prevention councils— effectively pro-police lobbies that also campaigned for their favored politicians—were calling for more hard-nosed tactics.

To impart this lesson about how he felt Oakland should be policed, Mabanag turned field training into a showcase of OPD methods. On their first night out that summer, Mabanag promised Batt he'd get him into a street fight. Batt initially thought his FTO was joking but soon found out that Mabanag was dead serious.

All police academy graduates are permitted to take a well-deserved short vacation before their first official day in uniform. On June 18, a rested Batt showed up at the Police Administration Building ready to work his first "dogwatch" shift—the inherently dangerous hours from dusk to dawn. He was riding with Mabanag in a well-worn Ford Crown Victoria, the OPD's standard patrol car. A call came over the radio for a 10851: California police code for a stolen vehicle.

When they arrived at the Adeline Street address given to them, they were greeted by two men. The owner of the stolen car stood in his front yard, clutching his vehicle's paperwork and ready to give the officers a report. The man's cousin, Kenneth Soriano, was there, too, with his pet Rottweiler tied up behind a waist-high chain-link fence. The dog was barking at the officers.

Mabanag began by asking about the missing car, but then switched his line of questioning to the Rottweiler. "Is that dog tied up?" Before either man could answer, he provided his reason for asking: "I don't want to have to shoot your dog if he bites me. I've done it before."

Soriano, confused and wanting to discuss his cousin's missing car, took offense and told Mabanag in a slightly slurred voice, because he was drunk, "I wouldn't do that if I were you. If you did that, I'd do you, too."

De-escalation was not in Mabanag's vocabulary. He responded by telling the twenty-year-old that he was under arrest for public intoxication, even though he was standing on his family's property. Soriano refused Mabanag's questionable orders, so the officer began wrestling with him. By this time, a small group of neighbors had gathered; they seemed stunned at how what was supposed to be a routine stolen car report had erupted into a physical confrontation. Batt, too, was surprised by the speed at which Mabanag moved to arrest Soriano, but he knew he had to protect his partner, so he tried holding back the onlookers from approaching. Mabanag, meanwhile, was still grappling with Soriano and barking, "Forty-eight!" into his shoulder radio—the code for requesting backup.

The owner of the stolen car pleaded with Mabanag to stop, but this was the fight the seasoned FTO had promised his rookie, and he wasn't about to back down. Taking cues from his supervisor, Batt attempted to help Mabanag restrain Soriano. Not that the young man was fighting back. Instead, he tried to avoid being arrested by going stiff and holding on to the fence. Mabanag wrapped his arm around Soriano's neck and attempted a carotid hold to cut off the flow of blood to his brain, but the hold slipped, choking off Soriano's breath. He released his grip on the fence and sputtered, "I give up, I give up." Mabanag responded by throwing Soriano to the ground face-first. The young man's head and chest slammed against the pavement.

Swiftly, two other officers appeared. Francisco "Frank" Vazquez and Jude Siapno ran up from their patrol car and immediately began punching and kicking Soriano as Batt attempted to cuff him. After pummeling him, the officers stuffed him into the back seat of a patrol car.

Mabanag, dusting himself off, ordered Batt to write the arrest report and to be sure to add that Soriano elbowed him, even though the detained man hadn't thrown a blow at any of the four officers. Nevertheless, the trainee complied and scribbled the report. In a separate arrest report that Mabanag later wrote himself, he withheld the fact that he, Siapno, and Vazquez forcefully subdued Soriano. Mabanag showed this passage to Batt, explaining that the omission would help them avoid scrutiny from supervisors and the Internal Affairs Division. This was how you did the job and avoided the paper pushers and rats in the PAB: Oakland's Police Administration Building.

Mabanag and Batt then drafted a statement for Soriano to sign. The two officers then drove Soriano to the Oakland City Jail on Seventh Street next to the Police Administration Building for booking. Not long after, Mabanag pulled over, parked the car, and took out his clipboard with Soriano's signed statement. He looked over at Batt and said, "Hey, kid, let me show you a trick."

At this point, Soriano's partially filled-out statement said only that he had resisted arrest. On several blank lines at the bottom, just above the man's signature, signed under duress, Mabanag wrote in Soriano's voice the following: "I'm sorry for giving the police a hard time. The officers were not the ones who beat me. I guess I was just mad cause somebody threatened my family earlier, and my temper got the best of me. That's why I took it out on the police. This is a true statement."

It was utter fiction, but Batt understood immediately that this was his FTO's way of concealing the brutal beatdown and humiliating Soriano by forcing him to sign a false confession exonerating the officers. The large cut and bruise on Soriano's forehead, caused when Mabanag threw him to the sidewalk, and any other injuries he might have sustained from both the chokehold and Vazquez's and Siapno's punching him, were explained away as being due to a fight earlier in the evening with someone else.

This was Batt's very first taste of the real OPD, and it didn't sit well with him. Although Soriano was never charged with a crime, seeing him prosecuted was never the point. The punishment the OPD officers wanted to exact was meted out on the street in the form of a demeaning assault. It was a stark warning to Soriano, his family, and the entire neighborhood that someone like him—a Black man offended by a threatening remark—should never challenge an Oakland police officer.

———————

A few nights later, Mabanag decided that he and Batt would accompany a group of officers to serve a search warrant on a Chestnut Street house where a drug dealer had reportedly set up shop. Frank Vazquez wrote the warrant and led the raid. He pounded on a metal security door. Then, without giving anyone inside a chance to open up, officers used "the hook," a large pry bar–like tool, to force it open.

A woman inside the house, Janice Stevenson, began screaming, asking the police what was happening. The hook failed to rip the door off, and she opened it. The officers poured inside. Vazquez promptly drew his gun and pressed it against Stevenson's head.

"Bitch, we got you now," one of the cops gloated.

The officers tore through the house and threw the occupants' belongings on the floor. Batt was stationed out front in case anyone inside the house tried to escape. Beside him was Jerry Hayter, a grizzled sergeant who was in charge of overseeing the dogwatch squad. Not much time had passed when a single gunshot from behind the house pierced the air. Batt was alarmed. Even Hayter raised his eyebrows at the noise, but moments later, Officer Jude Siapno's voice came over the radio stating that the "K3," police code for shots fired, was a dog he had just killed.

Siapno and Mabanag had found the woman's dog tied up to a post in the basement. It wasn't threatening anyone. However, Siapno wrote in his report that the animal was untethered and lunged at him, and that he fired a single hollow point bullet into its brain in self-defense.[4]

Batt's discomfort with the senseless killing of the dog was evident to others at the scene. But Mabanag bragged to Batt that he'd shot six dogs before. The remarks were a none-too-subtle way of telling the trainee that he should get used to putting down dogs. All through the 1990s, OPD officers frequently killed dogs in what can be described only as sport. Occasionally, they were justified in killing an unleashed and menacing pit bull. But many times, the animals were leashed. Cops were often accused of cutting the leashes afterward to cover up the needless loss of life. The animal killings served another purpose: as punishment for people the officers suspected of operating drug houses or hiding fugitives.

Batt and another rookie, Steve Hewison, were made to dispose of the dog's carcass later that night. The officers, having discovered crack cocaine and a sawed-off .22-caliber rifle in the basement, arrested Stevenson. Frank Vazquez stole some of the crack, which he used later to pay an addict for information about another drug supplier—this, according to a conversation that Keith Batt witnessed. The drugs were used to make yet another controlled drug purchase that served as the basis for another search warrant.

At a lineup the next evening, before they started their shift, Sergeant Hayter joked in front of the assembled group of officers, including Siapno, Vazquez, Batt, and Mabanag, that there were "two versions of the story" regarding the killing of the dog. One version, he chuckled, was that the dog was just "licking Jude's hand" when Siapno put a bullet between its eyes. The other was that the dog had growled and lunged at him.

Batt's first week on the force continued like this, filled with vulgar displays of power, impunity, and dishonesty by his training officer and half the other cops they worked with. He followed Mabanag around West Oakland, sometimes just the two of them, but often with others, chasing down narcotics suspects in chaotic pursuits that frequently ended in beatings. In the small hours of the morning before the sun came up, Batt and the rest would change out of their uniforms and drive home to sleep away the first half of each day. However, the newbie cop was losing sleep over the transgressions he witnessed. It wasn't just that officers were brutalizing people and filing false reports; some of them appeared to take pleasure in these crimes.

On the night of June 26, Mabanag and Batt were driving along Thirty-Fourth Street in West Oakland when they spotted a man who seemed to be acting strangely. In Ghost Town, the mere fact that he was walking down the street at ten thirty was enough to raise suspicion. During the height of the OPD's version of the stop-and-frisk policy, simply being Black was cause enough for officers to detain a person and search for weapons and drugs. Mabanag pulled up alongside the pedestrian and hit the brakes.

"Grab that guy," he ordered his trainee.

Batt rushed from the car and cuffed the man, who was already protesting that he'd done nothing wrong. They placed him in the back seat, then searched the area for drugs. Mabanag explained that panicked suspects usually tossed their contraband into weeds or over fences. After briefly scanning the ground and bushes, he came up with two small rocks he claimed were crack cocaine. The patrolman took out his notebook and began scribbling a report as Batt looked on. Then Mabanag handed the rookie his notes and told him, "Copy it."

It was a strange command, but Batt dutifully began copying the report word for word in his own handwriting. However, when he got to the part that said that he had witnessed the man throw contraband on the ground, Batt paused.

"I didn't see that," he said.

To write it would be a lie. Cops are supposed to tell the truth, even if it means not having the complete, ironclad evidence needed to charge someone for a suspected crime.

Mabanag ignored the rookie's complaint and explained that in order to send the man to prison, they needed to link him directly to the narcotics. The best way to do that was for Batt to write that he'd seen the man drop the crack cocaine that Mabanag recovered almost immediately.[5] If his decade on Oakland's streets had taught the veteran anything about the law, it was that prosecutors needed particular kinds of evidence and statements in order to secure a guilty plea or conviction, and Mabanag was eager to provide these gifts.

But Mabanag's dishonesty bothered Batt in a deeper way. It wasn't even clear to Batt whether his superior had actually discovered the narcotics on the ground that night. He could have planted the evidence there. Mabanag and many other officers would later be accused of having planted drugs on numerous suspects over the years and also paying informants with drugs they'd confiscated from others. Batt hadn't been on the job for even a week, but his mind swirled with suspicion.

Mabanag certainly wasn't the only FTO who had trainees copy falsified police reports. Frank Vazquez had also recently ordered Hewison, another graduate of the 146th police academy, to copy an arrest report stating that he'd observed a suspect toss a bag filled with forty-eight crack rocks between two houses just before he was captured. Hewison had seen no such thing, but, fearing a bad write-up, which could put a quick end to his police career, he agreed to falsify his report.

Much of what the Oakland PD did in Ghost Town and other predominantly Black and Latino areas of the city in the late 1990s and early 2000s involved this kind of policing. Between responding to calls such as car thefts and domestic violence, cops would jump out on anyone who might be buying or selling weed, cocaine, and heroin or other narcotics. Anyone they recognized as being on probation or parole was also an immediate target for a stop-and-frisk.

West Oakland cops such as Mabanag, Siapno, Vazquez, Hayter, and many others had become so zealous in their mission that, by the late 1990s, they'd earned a nickname: the Riders. It came from a favorite story that was told and retold in OPD locker rooms and went something like this: A Black man was driving through West Oakland one day when a policeman stopped him and cited him for a traffic violation. Pleasantly surprised by the officer's courteous and businesslike demeanor—no insults, no brutality, no requests to search the car, just a simple ticket—the driver thanked him for being "nice."

This puzzled the officer. "Why are you thanking me for being nice?" he asked.

"Because you all aren't always so nice," the man explained. "Like at night. This isn't at all what it's like at night. At night, the Riders come out."

––––––––

The Riders—Mabanag, Siapno, Vazquez, another officer named Matthew Hornung, and multiple other Oakland cops—might have gone on with their illegal and brutal tactics for years to come had they not stopped Delphine Allen, an unassuming twenty-one-year-old Black man with a thin criminal history. But arrest him they did, and what unfolded from this encounter on June 26, 2000, would go on to change the course of Oakland history and ignite the longest sustained police reform effort in the United States.

Allen was simply walking home at the wrong time: a quarter to two in the morning. He had no drugs or weapons on him. He claimed he was tired and just wanted to go to bed. But Vazquez, a passenger in a green minivan that the OPD used for undercover operations, spotted him. Siapno was at the wheel, and Batt was in back, poised to jump out and apprehend the suspect if necessary. Meanwhile, Mabanag drove behind them in a patrol car equipped with an arrest cage in back for detainees snagged by the van. This was part of a "special narcotics enforcement project" that Vazquez, Siapno, Mabanag, and other officers had been running on their own initiative, without supervision, for some time. Their strategy wasn't sophisticated. They simply cruised around West Oakland in the minivan, or other unmarked cars, and then bum-rushed anyone who so much as fit the description of a drug dealer.

"There goes one of those motherfuckers right there," said Vazquez, pointing to Allen's silhouette as he crossed under a streetlight on Market Street and headed toward Thirty-Fourth Street, where his mother lived.

Siapno pulled up alongside Allen and ordered him to freeze, but the young man continued to walk away from the officers, dodging between gaps in a boarded fence and slipping into a yard. It's possible Allen didn't even know the van was filled with police.

"Get him," Vazquez ordered Batt, and the two of them scrambled out of the vehicle. They chased the suspect a short distance before catching him. Allen didn't really try to run once he realized they were police.

Vazquez threw Allen to the ground and slapped him hard across the head before cuffing him. Allen knew who Vazquez was and wanted nothing to do with such a dangerous and corrupt cop. Vazquez's pockmarked face and pronounced scarring on the left side of his profile made him easily recognizable. Stocky, muscular, built as solid as a football running back, he was well known in the community as a crooked officer with a penchant for random violence.

Vazquez had spent the 1990s patrolling East Oakland, a vast expanse of neighborhoods far from the nascent gentrification of downtown and West Oakland. His abusive behavior came to the attention of one sergeant, Ricardo Orozco, who kicked Vazquez out of his squad because, too, many of his prisoners showed signs of having been slapped, kicked, punched, and choked. Vazquez also failed to show respect for commanding officers. Like Mabanag, he had a long list of IA complaints against him: twenty-six separate incidents alleging brutality and dishonesty. And he too had been decertified as a field training officer, only to regain his certification under Chief Word. Vazquez had recently been transferred to West Oakland, where he quickly made friends and allies with Siapno, Mabanag, and other aggressive officers who were part of the Riders clique.[6]

Batt took hold of Allen and led him in handcuffs back to the street, where Mabanag and Hornung were waiting to transport him to the city jail. Vazquez and Batt placed Allen in the back of the car, but the young man, in frustration, mouthed off and told Vazquez that one day he would "slip."

Vazquez, wise to the street meaning of that word (to let your guard down), paused and asked Allen, "What's your problem?" Once again, a seemingly routine arrest was about to spiral out of control. "Do you want to fight me?" he demanded. "I'll whip your ass right now. Do you want me to take those handcuffs off and whip your ass right now?"

Allen didn't back down from the challenge, so Vazquez hauled him out of the car and began marching back toward the dark yard, away from the streetlights, so that neighbors peeking from behind curtains wouldn't be able to see what was about to happen. Allen, perhaps sensing that the handcuffs weren't going to come off before Vazquez decided to unleash on him, began to panic. A woman walking by on the sidewalk glanced their way, and Allen pleaded with her to intervene somehow. "They're going to beat me," he stammered.

The pedestrian's mere presence may have spared him—momentarily, at least. "Oh, you pussy, you're a piece of shit," Vazquez muttered. He promptly turned Allen around and put him back in the car.

Vazquez then suggested the other officers start searching the area for drugs, so Batt began scanning the ground where Allen had been standing. "Why don't you look right over there?" Vasquez said, pointing to a patch of sidewalk. The young trainee knew already what was expected of him: to pick up a crumpled ziplock bag filled with fragments of crack rock that Vazquez had taken from his breast pocket and dropped there for him to find. Sure enough, there it was. Batt noticed immediately that the rocks were broken into small pieces and powdery—a clear sign that they had been handled by someone for a long period of time. He doubted that any dealer would have such poor-quality product on him. The implication was especially clear this time. Frank had "put a case" on Allen: planted drugs for the rookie trainee to recover and justify the illegal stop and arrest.

Meanwhile, Vazquez was standing behind the locked patrol car. When he told the young man in back that he would be taken downtown and booked for possession of crack, Delphine lost his head.

"I didn't have no motherfucking rock!" he yelled, kicking the patrol car's rear seat divider with both feet. As Allen would later claim at a pretrial hearing, this was at least the fourth time that an OPD officer had planted drugs on him.[7] Handcuffed, he spun around on the seat and kicked the side windows and back window. Vazquez yanked open the passenger-side door and shoved his right thumb into one of Allen's eyes like a bowling ball, while using his other hand to empty the better part of a can of pepper spray into Allen's face and mouth. With that, the others piled on; first Mabanag, then Matt Hornung, a three-year veteran of the force who'd been one of Mabanag's trainees, pummeling Allen with fists and boots. Siapno, not to be left out, beat the soles of Allen's bare feet with his baton.

The one-sided melee took place in full view of concerned neighborhood residents. Four cops looming over a handcuffed prisoner half hanging out of a police car, howling in pain and gasping for breath, batons, boots, and fists raining down. One woman, Danielle Keller, tried to intervene. "They were punching and kicking, grabbing him by the throat," she recalled.

"I stepped off the curb to ask one particular officer, 'Why are you guys hitting him, and what is the problem?'"

The officer told her to "'step back onto the curb before I split your head,' and then he drew his flashlight."[8]

Even Batt joined in the violent ritual. He crammed the planted drugs into a plastic evidence bag, taking care not to spill anything. Then he ran to the back of the patrol car and kicked Allen a couple times, to placate Mabanag. Batt would later testify that he feared his FTO and felt immense pressure to take part in the casual violence. It was like he was joining a violent gang, and his initiation required participating in criminal brutality to show he was one of them. But apparently it still wasn't enough to prove Batt's mettle.

"Why did you stop?" Mabanag asked him later on, disappointed in how Batt "held back." Chuck had threatened his trainee while they drove through West Oakland's streets. In one of their first conversations, he warned Batt not to be a snitch, and that "what goes on in the police car, stays within the police car." The FTO also hounded him about his enthusiasm for the job. If Batt wasn't prepared for a shift, Mabanag told him, "I'm going to stick a hanger up your ass and give you an abortion like your mother should have."[9]

Hornung, the youngest of the Riders, had already earned a reputation for violence in just three years as a cop. In his first year on the job, Hornung, a tall, blond, athletically built Union City native who'd gone to college in Chico before joining the OPD, stopped a driver on Shattuck Avenue near the North Oakland nightclub Dorsey's Locker. In Hornung's mind, the man was furtively swallowing something, so he reached into the car and grabbed his face and throat and choked him in the hope that a bag of rock cocaine or other contraband would pop out of his mouth.

Hornung's victim, D'Wayne Wiggins, had actually just taken a sip of water. The assault might have passed without much notice; after all, it was just another Black man being harassed by an officer. Except that Wiggins, cofounder of the popular R&B/soul/hip-hop trio Tony! Toni! Toné! along with his brother Raphael, was well known and respected far beyond Oakland. Using his stature as an artist, Wiggins filed a lawsuit and forced the city to pay a $25,000 settlement, including a $10,000 scholarship for local high school students.

Siapno, too, was feared by West Oakland residents. His fellow police officers had even nicknamed him "the foot doctor" for the torture technique he employed with relish, and not just on Delphine Allen. After removing victims' shoes, Siapno would allegedly beat their soles with the tip of a telescoping baton, ensuring that they'd bruise so badly it would be hard or impossible to walk for several days. Siapno had a fatal shooting on his record, killing a twenty-six-year-old West Oakland man after a chase in 1997. Police reports claimed the man was armed with two guns. Like the other Riders, Siapno had an unusually large number of complaints lodged against him with the Citizens' Police Review Board, the city's mostly toothless civilian oversight body. However, in the late 1990s he was viewed within the OPD as one of the courageous officers helping impose order on the chaotic streets. Officers who weren't proactive like Siapno were derided as "slugs."[10]

But Vazquez was by far the most sadistic and dangerous of the Riders. He was also the most willing to threaten other cops. He menaced Batt and other rookies who were visibly uncomfortable with the extralegal tactics being used, telling Batt bluntly that if he informed on another officer, "If you are a coward, I'll terminate you. I'll beat you myself. And if you're a criminal, I'll put you in handcuffs, put you in the back of the car, and take you to jail myself." This was a speech he'd rehearsed and given before. When he laid down these rules for Batt, he added, "Snitches lie in ditches," then repeated the warning dramatically to make it abundantly clear that he meant it.

Vazquez was straightforward about what Oakland police were really doing when the sun went down on the Black part of town. "Fuck all that shit you learned in the police academy," he said to Batt. "Fuck probable cause. We're going to just go out and grab these motherfuckers."

Like Siapno, Vazquez had a nickname within the OPD: "Choker," on account of his penchant for throttling suspects or getting a viselike grip on their faces to prevent them from swallowing drugs. Keith witnessed one incident where Vazquez expertly grabbed a young Black man by the windpipe with one hand, cutting off his breath.

Delphine Allen had the bad fortune of falling into Vazquez's clutches. After they'd finished battering the young man, he and Siapno forced Allen back into the cage car. By now, neighbors were poking their heads out of windows and calling out to the police, "Why are you beating him?" The

Riders knew they needed to leave before a crowd gathered or someone phoned in a complaint. So, Vazquez and Siapno hopped into the car with Allen and told Mabanag, Batt, and Hornung to drive the minivan and meet them at a nearby Arco gas station, where they could write the arrest report and rendezvous with their sergeant.

But Vazquez and Siapno weren't finished. Instead of heading to the gas station, they drove to a deserted dirt lot beneath the Interstate 880 bridge near the West Oakland Bay Area Rapid Transit (BART) station. The two cops had taken other prisoners there when they wanted to torture them under the cover of darkness, away from prying eyes. There were no houses or apartments nearby. There was no community staring from behind curtains or passersby whom a prisoner could beg for help. The roar of traffic above drowned out the terrified screams of their victims. Vazquez and Siapno pulled Allen out of the car and beat him savagely while he was handcuffed. Siapno brought his elbow crashing down on Delphine like a professional wrestler while Vazquez punched and choked him. After roughly rubbing Allen's face into the dirt, they threw his sagging and bloody body back into their car.

While Allen was being brutalized, Mabanag, Hornung, and Batt were driving in circles like the Keystone Kops. First, they made a beeline toward the Arco gas station on West Grand Avenue as instructed. But when a speeding car came up behind them, Mabanag decided he didn't like the way this person was driving, so he slammed on the brakes, nearly causing an accident. All three officers leapt out and ran toward the car, which had swerved around them but then stopped about twenty feet ahead. They pulled two men out of the car, and Mabanag got straight to the point.

"What the fuck is wrong with you? What are you speeding for?" Mabanag asked.

The driver said he didn't know, and he didn't realize the van was police, but he stopped once he saw their uniforms. Mabanag noticed an open beer container in the car and questioned the driver about it, but despite soliciting a confession that he'd been drinking and driving, Mabanag decided that the meeting at the gas station was of the utmost importance. He had Batt and Hornung release the two men. "Okay, get out of here. Uncuff him," Mabanag ordered. The men drove off, drunk, into the night.

A minute later, they made it to the gas station, but Vazquez and Siapno weren't there. Thinking they might have gone to a different Arco farther north on San Pablo Avenue, the three piled back into the van and headed there, but that gas station was empty, too. They tried the radio. Vazquez's voice came back over the air, saying only "Quit calling on the fucking radio," and "We'll be there, just hurry."

They returned to the first gas station and waited. Finally, Vazquez and Siapno appeared with their prisoner. As they pulled into the gas station lot, Batt was alarmed to see Allen's swollen, bleeding face covered in dust. Snot dripped from his nose. His eyes were tearing and red from the pepper spray.

Vazquez and Siapno got some alcohol hand wipes and ice and offered them to Allen to clean himself up, but the young man just sat there stone quiet, except when he would cry. The officers had learned to clean up their prisoners following a beating in order to not raise suspicions. In a similar incident just a few weeks earlier, Vazquez and Siapno arrested a Black seventeen-year-old named Matthew Watson, whom they accused of selling drugs. Under the same freeway bridge, Vazquez used his metal flashlight to club the boy in the face. He grabbed Watson by the Adam's apple and choked him. Then Siapno allegedly threw the teenager down into the dirt and drove his knee into his back, cutting off his breath. Later, they had the boy clean his wounds with napkins in a Taco Bell parking lot before they drove him to the city jail. Even so, intake staff questioned the boy about his injuries and the dirt on his clothing. Watson lied and said he'd been in a fight with someone else before the police caught him. As he spoke, Siapno and Vazquez loomed behind the teen. The jailer was suspicious but didn't press the point.

Jerry Hayter eventually arrived at the gas station and interviewed Allen as he sat in the police car. The sergeant didn't raise any questions about his injuries, and the young man didn't offer any answers. As Batt would later tell investigators, "Even if he wanted to talk about it, how is he going to talk about it with, uh, Officer Vazquez and Mab—Mabanag—standing there next to the car, in his view, looking at him while the sergeant's talking to him?" Surviving was probably all that Allen was thinking about.

When Hayter asked what happened, Allen told him, "They bounced out the car and grabbed me." The sergeant replied, "It says here you ran," pointing to the statement Vazquez had written up and forced Allen to sign. Delphine's face fell, realizing that even the officer in charge wouldn't intervene on his behalf. "What it says there is true," he replied dejectedly.

Hayter made no effort to figure out the truth. He accepted the reports from his subordinates, and they all parted ways. Mabanag and Batt drove Allen to Oakland's Highland Hospital, the big public hospital where the indigent crowded the emergency room and police routinely took suspects as well as gunshot and stabbing victims to be treated by some of the best trauma surgeons in California. Allen, however, couldn't even walk from the car into the ER. Something, perhaps Siapno's club, had worked over the bottoms of his feet. They had to roll him into the hospital in a wheelchair so that a nurse could treat his injuries. All the while, Batt was taking in the degree of violence that had been inflicted on the young man.

Later that morning, Allen was booked into Oakland's city jail. The Riders had made him sign a statement that he had used crack cocaine, possessed drugs with intent to sell, resisted arrest, and destroyed police property by kicking the inside of the patrol car. Allen faced years in jail or possibly even prison and would suffer physically and psychologically from the assault for many years to come. To the Riders, it was all a joke.

Later that morning, as the squad ate their end-of-shift breakfast at the ButtercuP diner, Vazquez mused about the beating. "They're going to have to peel his cornea off Jude's elbow," he said, laughing. The officer repeated the line over and over, relishing the image.

Days later, with Allen in jail, Vazquez and Siapno were still joking about the beatdown in the locker room and on lunch breaks. Siapno, trying to provoke Batt, told him, "If you had been there, it would have shocked your conscience, and you would not have known what to do."

———————

From the start of his training, Keith Batt was deeply troubled by the behavior of Mabanag, Hornung, Vazquez, Siapno, and other senior officers on his shifts. The beatings, the lying, planting evidence—none of this was what he expected, even after repeated warnings about what field training under Mabanag would entail.

"I just knew there was more that I didn't know they were doing, and I was starting to see what that was," Batt reflected.

He'd even witnessed his field training officer lie about a shooting: during a foot chase involving Officers Kwang Lee and Cory Hunt, a suspect sought cover in a clump of bushes. Lee fired a shot at the man, who was unarmed, but missed.[11]

"Then Chuck falsified his OIS report, saying that the suspect was trying to do a gun takeaway," recalled Batt, referring to a fabricated struggle in which the suspect attempted to take control of Lee's gun. (OIS is the acronym for officer-involved shooting.) At the time of the incident, he thought to himself, *Okay, so now we're lying about shooting people. When they're saying, "Do you want to see the dark side?" and they're lying about shooting people, if this isn't the dark side, if I haven't seen it yet, what is it?*[12]

Seeking guidance, Batt turned to other cops he knew, including Eric Rosenoff, a neighbor who worked for the California Highway Patrol's Oakland office, and two friends who were officers in Sacramento and Rohnert Park, near Keith's hometown in Sonoma County. They all gave him various versions of the same pep talk, encouraging him to stick with the job so that he could do it his way eventually. "I know you're a good guy and you can do things, you know, your own way, the right way, but you're just kind of stuck with this guy right now," Rosenoff advised.[13]

On two occasions, Batt called Mary Guttormson, the gruff officer who'd supervised Batt's police academy class, and told her that he was struggling with field training. The rookie recounted Mabanag's unethical behavior, instances when drugs and evidence had been planted, and unwarranted uses of force he'd witnessed or taken part in. In their conversations, Guttormson tried to help Keith find a way forward, but also suggested that if things were as bad as he made out, he should report the issues to his supervisors.[14] However, she did not relay her conversations with Batt to Internal Affairs or any other supervisor at the OPD, as she was supposed to do.

Batt's closest friend at the OPD was Kristofer "Kris" Jenny, a Marine Corps veteran who bonded with Keith over their shared love of fast cars and their prowess with firearms. Jenny had a bit more street smarts than Keith, having grown up in Vallejo, a racially and ethnically mixed city north of Oakland that had experienced serious urban decline and a concurrent influx of hard drugs and violent crime after the Mare Island naval base shut down in 1996.

Early in his training, the pair had spoken about Keith's first few nights out on patrol, and the adrenaline rush that came with serving the search warrant, getting into a fight with Kenneth Soriano, and the shooting of the dog.[15] "That doesn't happen all the time," Jenny recalled during a court hearing years later. "He was pretty excited about everything that went on."

But when Batt called his friend a week and a half later, "his demeanor was exactly the opposite," Jenny said. "He was sort of depressed and almost sick." Jenny, concerned about Keith's sudden change in behavior, agreed to meet him at a Denny's in Emeryville one Saturday morning. Keith talked about problems he was experiencing in field training. At Jenny's request, he spoke about misconduct in general terms, for if Batt gave specifics, OPD guidelines obligated Jenny to report it. That decision needed to be Keith's—especially since he told Jenny that some of the behavior was potentially criminal. Also, neither man wanted to be labeled a snitch in the department, which could potentially lead to other cops harassing them, not backing them up in dangerous situations, or worse.

"He talked about making a walking stop and throwing somebody to the ground and being told that he has to drive a knee into the suspect's back in a certain way," Jenny recalled. Batt also confided that he was "directed to add on to a statement after it was signed by a suspect."

Jenny knew how crucial an FTO's opinion of a trainee was to a young officer's keeping his or her job. In fact, he'd experienced this dynamic first-hand as a police cadet in Vallejo prior to joining the OPD. Trainers could "pen fuck" a rookie by inflating or falsely documenting missteps.[16]

He advised Keith to first try talking to Mabanag—away from other officers—and ask why he was being asked to behave this way on the job. If that didn't help, Jenny said, Keith might try speaking with Officer Guttormson about getting reassigned. "I told him that if the event or events were as serious as they seemed—or that was the impression I got, that they were pretty serious—he'd have to go to Internal Affairs or just quit," Jenny said.[17]

The reality was, speaking out almost certainly meant that Batt would have to resign. Life at the OPD would be far too fraught for him—a hard reality that both men, less than two weeks into their police careers, recognized as an incontrovertible truth.

———

The casual violence that so unsettled Batt was no exception; it was how the Riders carried themselves every day. They felt at liberty to use brutality to clean up Oakland's streets for Mayor Jerry Brown's shiny new vision of the city. Although none of them was assigned to the downtown district targeted for renewal with new condos and apartments and chain stores like the Gap, it was alleged that the officers would often drive out of their district to essentially kidnap homeless residents off the streets of the city center, work them over, and dump them on a corner far from the towers and construction sites of downtown Oakland. They would jokingly refer to these extracurricular attacks as the "Beat and Release" program.[18] They relished any chance to satirize their own department's technical language and subvert the notion of professional standards. Vazquez spoke often of using a "knee drop distractor strike" on suspects; Mabanag told Batt that "academy bullshit" didn't work on the streets. The Riders had their own moves and crude language to describe them.

Siapno's comments about Batt's conscience were also no joke. He'd said it with a serious look in his eye. He was the one who'd asked the rookie if he was ready to see the "dark side," which Batt took to mean the things that had been withheld from him so far, the things that happened to Delphine Allen when he was kidnapped and tortured under the bridge.

Batt's conscience was already beyond shocked. During his few weeks on the job, he confided in several senior officers in the training division. He told them he'd taken part in some things that made him uncomfortable. They pressed him for specific examples, but Batt held back, realizing how dire the situation had become, and what repercussions—physical harm to him, massive reputational damage to the OPD—could result if he told the truth. He also spoke to a few other peers in the department besides Kris Jenny, but, again, without specifying the misconduct he'd witnessed out on patrol. He didn't know what exactly to do, but felt a growing conviction to take action.

There were signs that others within the OPD knew about the pattern of brutality, false arrests, and forged paperwork. One day at the Police Administration Building, Batt was writing a report for a drug arrest on behalf of Mabanag, who'd gone home early and let his rookie handle the paperwork. An older cop whom Keith didn't know walked by and glanced over his shoulder at the bagged-up crack rock and the police report. "Oh, another dropsie case, huh?" the officer remarked sardonically, his tone implying familiarity with the Riders' evidence-planting practices. That interaction, Batt said years later, "made me realize that no one's fooling anybody; everybody knows this is what's going on. It's no secret."

As he reflected on the nights he'd spent with Mabanag, Batt realized that if he had been specific in talking to Jenny or other officers, he would have confessed that he had witnessed a Rodney King–style beating of a Black man. He'd seen cops plant drugs on people. He'd been ordered to write false police reports and to lie. A dog was wantonly executed. He'd seen cops pay informants with cocaine. And he was being told that this was routine: this was how officers did the job in West Oakland, and that he was observing the OPD's "cream of the crop" in action.

If he had been specific, Batt realized he would have blown the whistle. But first, he knew he had to confront the Riders.

––––––––––

Batt showed up for work on the evening of July 3 unsure of what he would do. Mabanag and several other senior officers had to take their annual firearm qualifying tests, so the pair drove to an indoor gun range in the city of San Leandro used by the department. On the way there, the mounting tension came to a head. Mabanag casually told Batt how much he'd improved in just ten days. "You're doing a good job," he said. He praised his trainee as less timid and more assertive. Then he turned the questioning to Batt.

"What do you think of my training?"

Batt was candid, telling his FTO he felt berated, talked down to, and ridiculed. Mabanag said he didn't appreciate the comment, but brushed it off. Then Batt said obliquely that he also didn't agree with the way Mabanag and others conducted themselves. He disagreed with the "use of force" and the "dishonest" conduct he'd witnessed. Mabanag's mood darkened at once. "This is a major setback in your training," he warned. "We are going to have to have a big talk about this later."

When they arrived at the gun range, Mabanag left Batt behind to go shoot. Keith spotted Steve Hewison, and the two rookies decided to go sit outside in a patrol car and wait for their FTOs to finish their weapons certification. He opened up again, telling Hewison that he felt "miserable."

"I'm not having any fun at all," said Batt. "I can't deal with this. I don't know what to do."

Hewison didn't press for details, and, after a short while, Sergeant Hayter ambled out and waved for them to come inside. They were directed to the back of the building, where, inside a small classroom, the two rookies were ordered to clean several shotguns that had just been fired. It was the kind of grunt work they were expected to do, but as they were in the middle of this task, Mabanag, Vazquez, and Siapno came into the room and closed the door behind them. Frank stared piercingly at Batt and said, "I'm really angry with you. I'm hearing you feel bad for these suspects." Keith tensed. He didn't know what these men were really capable of, but he feared them. Before he could say anything, and before they said much more, the three senior officers turned and left.

Batt and Hewison sat there cleaning more weapons and dreading the return of their FTOs. When they came back, Vazquez and Mabanag resumed the questioning, but with a surprisingly softer tone. They asked Batt why he was having problems. Keith explained again that he disagreed with the force he'd seen them use against suspects, adding, "Look, I'm not like you." Frank smirked.

"Oh, you could never be like me," Mabanag responded. "But you know, I want you to do your fucking job."

The discussion ended as quickly as it started. Hewison left with Vazquez and Siapno, and Mabanag escorted Batt to their car. They drove back into Oakland, now completely at odds. Chuck continued questioning Batt, asking what specifically he objected to, probing the rookie's feelings, trying to figure out how deep his convictions were and just how big a problem he had on his hands.

Batt recalled the instance, just the prior week, when he asked Mabanag what to do when someone he'd detained refused to divulge his name. The FTO had responded, straight-faced, that Batt should threaten to put drugs on the suspect. What about that? asked Batt.

"You think I was serious?" Mabanag told Batt now. "I was just kidding."

Next, Batt brought up a car chase where two men "foot bailed." One ran into a backyard. The officers who discovered him hiding in a doghouse, including Siapno and Vazquez, clubbed him mercilessly with their flashlights, which they laughingly called "lightsabers." They joked about the sound of the flashlights cracking against the man's skull for days afterward.

"Why do you want to know?" Mabanag asked dismissively.

"Because it seemed wrong," replied Batt.

He then asked his FTO about instances where Vazquez had given crack to informants or obviously planted drugs on the ground where a suspect had been cuffed. "Well, you know," Mabanag said ominously, "you're gonna have to ask Frank."

They exited the freeway and drove to a twenty-four-hour parking garage nestled under a glass-fronted midcentury office building on Twenty-Seventh Street, just behind an old Gothic church. The Riders, having claimed it as one of their retreats from the street, called it the Light Cave because every inch of concrete was illuminated with pale fluorescence. Mabanag parked outside and ordered Batt out of the car. Vazquez was already there with his trainee, Hewison. Standing between their cars, Mabanag demanded that Batt tell Vazquez that he knew he was planting drugs on suspects.

"You're going to be a man," Mabanag said. "You're going to ask Frank. You're going to tell him what you think, to his face. Go ahead. Be a man."

Batt was panicking. In Frank Vazquez, he saw a stone-cold criminal in a cop's uniform, someone whose face broke into mirth when he recounted incidents of brutality, and was certainly strong and unpredictable enough to seriously hurt him. In the back of his mind, a dark thought coalesced. What might these men do to him?

"I remember thinking, *These guys are going to fucking kill me, and I think I can probably draw my pistol and kill both of them before they shoot me,*" Batt recalled more than twenty years later. "*Can I draw fast enough to get both of them, and what is this gonna look like if I get into a shoot-out with two cops?*"[19]

Instead, Batt stammered out a few words. He told Vazquez he disagreed with the beatings, planting drugs, and false reports. Without naming him, Batt made it clear that he knew what had happened to Delphine Allen, and it sickened him.

Vazquez's response was denial. "I don't plant drugs on people," he said firmly. "That's one thing I won't do. I won't risk my job, Chuck's job, or your job." But Vazquez admitted to slapping suspects. Like Mabanag, he argued that it was a form of defensive offense; a way to avoid being caught flat-footed. Keith felt insulted. If he didn't have to be worried that the Riders might assault him, he would have laughed in Vazquez's face.

"We're not riding with you anymore," Mabanag told Vazquez, putting an end to the conversation. Vazquez gave a knowing nod, and he and Hewison drove off. With that, Mabanag's whole demeanor changed. Whereas before he'd been condescending and outraged that his trainee would say such things, now he was calm—even compassionate. In the car, the hostile, ironfisted FTO turned to Batt and said in a soft, almost sweet voice, "You look like you're about to cry."

"I am," Batt admitted.

"Well, just let it out. You're not the first trainee to cry in my car."

Mabanag slowly reasoned with the rookie, telling him this wasn't going to work—that he'd tried to protect him, to show him the way of the streets, to teach him how to survive—but Keith's true colors had shown. He was soft; a naïve recruit from a small town who simply wasn't ready for Oakland. "These fuckers are trying to kill you," Mabanag said. "If you don't act first, they're going to turn on and kill you."[20]

"This is what we're doing, this is what it is," Chuck told Batt, referring to the "proactive patrols" where the rookie had witnessed his supervisor plant evidence, beat up suspects, and slay a dog.[21]

Mabanag methodically ruled out Batt's options. He couldn't continue as his trainee. He couldn't keep riding with the likes of Vazquez, Siapno, Hornung, or a dozen other cops they'd backed up. He couldn't switch FTOs because nobody was going to teach him right. Batt wouldn't be able to patrol the streets with any of his classmates if he was constantly questioning their use of force on suspects. Mabanag spoke slowly, maintaining his kind, understanding tone, building reason upon reason, and weaving key questions into his monologue, giving Batt just a few seconds to answer each time.

"You're not going to go upstairs and get anybody in trouble, are you?" Mabanag asked, referring to the sixth-floor Internal Affairs Division.

"No," said Batt.

"Well, what do you want to do? We can't just sit here all night."

They sat in silence for a moment outside the Light Cave. Batt asked: "Can't we just go take calls?"

Mabanag made it clear that was no longer an option. He had to quit.

"Fuck it, let's go," said Batt.

Mabanag had one more thing to say, though. He asked what Batt planned to tell Sergeant Hayter and other supervisors about why he was quitting. Before Keith could answer, his training officer supplied a script: "You're going to tell them that the city was a little too much for you. That it was overwhelming and that you're quitting for personal reasons."

They drove down Broadway to the Police Administration Building. There Mabanag had Batt type out his letter of resignation and then change out of his uniform. Mabanag told Keith he'd take him out to breakfast, and they could talk some more, but, as they were about to leave, a call came in over the radio. An officer was pursuing someone on foot, panting heavily, and yelling for backup. It was Frank Vazquez. Chuck nearly took the call but then decided he'd rather talk more with Batt, perhaps to assuage the moral misgivings of his now former trainee. As it turned out, the two never made it to breakfast because their usual diner was closed. After driving around, they ended up back under the I-880 freeway near the PAB, next to the Oakland Police Officers' Association building and the parking lot where cops kept their personal cars. Mabanag unceremoniously dropped off Batt at the gate at four in the morning and told the rookie good-bye.

On July 5 Batt walked into the lobby of the PAB to turn in his badge and gun.

Racked with disappointment and hopelessness, he called his police academy supervisor, Mary Guttormson, whom he looked up to and had spoken with twice before about his nightmarish two-plus weeks on the force. He told her that he'd written a letter of resignation stating that the job was too much for him.

"Well, you can let them believe that load of bullshit you wrote, or you can go up there and tell the truth," Guttormson told him. There was no avoiding Internal Affairs now.

Sergeant Anthony Banks, an eighteen-year department veteran who coordinated the police academy and field training program, was surprised by Batt's resignation. Chronically understaffed, the OPD needed cops, and Keith had shown promise in the academy. Why suddenly give up? The fact was that many trainees washed out during their first few weeks on the job; for some, police work wasn't what they imagined it would be. But Batt hadn't exhibited any signs that he wasn't up to the job.

Batt opened up and described to Banks the June 26 assault on Delphine Allen and the subsequent cover-up. This left the sergeant with no choice but to walk Batt up to the OPD's Internal Affairs Division. As a supervisor, it was his duty to report any allegation of misconduct immediately. The claims of excessive force and lying were among the most serious misconduct an officer can be accused of.

Later that day, Batt sat down with Sergeant Jon Madarang, an IA investigator, for a five-hour taped interview. He described Mabanag's illegal tactics; the violence he witnessed Mabanag, Vazquez, Siapno, Hornung, and others instigate; and the fraudulent reports they filed. In all, he described eleven separate incidents involving lawless and brutal behavior by his field training officer and other cops.[22]

Batt wasn't the first person to inform Internal Affairs of what happened that night. On June 30, Delphine Allen posted bail and then immediately filed a complaint that described everything Batt said about Vazquez's and Siapno's actions and more. Other victims had also gone to IA in the preceding weeks to file official complaints against Mabanag, Vazquez, Siapno, and Hornung. For example, Matthew Watson, the seventeen-year-old who accused Vazquez and Siapno of assaulting him under the freeway in early June, was released after spending three days in juvenile hall. He wasn't charged with any crime. Two weeks later, he went to IA and reported that he'd been kidnapped by the Oakland PD, beaten, and framed.

But Keith Batt changed everything. Here was an extremely credible witness: a police officer willing to break the code of silence. Batt's actions also caused a second rookie to step forward. Steve Hewison, realizing that the events he'd been part of were now the subject of an internal investigation—and, faced with a subpoena from prosecutors about a report he'd falsified—told Internal Affairs about some of the things he'd observed while patrolling with Vazquez, corroborating several of Batt's allegations.

Mabanag, Vazquez, and Siapno were placed on administrative leave on July 7. Hornung remained on duty, but the fast-moving investigation would lead to the same fate for him by September. The allegations were quickly leaked to the press. The Riders became an instant scandal comparable to the Los Angeles Police Department's Rampart Division saga of evidence planting, brutality, cover-up, and attempted murder by antigang officers, though it differed in key ways.

After interviewing Batt, Hewison, and some of the Riders' victims, Madarang contacted the accused officers and directed them to appear at Internal Affairs for an interview. All declined to comply with the order. The reason for the Riders' refusal soon became clear. As Mabanag's attorney explained in a September 12 letter to the OPD, "I have advised my client to be insubordinate" and "not to make a statement in connection with this investigation." Attorneys for Siapno and Hornung sent similar letters stating that their clients would not cooperate, either. Hornung's attorney also requested assurances from the OPD that the IA case wouldn't be used in any way to criminally prosecute Hornung. Otherwise he would advise his client to remain silent.

The Riders' lawyers knew that the misbehavior under investigation would not only be cause for dismissal from the force but also serve as the basis for criminal charges. In the early days of the scandal, community activists and the Riders' victims called for the officers to face trial and jail.

In late September Madarang met with prosecutors about the case. Although the Internal Affairs probe was formally separate from District Attorney Tom Orloff's criminal investigation, so many crimes were described in the interviews and came to light through examination of evidence that it became a key building block for the prosecutors, who announced they would be filing charges.

What's more, the DA's office was forced to review hundreds of criminal cases, going back several years. These were cases where Mabanag, Hornung, Siapno, and Vazquez had made arrests, served as witnesses, wrote warrants or police reports, or were connected to in any way.[23] Most immediately, the case against Delphine Allen was thrown out. Ultimately hundreds of cases would be dismissed or reversed due to the Riders' misconduct.

2

NOBODY WILL LISTEN TO JERRY AMARO

To understand the corruption and brutality that Keith Batt witnessed during his seventeen days as an Oakland police officer, one has to step back and look at the entire city, its deeply rooted problems, and the dreams of its political leaders around the turn of the millennium.

As in many American cities, the 1990s were a turbulent time in Oakland. Deindustrialization and white flight ravaged its economy, starting in the 1970s and culminating in the 1980s with the bankruptcy and dissolution of several big employers, including the headquarters of the industrial metals manufacturer Kaiser Steel and the closure of factories such as the Del Monte cannery. Perhaps the biggest hit was the demise of Oakland's retail economy. By the late 1980s, dozens of major department stores located downtown and along East Fourteenth Street, the major thoroughfare spanning East Oakland, had closed. In West Oakland, the construction of the BART commuter rail decimated Seventh Street, a historic Black business district. But these were only the most glaring examples of a citywide phenomenon: entire boulevards became galleries of empty storefronts and run-down homes filled with unemployed families cut off from the American dream.

For decades, Oakland's leaders tried to reverse the city's fortunes, but their efforts were futile. State and national policies that disinvested in Black and low-income communities left Oakland economically drained. Surrounded by wealth, from San Francisco's finance and real estate sectors to the white-hot tech industry expanding in Silicon Valley, Oakland was viewed as the regional backwater.

By the time that crack cocaine arrived in the 1980s, Oakland's social fabric was already ripping under economic pressures. Violent crime hit its apex in 1991, when 165 Oaklanders were murdered, mostly in turf wars between competing drug organizations.[1] Large stretches of the West and East Oakland flatlands, where the drug trade and underground economy flourished for years in symbiosis with the Port of Oakland, military installations, and the growing logistics industry, were now home to open-air bazaars where hustlers sold crack and heroin.

Oakland voters had moved significantly to the left in the mid-1970s, when the city's Black community united with white liberals and Latinos to overthrow the conservative Republican business community that had dominated city hall for decades. Starting in 1977, Black mayors and liberal majorities on the Oakland City Council reached a consensus that structural racism and widespread poverty could be addressed best through jobs programs. But the economic calamities affecting Oakland and other urban communities throughout the nation were simply too enormous for the city's liberal leaders to tackle. Black power in Oakland was achieved and given a chance to change the city only at precisely the moment that the federal government began dismantling the welfare state's Great Society programs, and at the same time that California's white suburban voters—a solid majority—were enacting strict constitutional limits on the ability of the state and cities to raise taxes. Crime in Oakland tracked the rise in violence nationally and the steady upsurge in shootings became a crisis. By the mid-1990s, many Oakland residents, including white middle-class hills residents and low-income people of color in the flatlands, were withdrawing their support from root-cause programs offering jobs and services to the city's poorest residents. Instead, they now gravitated toward law-and-order policies that filled prisons. This was the latest swing of the pendulum in the city's long, contradictory political history.

Into this atmosphere came a new mayor with a familiar face: Jerry Brown, California's governor from 1975 to 1983 and a two-time presidential contender. The son of Edmund "Pat" Brown, the state's liberal Democratic governor in the 1960s who built its massive water systems and expanded the University of California, Jerry grew up in San Francisco and adopted some of his hometown's midcentury eccentricity. He started out wanting to be a priest, but, upon leaving the seminary, decided to become an attorney instead. Then he embraced his father's profession, but with greater ambition.

Brown's first successful political campaign was for California secretary of state, and he established his reputation as a principled reformer. Mercurially, he ran for governor in 1974 and won. His administration peeled away from the rock-ribbed social conservatism of his predecessor, Ronald Reagan. The media portrayed him as a young radical with progressive visions for the future. He earned the nickname "Governor Moonbeam" after floating the idea that California should form its own NASA-like space exploration agency and starting a short-lived agency, the Office of Appropriate Technology, geared toward the technical aspects of a transition toward a greener, space-age future.[2] But Brown's star fell after he unsuccessfully ran for president as a left-liberal alternative to the centrist Democrat Jimmy Carter in 1976 and 1980. A failed Senate campaign and another reach for the presidency in 1992 seemed to be the nails in Brown's political coffin.

While he was in the political wilderness in the early and mid-1990s, Brown made the unlikely move from San Francisco's Pacific Heights neighborhood, a bastion of wealth, power, and privilege fit for political royalty, to blue-collar Oakland. It was a seemingly improbable embrace given by one of California's most celebrated native sons to a city that had become synonymous with high rankings on the FBI's annual violent crime index.

Whatever his original reasons, Brown's relocating to Oakland soon became the seed of a new campaign by a canny politician to rebrand himself as more in touch with the problems afflicting a working-class, postindustrial city. Years later, Brown told interviewers he picked Oakland for his political metamorphosis because it was away from the media spotlight and scrutiny of larger stages such as Los Angeles. From his $1.3 million work-live loft in the city's Jack London district, which included a studio, auditorium, and rooftop garden, Brown hosted a weekly show, *We the People*, on Berkeley's independent radical radio station KPFA-FM. The building also served as the hub for his We the People nonprofit, which promoted free-spirited lectures on everything from Tibetan monasticism to nuclear abolition. Brown's identity morphed again, and he became a quirky leftist thinker who jogged Lake Merritt, practiced Tai Chi, and held conversations with the likes of author Gore Vidal and Ivan Illich, the theologian and philosopher known for his critique of education.

His political ambitions soon reemerged. In 1998 Brown confirmed rumors and announced his campaign for mayor of Oakland. At first, he ran on the progressive, environmentally minded ideals that he and his intellectual coterie had developed through his nonprofit and radio show. Oakland could be an ecopolis, Brown proposed, a Mediterranean-style sustainable city of greenery and low-emissions transit, alternative energy, recycling, and biointensive urban food gardens. Brown described Oakland as a "place of hope." Progressives, who controlled the city's influential local Democratic Party and progressive clubs, ate up his message and mobilized for him in droves.[3]

Brown's manifesto, written by several college professors, promised: "In place of quantitative economic growth that rewards the few and impoverishes the many, Oakland Ecopolis substitutes environmentally benign sustainable development that enriches the social lives of the body politic and enlarges the public treasure of the commonwealth."[4]

But as the candidate toured Oakland and spoke with voters, his ecotopian message did not resonate. Many Oaklanders prodded Brown about decades-old problems: jobs, housing, crime. He absorbed these conversations and the fears many conveyed to him about street violence and the drug trade.[5] For much of the twentieth century, Oakland's leaders, mostly white Republicans, had addressed crime by putting more police on the streets. And crime *had* been lower before the 1990s. However, conservatives had run the city at the peak of postwar prosperity, before heavy industry withered away, mass white flight, and the explosion of the crack cocaine trade. Now the economy was in tatters. Residents had lived through two decades of Black mayors and Black-led city councils that proved powerless to stop the economic collapse while the violence metastasized.

In an interview with historians from the University of California, Berkeley, two decades after his successful first run for mayor, Brown acknowledged that his initial green dreams for Oakland fell flat. "There were a lot of these ideas," he reflected. "When you try to apply them to the world of teachers unions, highway construction, prisons, the budget, the tax system, Medi-Cal [California's safety net health insurance program], then it becomes quite a gap between these ideas."[6]

Ever the nimble politician, Brown didn't try to bridge this gap. Instead, he quickly abandoned his leftist agenda and ran on a program that had already worked for a generation of Democrats in the 1990s, especially the current president of the United States, Bill Clinton. Brown decided he'd be even tougher on crime than Republicans and would emphasize neoliberal economic development whereby the government spurred the private sector to create growth that would trickle down. His own family background hinted at this pro-police turn: Brown's paternal grandfather had been a captain in the San Francisco Police Department, while his father served as San Francisco's district attorney prior to winning the governor's office in 1958.[7]

Voters, ready for a change, and possibly starstruck by the local involvement of a national politician, gave Brown a mandate with 59 percent of the vote. In January 1999 he took office. The new mayor conspicuously signaled his metamorphosis by hosting $500-per-ticket events at which he would praise real estate developers and their lawyers and assure them they'd soon be able to invest comfortably in a future downtown Oakland where ten thousand future residents would live in yet-to-be-built sparkling apartment towers with hip nightlife and chic restaurants on every corner.

But it was Brown's approach to public safety that was most abrasive and decoupled from the philosophies he'd espoused just a few years before on his KPFA radio show. The new mayor advocated NYPD-style quality-of-life policing that targeted street-level drug dealing, homelessness, and petty crime. William Bratton, the reactionary, data-obsessed commissioner of the New York City Police Department in the mid-1990s, consulted with Brown on Oakland's crime problem, meeting with him in a Jack London Square hotel in March 1999. At this "crime strategy retreat," Brown set the agenda by telling attendees that his election was "an expression of discontent" from voters and that Oakland needed to drastically change its crime fighting strategy. "I was reading a speech by Martin Luther King last evening," Brown said. "In the speech, he spoke about there being a time for gradualism and times that call for swift change. There has to be a shift in our paradigm, and it is the opposite of gradualism."[8]

At neighborhood meetings, Brown, carrying crime stats fresh from the police department's analysts in his shirt pocket, rattled off numbers of shootings, homicides, and arrests. Where he had once railed on his radio show against the "prison industrial complex" as a punitive means of removing "capitalism's losers" from society, as mayor he not only advocated arresting people, even for low-level drug possession charges, but even personally reported a drug user and had the woman arrested.[9]

Brown also took his neoliberal, clean-up-the-streets politics to a wider audience, currying favorable press in national publications at opposite ends of the ideological spectrum, such as the archconservative *City Journal* that had cheered Mayor Rudy Giuliani's militarized Disneyfication of New York

City, and the *Nation*, a left-wing magazine founded by abolitionists in the mid-nineteenth century.[10]

The new mayor's pro-police agenda rattled Black leaders who had worked hard in the 1980s and 1990s to try to temper the OPD and bring about a modicum of trust between the department and Black and Latino residents.

During Brown's first year in office, the Reverend J. Alfred Smith, an influential activist who led one of the city's biggest African American churches, asked at a protest outside the mayor's home, "Is Oakland going the way of New York under Giuliani, and does that mean we're going to face what's going on in New York City right now?"[11] In February 1999 four New York City policemen mistook a West African immigrant named Amadou Diallo for a suspected rapist and shot at him forty-one times outside a Bronx apartment building. The cops believed the twenty-three-year-old was reaching for a weapon, when, in fact, he was unarmed—Diallo was taking out his wallet. The massive local protests that followed ultimately led to the disbanding of the elite Street Crime Unit responsible for his murder and exposed the broader systemic brutality by NYPD officers marching to the tune of Giuliani's crime reduction mandate. At the same time, Brown was busy giving his police department the go-ahead to assemble specialized teams to crack down on street crimes.

Brown boosted the agency's budget by 22 percent his first year and hired fifty-six new officers. He also ordered Police Chief Joseph Samuels to permit more aggressive tactics.[12] While the OPD was certainly accused of more than a few abuses in the mid-1990s, Samuels, the city's first Black chief, was politically accountable to a Black mayor, Elihu Harris, Brown's predecessor. Harris was a pro-business moderate and not at all a police critic, but his main constituents, the city's Black voters, asked for clear limits on police tactics that had prevented some abuses and helped smooth things over when an incident of aggression did surface. Brown's election signaled not only the end of an era of Black leadership but equally an end to any restraints on the OPD. Not long into his first term, Brown forced Samuels out of the job after the chief pushed back on the force's new direction.[13]

Having ditched the "ecopolis," Brown adopted a new slogan: he was running a "campaign against crime and grime," and he spoke about public safety in terms of zero tolerance and numbers.

In his inauguration speech, he told Oaklanders, "Crime and disrespect for the rights of others won't be tolerated. By the time we get finished, there'll be a lot less crime in Oakland than in Walnut Creek." This drew a militant cheer from the audience in the Paramount Theatre.[14] The new mayor went on to say, "We need to bring down crime significantly. We need to develop numerical targets and timetables for the reduction of crime."[15]

Among these numerical targets were arrests of drug users and dealers, the kind of arrests the Riders excelled at making, albeit often in extralegal fashion. This was the context in which the Riders emerged. They were by no means a "rogue" squad. Others in the department became equally aggressive upon Brown's takeover of city hall. Like the Riders, these officers would commit heinous acts of violence and deception. One case stands out among the cacophony of misconduct for its brutality and callousness. But unlike the Riders scandal, this incident would remain a secret for nearly a decade.

It was March 23, 2000, and thirty-six-year-old Jerry Amaro was looking to get high. Amaro wasn't a violent person, but because he was addicted to heroin and crack, he was one of the "criminals" Brown had sworn to run out of town. Amaro lived with his mother and sister and supported them through a series of odd jobs. His father had suffered mental health issues after he was discharged from the military, and his mother had similar psychological problems that made it difficult for her to handle her finances and raise her kids. As a result, Amaro was effectively the caretaker of his fifteen-year-old sister, Stephanie. He'd kept her fed and clothed, helped her with schoolwork, and encouraged her to pursue her education.

But this evening, Amaro wasn't thinking about his family. He was cruising on a red Schwinn Sting-Ray bicycle past sidewalks that dealers frequented, including side streets along Seventy-Third Avenue, deep in Oakland's eastern neighborhoods. On Holly Street, Amaro spotted several Black men standing around in a businesslike manner. One was wearing a dark puffy jacket; the other, a hooded sweatshirt. He approached them, parlayed, and bought some crack cocaine.

Unbeknownst to Amaro, the men he'd just scored from—Eric Karsseboom, Clifford Bunn, and Marcel Patterson—were undercover cops from one of the OPD Crime Reduction Teams. This particular CRT had set out that afternoon to run reverse narcotics stings: fishing expeditions to lure in drug users, sell them a fake bag of rock or a bump of heroin in a balloon, and then arrest them. CRTs and similar specialized units were newly energized under the leadership of Brown and Chief of Police Richard Word. Arrest as many people as possible, they'd been told. Disrupt the drug trade at all levels. Take back the streets. Users were the lowest-hanging fruit. Easy arrests, quick stats.

Lieutenant Edward Poulson led the operation. Despite his rank, Poulson lacked street experience. He'd mostly held administrative jobs and put in a stint in Internal Affairs before his promotion. He'd never even worked, let alone supervised, a drug sting using plainclothes officers before. What's more, several of the officers on his team were inexperienced rookies. Even his undercovers were relatively new. The most seasoned officer, Marcel Patterson, had just two years with the OPD.[16]

Poulson did not plan the operation ahead of time. Instead, he ran it on the fly. His undercovers, dressed as exaggerated dope boys in sagging pants, oversized hooded sweatshirts, and plenty of bling, put down roots on the sidewalk, waiting for customers. Meanwhile, a uniformed arrest team lurked in a van nearby, prepared to rush in and make arrests as soon as the signal was given. Poulson also ordered his undercover cops to participate in arrests, a decision that had dangerous consequences because then they'd be perceived as "jacking," or robbing, people. The lieutenant may have settled on such a plan because in addition to arresting drug buyers, the officers wanted to recover the fake drugs before they might be tossed or swallowed, and uniformed cops often arrived too late to do this. Many of these decisions contravened OPD policy, but officers and high-ranking supervisors alike routinely ignored department rules. This, according to Poulson, was also an "experimental program" to boost drug busts.[17]

Perhaps his most significant decision was to personally participate in the arrests. Being part of the three-person squad tasked with grabbing and cuffing suspects meant that the inexperienced lieutenant would have to get physical, thus impairing his ability to properly supervise his team.

It was Amaro's bad luck to walk into this trap. As soon as he took the drugs and handed over his cash, the arrest team piled out of the van and chased him.[18] Poulson and two officers, rookies Roland Holmgren and Tai Peña, just six months out of the most recent police academy, caught up with the suspect. Amaro may not have even known that the people rushing toward him were police; after all, they were disguised as drug dealers.[19] Amaro lost hold of his bicycle and was tackled to the ground, landing painfully across the curb, half on the sidewalk and half in the street. Holmgren and Peña pinned the man against the concrete by kneeling on his back and restraining his legs, while other officers—either the undercovers Patterson or Bunn, or Poulson, who was uniformed, or all three of them—kicked Amaro in the ribs and punched him in the face.[20] As Holmgren, a lanky Marine Corps veteran, restrained him on the ground, he felt his detainee's "body jolt" from a series of blows.[21]

Witnesses later recalled seeing Amaro pinned by a "rat pack" of cops, pummeled and kicked while curled up in a defensive posture. After the beating, the cops hauled him off to a squad car and dumped him—bleeding from the nose and mouth and crying in pain—into the back seat.[22]

"Why did you slam me?" Amaro asked the cops.

"You slammed me first," one of them replied. When Amaro complained about pain to his ribs, Lieutenant Poulson lifted up the man's T-shirt, looked at his torso, and replied, "You look fine to me."[23]

Tim Murphy had been arrested earlier that night in the same sting operation, thrown to the ground and pummeled so forcefully that his dentures were dislodged. He was already sitting in the patrol car when Amaro was stuffed into the back seat next to him. Murphy, who hadn't been hurt as badly, noticed that Amaro was in pain.

"Serious, man, I'm having difficulty breathing, it's hard for me to breathe," Amaro said, his voice rasping audibly. "I think you guys broke my ribs."[24]

The two uniformed officers in the front seats, who hadn't been involved in the arrest, also noticed Amaro's distress. Amaro immediately began asking to see a doctor as Steven Nowak and Mark Battle drove them away from the arrest scene to a nearby street, stopped, and searched the pair for drugs, weapons, or contraband the arresting officers may have missed. The entire time, Amaro repeated his plea to see a doctor. Nowak and Battle told him it could be arranged, but it would delay his booking into a jail and result in him being held in custody longer.

After completing their search, Nowak and Battle drove their prisoners back to Holly Street, where yet another drug buyer had been tricked, tackled, and cuffed. Poulson's team deposited this man, James Garry, into the cramped back seat of the car alongside Amaro and Murphy.

Garry had been "trying to cop a dime bag of hop [heroin]" and had also been beaten, but his injuries weren't serious. He looked over at Amaro, who was crying out in pain and sweating profusely. Even though he feared Amaro might have some sort of illness, Garry, who had slipped out of his plastic flexicuffs, wiped the perspiration off Amaro's brow out of pity.[25] He felt there was no way the officers couldn't have known their prisoner was in desperate need of help. Murphy felt the same. Years later, when attorneys interviewed him about that night, he contended that Amaro was "screaming for medical attention" and "hobbling like a horse," adding, "Ray Charles could have seen he was beat up."[26]

As the police were loading Garry into another car, Murphy noticed something else concerning. Like Amaro, Murphy had ridden his bicycle up to the undercover officers, believing them to be peddling drugs, and was pulled off the bike and tackled. He saw one of the undercover officers now riding his bike playfully, and a second undercover having fun with Amaro's Schwinn. Murphy didn't know it, but OPD rules were that the bikes should have been impounded. Instead, the undercovers basically stole them.

As they were leaving, Murphy appealed to the two officers once more to help Amaro, but they'd lost interest in the prisoners' welfare. "If you don't be quiet, you'll end up in worse shape," one of them threatened.

Amaro, who was booked into a cell in the North County Jail, an imposing beige tower attached to the Wiley Manuel Courthouse and OPD headquarters by a series of skybridges, continued to complain about chest pain. One jailer noted in his intake report that Amaro said his ribs hurt and that the police had beaten him up.[27] But this was a common complaint, one that police and jailers often brushed off. Later that night, a jail nurse examined him, but she claimed she found no visible sign of injury, and so she gave Amaro only a mild over-the-counter pain reliever, ibuprofen, and sent him back to his cell. The next day, after another sick call, a nurse wrote that Amaro had "pain in back of neck, ribs, and chest," and they noted some swelling on the right side of his rib cage. They gave him another 200-milligram ibuprofen pill.

During sick calls over the next several days, Amaro kept telling jail nurses that his chest was aching and that he'd been beaten by the cops who arrested him. Still, all he was offered was the ibuprofen. Murphy, who was bunking in the same cell, pitied him and recognized the poor treatment. Some mornings, Amaro couldn't raise himself out of his bunk and make it to lunch and dinner, so Murphy and others snuck sandwiches back to him.

Amaro and the others were eventually transported to Alameda County's massive Santa Rita Jail in Dublin, where they were separated. Five days after his arrest, Jerry Amaro was finally released. Though still in pain, he managed to visit his mother, Geraldine Montoya, at her home in East Oakland's Sobrante Park neighborhood. He told her he'd been beaten by OPD officers. Geraldine, seeing the bruising on her son's face and other parts of his body, was worried about him, but Jerry told her he'd get help.

Still racked with pain weeks after the incident, Amaro finally went to a clinic on April 18. X-rays revealed that he had five broken ribs, one of which had punctured his right lung, causing it to fill with bloody fluid and collapse. The clinic doctor told Amaro that he needed to go to a hospital immediately, but Jerry had other things to do first, such as pick up his paycheck and handle other personal business. He took a copy of the X-ray and his medical file and put them in a small stack of documents that included his arrest report, carrying these around town in a manila envelope the next couple days.

Two nights later, Amaro showed up at Gilbert Becerra's home in rough shape, asking his friend if he could spend the night there. He was displaying worrisome symptoms, including shortness of breath. Becerra told him he could sleep on a mattress in the basement.

The next morning, his friend found Amaro in an agonized pose, crouched on his knees, motionless, his body cold, with blood trailing out of his nose and mouth. Becerra called the police.

Amaro might have injected heroin that night to dull his agony— hypodermic needles and other drug paraphernalia were found next to his body. He also had a weakened immune system due to being HIV positive. But his drug addiction and the virus were not the cause of death. An autopsy would determine that Jerry Amaro had died of pneumonia caused by his collapsed lung and broken ribs.[28]

OPD homicide investigators Sergeants Gus Galindo and Derwin Longmire were sent to the friend's home in Oakland's San Antonio neighborhood to look into what was being categorized as a suspicious death. The detectives stepped under crime scene tape in front of the little yellow house and walked down a steep driveway to the back, where an exterior door opened into the small basement. Inside they saw Amaro's corpse on the mattress, legs bent at the knees, arms bent at the elbows, blood on his face. Jerry's friend offered immediately that before he died, Amaro told him about being beaten by police in East Oakland. Evidence to back this up was readily available to Galindo, who took lead on the case. Near Amaro's body was his manila envelope containing his medical and arrest records.

Galindo spent the rest of the day piecing together Amaro's case. He made swift progress.

A records check showed that Jerry Amaro had been arrested a month before in Lieutenant Ed Poulson's sting operation, but the arrest reports were written by Eric Karsseboom, the undercover who sold Amaro crack, and Steven Nowak, who drove him away in the patrol car. Critically, both reports made no mention of Amaro having been struck by police. Not one report mentioned Amaro's requests for medical attention.[29]

Galindo called Poulson as well as Acting Lieutenant Mike Yoell, who worked in the same area and supervised several of the officers involved in the sting operation. The sergeant asked the two men to come to his Homicide Division office and brief him about what happened on the night in question.[30]

Poulson told Galindo it was a simple buy-bust operation. Amaro resisted arrest and was restrained, but no one struck him. The lieutenant's statement contradicted not only what the victim's friend had said but also the X-rays that Galindo now had. Soon the homicide investigator would uncover more evidence that the police were at fault.

After meeting with Poulson and Yoell, Galindo called the physician who'd examined Amaro, Angelica Green. She recounted how Amaro had come to her clinic in obvious distress, and she diagnosed his fractured ribs and collapsed lung. Dr. Green also related that the patient had told her he'd been beaten by cops. Next, Galindo interviewed one of the jailers to whom Amaro had complained about his shattered ribs. Same story: he'd told the jailer that OPD officers had kicked him in the side and that he needed a doctor.[31]

By four in the afternoon, Galindo and Longmire were driving across town to Seventy-Third Avenue and Holly Street, the scene of the sting operation. Several other OPD sergeants were already there canvassing door to door, asking residents if they'd seen police beat up anyone. One witness, Laureen White, told the officers that she'd heard a scuffle from her second-floor apartment and looked down just in time to see a "Hispanic male" struggling with two undercover officers and at least two uniformed officers during what she knew was an undercover operation. The undercover officers punched the man, she said.

Galindo now had a wealth of information pointing toward Poulson's sting operation as having caused Amaro's death. But the sergeant's next move wasn't what a competent investigator would do under the circumstances. Instead of confronting Poulson with the numerous contradictory statements and evidence that impeached his version of events, Galindo and Longmire drove to Geraldine and Louis Montoya's house late that afternoon. The Montoyas, who weren't yet aware that Jerry was dead, greeted the officers and stepped into their front yard, where Galindo broke the tragic news to them. However, he concocted a wholly fictional account of how Jerry died, saying that he was killed "in the street" during a gang fight over drugs.[32]

There was no evidence in Galindo's chronological report, or anywhere in the investigative file, to support this claim.

Geraldine grew suspicious immediately. Her son had shown her his wounds and told her that the police had beaten him. And on April 18, after seeing Dr. Green, he shared his X-rays with his mother and his sister, telling them that he intended to sue the Oakland Police Department for excessive use of force. The Montoyas told Galindo that his account of Jerry's death was wrong and that he needed to look closer at the police's involvement.

As Louis Montoya recalled later, "It appeared that Sergeant Galindo did not want to hear this and continued to insist that my stepson had been killed as a result of gang or drug activity."[33] According to the Montoyas, Galindo even became angry and yelled at Geraldine to "stop talking about the police involvement!" Then he ordered her to get into his car alone with him to make a statement.[34] The content of the ensuing conversation remains a mystery. Although Galindo recorded it, the tape was never provided to the Montoyas or anyone else, including the authors, who obtained files about the case through a lawsuit.[35]

Geraldine, hysterical and sobbing that night, wouldn't remember much about the upsetting encounter many years later, but she would recall forever how Galindo's actions that afternoon set in motion the OPD's stonewalling to prevent her from finding out the truth.

As for Sergeant Galindo, even though he'd adamantly tried convincing the Montoyas to dismiss the idea that the police had killed their son, his investigation zeroed in on Poulson's squad and revealed evidence of a cover-up in the making.

Two days after Amaro's death, Galindo conducted a lengthier interview with witness Laureen White. She retold the same story as before, but in more detail, describing the two undercover cops punching Amaro.

Perhaps the most damning account—one that implicated Poulson directly—came from another friend of Amaro's, Anthony Gonzales. There had been a party at a house just around the corner from where the buy-bust operation was set up. Gonzales said that shortly after Amaro left the party, several guests arrived saying that Jerry had "got beat up pretty bad by the police" down the street. About ten days later, Gonzales randomly saw Amaro hobbling along with a bicycle—not his Schwinn, but a cheaper ten-speed. Gonzales offered to give his friend a ride in his truck, but "Amaro couldn't even lift the bike up" to put it in the truck.

"I asked him, 'Hey, man, what happened to you?' And he goes, 'I got beat up by the OPD, man.'" According to Gonzales, Amaro's face "looked kind of messed up," and he had a "nasty bruise" on his side. "He said when he was handcuffed, they were picking him up off the ground, and this one police officer came and booted him in the ribs."[36]

That same afternoon, Galindo also obtained Amaro's complete medical records with a search warrant. Another doctor at the clinic where Dr. Green had seen Jerry told the detective that the man said he'd been struck by the police. Over the next several weeks, other witnesses to the sting operation came forward to say that they'd seen the police tackle and beat arrestees. One of them, Theresa Batts, would later tell the police that she saw the narcotics unit take several other men into custody that evening in similar fashion, by "bum-rushing" them. The arrests, not uncommon in that rough area of East Oakland, shocked Batts because of their excessive violence. She would later tell investigators that one man, perhaps Amaro, was tackled so hard that you could hear his body hit the ground. The sharp noise may have been Amaro's ribs cracking as he was slammed into the concrete.

On April 25 Poulson and his squad arrived at the OPD's Homicide Section for interviews. It was routine for officers to be interviewed by homicide detectives after they'd killed someone in the line of duty, usually right after a fatal shooting. The outcome of these interviews had always seemed preordained, with homicide detectives virtually always clearing their fellow officers. However, it was less common for cops to be interviewed about a death that had taken place weeks before. And rarely were so many officers potentially culpable for one fatality.

Several homicide investigators helped Galindo interview the officers. He, Longmire, and Lieutenant Paul Berlin, head of the Homicide Section, questioned Karsseboom about the fateful evening the month before. The undercover cop told them he sold the rocks to Amaro and then two uni-formed arrest team officers "jogged" to make the arrest. Amaro spotted them, ran, and the officers "tackled" him. Karsseboom claimed he saw the two uniformed cops "wrestling"—his word—with Amaro, but he did not see anyone throw punches or kick him.

An hour and a half later, the same three homicide investigators sat down with Poulson in an interview room. Poulson told a similar story, which Galindo later summarized in his homicide report: "Amaro was forced to the ground," and he "did not strike Amaro," nor did he see anyone else hit him. All the officers repeated that same detail: they didn't hit Amaro, and they didn't see anyone hit him. Their memories and perceptions were all equally blurry during the moments that Amaro was tackled and cuffed. Their rec-ollections echoed the Riders' reports. No officer ever seemed to see another officer use force. Poulson and the officers were thanked and returned to work at the Eastmont Substation on Seventy-Third Avenue.

Alarmingly, the next day, Galindo was called into a meeting with Lieu-tenant Berlin. In the room were Sergeant Mike Reilly and Lieutenant Mike Yoell, two older cops who commanded squads out of the Eastmont Substa-tion alongside Poulson. Reilly, Yoell, and Berlin told Galindo that some of the officers he'd interviewed the previous day were being less than truthful. "They may change their story," the three commanders said. But the sergeant would never follow up on this tip. The following day, Galindo was sent to brief Richard Word about the unfolding situation. The chief listened but then ordered him to forward his report to Internal Affairs.

Galindo never called Poulson and his squad back in for second inter-views. There was never any attempt by the OPD to call out the officers for lying and seek the truth about Amaro's killing.

On May 1 Galindo presented the case to Alameda County deputy dis-trict attorney Sandy Quist, a senior prosecutor who had been described as one of District Attorney Tom Orloff's "right hands" partly because of her role in cases with major political implications. Based on Galindo's incomplete investigation, Quist determined the Amaro case involved no foul play.[37]

But suspicions about Amaro's death within the Oakland Police De-partment itself were not laid to rest with the closing of the criminal case. Rumors began swirling through the ranks that Poulson had walked into Eastmont the night of the operation bragging about kicking an arrestee during a buy-bust, and that the man had subsequently died. Another rumor had it that Officers Patterson and Karsseboom delivered the blows that would later kill Amaro.[38]

But while the Internal Affairs case got under way, key evidence from the Amaro homicide investigation disappeared mysteriously from police records, including his X-rays, his booking photos from jail, and witness Laureen White's written statement.[39] What followed was a Gordian knot of an IA investigation that plumbed new depths in the corrupt, politicized, backstabbing, old boy culture of the Oakland Police Department. The truth, and a shred of justice for Amaro's family, would not emerge for almost a decade.

———————

Yoell and Reilly, the East Oakland supervisors who tried to push Galindo's homicide investigation forward by telling him about the apparent lies the officers were telling, weren't through trying to expose the truth. The killing and cover-up bothered Reilly for several reasons. He'd been preparing his own reverse drug sting for the same night of March 23, when Poulson pulled rank and told him to stay at Eastmont and file paperwork for the squad. The lieutenant said he'd take over and work with "my guys tonight." This unsettled Reilly because he was unsure how much experience Poulson had with buy-bust operations—and Poulson was pulling some of the officers under Sergeant Reilly's command into the sting. Poulson had only recently been put in charge of the Crime Reduction Team that Reilly ran on a daily basis.[40] Within the department, Poulson had a reputation as a well-connected administrator. He was anything but a seasoned street cop, let alone a narcotics officer.

Yoell and Reilly decided to come forward and tell Paul Berlin about the apparent lies Poulson and his squad were telling after Reilly was approached by one officer who took part in the buy-bust. The officer told Reilly in confidence that Poulson may have kicked Amaro.[41] Based on this, Reilly and Yoell called in Officer Marcel Patterson, one of the undercovers, for a meeting on April 26. They'd picked him for a one-on-one because he was the officer with the most street experience and therefore would be most likely to be able to influence the others who'd lied to cover for Poulson and whoever else may have kicked or punched Amaro.

In Reilly's office in the cramped, dingy Eastmont Substation, Patterson listened nervously as the sergeant told him that the Homicide Unit did not believe the accounts of any of the cops who'd taken Amaro into custody. "The homicide investigators think that you're all a bunch of liars and that you need to go in there, and someone needs to fess up to hitting this guy," Reilly said bluntly.[42]

This was Patterson's first conversation with anyone outside his arrest team about Jerry Amaro. Reilly's patient line of questioning and rapport with Patterson, who was reticent to admit anything had gone wrong, shook loose enough information for Yoell to determine that serious misconduct had taken place and that Poulson was likely to try to shift blame for Amaro's death onto his subordinates.[43]

Immediately after speaking with Patterson, Yoell and Reilly drove downtown to police headquarters and met with Lieutenant Berlin in Homicide. They informed him that there were problems with the circumstances around Amaro's arrest and death.[44] Yoell and Reilly, who were no strangers to street violence and excessive-force complaints themselves, told Berlin that "the whole truth" of the incident had not come out.

These attempts to crack the code of silence couldn't be pursued in secret. Poulson, the last officer to be interviewed by Homicide on April 25, soon caught wind that his account wasn't being accepted as the truth. As the hours ticked by, the lieutenant began to feel increasingly uncomfortable with his interview.

On April 26, while Yoell and Reilly were downtown briefing Berlin on the situation, Poulson, who was off duty, paged Patterson and Bunn.[45] This was barely a half hour after Patterson's sit-down with Reilly and Yoell.[46] Poulson drove from his suburban home to the Eastmont Substation and convened a risky emergency meeting with his two subordinates—but not inside. The trio walked around the building to a secluded spot "in the cut" near a line of waste bins, where they could speak privately.[47]

Both Bunn and Patterson were perplexed: they'd never been summoned to a meeting like this by their supervisor, who was on his day off. "This is Ed speaking," Poulson said, adding that he wished he could have this friendly man-to-man conversation "over a couple of beers."[48] The workback on the Amaro investigation, he told Bunn and Patterson, would continue to drag on, they would have to "ride it," but everything would be fine. In the lieutenant's opinion, there was no use of excessive force, and he had no regrets about how the operation went. He told his subordinates—in that same chummy tone—that they should "tell the truth" about what happened and the "K-4" (use of force) investigation was entirely unnecessary.

Toward the end of the one-sided conversation, Poulson mentioned that he would be taking time off to study for the captain's exam, and that both Bunn and Patterson should consider his future position in the department.[49]

"You be loyal to me, and I'll be loyal to you," Poulson told them. Patterson thought that the lieutenant was implying that if he got promoted, his two subordinates would be in a better position to get favorable days off or overtime assignments. Bunn's reaction to this encounter was stronger: for him, Poulson's remarks were an inappropriate attempt to influence the Amaro investigation and to cover for their supervisor's misconduct in exchange for preferential treatment.[50]

Just then, Reilly and Yoell, returning from their downtown powwow with Paul Berlin, pulled into the Substation parking lot. They spotted Poulson, in civilian clothes, huddled with Bunn and Patterson, and immediately grew suspicious.

"Whoa, what do you think's going on?" Reilly said to Yoell.

"I don't know, but go get your guys," Yoell replied. "I'm going to talk to Ed."

Yoell caught Poulson's eye and waved him over to his car. Poulson came over and sat in the front passenger seat while Reilly walked back into Eastmont with his subordinates, Patterson and Bunn.

"Hey, Ed, I know what's going on, and I know what you did," Yoell told his colleague bluntly. "You need to take accountability for this." He warned Poulson that the meeting with Bunn and Patterson reeked of a cover-up.[51]

Poulson stared at Yoell blankly. "I don't know what you're talking about," he replied before getting out of the car and walking away across the parking lot.[52]

———

If Lieutenant Poulson was worried about being criminally prosecuted, he shouldn't have been. When Chief Word had Sergeant Gus Galindo close the homicide case, he effectively ended any chance at holding the officers criminally liable: under California law, compelled statements during Internal Affairs interviews cannot be used in criminal investigations.[53] Even so, the possible consequences of the IA case could be career ending for Poulson and other officers.

The case was assigned to Sergeant William Wallace, a twenty-seven-year veteran who joined the OPD in the late 1970s. Wallace found and interviewed several new eyewitnesses who were either unknown or never contacted by Sergeants Galindo and Longmire, including Tim Murphy, James Garry, and three other men arrested during the March 23 reverse sting. Their consistent recollections all implicated Poulson, Patterson, Bunn, Karsseboom, Holmgren, and Peña in Amaro's death.

Wallace reinterviewed Laureen White. One detail about her underscored her credibility as a witness. White was a police supporter, one of many flatlands residents who welcomed the OPD's aggressive presence and operations to shut down street narcotics dealing. Nevertheless, she didn't hesitate to say that Amaro was tackled to the ground and hit by the officers.

Wallace also located Theresa Batts, the resident who saw the brutal encounter with her own eyes.

"It wasn't no cop that stood by and watched everything. All of them had a piece of the action," Batts recalled.[54] "These people beat this man. It was no tug of war. There was no, 'Okay, you're under arrest, let me handcuff you'—there was none of that. The first thing they did was tackle this man; the second thing they did was starting whooping they ass."[55]

But decisions from the department's highest levels kept tamping down the investigation. In a highly unusual move that raised eyebrows among some senior OPD brass,[56] Chief Word issued an order that officers would not be punished for their previous lies if they came forward to give IAD investigators a truthful account of the Amaro incident.[57] Captain Anthony Rachal, who ran the Internal Affairs Division at the time, could not recall another case where such leeway was granted to officers under investigation for lying, which is a fireable offense in the OPD.[58]

Rachal also received a disturbing anonymous letter that spelled out a blatant attempt by Poulson to influence the outcome of the criminal probe into Amaro's death:

"Lt. Poulson definitely did try to manipulate officers [sic] testimony. He called everyone into a room and said, this is a quote, 'I am studying for the next captains exam, so if you are loyal to me I will be loyal to you.' He let everyone know he would be a Captain, which also meant if he wasn't supported, they would be going against a future Captain."[59]

But the Internal Affairs Division's investigation was limited only to the question of lies and a cover-up. IAD had received only a complaint about possible lying by officers about Amaro's arrest, not allegations that he had been beaten so severely as to bring about his death. No OPD officers were ever investigated for a lethal instance of excessive force.

Even so, the findings were initially damning. In his final report, Wallace concluded that Poulson had failed to properly supervise the buy-bust operation, had not drawn up an operations plan in advance, signed off on reports that excluded the use of force on Amaro and three other men taken into custody that afternoon, and attempted to influence the homicide investigation by meeting with Officers Bunn and Patterson outside the Eastmont Substation. The incident, Wallace wrote, "has brought the department into disrepute."[60]

The discipline recommendation for Poulson fell to Captain Ron Davis of Patrol Division, a twenty-year OPD veteran who would later run the East Palo Alto Police Department in addition to the US Department of Justice's Community Oriented Policing Services (COPS), a government think tank that awards grant money and conducts reform-oriented trainings for police and community organizations. At the time of the incident, Davis was in charge of CRT teams in his area of East Oakland. The captain wrote a scathing confidential report summing up the Internal Affairs findings, accusing Poulson of a "blatant attempt to influence the testimony" of Bunn and Patterson, undermining the OPD's chain of command in the Amaro investigation, concealing the victim's injuries, and failing to properly supervise his subordinates.[61] Davis added that this was not the first time Poulson had been formally cautioned about failing to report "incidents that could bring the department into disrepute."[62] Poulson did not plan for or even brief his officers prior to beginning the drug sting, and also allowed a subordinate, Karsseboom, to write and sign off on inaccurate reports for all five men arrested that day on Holly and Seventy-Third Avenue. The reports omitted any mention of force used during the arrest, which investigators confirmed through the statements of witnesses, arrestees, and even Officer Holmgren.

Davis explained his feelings about the case in a deposition taken nine years later: "Interfering with a criminal investigation and even an internal investigation in my opinion is compromising [the] integrity of the department, brings into question our ability to investigate ourselves. It just destroys public trust and confidence."[63]

Davis recommended that Poulson be demoted to sergeant, in order to set an example for zero tolerance of such behavior by any member of the

Oakland Police Department. He'd been considering asking Chief Word to fire Poulson for his actions, but eventually decided on the lesser penalty.[64]

However, Davis's views weren't shared by his superiors. When he went to Deputy Chief Pete Dunbar's office to hand over a folder with his report and findings, Davis was stunned to learn that Word had already decided to give Poulson a ten-day suspension—a slap on the wrist—for his role in Amaro's death. "When I handed my recommendation to Deputy Chief Dunbar, he basically responded to me and said, 'Well, don't worry about it, the chief decided to give him ten days.'"[65]

At the bottom of Davis's report, Dunbar wrote, "Although violations are serious, I do not believe they support demotion." Poulson received the lighter penalty and kept his rank and reputation intact—for the time being.[66]

Word's decision to let Poulson off the hook surprised and angered Davis. "To make a decision without hearing the recommendations of the commander was inappropriate," he would recall in a deposition taken nine years later.

Throughout the department, Lieutenant Poulson was known to have political connections to the very top. His best friend, Dave Walsh, was Richard Word's chief of staff. Poulson and Walsh had served as each other's best man at their weddings.[67] The sense among senior Oakland cops in the know was that Poulson had been shielded from serious consequences by the powers that be.

When Lieutenant Yoell learned of Poulson's light punishment, he blew his stack. A ten-day suspension for a supervisor after kicking a suspect, lying about it to Homicide and Internal Affairs, and leaning on his subordinates to cover up the misconduct was beyond the pale. Yoell called a friend in the City Attorney's Office whose husband also happened to be an OPD captain. "I'm extremely upset about this," Yoell told her. "I think Ed's getting taken care of. I want you to look into this. He's getting a ten-day suspension—and this guy died—and he tried to throw all these guys under the bus and not accept accountability for this. I want you to say something to somebody."

As Yoell recounted years later, "And she said, 'I'll look into it,' and that's the last I ever heard of it."[68]

The callous brutality of Amaro's death and Chief Word's decision to give Ed Poulson a pass for outrageous misconduct occurred against the backdrop of

Mayor Jerry Brown's development-driven agenda for Oakland's economic revitalization. Brown gave his full-throated support to the police, appearing alongside Word in front of dozens of cops at lineups before their shifts, urging them to "hit the corners."

Complaints against Oakland cops filled thick files in IA's offices. There was nothing new about suspects telling stories of being beaten up and framed by the police, but brutality complaints had risen sharply since Brown took office in 1999. By the OPD's own count, there were 83 complaints in all of 1998 and 154 in 2000.

But these allegations, coming mainly from Black people, many of them working-class flatlanders with prior criminal records, were easily dismissed or ignored. To OPD investigators, they were drug addicts, criminals, and unreliable witnesses. Their stories were genuinely hard to corroborate—not that IA investigators really tried. The reality was that the Oakland Police Department's violent and corrupt officers were seen as inherently more trustworthy than their accusers.

Moreover, the OPD had its own methods for weeding out individuals who did not conform to the agency's internal culture. Under George Hart, Oakland's longest-serving chief of police, from 1973 to 1992, the emphasis on recruitment revolved around professionalism and building large cadres of African American officers to connect with Oakland's most heavily policed population.[69] But by the mid-1990s, the department's new hires had begun to skew heavily toward veterans with active-duty military experience.

The main juncture for pushing out cops who wouldn't get with the program was during their academy and field training. Aside from the punishing physical training cadets were subjected to during Hell Week in order to "weed out the weak ones," would-be officers were bullied mercilessly if they deviated from heteronormative culture.[70]

Scott Hoey-Custock, a gay man and San Francisco resident who moved across the San Francisco–Oakland Bay Bridge to pursue a career at the OPD, received the full treatment during his time in its 137th academy class in 1996. The thirty-year-old was verbally and physically abused by both fellow trainees and academy instructors for his sexual orientation. During classroom instruction, he was mocked by cadets Sean Moriarty, Joseph Antonacci, and Donn Campbell, who would roll their eyes, bat their eyelids, pucker their lips, bend their wrists, and place their tongues inside their cheeks when they were near Hoey-Custock, all direct allusions to his sexuality. Campbell openly called Hoey-Custock a "stupid faggot" in a break room. During a running drill, Moriarty pummeled Hoey-Custock across his crotch with a baton, later apologizing and asking him to keep quiet in order to avoid discipline.[71]

The academy supervisors weren't much better. Sergeant Dan Endaya, a weaponless-defense instructor, asked Hoey-Custock with a smirk, "Where are you from, San Francisco?" Another sergeant, Jim Martinez, told war stories of rousting "queens" engaged in sex from public bathrooms in Oakland.

Eventually the harassment proved too much. Fellow cadet Kyle Thomas filed an Internal Affairs complaint on October 11 about the abuse of Hoey-Custock from Antonacci, Moriarty, and Campbell.[72] On October 14 all three trainees were placed on administrative leave pending sexual harassment allegations and kicked out of the OPD's academy. Hoey-Custock was pulled out of class—for his "own safety," he was told—by Sergeant Ramon Paniagua and escorted off the premises. On their way out, Paniagua apologized for the poor treatment the cadet suffered during the academy, but said there was nothing anyone could have done to make it better.

Summoning him from the classroom made it abundantly clear to his peers that he was the victim of the complaint, and he soon became known as the "snitching faggot." The very next day, as Hoey-Custock stood in the locker room, an officer walked in and yelled, "Who's the fucking faggot who had the trainees removed from the academy?" When Scott complained to Recruit Training Officer Mary Guttormson, who ran the academy, she replied that he would "have to develop a thicker skin."[73]

Training became much more difficult from that point on. Recruits and officers alike picked up on the harassment. Sergeants Martinez and Endaya openly challenged the IAD investigation, stating, "This year's academy is the worst class because everyone tells on one another." In November, as the academy drew to a close, Hoey-Custock got a premonition of what was to come when he received two formal notices of subpar performance.

Then, on January 3, 1997, the OPD fired cadets Moriarty, Campbell, and Antonacci. Sergeant Paniagua pulled Hoey-Custock aside yet again and warned him that he would not receive backup from other officers in the field once he graduated from the academy, a dangerous but common retaliation within the department for officers viewed as untrustworthy.

Two days later, Martinez and Endaya flunked Scott out of the academy for failing to find brass knuckles and a butterfly knife hidden on another officer during a patdown exercise. Hoey-Custock filed a wrongful termination lawsuit spelling out his mistreatment and solicited the testimony of other officers to support his account. This included Ron Riveira, a former Marine Corps medic and jiujitsu enthusiast who'd befriended Hoey-Custock during the 137th Academy.

In his February 2001 testimony during the civil trial, Officer Riveira confirmed that, when questioned by Internal Affairs, he had supported Kyle Thomas's allegations about the abuse Hoey-Custock endured. Riveira spoke up because Hoey-Custock should be "justly treated, just like we're supposed to treat the citizens when we go to the streets."[74] As a result, Riveira was branded "the snitch of the 137th" and insulted to his face. Among the officers who taunted Riveira as an informant, he testified, were Chuck Mabanag and Jude Siapno, two of the Riders facing a raft of criminal charges at the time. Prior to his appearing in court, Riveira had been well accepted by the pair because of his martial arts background, even receiving an offer from Siapno to train with them for an upcoming police Olympics-type tournament called the California Police and Fire Championships.

In addition to laying out Hoey-Custock's mistreatment in the academy, Riveira also gave a glimpse into another sordid aspect of the OPD's internal culture: a clique of officers who, like the Riders, reveled in their physical prowess. Siapno, Mabanag, Endaya, and Martinez, along with Officer Sammy Faleafine, another weaponless-defense trainer, were allegedly part of a group called West End Law that treated him like a snitch. According to Keith Batt, Faleafine, Endaya, and Frank Uu, who all instructed his class during the academy, frequently cracked jokes about using force in the field. "I didn't have the context to know what that meant until my two weeks in the field with some of those guys," he recalled, noting that all three were close to Mabanag and Siapno.[75]

City attorneys protested vociferously, but unsuccessfully, to prevent Riveira's testimony from being entered into the record.[76] The former US Marine medic told the court that his being branded a snitch by West End Law resulted in him not receiving backup in the field, a huge safety issue in a city where firearms were plentiful and police were fired upon not infrequently.

The Riders and similar cliques were so influential and notorious within the department that even fresh academy cadets would do anything to avoid having to train with them. Batt's close friend Kris Jenny, who stayed at the OPD for four years before joining the Napa Police Department, experienced this atmosphere firsthand.

Although Jenny had not blown the whistle on the Riders, his friendship with Batt forever tarred him within the force. When they met at the Emeryville all-night diner just days before Batt decided to quit, Jenny asked his friend not to tell him specifics about the awful things he witnessed while on patrol with the Riders because he, too, would then be required to report them to his supervisor. The very real fear, he reflected years later, was that he "could be labeled a snitch" and "might not get cover while out on the street."[77] Even less than two weeks on the job, Jenny knew the consequences for breaking the OPD's code of silence.

As an officer, Jenny would see how fellow cops delayed their response to radioed requests to back up certain officers considered undesirable or loose-lipped. "I'd be standing with them, and they are, like, 'I'm not going,' or 'I'm not in a hurry to go help them,'" he said years later in court testimony.[78] It wasn't long before he was on the receiving end of this slow-roll practice himself. Certain cops, he said, "had no problem looking me in the eyes, telling me they didn't like me, and telling me I should find somebody else to work with me so they don't have to keep calling them for cover."[79]

The intimidation of recruits and young officers prompted some prospective cops to clear out as soon as possible. Chris Austria, another of Jenny's friends in the 146th Academy, had been a fellow cadet in the Vallejo Police Department. Austria was so committed to joining the OPD that he purchased a house in Oakland. However, he made the stunning decision to quit the force before he'd even started field training. It took just one conversation with his field training officer.

The first thing the supervisor asked him was that familiar refrain "Are you a snitch?"

Chris Austria's FTO was Officer Frank Vazquez.[80]

3

"REAL GANGSTER GUNSLINGERS"

The Oakland Police Department's Internal Affairs investigation turned up plenty of evidence of criminal wrongdoing by the Riders. So much, in fact, that Chief Word personally called District Attorney Tom Orloff's deputy, Nancy O'Malley, to give her a heads-up: not only might hundreds of criminal cases be tainted, but also the DA would soon have to consider prosecuting the four officers themselves.[1] In late September 2000, two months after Mabanag, Vazquez, Siapno, and Hornung were placed on leave, the IA file was formally handed over to the district attorney's office.

Deputy DA David Hollister, an experienced prosecutor working gang-related murders and shootings at the time, was assigned the Riders case. Hollister, a tall, bespectacled fishing aficionado, had pretty much seen it all while pursuing some of Oakland's most violent offenders, but the Riders scandal still managed to surprise him. Years before, he'd handled cases brought to the DA's office by Mabanag, Vazquez, and Siapno when he was prosecuting probation violations.

Joining Hollister was perhaps the one person who knew the most about the Oakland Police Department: Bob Conner. The retired Oakland cop grew up in Sacramento and joined the OPD in 1971. He had a storied career, serving in patrol and then rising through the ranks to become the lieutenant in charge of the Homicide Unit. Toward the end of Conner's time at the department, he ran the intelligence unit, reporting directly to the chief of police. He'd handled just about every other important investigative job in the department, too, but in 1994 he retired and joined the DA's office as an inspector. When the Riders scandal exploded in the newspapers in late September 2000, Conner still had many friends on the force. Hollister, reflecting on Conner's stature in the Oakland PD, said once that walking into police headquarters with the inspector was like "walking through Yankee Stadium with Babe Ruth."

For Hollister and Conner, it didn't matter that the Riders were police. If they broke the law, they'd pay for it. But they knew the case was going to be one of the toughest they'd ever worked. Their approach was to try to disprove everything that Keith Batt alleged. If the facts stood up against their efforts to knock them down, they'd likely convince a jury.

Hollister considered the Internal Affairs file to be the "trunk of the tree" of their criminal investigation. But the truth was that Sergeant Madarang's IA report was more like a heavily pruned hedge than a towering redwood. Chief Word had ordered IA commander Anthony Rachal and Madarang to investigate only allegations of misconduct that occurred during Batt's short time on the force—an inauspicious decision, considering the kinds of complaints that Mabanag and Vazquez had generated over the years. Madarang had also rushed to complete the case, working overtime through September to finish his report so that Word could notify the four Riders they were being fired.

Albeit truncated, the IA report gave Hollister and Conner something to start with. They walked the streets of Ghost Town, sometimes between midnight and three in the morning, asking people if they knew Delphine Allen or other victims of the Riders. Locals rarely wanted to speak with the prosecutor and the inspector right there on the sidewalk, for fear of being labeled snitches. Hollister and Conner would come back late at night in Bob's unmarked car and park on Telegraph Avenue outside a Casper's hot dog stand. Witnesses would walk out of the neighborhood by passing under the busy MacArthur Maze freeway interchange and meet with the two lawmen. Under the streetlights' yellow glare, they recounted what they knew of the Riders, Conner preserving it all on a cassette tape recorder.

"Our game plan," said Deputy DA Hollister, "was to interview all the civilian witnesses and review all the old CAD records, the radio purge, and the records." CAD is an acronym for computer automated dispatch. These computerized text summaries of calls for service and subsequent police action included the names, locations, vehicles, and other information of additional potential victims and bystanders. Hollister and Conner worked fast to collect every scrap of potentially useful information. In time, their casework put the OPD's cursory Internal Affairs investigation to shame. Where the department didn't pursue leads or interview additional victims, the prosecutor and inspector did. Where it didn't track down physical evidence, they did.

The two men concluded that the four officers had engaged in a spree of criminal misconduct. They knew the Riders' exploits went back at least as far as the mid-1990s and touched other areas of West and East Oakland, but they focused on incidents that could be proved beyond a reasonable doubt. These were the crimes that Keith Batt was forced to take part in, as well as a few incidents, involving another rookie cop, for which there was unambiguously fraudulent paperwork. In October they met with their boss, Tom Orloff. A by-the-book district attorney, he wanted to send a clear message to law enforcement officers: criminal behavior under the color of law wouldn't be tolerated. In Orloff's office on the sixth floor of the René C. Davidson Courthouse, Hollister and Conner presented their findings.

Hollister's recollection is that Orloff "looked it over and said, 'Do it again.'" Pull their investigation apart, break it back down to the original components, and run the rule over every single fact a second time.

So, they did. And, crucially, they built a relationship with Batt, whose eyewitness accounts and ability to connect specific crimes with records and evidence would make him the lynchpin of the case.

———

On November 1, 2000, Deputy District Attorney Hollister filed criminal charges. Hornung faced three felony counts of conspiracy to defraud and two counts of impersonating a police officer. Mabanag was looking at twenty charges, including multiple counts of filing false reports and documenting false evidence, plus impersonating an officer and conspiracy. The most serious charges were leveled at Siapno and Vazquez, including kidnapping, assault with a deadly weapon, and false imprisonment for their treatment of Delphine Allen. If convicted, all four were looking at years of prison time, with Siapno and Vazquez facing more than a decade behind bars.

The Riders made their first appearance in court on November 2, 2000, four months after Batt blew the whistle. They stood expressionless and silent, dressed in suits and ties, as a judge read out sixty-three felony and misdemeanor counts listed on the massive sixteen-page complaint. All the crimes stemmed from mayhem between just June 13 and July 2. Hollister and Conner had decided to build their case around ten of the Riders' victims, including Kenneth Soriano, the man Mabanag beat up and arrested on Batt's first night on patrol, and kidnapping and assault victim Delphine Allen.

But day one in court came with a surprise: Frank Vazquez was a no-show. Described by other officers as "distraught" about the scandal, his whereabouts were unknown. William Rapoport, the attorney representing Siapno, said Vazquez was "terrified" he wouldn't be able to receive a fair trial in Alameda County due to the widespread media coverage. Even before Vazquez absconded, however, there were hints that something was wrong.

In October, Vazquez signed over power of attorney to his wife, Pilar. He was in a bad way due to the criminal charges and his subsequent suspension from the OPD, and telegraphed his intentions not to face trial. Shortly before the scandal blew up in the Bay Area media, Vazquez was pulled over by police in Suisun City, California, a small suburb about forty-five minutes northwest of Oakland, where he lived. The officers noticed an assault rifle in his car but didn't know that Vazquez had stolen the long gun from the OPD's arsenal. Despite his suspension, he badged his way out of the encounter without consequence.[2]

By mid-November, it had become clear that Vazquez—despite being married, with a daughter, and owning a home—had gone underground to avoid prosecution. FBI records described the former cop as "armed and dangerous," likely carrying several handguns, including a .38-caliber Taurus revolver, a .25-caliber Raven pistol, and a 9-millimeter Sig Sauer pistol. Agents were warned Vazquez had "suicidal tendencies."[3]

As the FBI manhunt expanded, rumors swirled about Vazquez's whereabouts and how he'd managed to vanish. Several people with intimate knowledge of the Riders' investigation believe that one or more OPD officers may have alerted their ringleader that charges were about to be filed and possibly even helped him flee the country, but no one ever found evidence or made public allegations. FBI agents believed he left for Mexico, where he was born and still had family around the city of Mérida. Vazquez's decision to run made him a fugitive from justice. Although the feds pursued tips that the disgraced ex-cop was seen in Cancún, he remains a fugitive to this day.

On top of Vazquez fleeing, there was a brief moment in late 2000 when the other three Riders, and possibly other Oakland cops, were on the brink of facing federal charges as part of a larger corruption and civil rights case. Hollister had been temporarily cross-designated as a federal prosecutor by the US attorney for Northern California, Robert Mueller.[4] He was partnered with Melinda Haag, an assistant US attorney who would later run the Northern California office from 2010 to 2017.

During their investigation, Hollister and Conner kept the feds updated on their findings in case the US Justice Department decided to intervene. Had the criminal cases been taken over by the federal government, the Riders would have faced prosecutors with far more resources than the Alameda County DA, and the investigation could have delved deeper into the past actions of the Riders, as well as the histories of other cops.

But the feds backed out.

Mueller and other DOJ leadership made this decision against the backdrop of Los Angeles's Rampart police scandal. Two years before the Riders were exposed, the LAPD and the Los Angeles County District Attorney's Office assembled a secret task force to examine corruption within the police station in the city's Rampart section—especially the Community Resources Against Street Hoodlums (CRASH) antigang unit. Local prosecutors were digging into allegations of evidence planting, assaults, false arrest, and even murder involving more than seventy LAPD cops. As in Oakland, the majority of the Rampart victims had criminal histories, including drug dealing, which the cops' defense attorneys used to question their credibility.[5] Ultimately, three officers had their convictions overturned by a Los Angeles County Superior Court judge, while the cop who turned state's evidence, Rafael "Ray" Perez, served three years in prison for his crimes.

At the same time, federal investigators were carrying out a sweeping "pattern-and-practice" probe of systemic civil rights abuses by the entire LA police force. Under the authority of the Violent Crime Control and Law Enforcement Act of 1994, the US Justice Department can bring civil lawsuits against police departments and force them to reform. This investigation had begun in 1996, when allegations of violence by CRASH officers first became public.[6] In 2001 a federal judge imposed a consent decree, a binding reform program buttressed by the authority of the court.

Unfortunately, the same degree of federal interest in the Riders case and broader systemic problems in the Oakland Police Department never materialized. George W. Bush's questionable Electoral College victory in the 2000 presidential election ushered in eight years of a Republican Justice Department that refused to bring a *single* pattern-and-practice investigation into widespread police misconduct.[7] The absence of a full DOJ review of abuses by the OPD would have long-lasting consequences for both the department and the city.

It's unclear why Mueller and other federal leaders ultimately turned down the criminal case against the Riders and chose not to pursue a civil rights pattern-and-practice case. However, one could reasonably infer the decision had something to do with the victims. Black West Oaklanders with histories of drug use and sales, burglary, and weapons possession were "no angels" in the view of the American criminal justice system. Hollister remembers meeting with Mueller in his eleventh-floor office in the federal courthouse on Golden Gate Avenue in San Francisco, a towering glass-and-steel obelisk with commanding views of San Francisco Bay, to update him on the case. "Mueller asked me, 'Tell me more about the victims'—and these were people whose records went on forever; rap sheets that would stretch to the floor," Hollister said in an interview. "And he said, 'I wish you the best of luck.'"

Federal prosecutors also have a reputation for being risk averse and uninterested in cases that aren't slam dunks, particularly when it comes to prosecuting law enforcement. Batt was the only truly cooperative witness for the prosecution, and the only one with a sterling character. The other officers who would be called to testify, especially rookies and young cops who had worked alongside or under the tutelage of the Riders, weren't interested in cooperating. The code of silence was still very much operative, and they took every opportunity to say as little as possible. Some would go even further, perjuring themselves to defend the Riders.

Making no public statements themselves, Mabanag, Siapno, and Hornung were represented by several of California's preeminent police union lawyers. Mabanag's attorney, Michael Rains, was a Marine Corps veteran who'd served in Vietnam and joined the Santa Monica police. While working as a cop in the Southern California beach town and serving as the head of the SMPD's union, Rains attended law school at night and became a tenacious litigator. His Pleasant Hill law firm specialized in representing police unions and officers. Rains had personally defended dozens of cops throughout the state against allegations of wrongdoing. One of his more

infamous cases was the defense of eight Corcoran State Prison guards accused of orchestrating the notorious mid-1990s "gladiator battles" between
inmates, in which prisoners fought each other in bloody bouts for the en-
tertainment of the correctional officers. Rains won the guards an acquittal
in federal court, despite being up against a four-year FBI investigation and
lurid testimony from former inmates.[8]

Edward Fishman, a Petaluma labor attorney with many law enforcement
clients, represented Hornung, while Siapno retained William Rapoport, a
former Contra Costa County prosecutor turned private defense attorney
who specialized in representing cops in administrative hearings and civil
and criminal cases. The three lawyers were as close to a legal dream team as
the officers could have hoped for.

By December, the Riders scandal, and the OPD's long history of conflict
with Black and brown residents, were national news. One of Rains's first
moves was to try to stem the endless negative publicity by requesting the
preliminary hearings be closed to the press and public. Judge Leo Dorado,
an Oakland native who grew up in the city's Fruitvale neighborhood and
graduated from UC Berkeley's Boalt Hall School of Law, declined. Dorado
also shot down a request from the defense to move the case out of Alameda
County, a tactic that defense attorneys for police would deploy frequently
for years to come.

On December 1 the department fired Mabanag, Siapno, and the fugitive Vazquez. Hornung would be terminated two months later. As the case
headed toward trial, in what was widely perceived as a rebuke of the Riders, the Oakland City Council decided not to pay for their legal defense. "If
they violated the due process rights of residents, that is not in their scope
of duty," Jane Brunner, an attorney who sat on the council, said about the
decision. "If you're going to fire employees for misconduct and then turn
around and defend them, it seems to be a contradiction."[9]

Without both the city's deep pockets and their own paychecks, the
Riders had only one ally: the Oakland Police Officers' Association.[10] But
the union's support was more than enough. Many rank-and-file officers
believed the Riders were being wrongfully punished for following orders
from the mayor and the police chief, and that the city abandoned its cops
in the midst of a "fake" scandal. OPOA members rallied around their own,

and they backed the idea of putting the city, its police chief, mayor, and the rookie Batt on trial instead.

The police union was able to convince the powerful Peace Officers Research Association of California to dip into its legal defense fund to pay for the Riders' legal team.[11] Underwritten with union dues from roughly 46,000 members in 650 different police departments, it could bankroll years' worth of costly attorneys' fees, if needed. And Mike Rains's law firm already counted PORAC—arguably the most powerful state law enforcement lobbying group in the country—among its clients, alongside the Oakland Police Officers' Association.

In May 2001, witnesses began to take the stand for the preliminary hearing, a procedure in California courts in which a judge considers testimony and evidence to determine whether defendants should stand trial. The setting was the imposing 1930s Depression Moderne–style René C. Davidson Courthouse on the shore of Lake Merritt, where Supreme Court Chief Justice Earl Warren once presided as Alameda County district attorney, and Black Panther Huey Newton was tried for the killing of an Oakland police officer. In court, Mabanag, Siapno, and Hornung sat stoically next to their attorneys while David Hollister called forth witnesses who recounted their run-ins with the former cops.

Kenneth Soriano recalled the night of June 19, 2000, when Mabanag threatened to shoot and kill his Rottweiler. He identified Mabanag by name, saying the ex-officer put him in a "sleeper hold" and "slammed" his head into the pavement. "I have a little scar still there," Soriano said, showing it to the judge. He then explained how Mabanag made him sign an incomplete apology that was later altered to create a false statement.

When it was the defense's turn to cross-examine the prosecution's witness, Mike Rains revealed one of the foundational legal strategies of the Riders' defense: he asked Soriano whether the police report, actually written by Batt under the direction of Mabanag, contained false information. Rains appealed to Soriano: "Would this rookie be lying?"

"Yes," Soriano had to answer.

It was a point that Rains and his colleagues would pound away at in the coming trials: Batt had lied, so how could his word be trusted over other police officers' statements?

Another victim's testimony highlighted a similar challenge facing Hollister and Conner. The Riders claimed to have "found" drugs where Anthony Miller was standing when they arrested him, and wrote a false report. When asked to explain why the drugs couldn't have been his, Miller testified, "Well, if I had drugs on me, I would not have just dropped them. I would have thrown them."

Hornung's attorney, Fishman, pounced on the admission: "How many times have you thrown drugs down to the ground when being approached by the police?"

"Once that I recall," Miller answered honestly about a 1994 incident. Fishman then ran through a series of questions designed to showcase Miller's past as a drug addict with a clear implication: How can you trust a junkie with a lengthy rap sheet over the three officers?

Under questioning from Hollister, a man named Joshua Richardson recalled the night he was standing on Chestnut Street with his friend Jabaree Highsmith. The Riders rolled up in their unmarked minivan and seized the pair. Vazquez immediately started slapping Richardson's face as he was handcuffed.

"Did the slapping cause any injury to you?" Hollister asked in court.

"Busted lip," replied Richardson.

On cross, Fishman asked about Richardson's evident involvement with West Oakland's drug trade, making the young man squirm as though he were on trial. Highsmith's testimony took the same turn.

"He got out of the van, drew a gun, pointed it straight to my head, and he slapped me in the face a couple times, like twice," Highsmith said about Vazquez, who had abused him on several occasions. Jabaree then described how one of the officers made him sign a partly complete statement so that Richardson could go free—a statement that was later filled in to say he had stashed twenty-eight crack rocks in his Oldsmobile nearby.

Highsmith and other Riders victims did the prosecution no favors by trying to proclaim their innocence in the drug trade. Jabaree insisted that the car wasn't his and told a convoluted story about how the vehicle actually belonged to another man. But even if Highsmith was on Chestnut Street at one o'clock in the morning selling crack out of his Oldsmobile, the obvious problems with the Riders' behavior were on display for the judge. They'd rushed two men for simply being Black and on the street at the wrong hour, cuffed them, slapped them, pointed guns at them, and carried out a potentially illegal search of the car where the drugs were purportedly found. Highsmith summed up his feelings about the police officers' procedures:

"I bet if we was Caucasian or Chinese or another race besides Black, I bet we wouldn't have got stopped," he told the court. "I tell police officers in his face, I got no ID, I'm not on probation, that no reason for you to be searching on me."[12]

The same dynamic played out with other witnesses. Hollister asked about the Riders making illegal stops, planting drugs, falsifying reports, hitting and choking people, and the Riders' attorneys undermined their testimony by making each victim admit to using or selling drugs, having been shot in the past, and being involved in West Oakland's midnight-hour violence.

On June 7 the one witness the prosecution hoped could withstand this legal strategy took the stand. Keith Batt's appearance was a dramatic turn in the proceedings. Sworn in, he sat upright in the witness box, wearing a neatly pressed, long-sleeve wool dress uniform with a gleaming golden badge pinned over his heart. After quitting the OPD, Batt left Oakland and returned to Sonoma County for a few months, working at a Healdsburg winery and a mechanic's garage at the Sears Point Raceway. But, undaunted by his traumatic experience in Oakland, he was hired as a cop in Pleasanton, a small middle-class suburb east of Oakland.

Hollister had Batt identify Mabanag, Siapno, and Hornung, as well as a photograph of Vazquez. Next, the prosecutor asked about Batt's time on the streets with the Riders, starting with the Soriano assault and culminating with Delphine Allen's abduction. Batt recounted how Siapno asked him repeatedly if he was ready to take part in the "dark side," a crude *Star Wars* reference meaning "illegal activities committed by police officers, excessive use of force, lying in police reports, things of that nature." He also retold some of Siapno's and Vazquez's jokes about the vicious assaults they'd perpetrated. Batt's recollection was still crystal clear, and his testimony seemed unimpeachable.

Rains wasted no time attacking Batt's credibility. The tenacious attorney pointedly asked Batt why, if he knew what was happening was wrong, he didn't immediately go up the chain of command and report it. Next, Rains made Batt admit that he'd taken part in the alleged crimes, including striking Allen twice and signing his name to false police reports.

Hollister and Conner, of course, had seen this coming. On redirect, Hollister asked the officer again why he'd waited two weeks to report the lawlessness and abuse of authority he'd witnessed. Batt laid out a candid portrait of a police department where supervision was cursory at best. His sergeant, Jerry Hayter, was virtually absent while his subordinates either slacked off or went berserk. Hayter, who by this point had been notified that he would be demoted to the rank of officer for failing to supervise his men and for lying to investigators, had ignored egregious uses of force by his squad members—the most obvious example being his lack of interest in determining how Allen ended up bleeding from the head, his eyes swollen shut, and barely able to walk after being allegedly stopped for drinking out of an open container and arrested for possessing a tiny amount of crack.[13]

"Officer Batt, why did you wait two weeks to discuss what had been occurring as you were being trained by Chuck Mabanag?" asked Hollister.

"Well, there are a lot of reasons," Batt replied. He didn't like the brutality and dishonesty he'd seen starting on his very first day in uniform, but he told the court he felt his "job was more important . . .

"I still wanted to be an Oakland police officer. I wasn't ready to give it up just because of a few lies in a report," admitted Batt.

Reflecting on his decision to ultimately come forward and report the Riders, Batt said the biggest obstacle was his own self-doubt and revulsion at the contrast between what he'd been led to believe policing would be like and the ugly reality of his field training. "Looking back on it, there was a struggle," he explained thoughtfully. "I had this identity as an Oakland police officer—because this academy was not easy, and I had gone through it and succeeded, and I felt like I'd earned my place there. And I wanted to be there, but what I was doing, I didn't want to do at all."[14]

There were indicators that his field training officer's loose conduct was common knowledge around the department. Before Batt's first day out with Chuck Mabanag, Officer Ervin Romans and his girlfriend, Officer Nicole Elder, cautioned the rookie about what he would see. Elder told Batt to "keep his mouth shut and his eyes and ears open." According to Batt, they "told me that [Mabanag] is going to be rough, and they told me to let his comments slide off my back."[15]

Batt described the stress of feeling isolated and not being able to tell his friends and fellow trainees everything, fearing he'd put them in a situation where they could also face punishment if they didn't report immediately to Internal Affairs. He recounted how Mabanag told him not to snitch and made clear one of the informal rules of the police department's code of silence.

"Chuck Mabanag told me to never say what any other officer did, only what I did," said Batt. The rules he'd been ordered to play by from the start began with "What goes on in the car stays in the car," and no officer ever saw another officer strike a suspect. (Even if he or she did.)

This same behavior was part of what prevented the Jerry Amaro killing from becoming a major public scandal around the same time. All the cops who'd rushed, tackled, and struck Amaro obeyed the rule, omitting from their reports and statements to Sergeant Galindo any mention of force used by their fellow officers.

Solidarity among some Oakland cops ran deeper than the code of silence, however. Certain officers were willing to perjure themselves to defend the Riders. Alexander Conroy, a twenty-eight-year-old cop with a little over two years at the OPD, was present at the arrests of Jabaree Highsmith and another West Oakland resident named Phillip Miller. Called to testify for the defense, Conroy claimed that he saw Miller toss away some drugs and that Keith Batt had actually told him and other cops that he'd seen the same thing before offering to write up the report.[16] In Highsmith's case, Conroy contended that he heard Highsmith give Matt Hornung permission to search the yellow Oldsmobile, making it a legal search. That would make Batt either a liar or misinformed. Conroy's testimony directly opposed Batt's, undermining the prosecution's case.

However, Hollister, Conner, and the OPD's Internal Affairs unit absorbed Conroy's testimony with great interest. They determined quickly that the officer, who was actually a close friend of Mabanag's and had trained under him, had lied in order to discredit Batt. Conroy's testimony was filled with contradictions and false statements, and Hollister and Conner were able to show he'd also falsified reports, similar to the Riders.

"I think the testimony, particularly this morning, showed that Officer Conroy should not be believed, and that he was not credible," the deputy DA said in his closing argument during the July 2001 preliminary hearing. According to Hollister, Conroy had previously "lied as a police officer to help a friend; a circumstance very similar to what we're in today."[17]

Conroy was investigated by Internal Affairs, suspended from the force in August 2001 for lying on the stand, and fired in January 2002.[18] Jennifer Farrell and Aaron McFarlane, two other young officers, also testified in support of the Riders, but on cross-examination Hollister debunked their claims that Mabanag had taught them to write accurate reports.[19]

————————

In July 2001 Judge Dorado ruled there was probable cause to put the Riders on trial. After a flurry of motions and discussions about a potential plea bargain that went nowhere, a jury of six men and six women—most of them from the suburbs to the east and south of Oakland—were selected. In September Hollister delivered his opening statement. The prosecutor recounted once more the ten nights of violence. He pointed to the three defendants sitting in the courtroom and a large, blown-up photo of Vazquez. Although Choker's disappearance was initially a nightmare for the defense, it became something of an asset after Rains, Fishman, and Rapoport argued successfully that the mere knowledge Vazquez was a fugitive could incriminate the other three cops in the eyes of the jury. Dorado therefore ordered that neither side reference his conspicuous absence.

The trial, which would become the longest in Alameda County history, featured 115 witnesses for the prosecution. They included several of the Riders' victims, and numerous OPD officers of all ranks who were subpoenaed to testify about the department's culture.

Batt took the stand early on, telling the jurors about the beatings endured by Soriano and Allen, the drugs planted by Vazquez, the blatantly false reports, the cruel dog shooting, the routine brutality, and the code of silence. He was grilled on cross-examination by the defense, which, even more forcefully than during the preliminary hearing, portrayed Batt as a liar who betrayed his fellow officers and greedily filed a wrongful termination lawsuit against the city after he quit. Some of the Riders' allies within the force, such as Dan Endaya, showed up to watch Rains hound Batt, smirking at the young cop from the gallery.[20]

Rains's message to the jury was that Mabanag, Siapno, and Hornung were heroic, hardworking cops who put their lives on the line in a dangerous, drug-infested corner of Oakland. "Keith Batt is a sniper," the attorney stated, using a battlefield metaphor. "One who doesn't confront you face-to-face, man-to-man. One who doesn't look you in the eye. One who lays in the weeds and picks off his victims before he knows it."

Rains alternately portrayed Batt as a clever villain, but also a "naïve" kid from the tranquil suburbs who couldn't handle West Oakland's mean streets. Having resigned in defeat, Rains claimed, Batt sought revenge by fabricating a corruption case about his FTO and other officers and then sought a payday by suing Oakland. "It was a money grab," the attorney maintained. He then told the jury that they should view the whistleblower as a wannabe.

"Batt was taken up to IA. It would be a better story if he banged down the doors and pulled a Frank Serpico," Rains said, referring to the courageous NYPD undercover detective whose 1971 testimony before a panel appointed by Mayor John Lindsay of New York exposed rampant corruption among New York City's men and women in blue, at grievous risk to himself.[21] "That didn't happen."

Some of the jurors may have been swayed by this narrative, but Batt's testimony was merely one element of a raft of evidence against the Riders, including physical evidence that told the story of the Riders as a kind of gang that formed within the OPD in late 1999 and early 2000. One of the strongest pieces of evidence was, of all things, a softball. Officers Malcolm Miller and Bruce Vallimont both joined the force in 1998. They were partners on the job and good friends outside work who often commuted to Oakland together.

Vallimont and other cops had been teasing Miller about his sluggish pace in foot chases; other members of the force often left him in the dust while going after a fleeing suspect. Driving to work one day, Vallimont recounted a story about his kid's Little League team, and how several times that season his son had won the game ball—the ball given out as a trophy for the day's top performance. Vallimont was proud of his kid's athletic prowess. When the topic switched back to policing, he started giving Miller tips on how to win a foot chase. Inspired, his partner replied, "You know what? I'm going to get the game ball. I'm going to try real hard. If we get in a foot chase, I'm going to catch the suspect."[22]

In June 2000 the two were on patrol when Miller, true to his word, chased down and tackled a man. As they wrestled on the ground, another officer arrived and struck the suspect hard with a baton. One of the blows landed on Miller, breaking his leg. In the ambulance, an EMT gave Miller a shot of morphine. Vallimont was by his side, and as the drug kicked in, Miller cracked, "I got the game ball."

A few weeks later, Vallimont brought a softball into the locker room before evening lineup and passed it to the dogwatch squad to sign as a gift for Miller. As Batt recalled, Vallimont wrote "The Game Ball" and "The Riders" in giant letters all the way around the ball with a black felt-tipped pen. He then added his call sign, "1 Adam 7," and his nickname, "Big Country,"[23] and handed the ball to Mabanag, who scrawled "Chuck X" on its face. Siapno wrote "St. Jude, the Saint," and Hornung jokingly scribbled "Space Monkey Hornung." Rookie Samuel Armerding signed it "Ding-Ding," while Martin Ziebarth wrote "Z-Man." Vazquez simply scrawled "Frank Vazquez" on the white leather.

But when the ball was handed to Batt, Siapno grabbed it from him and snapped disapprovingly, "No, no, not yet. He's not a Rider yet."[24] Hewison and another trainee, Mike Legan, as well as officers Chuck Ilacqua and Bruce Garbutt, were not allowed to sign the ball, either, an indication that they were not considered part of the clique.

The softball signing was a seminal event; the Riders name wasn't known outside the West Oakland dogwatch shift until Batt recounted the locker room scene to Sergeant Madarang in his initial Internal Affairs interview.[25] The ball's significance became clear after Hollister and Conner showed up at Miller's home one day with a warrant for it. The Riders panicked. Mabanag, who by then had been placed on leave, learned from a friendly source at the OPD that the softball had become evidence. He called Vallimont and Miller and questioned them worriedly about the ball and other events.

With their nickname signatures scrawled under "The Riders," it became difficult for any of the dogwatch officers to feign ignorance. In court, Vallimont acknowledged having heard suspects shout, "Riders!" as the police entered a home to search it. Batt recalled on the stand Mabanag's telling two suspects in the back of their patrol car, "You know we're the Riders," in a threatening tone.

The defense made no effort to deny this. Other cops said they'd heard the term bandied about the locker room or on patrol. Most, though, downplayed its significance, a few of them even claiming that West Oakland's drug dealers referred generally to *all* police as the Riders, kind of like "5-0" or "rollers." However, it had now been established that the Riders existed, that they were a cohesive group of officers, and that they had an infamous reputation in West Oakland.

———

Keith Batt wasn't the only officer to testify directly and clearly about crimes committed by the Riders. Steve Hewison, the other rookie who turned state's evidence in the face of indictment for falsifying reports, also took the stand. He described the beatings and frame-ups he'd seen and taken part in under pressure from his substitute FTO, Vazquez. But most revealing was Hewison's testimony about the intense pressure he felt from Hornung and Mabanag not to go to Internal Affairs, not to tell the whole truth, and to follow the Riders' first commandment: the code of silence.

Hewison had originally been assigned to Chuck Ilacqua for field training, but when the sergeant went on vacation starting July 2, 2000, Vazquez was temporarily assigned as his FTO. Hewison testified that Vazquez and Mabanag schooled him in the practice of "jumping corners," where the officers would stop and detain a group of people congregated on a street and then search and question them.[26] Vazquez also advised him, "What is said in the car stays in the car."

But there were two incidents that simply couldn't stay "in the car" for Hewison. The rookie had participated in the search of a young man named Rodney Mack at Tenth and Center Streets in West Oakland, then was given a completed report to copy and sign by Chuck Mabanag. The report claimed that Hewison saw Mack drop several twists of crack rock, but that wasn't true at all, he admitted later to Conner and Hollister. He'd caved and forged the report, Hewison explained, because he "didn't have the courage" to refuse his superior's order.

Hewison knew that Batt had ethical concerns with the Riders. In multiple conversations, Keith told him about Mabanag and the other Riders beating prisoners and planting drugs. Hewison hadn't been exposed to the Riders except for the few nights when his by-the-book FTO, Ilacqua, was on leave. It wasn't until he received a subpoena to testify about Mack's bogus drug arrest that he realized his own complicity in the Riders' criminal exploits.[27] With the summons in hand, Hewison went to Ilacqua and confessed he'd falsified the report and couldn't lie about it in court. The sergeant promptly brought his trainee downtown to police headquarters for a conversation with Jerry Hayter about the true circumstances behind Mack's arrest.

At Sergeant Hayter's urging, Hewison called the DA's office to find out if the Mack case would be going forward. Much to his relief, at least temporarily, he was told that it had been put on hold. Hayter said he'd keep the report and take care of the problem.

Hewison felt "certain that Sergeant Hayter was going to handle the Mack matter with additional follow-up." However, Hayter never relayed the information about falsified reports to either the DA's office or Internal Affairs, nor did he inform IAD about the misconduct in his squad.[28] During the course of the criminal investigation, Conner made notes that he wanted to question Hayter about how he selected which officers would partner up for narcotics enforcement. "Did he ask for volunteers, or was it accepted that Chuck and Frank would run the show as they saw fit?" Conner wrote.[29] It appeared that Mabanag and Vazquez were running the show, and Hayter failed to supervise his squad.

Not long after Hewison came clean about the first false report, a second falsified report created by Vazquez turned up with Hewison's name and signature on it. The rookie had no choice but to return to Internal Affairs and make a second statement admitting the wrong he'd done. On the stand, Hewison came across as a less-than-enthusiastic witness for the prosecution, someone who hadn't wanted to come forward but was forced to and who'd paid a price for doing so.

Bob Conner and Dave Hollister dug into the circumstances around Rodney Mack's arrest to corroborate Hewison's story. Poring over documentation of that incident, they noticed a warrant check for a man who hadn't been arrested. Twenty-two-year-old Shumarr Doernners, a resident of the close-knit Campbell Village public housing development, was at a dice game on Tenth and Center when the cops arrived to break it up.[30]

A small man came sprinting toward Doernners, with the crater-faced, stocky Frank Vazquez on his heels. "Get down, or I'll shoot!" Vazquez yelled. The small man fell to the ground, and Vazquez dove on top, punching him in the face over and over before cuffing him. When Vazquez noticed Doernners, he ordered him to the ground at gunpoint and cuffed him, too.

"You saw what I did to your friend?" Vazquez said.

"Yeah," said Shumarr, who'd played tackle for the McClymonds High School football team and then for the San Francisco City College Rams.

"I'll do you worse cause you're bigger," he told Doernners. When Shumarr turned to look at him, Vazquez slapped him in the face. It wasn't the first time he'd been brutalized by an Oakland cop: at the age of fourteen, Doernners was stopped by Larry Robertson, an aggressive street cop known as "Dirty Rob," who grabbed him by the throat to check if there were twists of cocaine or heroin under his tongue.

What he witnessed on Tenth and Center was commonplace for West Oaklanders. The cops recovered crack rocks littering the ground beneath some bushes, although they hadn't seen who'd disposed of the drugs. Vazquez, Jude Siapno, and Chuck Mabanag discussed what to do. From the curb, Doernners overheard Vazquez say, "We're gonna pull each individual to the side, count their money, and if they tell us the exact amount in their pocket, we'll cut them loose." First they asked Rodney Mack.

"He said four hundred sixty-five," Doernners recalled. "When they counted it, he had six or seven hundred dollars. He was winning the dice game!"

The young man's recall impressed Conner and Hollister enough to put Doernners on the witness stand. Being the center of attention at a high-profile trial was unnerving, as were Mike Rains's attempts to discredit him. Shumarr wanted to hold dirty cops accountable. It felt good. But even as Doernners painstakingly recounted how Rodney Mack was framed, his faith in the legal process was beginning to wane.

"I took a look over at the jury box," Doerrners remembered, "and I saw the one Black guy on that jury. Everyone else was older, white. I'll never forget: I looked over at that jury box, and something in my mind told me, *Damn, man, this might not work.*"

The OPD's rank and file turned against the few officers who either cooperated with the DA's office or were thought to have put up too little resistance to the prosecution. The 146th police academy class that Batt and Hewison graduated from was reviled as the "One Forty Snitch." Cops loyal to the Riders initiated a campaign of harassment that lasted several years.

Hewison, who stayed on at the department for years, endured anonymous threats, including vandalism of his locker with warnings such as "Hewison, yours is coming" and "Hewison is a rat bitch." His car was keyed in the OPOA parking lot shortly after the Riders were placed on leave. One message written on his locker read "Yellow betrays blue." Unknown officers embittered by the effort to bring the Riders to justice also scrawled messages aimed at the district attorney's office on bathroom walls in the Police Administration Building.[31]

According to Hollister, the Riders case triggered a long-running rift between the OPD and the prosecutor's office. The harassment extended to officers who were part of the Riders clique but had been forced to speak to the prosecution and the IA. For example, Bruce Vallimont was in the bathroom at OPD headquarters when he heard the door creak open and a voice call out his name. He responded, and the voice said simply, "You're a rat!"[32]

Not surprisingly, Batt experienced the worst retaliation. As the DA's investigation was gaining steam in the fall of 2000, his friend and fellow rookie Kris Jenny phoned him to relay something he'd overheard in the OPD locker room. A few rows over, several officers were talking about the scandal. One said he knew where Batt lived in North Oakland. They should go there that night, the officer said, to "do a special project"—terminology that OPD officers used to connote a special enforcement task. Batt thanked Jenny for the warning. Fearing the worst, he had already begun the process of moving out of his apartment.

Batt found himself carrying a concealed pistol wherever he went, first illegally as a civilian after he quit the OPD, and later while off duty as a Pleasanton cop. Jon Madarang had given him a blunt warning, especially about the fugitive Frank Vazquez. "Sergeant Madarang told me he knew why I had to leave. He told me he knew it would be extremely difficult for me if I had stayed; that it would be dangerous for me," Batt recalled in a 2005 deposition. According to Batt, Madarang even told him to pack the gun without a concealed carry permit and "deal with the arrest" if he was caught, "rather than get killed."[33] Madarang said as much in an interview a few years earlier: "Officer Vazquez is in my mind a serious criminal, and it was my advice to Mr. Batt that it was probably a good idea to arm himself and to be prepared to protect himself."[34]

But the threats followed Batt and became more random. One night at Crogan's, a bar in Walnut Creek frequented by cops from around the region, a man approached Keith, who was there with a friend, and identified himself as an OPD officer. "Hey, Batt, you got three other cops standing right behind you. You'd better leave before something goes down. They're right behind you, and they don't like you. You need to go." Batt pulled back his shirt to show his pistol and walked out as the OPD officers glared menacingly at him.

Batt found out later through the district attorney's office that an Oakland officer had unlawfully gained access to his Department of Motor Vehicles records, including his home address. The culprit was never identified, but Inspector Bob Conner petitioned the DMV to have Batt's information hidden and flagged for notification if there was any attempt to run it.

———————

In April 2003 Jude Siapno took the stand. Under questioning from his attorney, he described West Oakland as a battlefield into which officers had been sent by the chief and the mayor with orders to "harass drug dealers."

"Don't be afraid to put your hands on them." According to Siapno, that is what he and other officers were told at lineups by Chief Word and Deputy Chief Pete Dunbar, who oversaw the patrol division. "We'll back your play."

Siapno decided to testify to refute Delphine Allen's story. His attorney, Rapoport, asked him under oath how Allen's facial and head wounds came about. The ex-officer shrugged and said Allen must have hurt himself banging about in the back of the patrol car after he was arrested. He denied that anyone used excessive force and said he never saw Vazquez empty a can of pepper spray into Allen's mouth.

"Did you ever kick, punch, or elbow Allen?" Rapoport asked.

"No, sir. You could get fired for kicking someone," Siapno told the judge and jury.[35]

The former cop's claims flew in the face of physical evidence and everyone else's testimony, including that of an ambulance technician who treated Allen's eyes, inflamed by the pepper spray.

Hornung, the youngest of the Riders, chose not to take the stand and sat silent throughout the trial. But Mabanag, whom David Hollister viewed as the brightest of the group, took the stand next, describing for the jury his deep feelings for his work as a police officer and telling the court that he was motivated in part by a shrine within OPD headquarters to fallen officers. He wanted the jury to comprehend how dangerous the job was and to therefore understand that the violence the Riders meted out was necessary. Echoing Siapno, Mabanag spoke of the pressure beat cops were under from police brass to suppress drug dealing and burglary.

———————

The defense called Chief Richard Word to the stand on May 1, 2003. His testimony represented a strange capstone to his career. At the time of the Riders trial, Word had been an Oakland cop for just fifteen years, a remarkably short time for someone to rise through the ranks to chief. The experience was an emotional one. "It's painful to see this whole thing unfold," he said about how the Riders scandal affected the department.[36] The chief was unequivocal in the press about how he felt: the Riders had given the rest of the OPD a bad name. He thanked Batt for blowing the whistle and pledged to undertake reforms.

But Word put out mixed messages, especially within the department. His daily departmental bulletin of November 17, 2000, sent to the department's entire staff of more than a thousand cops and civilian employees, included an item about the role of the OPD's Fugitive Unit in attempting to locate and arrest Vazquez. He requested all information be forwarded to a particular officer, but on the following page, under the "Nonofficial" heading, Word included another message: "There is a collection box located at the Patrol desk for persons who wish to donate money to Chuck Mabanag and Jude Siapno to help w/their legal fees. All donations are welcome."[37]

Rains's goal was to have Word describe the city's broader political atmosphere at the time the Riders were prowling West Oakland. He had the police chief explain Mayor Brown's 20 percent crime reduction plan they'd promised the city. This audacious target was double the previous record for an annual decrease in Oakland's crime rate, around 10 percent in the mid-1990s.[38] The strategy, he continued, was to move away from older methods that relied on specialized narcotics squads, such as the Special Duty Unit that Word himself had served on in the 1980s, and to employ an aggressive new model of "directed patrol." Instead of responding to calls, officers went out proactively in search of drug dealers and other suspects. And in a break from the past, officers from third and first watch (dogwatch and daytime watch, respectively) overlapped their shifts and flooded neighborhoods where complaints were common, effectively doubling the OPD's manpower for a few early morning hours. The name of this crime fighting plan was Project SANE: Strategic Application of Narcotics Enforcement.[39]

"It means you're active, you're making car stops, you're talking to people, you know people that live and work and visit your beat," Word told the courtroom. The overall concept was to "really get at what we call the root of crime in the city, which was drug use, drug abuse, drug sales."[40] Project SANE drove "directed patrols" toward drug hot spots: areas with high numbers of complaints, arrests, and drug seizures. District 1, which encompassed West Oakland, and Beat 7, where the Riders and Batt patrolled, had twenty-six such hot spots.[41]

According to a December 1999 memorandum by Word, the OPD would "work to create an environment in Oakland that is hostile to criminals and those contemplating criminal activity."[42] But the chief condemned excessive force and frame-ups by his officers: that September, he authored another bulletin urging the department to treat residents "with the *utmost dignity and respect*." If cops conduct themselves in an upstanding manner, "people are more likely to talk to us and share information about crime when they are treated respectfully."[43]

But officers had ample incentive to be aggressive and little to be respectful. Project SANE tracked and evaluated police by how many arrests and contacts they made. The level of activity was frenetic: from October 2 through October 29, 1999, OPD officers made 1,955 field contacts.[44] If the same rate of contact was kept up for the entire year, 5 percent of Oaklanders—twenty thousand people—would be stopped by the police on an annual basis.

Although the Riders' legal team had failed in its effort to make Mayor Jerry Brown testify, his police chief suited them just as well. Rains slightly reframed Word's description of the OPD to show the jury a picture of a city where cops had been told to be aggressive, put their hands on suspects, hit the corners, and attack the drug trade head-on. Their actions, no matter how egregious, were all in the name of public safety and hitting the mayor's magic 20 percent crime drop. Moreover, the proactive policing program was popular among the rank and file. "They enjoyed the work," Word said on the witness stand.[45]

Rains, Fishman, and Rapoport interpreted this for the jury through a different lens. Hornung, Mabanag, and Siapno weren't rogue cops; they were following orders. If anyone should be on trial, it should be the city's political leaders, not a few hardworking men in blue.

———

The defense rested in May 2003. However, by July, it became clear that the jury was deadlocked. Some were in favor of finding the cops guilty on multiple counts, but not all of them. Several jurors refused to convict on anything. At one point, jurors passed a note to Judge Vernon Nakahara, who was filling in for Dorado while he was on vacation, complaining about the conduct of several of their peers. Nakahara, and then Dorado, considered the note but refused to make its contents public. Dorado admonished the jurors in open court not to insult or ridicule one another. Things had become incredibly tense, with reports of crying and shouting in the jury room. The trial had consumed a full year. Having sacrificed all that time, no one on the jury wanted to come away thinking he or she had made the wrong decision.

As the weeks dragged on, Hollister told reporters hanging around the courthouse that some jurors may have been hung up on the concept of "noble cause corruption": the idea that the Riders were actually guilty but should be found innocent because they were not out for personal gain. They were simply trying to fight crime.

Three times the jurors told Judge Dorado they were hopelessly deadlocked. Each time, he sent them back to deliberate some more. Finally, on September 30, 2003, Dorado relented. The jurors deadlocked 10 to 2 on most of the counts; the judge declared a mistrial.

Mike Rains celebrated the news. "It was my view from the get-go they would fight, they would feud, and they would hang, and I thought that was probably the best we could see," the defense attorney said of the jury.[46]

Hollister's boss, Tom Orloff, vowed to retry the case, and the second trial began the next year. But while prosecutors pared back the number of charges and focused more on the brutality and fraudulent reports, the trial proceeded much like the first. Again, Rains, Fishman, and Rapoport managed to convince enough of the jury to side with the ex-cops. In June 2005 the second jury deadlocked on the charges against Mabanag and Siapno, and acquitted Hornung.

Shumarr Doernners, who'd testified at both trials, was disappointed but not surprised at the result. He understood the jury's difficulty in believing him and the other victims of the Riders, whose criminal histories were aired repeatedly during cross-examination. "It gives people not in the street life a different perspective on that individual—'He deserved to go to jail, no matter what.' The ends justify the means," Shumarr observed. What did he think of Rains? "You had to give him props, he definitely did his job both times."

However, Doernners couldn't believe the jury's dismissing Keith Batt's testimony. "It wasn't street folk who turned the Riders in. It was one of their own. That's what was mind-boggling to me," he said. "If you don't believe us, then at least you can believe [Batt]. He's under oath. He's a sworn officer."[47]

After the second trial, Mabanag, Hornung, and Siapno sued Oakland, hoping to force the city to reinstate them as police officers and win hundreds of thousands of dollars in back pay. Hornung also filed a wrongful termination lawsuit against the city, seeking $5 million. In 2007 Oakland settled, agreeing to pay Hornung $1.5 million. The two other Riders' terminations were upheld, however, and all three ex-officers were forced to move on with their lives.

Mabanag moved to Southern California, where he was hired by the city of Indio as a police officer. He later took a job with the Community College District in Rio Vista, near Sacramento, again as an officer. He was joined there by his former trainee Alex Conroy, who'd been fired by Oakland for lying during the trial to protect Mabanag.

Hornung and Siapno both went into private security. Matt, married to another Oakland police officer, Tai Peña-Hornung, would maintain close ties to the OPD for years to come, as would Mabanag, especially when he returned to Northern California. Jude left the Bay Area and became a mercenary with the contracting firm SOC. He was deployed to Iraq, where he patrolled desert cities in night-vision goggles while wielding Uzis.

The criminal trials of the Riders didn't send a message to Oakland cops, as prosecutors had hoped. If the case had any lasting impact, it established a narrative inside the department that the Riders were innocent, and that the scandal was really about politicians giving cops marching orders and then abandoning those same officers once their ugly methods became public. Fatefully, anything related to the Riders scandal was viewed as illegitimate, including the broader civil rights lawsuit and reforms that the city of Oakland and the OPD agreed to in 2003 in the heat of the first trial. The result was that there would be incredible resistance to reform from the very start.

In 2012, seven years after the end of their second trial, Siapno and Mabanag would joke on Facebook about their reputations as the Riders. Below a photograph Siapno posted of himself holding an AR-15-style rifle somewhere near Camp Ramadi in Iraq, Mabanag commented, "That's a pretty gangster photo," to which Siapno replied: "Chuck, I used to ride around with real gangster gunslingers."

4

ONE HUNDRED NINETEEN
BLACK MEN V. THE CITY OF OAKLAND

Early in the summer of 2000, before the Riders scandal erupted in the press, two Oakland civil rights attorneys noticed something strange.

John Burris and Jim Chanin were accustomed to walk-in clients complaining about the Oakland police. Over the years, a steady trickle of men, most of them Black or Latino, or their mothers, wives, and girlfriends, had made the trip to Chanin's office in South Berkeley or to Burris's office near Oakland International Airport to complain about violent encounters or frame jobs. Most of the time, each lawyer listened intently and respectfully, but, lacking strong evidence to back up a person's claims, had to tell potential clients there was only so much he could do. That summer, however, the number of walk-in clients increased noticeably, and a pattern emerged in their stories.

In August a man named Rodney Mack walked into Chanin's office with a familiar-sounding tale. He'd been out on the night of July 2 in West Oakland. Sometime just after midnight, a squad of hard-charging cops broke up a street corner dice game and arrested Mack. He alleged that one of the cops planted a few rocks of cocaine on him. Mack spent eight weeks in jail before the DA dismissed his charges. Chanin thought Mack's account sounded legit, and the district attorney's decision to drop the case signaled that prosecutors knew the police work was tainted. However, there wasn't much evidence to show that the arresting officer, Frank Vazquez, had violated Mack's civil rights. It would be a difficult case, but Chanin agreed to file a claim. Soon after, another man walked into Chanin's office with a very similar narrative, about the same group of officers, in the same part of Oakland.

Around this time, Chanin received an unusual request from a deputy city attorney who represented Oakland in police brutality cases: What might it take to settle the Mack case quickly? Was there a satisfactory dollar amount? The question set off alarm bells in his head.

"I've been litigating against Oakland now for twenty years, and no one has ever asked me to settle a case," Chanin reflected two decades later. "Here's this guy with no evidence, no corroboration, who says this officer planted drugs on him. Why do they want to settle?"[1]

Chanin called up Burris to get his impression of the city attorney's request. Burris, it turned out, was seeing the same cascade of complaints about a squad of cops in West Oakland running roughshod. The two chewed over the meaning of the allegations but weren't certain they were linked. The puzzle pieces didn't fit together until Keith Batt's story made headlines in September. Suddenly the two attorneys saw how the scattered complaints made up a larger, systemic problem. These were the Riders' victims. Dozens came forward, and Burris and Chanin knew there were many more.

"The high-visibility arrest of the Riders was really the impetus for clueing us in on this," Burris said. "Jim had a couple, I had a few, and we started saying, 'Why don't we start doing this together?'"

Chanin and Burris got to work. Their inquiry would have more far-reaching consequences for the Oakland police and the national debate around police accountability and reform. Whereas Deputy DA David Hollister and Inspector Bob Conner's criminal case had to prove beyond a reasonable doubt that the Riders committed specific crimes, Burris and Chanin's civil rights case had to show only, through a preponderance of evidence, that the Riders had violated the civil rights of the men they'd beaten and framed. Because of this lower evidentiary bar and the introduction of findings beyond the Internal Affairs and criminal investigations, the civil rights case could expand well beyond the few incidents to which Keith Batt was a witness, or the handful of events where Hollister and Conner could find physical evidence and impeaching records. Chanin and Burris soon tracked down more than a hundred people who'd been ambushed, abused, or imprisoned by the Riders—all but one of them Black, most of them West and East Oakland flatlands residents. They also found victims who had been attacked by other officers beyond the four who were charged, showing that the Riders weren't "rogue," as city officials claimed.

Burris was already familiar with Siapno, Mabanag, and Hornung, defendants in brutality suits he'd brought against the OPD years before.[2] One incident that particularly haunted Burris was the 1997 police killing of twenty-six-year-old Vernon Dykes, a Black man who was shot twice in the back by Jude Siapno during a foot chase in West Oakland. The department justified the killing by pointing to two handguns allegedly found on Dykes.[3]

"The community was telling me that that gun was a drop gun," said Burris. Though the attorney couldn't ultimately prove that the OPD planted the firearms, the incident left him with a distinctly negative impression of Siapno.

Regarding Matt Hornung, Burris had sued the police department and won a civil settlement on behalf of musician Tony Wiggins of the trio Tony! Toni! Toné!, whom Hornung had accosted and choked outside a North Oakland nightclub. And Burris had dealt with Chuck Mabanag in several previous matters, including an incident where he allegedly beat and manhandled a teenage boy.

Some of the abuses the two lawyers unearthed happened *after* Keith Batt blew the whistle and the four officers had been put on leave, indicating that disciplining the Riders hadn't sent a message to the rest of the department. One man told Burris and Chanin that he'd been ordered by a pair of OPD officers to move his double-parked car outside his girlfriend's house on Mead Avenue in West Oakland. The officers thought he'd talked back. One cop beat him with a flashlight, dragged him to the ground, and cuffed him. The victim's girlfriend protested, only to be punched in the face and called a "fat bitch" by the second cop. When a bystander came out of his house to protest the officers' brutality, he was knocked out with a flashlight blow to his temple.

Many of the stories centered on Frank Vazquez's long tenure as a poorly supervised East Oakland beat cop. These incidents, on top of Vazquez's ever-present role in the mayhem that Batt recounted during his short time at the department, bolstered the impressions of David Hollister and others that Vazquez was the "heavy," or ringleader, of the Riders.[4]

An East Oakland man came forward with a story from May 1999. That morning, he was walking home from a bakery when he was stopped by Vazquez, who was patrolling Oakland's Fruitvale neighborhood. Vazquez told the man he was detaining him because he'd been seen walking away from a drug deal. The cop then pulled a baggie of heroin out of his shirt pocket next to the OPD insignia on his chest and told his victim he'd found it on him. The man would end up spending forty-one days in jail and being sentenced to five years' felony probation.

A high school senior told of a 1998 encounter in which Vazquez slammed him against a wall and then planted rock cocaine on him during an illegal search. The boy's family was then shocked when the cop lied on the stand in juvenile court. Although a judge acknowledged this conflicting testimony, he still convicted the boy.

Some of the complaints against Vazquez went as far back as the mid-1990s. Five of the incidents took place in the Deep East Oakland district Vazquez patrolled before being reassigned to West Oakland. One of the oldest was from 1995, when he stopped an off-duty postal service worker for drawing on a sidewalk with chalk. The woman had been injured on the job and was preparing to file an insurance claim. Vazquez told her nobody drew on the sidewalks on *his* patrol beat, and he arrested the woman on prostitution charges.[5]

That fall, Burris and Chanin submitted a lengthy claim letter to Oakland's city attorney. In it, they named Chief Word, officers Mabanag, Siapno, Vazquez, Hornung, their supervisor Sergeant Jerry Hayter, and dozens of other police officers—including Roland Holmgren and Eric Karsseboom, who'd taken part in Jerry Amaro's violent arrest—alleging they had engaged in violent misconduct, covered up for others who did, or managed the OPD so poorly that these outrageous abuses were allowed to happen repeatedly without consequences. The claim, seeking a huge financial award for their clients, was something the two attorneys knew Oakland would reject. However, it was the first step toward filing a civil rights lawsuit that could show that the entire Oakland Police Department—from the command staff down to the lowest-ranking officers—had perpetrated a sustained pattern of denying African American Oaklanders their civil rights.

This was *the* lawsuit Burris and Chanin had been hoping to bring against Oakland for nearly two decades. The attorneys saw it as their best chance to force lasting changes on the city's police force.

———

Intellectual and intense, Jim Chanin was an unlikely advocate for police reform. He grew up in a middle-class Jewish family of moderate Democrats in a conservative, Republican-leaning town in New York State. Chanin viewed the police as friendly members of his community. His only run-in with the law was a fistfight that resulted in him and a group of boys having their parents called to the police station. The police chief let them go after a lecture. It impressed Chanin that a police officer used his discretion to teach them a lesson without throwing them in jail. (It would take other experiences later in life with California's police to show him that this was an exception, not the rule, and that people of color were seldom afforded this privilege.)

In 1964 Chanin traveled to Berkeley to attend the Ethical Culture Society's Encampment for Citizenship, a liberal, nonsectarian youth gathering meant to foster democratic values. Staying at Barrington Hall near the University of California campus, he met Black Southerners, white Midwesterners, and immigrants whose lives were far different from his.

"They believed that we should be exposed to as wide a variety of different thoughts as possible, not only leftist thoughts," Chanin recalled of the society's philosophy.

Over the summer, Jim changed his mind about the Vietnam War. During his intellectual awakening and immersion in New Left politics, the onetime National Rifle Association youth member absorbed broader criticisms of the American power structure. Had the war in Southeast Asia been a fight against Fascism, he would have gladly enlisted—his father fought against the Nazis and helped liberate a concentration camp—but Chanin felt "betrayed" by the imperialist overtones of American foreign policy.

He ended up enrolling at UC Berkeley a couple years later. He described himself as "more of a hippie," and lived on Haight Street in San Francisco during the 1967 Summer of Love, soaking up the counterculture before moving into a little apartment overlooking what would become People's Park in Berkeley.[6]

In October Chanin decided it was time to quit being just a hippie and do something to help stop the war. He attended a massive rally at Sproul Plaza on the edge of UC Berkeley's campus and marched to Oakland's US Army Induction Center, where each week thousands of men underwent physicals and then were bused to military bases for combat training. Chanin decided he would join hundreds of other students and sit down on San Pablo Avenue, blocking the induction center. He assumed it would be a disruptive act of civil disobedience, and that the police would calmly arrest and cite them.

"We sat down, and Joan Baez was there," Chanin said about the start of the protest. "She gave the wave as she was led away by OPD.

"And then they just beat the hell out of the rest of us."

Archived newsreel footage shows dozens of Oakland cops and California Highway Patrol officers marching through downtown streets while escorting buses full of draftees. "It was the first time that I understood that the police weren't the same for everybody."[7]

Over the next several years, Chanin witnessed and experienced police brutality. He was shot with unknown ammunition, possibly rock salt, during the People's Park protests, and he saw fellow demonstrators gruesomely wounded. He also observed the Oakland Police Department's war against the Black Panthers and Chicano activists such as the Brown Berets. At a rally for Jose Barlow Benavidez, a Latino man whose head was blown apart "accidentally" by an OPD officer making a traffic stop in 1976, Chanin witnessed a carload of Oakland cops roll by and point guns at protesters.

"They were not playing around in those days," he said.

At some point, Jim felt the demonstrations against the war and the stifling of dissent had reached the limits of what they could achieve.

"By this time, I'm pretty alienated from the police, the United States government," Chanin explained. "They were putting us in jail for resisting the war, and kids I knew from high school were dying [in Vietnam]."

In 1972 Chanin, who by this point was a doctoral student in South Asian studies, got involved with a group of Berkeley activists hoping to create a civilian police review board. He was appointed to the new Berkeley Police Review Commission by the city council. Almost immediately, the Berkeley police union started filing lawsuits to eviscerate the powers of one of the first independent police oversight agencies in the nation. Chanin, a frequent target of those lawsuits, made a decision that changed the course of his life. He turned down a Fulbright scholarship that would have allowed him to travel to India, and instead enrolled in the University of San Francisco School of Law.

"It was too much what they did to me, what I saw them do to other people, like what I knew they were doing in the Black community, what I knew they'd done to Barlow Benavidez."

Over the next five years, Chanin fought to rein in Berkeley's cops by eliminating their Mobile Unique Situation Team—a precursor of the now ubiquitous SWAT teams—and prohibited BPD officers from attending a controversial "crisis training" program that portrayed activists such as the late Dr. Martin Luther King Jr. as having links to terrorist groups. In 1977 he graduated with his law degree.

John Burris, born in 1945, grew up in Vallejo, a small working-class city with a major US Navy base north of Oakland. After graduating from Golden Gate University, he became a licensed public accountant at one of San Francisco's most well-respected firms. But he abandoned a career in corporate America to enroll in UC Berkeley's Boalt Hall Law School.

Burris spent his last law school summer interning with Chicago's prestigious Jenner & Block firm, where one of his assignments foreshadowed his future. Congressman Ralph Metcalfe represented Chicago's African American South Side and, by the early 1970s, had become a leading critic of the city's thuggish, racist police department. Metcalfe's 1972 Blue Ribbon Panel report, *The Misuse of Police Authority in Chicago*, was a major achievement in a city dominated by the staunchly pro-police family of Mayor Richard J. Daley. Burris helped compile the stories of dozens of people, nearly all of them Black, and produce the final report, which described a violent, secretive, and poorly managed police department that could just as easily have been Los Angeles, New York City, or Oakland.[8]

As a young prosecutor, the thirty-two-year-old cut his teeth with the office of the Cook County State's Attorney. But California drew him back: in 1977 Burris, mercurial, dapper, and talented, returned to the Bay Area and took a job as an assistant district attorney in Alameda County. What struck him about the work was his impression that Alameda's DA was too focused on putting people in jail, including those who didn't belong there. He was also "profoundly impressed" by how much the Black community in Oakland hated the police department.[9]

In the 1980s and early 1990s Burris and Chanin would both gain fame (or notoriety, depending on who you asked) for watchdogging Bay Area police, often with devastating results. Burris sued the OPD on behalf of rap artist Tupac Shakur and a long roster of less famous clients, often winning large settlements. Chanin played a key role in forcing through changes in the Richmond Police Department, where a violent and racist gang of seven white officers known as the Cowboys terrorized residents in the predominantly Black oil town.[10]

The two attorneys began their informal partnership in the late 1990s. As successful as they were in suing violent and dirty cops, reform was a goal that had mostly escaped them, especially in Oakland. The city paid out millions each year to settle police misconduct cases, but, unlike smaller cities, the price tag never threatened to upend Oakland's finances. Chanin and Burris's theory that elected officials would pressure the police to change only under threat of a constant drip of costly litigation—a theory that had partly worked fifteen years prior with the Richmond Cowboys—turned out to be wrong. Mayors and council members came and went, and Oakland paid off plaintiffs alleging police abuses. There was enough of a law-and-order constituency that viewed hard-nosed, abusive policing as a necessary evil. Lucrative as it was, the work took a psychological and emotional toll on the two civil rights attorneys, who had started off as idealists seeking to change systems, not to exploit them for personal gain. It was time to stop making taxpayers foot the bill.

"We'd gotten tired of feeling like we were part of this assembly line," explained Chanin, "where the police would beat someone up, and we would sue and win a bunch of money."

The better path, both men decided, was to sue entire departments and to eliminate bad policies, procedures, and toxic aspects of police culture.

———

Burris had unsuccessfully tried several times over the years to apply the Monell doctrine to the Oakland police. Named for a 1978 federal civil rights lawsuit brought by women forced to take unpaid maternity leave from their jobs at the New York State Department of Social Services, the US Supreme Court ruled that employers, including local governments, could be held liable for the actions of their employees who violated anyone's civil rights. In *Monell*, this meant that New York State was responsible for allowing a pattern and practice of gender discrimination against pregnant women. In the context of policing, the decision meant that when officers engaged in a pattern or practice that violated the civil rights of a group (in Oakland's case, Black residents), the city could be sued and forced not only to pay damages but also reform itself under court order. But *Monell*, as the Supreme Court designed it, was a high standard. Courts were often skeptical of claims that specific cases of police brutality were part of some broader problem.

In the mid-1980s Burris tried to target the Oakland Police Department's arrest quota system in a class action lawsuit with two dozen clients, only to have a judge bat down his claim.

"The quota system is kind of the underpinning of the Riders case. Go out there, get complaints, it doesn't matter how you get them, just get them," Burris recalled.

In 1994, Oakland cops responded to a fight among some attendees at Festival at the Lake, a popular annual street fair near Lake Merritt. Officers beat up and pepper-sprayed not only the combatants but innocent bystanders as well. Burris filed suit, alleging that the OPD's response was shaped by racial discrimination (most of the festivalgoers were Black), and that other deep-seated problems, such as poor supervision, training, and the department's Vietnam War–era crowd control policy, resulted in the unnecessary police violence. While he did manage to win monetary damages for his clients, the lawsuit was also unsuccessful under the *Monell* doctrine.

The missing link, Burris said, was that the cases didn't have sufficient "volume"—that is, there weren't enough plaintiffs to convince a judge of a profound pattern of abuse by Oakland cops that needed rectifying. The absence of statistics documenting police stops, citations, arrests, and use of force by race further compounded this problem. The departments that did gather such information rarely made it public. Judges mostly viewed beatings and shootings of unarmed people of color as unfortunate, isolated examples of misconduct rather than a systemic reflection of law enforcement's inherent biases.

"It was always my plan and desire in life to do this Monell case against the city of Oakland to deal with this whole question of culture change," said Burris.

With the Riders case, Burris and Chanin had more than a hundred clients. The volume was overwhelming, and the department's firing of the four implicated officers undermined the city's potential defense. Furthermore, the civil rights attorneys didn't have to stay mum about Frank Vazquez's status as a fugitive.

Most promising of all, the Riders scandal had something that previous police outrages didn't: "The real difference here," Burris said, "was there was an officer who told a story of police misconduct."

———

One other development that made the moment ripe for a reform lawsuit was the nation's shifting mood on police misconduct. After the eruption of protests and demands for systemic change in police-community relations in the 1960s and early 1970s, much of the nation cooled to the idea of police accountability in the 1980s. But the videotaped beating of Rodney King in March 1991 by four LAPD officers—fifty-six baton blows and six kicks played on repeat on the nightly news—rocketed the issue into the national consciousness again.

In response, Los Angeles mayor Tom Bradley appointed former US secretary of state Warren Christopher and a panel of independent experts to examine his police force's training, recruitment, and command structure. The Christopher Commission's landmark final report found that a small number of cops accounted for a disproportionate amount of all allegations of excessive force. Future studies elsewhere would reach similar conclusions: while a small number of "problem" officers committed most of the violence, other "good" officers looked the other way. Police supervisors often wrote glowing performance recommendations for violent cops because they provided the performance statistics—felony arrests, and so on—that both appeased politicians and helped advance their commanders' careers. Ultimately, the commission recommended that Los Angeles reframe the problem of police corruption and violence as one of mismanagement by department and city leaders, rather than of rogue cops who needed to be punished. The Christopher Commission's report would set the tone for the next three decades of police oversight and reform, including in Oakland.[11]

The commission also called on LAPD's chief, Daryl Gates, to resign so that the department's culture could transition away from a "warrior" mindset and toward a community-policing paradigm. But Gates resisted calls to step down, and Los Angeles's political class did not commit to making substantial changes. In April 1992, when a suburban Simi Valley jury failed to convict the four officers for savagely beating King, Los Angeles and other cities erupted in days of deadly riots that caused unprecedented destruction. In the aftermath, more systemic problems within the LAPD were uncovered, still other Black and Latino people were beaten and killed in questionable police encounters, and a former LAPD officer came forward with credible allegations of police spying, all of which made reform seem a distant mirage.[12]

Into this morass of local politics and civil unrest stepped the federal government. The Department of Justice filed criminal civil rights charges against the officers involved in the King beating, but enduring federal involvement came in 1994 when Congress passed and President Bill Clinton signed the Violent Crime Control and Law Enforcement Act. The crime bill was the largest package of criminal justice laws passed in US history, designed mostly to free up the hands and fill the coffers of the police and state prisons. It set the stage for the prison boom of the 1990s and early 2000s, as well as the further militarization of police through block grants and the transfer of surplus federal vehicles, firearms, and body armor to local agencies.[13]

But one provision in the crime bill authorized, for the first time, the US attorney general to investigate police brutality and misconduct in any local or state agency, and to bring a pattern-or-practice lawsuit. Where the DOJ's prosecutors found constitutional violations, they could seek a binding legal agreement to force a poorly managed, brutal, or corrupt agency to reform itself under the supervision of a federal judge.

In the twentieth century, consent decrees were used mostly to combat racism and gender discrimination in state and local education, health care, welfare, housing, and jobs programs. Only a few consent decrees were issued by federal judges in the 1970s against police forces, and these measures focused more on hiring practices. For example, after women and Black and Latino officers filed suit against the San Francisco Police Department and showed a pattern of its hiring mostly white males as officers, the SFPD was placed under a consent decree and made to diversify its ranks—a requirement that has met with mixed results due to entrenched resistance from the department's legacy families and poisonous relations with San Francisco's dwindling Black community. A few sheriff's departments were also hit with consent decrees for employing cruel and unusual punishment against prisoners in the 1970s and 1980s. But because of the 1994 crime bill, police departments, which largely escaped the legal battles of the civil rights movement era, were now explicitly subject to federal intervention.

The Clinton administration used this new authority sparingly, opening the first pattern-and-practice investigation into the Pittsburgh Police Department in 1996 after years of brutality-related complaints, mostly from Black residents.[14] A reform agreement, reached in 1997, lasted eight years before a federal judge determined that the agency had met all its goals for change.[15] Smaller departments in Maryland and Ohio, and the New Jersey State Police, were forced into consent decrees by federal prosecutors in the late 1990s. And in 2000, capping the Los Angeles Police Department's decade of crisis that began with Rodney King and ended with the Rampart scandal, the LAPD was placed under a consent decree that would last thirteen years.

While consent decrees prevented reform experts from being bogged down in local political squabbles, unfortunately they proved to be subject to the alternating priorities of Democrats and Republicans in the White House. From 2001 through 2009, the George W. Bush administration downsized the DOJ's Civil Rights Division and actively discouraged pursuing new consent decrees.[16] During Bush's presidency, only one law enforcement agency was sued and placed under a new federal consent decree.[17] Barack Obama reversed course, opening a record number of investigations, leading to fifteen new consent decrees with agencies, including the New Orleans Police Department, Arizona's Maricopa County Sheriff's Office, and the police department in Ferguson, Missouri.[18]

However, despite the clear pattern of police misconduct in Oakland in the late 1990s and early 2000s, and the grievous consequences of the Riders scandal on the OPD's reputation, as well as for active criminal cases and convictions, there was no serious federal interest in pursuing systemic oversight and reform.

John Burris, like David Hollister, had some insight into the Justice Department's thinking. He recalled his conversations with staffers from the DOJ's Civil Rights Division in the winter of 2000, the waning days of President Bill Clinton's lame-duck second term, and the expectation that incoming Republican president Bush would put a lid on police accountability initiatives.

"They were telling me, 'Hell, man, we're burning our emails here. We're not taking on new work; we're trying to get the hell out of Dodge,'" Burris said.

The feds' disinterest in Oakland didn't deter Burris and Chanin. In fact, the DOJ's absence freed them up to pursue a novel solution of their own.

Their plan of attack was data driven. In order to establish a pattern and practice of civil rights violations, Burris and Chanin focused on finding felony arrests by the four Riders officers for drug offenses with small amounts of narcotics. "Those were the kind of cases I was most interested in having a handle on," Burris said. These were the most likely instances of a false arrest or planted evidence. They scoured the arrest records of Vazquez, Siapno, Hornung, and Mabanag and compiled records on other

OPD officers. Contacting arrestees, some of them in jail and prison, the two lawyers built out a lengthy list of misconduct.

On December 7, 2000, Burris and Chanin filed suit on behalf of 119 individuals, all of them Black except for one white man. The lead plaintiff was Delphine Allen.

———————

It was John Russo's job to strategize the city's response to the Delphine Allen lawsuit. While the city council would ultimately decide whether to fight Burris and Chanin or reach some kind of settlement, Russo, as Oakland's city attorney, was in a position of influence. In closed-session meetings with the council, he advised what the best course of action might be.

Russo didn't think fighting was a good idea. Before he became city attorney, Russo served on the city council from 1994 to 2000 and had several run-ins with the Oakland Police Officers' Association and OPD brass. He tried pushing management reforms on the department that he thought would create a police force better at fighting crime and less likely to harm residents. Russo knew the OPD's troubles firsthand. He supported the goals of Black police officers to diversify its ranks and pushed for years to remove commanders, including deputy chiefs and captains, from the OPOA. He felt that commanders' participation in the union weakened disciplinary decisions because supervisors had to get along with their subordinates—and union colleagues. Russo was an ally of progressives who pushed, successfully, in the mid-1990s to strengthen Oakland's police civilian oversight board.[19]

So, when the civil rights lawsuit landed on his desk, Russo's instinct was to cut a deal that would help overhaul the OPD. He also sought to prevent a massive hit to the city's budget. Los Angeles's Rampart scandal ended with the city paying more than $140 million to victims. LA could handle such a financial blow, but in Oakland, that was $20 million more than the police department's annual budget. And it was possible that the city would have to pay nearly as much if it rolled the dice on a jury trial.

"It was obvious we had to settle," Russo recalled in an interview. "There were a hundred nineteen plaintiffs; the ringleader, Vazquez, had fled the country—I believe to this day with the assistance of the OPOA. I can't prove it, but I believe it to be true, knowing the culture there."

He'd done the math: Oakland would have to spend at least $6 million on attorneys' fees. There would be multiple trials even if many of the plaintiffs were consolidated before a single jury, and each jury would be drawn from what Russo called "the most liberal jury pool in the country." The Riders' victims could point to more than twenty-five years combined they'd spent in jail or prison on cases cooked up by the West Oakland squad, and a few, such as Delphine Allen, Kenneth Soriano, and Matthew Watson, had sustained physical and emotional trauma, all of it adding up to millions in damages.[20]

"We'd have to hope we go one hundred nineteen for one hundred nineteen in trial, and that one liberal jury does not get pissed off and nail us for $100 million," said Russo. "All this when the insurance companies said they were willing to go as high as $8.9 million on a settlement. It was a no-brainer."

The city council agreed, and Russo's team sat down earnestly with Burris and Chanin to hash out some kind of solution. The two civil rights lawyers were more than willing to talk settlement. Although they could shake tens of millions of dollars from the city, at minimum, they had calculated a fair payout to their clients at around $7 million. But to let Oakland off the financial hook, Burris and Chanin wanted a unique settlement that would use the consent decree model created by the 1994 crime bill to reform the police department. The difference would be that Burris, Chanin, a federal judge, and a court-appointed monitor—not the federal Department of Justice—would hold OPD leaders to their promises.

The two attorneys hired their own experts, including Jeffrey Schwartz, an expert on law enforcement and prison regulations, and a retired San Jose police officer, while the city brought in its own advisors—namely, a former police chief from Dallas—to help craft the settlement from its side.[21] The attorneys and experts drew liberally from the consent decree signed in Los Angeles in 2000, and from those in Washington, DC; Pittsburgh; Steubenville, Ohio; and New Jersey.

On February 19, 2003, after eighteen months of negotiations, Russo, Chief Word, and two members of the city council—Ignacio De La Fuente, from Oakland's heavily Latino Fruitvale district, and Larry Reid, from predominantly Black Deep East Oakland—stood before a crowd of reporters in Oakland City Hall. A settlement had been reached.[22] The city agreed to put the Oakland Police Department under the watchful eyes of an independent monitor who would ensure, over a five-year period, that the police accomplished fifty-two distinct reform tasks.

The core requirements were that the OPD deploy more sergeants and lieutenants on each shift so that no officers went unsupervised. The failure of Sergeant Jerry Hayter to control his officers, including the Riders, and his unwillingness to ask why some arrestees were bleeding or unable to walk, led the city to fire him, but the settlement agreement underscored that this wasn't just the sergeant's fault; the department was structured in a way that allowed officers to go without supervision.

In the next half decade, the OPD would also have to strengthen its Internal Affairs Division and see to it that police misconduct investigations were completed swiftly and rigorously. Per the settlement, all uses of force would be documented, regardless of whether anyone complained.

OPD academies and field training programs would also need to be overhauled. Echoing the findings of the Christopher Commission, the department was required to create a system to track and analyze police officers' behavior, especially how often they engaged in risky conduct such as using force, firing a gun, or high-speed chases. This "early warning system" was meant to be a tool that the OPD could use to intervene and help officers avoid getting into trouble and to keep the public safe.

The Oakland Police Officers' Association opposed the settlement from the start. The union, represented by Rockne Lucia, a partner in the same law firm with Riders defendant Clarence Mabanag's attorney, Michael Rains, feared it would be used to punish officers rather than change OPD management. The Officers' Association also feared it was the camel's nose under the tent of its collective bargaining agreement, but the union managed to safeguard its labor agreement with Oakland under the terms of the settlement agreement.

The police officers' union had one other major objection, one shared by some police brass, as well as some of the city's civilian leaders. It strongly opposed appointing anyone other than a former police chief as the independent monitor of the department. How could anyone without law enforcement experience understand the complexities and demands of policing? Another fear was that an academic or attorney would turn the settlement agreement into an impossible list of goals. To community activists, however, these concerns seemed more like resistance to actually being held accountable by someone who wasn't also tainted by a virulent police culture.

The first monitoring team selected was to the OPD's liking. It included Rachel Burgess, a retired Los Angeles Sheriff's Department division chief,

Police Chief Charles Gruber of South Barrington, Illinois, and two former US Justice Department Civil Rights Division attorneys, Kelli Evans and Christy Lopez. Under the terms of the settlement agreement, this team reported to only one person: US District Judge Thelton Henderson, a Shreveport, Louisiana, native and former UC Berkeley running back who later graduated from Cal's renowned law school. Henderson, the first African American lawyer hired by the Civil Rights Division, investigated the September 1963 bombing of the all-Black Sixteenth Street Baptist Church in Birmingham, Alabama. On a peaceful Sunday morning, a bomb planted by a back staircase detonated, killing four young girls attending Sunday school and injuring more than twenty other members of the congregation. Justice would be slow in coming, but eventually three members of the Ku Klux Klan were convicted of the crime and imprisoned for life. (A fourth man, suspected of participating in the bombing, died without ever being charged.)

Appointed to the US District Court of Northern California by President Jimmy Carter, Henderson had already carved out a reputation as an independent thinker whose decision in a 1995 civil suit forced groundbreaking oversight of California's supermax Pelican Bay State Prison.[23] Looking over this complicated arrangement (the settlement agreement was fifty-seven pages long and touched on almost every aspect of OPD operations), Henderson signed off on the plan.

Even after the first Riders mistrial in 2003, there was a broadly shared confidence that the settlement agreement had put the OPD on course for success. In the first report to Judge Henderson that December, the monitoring team wrote, "Although there is no question that cynicism, fear and even obstructionism regarding the Settlement Agreement exist within OPD," they characterized their interactions with Oakland police leaders as mostly positive. Despite concerns that the department was slow to meet some of the earliest deadlines, they noted cheerfully that the OPD had already set up its own inspector general office to promote greater internal accountability and change, and that Chief Word seemed personally invested in fulfilling Oakland's unique consent decree.

"To OPD's credit, we have observed, for the most part, recognition of its own shortcomings and good faith efforts towards compliance with the

Settlement Agreement," the monitors reported to Henderson. "It is clear, however, that the successful implementation of the Settlement Agreement will require the sustained efforts of officials throughout the city, not just the efforts of the Oakland Police Department."

But there were clear indications that many inside the department were hostile to the reform push. No sooner had Oakland officials signed the set-tlement agreement than a squad of OPD officers attacked protesters and longshore workers at the Port of Oakland in a vicious display of force. And in 2004 the monitors would learn that cops as well as commanders were willing to "flout" the agreement, deriding as "bullshit" core tenets such as collecting stop data to reduce racial profiling. In a report that December, they wrote to Judge Henderson: "Through lackadaisical supervision and little to no accountability, OPD has fostered an environment where scores of officers and their supervisors feel comfortable simply disregarding OPD policy and the Settlement Agreement in this area."[24]

Signaling the long road ahead, one filled with future tragedies and injus-tices, was a killing on a West Oakland street.

Matthew Watson, the young man who was kidnapped by Siapno and Vazquez and beaten under a freeway bridge, was awarded one of the larg-est civil settlements. But money couldn't save the nineteen-year-old from Oakland's streets. With his windfall of more than $100,000, Watson bought a 1990 Cadillac Seville. In June 2003, just after he took the stand in superior court to testify in the criminal case against the Riders, he was gunned down by an unknown carjacker.

Burris, who had become something of a father figure to Watson, tak-ing him to McDonald's and chatting with the young man about his life, mourned the loss. While Oakland faced a serious challenge reforming its violent police department, residents also suffered incredibly from violent crime. To reformers like Burris and Chanin, police misconduct and violent street crime weren't separate issues: they were two sides of the same coin. Reforming the OPD would also create safer streets in the long run, foster-ing trust and preventing tragedies such as Watson's killing. But not all city leaders were on board.

Mayor Jerry Brown, who ran on a tough-on-crime platform and en-couraged cops to be more aggressive, emerged virtually unscathed by the Riders scandal. He told the *Los Angeles Times* that it was "preposterous on its face" to suggest that this had fostered brutal policing.[25]

Within the department, very little actually changed in the short term. During the Riders trial, rookie cops in field training were still jumping out of squad cars and stopping Black and Latino residents, in order to meet their supervisors' demands for the mayor's quota of "goldenrod" felony arrests.[26] ("Goldenrod" was a term OPD officers used to refer to the yellow carbon copies of arrest reports that line cops turned in to their supervisors at the end of a shift.) In the three years following the settlement agreement, Brown continued to talk about public safety as the city's greatest need, while neglecting the reform mandate. The fact that Oakland's police force had been put under a consent decree almost went unmentioned in 2006, when Brown, his second and final term as mayor coming to an end, ran for state attorney general, steamrolling his Republican opponent. Instead, his critics tried to paint him as someone who hadn't done enough to crush violent crime.[27] That year, Oakland recorded 148 murders, the highest death toll since the early 1990s and a harrowing sign that Brown's OPD had not made the city safer in the long run. One of the hallmarks of this period was gang members and other criminals targeting witnesses who cooperated with law enforcement and a pervasive stop-snitching culture that drew on generational mistrust of the police.[28]

As real and dire as the city's violent crime situation was, few at the time directly connected the need to reform the OPD with the goals of preventing gun violence, rape, and robbery. And nowhere was this siloing more apparent than within its ranks. Despite the optimism of the first monitoring team, and the hopes of Burris, Chanin, and Henderson for the settlement agreement, it soon became apparent why the department had signed the reform contract: few in the police department and city hall took it seriously. They assumed the settlement would expire in five years after they'd checked off its procedural boxes by issuing paper policies and that the two civil rights attorneys, monitoring team, and judge would move on.

Nothing would be further from the truth.

5

THE ORIGINS OF WEST COAST COP CULTURE

The brutality and corruption that rocked Oakland's police department in the early 2000s was not the by-product of one group of "bad apple" officers. These features were part of the OPD's internal culture, forged over 150 years by broad currents in American history, but also shaped by local personalities who would go on to influence the course of the nation.

In its early years, OPD leadership encouraged violence and corruption. During the first century of the department's existence, custom and practice condoned the quick use of the nightstick and revolver to control restive populations: labor unions, the Chinese, and white ethnic immigrants who upset the city's image of itself as a pious, middle-class, Anglo-Saxon settlement. As an urban agency, the Oakland police had much in common with law enforcement in eastern and Midwestern cities such as New York, Boston, Chicago, and Cincinnati. Oakland cops operated in a highly politicized environment as one component of the municipal machine government. Badges were handed out to allies of mayors and council members. This favoritism often had an ethnic cast, with Irish, Italian, and other immigrants looking out for their fellow countrymen.

From its founding in 1852, Oakland was a West Coast boomtown drawing huge investments of capital thanks to the siting of the first transcontinental railroad, which terminated at the city's port in 1869. This drew labor, including European immigrants and white workers from the East Coast who settled in West Oakland and the downtown area. As in the rest of the nation, Oakland's workers were frequently pitted against one another by the railroads, major shipping companies, and factories. These conflicts often had racial fault lines. During depressions such as the one that crippled America's economy in the late 1870s, white workers lashed out against California's Chinese, whom they blamed for mass unemployment. Embittered by the Port of Oakland's use of Chinese workers to build roads, Oakland's white laborers threatened violence. Although the city avoided full-blown race riots like San Francisco's multiday mob assault on the Chinese in 1877, Oakland still came to the brink of a pogrom. Police were deployed several times to preemptively put down xenophobic riots.

But the Oakland police were also the chief exploiters of the city's Chinese population. In the 1880s and 1890s, the OPD regularly raided Chinatown, arresting locals on charges of gambling, opium possession, and prostitution.[1] During its first fifty years, the force controlled Oakland's Chinese population so frequently that it was arguably the department's first order of business. Mayor Washburne Andrus described the police department's central function in his annual message to the city in 1879. Pointing across the bay to San Francisco, which by then had the country's largest Chinatown, Andrus said "no greater calamity" had befallen that city than the Chinese putting down roots, and that Oakland "should take proper precautions, if possible, to prevent such a misfortune from occurring here." The mayor, a member of the proto-Socialist Workingmen's Party of the United States (WPUS) that had rampaged against Chinese immigrants a few years before and backed the soon-to-pass federal Chinese Exclusion Act, advocated that Oakland ban occupations that drew Chinese workers and redline the Chinese out of every neighborhood except the crowded district they already occupied just east of Broadway.

"The presence of these people is in every way undesirable and should be discouraged by every legal method, direct and indirect," Andrus railed. Although the Chinese comprised a mere 10 percent of Oakland's population, he blamed them for one-third of the city's murders and thefts. However, because of California's insatiable need for labor, the Chinese continued to immigrate and settle in places such as Oakland's Chinatown—that is, until President Chester A. Arthur signed the Chinese Exclusion Act of 1882 into law. A disproportionate number of Chinese filled Oakland's jails. Pursuant to an 1875 order from the city council, the OPD put Chinese inmates to work on chain gangs. The prisoners regularly cleaned the streets and were forced to lay out the city grid, build Jefferson

Square, and grade roads around Lake Merritt and from Peralta Street to the bay in the 1880s.[2]

By the early 1900s, reports of Oakland police officers routinely mugging and extorting the Chinese were commonplace. In 1906 prosecutor Francis Heney, who had been brought to the Bay Area from Oregon to root out corruption in San Francisco, turned his attention to Oakland. China's ambassador to the United States complained about the behavior of the police there, handing federal authorities a list of corrupt officers.[3] However, these allegations were never acted upon, and cops continued to shake down the vulnerable community.

Over the span of a few years, hundreds of Chinese men were arrested on gambling charges. Dozens eventually hired attorneys to fight the accusations and object to the obvious targeting of Asians, while other groups, including Irish, Italian, and native-born whites, ran saloons where games such as bunco and poker were played in the open. Few white men ever went to jail or were deported for vice crimes, whereas the Chinese were under constant threat of arrest and removal.[4] But in 1909 multiple Oakland patrolmen were fired for extorting the owners of cafés where Chinese men played fan-tan, a game similar to roulette.[5] Occasional revelations of police abuses and discipline meted out in particularly glaring cases of Oakland police bribery and extortion signaled a deeper rot.

By 1914, Heney was warning East Bay residents of Oakland's "honeycombed" graft, a system of payoffs with police at the center. One November evening, the special prosecutor told a rapt audience of five thousand gathered in the Piedmont Pavilion near Lake Merritt that San Francisco's gamblers had simply relocated to Oakland after that city's famous corruption trials two years before. Now they were operating out of nightclubs on Broadway in full view of Chief Walter Petersen and District Attorney William Hynes. To keep up appearances, local authorities would authorize an occasional raid but otherwise left the gambling industry largely untouched. Captain Charles Bock, Heney claimed, was a frequent guest at a particularly notorious Broadway saloon, and other officers were seen partaking in vice. A newspaper reporter who witnessed the accusatory speech wrote that Chief Petersen, who was in attendance, "grinned sardonically" from the back of the crowd as the payoff system was exposed.[6]

Five years later, Hynes's successor, Ezra Decoto Jr., indicted Petersen's replacement, Chief John Nedderman, on fourteen counts of extortion. Nedderman resigned, while Decoto and former chief Petersen—who had been demoted to the rank of captain after an election put his opponents in charge of the city council—finally built a significant case against police corruption.

In a mere fourteen months as chief, Nedderman allegedly amassed a small fortune in bribes, part of the monthly sum that was extracted by the police, primarily from Oakland's Chinatown. Gee Sam Kee, a Chinese businessman who owned eight Oakland nightclubs, testified that the police racket was imposed upon him first by a gambler and intermediary for the police named David Cockrell. In order to keep the clubs open, Cockrell told Kee, he'd have to pay "the head man at the city hall." Kee paid until late 1918, when OPD captain Thorvald Brown sent a squad to raid one of his establishments. The intrusion, Kee told a jury, was a message that the OPD's price of "protection" was being upped from $40 to $100 per club.[7]

Nedderman faced several trials, but Decoto, citing the impossibility of impaneling a "jury sufficiently free from misguided sympathy and self-interest," failed to win a conviction. Nedderman eventually won his job back at the rank of sergeant, and Oakland's carousel of corruption took another turn.

In the meantime, the on-and-off-again police chief Walter Petersen was again accused of associating with gamblers, as his political foes sought to drive him from office. The county grand jury, which had been investigating the city's landscape of graft for years, reported in 1917 that police were permitting gambling and prostitution in a half dozen saloons and clubs frequented by white men, including police officers, all of them owned or mortgaged to local crime boss Jack Woolley. The grand jury also uncovered a bizarre stock scheme in which Captain Thorvald Brown and an OPD corporal sold stocks in a land development company to gambling house operators, sex workers, and other underworld figures.[8]

The blur of graft accusations signified how complicit many of the city's officials were in on OPD's thriving rackets: patrolmen relied on the patronage of their sergeants for cushy assignments, and lucrative payoffs from saloons and club operators lined the pockets of sworn officers.

———

Oakland's saga of flagrant corruption, watched over by authorities who seemed indifferent or incapable of stopping it, helped give rise to the Ku Klux Klan in Northern California. The Klan had a substantial chapter in

Oakland, setting up a downtown storefront office in 1921 and hosting huge rallies at the Oakland Civic Auditorium by Lake Merritt. More than eight thousand people attended one such gathering in 1925 to watch white-robed Klansmen burn crosses.[9] That same year, two thousand hooded Klansmen in full regalia massed around a ten-foot-tall burning cross that lit the night sky a terrifying orange at an admission ceremony for five hundred new members in the Oakland Hills.[10] The ceremony's location, a remote canyon northeast of downtown, was an indicator of Oakland's emerging racial and class geography. Conservative, Protestant, native-born whites were a fast-growing demographic, and they viewed the city's ethnic communities—Italians, Greeks, Portuguese, Catholics, Jews—as their enemies. New housing tracts were being built in the hills and East Oakland. It was in these areas, far from the multiethnic hubbub of downtown and West Oakland, where the white middle class settled. Although the city's political landscape would change significantly in the coming decades, the racial and class delineations—with Oakland's white conservatives flocking to new hills neighborhoods—became a lasting feature.

In the South, during Reconstruction, the Klan terrorized Black people and white Republicans who supported the expansion of democracy. But the KKK that rose to prominence in Oakland and the West in the early twentieth century was a different beast. Although its members were white supremacists, this Klan was focused more on the "purification" of America by attacking immigrants, particularly Catholics and Jews. It waged a holy war against perceived immoralities such as alcohol, gambling, and sex work. Black people weren't the focus of the California Klan, partly because the Black population was still minuscule.

In 1922, to press their case against vice, Klan members sent Oakland's public safety commissioner as well as District Attorney Decoto letters warning of a "moral crusade" against bootleggers, saloons, and gambling houses.[11] Vigilante violence was more than implicit in their communiqués. Across America, Klansmen were assaulting public officials and private citizens who did not accede to their demands.

Oakland's police chief, James Drew, appointed in 1921, denounced the Klan as un-American and said the group "should not be permitted to exist" because of its racism. But the East Bay KKK's members included perhaps as many as thirty Oakland police officers. Even high-ranking law enforcement officials in the region, such as Piedmont police chief and future Alameda

County sheriff Burton Becker, wore the Klan's white robes. Becker had lied by speaking out against the KKK alongside Chief Drew. In actuality, he was a sworn adherent of the organization's violent creed.[12] Up and down California, law enforcement enthusiastically joined the KKK. Nathan Baker, the Klan's California recruiter (a kleagle, in KKK parlance), was a Los Angeles County deputy sheriff who personally recruited many prominent public officials. Louis Oaks, who ran the Los Angeles Police Department in the early 1920s, was also an open Klan member.[13]

One official who was not a Klansman, Los Angeles district attorney Thomas Woolwine, raided the terrorist group's offices in 1922 following deadly KKK attacks against Mexican "bootleggers." Woolwine's men confiscated membership lists, then leaked the identity of Klansmen to the press and in letters to mayors and police chiefs to encourage a crackdown. This meant confronting some of California's most powerful law enforcement leaders. Among the Klan's members were Sheriff William Traeger of Los Angeles County, LAPD chief Oaks and at least a hundred of his officers, Bakersfield's police chief, Charles Stone, and a Kern County judge. At least twenty-five San Francisco police officers were known Klansmen, as well as seven Fresno police officers, seven Sacramento deputy sheriffs, and three Kern County deputy sheriffs.

The Klan made a point of recruiting police officers. In many cities, the "invisible empire," as the KKK branded itself, set up terror cells initially by recruiting cops. The police chief in Long Beach, California, Benjamin McLendon, warned his officers in a 1922 bulletin of the Klan's "sinister motives in seeking peace officers as a nucleus of each newly organized lodge," which was "for no purpose other than to shield violence, un-American and unlawful acts."[14]

Perhaps the involvement of so many police officers—in addition to doctors, attorneys, and businessmen—with the Klan explained Bay Area law enforcement's initial reluctance to pursue the vigilante group. In 1922 DA Ezra Decoto declared membership in the Klan was "no crime." He said there would be no effort by his office to prosecute the terror group.[15]

Many of the Oakland KKK's goals were adopted by local government and the white middle class from which the Klan drew its night rider membership. The Klan's thirstful hatred of Oakland's old ethnic political class, with its relative tolerance for immigrants, was slaked in the late 1920s as the machine unraveled and was replaced by a Progressive movement–era city administration and civil service. While the group's dream of eradicating Catholics, Jews, and anyone partaking in the vices of alcohol and gambling from public life in California would not be achieved, the Klan's crusade against corruption and vice was advanced by Alameda County law enforcement leaders and another rising political faction: Oakland's downtown business elite.

––––––––––

From 1925 to 1939, a young, energetic district attorney determined to clean up municipal government successfully transformed policing in Alameda County, sweeping away the patronage system and culture of graft. Born in Los Angeles, raised in Bakersfield, and educated at UC Berkeley, Earl Warren would become a towering figure in American law enforcement and politics. But in his early years, Warren was an outsider to Oakland's complex political machine. He settled in the city intent on practicing law on his own, but he took a job in the DA's office and eventually decided to make a career of it.

As an assistant district attorney, Warren caught the attention of Oakland's downtown business leaders, including Joseph "J. R." Knowland, the publisher of the *Oakland Tribune* newspaper and the son of Joseph Knowland Sr., a forty-niner (i.e., a Californian who migrated west with the gold rush of 1849) who gave up prospecting and made a fortune in the lumber industry. Knowland Senior's fortune grew with investments in banking, mining, manufacturing, and East Bay public utilities. By the time J. R. Knowland purchased a controlling interest in the *Tribune* in 1915, the family was synonymous with the conservative faction of the Republican Party in Northern California. Knowland and Oakland's business magnates took advantage of the collapse of the city's polyglot ethnic machine to exert their control over city and county government, including law enforcement.

With the support of the Knowland circle, Earl Warren waged a fourteen-year battle against corruption and vice. Most famously, he crushed bootlegging operations in Emeryville, a tiny city bordering Oakland, where a horse-racing track anchored a red-light district and a cluster of mob-affiliated speakeasies. In 1924, with Prohibition in effect, a federal agent said that his men had received no cooperation from Emeryville's notoriously corrupt police to enforce anti-liquor laws. Warren labeled the city "the rottenest spot on the entire Pacific coast, if not the entire country," adding, "Alameda County would be a decent county if we could get rid of Emeryville."[16]

Building on this success, in 1931 Warren uncovered what he described as a "colossal" bribery ring in the Oakland Police Department. Utilizing the services of federal agents who spent months burrowing their way into the city's criminal underworld, he revealed that as many as 150 cops were providing paid protection to local bootleggers. The scheme netted more than $3 million over four years, an immense sum equivalent to more than $50 million today. One officer was accused of buying a house, a luxury car, and a yacht with his spoils. Another deposited $20,000 into a bank account in a relative's name. Others were raking in as much as $1,000 a month in pay-offs.[17] Oakland cops were skimming so much of the lucrative alcohol trade's profits that local bootleggers formed a Bootleggers' Protective Association to collectively resist the extortion.

"I doubt whether there is any 'czar' in charge of graft collections," Warren said of the OPD's protection scheme. It was the department's culture to accept bribes or to look the other way, and the DA judged that "it seems to be handled by individual officers or small groups in each district, without any special organization or 'higher-up' to direct operations."

In fact, there *were* higher-ups directing corruption in the East Bay. Warren eventually found their leader in Burton Becker. Despite railing against the corruption of Oakland's old ethnic political machine, the Klansman and county sheriff benefited from the graft. He installed an undersheriff, fellow KKK member William Parker, to sit on Oakland's road commission and ensure that the two men could profit from the city's lucrative paving contracts. Becker and his deputies, along with police officers in Emeryville, Oakland, and other neighboring cities, also allowed gambling at clubs that paid protection fees. Gamblers received tips on impending raids or were entirely spared the nuisance of having to hide craps games and slot machines; Becker's office ignored hundreds of search warrants issued by the district attorney and judges.[18]

For three years, Warren hammered away at Becker through the county grand jury by calling witnesses who described the sheriff's protection racket. Newspapers ran photos of county inspectors busting gambling halls and posing with confiscated roulette wheels linked to the sheriff. In 1930 Warren indicted Becker and three of his deputies on charges of conspiracy and soliciting bribes. A jury convicted all four, landing them in San Quentin State Prison.

Warren's toppling Burton Becker and other local graft prosecutions in the 1920s and 1930s had a lasting effect on police culture in Alameda

County. The Progressive movement's goals of professionalizing law enforcement and rooting out avarice from public office advanced further in California than in other parts of the nation. Although smaller corruption scandals would crop up periodically in Oakland and elsewhere, the East Bay became something of an outlier, especially compared with eastern cities. Protection rackets, extortion, and bribery became uncommon.

But as police graft in Oakland and the rest of California waned, another violent creed took hold. From the 1940s on, overtly hostile racism became one of the dominant features of Bay Area law enforcement, after Black people arrived in large numbers during World War II. Such bigotry wasn't viewed as aberrant but rather was tolerated by the district attorney, mayor, city council, state officials, and much of the region's white population. The downtown business elite, including the Knowlands, viewed police repression of Black people as normal and necessary, given what they imagined were the Black working class's natural tendencies toward vice and crime.

This acceptance of racial violence would piggyback onto a police force with a deeply reactionary worldview shaped by a long war against the American labor movement and other political radicals.

———

From its earliest days, West Coast law enforcement worked hand in glove with business interests during labor conflicts. Repeated clashes from the late nineteenth century through the 1940s saw attempts to organize California's major industries, including the railroads, ports, shipping, canneries, factories, and fields. Police were used to break through picket lines, neutralizing labor's ability to take industrial action. During the heyday of the Industrial Workers of the World (IWW), a radical wing of the labor movement that sought to organize California's logging and construction camps, farms, and industrial plants, police did far more than crack skulls: they set up special intelligence units to spy on labor leaders. Police across the nation carried out coordinated raids on "Wobbly" offices and looked the other way while vigilantes assaulted strikers and organizers.

Law enforcement's alliance with business went all the way to the top: prosecutors in Los Angeles, San Francisco, Sacramento, and Alameda Counties enthusiastically used anti-labor laws to imprison working-class leaders and chill the speech of labor's allies. Nowhere was the law enforcement war against labor more apparent than in LA, where the city's Merchants and Manufacturers Association and *Los Angeles Times* owner, Harry Chandler, used the LAPD to wage a scorched-earth campaign against unions.[19] Chicago and New York City police also dispatched large, well-resourced intelligence units to spy on unions and any other "subversive" threats to the status quo.

The Oakland police were no different. A "Loyalty Squad" was established during World War I to investigate potential terrorists and saboteurs who sought to undermine the war effort. Like anti-Socialist/Communist Red Squads in other cities, Oakland's went after anyone who criticized the war or advocated for a more strident labor movement.

California lawmakers passed the Criminal Syndicalism Act in 1919, which outlawed "acts of force and violence or unlawful methods of terrorism as a means of accomplishing a change in industrial ownership or control, or effecting any political change." The law also made it a crime to espouse revolution by these means. The Syndicalism Act, which wouldn't be ruled unconstitutional for more than forty years, was one of dozens of similar bills passed in other states with the purpose of wiping out the IWW and policing other radical ideas out of existence.

The OPD's Loyalty Squad, led by Inspector Fenton Thompson, who joined the force in 1903, was ordered by Chief Petersen to carry out an "IWW cleanup in Oakland." One of Thompson's first actions was to raid the group's local headquarters. After ransacking the offices, he arrested James McHugo, the Wobblies' local secretary. McHugo's subsequent trial, the first under the new anti-syndicalism law, was watched closely by police and prosecutors throughout California, as well as by labor movement leaders, who feared its outcome. Featured as evidence were pamphlets and items taken during the raid, such as activist Elizabeth Gurley Flynn's book *Sabotage: The Conscious Withdrawal of the Workers' Industrial Efficiency*, political stickers and buttons, and a wooden shoe that hung on the wall near McHugo's desk.[20] Sentenced to fourteen years in San Quentin, McHugo said in court that his conscience was clear: "My fight has been for the workers."[21]

The McHugo case showcased the efficacy of the criminal syndicalism law as a potent weapon against radicals. Soon police throughout California would use it to dismantle leftist unions and political groups. In Oakland, this campaign was heartily endorsed by the Bay Area's biggest employers and all the major newspapers.

One paper that did not endorse the crackdown was the *World*, a daily of the Socialist Party, which by 1919 had become Oakland's branch of the

Communist Workers Party. The *World* catered to recent immigrants from central, eastern, and southern Europe.

The Oakland police raided the *World*'s offices in November 1919, arresting publisher John Snyder for syndicalism. Snyder attempted to restart printing while out on bond, but members of the American Legion, with tacit approval from Oakland's highest officials (OPD chief Petersen himself was a Legionnaire), threatened to destroy the press. Just the week before, the Legion, a veterans' organization founded with xenophobic and anti-Communist views, stormed Loring Hall in downtown Oakland, where several German immigrant aid societies and the Communist Workers Party leased space alongside Snyder's newspaper. The Legion, which claimed many Oakland cops as members, would offer its services repeatedly to the police as an extralegal shock force.[22]

"I am of the opinion that the American Legion boys were thinking that they were doing justice," said Oakland council member and commissioner of public safety Fred Morse, dismissing complaints about the Loring Hall attack. "As yet I have no reason to say whether they were or not."[23]

That same month, the OPD carried out its own raid of the Communist Workers Party's headquarters in Loring Hall, carting away all of the organization's literature and files and confiscating membership rosters and other records.

Within a few weeks, Snyder was indicted in state court on syndicalism charges, and by the US attorney under the Espionage Act of 1917, which criminalized opposing the American war effort and established a censorship regime for news publications. Nine members of the jury that would convict Snyder of criminal syndicalism were members of the Oakland Chamber of Commerce. Seldom would the collusion between police and business in Oakland be so blatant.

At the same time, District Attorney Decoto, Earl Warren's predecessor and friend, impaneled a grand jury with the goal of obtaining at least a half dozen indictments under the Criminal Syndicalism Act. On January 2, 1920, Decoto indicted nine other Oaklanders for syndicalism based on their membership in the Communist Party, their distribution of political literature, and for an alleged act of provocation: *draping* a red flag over the Stars and Stripes during a meeting. (One witness would later say it was a provocateur from the OPD's Loyalty Squad who draped the flag to frame the group.)[24]

Dozens of Oakland residents were arrested and tried in 1919 and 1920 under the syndicalism statute and sentenced to San Quentin.

Finally, on the night of January 3, 1920, the police orchestrated a massive raid to arrest twenty alleged Communists, most of them immigrants, and sent them to a detention camp for eventual deportation. It was all part of the notorious Palmer Raids, a coordinated national crackdown involving police in forty cities. More than 4,500 accused radicals were jailed. The Loyalty Squad was praised by the *Oakland Tribune* and the *San Francisco Examiner* newspapers for giving the US Justice Department a long list of names obtained during the Loring Hall raid in 1919 that helped identify subversives across the nation.[25]

California law enforcement agencies succeeded in putting labor on the defensive. By the late 1920s, the IWW was no longer a factor in the Bay Area. But the turmoil of the Great Depression touched off an unprecedented wave of strikes. In Oakland, the police responded again with force. On May 1, 1930, fifty Oakland police officers assaulted a gathering of unionists and Communists hoping to celebrate May Day and march in support of programs that would later become part of the New Deal. The police sent ten demonstrators to the hospital with concussions. One OPD officer revved his motorcycle engine to drown out a woman delivering a speech about workers' rights.[26] The next year, Police Chief James Drew prohibited any marches of "Reds."

In 1934, Oakland workers joined the masses of dockyard laborers in San Francisco, who led a historic waterfront strike up and down the West Coast that crippled the shipping industry. More than twenty thousand East Bay workers walked off their jobs, halting the region's streetcar system and shuttering factories, restaurants, and shops. During the strike's peak, police raided union offices, where alleged Communists were rumored to be plotting radical actions. The cops smashed equipment and destroyed files, while members of the conservative teamsters union were allowed to attack strikers on the street under police protection, fulfilling the same auxiliary role as the American Legion decades earlier.[27]

Waterfront unions prevailed in the 1934 strike, and President Franklin D. Roosevelt's New Deal tempered some of the reactionary vitriol toward organized labor. Unions were finally legitimized as vehicles for working-class prosperity. However, the OPD continued to gather intelligence on those it branded as Communists or radicals. East Bay law enforcement still went after workers who threatened to seriously change the local balance of power.

Two years after the West Coast dock strike, Alameda district attorney Earl Warren made an example of three influential labor leaders after an anti-union chief engineer was found murdered on a ship. Arrested on the questionable testimony of informants was Earl King, secretary of the powerful Marine Firemen, Oilers, Water Tenders, and Wipers Union. King was viewed as the second most important organizer on the Bay Area's waterfront after Harry Bridges, who led the 1934 waterfront strike. Warren and his prosecutors threw themselves at the case. King and three other defendants were convicted and sentenced to five years to life. The case transformed Warren into the highest-profile law enforcement figure in California and positioned Alameda County as the tip of the law enforcement spear against so-called Communist forces.[28]

When World War II broke out in Europe, the global tensions between Socialism and Fascism rippled through Oakland, with many workers rallying in solidarity with the Soviet Union against Nazi Germany's aggression. One such workers' rally in July 1941 was broken up by sailors and army privates at the behest of the police. According to a leader of the culinary union who organized the street corner protest, Oakland police officers "went to taverns and got together servicemen to break up the Reds meeting." One sergeant assaulted several unionists.[29]

Even after the Japanese attack on Pearl Harbor catapulted the United States into a two-front war against not only Japan but also the Fascist powers of Germany and Italy—and even though the Soviet Union had suddenly become a vital ally—the federal government intensified its war against Communism at home, sweeping up dissenters of all stripes.

Warren, who did so much to crack down on police corruption in Oakland and the East Bay, was one of the architects of the Bay Area's police spying programs. In the 1930s he had drawn on FBI director J. Edgar Hoover's assistance in establishing the Anti-Racket Council to target organized crime, providing the FBI access to the Alameda County district attorney's extensive files on "radicals" and "subversives"—mostly labor leaders, but also anyone branded either an anarchist or a Communist. During World War II, the list of subversives grew to include those who spoke out for the rights of the Bay Area's Black, Chinese, and other nonwhite residents.[30] Much of the intelligence in these files was gathered by Oakland cops, in addition to Warren's inspectors from his office's Political Intelligence Unit, which was among the oldest and most aggressive spying operations in California—no mean feat, given the reactionary nature of contemporaneous Los Angeles authorities.[31]

The Cold War reinvigorated US law enforcement's antisubversive mission, but this time the Oakland police would be enlisted by conservative business interests not just to put down union agitators but also to respond with violence to the new political reality created by the migration of millions of Black Americans from the South.

––––––––

Oakland's racial composition changed remarkably during the Second World War.[32] Between 1940 and 1950, its Black population mushroomed from just over eight thousand to forty-two thousand. These new migrants were met by a predominantly white city that had fought for nearly a century to shut the door on Asian immigration and tamp down its working class.

Black people discovered all too quickly that, in many respects, California resembled the Jim Crow South they had fled. "There's very little difference between the segregation here in California and the blatant things that go on in the South," one Black resident told an interviewer in the 1940s. Complaints of police brutality, racism, employment discrimination, and segregation in public accommodations were rife.[33]

Suddenly, with intense purpose, the Oakland Police Department adopted a new mission: enforcing white supremacy against Black people. Black Oaklanders and their allies in the radical wing of California's labor movement wasted no time in pushing back against both the cops' attack-dog tactics and the tolerance that city leaders and wealthy industrialists showed for police violence. The response from the establishment was to denounce anyone aiding Black people in their freedom struggle as a Red. The region's mainstream media and political class portrayed white radical solidarity with Black people as a treasonous plot to weaken the United States in the early days of the Cold War.

This Far Right worldview, which saw Blacks, labor unions, and radicals as existential threats to the American way of life, was embraced by Oakland's cops—who, in turn, saw themselves as righteous defenders of the nation against subversive elements. This would become a foundational component of the Oakland Police Department's internal culture as it headed into the turbulent 1960s and a virtual war against the Black Panther Party and student antiwar protesters. But before it animated the political battles of the 1960s, the OPD's reactionary tradition justified the brutality and indifference that its cops showed Oakland's Black community in the postwar years.

English journalist Jessica Mitford and her husband, attorney Robert Treuhaft, moved to Oakland in 1947 and plunged into the city's restive atmosphere. Mitford described Oakland as a place where the local Communist Party chapter was predominantly Black, led by a Spanish Civil War veteran, and "there was nothing abstract about the class struggle." The city "seemed a microcosm of some Alabama or Louisiana town, replete with white prejudice in its most savage form."[34]

During the first week of June 1947, West Oaklanders were handed fliers on street corners that read: "Attention, citizens, do you know what is happening in our community? Do you know that the police are beating and arresting people of our community—because they are Negroes???"

The fliers, by now making a familiar appeal against police racism, encouraged people to attend the next city council meeting to "demand the city start a course in race relations for all police officers." On June 5 about fifty people appeared in Oakland City Hall. Among them was a Black former shipyard worker named Raymond Thompson. He led the local chapter of the National Negro Council, a group that sought to unite the Black civil rights movement with the labor movement. The organization's local chapter had also recently set up the Committee Against Police Brutality, one of the first Black-led groups of its kind in the nation.[35]

Thompson, a well-known activist who led protests in 1945 against white-dominated unions over racial equality, implored Oakland's legislators to address numerous complaints of bigoted police brutality. At the city council meeting, he singled out one recent incident to make his case. A week before, Mrs. Ceda Cowan, a Black woman, was violently arrested—dragged in the street and her blouse torn, by one account—by an OPD officer after she complained about a traffic ticket her brother was being given. Another account indicated Cowan also tossed cherry pits at a cop. Officer Lloyd Hunt's version of events was printed several times in local papers, casting Cowan as the aggressor and Hunt as a patient, gentle traffic cop. But Cowan and Thompson said the humiliating arrest was only the latest outrage by an unaccountable police force. The incident nearly triggered a riot as Black people gathered around the six-foot-tall, heavyset police officer and the diminutive Cowan, who was screaming.

Next-day newspaper reports of the council meeting in the *Tribune* and the *Examiner* told straight accounts of what appeared to be racially motivated police brutality. But subsequent coverage in both papers alleged that sinister "Communists" were behind the allegations in an effort to weaken law and order in Oakland. As the Black-owned *California Eagle* newspaper of Los Angeles observed, "in the second editions, an alleged case of brutality became within the short space of a few hours 'a routine incident.'"[36]

Rather than investigate Officer Hunt's actions, Alameda County district attorney Ralph Hoyt—Warren's number two, who took over after the future chief justice of the US Supreme Court became state attorney general—investigated Thompson. In what appeared to be information delivered to the DA's office straight from Hoover's FBI, Thompson was charged with five counts of voter fraud for participating in local elections after an alleged felony conviction twenty years prior when he was a young man. One week after the city council meeting, the *Oakland Tribune* published a raft of other allegations sullying Thompson's character, including records claiming he'd been jailed in four other states and that he'd declared membership in a Communist group when applying for a shipbuilding job at West Oakland's Moore Dry Dock Company in 1941.[37]

By 1949, Police Chief Robert Tracy was viewing any criticism of his men for beating up Black people as part of a "Communist plot to discredit and harass the OPD." An *Oakland Tribune* editorial relayed Chief Tracy's paranoid claims:

"Tracy maintains that he has evidence Communist agents have contacted persons involved in police troubles. Most of them have no complaints and just want to forget their stray off the straight and narrow path. But some are susceptible, are swayed by Communists' claims of an interest in the 'downtrodden.' They were the ones who allow themselves to be used in trumped-up charges of police brutality."[38]

East Bay activists pressed the city to examine the police department's treatment of Blacks. Reluctantly, council members referred the problem to the mayor's civic unity panel for recommendations about bridging the growing divide between cops and community. One white panel member, civil rights and defense attorney Bertram Edises, told city leaders that evidence of police brutality and racism was apparent. "I cannot but believe that some of the attitude of the Deep South has seeped into the department,"

Edises said. "The [police officers] arrogate to themselves a judicial function, and I think it starts at the top."[39]

The panel's damning report in June 1949 met a predictable fate: Oakland's elected officials took no action.[40]

Following several other controversial arrests and beatings and lawsuits,
the multiracial Civil Rights Congress (CRC) and the National Association
for the Advancement of Colored People (NAACP)—with the support of the
International Longshore and Warehouse Union (ILWU), white radicals, and
progressive Black ministers—asked Los Angeles assemblyman Vernon Kilpatrick to open a state investigation. It is one of the earliest examples of outside
oversight hearings on law enforcement in the United States.[41] Robert B. Powers, a former Bakersfield chief of police who had unsuccessfully investigated
the 1938 murder of Earl Warren's father and was recruited to state services as
Warren's statewide coordinator of law enforcement in 1944, was appointed by
California attorney general Bob Kenny (by this point, Warren was governor)
to oversee the state's examination of Oakland police complaints in 1949.

A key investigative source for Powers was the investigations and lawsuits
that the Civil Rights Congress had filed in recent years against the OPD.

"They became aware of extreme police brutality," Powers said about the
CRC, "and I don't use the word lightly: I mean murders, beating a man until
he had ruptured kidneys because he was Negro, locking people up who
were never heard from again."[42]

Working alone, Powers dug into the allegations, but was met with blan-
ket obstruction from police and the city administration. "I couldn't have
gotten near a police record," he said. "I found the mayor [Clifford Rishell]
particularly to be the most bigoted racist that I'd ever seen. The city manager [John Hassler] wasn't going to drop out from behind his police chief.
The police chief [Lester Divine] was beginning to hate my guts."[43]

With the assistance of Treuhaft and Mitford, labor leaders such as C. L.
Dellums, an organizer with the Brotherhood of Sleeping Car Porters, and
local clergy, Powers located relevant documents and interviewed reluctant
witnesses. He was convinced that the allegations about the OPD's "sadistic"
practices were all true, and that they were a result of policy decisions from
on high.

At the time, the CRC was the largest civil libertarian group in the East
Bay: five hundred members strong, predominantly Black, and ten times
larger than the local NAACP chapter. Mitford and her husband—the John

Burris and Jim Chanin of their day with respect to how they used the legal system—were deeply involved in the organization's initial investigations into the OPD's abuses, which prompted the initial city council inquiry.

Mitford wrote in her memoirs: "I found it hard to describe adequately the sense of monstrous beastliness, authority clothed in nighttime garb, that our investigations disclosed. We discovered that on Fridays, pay day for most workers, police would regularly lie in wait outside the West Oakland bars which served as banks for the cashing of paychecks, arrest those emerging on charges of drunkenness, and in the privacy of the prowl cars en route to the West Oakland police station, beat them and rob them of their week's pay."[44]

Over three days in January 1950, in the Alameda County Courthouse, the Assembly Interim Committee on Crime and Corrections, led by Assemblyman Kilpatrick, heard testimony from dozens of people about their mistreatment by Oakland cops.[45]

The key incidents at the heart of the hearings were the April 1949 shooting of unarmed Andrew Lee Hines by Officer Spencer Amundsen; the station house beating of George B. McDaniel by Inspector Charles Wood, when McDaniel walked in to report a robbery; the beating of Melvin Cunningham by two cops that left him with a ruptured bladder; and a New Year's Eve incident where a cop smashed a wine bottle into the face of amateur boxer Johnny Ortega, sending him to the hospital.[46]

Hines's killing took place on April 17, 1949, while Oakland was conducting its initial review into police violence. According to contemporaneous news reports, Hines was standing outside his rooming house shortly after midnight when he caught Amundsen's attention. The cop claimed later that Hines, a cannery worker, appeared suspicious. Amundsen forced the man into the rooming house at gunpoint and began to interrogate him in front of three witnesses. At one point, Hines's hands may have dropped; Amundsen fatally shot him through the heart. The officer would say later that he thought the victim was reaching for a gun and that he was aiming at his arm. Inspector Howard Sorrells determined that Amundsen's actions were reasonable, and the officer returned to duty even though a separate inquiry by the Oakland City Council found that he had "shot prematurely."[47]

In his remarks at the hearing, attended by an overwhelmingly African

American crowd of two hundred, C. L. Dellums condemned the OPD's "lawlessness of the law," and explained that in Oakland, "generally, Negroes regard the police as their natural enemies."[48]

Bertram Edises told the committee, "Oakland has the second largest Negro population west of the Mississippi. Yet the Negro citizens of Oakland live in daily and nightly terror of the Oakland Police Department." He dismissed the US attorney general's designation of the Civil Rights Congress as a "subversive organization," calling the label an "old red herring" used to obscure egregious abuses and discrimination. "The important thing is to end police brutality in Oakland," Edises said.[49]

City Manager John Hassler, Mayor Clifford Rishell, OPD chief Lester Divine, and multiple officers also testified. To a man, they denied the allegations put to them. Although Divine admitted he had never suspended an officer for using excessive force during his entire tenure, he defended the department's practices wholeheartedly, even the "custom" of illegally booking suspects for seventy-two hours without charge. "I would say the character of the Oakland force compares favorably with that of any police department in the country," Divine told the state lawmakers.[50] His agency was "as clean as a hound's tooth."[51]

San Francisco Chronicle reporter Robert de Roos, sitting among the spectators, noted the instantaneous reaction to the chief's comments. "Thereupon there was laughter from the audience of about 100 people, about half Negroes," he wrote.[52]

For attempting to conduct an evenhanded and clear-eyed examination of the Oakland PD, Powers himself was branded a Communist by the American Legion in the organization's magazine. Two decades later, the former police chief and respected special investigator paid tribute to the work of Mitford, Treuhaft, Edises, and the rest of the Civil Rights Congress. "Thank God for the Communists when you're in a pinch," he recalled in an interview with UC Berkeley historians. "They sure don't scare easy."

But the Oakland investigation left Powers "sick spiritually." He would later tell interviewers that he "had plumbed the depths of degradation" while examining the abuses of the Oakland police.

Despite the furor, the OPD remained unchanged after the Kilpatrick Committee hearings. Minor adjustments were made in response to discrimination claims, but no one in the city's government admitted to the department's institutionalized racism.[53]

In 1955 Chief Divine stepped down to be replaced by Wyman Vernon, the former head of the department's traffic division, who held a degree in business administration from UC Berkeley. While still a lieutenant, Vernon took a leave of absence and was appointed acting police chief in Richmond in order to reorganize that agency amidst a top-to-bottom corruption scandal. Vernon restructured the OPD similarly, adopting the LAPD's full-time Internal Affairs structure to ensure more professional investigations and placing the IA unit outside the regular chain of command to allow for more independence. A ballot initiative also created three deputy chief positions to oversee the bureaus of investigation, patrol, and administration. For the first time, records were systematically kept. Precinct houses were eliminated to centralize patrol operations and address the payoff corruption rife among beat cops.[54]

While Vernon did professionalize the OPD and crack down on the most flagrant instances of misconduct (sixteen officers quit or were terminated during his first year in charge), some graft persisted. More tellingly, institutional racism and overt bigotry continued to fester. Gwynne Peirson, a former Tuskegee Airman turned police officer, was one of fewer than twenty Black cops out of six hundred men on the force in the mid-1950s. African Americans were routinely denied promotion, verbally abused by their white coworkers, and, as Peirson viewed it, generally used as a public relations front.

"The primary purpose for hiring Blacks as police officers was to soothe the feelings of groups who were pressing for full integration," he wrote in his UC Berkeley sociology dissertation decades later.[55]

While Vernon did make an effort to hold Oakland police accountable to the law, other elements of the criminal justice system were reluctant to follow suit. Officers convicted of theft and extortion during the mid-1950s had their offenses downgraded from felonies to misdemeanors. Sympathetic judges converted their prison sentences to probation or time served.[56] This pattern of leniency for police facing criminal allegations would be a feature of the Alameda County courts for decades to come.

Incremental progress toward professionalization dissipated upon Vernon's retirement in 1959. His successor, Deputy Chief Edward Toothman, comported himself in a "paternalistic" fashion, ensuring that a Black officer was alongside him whenever he interacted with Oakland's African American communities. But within the OPD, there was no progress whatsoever on racial bias or equitable treatment and promotions for Black cops. Racist leaflets and fliers circulated widely throughout its ranks, reappearing even after the brass issued cautionary departmentwide bulletins.[57] According to Peirson, new Black officers learned instantly "that institutional racism was a functional part of the police department."[58]

Chief Toothman, a conservative with a reactionary streak, also set in motion a chain of events that would have dramatic repercussions in Oakland and beyond: he placed a small study group of Black radical students at Merritt College in North Oakland under heavy surveillance after they began handing out fliers and conducting their own traffic patrols at intersections where children had been struck by speeding drivers.[59] Spying on the group was perfectly in line with the practices handed down since the early 1900s, when Oakland cops and prosecutors gathered intelligence on other radical groups suspected of upsetting the social order.

Over time, these Black activists would start free breakfast programs and health clinics in Oakland's ghettos, and publish a nationally distributed radical newspaper. They also began conducting their own armed patrols, confronting policemen they believed to be harassing African Americans. Toothman grew so concerned about the group that he created a special radio code to inform the entire force whenever one of its members had been pulled over. The department quickly compiled a list of all suspected members that was distributed to every Oakland cop.

This was the Black Panther Party for Self-Defense.

6

NOTHING WILL GET DONE UNTIL OAKLAND BURNS TO THE GROUND

It made sense that a pair of students founded Oakland's Black Panther Party. The city was a center for youth activism, first coalescing around struggles over integration of local high schools, then eventually erupting against police violence.[1]

The 1959 construction of Skyline High School, zoned so that only residents of the predominantly white and wealthy hills neighborhoods could enroll their children there, was a flashpoint in debates over segregation. When it opened in 1961, Skyline had no Black students. At the same time, McClymonds High School in West Oakland was nearly 100 percent Black and hurting for resources, while Castlemont High School in Deep East Oakland had become a battleground. In the 1950s, whites made up the majority of its student body, but by 1966, Castlemont was 72 percent Black. Skyline absorbed some white pupils from these flatlands schools, but thousands of white families left Oakland entirely in the 1960s, chasing after good jobs and spacious homes in lily-white suburbs.[2]

Black parents and students protested this state of affairs. They lit up the Oakland Unified School District's phone switchboard with protest calls, asking, "Do you practice segregation?"[3] The district's all-white school board denied the obvious fact that the Black population, which had grown by a factor of ten in just twenty years, was being hemmed into ghettos and its kids shunted into subpar schools.

In 1966 two activist groups organized a school boycott to demand rapid desegregation, busing, smaller class sizes, and free school lunches:

the Oakland Direct Action Committee (ODAC), founded by an African American, Mark Comfort, and the Ad Hoc Committee for Quality Education, established by Black civil rights attorney John George. One-third of Oakland high school students participated, but the school district, city council, mayor, and county board of supervisors did their best to ignore their demands. The boycott also coincided with violent clashes between youths and police.

On the eve of the walkout, a group of Black youngsters gathered near the scene of a hit-and-run on MacArthur Boulevard. Cops ordered them to leave. Some refused. Officers roughed up and arrested seventeen-year-old Shirley Jones and her nineteen-year-old brother, William, who came to her defense. Hundreds of outraged teens took to the streets. OPD officers peppered them with shotgun blasts from afar and bludgeoned them with batons before filling wagons with arrestees. Some of the youngsters broke into Castlemont High, vandalized school buildings and surrounding commercial properties, and fought with school authorities and white students.[4]

Although the political nature of the violence was apparent, the local media portrayed the brief uprising as "roving Negro teen-age gangs" who senselessly "rampaged." School board members wondered aloud if they should ask the district attorney to prosecute the boycott leaders for instigating the riot. DA Frank Coakley said they were certainly "liable" and that youth participants should also be criminally charged. "Blatant intimidation," replied George as the boycott pressed ahead.[5]

City Manager Jerome Keithley's views represented those of most of the city's white leadership. He denied serious problems existed in the schools or that Black Oaklanders had legitimate complaints about poverty, segregation, and the routine police violence they suffered. "There has not been, as a matter of fact, any voiced discernible grievance by juveniles or others to rationalize the window breaking or other malicious lawless acts," Keithley told the press.[6]

Oakland's power structure had done its best to tune out two decades of complaints about police brutality and the city's racial caste system. They all but ignored the obvious links between the city's small-scale riot and the deadly 1965 Watts rebellion or the recent uprising in San Francisco. After San Francisco cops killed a Black teenager running from a stolen car, the Hunters Point neighborhood exploded in protest, looting, and fires. Given the intransigence of Bay Area authorities in the face of peaceful pushback to the racialized status quo, violence grew increasingly likely. The rise of the Panthers was inevitable.

The Black Panther Party's founders personified Oakland's postwar transformation. Huey Newton's father, Walter, a sharecropper and railroad brakeman who was almost lynched for talking back to his white bosses, left Louisiana during the war years for California to seek work. His family, including Huey, the youngest of seven siblings, followed during the Great Migration. Likewise, Bobby Seale's family moved west from Texas in the mid-1940s so that his father could work as a carpenter in the booming Bay Area. Young Huey and Bobby were intimately familiar with California's particular brand of white supremacy by the time they were in their late twenties and early thirties, studying at the two-year Merritt College in North Oakland's flatlands. They'd seen their parents escape Dixie, only to be immiserated in the Golden State.

The duo met in 1961 while attending a gathering of the Afro-American Association, a political group founded by a UC Berkeley Boalt Hall Law School graduate named Donald Warden, one of the Bay Area's few Black attorneys. Warden's group had a foothold on the Merritt campus, which had a sizable Black student population. Afro-American Association members studied W. E. B. Du Bois and Malcolm X and advocated a version of Black nationalism critical of the mainstream civil rights movement—specifically, its goal of integration. "Black people should uplift themselves by building their own institutions and businesses, pushing back against white racism whenever necessary," they reasoned.[7]

When Newton and Seale founded the Black Panther Party in 1966 and penned their Ten-Point Program for liberation later that year, the two drew liberally from the ideas to which Warden had introduced them, as well as the positions of Comfort and ODAC. Comfort had lived in the South and was familiar with the armed self-defense initiatives of Black people in Alabama's Lowndes County and Louisiana's rural areas. Comfort also introduced the striking iconography of the black panther to the Bay Area radical scene, a visual Newton and Seale appropriated as their group's logo.

The early Panthers members were charismatic and had deep, organic connections to Oakland's Black community, particularly the burgeoning number of youths who were eager to live free of the city's racism, which intensified in the early 1960s as the region's white majority sought to exclude the Black community from economic prosperity, pinning them inside the West Oakland ghetto.

Newton and Seale's program was different from the existing Black nationalist and civil rights movements in several key respects. Whereas civil rights leaders led methodical, elaborately planned campaigns arcing toward change, the Panthers urged immediate action to strike against white supremacy. They projected a righteous impatience. They were also armed: not to defend themselves and shoot back at Ku Klux Klan night riders, as the Lowndes County Panthers and Louisiana's Deacons for Defense and Justice had done, but to proactively go out and patrol against the Oakland police, like a federally funded program in post-Watts Los Angeles that hired ex-gang members to monitor LAPD patrols.[8]

Meeting state violence with armed self-defense was inspired by anti-imperialist thinkers such as Mao Tse-tung, leader of the People's Republic of China; the Martinique-born author and psychoanalyst Frantz Fanon; and Che Guevara, a revolutionary leader in Latin America.[9] Black Americans, the Panthers believed, were a colonized people forcefully repressed by racist, segregationist law enforcement, and it was their duty to resist by any means necessary, like the Vietcong or Algeria's National Liberation Front. Their framing of Black America as a "colony within a nation" would leave a lasting mark on leftist ideology throughout the Western world. The decision by Oakland's white political and business leaders to respond to the increasing radicalism of Black activists with a militarized crackdown that brought home many of the counterinsurgency methods employed by the Communist enemy in Vietnam would leave a lasting mark on police culture in the United States.

The Black Panther Party released its Ten-Point Program on October 15, 1966, the same week that Black students walked out of Oakland schools and fought back against the police. Along with calls for decarceration, exemption from the military draft, full employment, housing, education, food, justice, and peace, they included freedom from police brutality:

"We believe we can end police brutality in our Black community by organizing Black *self-defense* groups that are dedicated to defending our Black community from racist police oppression and brutality. The Second Amendment of the Constitution of the United States gives us a right to bear arms. We therefore believe that all Black people should arm themselves for *self-defense*."[10]

Although the Panthers' work included children's breakfast programs, community food pantries, and freedom schools, arguably their most profound impact was through confrontations with the police. The party created an image of the Black urban freedom fighter who would stop at nothing until liberated, and it changed forever how many Americans, of all races, viewed the police. Panthers popularized the epithet "pigs" for cops among young people, and Minister of Culture Emory Douglas's caricatures of snarling hogs with guns and badges spread through the party's newspaper and on posters put up by chapters throughout the country.[11]

Carloads of armed Panthers drove around Oakland's flatlands seeking confrontation with the OPD, who systematically stopped, searched, and wrote them up for minor or nonexistent infractions such as loose license plates or broken taillights. A typical interaction on one of these patrols would involve a cop asking the beret- and leather-clad militants: "What are you doing with the guns?"

"What are you doing with *your* gun?" Newton would reply, stepping out of the car with a law book in one hand and a shotgun in the other. The "minister of defense" would expound in his high-pitched voice about the procedural violations the cops had committed in conducting their traffic stop, all in front of crowds of bystanders and his compatriots recording the clash with home movie cameras or portable tape recorders. When the police would retreat, as they often did in the early days, the spectacle served as prime recruiting material for restive Black youth.[12]

Oakland's political class was never going to accommodate the Black Panther Party. They were a cosseted, conservative Anglo upper crust from the verdant hills neighborhoods and the wealthy enclave of Piedmont—the self-proclaimed "city of millionaires"—purposefully carved out of its larger, more diverse neighbor. These men had one overarching goal: to revive Oakland's economic fortunes by making the region as friendly to business as possible. White-dominated labor unions were begrudgingly given a place at the table. Black and Latino Oaklanders, however, had no place in this vision, and the demands of leather-clad, gun-toting radicals would be met first with contempt, then with force.

Oakland, dubbed an "All-American City" by *Look* magazine in 1955, experienced an unparalleled economic boom during and just after World

War II. But by the mid-1960s, the outmigration of industry to nonunion cities, and extreme levels of poverty in the overcrowded flatlands, characterized a city suddenly in decline. In a famous 1966 article in the seminal, stridently antiwar Leftist magazine *Ramparts*, political journalist Warren Hinckle drew a stark picture of Oakland's civic landscape: "Decisions bearing on the future of the city are made by a small group of self-elected men—leaders in industry, some politicians, labor leaders, a few civil servants, members of social and civic boards. The mass of Oakland citizens is supine, apathetic, and impotent." This wasn't hyperbole: only a quarter to a third of registered voters participated in elections.[13] Many of the city's Black, Asian, and Latino residents weren't even registered.

Not that voting mattered as much as it should have. The city was run by seven council members and a mayor who appointed the city manager—a kind of super bureaucrat who called the shots on a day-to-day basis. Council members were elected through citywide votes, purposefully diluting the electoral strength of West Oakland's Black community, Chinatown, and Fruitvale's Latinos, ensuring that representatives were pro-business and pro-police.[14] Power was concentrated in Oakland City Hall, the *Oakland Tribune* newspaper—which dominated the East Bay's media landscape—the Chamber of Commerce, and the boardrooms of a few major companies. Neighborhood councils were forbidden from making policy decisions, in what Hinckle called an "anal-retentive form of municipal management" designed to keep power in the hands of handpicked council members—many of them, as per a time-honored Alameda County tradition, appointed to their post by other council members after one would quit midterm, usually to take some higher office or return to the full-time job of managing his corporation.

The few times when politics became competitive were when one or more council members adopted a liberal position that grated against the bigotry of the city's white middle class. In 1950 three council members faced recall after approving a three-thousand-unit public housing project that would benefit labor unions and Blacks. It amounted to "Socialism" in the eyes of the *Tribune* and white property owners. One of the council members was recalled, and the other two lost their elections the following year, with candidates opposed to public housing taking all three seats.[15]

One of Oakland's most influential leaders in the 1960s was William Knowland, son of Joseph "J. R." Knowland. After representing California in the US Senate for fourteen years, he succeeded his father as publisher of the *Oakland Tribune*, the newspaper that J.R. had purchased and turned into a voice of staunch conservatism. In 1945, when Earl Warren was California governor, he appointed the younger Knowland, then thirty-seven, to a vacant US Senate seat.[16] William and Joseph served as a northern corollary to Southern California's hardcore pro-business Chandler family, which controlled the *Los Angeles Times*. The two dynasties were closely aligned, trading intelligence about their political enemies. Like the Chandlers, the Knowlands used the *Tribune* to cheerlead the real estate industry and entrench Republican dominance in local and state politics, while shielding institutions—including the Oakland Police Department—from scrutiny.[17]

The *Tribune* proved crucial for Knowland's first Senate reelection campaign. He ran on an anti-union, anti-Communist platform that tracked with the newspaper's opposition to widespread labor agitation and a general strike that tied up downtown Oakland beginning on Monday morning, December 3, 1946. The citywide industrial action was the last general strike in American history, and although it stemmed from campaigns to unionize downtown department stores Kahn's and Hastings, Oakland's strike was the last of a wave of similar actions that swept across the United States from 1945 through 1946. The OPD played a key role in breaking the two-and-a-half-day strike by sending hundreds of riot police to escort scab laborers past furious picketers and setting up machine guns in the middle of Broadway to deter resistance.[18]

Senator Knowland might have remained in Washington, and been less influential in Oakland politics, had he not launched an ill-fated campaign for governor in 1958. Ignoring his advisors, he ran on a platform of transforming California into a right-to-work state, an anti-union measure that prohibited employers and unions from requiring all employees to pay union dues. After losing, largely because of labor's fear that he'd turn the state into the Mississippi of the West (the Southern state was notorious among organized labor types as an anti-union, right-to-work bastion), Knowland moved back to Oakland permanently. He took over the helm of the family media property and also assumed leadership of the state Republican Party.[19] In the *Tribune*'s editorial pages, William encouraged his writers to relentlessly red-bait progressives who dared to challenge the local political machine, often railing against the "Communistic" influence of the Alameda County labor movement's sporadically successful electoral campaigns.[20] This paranoid view that Communists were behind everything they opposed, including the Black freedom movement, trickled down to the Oakland Police Department, where recruits tended to be conservative white men already predisposed to this kind of right-wing worldview.

John Houlihan, another member of the political machine, was Oakland's mayor from 1961 to 1966. The son of an Irish San Francisco cop, he earned a law degree and elbowed his way into the mayor's office by accusing the folksy but bland incumbent, Mayor Clifford Rishell, of failing to prevent the suburban exodus of industry.

To reinvigorate Oakland, Houlihan spearheaded construction of the city's downtown art museum, new jet-age airport runways, and the Coliseum sports complex. But reviving the breakneck economic growth of the 1940s proved elusive, while addressing the plight of the poor was even more difficult. Oakland's forty-third mayor promoted "slum clearance," but tearing down the homes of the poor merely scattered families and did little to improve their economic conditions.

Houlihan was hostile to civil rights advocates' demands and scoffed at the idea of consulting with mainstream groups such as the NAACP, the Congress of Racial Equality (CORE), and the Civil Rights Coordinating Committee (CRCC) about his considerations for board seats.[21] The mayor made a few appointments to try to mollify the Black community.[22]

The city's leaders tended to ignore or ridicule serious proposals to uplift impoverished Oaklanders. For example, in 1963 the mayor's Committee on Full Opportunity (COFO), created to address housing and job discrimination complaints, published a report by UC Berkeley sociologist Floyd Hunter that blamed extreme discrimination for locking the Black working class into a cycle of poverty. Most Oakland real estate agents and white homeowners admitted to discriminating against Black renters and home buyers. This reflected many white Californians' hostility (bankrolled by the California Real Estate Association) to integrating their neighborhoods.[23] In Oakland, the Chamber of Commerce took no position on Proposition 14, the 1964 initiative that successfully repealed the Rumford Fair Housing Act. But privately, many in the business community cheered the demise of California's fair housing statute, which had been voted into law only the year before.

When COFO members presented Hunter's report to Houlihan in 1965 and asked for action to combat housing discrimination, the mayor deflected, quipping: "Stay in business, and I'll give you the staff and money if you'll dig into San Leandro and Hayward,"[24] referring to Oakland's whiter, less union-friendly suburban neighbors to the south.

Floyd Hunter had recommended pouring $123 million into affordable housing and $80 million in income subsidies for Oakland's poor, plus no-interest loans for Black businesses and home buyers. The esteemed sociologist also advised city leaders to place less emphasis on recruiting businesses to Oakland at the cost of slum dwellers' health. "These and a number of less urgent recommendations shocked the Oakland power structure and its civic machine," a disappointed Hunter observed after his report was buried and forgotten.[25]

The posture of Oakland's ruling class toward the city's restive Black population changed in 1965, sparked by events 343 miles to the south. The violent arrest of a young African American motorist named Marquette Frye by the California Highway Patrol in the Los Angeles neighborhood of Watts triggered protests that spiraled into six days of looting, arson, and running street battles with the LAPD. The uprising left thirty-four people dead, at least a thousand injured, and more than $40 million in property destroyed.[26]

The intensity of the Watts rebellion alarmed President Lyndon Johnson. His administration drew up a list of cities with similarly incendiary conditions that could potentially explode. Oakland topped the list. News coverage of the federal memo branded the city as a "racial tinderbox."[27] An elderly East Oakland resident sitting on the porch of a dilapidated home told Hinckle, the *Ramparts* journalist, "You are not going to get nothing done in Oakland until it burns to the ground."[28]

In the wake of Watts, Oakland's Black activists demanded that city leaders rein in the police; not only to prevent a riot but also to address decades of abuses. On August 31, 1965, they packed Oakland City Hall and pleaded for action on housing, discrimination, and jobs, asking for the establishment of a civilian board that could hear police misconduct complaints, something no city in America had.[29]

"What happened in Watts, I am not saying it's right, I'm not saying it's wrong," said Curtis Baker, a prominent Black West Oakland activist. "But one thing it did, it opened your eyes and those of a lot of cities in California."

Observing the meeting was Terence Lee, an assistant to former CIA director John McCone, whom Governor Pat Brown had appointed to study the conflagration in Watts. Lee's job was to prevent a similar flare-up in Oakland. The Governor's Commission on the Los Angeles Riot, known informally as the McCone Commission, would eventually conclude that the LA rebellion was a fire sparked by the thwarted dreams of Black people forced into Southern California's massive ghetto. Promised major social change by reform-minded politicians, the jobs and welfare programs Black Angelenos staked their hopes on in the early 1960s did not materialize.[30]

"What can be done to prevent a recurrence of the nightmare of August?" Lee and his colleagues wrote in their report, *Violence in the City—An End or a Beginning?* "It stands to reason that what we and other cities have been doing, costly as it all has been, is not enough." The commission recommended massive investments in jobs and education programs, and police reforms.[31]

Oakland's activists didn't need to wait around for findings. Elijah Turner, another local activist, warned against more blue-ribbon commissions, advisory panels, and sociologists. "The city has been studied enough," he said. "The statistics on Oakland will fill up this room. The problem is obvious."

But Oakland's conservatives weren't sympathetic, nor were they unanimous in feeling that Watts was a warning to heed. Sanford Kraemer, head of the powerful Oakland Real Estate Board, told the council, "The term 'police brutality' is a farce," and urged them to reject a police oversight commission. Notwithstanding Kraemer's comment, Mayor Houlihan told the council, "We've only heard from the minority, not the majority who pay the bulk of the taxes," before adjourning the meeting.

The following week, representatives of a Washington organization that advocates lowering taxes, the American Taxpayers Union, showed up to urge the city council to organize an official "Support Your Police" campaign, which was linked to a wider effort led by the ultra-right John Birch Society. Patricia Atthowe, a self-described housewife married to a sheriff's deputy, asked the council members not to allow themselves to be "blackmailed" by the "big stick" of a potential Watts in Oakland. (Unbeknownst to most at the time was Atthowe's role as the founder of a private intelligence firm that spied on East Bay activists and students and worked closely with Alameda County's district attorney, Frank Coakley.)[32] Without much deliberation, the council rejected the police review board idea.

In the spring of 1966 the same demand was back before the city council, now led by Mayor John Reading, a retired air force colonel and food company executive. Reading was more willing to listen to police critics. But he, too, rejected the police oversight board, after hearing from law enforcement and white "taxpayers" groups.

OPD captain Palmer Stinson railed against the oversight proposal during a speech at a Lion's Club meeting in 1966, claiming "nearly all critics of the police are from the radical Left," while a sergeant who was president of the Oakland Police Department Welfare Association (the police union's predecessor) said firmly that officers would refuse to cooperate and fight it all the way to the US Supreme Court.[33]

District Attorney Coakley told a conference of law enforcement intelligence units at police headquarters that police review boards were nothing more than a Communist conspiracy. "The seeds of revolution have taken hold in this country," he warned the men in blue ominously.[34]

Coakley had worked under Ezra Decoto and Earl Warren until 1943, when he joined the navy. As a judge adjutant general, or JAG, he led the controversial prosecution of fifty Black sailors accused of mutiny. The sailors were the survivors of the 1944 Port Chicago disaster thirty miles northeast of Oakland in which hundreds of men, mostly Black sailors, were incinerated after ordnance went off in a ship's hull. Survivors feared returning to work—under conditions the navy knew were unreasonably dangerous—and were branded traitors.[35] Coakley sent many of them to prison. The trial was observed by NAACP Legal Defense and Educational Fund executive director and future Supreme Court justice Thurgood Marshall, who accused Coakley of racial prejudice.

The DA, who believed that Black people were "brainwashed" by Communists to fixate on police brutality, as part of a plot to undermine America,[36] led the powerful California District Attorneys Association. His right-hand man, Richard Chamberlain, state leader of the American Legion, served as one of the CDAA's main lobbyists. Chamberlain frequently pushed to maintain rules of jurisprudence that, decades later, would be ruled unconstitutional. This included Coakley's opposition to the idea that exculpatory evidence discovered after a trial could be used to exonerate someone. Coakley's staff also faced accusations of systematically removing Black people from juries, especially in cases where the defendants were Black.[37] Regarding the Watts riot and other urban rebellions, Coakley's position was that the Oakland police would crush any attempt at upsetting the status quo, a position the police were happy to endorse.

Nevertheless, no matter how much Oakland's power structure wanted to ignore the looming specter of civil unrest, poverty and racism were tearing Oakland apart. No degree of police repression could keep a lid on those volatile forces.

President Johnson sent a team to Oakland in 1966 to ease racial tensions and avert a riot.[38] The situation, according to one bureaucrat, was a "powder keg."[39] The Great Society initiative launched countless social welfare programs and community and economic development initiatives across the United States to treat what many sociologists believed were the root causes of crime and strife in a manner rivaled only by the New Deal. Working under the auspices of the Oakland Economic Development Council (OEDC), federal anti-poverty warriors set up programs such as the New Careers Development Council in Oakland. With millions of dollars in funding from Washington, they hired the chronically unemployed, formerly incarcerated, and disillusioned, paying them living wages to attend college and train for careers.[40]

At first, Mayor John Reading and a handful of other powerful Oakland conservatives were cautiously optimistic about the War on Poverty programs. His own philosophical view, Reading said in interviews, was that jobs were the solution to crime and civil unrest. If the federal government was footing the bill, all the better for Oakland's taxpayers.

However, it didn't take long before the federally funded agencies conflicted with the city's white leadership. Once again, one of the biggest disagreements was about police oversight.

OEDC, the local steering committee that disbursed millions in federal anti-poverty funds, voted in February 1966 to recommend that the city create a civilian police oversight board with the power to hear complaints about police brutality. Dissenting OEDC member Philip Ennis, who led the *Tribune*-dominated downtown Retail Merchants Association, said he didn't believe "the great majority of Oakland citizens have voiced any legitimate complaints against the Oakland Police Department," but a majority of the committee endorsed the idea. "It is a fact that considerable hostility exists between the low-income and minority residents of Oakland and the Oakland Police Department," the OEDC majority wrote in a report to the city council. "Stories about 'police brutality' and 'police harassment' are common, yet the existing channels for filing complaints are seldom used."[41]

The split on police oversight contributed to the eventual position taken by Oakland's white power structure to run the federal government out of town. Oakland's hostile approach to the War on Poverty foreshadowed the direction the United States would eventually take when it turned hard to the right during the administration of President Richard Nixon and rejected social and economic transformation that could structurally eliminate the root causes of crime. Instead, the country embraced police violence to contain poverty.

One telling episode involved an East Bay congressman's discovery that Panther Party cofounder Bobby Seale was employed by a North Oakland youth center, one of the War on Poverty programs. Federal officials quickly had Seale fired. William Knowland's *Tribune* and Mayor Reading lambasted the program and others like it as pernicious "Socialist" interventions. As radicals increasingly took on roles in the Great Society, attempting to use federal funds to try to transform Oakland's ossified social and political structure, the *Tribune*, Reading, and the rest of the business community branded the initiative a Washington-run "shadow government" that ferried radical Black and Latino organizers to power.[42] The feds would eventually tax the city's businesses and middle class into oblivion, warned the conservatives.

In the end, the War on Poverty didn't recast American society; tremendous resistance from local authorities across the United States saw to that. Entrenched state and municipal power structures, like the one in Oakland, realized that such restructuring according to the demands of people of color and white progressives meant relinquishing their own power and privilege.

Oakland's civic fathers declined to use federal resources to reshape the local economy more equitably. Many of Oakland's political elite gravitated to the hard-line law-and-order and anti-Communist politics championed by California governor Ronald Reagan and President Richard Nixon during their ascent in the 1960s and early 1970s. As governor, Reagan and Oakland attorney Edwin Meese killed the Oakland Economic Development Council, the nonprofit that had channeled more than $20 million in federal grants to the city's poor, when they vetoed its 1971 block grant.[43] As president, Nixon would complete the demobilization of the poverty war's foot soldiers while ramping up federal spending on police and prisons as part of his nascent War on Drugs.[44]

Instead of doing their best to reshape the local economy and provide opportunities for the poor to thrive, Oakland's leaders chose to have the police contain the increasingly destitute and frustrated Black masses. But with the Panthers now on the prowl, the struggle for racial justice would become increasingly violent and desperate.

————————

In the predawn hours of October 28, 1967, Officer John Frey watched from behind the wheel of his patrol car as a tan Volkswagen cruised through the intersection of Willow and Seventh Streets in West Oakland. Frey glanced down at a list of vehicles belonging to Black Panther Party members. Second to last was the car's description and a matching license plate number. The rookie cop radioed for backup using the OPD's Panthers incident code and pulled out behind the VW, hitting his lights.

The vehicle list was a product of the major counterinsurgency operation run by Oakland police against the Panthers and other radicals. The department created a special unit, active from 1967 through 1972, responsible for tracking, documenting, and suppressing the Panthers.[45] The unit was commanded by Captain Ray Brown, a military veteran who joined the OPD in 1947. Brown was a key point of contact with statewide law enforcement, serving as a liaison to Governor Reagan on law enforcement issues, and instructing other agencies on crowd control tactics used against labor and civil rights protesters. He made his views on protesters known in public speeches, disparagingly telling a gathering of Monterey County officers in 1965 that "there are two things that scare most professional pickets: the threat of getting a job, and a bathtub."[46]

Brown's anti-Panthers unit had compiled a list of twenty cars owned or used by the group and instructed patrol officers such as Frey to use any excuse to jam up the Black militants. Pull them over, question them, harass them, ticket them, and arrest them if possible. Give them no rest.

Frey didn't know it, but he was tailing Huey Newton and Gene McKinney through West Oakland's early morning mist. The pair were on their way to breakfast after a night of carousing at Bosn's Locker, a bar and restaurant on Shattuck Avenue in North Oakland. Just twenty-three, Frey already had a reputation as a head-cracking cop. In a visit to a Clayton Valley High School class in rural Contra Costa County, he told the teenagers that the "niggers" he policed were "a lot of bad types." In one well-known incident, a

Black insurance agent claimed that Frey racially abused him during a traffic stop. When he protested, the burly young cop placed his hand on his pistol and said, "I am the Gestapo."

The Panthers knew about Frey and plastered his photograph on lamp poles as an alert.[47] Just hours before he stopped Newton and McKinney, the officer had responded to a call from a grocery clerk accusing a Black man of theft. Frey, according to the suspect, called him a nigger and held him down so the white clerk could rough him up.[48] He was the exact type of cop the Panthers wanted to confront.

Newton pulled to the curb around Seventh and Campbell, on West Oakland's main drag, where concrete pilings for the new Bay Area Rapid Transit elevated train line were being erected opposite a nondescript row of shops and nightclubs. Frey walked up to the driver's-side window, and when he got a clear look at the car's occupants, he sneered, "Well, what do we have here? The great, great Huey P. Newton."

Newton handed over his license and the car's registration, and readied himself for a legal standoff.

The past year and a half had seen one tense encounter after another between the Panthers and the police. In May, the Panthers had descended on the state capitol with guns to protest Oakland's hard-line conservative, Anglo assemblyman Don Mulford's bill banning open carry of firearms, in a direct response to their armed patrols. Later that month, Newton was arrested by the OPD after showing up at the scene of a raid and demanding to know if the officers had a warrant. When Seale went to bail out Newton, *he* was arrested on an antiquated law outlawing firearms possession near jails. Just before Frey pulled them over, Newton and McKinney had attended a fund-raiser to pay for the legal defense of Seale's charges related to the capitol protest. The Panthers' Oakland headquarters on Grove Street was under constant police surveillance, and Captain Ray Brown was advising other departments in cities with new Panthers chapters how to create suppression squads.

While Frey went back to his car to check for open warrants over the radio, Patrolman Herbert Heanes pulled up.[49] The two officers conferred, walked back to the VW, and ordered Newton and McKinney out. Newton, with a criminal law book in hand, stepped out, and Frey told him to place his hands against the roof of the car. After patting down Newton, he walked him back to his squad car.

Though the following events have always been highly disputed, here are Newton's claims about what transpired, as told in his 1973 autobiography, *Revolutionary Suicide*, and testimony during his subsequent trial: With his free hand, Newton opened his law book and told Frey, "You have no reasonable cause to arrest me." Allegedly, the officer replied, "You can take that book and shove it up your ass, nigger," before belting Newton in the face and drawing his revolver.[50] Later on, Newton gave conflicting accounts of the incident. In one version, he claimed that Frey groped his genitals during a patdown, and the two began fighting.[51] In his memoir, Newton's story was that he blacked out after being shot, and that Frey and Heanes shot each other in a cross fire.

However, a witness to the incident said that Newton wrestled away Frey's revolver and shot him. The gun was never recovered. Newton was left with a gunshot wound to the abdomen, Frey lay dying on the pavement, and Heanes climbed back into his car, having suffered a gunshot wound.[52] Despite his injury, Heanes got on the radio and put out a "940B" alert for an officer in need of immediate assistance. Fellow Panther David Hilliard drove Newton to the hospital, where he was quickly tracked down by OPD officers, cuffed to the gurney, and allegedly beaten.

"If you don't die in the gas chamber, then when you're sent to prison, we'll have you killed there," one cop sneered. "If you're acquitted, we'll kill you in the streets."[53]

District Attorney Coakley indicted Newton for Frey's murder. The Panther was arraigned bedside in Highland Hospital by a judge as a shotgun-toting police officer stood guard at his door. Coakley assigned the prosecution to Lowell Jensen, the trusted assistant he'd been grooming to take over the reins of the DA's office.

Newton's case became a cause célèbre. From the stand, the Panthers' co-founder used questions from his lawyer, Charles Garry, a white civil rights attorney, not just to deny murdering Frey but also to expound on the impoverished conditions of Black people and the role law enforcement played in undermining their attempts at self-improvement.

A jury of eleven whites and one Black person convicted Newton of voluntary manslaughter in September 1968 and sentenced him to two to fifteen years in prison. However, his conviction was reversed on appeal in 1970. Jensen retried Newton twice, but each time the trial ended in a hung jury.

Although Frey was, in the words of one veteran officer, "not what I would categorize as a good cop," law enforcement viewed his killing as a declaration of war. The Seventh Street gun battle precipitated a period of armed conflict between the Panthers and the police.[54] As the FBI's counterintelligence program, or COINTELPRO, circulated poison-pen letters seeking to drive a wedge between the Black Panther Party chapters and their allies, the department actively sought to destroy the Black militant group by raiding churches where Panthers held their weekly gatherings and stepping up their daily harassment, including traffic stops.[55]

For their part, the Panthers didn't shy away from taking the fight to the police. On April 6, 1968, two days after the assassination of Martin Luther King Jr. in Memphis, three cars filled with Panthers, including Eldridge Cleaver, David Hilliard, and seventeen-year-old Bobby Hutton, the party's first-ever recruit, pulled over in a mixed stretch of single-family homes and warehouses. Cleaver got out of the lead car to urinate and found himself illuminated by a spotlight: several patrol cars from the OPD's Panthers squad pulled up and surrounded the militants. Words were exchanged, then gunfire.

Decades later, Cleaver would admit that he and his comrades had gone out looking for a gunfight that evening, and they initiated the shoot-out.[56] Richard Jensen, one of the cops wounded in the initial exchange, said that while they had a copy of the Panthers license plate list in their possession, he and Officer Nolan Darnell weren't out looking for the activists. Jensen claimed they came upon an empty car in the street, and when they stopped to investigate, they were ambushed by a barrage of Panthers gunfire.[57]

Whatever really happened, the Panthers fled into the neighborhood, seeking cover from the small army of law enforcement after them. The police cordoned off a two-block area, lobbing tear gas and incendiary grenades to flush out the Panthers from a house during a ninety-minute gun battle. Cleaver and Hutton holed up in a basement, wounded and suffocating in the noxious air. Eventually Cleaver emerged with his hands raised, stark naked, and was arrested. Hutton, too, came out of the basement to give up, but was cut down in a hail of bullets.[58] The Panthers claimed he had surrendered naked, and that the OPD killed him in cold blood.

Months after the controversial shooting, Hutton's killers were identified. They included Owen Brown of the Emeryville Police Department and Oakland officers Robert Coffman and Robert Fredericks. Fredericks had a reputation for violence. Three months after gunning down Hutton, he and a group of officers hunted down Dallas Charles, an unarmed man suspected of stealing a gun from a gas station, who fled a traffic stop on foot. Fredericks killed Charles with a shotgun blast to the back of his head. In 1971 Fredericks blew out the ankles of a suspect with a shotgun blast. Fredericks was involved in at least six shootings in his career.[59]

The OPD pushed back hard against allegations its officers had assassinated Hutton. Oakland cops testified that Hutton was shot while trying to escape, and the department's new chief, Charles Gain, vociferously defended his officers in the media, claiming at a press conference that the seventeen-year-old Hutton had been fully clothed and potentially armed. The Panthers' allegations were "ridiculous lies, ridiculous claims to create prejudice against the Oakland Police Department."[60] The OPD went on a media offensive, painting the Panthers not as a radical political organization but as a terrorist group bent on destabilizing society and manipulating the grievances of the poor for the purpose of sowing violence.

The Oakland Police Officers' Association even went after detractors in the media, with Fredericks, Coffman, and Brown filing a $26 million libel lawsuit against local ABC affiliate KGO-TV and Marlon Brando for broadcasting the actor's comments that Hutton's killing was "cold blooded." The officers, who contended that this defamed them by calling them murderers, filed an identical $26 million lawsuit against popular *San Francisco Chronicle* columnist Herb Caen for writing a story critical of the department and its actions.[61]

Not everyone within the OPD agreed about the Panthers. Two of OPD's Black officers—among the few employed by the department in the late 1960s—spoke up about what they witnessed the night Hutton was killed.

Gwynne Peirson was a decorated Tuskegee Airman who, in World War II, flew daring combat missions with the famed "Red Tails" 332nd Fighter Group during the Allied invasion of Sicily. He joined the Oakland PD in 1951, serving twenty-four years, mostly in Homicide, and capped his police career by documenting the department's systemic racism in a scathing UC Berkeley doctoral dissertation.[62]

Peirson was at the basement siege. So, too, was Eugene Jennings.[63] In depositions made to inspectors from the Alameda County District Attorney's Office, the two men contradicted claims that Hutton had tried to escape. He and Cleaver had both walked out of the basement with their hands raised, when Cleaver tripped over debris on the ground, causing Hutton to tumble over him. Jennings observed several of the officers on scene rush up, encircle the pair, and begin beating them with the butts of their guns.[64]

The cops stood Hutton and Cleaver up and shoved them down the street. Hutton stumbled, "and when he instinctively lowered his hands, he was shot several times," recalled Peirson. The Black officers stated under oath that his killing was unjustified.[65]

"I saw him stumble, and the shots were fired," said Jennings, who was positioned on a building directly across the street from the basement where Cleaver and Hutton had been taking cover.[66] "I've never seen a man shot before in my life. Naturally, it was a rather shocking experience to me, and I can only see in my mind one officer shooting."

Peirson's and Jennings's statements were prima facie evidence for criminal charges of perjury, manslaughter, or, potentially, murder against their OPD colleagues. None of that came to pass. According to Peirson, their depositions were never presented to the grand jury, nor were they called to testify.[67]

Once other officers learned that Jennings had given a deposition implicating fellow cops in a homicide, he was "badgered and tormented constantly,"[68] his assignments were shifted constantly by his superiors, and he was written up for the slightest error. In one instance, the threats to Jennings turned physical. One day he and several other officers were searching for a burglary suspect in West Oakland. A white cop handcuffed the man, put his revolver to the back of his head, and cocked the gun. Jennings, who had just arrived on scene, put his hand on his colleague's arm and told him to let the suspect get up. The officer swung the barrel of his revolver to bear on Jennings and said that if the Black cop ever touched him again, he'd end up dead. The white cop faced no discipline, and Jennings's ordeal intensified. He was transferred out of patrol to the Juvenile Division and retired a few years later.[69]

District Attorney Jensen's concealment of Peirson's and Jennings's testimony from the grand jury was not an aberration: in the widening conflict with New Left radicals, the Alameda County justice system carved out exceptions for police facing criminal culpability.

In September 1968, OPD officers Richard Williams and Robert Farrow were dismissed from the force and charged with felony assault after firing a dozen shots from their marked patrol car into the Black Panther Party headquarters on Grove Street in a brazen, drunken drive-by seen by several eyewitnesses.[70] One round passed through a poster of Huey Newton hanging in the window, a none-too-subtle message about the Panthers' leader on trial for the murder of John Frey.[71] After pleading guilty, both officers were sentenced to probation by the judge, who "found no traces of racist tendencies in either of the defendants."[72]

Racism and bigotry were endemic to the Oakland Police Department of the mid-1960s. In OPD vernacular, a nightstick was referred to as a "nigger knocker," and police generally treated Black Oaklanders as second-class citizens without rights.[73] From the 1940s until the early 1970s, the city's police and fire departments both discriminated systematically against Blacks, refusing to hire them in any significant numbers and barring the few who made it from being promoted to any senior level.[74]

Peirson laid out two ways that Black officers coped. Some ignored the bigotry, while others actively resisted, but neither approach was effective. He concluded that the only reason Black officers started to be hired in significant numbers in the late 1960s was for the purposes of social control.[75] "The black policeman was not hired because of greater freedom of opportunity," Peirson contended, "he was hired because he was black and was needed for a limited occupational role."[76]

The deeply entrenched racism of white Oakland cops—many of whom, like their more famous LAPD counterparts, were recruited either from the Deep South or straight off local military bases after demobilizing—was compounded by the placement of openly bigoted supervisors in key training roles, giving them a forum to impart their values to green recruits. According to Peirson, one motorcycle drill sergeant assigned to teach a course on race relations remarked repeatedly that "colored people were 200 years behind whites in intellectual development, and therefore could not be expected to compete with whites on an equal basis."[77]

Another instructor in race relations classes, a lieutenant, was an open member of the ultraconservative John Birch Society. He attributed the 1965 Watts uprising to an "alleged Communist plot." The militant anti-Communism of the Birchers found a very receptive audience among the OPD's ranks and California law enforcement at large.[78]

Command staff, too, shared these retrograde views. Until the early 1970s, captains in North and East Oakland refused to accept Black officers for patrol assignments. The Traffic Division was all white by design.

And Black cops were also barred from working in Internal Affairs. Sergeant Clarence Lucas, who ran the IA Division for several years, explained the reasoning: "Negros cannot be expected to be objective in any investigation of a Negro citizen or Negro police officer," he said.[79]

Radicals would occasionally attack authority figures and police in Oakland, feeding the OPD's paranoia and sense of mission that it was holding back the forces of anarchy. This included San Francisco's grisly so-called Zebra murders, in which victims—all white—were shot or hacked up with a machete by a group of Black extremists known as the Death Angels. Similar unsolved murders took place in Oakland and Berkeley from 1970 to 1973, including the assassination of a Berkeley motorcycle cop named Ronald Tsukamoto.[80]

In October 1973 the Oakland PD's helicopter lost power midflight over Fruitvale Avenue and plummeted to the ground, killing two officers. Initially, Chief Gain claimed the chopper was downed by a sniper, and a previously unknown guerrilla group, the August Seventh Guerilla Movement, claimed responsibility for the attack.[81] Although investigators would determine that mechanical failure caused the crash, the incident added to the police's sense of siege, which was further exacerbated four days later, when a patrol car took gunfire less than a mile away.[82]

One month later, Marcus Foster, the country's first Black school superintendent, was shot eight times with cyanide-laced hollow-point bullets in a parking lot after leaving a school board meeting. The assassins were members of the Symbionese Liberation Army, a tiny revolutionary cult that rocketed to infamy three months later with the kidnapping of heiress Patty Hearst. Foster had incurred the group's wrath by proposing a district-wide student identification card, which the SLA viewed as a "Fascist" tool of oppression.[83]

––––––––

Overlapping with Black resistance to police violence in Oakland was the anti–Vietnam War movement. Oakland, with its downtown Army Induction Center, where tens of thousands of young men were processed for eventual combat, became a battleground between radicals and Washington, DC.

The Vietnam Day Committee (VDC), an antiwar coalition formed in 1965 by several young radicals including Yippie and future Chicago Eight member Jerry Rubin, had blockaded troop transport trains in Berkeley and the nearby city of Albany, and picketed military commanders visiting San Francisco. They identified Oakland's induction center as a strategic location where nonviolent civil disobedience could slow down the intensifying war. For months, small groups of activists gathered outside the center on Clay Street, just behind Oakland City Hall, handing out pamphlets to inductees or symbolically trying to block its doors.

In October 1965, VDC organizers from Berkeley announced plans to march on the induction center. This escalation was interpreted by pro-war authorities such as the police and the district attorney as brazen, criminal insubordination. Police viewed the VDC's members and followers as unwashed masses of Communists and dupes. They vowed to do everything necessary to repel them from Oakland.

On October 15, fifteen thousand students and antiwar activists were turned back by a wedge of four hundred Oakland cops in riot gear at the Berkeley–Oakland border on Woolsey Street, as Chief Edward Toothman barked orders over a walkie-talkie. That evening, Berkeley's chief of police, William Beall, drove one of the march monitor captains, Robert Hurwitt, to the border and warned him that if they tried to reach Oakland the next day, the police there would likely respond with force. "We'll be right here," Beall said, "but we won't be able to control the OPD."[84]

Oakland's cops were intimately familiar with the Vietnam Day Committee: in the same way that they spied on Black activists, Toothman embedded three rookie officers in the local antiwar movement as undercovers.[85] It was no surprise to the department that the following day, five thousand people again attempted to cross into Oakland. Stopped by a mass of riot-ready police, the front of the march sat down while the VDC monitors formed a line around them. The Oakland cops had a surprise in store: they stepped aside for eighteen Hells Angels outlaw motorcycle club members to charge through and attack.

Screaming, "Traitors!" "Communists!" and "America first!" the burly bikers shredded an antiwar banner and pummeled the students.[86] Sonny Barger, the Oakland chapter president, brained Hurwitt in the head with a metal pipe. The protesters couldn't relay word of the attack to their comrades or request support or medical attention because FBI agents were jamming their walkie-talkie system.[87]

"When push came to shove, the Hells Angels lined up solidly with the cops, the Pentagon, and the John Birch Society," "gonzo" journalist Hunter S. Thompson wrote about the melee in his 1967 book *Hell's Angels: A Strange and Terrible Saga*.

The biker assault was beyond the pale for the Berkeley cops who had escorted the march to the border. BPD officers rushed in with clubs flailing, trying to collar as many Angels as they could. Two bikers knocked a sergeant to the ground and began kicking him, breaking the officer's leg. Berkeley cops arrested several Angels. Their Oakland counterparts? Not a single arrest, even though Toothman observed the assault firsthand. He would later deny that his officers had permitted the Angels, a lawless, violent criminal enterprise, to wreak havoc. "The Hells Angels also have civil rights," he said weakly. "You can't just arrest people unless they violate the law, even though they are a bunch of persons of bad repute."[88]

The brutal attack wasn't unexpected. The motorcycle gang was openly tolerated and even weaponized in the same manner that the OPD had used the American Legion's right-wing extremism against unionists and other left-wingers earlier in the century. They were the Proud Boys of their day. A four-man detail was assigned to keep tabs on the Angels in the 1960s, but in amicable fashion. The Oakland Police Department's light hand regarding Hells Angels activities stood in sharp contrast to crackdowns on the motorcycle gang by other California cities.[89] The Oakland chapter, according to Barger, was viewed as a counterweight to a potential Black uprising in East Oakland, which in the sixties still had a significant working-class white population. The local police, Barger told Thompson, counted on the Angels to "keep the niggers in line—they're more scared of the niggers than they are of us."[90]

Two years later, OPD would again target the antiwar movement. When the student protesters descended on the Army Induction Center on October 16, 1967, police drove away a few hundred and violently arrested several dozen, including folk singer and peace activist Joan Baez. The next day, thousands more marched from Berkeley and joined hundreds walking north from Oakland's Lafayette Square Park. They were intercepted by platoons of helmeted OPD officers, Alameda County sheriff's deputies, and highway patrolmen. Captain Ray Brown made an announcement: the protest was an unlawful assembly. In the predawn light, as buses filled with enlistees were making their way along city streets toward the center, the police attacked. One newspaper account of the day called it a "seven-minute blitzkrieg." Enraged officers clubbed protesters, beating at least one hand-cuffed man in plain sight of newspaper reporters.

"Another was pushed, stumbled, struck on the head, and went down twice," the *San Francisco Examiner* reported. "He rose with his face bloodied, surrounded by Oakland police officers."

When a few of the protesters defended themselves, the police became even more savage. "One demonstrator threw a road flare at a California Highway Patrol officer. He was knocked unconscious and was still laying in the gutter fifteen minutes later."[91]

Governor Ronald Reagan praised the police riot, stating it was "in the finest tradition of California's law enforcement agencies."[92]

District Attorney Coakley hit arrestees with maximum bail to keep them jailed as long as possible. Chief Charles Gain defended the OPD's harsh tactics, which he witnessed from a nearby rooftop: "I take exception to the use of force being described as a beating," he told reporters. "When people violate the law, they have no reason to expect police to act a certain way."[93]

The extraordinary violence might have been glossed over were it not for the fact that a couple dozen newspaper reporters and photographers were clobbered.

"There was a hostility this day—and throughout the week—on the part of the Oakland police which I have never encountered before," wrote Charles Howe, a military correspondent for the *San Francisco Chronicle*.

Reporters suffered broken ribs and lacerations and said they'd never experienced such a callous attack, even after having covered civil rights protests in Alabama and Louisiana. Charles Braverman, a young CBS cameraman, said a row of CHP officers contemptuously flicked lit cigarettes at him from the second story of a parking garage, and that this was after he witnessed an OPD officer "beating a young girl lying in the street." Police clubbed radio reporter Michael Forrest several times despite his press card dangling around his neck. He wrote afterward:

"I have been shot at in the Dominican Republic and received an award of appreciation from the Eighty-Second Airborne for my coverage there. I have covered shoot-outs while the shooting was still going on. I have never been treated like this—and especially had no reason to be at a time when no one was being abusive and there was no threat of violence toward the police."

Weeks after the riot, veteran *San Francisco Examiner* photographer George Place was chatting with an SFPD officer he was friendly with. The officer had been called over to Oakland during the draft week protests to back up the OPD. He asked Place, "What do you make of those hooligan cops in Oakland? What's the matter with those guys?"[94]

Chief Toothman, who collaborated with DA Coakley and the FBI to conduct intense surveillance against the Left, stepped down in 1966. His replacement, Robert Preston, wasn't much different.[95] Preston, forty-seven, held regressive views on race and saw the police as a force to contain social movements that agitated for change. For Gwynne Peirson, the outspoken Black officer, the department adhered to a practice of "white suppression."[96]

However, by the late 1960s, calls for police reform were gaining traction. Preston wasn't fit to lead the OPD if the city was to avoid chaos. His beliefs were "naïve, stupid, or insincere," as Lionel Wilson, the county's first Black judge, said in 1966. The same year, the attorney and activist John George called Preston's police force "the frontline troops to keep down the rising tide of Negro hopes."[97]

In September 1967 Preston died suddenly of an apparent heart attack after just a year and a half as chief. His passing created an opening for reform. Deputy Chief Charles Ray Gain, born in Texas and raised in Oakland since he was five by a family of dust bowl migrants, was suddenly thrust into the role. Gain was more scholar than cop. He had an inquisitive mind and enrolled constantly in behavioral sciences and management courses as he rose through the ranks. He never felt comfortable at the OPD. Early in his career, he attended a police union meeting but walked out after hearing "derogatory remarks" against racial minorities and commanders.[98] The force urgently needed modernization, and he thought the latest research in sociology could be mobilized for good. Like many liberals of his era, Gain believed poverty to be the root cause of crime and violence and that the police could do little to bring down crime rates. But they could at least stop abusing the poor.

Gain ordered that stops and searches of pedestrians and drivers be reduced, particularly in Black neighborhoods. The new chief also ordered all officers to undergo training on race relations. He hired a female legal advisor, created a family crisis intervention program, a landlord-tenant in-

vestigation program, and a consumer fraud unit.[99] Underscoring how reactionary most American police were at the time, and how liberal Gain
was by comparison, was a 1970 hearing before a US Senate subcommittee
on internal security regarding a rash of sniper attacks against police officers. Chief Edward Davis of the Los Angeles Police Department told the
senators that the shootings were certainly part of a vast Communist insurgency using Black Panthers as "shock troops." Gain, who also testified at the
Senate hearing, acknowledged seventeen such shootings in three years but
dismissed Davis's outlandish claims as a "disservice" to the truth. Oakland's
chief of police reasoned that the attacks were caused by racial strife, the
Vietnam War, and social inequities.[100]

One of Gain's most profound actions was overhauling the OPD's use-of-
force rules. Just before midnight on February 5, 1968, twenty-three-year-
old Charles De Baca ran from officer Walter Gibbons, who suspected the
Latino man of breaking into a car. Gibbons shot De Baca in the back, killing
him. This case, on top of Charles Dallas's grisly killing by Officer Robert
Fredericks the previous July, pushed Gain into action: he banned officers
from shooting at fleeing burglary suspects and car thieves. The order was
far more restrictive than state law at the time.[101] Gain also restricted officers from shooting out of their patrol cars and shooting at juveniles. The
chief knew what he was doing: he had authored the department's earlier lax
firearms rules in 1958, when he was a lieutenant, but had come to see since
that "the use of deadly force to apprehend burglars cannot be conceivably
justified."[102]

Gain further raised the ire of OPD line cops over his attempts to impose
lasting discipline for misconduct and hold officers accountable for actual
criminal violations. Previous chiefs, such as Preston, followed a one-of-the-
boys approach in which officers were viewed favorably and rarely punished.
In six years, Gain terminated thirty-eight cops for misconduct following Internal Affairs investigations.[103] At one point, Oakland's top cop had become
so disliked by his rank and file that when he walked the halls of the Police
Administration Building, officers would turn away to avoid talking to him.

Speaking more than a decade following his retirement from policing,
Gain cited the Oakland PD's casual corruption as a motivating factor in his
rise in the profession. "In my younger years," he reflected, "I was very disillusioned by all the police corruption, and I hoped to have a higher rank and
do something about it."[104]

Gain also tried diversifying the force by hiring more Black officers. Larry Murphy, a retired Oakland police sergeant who served in the 1960s and early 1970s as a patrol and training lieutenant, recounted in a memoir, *Blackjack and Jive-Five*, the work he did for Gain—work that was frequently undermined by officers and the police union. When Murphy transferred to patrol in 1972, the OPD was still 90 percent white. At its academy, he supervised the training of many of the younger Black cadets recruited under Gain. That experience, plus academic training on subcultures that he and his partner, Jon Sparks, received at the University of California, Los Angeles, at Gain's insistence, led to his appointment running a squad of Black officers to prove they were just as capable as white officers. This resulted in OPD officers up to the rank of captain labeling him a "nigger lover" and a "Commie."

"There should have been some sort of riot in Oakland during that time," Murphy wrote about the deep well of fear and distrust Black Oaklanders had for the police who had abused them for a generation. "The anger and discontent were there—particularly the anger. I saw the hatred as I worked a police beat in those days, not fully understanding the hostility toward me as I learned to respond to my new name: 'pig.' "[105]

Murphy's patrol supervisor, a lieutenant he gave the tongue-in-cheek sobriquet "Dumas," made no secret about his antipathy toward Black cops and Chief Gain. "You and your liberal-assed partner have been working for that skinny-assed chief of police!" Dumas screamed at Murphy during one conversation, remarking that he had seen Sparks, Murphy, and Gain "swaggering around this police department in your fancy suits and colored shirts and faggy-looking ties."

Gain, Sparks, and Murphy were directly challenging the racist "stormtrooper" ethos to which Oakland cops had grown accustomed. Lieutenant Dumas's estimation was that "between the three of you, you have done more to fuck up this police department than the rest of us could do in a lifetime!" But Gain and the few who believed in him hadn't done nearly enough to change the culture.

"He did not want Oakland to burn, as other cities had," Murphy recalled. "He personally reached out to communities, giving assurances that insensitive or misbehaving police officers would be disciplined, fired, or jailed. Some of all three things happened. Oakland did not riot, but the police department damn near did."[106]

When Gain assumed office, the Vice Unit at the time was commanded by a captain named Tim Brown, who disliked having Black officers in his unit because "Negroes tend to be troublemakers." Gain successfully removed Brown from Vice and brought Black cops into the unit. Similar efforts to integrate other Jim Crow units, such as the Motorcycle Squad and the Traffic Division, produced still more resentment, culminating in a 1971 vote of no confidence in Gain by the Oakland Police Officers' Association. More than half the department voted against the chief, asking him to retire within three months.[107] Notably, though, the Oakland Black Officers Association, which represented the department's forty-eight Black cops, issued a statement after the vote calling it "without merit," and civil rights leaders rushed to back the city's police chief.

Gain retired from the OPD in 1973 after twenty-seven years. In 1975 he became San Francisco's police chief but was fired by Mayor Dianne Feinstein after refusing to allow his force to attack "rioting homosexuals" (per a contemporaneous news article), upset at the light sentence handed down to Dan White, a former SFPD officer and city supervisor, in 1979. The previous year, White had snuck into city hall and shot to death Mayor George Moscone and then supervisor Harvey Milk, a popular gay activist. Relying on a defense that he was depressed and distraught at the time he committed the murders, White was found guilty of two counts of voluntary manslaughter, not first-degree murder, and spent a mere seven years in prison.

Charles Gain's time in charge of the Oakland PD was notable for a number of reasons: it represented the first instance where the city attempted to deal with its police force's institutionalized racism. The police's autonomy within the city was also greatly reduced, and the department was, to some degree, made more accountable to the residents it served.

However, Gain's reforms didn't have much staying power. Gwynne Peirson, while appreciative of his former chief's attempts to break with the OPD's dark past, cast his former boss's achievements in the longer context of history. The reforms weren't institutionalized, and the virulent resistance to Gain's initiatives around race, use of force, and professionalization persisted as a major undercurrent among the department's rank and file.

In Peirson's estimation, the Oakland police still enforced a racist social system with the tacit approval of local government. "The police have been able to use the criminal law to avoid legal restraints on law enforcement," he wrote. "The discretion police are allowed to enforce social values of the larger society has aided in their own corruption."

———————

Recognizing the rapidly changing political and social landscape of his city, Mayor John Reading struck a conciliatory tone with his choice of Charles Gain's successor. George T. Hart grew up on a cattle ranch in Kings County, a rural, working-class corner of the Southern California desert. He earned a degree in criminology from UC Berkeley in 1956 and took a job at the OPD that would become his life's calling. Although he shrugged off comparisons, Hart kept with his predecessor's policies, challenging the force's previous "stormtrooper" incarnation and seeking a better rapport with Black Oaklanders.

"We want a police organization that services the entire community in a fair and impartial manner, and we want a police organization in which we can have confidence," Chief Hart told a documentary crew in 1974.

"People should never forget that policing in our society is, by definition, in my opinion, a negative institution. We exist, the police system—in fact, the entire criminal justice system—out of need. We need to help resolve people's problems; all of our problems. It is by definition, then, a conflict-ridden task. Our job," he said, "is not to be loved, our job is to accomplish what we have to as effectively and efficiently as possible with as much understanding, awareness, and, if you will, warmth, just human-to-human skills, as possible."

Instead of superhuman crime fighters, Hart wanted his officers to realize that a large part of their work would be helping people with everyday problems.

"There are all different ways to establish authority as a police officer," he explained. "You can establish authority by humor, you can establish by showing concern. Showing physical force is not an absolute—that's not the only way one controls the situation."[108]

In 1969 Charles Gain used a federal grant to bring in a sociologist who worked extensively with the California prison system for the purpose of helping Oakland cops involved in violent encounters review their conduct and discern alternatives. The practice was so successful that in 1972 the chief of police institutionalized the self-review session under a "conflict management section," which regularly held sessions at which cops listened to recordings of encounters with citizens to improve their "discretionary decision-making."[109] In contemporary parlance, this is called de-escalation.

In 1971 the OPD began using data and the filing cabinet–sized computers of the day to systematically track and document uses of force, utilizing a program that periodically flagged officers with high numbers of such incidents so that a nonpunitive panel of peers could provide guidance.[110]

The self-reflective programs helped cut the number of citizen complaints against Oakland cops in half, and there were 30 percent fewer arrests for resisting arrest or assault on an officer during the early 1970s.

But Hart wasn't as forward-thinking as Gain. Part of his reform-mindedness was born out of a desire to alleviate the controversies the department had been embroiled in for years and return to a simpler era of policing. He embraced a color-blind view and denied that racism was a systemic problem within the OPD, telling an interviewer in 1979 that he found it "mind boggling" that the public presumed his white officers couldn't treat Black people fairly.

"The average officer in Oakland works largely with Blacks," said Hart. "That's the part that I have so much trouble with. Why would people construe that we are prejudiced against the people we work with?"[111]

The police department was not the only Oakland institution undergoing change in the early 1970s. The city's growing Black population was tired of the political status quo. Sky-high unemployment rates, housing discrimination, and the razing of West Oakland's Black-owned businesses for the new elevated Bay Area Rapid Transit tracks and Cypress Freeway all contributed to a growing urgency to fundamentally change the city's state of affairs. And because Black people now accounted for a third of the population, community leaders realized that much more than resistance was possible.

Inspiration for greater things came in 1972 when Democratic representative Shirley Chisholm of New York, who four years before became the first Black woman elected to the US Congress, ran for president. In Oakland, a young Mills College student and volunteer with the Panthers named Barbara Lee invited Chisholm to speak at the all-women campus. The event set in motion a decision by Lee and a handful of other students, lawyers, and organizers to support Chisholm's campaign to become the first Black

female presidential nominee of a major political party. They started regis-
tering Black, Latino, Asian, and white working-class voters in Oakland's
flatlands, many of whom had never bothered to vote before.[112] Lee eventually recruited the Black Panthers to support Chisholm's campaign, and the
taste of electoral politics turned them into an actual party.

Panthers cofounder Bobby Seale decided in May 1972 that the time was
ripe for a local political revolution. In West Oakland's DeFremery Park, a
symbolic location the Panthers had rechristened "Lil' Bobby Hutton Park,"
Seale announced that he would challenge John Reading in the mayor's race.
In an important visual cue, the Panthers' cofounder appeared in a conven-
tional business suit and white dress shirt, forsaking the beret and leather
jacket he and Newton had elevated to global symbols of Black militancy.
Running alongside Seale was fellow Panther Elaine Brown, who sought a
city council seat.

Seale surprised Oakland by eking out second place in the crowded
nonpartisan primary of nine candidates, forcing Reading into a runoff.
Although the incumbent mayor's fifty-five thousand votes was more than
double his take, Seale confidently predicted his victory in the general election, if his party could register and mobilize the thousands of uninvolved
Black and Latino voters. While the Black Panther Party managed to register
thousands more, Seale ended up losing, but his tally of forty-seven thousand votes demonstrated the hunger of Black Oaklanders for more power.
And not all of Seale's votes were cast by people of color. A significant por-
tion of the city's white population also voted for the firebrand, a sign of the
increasingly liberal attitudes in formerly Republican hills neighborhoods
such as Montclair and Rockridge.

In 1976 John George, the civil rights attorney who had led campaigns
against police brutality and school segregation in Oakland, became the first
person of color elected to the powerful Alameda County Board of Supervisors. It was also noteworthy that he prevailed over William Rumford Jr., a
Black former Berkeley cop and the police chief of the regional BART transit
system who ran as a law-and-order candidate.

Two years later, a political earthquake struck when Lionel Wilson prevailed in the mayor's race. Although Wilson, a superior court judge, campaigned as a moderate, he benefited directly from the tens of thousands of
new voters registered by the Panthers and other activists, many of whom
endorsed him in the runoff against David Tucker, a white Republican stock-

broker and school board president who had Reading's backing. Like Rumford, Tucker ran on a law-and-order message; he pledged to add 150 officers to the police department, adding in his official nominating statement filed with the county, "My first priority will be an all-out *war on crime.*"[113]

The scare tactics didn't work.

When he walked into the mayor's office for the first time, in 1978, Wilson pledged to address Oakland's crime problem by treating the root causes of poverty, unemployment, and racial discrimination. He knew something about all three. Like Huey Newton, Wilson was born into a family of modest means in Louisiana before they moved to Oakland when he was a child. His father faced harsh racism in California's workplaces: his light skin had allowed him to pass as white, but toward the end of his career as a custodian, he was discovered to be Black and was shunned. Even as a judge, Wilson knew how his own Black skin (even though it was light) would affect his chances of buying a home in the leafy Montclair section of Oakland, so he had his white wife visit their dream house alone to deal with the real estate agent and sellers.

Now gazing out his city hall office window, Wilson could see the ramshackle sprawl of West Oakland's empty lots and crumbling Victorians and the imposing wall of the Cypress Freeway Viaduct. As a judge, he'd had the power only to apply the law, mostly to a rotation of Black and brown defendants, suffering from deindustrialization, joblessness, poverty, and racism. Now he held the power in his hands to make policy. The city finally seemed ready for a liberal mandate. Wilson and his team could bring to bear the tools the War on Poverty had brought to Oakland, however, this time using the levers of city government.

But forces far beyond Oakland's control were about to upend everything: first, in the form of California's statewide tax rebellion, which would eviscerate Oakland's finances and make ambitious social programs impossible; then later in the form of drugs and firearms, which flooded the city in the 1980s and 1990s, leading to a period of unprecedented violence.

7

SMALL WARS

On the evening of March 17, 1979, a squad of Oakland cops searched for a mysterious sniper who was aiming a gun at traffic on the Grove-Shafter Freeway in North Oakland. No one had been shot. It wasn't even clear there was a sniper, but the police were treating it as an emergency. Near the highway, fifteen-year-old Melvin Black leaned against a blue Plymouth sedan. The young man faced away from Fifty-Third Street.

An unmarked police car, a Chevy Camaro driven by Sergeant Joe Thomas of the Vice Squad, with Officer Steve Bunting riding shotgun, rolled by and turned into an apartment complex parking lot. A moment later, a second unmarked car, a Pontiac driven by Officer Kent Thornberry, entered Fifty-Third Street. Officer Glen Tomek, in the passenger seat, spotted the teenager and told Thornberry to make a beeline to him.[1]

The two officers bounded out of the car with guns drawn, Thornberry taking cover behind another parked car, and Tomek peering from behind the police vehicle.

"Freeze!"

"Turn around!"

"Put your hands on the car!"

When Black turned, the vice cops would later tell investigators and a civil jury, he drew a gun from his waistband and pointed it at them.

Thornberry and Tomek opened fire. One bullet tore through Melvin's abdomen, but the teenager was still able to run for his life. Both cops unloaded their .38s as Black fled toward his family's apartment building.

Gravely wounded, he stumbled to his hands and knees. By now, Thomas and Bunting had heard the shots, sprinted from their car, and rounded the corner in time to spot Black. Thomas fired at him. Black got to his feet and ran again, reaching a neighbor's door and banging on it in a desperate attempt to escape. No one answered. Stumbling into the dark, he made it to the stairs leading to his home, where he collapsed. Black died in a hospital hours later from a gunshot to the back of his neck. A pellet gun was later found on the trunk of the car where police first spotted him.

Melvin Black's family immediately challenged the police's version of events. Oakland's Black community found that, unlike in the preceding decades, many white Oakland residents were now on their side, demanding answers. Oakland was no longer governed by a tone-deaf white city council and mayor whose first instinct, as in every controversial shooting in the 1960s and 1970s, it seemed, was to circle the wagons.

That era was ending. Protesters converged on council meetings and marched from high schools to the police headquarters. Councilman Carter Gilmore, the first Black man elected to the position in 1977, joined the NAACP in calling for an independent investigation. Mayor Wilson pledged to take action. The US Attorney for the Northern District of California, G. William Hunter, the first Black person to hold the position, also announced an FBI investigation. Now led by men of color, Oakland seemed finally primed for a reckoning with police violence.

Eleven days after the shooting, the pot was stirred further when Thornberry and two other cops stormed into the NAACP's West Oakland offices to arrest a man and woman on pandering and prostitution charges. NAACP leaders denounced the intrusion and claimed the two arrestees had offered up information about Melvin Black's killing. At a press conference, President Libby Dyson of the NAACP's Oakland chapter called the teenager's death a "murder" and demanded the arrest of Thornberry and the other officers who "broke" into their offices with guns drawn. The raid, Dyson claimed, was a blatant attempt to intimidate.

The officers reacted by filing a $4.5 million libel lawsuit against the NAACP. For the next year, the police union and civil rights group traded accusations in court.

On Mayor Wilson's recommendation, the city council appointed John Burris as a special investigator. The young lawyer had been in private practice only a few months before he was tapped to conduct the Melvin Black investigation. If his background gave any hint about his predilections, it was that Burris had ample experience in finding fault in boys like Melvin Black. He was a former prosecutor in both Alameda County and Cook County, Illinois, who had once tried a fifteen-year-old boy charged with three murders. In other cases, he prosecuted three teenagers who murdered two witnesses to another homicide they'd committed, and a fourteen-year-old boy who kicked a girl to death. With the Melvin Black case, Burris was reinventing himself into a strident opponent of police abuses.

Even though Burris's report wouldn't have the legal weight of the findings of the Alameda DA or the US attorney, his appointment, and the possibility of discipline for the cops involved in Black's shooting, riled Oakland police officers. Thomas, one of Black's killers, and his partner, Steven Bunting, left the OPD in protest for other law enforcement agencies. Chief Hart defended the shooting publicly, and the OPOA spoke up vociferously in defense of Thornberry and Tomek. Only the Oakland Black Officers Association held back from publicly supporting the cops.

Burris methodically reviewed police documents, interviewed witnesses, and took in the scene of the shooting to discern what happened. As his probe was under way, the police department and the district attorney completed their investigations. Predictably, the OPD exonerated its own, and DA Lowell Jensen also cleared the officers of criminal culpability. These findings were dismissed by many in the Black community, which awaited word from the special investigator.

In September, six months after the shooting, Burris submitted his report. Thornberry, Tomek, and Thomas, he found, all exhibited "faulty judgment and poor police tactics." The two-hundred-page analysis made clear that Melvin Black could have been stopped, questioned, and, if necessary, arrested without resorting to deadly force. Burris noted that Thomas and Bunting initially passed by the teenager while searching for the sniper, properly assessing Black wasn't a threat. Thornberry and Tomek leapt to the conclusion that the boy was their suspect. They needlessly and recklessly emptied their revolvers at the terrified youth. According to Burris, Melvin Black most likely took the pellet gun out of his pants and put it on the car as Thornberry and Tomek surrounded him. He was in the process of surrendering when the two cops opened fire and was fleeing a lethal threat when he was killed.

George Hart dismissed Burris's report. DA Jensen echoed the police chief: he was confident the officers acted in self-defense. OPOA president

Robert Foster, a fourteen-year OPD veteran who viewed the new mayor as a cynical politician using the police killing to grab more power, was more blunt: "The Burris investigation was clearly prejudiced from the beginning," he told the press. "We don't recognize this investigation as authentic."[2]

The city administration, which faced a wrongful death lawsuit from Black's mother, Oretha McKinney, and was concerned the report would be used to convince a jury of the officers' fault, declared the report confidential and tried withholding it from the media and the public. But McKinney's lawsuit would further expose the injustice of the killing. After a difficult trial in a Sacramento court—the case was relocated because of extensive press coverage—a jury awarded McKinney $693,000. "When you're shooting at someone who is not shooting back, don't you stop shooting?" McKinney's attorney, J. Gary Gwilliam, asked the jury in his closing argument. "What are you doing? Hunting someone?" After the trial, one juror said it was clear that the officers violated their own regulations and had broken the law.[3]

It would be thirty years before a police shooting—even one as obviously wrong as Melvin Black's—would lead to criminal charges. But the brazen police killing, and the city's refusal to fire the officers, galvanized Oaklanders to try one more time for something they'd sought since the 1940s: a civilian-led oversight board.

Melvin Black wasn't the only person killed by the Oakland PD that year. From January 1, 1979, to January 10, 1980, the city's cops killed nine people—all Black. Officers shot and wounded another eight people, six of them Black, an Asian teenager, and a white man. Two officers were shot and wounded in the same violent year, but for many Oakland residents, the increasingly dangerous streets weren't an excuse for police having a heavy trigger finger. The fact that there was a Black mayor who owed his position partly to the Black Panthers' influence emboldened activists. If the city's Black residents and progressives couldn't achieve the goal now, could they ever?

The Oakland NAACP united with the powerful Central Labor Council of Alameda County and the Oakland Citizens Committee for Urban Renewal to demand the establishment of a police oversight commission. They were joined by County Supervisor John George, who challenged Mayor

Wilson and his colleagues during a council meeting: "The question is, who rules Oakland? The city council or the police?"[4]

Wilson established a task force to explore the idea of an oversight entity. John Sutter, a white liberal council member representing a hills district, chaired the panel, whose other ten members included representatives of the downtown business community, such as David Way, president of the Clorox Company Foundation; civil rights leaders, including attorney and NAACP member Oliver Jones; and activists like Geoffrey Carter and Margaret Pryor.

The task force met for months to refine three different options. The Oakland chapter of the American Civil Liberties Union (ACLU) offered a model whereby a new Office of Citizens Complaints—employing civilian staff with no links to the OPD—would conduct investigations and hand off its recommendations to the police chief and the city manager for discipline. Crucially, the ACLU advised shuttering the department's Internal Affairs Division, to avoid wasteful duplication and prevent biased investigations.[5]

The NAACP's proposal went further. It called for the creation of a more robust Police Review Commission, modeled after the commission that Berkeley voters established in 1973. Jim Chanin, by then an attorney and colleague of Oliver Jones, closely advised Jones about the inception of the Berkeley Police Review Commission, which Chanin chaired in its early days. Oakland's version would not only investigate complaints but also examine all policy matters affecting policing and public safety and make recommendations for changes to the city manager and council. Its staff and commissioners would be paid, creating a professional counterforce to the OPD. Predictably, Chief Hart opposed any new "bureaucracy," as he called it, but especially the NAACP and ACLU plans.

Ultimately, it was Councilman Sutter's plan that gained the most traction. Sutter's vision was to set up a smaller oversight board staffed by investigators from the city attorney's office. They would have the power to investigate misconduct complaints and make advisory findings. Disciplinary and policy-making power would remain in the hands of the police chief and the city manager.[6]

A majority of the task force voted for Sutter's vision with a few modifications: the five-member commission, picked by the mayor and confirmed by the council, would have subpoena power to compel officer testimony and obtain records, but it would only be able to make recommendations.

The NAACP and other activists opposed Sutter's plan. Oliver Jones called it an "illusion" of reform. Bob Foster objected, but for the opposite reasons, arguing that the plan would create just one more layer of bureaucracy during a time in which the city's finances were suffering from the 1978 passage of Proposition 13, a statewide real estate tax cut benefiting homeowners and large corporations but curtailing property tax revenue. The OPOA president also accused Mayor Wilson of trying to wrest power away from the council and the city manager.[7]

Public debate on the issue reached a boiling point by the time the city council assembled on January 10, 1980, in the Oakland Civic Auditorium, a massive Beaux Arts stone building on the southern tip of Lake Merritt. More than 1,500 people packed the theater and heckled the handful of public speakers who favored the status quo, including Earl Hunting, the president of Citizens for Law and Order, a once-influential voice in public safety debates who dredged up the claim used by police chiefs and the Far Right American Legion over the previous fifty years that an oversight board was a conspiracy by "leftists groups" to weaken America's defenses.

When Sutter read the task force's plan into the record, the crowd jeered, and Wilson announced a short recess for "cooling off." Members of the Revolutionary Communist Party took over the hall, hung banners, and gave speeches while a young Black man "paraded throughout the hall carrying a large, freshly butchered pig's head atop a pole bearing a silver paper-star badge similar in design to the OPD badge."[8]

The council approved a version of the Sutter plan. In 1980 Oakland became the second city in California, after Berkeley, to set up a civilian police oversight commission. Over the coming two decades, the Citizens' Police Review Board, as it was known, would serve a small but important role for Oaklanders who felt abused by police. This was Oakland's first major structural reform to rein in the police. It would also be the last for decades.

———

Just as Huey Newton's early life personified the changes sweeping through Oakland and other American cities—from the Great Migration, to the civil rights struggle, to Black power insurgency—he continued to swim in the major currents reshaping America. After his 1971 release from prison, Newton, then twenty-nine, consolidated the Black Panther Party in Oakland, shutting down other chapters and ordering the remaining faithful to come serve in Northern California to establish "community control" in his hometown. Huey designated his bodyguards as the sole armed element of the party. This cadre, called the "Squad" by other Panthers and "Buddha Samurai" by Newton himself, enforced the BPP leader's mandate through strict discipline and corporal punishment.[9] Publicly, Newton spoke of "regulating" Oakland's "illegitimate capitalists"—the numerous drug dealers and small-time criminals—in order to stabilize the city's poorer communities.

But in secret, and later brazenly, Newton and his posse took part in Oakland's underworld. He'd started out as a self-admitted burglar, but as the leader of dozens of armed men, he became a crime boss.[10] Newton took over the management of the Lamp Post, a Telegraph Avenue lounge nominally owned by his cousin Jimmy Ward. The bar provided steady income and ample opportunity for Huey's bodyguards to extort protection money from the gamblers, pimps, sex workers, and drug dealers who frequented it.[11] Newton's other base of operation was from the twenty-fifth-floor penthouse of 1200 Lakeshore, a 1960s-era luxury apartment building from which he could gaze down on the courthouse where he'd been put on trial years earlier.

Newton's Squad members had no compunction about backing their threats up with consequences. On occasion, its members would burn down recalcitrant nightlife establishments that wouldn't pay the levy. In 1973 Newton's bodyguards were suspected of torching the iconic Fox Theater in downtown Oakland twice.[12]

Whereas the Panthers were hounded by local authorities in the late 1960s, legal consequences for their criminal transgressions in the 1970s never seemed to materialize. There were widespread suspicions that the party's post-1972 arrival as a potent political force had something to do with its local impunity. Mayor Wilson and Alameda County Supervisor John George both acknowledged they won office with the endorsement and organizing strength of the Panthers, developed during Bobby Seale's and Elaine Brown's campaigns. Although Seale was purged from the party by Newton shortly after, Elaine Brown's power grew. A classical piano player and soul singer turned radical powerhouse, she became a close confidante of Governor Jerry Brown's advisor J. Anthony Kline, lobbied successfully for millions of dollars in state grants, and helped appoint at least one local judge. Brown also served as a delegate for Jerry Brown at the 1976 Demo-

cratic National Convention. Mayor Wilson served on the board of the umbrella nonprofit responsible for the Panthers' Oakland Community School,
which was funded with hundreds of thousands in city and state grants.[13]

But rumors swirled that there was something more pernicious about
the aura of invincibility that surrounded Newton and his Buddha Samurai.
"They knew about all our clandestine activities," a former Panther told journalist Hugh Pearson in 1992. "We had politicians, judges, police, respected
businessmen in our pockets. There were members of the police force who
would call us up and tell us when someone in the department was going to
move on us."[14]

There was some veracity to that statement: in 1973 Police Chief Charles
Gain called Huey Newton to warn him that a contract on his life bankrolled
by Oakland pimps was circulating in the city's underworld. Whether vice
or narcotics officers ever called to offer more inappropriate warnings has
never been proven.

During the 1970s, the OPD's approach to the Panthers changed noticeably. The department no longer had a Panthers-specific squad gathering and
disseminating intelligence. Part of this was due to Huey's turning the party
toward "survival programs" rather than open confrontations with police.
From the mid-1970s onward, the Oakland police and the Alameda County
District Attorney's Office were also chastised following the exposure of the
FBI's COINTELPRO counterintelligence program and the revelations that
became public during US Senate hearings in the fall of 1975. The Senate Se-
lect Committee to Study Governmental Operations with Respect to Intelligence Activities, referred to informally as the Church Committee, chaired
by Idaho Democrat Frank Church, laid bare J. Edgar Hoover's covert efforts
to destroy the Black Panther Party—often with the assistance of local cops.

There was also a high degree of difficulty getting witnesses to cooperate
against Newton and his Squad.

In 1974 Newton brutally pistol-whipped tailor Preston Callins in his
Lake Merritt penthouse. The DA charged Newton with assault, but Callins,
seen sometimes near the courthouse in the menacing presence of Panthers
bodyguards, refused to testify. The Squad was also implicated in a series of
tit-for-tat shootings resulting in the murders of the doorman and the owner
of the Brass Rail restaurant in Berkeley.[15]

Most egregious was the 1974 murder of seventeen-year-old sex worker
Kathleen Smith, whom Newton allegedly shot in the face after she called

him "Baby," a nickname he'd detested since childhood. Smith's friend Crystal Gray, another sex worker who witnessed the shooting, gave sufficient evidence for the Alameda County district attorney to file assault and murder charges against Newton, causing him to flee to Cuba in 1974 and leave the party in the hands of Elaine Brown. In his absence, the Squad continued to flex its muscle in Oakland's underworld and diverge from the radical politics the Panthers once espoused.

The most notorious example of this devolution involved the murder of the Panthers' accountant. On January 17, 1975, forty-five-year-old Betty Van Patter's beaten and decomposing body was found floating in the bay. Van Patter, a white woman sympathetic to the Panthers' cause, had been recruited by Elaine Brown and *Ramparts* magazine editor David Horowitz to straighten out the books for the Panthers' school, Lamp Post bar, and various limited liability corporations controlled by Newton and the Squad. According to her family and close friends, Van Patter discovered a massive fraud. She was last seen having a drink alone at a Berkeley bar when a tall Black man handed her a note. She left shortly after reading the message, disappearing for thirty-five days before her badly beaten corpse turned up. Police suspected Newton and Brown silenced Van Patter, but the Panthers denied the allegations. No charges were ever filed.

On October 23, 1977, a little more than a year after Newton returned to the United States to stand trial for Smith's murder and the tailor's assault, an incident in Richmond cemented the party's downfall. Mary Matthews, a fifty-six-year-old Black woman, was lying in bed around five in the morning when she heard the unmistakable sound of someone tampering with her door. She called Richmond Police and grabbed the .38 revolver she kept for protection. While reciting her address to the police dispatcher, Matthews heard the screech of her metal screen door being torn from its hinges. She dropped to the floor and fired a single shot, only to be met by a fusillade of return fire. Miraculously unscathed, Matthews hid behind a pile of furniture until the police arrived. Outside her door was a pool of blood, a 12-gauge shotgun, and the body of Louis T. Johnson, a twenty-seven-year-old Black Panther who had been shot once in the back of the head.[16] A search of Matthews's neighborhood turned up a second shotgun, an automatic rifle, ammunition, and two sets of blue overalls and watch caps like the clothing Johnson wore. The shooting was clearly an orchestrated hit, but why target a law-abiding citizen like Matthews?

It turned out that the intended target lived in a pink clapboard house in the rear of Matthews's property. The two apartments were rented out to single mothers, including Crystal Gray (real name, Raphaelle Gary), the sex worker who'd witnessed Kathleen Smith's murder. She was scheduled to testify against Newton in court the very next day. Gray never testified against the Panther leader, and the murder case against Huey went nowhere.

News coverage of the blundering violence blew a hole in the Panthers' support in Oakland, leading former ally John George to voice public concerns about the party's direction. Elaine Brown, who had run the Panthers during Huey's absence, suddenly relocated to Los Angeles in the middle of the night after a rumored beating by Newton. The state soon opened up investigations into the Panther's nonprofit foundation that served as a fiscal vehicle for the BPP's school, the Educational Opportunities Corporation, after news broke that public funds were being used to pay for expensive apartments and other luxuries for Huey's bodyguards.[17]

The fall of the Black Panther Party was only the most acute symptom of the tide receding on the social activism of the 1960s and early 1970s. As radicalism cooled, a tsunami of poverty, drugs, and violence washed over Oakland and other American cities.

Factories continued to close, and the few jobs Black Oaklanders managed to secure at the Port of Oakland and adjoining warehousing sector were thinned by the rise of containerized shipping and long-haul trucking. The city's population dropped from 361,561 in 1970 to 339,337 ten years later, with a 39 percent reduction in the white population, as affluent residents decamped to the suburbs. Latino and Asian immigrants, many of them refugees fleeing the aftermath of US military interventions in their countries, began arriving in large numbers.[18] By the 1980s, Oakland was one of the nation's first "majority-minority cities," with nearly 160,000 Black residents holding the largest share of the demographic pie.

The passage of Proposition 13 had further eviscerated Oakland's coffers. By the early 1980s, the city budget was cratering, and President Ronald Reagan's decision to cut federal aid to cities left Oakland in trouble. Not only was the city unable to support 1960s-era social and economic programs, but it also cut basic services such as libraries and sanitation. Mayor Wilson's administration was forced to devise complex financial deals, selling off or leasing city assets such as buildings and renting them back for infusions of cash.

The illicit economy filled the gaps for many of Oakland's unemployed and desperate ghetto residents. Many became involved in the drug trade from the early 1970s onward, supplied with tons of heroin lugged home by demobilized Vietnam veterans and sailors smuggling product in through the burgeoning West Oakland docks.[19] In Mexico, production of the old narcolero staple of brown tar heroin increased to meet growing demand in El Norte.[20] Along with Los Angeles, Oakland became one of the West Coast hubs for the trade.

The Port of Oakland, the fifth biggest in the United States, was the first West Coast port to move from break-bulk shipping—that is, loose cargo loads—to containers, in 1962. The new process made trade faster and simpler but also complicated customs inspections. In 1991 the US Drug Enforcement Administration (DEA) and US Customs broke up a heroin trafficking network that moved tons of high-quality "China White" from Thailand, seizing a then-record 1,200 pounds from a Hayward warehouse.[21] "The Port of Oakland pretty much goes unchecked; I don't know of any other large port that doesn't have a police department," said Vic Bullock, an Oakland native who joined the OPD in 1981.

According to DEA estimates, by the early 1980s, there were 15,000 heroin addicts in Oakland.[22] Federal policies of abstinence and prohibition meant that the city was becoming poorer, more diverse, and exponentially less safe. In 1960 the city saw 20 murders, 59 rapes, 539 robberies, and 437 aggravated assaults. Nineteen years later, well into America's War on Drugs and incarceration boom, all those crime categories had increased by *500 percent to 700 percent*: in 1979 Oakland suffered 124 murders, 444 reported rapes, 3,572 robberies, and 2,513 aggravated assaults.[23]

One of the locals who rode the heroin wave to prosperity was Felix Mitchell, a Castlemont High School dropout and former member of the Black Panther Party's youth auxiliary group who sold marijuana and speed in the Sixty-Ninth Avenue housing projects where he grew up.[24] In the mid-1970s Mitchell landed a brown tar connection in Los Angeles. With this supply, his operation, named the 69 Mob, consolidated control of the drug trade in East and West Oakland.

Mitchell's organization was the first in Oakland to industrialize the drug trade. The 69 Mob pioneered an assembly-line system of street dealing in housing projects and apartment complexes: school-aged "spotters" kept an eye out for police, while addicts would walk into the projects and be verified as legitimate buyers by their telltale track marks from needle usage. After paying a "collector," they'd be pointed to yet another kid, the "spitter," who'd pass off a balloon of heroin hidden inside their mouth.

The profits were outrageous: youngsters could earn $300 a week as a lookout or $450 as a spitter. Mitchell's lieutenants minted small fortunes, raking in up to $12,000 a day. Of course, this came with risks. They defended their turf against rivals and rip-off crews with small arsenals—at first, revolvers and shotguns, but soon more powerful pistols and military-grade rifles and machine guns. Heavy-duty firearms were easy to find legally: in the late 1970s and early 1980s, Traders, a San Leandro sporting goods store just a couple miles from ground zero of the heroin and cocaine trade, advertised Beretta semiauto pistols, easily concealed .38-caliber snub-nosed revolvers, and Israeli-made Uzi submachine guns, all at bargain prices.[25] Oakland police frequently spotted drug dealers, enforcers, and jackers inside the shop, having their girlfriends and others with clean records "straw buy" them more firepower.

Mitchell's 69 Mob gained dominance through a murderous show of force. Some of its early opposition came from Newton's bodyguards, who sought to extort the drug gangs. Oakland police suspected Panthers gunmen in several fatal attacks on local dealers. One of them, Vernon "Preacher Man" McInnis, was murdered after he got into an argument with Squad members Robert Heard and George Robinson at the Lamp Post, claiming loudly that the Panthers "rip people off." Robinson was convicted for McInnis's murder, but the verdict was overturned after OPD officers were found to have improperly searched his car.[26] But the Panthers, already unraveling, found that they were not the dominant force on the streets. By 1977, Mitchell's 69 Mob had decided to take on Newton's men.

"Those are Huey's people—there they go, get them!" Mitchell ordered his lieutenant, Fred Sanders, one day in August 1977, just before the 69 Mob opened fire on Newton's bodyguards. In a separate instance, Mitchell's enforcers raked a van with a fusillade of bullets, killing an innocent man they mistook for a Panther.[27]

As the 69 Mob's reputation and lethality increased, Mitchell's gang expanded beyond its home turf near the Oakland Coliseum, running open-air dealing operations in West Oakland's Acorn housing project and farther afield in Berkeley and Sacramento.[28] They netted tremendous profits, on the order of $12 million to $50 million a year, according to law enforcement estimates.

"Felix could have been a CEO," FBI agent John Steiner told a newspaper years later. "He had a knack for business. Unfortunately, that business was heroin."[29]

Still in his mid-twenties, Mitchell became a millionaire and splashed the cash, purchasing two homes in Los Angeles and a limousine company and auto-detailing shop in Oakland. The 69 Mob's flashy displays of luxury cars, mansions, and designer clothes, and Mitchell's ostentatious persona— he was known to wear a small diamond-filled hourglass on a necklace— attracted admirers and elicited violent envy from rivals.

Milton "Mickey" Moore, a former soul singer and Oakland High School graduate, formed "The Family," modeled on the 69 Mob, in the late 1970s after linking up with a Los Angeles heroin supplier. In 1980 Moore's gang unsuccessfully challenged Mitchell, touching off a war that left six dead in the span of a week.[30] The Family was on the losing side of the conflict, and the gang fractured further in 1982, when Moore's nephew Andre Piazza shot one of their own dealers named Harvey Whisenton in the back during a feud. Whisenton survived and founded his own rival drug gang called Funktown USA.[31]

Although Moore was eventually vanquished, he did manage to stay one step ahead of the law for a time by paying off two Oakland cops, Carl Gayden and Wayne "Downtown" Brown, to tip him off about impending raids. Gayden and Brown were caught by federal DEA agents and prosecuted; it turned out that they were extending the same "service" to other drug dealers.[32]

Crack cocaine's emergence further inflamed Oakland. Though it is difficult to pin down precisely when crack first appeared, by 1984, OPD had noticed rock's soaring popularity. A street dealer and preacher named Roosevelt Taylor claimed the practice of smoking cocaine "base" was first concocted in Oakland in the late 1970s to accommodate customers with damaged septums.[33] The variant didn't spread widely until the mid-eighties deluge of cocaine on the streets of US cities, facilitated partly by the Central Intelligence Agency's alliance with drug-runners (some of them prominent Bay Area figures, such as Norwin Meneses and Oscar Danilo Blandón, outed by reporter Gary Webb as key links between the

CIA, the Contras, and American drug dealers) to fund the Nicaraguan guerrilla group the Contras in its fight against the country's Sandinista government, with its strong ties to the Soviet Union and Cuba.[34]

Competition to control Oakland's drug trade played out in a cycle of murders, investigations, mass arrests, and the emergence of new players.

Felix Mitchell, whose organization held the most territory, generated the most profits, and dropped the most bodies, was the primary target for Oakland cops and the feds. In 1981, federal agents arrested Mitchell at one of his LA mansions. He was charged with four murders, including three rivals belonging to the Family.[35] The 69 Mob fell two years later when federal prosecutors hit Mitchell and his crew with a separate indictment for tax evasion and racketeering. Sentenced to life without parole, Mitchell was stabbed to death at Leavenworth Penitentiary in 1987.

Mitchell's passing near the apex of the booming drug economy was marked by an unprecedented ritual of mourning and respect by thousands of Oaklanders who viewed him as a hero for bringing jobs and capital to neighborhoods otherwise abandoned by corporate America and the white middle class. His body was laid in an ornate bronze casket and set in a church, where two thousand people paid their respects. The next day, a procession formed in front of his mother's East Oakland home. Mitchell's corpse was paraded in a horse-drawn hearse across the the entire city, through the neighborhoods his gang controlled, trailed by an eight-mile-long procession of Rolls-Royces, Cadillacs, and sports cars, cheered along the route by admirers, and bemoaned by some ashamed locals. After services in North Oakland's Star Bethel Missionary Baptist Church, the singer Sade's jazzy hit record "Smooth Operator" was played as Mitchell's family and close associates filed past his casket for a final good-bye.

Several crews vied for the 69 Mob's crown, warring over five square miles of East Oakland's flatlands.[36] By the late 1980s, Darryl "Little D" Reed, a Brookfield Village dealer who came up under Mitchell, seized a commanding position.[37] "He had the whole city," said Ken Scott, an OPD narcotics detective who investigated Reed's operation.[38] The Fremont High School dropout's zenith didn't last long, though: federal agents wiretapping Reed's phone overheard him arranging multi-kilo deals and raided his apartment near Lake Merritt, where they found Little D in his kitchen "rocking up" thirty pounds of cocaine in a soup pot.[39]

Yet another small war erupted in 1989 when ex-lieutenants of Little D's crumbling empire gathered for a barbecue in Dimond Park in the East Oakland foothills. Anthony "Ant" Flowers, who now ran his own organization, got into a fistfight with Eric "Squeeze" Smith, a dealer in Timothy "Black" Bluitt's organization, which had also spun off from Little D's drug ring. Squeeze got the best of Ant. Humiliated, Flowers sought revenge. Over the next three years, the two sides raged against each other, leading to at least sixteen murders and dozens of shootings. Federal prosecutors eventually caught up with Bluitt, indicting him and fifteen associates, effectively ending the so-called BBQ War.[40]

Oakland's drug trade and lawlessness were fueled also by the predominantly white Hells Angels. In the early 1980s Australian Hells Angel Peter Hill flew to the United States to visit Oakland chapter member Kenny Walton in prison to swap Walton's speed recipe for five hundred liters of methamphetamine precursor worth $50 million, shipped stateside in pineapple juice tins.[41] The Angels were suspected to have Swiss bank accounts, small businesses like auto garages used to launder money, and girlfriends who worked for police agencies and could pass along information, keeping them one step ahead. At the Oakland PD, the Angels had a deal to provide intel and weapons recovered from the streets in exchange for favors.[42] Repeated efforts to prosecute them in the Bay Area and beyond failed. By the 1980s, the Angels' clandestine meth labs were thought to supply between one-quarter and one-half of the speed dealt in California.[43]

The escalating drug-related violence taxed officers whose ranks thinned as the city budget shrank. "You'd go from call to call to call; it was no break in between," said Rick Hart, a retired lieutenant who patrolled Deep East Oakland from 1978 through 1987. Hart, an Oakland native (no relation to George Hart), logged his daily experiences in a diary. "I got the feeling like we were on the treadmill."[44]

Some Oakland residents still filed police misconduct complaints. Occasionally, the OPD took public criticism for systemic problems. However, the era's bloodshed effectively silenced law enforcement critics. Instead, neighborhood watches and church groups lobbied for more cops and tougher approaches to crime.

The OPD was also a dramatically different department. As a result of changes initiated by Charles Gain, George Hart, and a 1974 affirmative action hiring mandate, it had diversified to the point where, by 1985, 39 percent of its officers were people of color, up from less than 1 percent in the mid-1960s.[45] With more Oakland-raised Black and brown cops on the job, the force finally had genuine community connections.

However, the fiscal crisis did not spare the police department. Chief Hart struggled with budgetary constraints, refocusing his officers on the drug turf wars while bolstering security downtown.[46]

A consummate personnel manager, described by one observer as "a quiet, thoughtful man with firmly held values, tempered by a deep appreciation of realpolitik," Hart knew every officer by his or her first name, was deeply involved in hiring, and negotiated deftly with the Oakland Police Officers' Association, which still held power over policies and assignments.[47] Veterans of the 1980s claim the rank and file's intense loyalty to Hart helped hold together the agency amidst protracted austerity and unprecedented bloodshed.[48]

Still, some programs were axed, including the "critical incident" peer review panel implemented in the early 1970s by Gain to improve de-escalation skills. "The peer review panels usually occurred on days off, and the union required that we pay each panel member time and a half," Chief Hart told an interviewer in 1986, pegging the price tag at $3,000 per panel. "It's tough to have innovative programs during a period of economic austerity." The tenant-landlord dispute program, the white-collar-crime section, and the OPD's in-department computer analytics also fell by the wayside.

Jerome Skolnick, a sociologist and law professor who studied the Oakland PD's navigation of austerity and surging violence, made the following observation: "The Oakland Police Department used to be considered one of the most, if not the most, innovative in the nation. Hart is not much interested in novelty and experimentation," he wrote. "Thus, there is little taste for new programs. Hart does not enjoy a high profile in the community, trips around the country, meetings, seminars or jaunts to Washington. He sees his job as maintaining a functioning department."[49]

The changes in the force's posture from Gain's innovations to the mid-1980s triage operation of Hart were in line with the broader shifts in the United States, away from the remnants of Great Society social programs and toward a neoliberal, militarized model of government under President Ronald Reagan. The former California governor (and FBI informant from the early 1940s through the McCarthy era) labeled narcotics as a national security threat in 1982, doubling down on Richard Nixon's 1970s enforcement efforts, and pushed through a package of get-tough legislation that funneled money and military surplus equipment to local law enforcement.

Edwin Meese, the Oakland native, former Alameda County prosecutor, and military intelligence officer who once terrorized 1960s Bay Area radicals with groundbreaking mass-arrest techniques, now served as the US attorney general. A hardcore conservative who characterized a peaceful Free Speech Movement sit-in at UC Berkeley as "a paramilitary operation," sardonically collected pig statuettes for his office, labeled the American Civil Liberties Union a "criminals' lobby," and routinely rode along on police operations, Meese devoted considerable federal resources to his hometown's War on Drugs.[50]

Nancy Reagan had made drug abuse her pet crusade, crystallized in an overly simplistic but memorable appeal to the young: "Just Say No." Oakland found itself in the glare of the Drug War spotlight when the First Lady promoted her antidrug program at the Henry J. Kaiser Auditorium in 1985. Two years later, the city received substantial federal money to establish a task force to suppress open-air crack markets.[51] The new units complemented OPD's Special Weapons and Tactics (SWAT) unit, formed in 1983.

Even more consequential was the formation of three Special Duty Units. SDU I pursued suspects on probation and parole, who could be locked up on lower-level infractions, while SDU II and SDU III were trained to target street-level drug dealers in buy-and-bust operations.[52] Unlike the standard "reactive" policing style of patrolling neighborhoods in marked cars and responding to calls for service, SDU officers went out looking for action in plain clothes and unmarked vehicles. They used pretextual walking and car stops for low-level offenses in order to try finding weapons or narcotics on suspects, the overwhelming majority of whom were African American or Latino.

Unlike the Vice Unit, which used informants, wiretaps, and federal cooperation to work "up the ladder" from street dealing to major traffickers such as Felix Mitchell and Rudy Henderson (another wholesale trafficker once referred to as Oakland's "cocaine kingpin"), SDU's work started and stopped on the street corner, suppressing the most visible part of the problem with force. The unit attracted officers who favored irregular hours and the adrenaline rush of undercover stings. Richard Word and Ron Davis, both of whom would rise high in the OPD a decade later, served in SDU, as did legendary and notorious officers like Barney Rivera, Ersie Joyner III, Frank Uu, and Sammy Faleafine.[53]

"Proactive policing is crime prevention," explained Sergeant David Krauss, Hart's chief of staff. "It means identifying suspicious persons and making field contacts. If the department wants crime to fall, it can't just wait for the phone to ring."[54]

Oakland was not alone in the shifting approach to law enforcement. As New York City's murder rate climbed in the 1980s, peaking at 2,154 in 1991, the NYPD formed a Street Crime Unit of plainclothes and undercover officers to catch would-be muggers and robbers.[55] Likewise, Los Angeles police established the Community Resources Against Street Hoodlums units in 1979. Each of the LAPD's eighteen patrol divisions had its own CRASH team, which led Chief Darryl Gates's all-out offensive against street gangs. With CRASH and SWAT as the spearhead, the LAPD "created an occupational army, the Hammer, antigang task forces, sweeps in which we'd arrest a thousand people," recalled former chief Bayan Lewis. "By God, if you even look like a gang member, you're going to jail."[56] Gang members were likened to the Vietcong by state lawmakers, who passed a draconian Street Terrorism Enforcement and Prevention Act in 1988 that lengthened prison sentences for those branded with the gang label.[57]

Decades later, both SDU's and CRASH's hard-charging—and occasionally lethal—methods and lurid extracurricular activities brought both the NYPD and the LAPD into disrepute, poisoning community relations.[58] But during the surge of street violence in the 1980s and 1990s, their oftentimes extralegal tactics, which were being used in Oakland, too, were viewed as the gold standard.

Oakland's aggressive shift was not just confined to the specialized units. Hart's directive to all officers was to invest in "beat health" and deal with conditions contributing to blight, building security, and sanitation. Many officers adopted a territorial attitude about their sectors and bristled when other cops responded to calls there.

Another component of the Oakland PD's proactive policing was a renewed focus on the downtown business district. The few remaining big businesses were alarmed at the influx of a class of residents Yale sociologist Albert Reiss disparagingly referred to as "mental offenders," "drifters," and "grate people" living rough on the streets, as well as the single-room-occupancy hotels used by parolees. They pushed for a harder-edged approach to "soft crime." This meant cracking down on loitering, panhandling, and public intoxication just as hard as on drug sales and prostitution.

Hart assigned Lieutenant Peter Sarna to work with businesses, developers, and community groups to put uniformed and plainclothes foot patrols and cops on dirt bikes on the streets. They overhauled municipal codes to ban loitering in certain areas of downtown. An entire new platoon, including a full Special Duty Unit (SDU III), was created to shore up Oakland's unique version of what is known as the broken-windows theory of policing.[59]

Despite the SDU's high levels of arrests, the OPD acknowledged that it was merely conducting triage. Suppressing the drug trade and preventing another Mitchell-like empire from emerging was the best it could do.[60] Conversely, the department's campaign against street dealing and quality-of-life offenses prompted sustained complaints from some African American residents about harassment, and a series of racial-profiling lawsuits filed by Jim Chanin and Oliver Jones.[61] Officers were "given a mandate to pounce on anything that even smelled of violence or criminal activity," according to one newspaper account.[62] Black and brown Oaklanders took exception and complaints about police conduct increased sharply, from forty-seven in 1988 to sixty-two in 1991.[63]

"The department's main problem is with its strategy of so-called proactive policing," wrote the scholar Skolnick. "It finds itself in the catch-22 position of being damned if it does and damned if it doesn't. To the extent that officers patrol aggressively in response to community demands to keep the streets safe and attractive, the department is liable to invite accusations of harassment and even brutality."[64]

By the end of the 1980s, violence had become endemic despite (or perhaps because of) the massive Drug War investment to dismantle trafficking operations. West Oakland, in particular, had been transformed by the steady outflow of industrial jobs and deepening poverty. It was on a West Oakland street in the heart of the Lower Bottoms neighborhood near the port where the drug trade claimed the life of the man who'd arguably done more than anyone to break down Oakland's mid-twentieth-century social order and the police department's iron grip on the Black community. At five o'clock in the morning on August 22, 1989, forty-seven-year-old Huey Newton was found lying in a pool of blood, dying from three gunshots to the head.

Since the demise of the Black Panther Party in the late 1970s, Huey had drifted further into alcohol and cocaine addiction, cycling in and out of prison and relying on his reputation to score from Oakland's dealers.[65] Although he had completed a doctorate at the University of California, Santa Cruz, and had moments of clarity, by all accounts, the onetime scourge of the Oakland PD and Hoover's FBI had become politically irrelevant. Oakland, where the Black middle class now controlled the levers of power, was consumed by the carnage of drug addiction and the kaleidoscopic universe of drug gangs that had been violently splintering since the 69 Mob's demise.

Huey developed a crack addiction that he fed by extorting free rock from dealers. This put him on the wrong side of powerful organizations such as the Black Guerrilla Family, an African American prison gang started by the imprisoned Black radical George Jackson in 1966 that entered Oakland's drug game as muscle for Funktown USA. A 1989 stint at San Quentin State Prison for a parole violation brought Huey into contact with BGF leadership, some of whom still blamed Newton for refusing to assist Jackson in his failed prison break in 1971;[66] the twenty-nine-year-old author of *Soledad Brother*, who'd spent much of his life behind bars, made it as far as the prison yard before he was shot dead from a guard tower.

The crack dealer who ended up murdering Newton, twenty-five-year-old Tyrone Robinson, was affiliated with the Black Guerrilla Family and later claimed the killing would help him "make rank" within the gang. However, he told police he'd shot Newton in self-defense, knowing that Huey, who'd ripped him off months earlier, had a history of assaulting dealers. Despite Robinson's confession and specious rumors that Huey had been set up by law enforcement, the Oakland Police Department's investigation held up. Robinson was convicted at trial two years later.[67]

Given that Huey Newton was once lauded worldwide as a symbol of resistance against imperialist and capitalist repression, his demise on a West Oakland street was profoundly depressing. In death, Newton's critics did not mince their words. "The Newton I dealt with in the seventies was basically a gangster," said Tom Orloff, the prosecutor who failed to convict him for teenage sex worker Kathleen Smith's 1974 killing.[68]

Nevertheless, more than six thousand people of all races turned up at the Palmer D. Whitted Funeral Home on Foothill Boulevard to pay their respects to the slain Black Panthers leader.

Reader Carl Miller, in a letter to the *East Bay Express*, an alternative weekly newspaper serving Berkeley, Oakland, and Richmond, defended Newton's legacy:

"Sure the Huey Newton some riff raff shot was probably a murderer, thief, alcoholic and drug addict. . . . But the man we remember was much more than just another thug. We remember the Huey Newton who stood up strong and black, who faced down the pigs and scared shit out of racists whose worst nightmare seemed about to come true. . . . The Huey we remember was a tonic that at the time our community sorely needed, so pardon us if we pay tribute to one of our own."[69]

Newton's lasting contribution to Oakland was his unapologetic militancy in the face of the oppressive, mid-twentieth-century segregation. By confronting the OPD on equal footing, armed with guns and the letter of the law, the Panthers forced police and local politicians to recognize that the status quo had to change in order to avert all-out conflict.

By the time of Newton's death, Oakland was one of a number of cities where African Americans had won control of the mayoralty and local government; others included Cleveland, Cincinnati, Los Angeles, Washington, DC, and Newark, New Jersey. However, the country's neoliberal restructuring, with capital draining from urban centers and pouring into white suburbs and right-to-work states—coupled with the Reagan administration's shredding the social safety net and the ravages of the crack era—scarred cities deeply and left them almost unrecognizable from merely twenty years prior.

Oakland was forever altered at the end of the decade by literal shifts in its landscape. As the brash Oakland Athletics of local heroes Rickey Henderson and Dave Stewart warmed up for Game Three of the World Series against the San Francisco Giants in Candlestick Park on October 17, 1989, a section of the San Andreas Fault slipped. A 6.9-magnitude earthquake rippled across Northern California, causing the most damage since the 1906 temblor that leveled San Francisco, while triggering Oakland's rapid twentieth-century expansion.

The Loma Prieta quake, as it would come to be known, brought down buildings from Monterey County to Oakland, killing sixty-three and injuring almost four thousand. A fifty-foot section of the Bay Bridge's upper level collapsed onto the lower roadway. In West Oakland, less than a mile from the corner where Huey Newton breathed his last gasp of diesel-tainted air, the upper deck of the Cypress Freeway Viaduct pancaked onto the lower level, crushing forty-two motorists to death. Firefighters and West Oakland residents swarmed on the wreckage, desperately trying to free trapped drivers and passengers. Oakland's thirteen-story, seventy-five-year-old city hall withstood the shaking but suffered structural damage, necessitating $90 million in repairs and remaining uninhabitable until 1995.

The natural and man-made tumult buffeting Oakland peaked in the early 1990s. Lionel Wilson, then seventy-six years old and in office for thirteen years, could count $1 billion in new construction among his accomplishments, including the gleaming new City Center project on what had been empty lots next to city hall. Oakland also underbid San Francisco with free land to convince the federal government to build new offices downtown. A state office building soon followed. Wilson's first term mostly satiated liberal and even radical aspirations; in addition to supporting the Citizens' Police Review Board's creation, he upended Oakland's system of contracting and city jobs, ramming through an affirmative action measure that gave Black businesses a leg up. In his last two terms, Wilson used his reputation as a civil rights advocate to stave off criticisms that he'd grown too cozy with the downtown business community and neglected the poor.[70]

But by the late 1980s, progressives and Black people were defecting from the coalition that had elected Wilson to three consecutive terms, citing the worsening poverty and violence in East and West Oakland. In the 1990 election, voters abandoned the incumbent in favor of state assemblyman Elihu Harris, who raised a record $1 million for his campaign, and Councilman Wilson Riles Jr., a voice of conscience in city hall. Harris, who briefly counted John Burris as a partner in his law office in the 1970s and was a confidant of one of the most powerful men in California politics, Assembly Speaker Willie Brown, beat Riles in the runoff. Harris announced that his administration would pursue economic growth like Wilson's, but he would also tackle crime with a mix of policing and social programs to treat root causes.

The next year, another disaster would reshape the wealthy hills to which Oakland's remaining white population had retreated, along with the city's ascendant Black professional class. Firefighters thought they had extinguished a small blaze on a brushy hill near the Caldecott Tunnel, but on October 20 a hot Diablo wind—hot hurricane-force winds from the northeast that stoke late summer and fall fires in Northern California—whipped embers into a roaring conflagration that ripped through the hillside neighborhoods, fueled by bone-dry chaparral and conifers that had gone without rain for five months. The firestorm killed twenty-five and destroyed more than three thousand homes and apartments.[71]

Reagan-era austerity and the city's continued commercial decline took a toll: one in six Oaklanders were on welfare, including more than half of public school students. A quarter of high school students dropped out annually. Black infant mortality rose 22 percent in a decade.[72] White flight and disinvestment reached a nadir: by 1990, fewer than 9 percent of the Oakland Unified School District's fifty thousand students were white. Families that declined to join the white suburban exodus opted increasingly for private hills schools such as Bishop O'Dowd and Head-Royce. Approximately one in five Oakland residents lived below the poverty level, rising to two in five in sections of East Oakland.[73] In 1991 J.C. Penney shut its store at the Eastmont Mall, East Oakland's shopping mecca. The next year, anchor store Mervyn's closed, beginning Eastmont's long slide into decrepitude. Soon the county would relocate its safety net health care services, unemployment office, and social security offices, transforming Eastmont into a poverty alleviation mall.

Meanwhile, murders and shootings continued to skyrocket. There were 148 killings in 1989, 165 in 1990, and 175 in 1992—an all-time record. Young Oaklanders flocked to the drug game, attracted by the promise of fast money in a city where paths to gainful employment were disappearing. The allure of the drug trade caught up to many promising young Black men and women, including Wilson's own son Stevie, charged by federal prosecutors with cocaine trafficking in 1988.[74] From 1980 to 1990, local juvenile courts saw a staggering 2,200 percent increase in drug cases.[75]

Like other impoverished Black and Latino communities nationwide, Oakland's flatlands bore the brunt of both the violence and the metastasized street trafficking, with "rock houses" serving as hubs of dealing and violence. Following the lead of other California municipalities, the city responded by shuttering more than eight hundred houses for alleged drug activity from 1988 through the early 1990s.[76]

Homeless residents were also targeted in efforts to "clean up" the downtown business districts. The sweeps reached the point where unhoused Oaklanders pushed back: fifteen people sued over a 1992 sweep of a downtown freeway overpass in which police destroyed their possessions and sleeping gear.[77]

As Oakland struggled with natural disasters, the cycle of violence begun in the late 1970s intensified. In the first four months of 1992, fifty-six people were killed, an ignominious record for bloodshed that still holds today. Mayor Harris's public safety plan was to hire more police, increase nuisance prosecutions, and divert $500,000 to youth athletic and jobs programs.

George Hart, fifty-seven and in his nineteenth year as chief, emphasized that the OPD's ranks had shrunk by 5 percent since he assumed office in 1973, even though calls for service had more than doubled in the same period. Most of Oakland's violence was, he believed, interpersonal conflict made deadly by the availability of cheap firearms. "People are operating with a mentality of 'bang-bang you're dead,'" he said. "They assign no sense of value to human life. And there is no sense of there being a consequence to their actions; they are willing to blow people away over issues that aren't really important." Police couldn't prevent this sort of violence. Where the OPD could have an impact, Hart believed, was on drug-related violence by having officers engaged in proactive patrols.[78]

The dangers of the 1980s and 1990s didn't leave the police department unscathed. Eight officers were killed in the line of duty during the two-decade period, including Ramon Irizarry, shot in the head during a 1983 drug house raid; John Grubensky, who burned to death while saving hills residents fleeing the firestorm; and Keith Konopasek, killed by a security guard—a two-time OPD applicant—who said he didn't recognize the uniformed officer searching a car near his house. Officer James Williams Jr. was killed in 1999 by a sniper firing from an overpass on Interstate 580.[79]

When Hart announced his retirement in November 1992, Oakland had already experienced 165 homicides. Mayor Harris was faced with a challenge that none of his predecessors had to deal with in twenty years: selecting a chief to run the police department. City Manager Henry Gardner led a nationwide search for Hart's replacement, no small task in a profession where most chiefs last three to five years on average. After a six-month search, Gardner selected Joseph Samuels, a former OPD captain then running the Fresno Police Department.

Samuels was Oakland's first Black chief. He had a reputation for engaging community groups in public safety efforts. Gardner's choice was seen as a response to calls for a more public-facing, cooperative police chief. However, Samuels's appointment was greeted negatively by rank-and-file officers and command staff, including three deputy chiefs—Robert Nichelini, Marvin Thomas, and Thomas Donohue—all of whom had been finalists to replace Hart.[80] "I'm terribly disappointed," said OPOA vice president Bob Muszar. "Any of the three deputy chiefs would have been better."

The subtext to the strife over Samuels's appointment was the decades-long struggle over who ran the Oakland PD: the city administration, which had regained control in the 1960s with Chief Gain's contentious, reform-oriented appointment, or the Officers' Association, which had been mollified for twenty years by Hart. Nichelini, a native who graduated from Oakland High School in 1960, served in the air force, and became an OPD officer in 1971, had been the OPOA's favorite. Two years later, he would leave Oakland to run the Vallejo Police Department in the North Bay.[81]

The other subtext to Hart's departure was that he had been slow to implement the community-policing model at the core of Harris's plan to hire more officers. Samuels shared this vision. The idea was to shift officers away from 911 response and SDU assignments to neighborhood beats, where they would address complaints about crime and quality-of-life issues. In theory, bringing police in closer communication with locals would foster greater cooperation with police, and ultimately result in less crime. By December 1992, Hart had reassigned only one officer to the community-policing plan instead of the twenty-two the mayor desired.[82]

From within the department, the perception was that clueless city politicians were micromanaging police work. Chief Hart had shielded the agency from political influence, but now "city council members were contacting captains, lieutenants, and officers to get things done," said Rick Hart, who balked at the requests in the 1990s in his new role as a sergeant. "Wait a minute, you're not in my chain of command!"

Samuels found eight more community-policing officers by disbanding Special Duty Unit III, the hard-charging street narcotics team responsible for three thousand annual arrests. Sergeant Barney Rivera, SDU III's commander, predicted that Oaklanders "are going to get half the service they got before" and that the city would "see a big increase in street-level activity on the corner."[83] The OPD's aggressive, manpower-intensive enforcement style was further altered by Oakland's fiscal constraints, with the city council pressuring Samuels to reduce his agency's overtime expenditures and establish an annual cap of $4 million.[84] When twenty-two-year veteran officer Miguel Soto was shot in the head in 1994 while patrolling West Oakland alone, OPOA president Bob Valladon laid blame partly on the community-policing program, saying the walking officer could have survived if he were in a patrol car with a partner.[85]

In spite of dire predictions that the streets would run red, Samuels's term witnessed a slow but steady decline in violent crime.[86] Killings decreased steadily in the mid-1990s. The new chief assigned twenty-six officers to neighborhood beats along with sixteen foot-patrol officers, a thirteen-person tactical unit, and five civilian neighborhood coordinators. An additional dozen "Beat Health" cops worked with landlords to deal with properties that attracted drugs and crime. In 1996 Oakland saw ninety-eight murders, the lowest in eleven years.

"We feel safer," Debbie Acosta, a member of a citizens' group called the High Street Neighborhood Alliance, told the San Francisco Chronicle in 1996, citing efforts to clean up graffiti, rehabilitate creek beds, and keep tabs on drug crews. "The areas that we see as a locus for crime, because of the efforts we've made, they're not hanging there anymore. . . . They continue to pop up, but we're watching them now. We know who they are; when they pop up someplace else, we're immediately on them."[87]

But Oakland's falling crime rate was directly in line with a nationwide trend that has never been convincingly explained by social scientists and historians. It wasn't clear if any particular policing policy caused the decline.

Law enforcement certainly became more proficient at identifying and dismantling criminal organizations, thanks to billions of dollars in federal Drug War assistance and new laws that lengthened prison terms for alleged gang members and drug offenders. Federal agencies found plentiful targets for mass arrests and conspiracy indictments in Oakland. California's prison population exploded, with 248,516 inmates serving state time in 2000, up almost fivefold from 54,300 in 1980.[88] Starting in 1995, Alameda County jailed more than 4,000 residents per year, the overwhelming majority of them Black and Latino, a rate that wouldn't decrease substantially until criminal charging and sentencing reforms began in 2012.[89]

The OPD's raw focus on statistics, combined with pressure from politicians to meet certain benchmarks, proved detrimental to Oakland at large, and seeded the culture that would produce the Riders. Some of the force's more experienced cops recognized the damage.

"When you put pressure on officers to reduce crime, you have to have more of a strategy than to go out and make arrests," explained Rick Hart. "You can't have that scorched-earth policy where 'Everybody's going to jail, we've gotta clear the corners.' It doesn't work because guys you arrest end back up on the street, and you'll end up dealing with them again."

When the brass would give laudatory announcements tallying arrests, guns seized, and dope taken off the streets, Hart felt like he was listening to replays of the misguided "body count" stats touted by US generals during the Vietnam War.[90] "You'd go to lineup, and you'd get commanders saying, 'You need more FIs [field interviews].' They can't give you a quota, but they can give you a negative rating. You'd have pressure to get arrests and dope."[91]

In the mid-1990s Oakland turned a corner. The two-decade-long tide of violence ebbed. Employment rates started to rise, as did tax revenues bolstered by the overflow effects of Silicon Valley's and San Francisco's red-hot economies that drove some firms to seek bargain offices and warehouse space in the East Bay.

The era altered public attitudes about public safety. It had started off in Oakland and many other cities across the nation with one final push for greater police accountability, but the climate shifted rapidly to a politics of fear and tolerance of aggressive police tactics.

Leaders such as Lionel Wilson and Elihu Harris attempted to walk a tightrope, showing their communities that the gains of the civil rights movement and Black power would be realized through social uplift, while also cracking down on a largely Black and Latino population rendered superfluous by deindustrialization, white flight, and the federal government's abandonment. Federal and state leaders passed unforgiving crime bills, culminating in 1994's federal Violent Crime Control and Law Enforcement Act, which poured billions into police and prisons. California lawmakers went on a prison-building spree as Democratic and Republican politicians tried to outflank each other by taking ever-harsher stances on drugs and crime.[92] Drug War critics, prison abolitionists, and police accountability activists were drowned out by the chorus of voices demanding punitive solutions.

By the time Jerry Brown ran for Oakland mayor in 1998, the contradictions of the nineties had reached a breaking point. It was a decade that brought America the crack epidemic and superpredators but was also bookended by LAPD's vicious videotaped beating of Rodney King and the NYPD's firing squad execution of Amadou Diallo, two incidents that elevated concerns about systemic racism and brutality in law enforcement.

Oakland's Riders scandal was a corollary to King, Diallo, the 1994 Mollen Commission that examined systemic drug corruption in the NYPD, Ramparts, and countless other shootings, beatings, and human rights violations at the hands of police. The OPD's placement under federal court oversight in 2003 resulted from John Burris's and Jim Chanin's deep understanding of the Black community's complex feelings about law enforcement, especially frustration at having lived through the incredible violence of the 1990s and relying on an inveterate police force. Oakland's post-Riders mandate was also the product of a federal judge, Thelton Henderson, who understood this predicament: yes, Oaklanders had called for more police and better public safety in response to violence that had claimed thousands of lives over the previous thirty years, but the city's Black community wanted constitutional policing. They had cried out for it since the late 1940s, carried guns to "police the police" in the 1960s, and demanded civilian police oversight in the late 1970s, but the concept had never really come to fruition in Oakland.

This was why, in the early and mid-2000s, as the Oakland Police Department ignored the reform mandate it had been ordered to achieve, the city would experience the deadly consequences of an incorrigible police culture. It is also why the city would eventually explode in protest in the late aughts as the system's same fatal flaws continued to unjustly claim lives and thwart dreams of equality.

8

DEADLY CONSEQUENCES

It was a crisp late-September afternoon, the sweet spot of North Oakland's summer when the morning fog burns away before noon and the sun shines unwaveringly until the marine layer rolls onshore through the Golden Gate Bridge at dusk. BART trains gave off their atonal howl as they ran along elevated tracks above Martin Luther King Jr. Way—the boulevard formerly known as Grove Street, where the Panthers once organized at Merritt College.

The area had changed significantly in the interceding decades. Merritt College relocated to the Oakland Hills. The predominantly African American area, made up of single-family homes and two-story apartment buildings, had come to be dominated by the expanding footprint of Children's Hospital. White families, UC Berkeley graduate students, punks, and hipsters had also moved into the area in a process of gentrification fueled by speculative landlords and realtors intent on making a killing by flipping houses and charging exorbitant rents. It was 2007, the height of the real estate bubble.

Gary King Jr., a twenty-year-old Berkeley native whose family had moved to the neighborhood in 2002, walked out of East Bay Liquors at the corner of MLK and Fifty-Fourth Street, holding a soda and bag of chips. He and his friends were taking a break from playing video games. Two more of their group had gone into a nearby clothing store to try on sneakers.

At the same time, a black and white slick-top OPD Crown Victoria drove slowly north on MLK, with Sergeant Patrick Gonzales alone behind the wheel. The sergeant was in his ninth year as an Oakland cop and had already cemented his reputation as a hard charger in the hard-charging agency. In 2002 he and Officer Rudy Villegas killed a shotgun-wielding Norteño gang member committing a robbery in Eastlake. Gonzales had racked up complaints with Oakland's Citizens' Police Review Board for publicly strip-searching and beating a Black man he'd stopped, and for pistol-whipping another Black man being arrested for selling marijuana to an undercover cop.[1] In 2006 Gonzales paralyzed Ameir Rollins with a bullet to the throat after spotting the sixteen-year-old carrying a partially dismantled but functioning rifle. Only a handful of other OPD officers had used deadly force more times than Gonzales. The prematurely gray thirty-two-year-old was now a firearms instructor, a rifle officer, a member of the SWAT unit, and supervisor of a North Oakland Crime Reduction Team searching for high-risk suspects.

The four young Black men, wearing the oversized T-shirts, hooded sweatshirts, and low-slung jeans in fashion in the mid-aughts, caught Gonzales's eye. The East Bay Liquors lot was known to city cops as an occasional open-air market for weed and other drugs. One of the youngsters stood out to Gonzales. He homed in on Gary King Jr., whom the sergeant described in police lexicon as having "long braids to his shoulder and a caramel complexion."[2] Gonzales swung his Crown Vic across MLK and stopped in the liquor store's parking lot.

"Hey, can I talk to you for a second?" he asked King from his open car window.

From the start, Gonzales's intention was to identify King, per a request from homicide detectives to gather information for future photo lineups. Like so many young Black men in Oakland, King had been stopped and frisked without reason many times.[3] On one occasion, he and his brother, Jamayah, were detained by police near their house. The youths were released only after their father intervened.[4]

In his first interview hours after the incident, Gonzales told investigators that King walked away from him and handed his soda to an "associate" before turning and walking back. Gonzales asked the twenty-year-old if he had any identification on him. "No," King replied.[5]

King's friend, standing a few yards away, heard Gonzales ask King if he would consent to being searched. Gonzales then took the bag of chips out of King's hand and placed it on top of the Crown Victoria. "What is this for?" King asked.[6]

Gonzales wanted to position King between himself and his vehicle, radio in the stop, pat down King, verify his identity, run a warrant check, and fill out a field contact card. He placed a hand on the young man's shoulder. King "tensed up" and tried to back away. Gonzales grabbed King's right wrist, trying to spin him around against the cruiser. King pulled away, and a struggle ensued. When the fight broke out, one of King's friends ran into the clothing store, where another friend was trying on a pair of Air Jordans, and yelled out, "Five-oh is whupping on Gary!" They ran out of the store, one of them wearing a single Jordan on his right foot.

Gonzales clutched a fistful of King's braids with his right hand. Bystanders, motorists, and even passengers on a Berkeley-bound BART train passing overhead gawked at the sight of King trying to wriggle free, swinging at Gonzales's face, but missing. Gonzales kneed the younger man twice in the stomach and slammed him into the driver's side of the patrol car. King was fit and no stranger to confrontations: as a boy, he'd trained in tae kwon do. The fight spilled out into the street. When King slipped to the ground, Gonzales used his weight to try to pin him down. The radio squawked: backup was on its way.

"Why are you grabbing him? What's the problem?" one of King's friends yelled at Gonzales, while another begged King to stop fighting. None of the friends dared intercede.

"Tell him to let go of my hair!" King yelled, gripping the sergeant's arm that had held his braids.[7]

King leveraged himself back to his feet and began to wriggle out of his sweatshirt. Gonzales let King slip out of his hoodie and T-shirt, but still grasped his braids with his left hand while pulling a Taser from his belt. The two metal darts dug into King's sternum, shocking him for four seconds. When the young man still struggled, the cop pressed the device into King's back, electrocuting him again with more intensity.

"Help me!" King yelled to his friends. He was shirtless now, with his jeans sliding down his thighs and exposing the basketball shorts he wore underneath.

Here's where accounts differ: some witnesses, including King's friends, say he broke free and started to run across MLK Way with his hands holding up his pants.

Sergeant Gonzales and several other witnesses tell a different story. As they scuffled, the twenty-year-old reached into his pants and gripped the hard metal of a handgun concealed in his basketball shorts. Gonzales reached down and felt the weapon's outline. He threw away the Taser and pushed King away from him, drawing his .40-caliber Glock pistol. King sprinted westbound across MLK Way, in front of dozens of witnesses, including rush-hour commuters. Gonzales fired twice in quick succession, striking King in the back from ten feet. The bullets severed King's aorta, fatally wounding him.

King's friends screamed in horror and anger. Two of them started to run toward their wounded friend. Gonzales whirled, leveled his pistol, and said he would shoot if they advanced any farther. The store clerk from East Bay Clothing, who'd followed Gary's friends outside, held them back. As the backup units arrived, Gonzales walked forward and handcuffed King.

Gary's parents, Gary Sr. and Cathy, lived nearby. They ran out to the street, now full of additional OPD officers summoned to hold back an increasingly angry crowd. Cathy tried to get through to her son's inert body but was stopped by a police officer. The Kings followed the ambulance to Highland Hospital. Doctors there told them later that Gary had died, but refused to let them see his body.

For Cathy, being barred from her son's deathbed was an insult heaped on injury. "No one should stand in the way of a mother in the final moments of her son's life," she said at a February 2011 conference on police violence in Oakland.

In his interview with investigators, Gonzales claimed that he'd patted down King as the youngster lay dying on the pavement, recovering a .32-caliber revolver from the left pocket of his basketball shorts. "I handed it to Officer [Nick] Callan," Gonzales told Homicide sergeant Lou Cruz, adding that he then ordered other officers to give King CPR.[8]

The five-shot Hopkins & Allen XL revolver was in such poor shape it needed to be hand-cocked and required triple the normal pressure on the trigger to fire, according to forensic reports. Four live rounds were chambered in the double-action pistol. A loose round was found on the sidewalk near King's body, and four more bullets were found in a ziplock bag in his jeans pocket.

It wasn't unusual for young men in Oakland to pack firearms. King might have been carrying it for safety. Shortly before his death, the teenager was robbed twice at gunpoint. Though Gary Sr. was unaware of the incidents at the time, he'd noticed a change in his son's demeanor. Gary Jr. had also complained to his father about problems with local boys, telling him, "Dad, the kids are crazy around here."

One of the friends with King that day said Gary had shown him the revolver a few weeks prior. He'd obtained the firearm after a stranger in a passing van accosted his girlfriend while the couple were walking near his house. When Gary told off the driver, the man pulled a rifle on King. "What're you gonna do now?" he sneered. The friend told investigators he'd seen the Hopkins & Allen XL only that one time and didn't know Gary had the piece on him the day he was killed.[9] A friend of King's parents wrote a letter to the Oakland PD a few weeks after the shooting, saying, "I heard that prior to his death, Gary Jr. was mugged. If his thought patterns mimicked mine at all, I can easily imagine why he may have been carrying a concealed weapon. Oakland is a big city, with big-city problems. I can't blame Gary Jr. for being scared."

There were discrepancies between Gonzales's statements about recovering the weapon and the recollections of the first officer responding as backup, as well as witnesses. Officer Richard Coglio, the first to arrive, wrote in his report that he saw Gonzales standing in the center divider of MLK Way. Gary King Jr. was facedown and handcuffed in a northbound traffic lane. As a crowd of two dozen onlookers gathered, the sergeant ordered Coglio and another cop to perform CPR on King.

"As Ofc. Mausz and I rolled King over onto his back, I conducted a search of King's waistband and pockets," Coglio wrote. "As I grabbed the outside of King's left front pants pocket, I felt the handle and cylinder of a revolver. I advised Sergeant Gonzales of this, and Sergeant Gonzales removed a silver-with-wood-handle revolver from King's left front pocket."[10]

In his interview with Internal Affairs, Gonzales told investigators that he conducted the search of King's clothing just after the shooting and recovered the gun. Two of King's friends confirmed this part of the officer's account, stating that they saw Gonzales "pull a gun out from the inside of King's basketball shorts," according to police records.[11]

Sixteen people witnessed the incident: the clerk at East Bay Liquors, from the moment Gonzales pulled into the parking lot; a woman who observed King's struggle and death just yards away through her car windshield; passengers on a BART train overhead. While many expressed shock that King fought back against a police officer, all but one said he never reached for his waist in the manner that Gonzales claimed to justify the officer's unholstering and firing his weapon.[12]

For many Oaklanders, these details were less important than the bigger picture: a stop-and-frisk had ended with an Oakland cop killing a young man who hadn't committed any crime, except maybe carrying a gun for protection.

————

When the OPD convened its Executive Force Review Board (EFRB) months later, investigators were united in their opinion that Gonzales was right to use deadly force. In a presentation to the panel of captains who would decide the sergeant's discipline, the investigators, including Sergeants Caesar Basa and Lou Cruz from Homicide, and Donna Hoppenhauer and Nicole Elder from Internal Affairs, described Gonzales as an accomplished sergeant with nine years on the force, important assignments, recent training in firearms use, and "two prior OIS incidents"—a reference to other shootings, both "in compliance." King was identified one-dimensionally as the "suspect." Nothing else was mentioned except his date of birth and prior arrests, including allegations of car theft when he was eighteen and an arrest in May 2007 for a juvenile warrant.

The investigators told the EFRB panel that Gonzales's initial reason for stopping and detaining King was justified because he was a young Black man with long braids to his shoulder, and a caramel complexion. A man with similar hair and skin tone was wanted in connection with two murders.

As idyllic as this section of the North Oakland flats appeared to casual observers, it could be a treacherous place. Blocks such as Gaskill and Forty-Fifth Street near Market were still home to drug crews who would occasionally settle scores with exchanges of gunfire. Since the turn of the millennium, Oakland's violence had begun to creep back up year by year, a grim reversal of the mid- and late-1990s progress. The second most violent year in Oakland history was 2006, with 148 homicides.

The mayhem continued into 2007, much of it concentrated in North Oakland. In August, at a gas station on Fifty-Fifth Street and MLK Way, a block north of East Bay Liquors, Ronald Jimmey Spears Jr. was shot to death by a hitchhiker who pulled a gun on him and his two female passengers.[13] Spears, out celebrating his twenty-ninth birthday, had gotten lost on the way to a friend's house and stopped at the station to ask for directions. On September 4 fifty-year-old Tony Simon pulled his Mercedes-Benz convertible into a Beacon gas station at the corner of West MacArthur Boulevard and West Street, a mile from where Spears had been murdered. Two men approached Simon's car. One pulled a gun and demanded cash—a robbery resembling the fatal August rip-off—but Simon resisted and tried to speed away. The man shot Simon in the back, killing him.

Gary King Jr. had no connection to either killing, except that his hair style and skin tone were similar to the suspected killer's. On page eight of their presentation, the investigators put a photo of King up next to the photo of another man, Rafael Kevin Duarte. About the same weight, same height, age, both with shoulder-length hair, and light-skinned, the young men looked similar, except that Duarte had dreadlocks, not braids. The reasons for comparing King to Duarte, a drug dealer, were flimsy and convoluted, but they constituted the linchpin of the department's rationale for justifying the shooting.

On September 18, two days before Gonzales stopped and killed King, officers had arrested Duarte for a burglary. When homicide investigator Sergeant Tony Jones learned that Duarte had been brought in, he plucked the young man out of North County Jail and took him to an interrogation room. During a marathon four-hour interview, Jones got Duarte to confess to killing Simon at the West Oakland gas station earlier that month.[14] The second man at the shooting had fingered Duarte, and Jones let him know it. The sergeant then showed him surveillance video of the shooting from the gas station's cameras. Duarte acknowledged pulling the trigger but claimed he did it only because Simon resisted.

Having more or less solved the gas station murder, Jones and his Homicide colleagues were still stumped as to the killer in the Spears murder. Although they originally thought the same man might have committed both crimes, Jones was able to rule out Duarte, which left another suspect on the street: another suspect with shoulder-length hair and a "caramel complexion." While Jones had Duarte in the interrogation room, he let Sergeant Phil Green bring Gonzales over to meet him.

"I went in the interview room, took a look at him, spoke to him briefly, just said 'Hi,' to see if I knew him from any previous contacts, which I had not," Gonzales told IAD investigators six months after the King shooting in a follow-up interview about his brief encounter with Duarte.

It was with Duarte's face, hair, and skin tone imprinted in his mind that Gonzales went out in search of murder suspects and found King, a young Black man with no warrants and who was not on probation or parole.

The real culprit of the Fifty-Fifth Street shooting wouldn't be arrested for another six months and wouldn't be identified for another ten.[15] On March 30, 2008, two OPD officers spotted Eric Perry, a twenty-year-old North Oakland resident on probation for theft, riding a bicycle. They found a stolen pistol hidden in his coat. Perry pleaded guilty and was sentenced to probation. Four months later, cops stopped a car that Perry was riding in and found twenty-four twists of crack. Perry's arrest report described his physical appearance: about 170 pounds, five feet eleven inches tall, light-skinned, and wearing dreadlocks just long enough to cover his ears. He was booked on the drug charges and for violating probation. Jail guards found a gold chain in Perry's cell: Ronald Jimmey Spears's gold chain. The shooter had stolen it from the dying man's neck during the robbery back in August 2007. Connecting the dots, investigators matched Perry's fingerprints to those found in Spears's car. A jury sentenced Perry to life plus twenty-six years in state prison for the murder.[16]

King's killing infuriated North Oakland. His parents and friends turned the street where he died into a memorial, placing flowers and photos beneath posters filled with good-bye messages pasted onto the concrete BART column. The images and words served as a counternarrative to the OPD's character assassination of the twenty-year-old. Four days after the shooting, King's parents led a protest to Oakland City Hall. In December they rallied again at the unveiling of a mural painted on the column near where he died. Gary was depicted in black-and-white stencil, a gentle smile on his face, angel wings emerging from his shoulders, and the words "The children of Oakland need justice," in capital letters, sashed across his chest. The city and transit agency sandblasted the mural, but for years afterward, people would return defiantly to write longing messages of loss on the pillar and sidewalk.

The uproar caught the eye of the United States Department of Justice, which directed the Federal Bureau of Investigation's San Francisco field office to conduct a preliminary civil rights investigation.[17] The move was unusual: during President George W. Bush's two terms, the FBI's civil rights work had been deprioritized. However, the federal probe went nowhere, and Sergeant Gonzales went back to work after a three-day administrative leave. The police were already well on their way to clearing him, and the district attorney's office was similarly on track to exonerate the sergeant, though it would take six years for the DA to finalize his report about Gary King's shooting.[18]

Oakland's Citizens' Police Review Board, the independent oversight agency set up after Melvin Black's 1979 killing, represented the King family's last hope for forcing the city to hold Gonzales accountable. Only after receiving multiple complaints about the shooting did the CPRB open a case.

One of the people who filed a complaint about the shooting was Rashidah Grinage, a tireless police-accountability activist who came to the work through a profound personal tragedy.

In the early 1990s Grinage, fifty-one, taught at a private middle school and tutored in the evenings in Berkeley. Her husband, Raphael, was an accomplished musician who had played bass for the iconic folk singer Odetta, known as "the Voice of the Civil Rights Movement." But Raphael had a bad case of diabetes, lost both his legs, was unable to work, and used a wheelchair. Rashidah, Raphael, and her third son, Luke, lived in the family's home in East Oakland's Allendale neighborhood.[19]

In his late teens, Luke began having run-ins with the police. Sometimes officers stopped him for no good reason; sometimes he was detained for possessing drugs and other petty offenses. On one occasion, they impounded Luke's car, but charges weren't filed. For Rashidah, a white woman who grew up in a homogenous New York town, her Black son's experience with law enforcement taught her about the harassment Black men faced at the hands of law enforcement.

"I thought, *This is a Third World country kind of thing going on here*," she said, recalling how difficult it was to understand the mistreatment. Luke's group of friends had already been identified by the OPD as trouble, which put him under suspicion. After other brushes with local cops, Rashidah consulted an attorney to see if anything could be done to protect Luke from police harassment.

"I thought, *This cannot be constitutional. This cannot be sanctioned. There's something wrong here*," she said.

The lawyer's advice was to file a complaint with OPD Internal Affairs or write to her city council member. Rashidah filed an IA complaint, but her husband reacted negatively. "You've done it now," he told her, worried that more hounding would ensue.

A few weeks later, on December 15, 1993, officers William Grijalva and Michael Naumann showed up at the Grinage home. Luke's dog had allegedly bitten someone, and they intended to impound the pit bull. Luke argued with the officers and resisted. When the officers finally dragged the dog out to the street, likely leading it away to be euthanized, Luke reappeared with a shotgun. The young man and the officers exchanged fire. Grijalva and Luke were killed in the chaotic gunfight. Raphael, caught in the cross fire, died in his wheelchair.

In the anguished months after, Rashidah sought help from attorneys, including John Burris, Jim Chanin, and an activist civil rights lawyer named Tony Serra, but no one would take the case. Grinage believed that her son wasn't first to fire and that it was Naumann's shots that killed Officer Grijalva. And, according to Grinage, now a widow, police killed the dog as revenge for the policeman's death. The department's version of events was that Luke initiated the shoot-out, causing his father's death.

From that point forward, Grinage dedicated her life to police reform. Gerald Smith, a former Black Panther who moved west from New York City and gained renown as a local activist, suggested she join People United for a Better Life in Oakland, or PUEBLO. The scrappy group, with offices in an old Victorian house in the San Antonio neighborhood, had been organizing against police brutality for some time.

"They had a mansion on East Twenty-First and Thirteenth Avenue," said Grinage, who was impressed by the group's bilingual meetings and deep bench of committed activists, such as a grandmotherly African American woman named Gwen Hardy. Born in Birmingham, Alabama, she moved to California and went on to help found and grow PUEBLO into a potent grassroots political force.

Through PUEBLO, Rashidah met survivors of police violence, like the family of thirty-two-year-old Nathan Roy Cosby, shot in the back of his head in 1994 by a police officer as dozens of Oakland cops and federal agents raided his home for a credit card fraud case involving his estranged wife. Cosby allegedly pointed a gun at a cop before he was killed. She met Brenda Curry, the mother of Baraka Hull, fatally shot in the back by a rookie cop. The nineteen-year-old, carrying two concealed handguns from a drug deal, wasn't seeking a confrontation with the law; he was fleeing the officer, running away at full stride. To Grinage, the deaths seemed unnecessary, and accountability utterly lacking.

"Those days were horrific," she reflected. "I think at that point, Oakland was third in the nation, after Newark or Detroit, in terms of police killings."

Families impacted by police violence came together to pressure Oakland for a better system of investigating police misconduct complaints. While the CPRB provided some transparency, it had no real power to investigate and discipline officers. For example, the Review Board lacked subpoena power; it couldn't obtain OPD records or force officers to show up and testify. The board also lacked staff to carry out investigations and was limited to reporting findings to the city administrator, who still held the power to discipline officers. The administrator, second in Oakland's municipal hierarchy only to the mayor, rarely informed the board about the city's ultimate decisions.

In February 1996 PUEBLO rallied a hundred supporters to show up to a Public Safety Committee meeting during a thunderstorm. The activists' thunder pushed the city council to set up a task force to consider changes to the Citizens' Police Review Board. Later that year, the council granted the CPRB subpoena power, made officer attendance at evidentiary hearings mandatory, and required the city administrator to respond publicly to the panel's disciplinary recommendations. Furthermore, for the first time, the board had its own investigators as well as an independent lawyer, to prevent a conflict of interests in which the city attorney might softball police misconduct investigations that it would have to defend in civil court later.

Two years later, under still more activist pressure, the CPRB's power was further expanded. A simple majority now sufficed to sustain a misconduct complaint. The Review Board was given jurisdiction over all misconduct complaints, not just wrongful use of force or bias, and its members now had full access to personnel files. And, significantly, police officers would now face penalties for failing to show up to misconduct hearings.

Within a decade, however, the pendulum swung the other way. By the mid-2000s, the Citizens' Police Review Board didn't have much in the way of teeth. While Sergeant Patrick Gonzales and a dozen or so other officers were subjects of serious CPRB inquiries, they rarely faced discipline.

Gonzales was investigated for a 2000 incident where he strip-searched eighteen-year-old Andre Piazza and his older cousin George Moore in public, allegedly probing the teenager's anal cavity and fondling his testicles. When Piazza taunted Gonzales by saying that the search made him "feel like you're fruity," the sergeant grabbed him by the face and squeezed his mouth open, ostensibly to look for narcotics. Piazza protested, and Gonzales slapped him across the face. Moore then asked the officer why he'd struck Piazza. According to Moore and other witnesses, the cop growled that he "shouldn't be talking so much shit." With that, Gonzales and his partner, Chris Sansone, released the pair and drove away.

The CPRB didn't sustain Piazza's complaint. It wasn't that the allegations were false, but that the investigators couldn't prove them.[20] And even if they could, the OPOA's contract with the city and state labor law provided several avenues for cops to thwart discipline. In the rare cases where the evidence proved overwhelmingly that an officer had abused someone, cops could still demand a Skelly hearing, a procedure whereby their union-appointed attorney could argue against discipline at length in a private meeting with command staff. If this failed, the officers were afforded arbitration, a process in which a neutral third-party arbitrator heard from both sides and made a final, binding decision that overrode whatever discipline the city administrator wanted to impose. By its nature, arbitration steered the disciplinary process toward a "split the baby" outcome, where neither side got everything it wanted. It often resulted in fired cops winning back their jobs.

If the CPRB had one real power, it was the ability to publicly air the dirty deeds of police. But in 2006 that window was slammed shut by a California Supreme Court decision, *Copley Press v. Superior Court of San Diego*, which expanded the secrecy provisions of a 1977 state law known as the Police Officer's Bill of Rights. The POBR, which was part of a national wave of bills sponsored by police unions, made officer personnel files secret. The information contained in them couldn't be made public, including disciplinary records. The *Copley Press* decision deemed that all records held by external oversight agencies such as police review boards were also secret because the boards were part of the city government and therefore also the officer's employer.[21]

As a result, independent review agencies, such as Oakland's CPRB, Los Angeles's police commission, Berkeley's Police Review Commission, San Francisco's Office of Citizen Complaints, and a handful of other entities in

San Diego, Richmond, Long Beach, Santa Cruz, and other liberal California cities, could no longer publicly identify officers accused of misconduct and hold open hearings about their cases. Such information proved critical to many reporters, most notably a 2006 *San Francisco Chronicle* series that profiled the SFPD's most problematic cops.[22] *Copley Press* was a watershed in California law enforcement's decades-long campaign to push back against the incremental reforms of the 1970s, including the California Supreme Court's 1974 *Pitchess* decision, which allowed defendants to obtain the personnel histories of officers involved in their cases.

"They've been relentless over the past twenty-five years to create a tool for law enforcement agencies to work without public scrutiny," griped Tom Newton, executive director of the California Newspaper Publishers Association. "With *Copley*, they hit the jackpot."[23]

With the Citizens' Police Review Board entering the post-*Copley* era, the investigation of Gary King's killing wasn't likely to result in public disclosure of new facts. Many of the police files about Gonzales and the shooting would be kept secret for another fourteen years until an open records lawsuit filed during the reporting of this book uncovered decades of OPD discipline records.

Even with its own staff, the CPRB relied mostly on Oakland PD files to investigate the King shooting. At the end of 2008, the Review Board's labor-intensive case was floundering. In its 2009 annual report, staff noted that they had paused their investigation indefinitely because King's family had filed a civil rights lawsuit against the city. The next year, Oakland settled with Gary and Catherine King, agreeing to pay them $1.5 million, but never acknowledging that the shooting was wrong. The payout was one of many footed by Oakland taxpayers in the post-Riders era.

By 2007, four years into the Negotiated Settlement Agreement (NSA), the court oversight process initiated after the Riders scandal, the Oakland Police Department had done little to reform itself. One area where there had been the least change was the use of deadly force. As in the 1980s and early 1990s, a core of aggressive officers racked up a disturbing number of shootings and beatings. Supervisors and IA showed little interest in examining these violent episodes critically. Few cases stand out as much as Officer Hector Jimenez's killings of two unarmed Black men.

New Year's Eve in Oakland's flatlands neighborhoods is pure chaos. Processions of cars barrel down the main boulevards, turning high-speed donuts and "burning out" at intersections while onlookers roar their approval. Thousands of illegal fireworks light up the sky, their crackling intermingled with the hollow pops of celebratory gunfire. The police department annually calls most of its officers in to work on the final day of the year to try to keep the mayhem to a minimum.

On December 31, 2007, Officers Keith Souza and Jason Mitchell were on patrol when they saw a Buick Park Avenue with three occupants and an out-of-date registration sticker roll through a stop sign on Forty-Sixth Avenue. The pair followed in pursuit. Andrew Moppin-Buckskin, the twenty-year-old driver, had been drinking and wanted to evade the police. After speeding a few blocks, he pulled over and bailed out.

Mitchell and Souza detained the car's passengers, recovering a half-empty whiskey bottle from the vehicle's floor.[24] Their sergeant, Barry Hofman, pulled up to oversee the arrests. Souza and Mitchell indicated that Moppin-Buckskin had gone to ground in the 1100 block of Forty-Seventh Avenue, near some industrial buildings.[25] The tension in Officer Souza's voice as he called for backup was palpable enough for the dispatcher to "hold the air," prioritizing the channel for the car stop over all other incidents. At the lineup briefing that evening, Assistant Police Chief Howard Jordan and Captain Ed Tracey cautioned the entire New Year's Eve shift about the high probability of encountering armed suspects.[26]

Hofman got back into his cruiser and drove down Forty-Seventh Avenue, looking for Moppin-Buckskin. He noticed two feet sticking out from under a green Ford Explorer SUV parked on the sidewalk and shone his car spotlight onto the pavement. Moppin-Buckskin pulled his feet back under the car. Hofman killed his lights and drove in reverse toward East Twelfth Street, radioing for backup. Both passengers in the Buick appeared to be gang members, and Hofman didn't know if the man at large was armed, so he wanted to put distance between himself and the hiding suspect.[27]

Officers Hector Jimenez and Jessica Borello heard the call over their patrol car radio and arrived to give support. Both cops were green: Borello, eighteen months into her OPD career, while Jimenez, a Richmond native, received his appointment in February 2007 after enlisting as a youth cadet. The rookies spotted Moppin-Buckskin squatting fifteen feet away from

them between the Explorer and a brick industrial building.[28] They drew
their pistols and confronted him, yelling, "Stand up!"

"What the fuck, I'm just taking a shit!" Moppin-Buckskin replied. He
slowly stood up, ten feet away from the officers. "Walk toward me!" Jimenez
ordered. "If you don't walk toward me, I'm going to shoot you."

The admonition from that evening's lineup rang in Jimenez's ears.
"I believe he might have a gun or some drugs because I know that New
Year's usually brings out either drug dealers or guns," he said later of his
mind-set.[29]

"I don't give a fuck, I've been shot before," Moppin-Buckskin snapped
back. However, his hands were in the air.

"Walk toward me!" Borello ordered. Meanwhile, Sergeant Hofman snuck
around the front of the SUV to cut off Moppin-Buckskin's escape route on
the dimly lit street. The young man began to walk toward Hofman. "Dude,
get your hands up!" he yelled. As all three officers told it, Moppin-Buckskin's
hands suddenly dropped to his waist. "He's reaching!" Hofman yelled.

Twelve seconds after arriving on scene, Jimenez and Borello opened
fire.[30] Moppin-Buckskin fell forward on his face, bleeding from his chest
and arms. Jimenez eased toward the wounded twenty-year-old and handcuffed him. Borello searched Moppin-Buckskin as blood gurgled in his
throat. She came up empty-handed.[31] He was pronounced dead at 8:09 p.m.

Cops scoured the area for evidence, even searching rooftops for a gun
or other contraband that Moppin-Buckskin may have tossed. They, too,
came up empty. Despite the absence of a weapon and the extremely brief
time between Borello and Jimenez's arrival and the fatal shots, Internal Affairs cleared the pair of any wrongdoing: investigators noted that Moppin-
Buckskin was on probation for selling marijuana, which would have resulted
in a long jail sentence had he been caught for the DUI. Sergeant Randolph
Brandwood, a gang cop, identified Moppin-Buckskin as a Norteño. IAD's
only criticism of the officers was that they didn't have good cover or use
their flashlights on the darkened street.

The district attorney would clear Jimenez and Borello of criminal conduct, although it took six years for the report to be completed. Andrew
Moppin-Buckskin's death was one of several "awful but lawful" shootings,
police jargon for gruesome, lethal, and likely preventable incidents that attracted heavy press attention, but, according to the Oakland police and the
district attorney, didn't violate criminal law or warrant discipline or training.

In July 2008 an OPD officer responsible for forwarding legal claims and lawsuits against police officers to commanders wrote, "Here are this week's batch of tasty legal claims" in an email, including one by Moppin-Buckskin's family. In the poor grammar and misspelling common in police reports, he joked, "As usually if you choose not to except these complaints you will be severely beaten . . . just kidding." The city attorney rejected the claim, and not long after, like Gary King's parents, Moppin-Buckskin's relatives filed a wrongful death lawsuit, one of many during some of the department's deadliest years.[32]

In the eight years between the Riders scandal and the day in 2008 when Hector Jimenez and Jessica Borello killed Moppin-Buckskin, city cops opened fire on at least sixty-three people.[33] According to an extensive analysis by *Contra Costa Times* reporter Thomas Peele, from 2000 through 2013 the Oakland Police Department shot at a minimum of 117 people, striking at least 88. Thirty-nine individuals were killed by OPD bullets during this period. The rate of shootings placed Oakland ahead of similar midsize California cities such as Fresno and Stockton, as well as larger municipalities like San Jose and San Francisco. Every year, Oakland averaged eight police shootings.[34]

Just sixteen out of the department's roughly 750 officers accounted for about 40 percent of all shootings. Patrick Gonzales and Hector Jimenez were among this number. The involvement of a small cadre of officers in an outsized percentage of OPD shootings precisely fit the pattern outlined decades earlier by the Christopher Commission.[35]

"That often happens in departments where the 'proactive, productive' officers are rewarded because they're keeping crime down in their districts," said Christy Lopez, a former US Department of Justice attorney who was part of the OPD's first court monitoring team.[36] Lopez and her colleagues were deeply concerned about the number of times Oakland police used their firearms. They studied the OPD's officer-involved shootings and identified substandard tactics as one key cause of the fatal violence. What's more, they found the department's investigations of deadly use of force to be woefully inadequate.

Just a year into the NSA, the monitoring team reported that Internal Affairs investigations were characterized by a failure to track down independent witnesses and gather or even recognize relevant evidence. Investigators rarely acknowledged particular acts of misconduct or the inappropriate involvement of supervisors. Final determinations often didn't line up with evidence and statements.[37] "The poor quality of investigations is so pervasive that it diminishes the overall credibility of OPD's Internal Affairs investigation process," the monitoring team stated.

The findings floored Thelton Henderson, who scolded the OPD at a hearing on February 14, 2005. "I haven't seen anything like this in twenty-five years. This is so unacceptable that I've been spending my time deciding what I can do to get the attention of the defendant," said the judge. "This is contemptuous. I'm so angry at the slap in the face, the ignoring of this decree, that my question is 'Who is responsible, and how can I get them in front of me?'" It was the first, but not the last, time that Henderson would threaten the city with contempt.[38]

In May 2005 Henderson ordered the department to reopen 775 unaddressed Internal Affairs complaints, including twenty-six Class I complaints: offenses that could lead to termination, such as dishonesty, planting evidence, sexual abuse, falsifying reports, or excessive force.[39] The existence of these uninvestigated complaints was discovered by the monitoring team during a review of the OPD Internal Affairs database.[40]

One year later, the monitoring team noted in another report that historically, the Oakland Police Department hadn't bothered to open administrative investigations into officer-involved shootings. The department only had homicide detectives give shootings a look, shirking the responsibility of generating a case that could be used to suspend or terminate an officer who violated policy when firing on someone. An Executive Force Review Board composed of supervisors was convened to examine deadly use of force, but "the board met infrequently, and reviews were not timely or sufficiently probing," the monitoring team wrote.[41]

To better understand the problem, the monitors conducted their own audit of sixteen officer-involved shootings from 2003 to 2005. They found that important issues, such as the legality of a stop leading up to a shooting, or whether firing on someone was a proportionate response to a perceived threat, "routinely went ignored" during officer interviews, which were often cursory and held but once. Investigators showed little appetite for pursuing discrepancies in officers' statements.

"Many of the OIS files reviewed were generally disorganized and routinely lacked critical information. Documents were haphazardly spread throughout the investigative files, and there was no consistent order to them," the monitoring team found. "Investigators also made no effort to verify the claims of officers about whether they'd used alcohol or drugs recently, or how up-to-date their training was."[42]

Only the broadest takeaways from the monitors' report were disclosed to the public. The full report, filed with Judge Henderson, contained shocking descriptions of shootings and flimsy investigations. The department's examination of Terrance Mearis's killing was but one example.

At 12:40 a.m. on October 5, 2003, officers Ryan Gill and Richard Vass were hitting corners in Deep East Oakland. After knocking a drug suspect to the ground by sweeping his legs out from under him, they stuffed the man into their patrol car and proceeded to a nearby apartment where they knew he stayed. The two officers—among the department's most "active," with numerous use-of-force incidents and complaints against them—knew the man was on probation, allowing them to search his residence. They forced their way in and found Terrance Mearis fast asleep in a bedroom. Vass kicked Mearis's feet to wake him up. Mearis might have been startled. He got to his feet and picked up a pillow to cover his body. Both officers wrestled with Mearis, and Gill attempted a carotid hold to knock him out.

Reviewing the incident years later, the monitoring team noted that carotid holds are "categorized as deadly force," and that there seemed "to be no justification" for it. The officers would later claim that Mearis grabbed Gill's gun and pointed it at his partner. Vass unloaded into Mearis's body. Gill claimed he was then able to overpower Mearis and point his own weapon, which Mearis was still clutching, at Mearis's head. Then Gill forced Mearis's finger to pull the trigger multiple times.

Three months later, an OPD Firearms Review Board ruled the fatal shooting justified. They misidentified the number of times Mearis was shot. The context of the shooting wasn't mentioned. Gill and Vass had used significant physical force on at least four other suspects in the preceding six months, which should have prompted interventions by supervisors. "There is no documentation that indicates these officers were ever counseled or evaluated by superiors," the monitors wrote.

Worst of all, Vass's and Gill's versions of events were questionable. The department tested Gill's gun and Mearis's hands for evidence that the victim grabbed the officer's firearm. But according to the monitors, "a review of the investigation file indicated that Officer Gill's weapon was analyzed by forensic technicians for fingerprints. None were found. This brings into question whether or not the suspect actually had the weapon in his possession and whether or not the officer just lost the weapon during the struggle. The subject's hands were tested for gunpowder residue. Had he handled or brandished the weapon and fired it, there could have been gunpowder evidence. There is no record of results in the file."[43]

In the mid-2000s, the OPD's shoddy Internal Affairs investigations were exacerbated by the involvement of officers with conflicts of interest. Some were friends with the cops they investigated; others had been let off easy earlier in their careers. In addition, district attorney's investigators were often former Oakland officers who still socialized with current cops.[44] It is unclear why commanders didn't mitigate conflicts of interest. They certainly had a deep enough bench: by the late aughts, the city had only ten cops assigned to Homicide, roughly half the size of the Internal Affairs Division at the time, which had been expanded pursuant to the Negotiated Settlement Agreement in order to rectify the calamitous dismissal of complaints that let the Riders' misbehavior go unchecked.[45]

The department also failed to build an early warning system to flag officers with violent records, thus providing supervisors an opportunity to retrain or reassign them before a tragedy occurred. The system, known early on as the Internal Personnel Assessment System (IPAS), was a wreck in the mid to late-2000s. The data that it did produce went unused.

Just like the Rodney King–era Los Angeles Police Department dissected by the Christopher Commission, there was little will in Oakland to scrutinize cops with unusually high use-of-force stats. Even though the NSA called for a sweeping cultural change, the OPD still valued aggressive policing, as evidenced in Hector Jimenez's glowing evaluations and Pat Gonzales's steady rise to sergeant. The deadly tactics of other violent officers went mostly unscrutinized in the late 1990s through mid-2000s. Oftentimes these officers were celebrated.

For example, Marcus Midyett was renowned throughout California as a legendary street cop, arresting in some years more than twenty homicide suspects and recovering dozens of guns and evidence convicting over a dozen murderers.[46] His uncompromising ways, and the department's permissiveness, also led to numerous shootings, including his 1998 shooting of Michael Moore during a foot chase. The twenty-three-year-old victim was carrying a .45-caliber handgun, but Midyett shot him in the back while he was fleeing.

Lieutenant Michael Yoell had a similar reputation: In July 2000 he and Anthony Centeno shot and killed Maurice Esters, twenty-eight, as he was startled awake in his car with a gun in his possession. Three months later, Yoell shot and killed Ronell Johnson after the nineteen-year-old made a "furtive movement." In a similar 1995 shooting, Yoell wounded an unarmed robbery suspect. The lieutenant had been the subject of a sexual harassment complaint and other excessive-force allegations, including the 1990 beating of a youth counselor, and running over a juvenile with his car during a 2003 drug bust.

Officer Rob Roche made his reputation by killing three people in as many years. In 2006 Roche shot seventeen-year-old Ronald Brazier, who allegedly fired at police. In 2007 he killed unarmed Jeremiah Dye, twenty-two, who was hiding in a crawl space. In 2008 he killed teenager Jose Buenrostro, who was armed but allegedly surrendering. Oakland paid $500,000 to Buenrostro's parents but admitted no wrongdoing by Roche.

The dangers of Oakland's streets, the willingness of a nucleus of officers to use their firearms, and the department's reluctance to change tactics caught up with the OPD in 2001, when one of their own was killed by friendly fire. Willie Wilkins grew up in Union City in a Panamanian family. He dreamed of becoming a cop, and at twenty-two he became a patrol officer. By 2001, Wilkins was routinely working undercover. On January 11 he was surveilling an East Oakland drug house when he spotted a stolen car and gave chase in his unmarked Dodge Durango SUV. Although he lost the suspects when they bailed, Wilkins had a hunch he could find them on foot. On B Street near Ninetieth Avenue, Wilkins stopped eighteen-year-old Demetrius Phillips.

As Phillips recounted in depositions taken years later, he didn't know that Wilkins was a cop; the man confronting him wore a hooded sweater, jeans, and sported earrings. Wilkins knocked Phillips to the ground and aimed a chrome-plated pistol at his face. Just then, an OPD patrol car pulled up. Rookies Timothy Scarrott and Andrew Koponen, both white, got out and yelled at Wilkins. The patrol cops had no idea he was an undercover. They saw an armed assailant and fired at least twelve shots, striking Wilkins in the back. According to Phillips, the twenty-nine-year-old Wilkins's dying words were "Fuck y'all. Y'all killed me."[47]

The shooting tore apart the force. On the one hand, commanders felt pressure to punish Scarrott and Koponen for killing a popular and hard-working officer. On the other hand, the brass felt pressure to absolve the rookies for tactics they used every other day on Latino and Black men who didn't happen to be undercover cops. Wilkins's closest friends in the department, Torrey Nash and Randy Wingate, were devastated. Nash, who witnessed the shooting, said later in depositions that he'd tried to tell the rookies Wilkins was a cop, but perhaps they hadn't heard him. Wingate felt that Scarrott and Koponen were "overzealous rookies" who should be jailed.[48]

In the end, the shooting was ruled justified. But Wilkins's widow, Kely, sued the department for wrongful death and put together a scathing case that the OPD was recklessly endangering its own officers by sending poorly supervised white officers into high-crime communities of color without any training on how to recognize undercover officers, many of whom were Black and Latino. Echoing the arguments being made by Chanin and Burris in the Riders lawsuit, Wilkins's attorneys wrote in a court brief that "the need for generally accepted training, supervision, policies, and procedures" to prevent unnecessary harm at the hands of the police "was obvious to OPD command staff even before the Wilkins tragedy."[49]

––––––––––

Hector Jimenez returned to patrol after a few days of administrative leave in early 2008, standard operating procedure for Oakland cops involved in shootings. However, his eagerness also resulted in thirty use-of-force incidents over the next seven months, in addition to the twenty-seven he'd racked up prior to killing Andrew Moppin-Buckskin, an eye-popping number for a young cop.[50] This should have alarmed his supervisors. During a foot chase in 2008, a suspect threw a handgun over a fence, and the gun went off when it struck the ground. Jimenez grabbed the man and kneed him in the stomach before cuffing him. During a narcotics bust that same year, Jimenez allegedly slammed a handcuffed suspect on the ground and pummeled him while his partner, Joel Aylworth, held back the man's family at gunpoint.[51] Jimenez and Aylworth also tackled, kneed, and struck a shoplifting suspect with an expandable baton after the man tried to run. And when another man taunted, "Fuck the police!" Jimenez pulled him off the gate he was sitting on, pepper-sprayed him, and kneed him six times until other officers arrived and helped Jimenez cuff and arrest his victim for public intoxication.[52]

Jimenez racked up nineteen Internal Affairs complaints in just a couple years and was reprimanded twice, once for a preventable car crash in his police cruiser and again for refusing to accept a complaint after a stop-and-frisk.[53]

Yet the young officer always received positive performance evaluations from fourteen separate supervisors throughout the department, as well as two citations from his captain, Anthony Rachal.[54]

"You exceed some senior officers with the amount of work and arrests you make," Sergeant Paul Balzouman wrote in Jimenez's first annual evaluation, labeling him a "very proactive officer" on account of the forty arrests he made in the last quarter of 2007.[55] Jimenez earned enough of a reputation for aggression, according to one of his performance evaluations, to become part of one of Oakland PD's "go-to teams for targeted enforcement" in Fruitvale, where rivalries between street gangs frequently degenerated into violence and the neighborhood's high undocumented population was often targeted in robberies.[56]

Buoyed by this praise, by July 25, 2008, Jimenez and Aylworth were working the swing shift, afternoon to early morning. It was a busy evening for the two: they helped canvass the scenes of two earlier robbery attempts. A pair of murders also took place while they were on duty: a thirty-six-year-old man was killed at a homicide memorial at East Seventeenth Street and Seminary Avenues, and a twenty-four-year-old man was shot to death at Eighty-First Avenue and Plymouth Street.[57]

Around 3:40 a.m., Aylworth was driving on Fruitvale Avenue when a red Buick Regal ripped past in the opposite lane, straddling the stripe of the two-lane road while speeding toward the hills and Interstate 580.[58]

"Let's light him up," Aylworth said.

"Yeah," Jimenez replied, while notifying dispatch of the pursuit.[59]

Aylworth pulled a U-turn and sped after the Buick, which had turned off Fruitvale onto School Street. Less than a quarter mile from the freeway, the Buick slowed to a stop. Then it swerved back onto Fruitvale from the direction it had come. As it drove past, Aylworth and Jimenez got a glimpse at the driver: a thin, young Black man wearing a baseball cap and sweating in the cool morning air.[60]

The driver was Mack "Jody" Woodfox, a twenty-seven-year-old with a checkered past. In 2006 he'd been arrested by the SFPD in connection with a murder, but never charged. However, neither Jimenez nor Aylworth had any clue of his identity during the pursuit. Riding in the passenger seat was Woodfox's female friend Shamika Steele.[61]

Jimenez got on the radio and notified dispatch that they were in pursuit westbound on Fruitvale Avenue of a possible drunk driver. The Buick sped downhill on the two-lane thoroughfare, blowing through a red light. Aylworth and Jimenez's Crown Victoria was close behind at sixty miles per hour, freeway speeds for a narrow city street.

Their supervisor, Sergeant Brandon Wehrly, came over the radio and ordered Aylworth and Jimenez to break off: the speed and location of their pursuit threatened other drivers and pedestrians, and Woodfox hadn't given them any indication he was involved in or about to commit a violent crime. It's unclear if the young cops heard the order.[62] Three blocks later, the Buick swerved violently across both lanes, screeching to a stop. Aylworth was following too closely behind and was surprised by Woodfox's abrupt halt. He braked too late, bringing the front wheels of the patrol car level with the Buick's rear wheels.[63]

Jimenez jumped to his feet behind the V of the passenger door and drew his .40-caliber Glock 22. "Get your hands up! Let me see your hands! Let me see your hands!" he screamed.[64] Woodfox was still struggling with the car's gear shift and his seat belt. By now, Aylworth was also out of the car and had his pistol leveled at Woodfox and Steele, shouting for the driver to raise his hands.

Woodfox, for reasons no one will ever know, undid his seat belt, opened the driver's-side door, and broke into a run with the Buick still slowly rolling. To get around the car door, he ran at an angle, briefly heading toward the police cruiser's driver's side before straightening out his path to run away. Jimenez and Aylworth both claimed to see Woodfox's hands drop to his waistband. At this movement, Jimenez opened fire.[65] One of the bullets struck Woodfox's left arm. Two more tore into the left side of his back.[66] Jimenez's remaining six rounds sailed into the residential neighborhood or ricocheted off the Regal and sidewalk.[67]

As Jimenez handcuffed the dying Woodfox, Aylworth ran and stopped the car, which was slowly rolling down Fruitvale. He ordered Steele out of the vehicle, handcuffed her, and searched the interior, turning up nothing but empty liquor bottles.[68]

Woodfox was pronounced dead at Highland Hospital. Toxicology reports would reveal traces of cocaine, alcohol, and MDMA in his system.[69] Within days, his family and friends decried the shooting. "Our family is hurting. His friends are hurting. We believe that it was senseless, that it could have been avoided," Woodfox's sister, Kennitta Vaughn, told the *San Francisco Chronicle*.[70]

———

For the second time in a little more than a year, Hector Jimenez was under scrutiny for killing an unarmed man. In this instance, Jimenez alone fired his pistol, and he and Aylworth didn't heed their sergeant's radio command to break off the pursuit. Other problems with the shooting were obvious to the IAD and homicide investigators who interviewed Jimenez and Aylworth.

"As soon as his hands are in his waistband, that's when I hear shots fire," Aylworth told Homicide sergeant Tony Jones later that day during his initial interview. Once Woodfox was struck by the first volley, Aylworth could clearly see his empty hands "flailing back and forth," but Jimenez continued to fire.[71]

When it became obvious that investigators weren't going to dismiss this shooting like most others, Aylworth's attorney, Justin Buffington of the Rains Lucia Stern law firm, began interrupting the interview. Deputy District Attorney John Jay was doing what had seldom been done in reviews of police shootings: interrogating discrepancies in Aylworth's and Jimenez's statements; asking Aylworth if he feared for his life; whether he felt Woodfox needed to be shot; and, pointedly, why he himself didn't fire.[72] Buffington, who also represented Jimenez during his interview with Homicide and IAD investigators earlier that morning, understood that Jimenez might face criminal charges and termination.

Jimenez tried to explain why he thought Woodfox was either a drug dealer or an armed robbery suspect: "because of the way he was evading us in the vehicle and the way he fled once he jumped out of the car." The officer claimed that when Woodfox bolted from the Buick and began running, "his arms were in his waistband" rather than swinging freely in a normal running motion. In Jimenez's twenty foot pursuits since joining the OPD, there was only one chase where the fleeing person ran with a hand in his waistband: that person was holding a gun.[73]

"When I told him repeatedly, 'Show me your hands, get your hands up,' he didn't show me his hands," Jimenez said.[74]

By Aylworth's recollection, only two seconds passed between Jimenez's commands and the first volley of shots.[75] Aylworth also said that he saw Woodfox's empty hands twice: first when he got out of the Buick and after Jimenez's initial salvo. At several points in his interview, Jimenez claimed that Woodfox never threw his hands up after being struck, contradicting his partner.[76]

"Did it concern you at all that you did not see a firearm before you pulled your trigger?" asked Jay.

"No, sir. I wasn't," Jimenez replied. "I felt that my life was at risk, and I felt that my partner's life was at risk. So, I wasn't trying to wait to see a firearm before I pulled the trigger."[77]

———————

On February 11, 2009, Captain Sean Whent, an introspective officer who worked his way up the ranks to lead Internal Affairs, sent a report to Chief Wayne Tucker, a former Alameda County assistant sheriff appointed to run OPD by then mayor Jerry Brown in 2005, recommending Jimenez's termination.[78] Two days later, Tucker fired the officer. But this wasn't going to be a rare moment of accountability within the department.

Since its rise to power in the 1960s, the Oakland Police Officers' Association had vigorously contested officer terminations, particularly those of aggressive young cops like Jimenez. The union took up his cause, first through a Skelly hearing at which attorney Justin Buffington told OPD supervisors that Jimenez had learned—and the department had shown during the Moppin-Buckskin investigation—that killing an unarmed man was acceptable as long as an officer could articulate fear that his target *might* be armed. The police union attorney made a few other tactics-related points and bookended his argument with a claim that Whent's Internal Affairs team "may have succumbed to political pressures" to fire Jimenez due to negative coverage of the Woodfox shooting.

Buffington's mudslinging didn't fly. In May 2009, nearly a year after the tragic event, OPD Captain Ben Fairow and Acting Chief Howard Jordan signed off on Jimenez's firing. With the OPOA's support, the young cop continued to fight by taking his case to arbitration. In March 2011, two years after his formal severance, independent arbitrator David Gaba ordered the city to reinstate Jimenez with $200,000 of back pay. This was a godsend to Jimenez, who had returned to his native Richmond and found work as a pest exterminator. John Burris, who represented Woodfox's family in their wrongful death lawsuit and won a $650,000 settlement from Oakland, called Jimenez's rehiring "a kick in the stomach."[79]

Jimenez's saga was just one example of Oakland's woefully inadequate system of investigating misconduct and punishing bad cops. Burris and Jim Chanin hired a private investigator to rework the OPD's probe into Woodfox's killing. They located two witnesses never interviewed by police. They confirmed that Woodfox had his back to Jimenez when the fatal shots were fired. In 2014 US District Court Judge Thelton Henderson would highlight Jimenez's rehiring in an order demanding a review of Oakland's failure to uphold terminations during arbitration. By that point, only three of fifteen firings held up under arbitration, a result of incomplete investigations and slipshod litigation by the city attorney.[80]

Hector Jimenez's killings weren't aberrations. Patrick Gonzales's fatal methods weren't "bad apple" tactics. They represented the essence of a police department stuck in—or even regressing to—the hyperaggressive street policing, deteriorating community relations, and lack of accountability that were the cause and effect of the Riders.

The monitoring team led by Kelli Evans and Christy Lopez confronted these deep-seated problems from the start. Their job was complicated by the unusual nature of a private consent decree they were charged with enforcing. There were no formal findings or reports by the Federal Bureau of Investigation or the DOJ's Civil Rights Division outlining the systemic rot that precipitated the actions of Hornung, Mabanag, Siapno, and Vazquez, and led to corrupt episodes like the Amaro cover-up and the litany of problematic, fatal police shootings.

"There was never any touchstone for what was wrong with the department, what this agreement was meant to fix, and how," Lopez said in an interview at her Washington, DC, office at Georgetown University's

School of Law, where she now teaches courses on criminal justice, policing, and reform.

> Even if it's not a DOJ pattern-and-practice case that has a finding
> report, you will have a blue-ribbon commission or something docu-
> menting. You didn't really have that in Oakland. For example, with
> LAPD you had the Christopher Commission even before DOJ came
> in there. You didn't have any sort of official body that decided "this
> is the problem we are trying to fix." The criminal perspective is very
> different. It's focused on bad apples and individual wrongdoing, not
> on systems and systemic deficiencies, which is really what the con-
> sent decree is meant to correct. I think that was problematic.[81]

The NSA's foundation consisted of two separate but parallel inquiries: the
Alameda County district attorney's criminal investigation into the Riders,
and the allegations of 119 civil plaintiffs represented by John Burris and
Jim Chanin. The fugitive Frank Vazquez aside, the Riders twice avoided
accountability at trial, leading to a perception within the police department
that the West Oakland cops had been persecuted. The civil litigation never
went to trial. While the Negotiated Settlement Agreement was a lengthy
document, its pages were taken up with details about the fixes to technical
systems, timelines, procedural overhauls, and policy design. It was a series
of boxes to be checked. There was no authoritative account detailing the
force's cultural problems.

The obstructionist mindset within the Oakland Police Department
thrived at the highest echelons. "The NSA sat in a desk drawer for the first
two years," recounted Ben Fairow in 2013, then a deputy chief at the Bay
Area Rapid Transit Police Department. While at the OPD, Fairow worked
his way up to captain and was among a group of brass who labeled themselves "the other commanders," advocating for modernizing investigative
methods. Fairow was privy to high-level meetings and conversations about
the court reforms, which the department's old guard and police union
viewed as unnecessary.

"Especially the first couple years," Lopez said, "[OPD] was just intent on
not doing anything, and we had no power to break through that. You're supposed to have that power because you have a consent decree and a federal
judge." Her monitoring team witnessed many officers, including command-

ers and field supervisors, deride attempts to collect racial data on the pedestrians and drivers stopped. One commander called stop data "bullshit."[82]

In the police academy and field training for new officers joining in the first couple post-Riders years, the NSA didn't register. Holly Joshi, an African American Oakland native whose father, Rick Hart, patrolled beats in the Deep East and North Oakland for decades, was stunned at the level of racial profiling she encountered during field training in 2002, in the same West Oakland district where Keith Batt worked briefly.

"Field training was: forget everything you learned in the academy, you need to come out here and fucking survive and show us you can survive, show us you can get into some shit and make decisions," she recalled. At the René C. Davidson Courthouse, less than a mile away from her patrol beat, David Hollister and Bob Conner were building their case against Hornung, Mabanag, and Siapno. Yet, on the streets, nothing had changed. "They weren't talking about the Riders in the academy. They weren't running around scared. It was a nonissue," said Joshi.

"They wanted me to stop old-ass black dudes walking down the street at two a.m., search them for rocks, and take them to jail," she recalled. "I really thought cops were gonna help people. I wanted to help people. I had this image that I thought that we were gonna be more like social workers."

Instead, Joshi found that she was arresting "dudes that could be my uncle" because they had minuscule amounts of drugs on them. "This is not what I came to do," she said. "I would have been fine if we had been going after drug dealers or homicide suspects." But instead, "It really felt like I was fucking with people who were down on their luck or had a mental health problem."

The catch-22 for field training was that all rookie cops needed to play by those rules: they needed a certain number of felony arrests during their probationary period to show they were capable of policing the OPD way. In the early aughts, possession of rock cocaine was a solid felony arrest that the district attorney would charge.

Even though Oakland had diversified significantly from the overwhelmingly white police force of the 1960s, the climate for Black officers remained difficult. They were almost always assigned or recruited for high-risk undercover work in drug or prostitution stings, even more so if they were Oakland natives.[83]

"If you spoke out, while you were there, it was almost like the Gestapo would come get you," said a former Black Oaklander and OPD veteran, asking not to be named for fear of retaliation. "You'd get written up for insubordination."[84]

The agency's composition reinforced the Oakland Police Department's oppositional stance toward much of the city: legacy hires were fairly common, with fathers and siblings working alongside one another. OPOA president Bob Valladon was accused of nepotism after getting his son, Scott, into the police academy, despite a criminal history and health problems.[85]

Whereas in the 1950s and 1960s Oakland recruited from the Deep South because "the whites in the South knew how to keep their blacks in line," in the aughts the OPD pulled heavily from neighboring white-majority suburbs such as Walnut Creek, Pleasant Hill, Danville, and Castro Valley.[86]

"They were hiring a lot of people from suburbs," said another Black officer who joined during the 1990s and requested not to be named for fear of retaliation. "It was almost like a clique thing to come from the 'burbs to work in Oakland. Some white suburban cops would take on a harder, tougher facade, inking themselves with tattoos, adopting Oakland slang and diction, chewing tobacco, and trying to act hard."[87]

The atmosphere for female recruits could also be poisonous. During the academy, Joshi and a number of other women trainees were taken aside by Recruit Training Officer Mary Guttormson, who had once counseled Keith Batt during his moral quandary about blowing the whistle. According to Joshi, she told the newbies, "In this department, you can be three things: a whore, a bitch, or a dyke. You've got to choose."[88] The misogyny rampant in the OPD's mainline culture was made explicit during physical training, when Sergeant Dan Endaya, the defensive tactics instructor accused of railroading Scott Hoey-Custock out of the force and participating in a Riders-like officer clique called West End Law, accused Joshi of "doing Dolly Parton push-ups," in other words, training like a weak, effeminate woman.[89]

———

The court-appointed monitoring team in charge of making sure the NSA was being implemented eventually realized it wasn't dealing with the sort of pay-to-play corruption that characterized East Coast and Southern law enforcement agencies brought under consent decrees. Like the LAPD, Oakland's cops were paid generously enough that, for the most part, graft wasn't

an issue. The West Coast style of corruption, especially in the late 1990s and
early 2000s, was the abuse of power on the street, always shaded through a
racial lens.

There were instances of blatant venality, but they were the exception,
not the rule. In November 2001 Narcotics Officer John Gutierrez was suspended for stealing money and falsifying reports. Yet that year, "Johnny G"
was named the force's Officer of the Year for bringing in huge drug hauls,
including an eighty-kilogram cocaine bust.[90]

"While there were some straight-up corruption issues in Oakland," said
Lopez, "I was struck by the fact that it was kind of a brutal place. It was just a
lot about force and beating heads and very harsh treatment of people. That
was the thing that jumped out at me more than anything."

Unlike some other law enforcement and corrections agencies that
Lopez examined as a federal civil rights attorney, Oakland's cops were
not incompetent or ham-handed. The training was rigorous, the organizational standards were fairly high, and a number of senior officers were
educating themselves in contemporary management and criminal justice
techniques.

"There was actually quite a lot of capacity in the department, compared
to a lot of places," Lopez praised. "There were a lot of officers who had really
impressive backgrounds, really smart, who had advanced degrees, at a time
when that really wasn't the case."[91]

The caliber of OPD personnel, however, didn't alter the institutional intransigence toward change. Early on in the consent decree, Lopez and other
members of the monitoring team spoke at a public event with community
leaders and police brass. "I said during the meeting how we were going to
reform the police department, and this consent decree was meant to reform
the police department," she recalled. Afterward, she met with Captain Ron
Davis, a Black Oaklander who earned the sobriquet "Maniac" for his frenetic service on the Special Duty Unit. "He said, 'You've got to stop using
that word *reform*. It really makes people think that the changes here are
going to be much more disruptive than they're ready to accept.'"

It was a jarring moment that, in retrospect, foreshadowed the degree
of resistance put up by the OPD to the consent decree process. "They were
hoping to kind of do all this stuff without much impact on their day-to-day
work," observed Lopez. "The whole point was *to have* a dramatic impact on
your day-to-day work. It just didn't register with them."

The monitoring team initially approached its mission in Oakland delicately. In the first reports to Judge Thelton Henderson about OPD compliance, Lopez and her colleagues pulled punches. "We decided that because we came from the civil rights background, we didn't want to come out swinging. We would look kind of overly harsh, like we weren't willing to work with them," Lopez explained. Nevertheless, the initial report to Henderson, released in December 2003, called out the department's "cynicism, fear, and even obstructionism."[92]

The backdrop to this review was the October 2003 hung jury of the first Riders trial and the pending reindictment of Hornung, Siapno, and Mabanag. But the moderating tone of the inaugural oversight report had consequences. "I think that was a huge mistake because it played into the sense that we could have the wool pulled over our eyes, and they could just go along to get along," Lopez said in hindsight. "It didn't give the judge the ammunition he needed to really go hard after them from the outset. It's hard to know whether that would've made a difference, but I will always wonder whether it might have if we had come out just much harsher."

The subsequent reports, issued every three months, fell into a familiar pattern of highlighting "systemic delays at nearly every step of the process" and a breakdown of the Internal Affairs process.[93] One practice identified by the monitors was a failure to discipline officers with sustained allegations of misconduct, because the investigation took longer than the one-year statutory limit established by the 1977 Police Officer's Bill of Rights. This practice, known as "3304-ing"—short for California Government Code Chapter 9.7 Section 3304—would persist for years in Oakland as a back-door means for invalidating a misconduct complaint.[94]

By fall 2004, the monitoring team was reporting to Judge Henderson that they "observed commanders' open disdain of trainings required by the consent decree. Such attitudes have been directly and indirectly communicated to subordinate members and employees, and undermine the Department's reform efforts."

In Christy Lopez's view, it should've gotten a lot harsher from there. "But even then, again, it felt like a voice in the wilderness for saying this stuff. Consent decrees are a prophylactic for good leadership. That's always the answer, but you just need someone in there who's ready to take on that culture and is effective."

Some commanders did take the NSA seriously, but two departures in quick succession deprived Oakland of consistent leadership. First, Chief Richard Word left the department to take the top job in suburban Vacaville in 2004; the following year, Captain Ron Davis moved on to run the East Palo Alto Police Department. Pete Dunbar, the deputy chief ostensibly in charge of complying with the NSA, was demoted to captain because of his failure to advance the court-ordered reforms.[95]

The leadership vacuum provided an opening for the recalcitrant faction to tighten its grasp on the Oakland Police Department. "It just leaves every thing the same as it is," Bob Valladon, the OPOA's president, would tell the *San Francisco Chronicle*—which, of course, was the precise opposite of what the monitoring team, Judge Henderson, and Oakland's civilian leadership intended.[96] Word's replacement, Wayne Tucker, was an outsider from the Alameda County Sheriff's Office, and he struggled to put his imprint on the OPD's insular culture. ("I'm a fan of the POA and their president," Tucker quipped to the press.)[97]

In 2007, seeing that the Oakland PD was not going to successfully complete the NSA by the January 2008 deadline, Judge Henderson ordered the first extension of the agreement for an additional two years. It would be a precipitous decision.[98]

Keith Batt (*left*) and Steve Hewison graduated from the Oakland Police Academy in the summer of 2000.

Following Jerry Amaro's death, his mother, Geraldine Montoya, put up posters in East Oakland seeking witnesses to his violent arrest by a team of Oakland police officers.

WANTED-KIDNAP-ASSAULT

Date:	11/08/2000
Case #:	88A-SF-128717
Soc. Sec. #:	458-37-2096
Name:	FRANCISCO VAZQUEZ
Alias:	FRANK
Address:	1305 Willow Court
	Suisun City, CA 94585
Height:	5 Feet 6 Inches
Weight:	168
Age:	44
Sex:	M
Eyes:	Brown
Hair:	Brown
Complexion:	pockmarked face
Race:	Hispanic
BirthDate:	10/23/1956

OTHER INFORMATION BELOW

ARMED & DANGEROUS***SUICIDAL TENDENCIES***ARMED & DANGEROUS

VASQUEZ has been a Police Officer in Oakland, California since January 13, 1992. VASQUEZ was charged in U.S. District Court, Northern District of California with a violation of Title 18, USC 1073, Unlawful Flight To Avoid Prosecution for the underlying crimes of Kidnaping, conspiracy, false imprisonment, assault with a deadly weapon and false police reports. The Federal warrant was issued by U.S. Magistarate Judge Wayne D. Brazil on 11/07/00. The above mentioned offenses are alleged to have occurred while VAZQUEZ was acting in his official capacity as a Oakland Police Officer.

Subject owns several handguns to include 38 cal revolver, 25 cal Raven, and 9mm Sig Saur.

Subject is a Police Officer and Caution should be used. Subject speaks Spanish. Subject born in Merida, Mexico.

TATTOO: upper right arm "Pilar", upper left arm Indian band, chest tattoo possibly tiger

ARMED & DANGEROUS***SUICIDAL TENDENCIES****ARMED & DANGEROUS

DEPOSITION EXHIBIT

FBI - Oakland
(510) 451-9782 or (415) 553-7400 (24 hours)
TRAK (356 -> 11.1.6.48) This flyer produced on a TRAK System. For more information about TRAK see www.trak.org

Oakland police officer Frank Vazquez fled before arraignment in 2000. The FBI coordinated an international manhunt, but Vazquez remains a fugitive to this day.

Alameda County prosecutor David Hollister holds up a photo of Riders victim Delphine Allen. Allen later sued the city along with 118 other people who had drugs planted on them, were beaten, or were falsely arrested.

David Hollister and District Attorney's Inspector Bob Conner confiscated a softball that was a key piece of evidence in the Riders' trial. Hollister had copies made to reveal to the jury the identities of some of the officers who stood accused of abusing West Oakland residents.

Clarence Mabanag (*left*) celebrates with his attorney Michael Rains outside Oakland's René C. Davidson Courthouse on Thursday, May 19, 2005, after a jury acquitted him on three charges and deadlocked on thirteen more.

Attorneys John Burris (*right*) and Jim Chanin filed a civil rights lawsuit on behalf of many of the Riders' victims in federal court. Rather than seek a massive monetary settlement from Oakland, they pursued a consent decree to reform the department. In 2003, Oakland agreed to the Negotiated Settlement Agreement, the most ambitious reform program imposed on a police department at the time.

8

Huey Newton was arraigned in his Kaiser Hospital bed on murder charges in the shooting of Oakland police officer John Frey in October 1967. An Oakland police officer guarded his door with a shotgun.

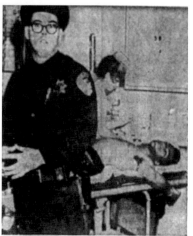

Anti–Vietnam War protesters tried to shut down the army's Oakland induction center several times in the 1960s. They were met with bone-crushing force by Oakland police officers.

Oakland's political establishment was upturned in the late 1970s as Black people rose to power. In 1978, Oakland's first Black mayor, Lionel Wilson (*right*), toured downtown Oakland with then governor Jerry Brown. Brown would reinvent himself two decades later by becoming the mayor of Oakland.

Felix Mitchell (*right rear*) on September 6, 1978. Mitchell built Oakland's most powerful drug trafficking organization. After his incarceration and death in 1986, street violence intensified in Oakland with the influx of narcotics and deadlier firearms.

A protester holds a severed pig's head on a stick during a January 9, 1980, City Council meeting where officials were considering establishing a civilian oversight commission.

A memorial at 53rd Street and Martin Luther King Jr. Way marked the spot where Gary King Jr. was killed by Oakland police sergeant Patrick Gonzales on September 20, 2007. The photo was taken in November 2008, shortly before BART and the city of Oakland sandblasted the mural.

Oakland police officer Hector Jimenez was photographed by OPD technicians shortly after he shot and killed Mack "Jody" Woodfox on July 25, 2008. It was his second controversial and fatal shooting.

Oakland youth dance on an OPD cruiser during the protests after Oscar Grant's slaying by a BART police officer on New Year's Day, 2009.

Lovelle Mixon murdered OPD motorcycle officers John Hege and Mark Dunakin on March 21, 2009, after a traffic stop.

Cephus "Uncle Bobby" Johnson speaks at a rally following the killing of Derrick Jones by OPD officers Omar Daza-Quiroz and Eriberto Perez-Angeles on November 11, 2010. The movement against police brutality that grew after Oscar Grant's murder would eventually help guide the Occupy Movement in Oakland.

Police fire tear gas and other "less lethal" munitions at Occupy Oakland protesters on January 28, 2012, during a failed attempt to take over the shuttered Kaiser Convention Center.

Scott Olsen in his Oakland backyard circa spring 2014, two and a half years after being seriously wounded in the head by an OPD "less lethal" projectile.

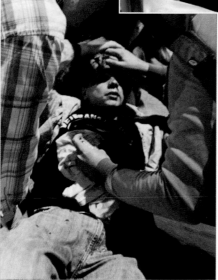

Occupy protesters attend to a wounded Scott Olsen in downtown Oakland on the night of October 25, 2011.

OPD's independent monitor Robert Warshaw spoke at a community meeting in Beebe Memorial Cathedral in 2014, just as OPD was starting to get back on track in completing the NSA's reforms.

22

Oakland police chief
Sean Whent in 2015.

23

Brian Bunton was one of multiple
OPD officers implicated in the
exploitation of the young woman
who went by "Celeste Guap." In text
messages, he warned her of supposed
undercover OPD operations on "the
blade"—Oakland's sex trafficking
strip on International Boulevard.

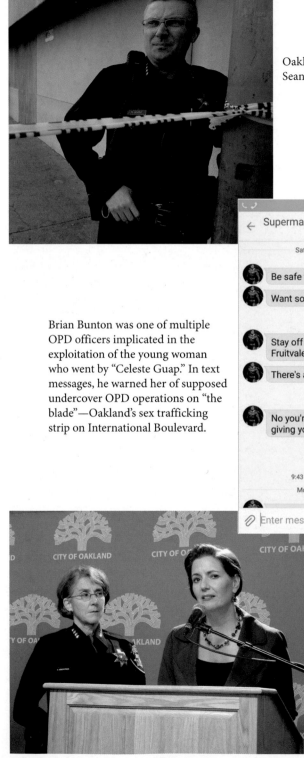

Superman ▼   CALL   MORE

Saturday, March 5, 2016

Be safe today!!   9:25 AM

Want some advice?   9:26 AM

9:27 AM   Tell me handsome

Stay off E14 from
Fruitvale to 42 tonight.   9:28 AM

There's a UC operation   9:29 AM

9:31 AM   Dam lol 😞😥

No you're not. Just
giving you a heads up.   9:36 AM

Thank u daddy 😞
I appreciate it ion
9:43 AM   wanna go to jail lol.

Monday, March 7, 2016

Enter message   SEND

24

Following the sex
exploitation scandal,
Mayor Libby Schaaf
(*right*) recruited Anne
Kirkpatrick to lead
OPD—the first woman
to do so. Kirkpatrick's
tenure would lead to
backsliding on the NSA
reforms, however.

"I FEEL I WAS BACK IN THE JIM CROW DAYS"

By 2008, five years had lapsed since Oakland began its court-ordered reforms. The monitoring team labored under the fiction that "significant progress" had been made, writing in a December report to Judge Henderson that "OPD will soon attain full compliance if it continues its efforts and adopts the recommendations made in our review reports." The reality, which the monitors were aware of but hesitant to state publicly, was that while the department had progressed on paper and plucked the low-hanging fruit of the NSA, the core reforms necessary to root out brutality and corruption were far from complete. Foot-dragging and outright resistance had stymied the consent decree's progress.

The monitoring team's increasingly technical reports no longer made headlines in the media, even though Lopez, Evans, and their colleagues consistently identified major problems: the department's Internal Affairs Division, its use-of-force investigations, and the span of control for supervisory officers were still in a state of disarray. In some cases, the dysfunction was as severe as during the Riders era.

As the Bay Area rode the boom-and-bust cycles of Silicon Valley and the Bush-era housing bubble, the Oakland police continued its well-oiled War on Drugs through undercover buys, surveillance, confidential informants, and joint federal operations to keep hitting the quicksilver trafficking organizations. Mark Candler's Acorn gang, named for the West Oakland housing development that served as its hub of operations, was wiped out in a 2008 sweep sardonically named Operation Nutcracker. Although Acorn was much smaller than Felix Mitchell's 69 Mob of the 1980s, the bust, over-seen by Jerry Brown, now ensconced in Sacramento as the state's attorney general, was a resounding success.[1] More than a hundred law enforcement officers, from Oakland and elsewhere, descended on nearly three dozen gang sites in the East Bay, netting fifty-four arrests.

The majority of drug arrests, however, were small fry: down-on-their-luck addicts or corner boys caught with a few rocks or bindles, or a bottle of the Ecstasy pills that fueled the hyphy cultural movement of the mid-aughts. Even cannabis, still years away from state legalization, led to arrests. "The War on Drugs did not slow down at OPD until probably 2013, 2014," recalled Holly Joshi, who, like many other Black cops and native Oakland-ers on the force, was drafted into undercover work.[2]

The humiliation of having the monitoring team uncover hundreds of uninvestigated civilian complaints jolted Internal Affairs out of its torpor and forced the in-house watchdog to professionalize. By the late 2000s, this half-awakened division would snag dozens of officers for all kinds of mis-conduct. Even the IAD's own commander would be ousted as one of the Oakland PD's most egregious cover-ups unraveled.

Karla Rush signed on as an Oakland police officer in 1999. The petite, light-skinned Black woman worked patrol for a few years before she was assigned to largely African American areas of East Oakland as a "problem-solving officer," a friendly term for a beat cop who worked closely with neighbors to root out street crime. In practice, Rush and other PSOs were narcotics officers.[3] Most neighbors who engaged with Oakland police through the city's Neighborhood Crime Prevention Councils—civilian groups designed to gather information about disorder and crime to share with OPD—leaned on PSOs to shut down trap houses and dope boys working the block.

As part of her work, Rush developed informants who fingered potential dealers in neighborhoods where the trade in cocaine, crack, and heroin flour-ished for decades amidst generational poverty. Based on information from her network, Rush wrote up search warrants for suspected trap houses, got them authorized by a judge, and enlisted other officers to bust down doors and make arrests.[4] Rush worked efficiently and was praised by her supervisors.

But in the spring of 2007 a suspicious pattern began emerging in court. Private defense attorneys and public defenders representing Oaklanders arraigned on charges based on Rush's casework uncovered discrepancies. The addresses on the warrants didn't match the actual residence that had been raided, or the informant's information didn't implicate the defendant, but rather someone else. Prosecutors began dismissing cases, starting with the March 2008 arrest of Reginald Oliver, a convicted drug dealer sent back to state prison on a parole violation after a falsified warrant led to a raid on his Douglas Avenue home, where officers recovered an assault rifle magazine and ammunition.[5]

The most consistent flaw in Rush's casework was the absence of chemical tests from the OPD crime lab of the substances purchased by her informants. The supposed drugs hadn't been confirmed as heroin, crack, or methamphetamine. Rush lied to superior court judges to get her warrants, telling them the tests had been completed.[6]

During this period, Rush was a familiar face in the downtown Oakland courtrooms, testifying at preliminary hearings about raids. Under oath, she swore again and again that the substances seized were methamphetamine, cocaine, or heroin. In her seven years on the force, Rush worked undercover while posing as a drug dealer, as a buyer, or providing cover for other cops playing those roles. She'd taken part in 250 drug investigations, 75 as the primary officer. She authored dozens of warrants and testified at least twenty times as an expert.[7]

Alarms began sounding inside the department in December 2007, when Rush and a team of officers burst into a little East Oakland bungalow. Their search warrant was based on a controlled buy. An informant had copped drugs on the street from a young Black man who'd retrieved the dope from a basement vent. Rush ordered the arrest of two people who lived in the house, both Vietnamese. One of the people, Belinda Le, was arrested solely on the basis of having little "baggies" in her kitchen, the kind you would put a sandwich in, and $10 in her bedroom. Rush claimed this was sufficient evidence to charge Le with dealing narcotics. Le complained, and after IA investigators reviewed the incident, they determined that Rush had committed false arrest.[8]

While Le's arrest was under investigation, other victims stepped forward. In February 2008 Rush prepared a search warrant for an apartment near the Oakland Coliseum based on information provided by another informant who claimed to have bought Ecstasy from a person associated with the address. Two days after Rush and a team of officers raided the apartment, the tenants filed a complaint, alleging that the suspect named on the warrant didn't live at their home, and that the officers illegally ransacked their place. Sergeant Ed Juarez, the Internal Affairs investigator initially assigned the case, tried pulling the crime report describing the informant's drug buy that Rush cited in her warrant affidavit. He couldn't find it. Juarez then went to the OPD crime lab to find the Ecstasy bought by Rush's informant. To his surprise, the envelope containing the supposed drugs was sealed. The technician who retrieved it "just happened to mention that the crime lab never tested the contents," Juarez wrote in a report, contradicting Rush's sworn search warrant affidavit that was signed off on by a judge.[9]

Realizing that Rush's shoddy police work might be a pattern, Juarez told IAD supervisor Lieutenant Sean Whent. The case was soon reassigned to Sergeant David Elzey, who was given another officer, Mark Rowley, transferred from patrol, to help dig through the voluminous paperwork. Three more officers soon joined. Whent wanted Elzey and Rowley on the case because they "were able to make hard decisions." Over the years, Whent saw too many other IAD investigators help exonerate the officers they were supposed to be dispassionately holding accountable. "Some investigators have a hard time saying something that sustains misconduct," Whent noted.[10]

Sergeant Elzey contacted the head of criminal records at the Wiley Manuel Courthouse, a utilitarian courthouse connected to OPD headquarters by a skybridge. That was where most officers went for warrants. His team gained permission to dig through the filing cabinets brimming with approved search warrants. First, they looked through warrants obtained from 2006 through 2008 in which officers used "x-buys." In an x-buy, an officer would typically give a confidential informant a small amount of money to buy drugs. Then the informant would tell the officer who sold him or her the drugs and where the deal went down, which the officer would put in a warrant application and send to a judge for approval. Elzey and Rowley compared the language on the warrant application with the drugs submitted to the OPD's crime lab, looking for false claims that drugs had been tested.

The results of the audit were cataclysmic. From 2001 through 2008, 57 percent of all Oakland police narcotics warrants in which an informant was used to buy drugs contained false information. Of the sixty-seven officers who filled out the 225 x-buy narcotics warrants in those years, nineteen were singled out as having authored "bad" warrants. The 129 x-buy warrants these nineteen cops wrote were picked apart line by line by Internal Affairs.[11] Elzey concluded that thirteen officers, Rush included, knowingly falsified drug test results. The cops didn't come from just one unit or one geographic area: copying and filing boilerplate warrants was common practice among problem-solving officers, Crime Reduction Teams, and even the Tactical Enforcement Task Force, which often worked with federal agencies on long-term drug and organized crime investigations.

Rush's warrants were by far the most problematic. In reviewing the forty warrants she authored during her career, IA found an alarming similarity. Rush relied consistently on three variations of the following phrase: "a presumptive test was conducted on the narcotics . . . which yielded that it indeed contained cocaine base."[12] The affidavits read as if they were written off a template: only the names and addresses differed.

The term "presumptive test" in the search warrants also posed problems: when questioned by the IAD, Rush said she believed a presumptive test meant she observed the suspected dope with her own eyes, rather than using a chemical field test kit or waiting for crime lab results.

The addresses of homes to be raided on Rush's warrants often didn't match up to the locations her team ended up tossing. Nor did some witness descriptions of alleged dealers. Rush admitted in IA interviews she hadn't seen her informants enter suspected crack houses or buy drugs in four separate cases.[13] In short, Rush repeatedly perjured herself in court and falsified dozens of reports. Some of the discrepancies appeared to come from bad intel from an informant that Rush didn't bother to verify.

East Oakland resident Claudette Washington and her two young grandchildren cowered in fear as police broke down the door to their Eighty-Third Avenue apartment on January 29, 2008, based on one of Rush's warrants. Washington, who got around with the use of a walker, was forced to the ground in her living room at the muzzle of an AR-15 rifle. Realizing they had the wrong address, the cops entered the neighboring apartment without a warrant, arresting Washington's neighbor, Cunnery Nelson, for large amounts of crack and marijuana.[14] The apartment building on Eighty-Third Avenue was undoubtedly used by drug dealers: the $1,102 in cash, scales, and sixty-something crack rocks recovered from Nelson's unit, and hiding spots around the property, made that abundantly clear.[15] However, Rush's corner cutting, reliance on unverified information, and lies led to arrests of drug dealers that couldn't hold up in court, and the wrongful arrest of innocent people. Washington's grandson was traumatized by the police raid, unable to sleep for nights after.[16]

Lieutenant Whent rejected an informal resolution of Washington's complaint in late July because Rush already had a sustained untruthfulness complaint that closely mirrored Washington's allegations.[17] Instead, Whent ordered a full investigation of the incident.[18] When she was interviewed, Rush admitted she had not field-tested a yellow dime bag of suspected cannabis stamped with the Batman logo turned over by her informant. The "presumptive" test referenced in her search warrant, Rush told Internal Affairs, was a visual inspection of the substance.[19]

In other instances, it was alleged Rush and other cops destroyed evidence, including potentially exonerating information. She and other officers destroyed a video surveillance system during the search of an East Oakland liquor store and made no attempt to recover footage of any suspected drug deals. An employee charged with drug dealing alleged he'd been framed by the Oakland police.[20]

In the end, sixteen criminal cases were dismissed and two people's convictions overturned.[21] Most of the cases involved alleged marijuana dealers, a glaring bit of cognitive dissonance in progressive Oakland: in 2004, voters passed a ballot measure making cannabis-related arrests the police's lowest priority.[22] While predominantly white and wealthy residents of Rockridge and Temescal freely bought weed from private storefront "clubs," the OPD ran buy-bust operations for small-time Black, Latino, and Asian dealers like it was still 1982.

At least two Oaklanders arrested as a result of bad warrants, Maceo Waqia and Nichole Pettway, served almost a year and a half in prison each.[23] Both were freed and their convictions voided once the nature of the OPD's involvement in their arrests became clear.

Deputy Chief Jeff Israel, one of the brass promoted when Wayne Tucker took over from Richard Word, twice asked Alameda County district attorney Tom Orloff to charge Rush for perjury. Orloff declined.

In April 2009 Oakland fired Rush. But with the backing from her police union attorney, Mary Sansen, Rush fought the decision. In a Skelly hearing, Sansen presented the OPOA's position: the city and police department were obsessed with meeting the federal court reforms and proving they "are not the bad guys." This caused the police to overreact against cops just trying to make Oakland a better place. Three years earlier, Sansen's colleague Mike

Rains outlined this argument in an essay titled "Reign of Terror,"[24] written for police officers and attorneys. The trade-off, Sansen claimed, was a lack of focus on public safety and little support for officers fighting crime.[25] Sansen also speciously attacked the Internal Affairs Division, calling Sergeant Elzey the "least qualified" person to investigate the cases because he'd never worked x-buy narcotics cases himself. (However, Elzey's partner, Mark Rowley, had, a fact that Sansen omitted.)

To Ed Kreins, the Beverly Hills police captain serving as the neutral Skelly hearing officer, these arguments weren't convincing. He upheld Rush's firing. Later, a labor arbitrator would also rule against her.[26]

Of the nineteen officers who wrote falsified warrants, the department sought to discipline only eleven of them because there was strong evidence that they knew their actions were wrong. Ultimately, only four would be punished. Seven of the cops argued successfully that they'd lied on warrants because they were poorly trained by the OPD. In addition to Rush, officers John Kelly, Ramon Alcantar, and Francisco Martinez were sustained for dishonesty and terminated. Rush and Kelly were rejected by several other police agencies when they tried to find new jobs, but the pair eventually landed as University of California police officers in neighboring Berkeley. Their dishonesty on search warrants and in court apparently didn't dissuade the UCPD from hiring them.

One cop who went unpunished was Sergeant Sekou Millington, Karla Rush's supervisor. Millington trained Rush and other officers on drug busts, warrant writing, and managing informants. He signed off on a falsified warrant affidavit by Officer Trainee Daniel Vaquero.[27] The faulty warrant led to the arrest of seventy-two-year-old navy veteran Edwoods Fields. Though no drugs were discovered in the illegal search of Fields's home, he was arrested for possessing two antique rifles. After Millington and Vaquero were turned away by the jail because Fields's elevated blood pressure and age placed him at high risk of dying, they drove the veteran home. Fields was never charged with a crime. Millington went on to have a good career at the OPD, leaving in 2019 to take the post of police chief of Tracy, a small Central Valley bedroom community on the fringe of the Bay Area.

Had the department learned from the Riders, it would have taken steps to make sure that cops were writing truthful police reports, including warrants. The involvement of so many officers was a clear sign that the reforms were being neglected. Ed Poulson, who was now the captain in charge of

Internal Affairs, labeled the cases "Warrantgate," a reflection of how badly it damaged the Oakland police's image. In a deposition years later, Chief Wayne Tucker recalled the use of falsified warrants by the department as a "colossal" management failure. "I'm talking about myself as the colossal failure," Tucker confessed. "Command staff, supervisors, and officers."[28]

The monitoring team run by Lopez and Evans also tracked the warrant scandal closely and noted various ways in which the department was setting itself up for failure. In mid-2007 they highlighted the stress that Oakland's push to hire seventy more officers by the end of the year would have on the OPD's academy. There simply wasn't enough classroom space or instructors to fully train that many recruits.[29] Without proper training, those rookies would likely make preventable mistakes. Before the systemic warrant falsification became public, Lopez and Evans raised the alarm about internal audits showing that OPD personnel "did not sufficiently understand the operative policies" they were trained to follow.

"It is not yet clear whether OPD will be able to make the hard decisions necessary to ensure that the positive changes OPD has undergone will be reinforced by training as the department moves forward," they wrote.[30] Another example of systemic policy failure that surfaced during the warrant scandal was the misuse of confidential informants, or CIs. Karla Rush had sloppily used information given to her by informants, leading to false arrests and raids on innocent people's homes. In early 2009, as the OPD prepared to fire her and others, the department's inspector general wrote that most supervisors were "not aware if their subordinates were using confidential informants," and that policies with respect to CIs weren't being followed.[31]

Rather than view the hundreds of bad warrants as a glaring sign of Oakland's failure to make fundamental changes since the days of the Riders, the monitoring team avoided what it thought would be a knee-jerk reaction. It praised the assiduous work of the OPD's Internal Affairs Division in discovering Rush's misconduct pattern and expanding its review to a department-wide scope.

Even before Internal Affairs completed its investigation into Warrantgate, John Burris and Jim Chanin jumped into the fray. They filed a class action lawsuit on behalf of dozens of Oaklanders caught up in the imbroglio. In their case, which involved 109 plaintiffs and settled for $6.5 million, the two attorneys linked the failings of Rush, Kelly, Alcantar, Martinez, and the seven others who weren't disciplined directly to the OPD's wasted half decade of resistance to the Negotiated Settlement Agreement.

"Oakland has been unable to fully implement the NSA, and the warrant scandal is a prime example of this failure," the pair wrote in their civil complaint.[32]

Whereas the police union viewed insufficient training as a means to exonerate most of the officers accused of falsifying warrants, Chanin and Burris viewed it as a systemic failure that resulted in racially biased drug enforcement. They also noted a paradox that stymied police reform: "Just as in the Riders case, where the officers' criminal attorneys successfully argued to a jury that the officers were poorly trained and supervised and should not be held criminally accountable for their own conduct, 7 of the 11 officers recommended for termination by the OPD for their false and misleading warrant affidavits had their terminations rescinded because they were able to successfully argue that they should not be held accountable for their own actions, which they contended were the product of poor training and/or poor supervision."

In other words, cops caught engaging in bad behavior blamed the day-to-day OPD's bad policies and lack of leadership. Accountability was limited, and the cycle of abuse continued.

———

Another contemporaneous practice by Oakland's drug cops made clear the consequences of business as usual. In 2007 dozens of Black Oaklanders, almost all of them men, kept turning up with similar stories at the law offices of John Burris and another civil rights firm run by Michael Haddad and Julia Sherwin. They'd been stopped by Oakland police, accused of using or selling drugs, and strip-searched in public.[33] In 2007 the attorneys filed over two dozen lawsuits with graphic allegations.[34]

One night in May 2007 welder John Smith took a female friend, Fidela Arrizon, out to eat at Art's Crab Shak in North Oakland. After dinner, the pair were heading back to their hotel when four Oakland cops stopped them. Smith knew two of the officers, John Koster and another whose last name was Brown, because he'd had previous run-ins with the duo. Koster and Brown handcuffed Arrizon, patted her down, and then allegedly reached into her underwear. Two other cops, Evan Frazier and Richard Holton, cuffed Smith and walked him over to the back seat of a patrol car. One officer doused Smith's eyes with pepper spray, temporarily blinding him.

According to Smith's lawsuit, Koster then got into the rear seat of the patrol car and allegedly grabbed the handcuffed man's throat with his latex-gloved hands. "Spit it out!" the cop yelled, believing that Smith had secreted a twist of drugs in his mouth. "Search his ass!" Brown suggested, laughing as he pulled on a pair of latex gloves. Two cops allegedly held Smith down as Brown pulled down his pants and boxers. "He's got it in his ass," one cop said. As the laughter of the other cops filled his ears, Smith could feel a hand running up and down his posterior. Then he felt a sharp jolt of pain as an object, most likely a finger, penetrated his anus three times in quick succession.

"Didn't I say I was going to fuck you?" Koster allegedly taunted Smith. "I'm fucking you now."

That was the last thing Smith remembered. Bleeding from his anus and blinded by the OC spray, he passed out in the patrol car. Smith woke up in a cell at the North County Jail, and reported his ordeal and injuries at the hands of Oakland officers to jailers and medical staff. His bleeding continued for another three days. It would be another three weeks before he was released.

No drugs were found on Smith.[35]

Kirby Bradshaw and his friend Spencer Lucas were accosted in a similar manner one morning in December 2005 while driving through Ghost Town with their friend Marty Robinson. They'd just picked up breakfast from the Koffee Pot diner on Telegraph Avenue and were heading to a friend's house to watch him fix a car. Lucas's gold 1972 Cadillac caught the attention of the Parole and Corrections Team, a task force charged with finding parole violators. Oakland police officers Ingo Mayer and D'Vour Thurston pulled over Lucas on Thirty-Second and West Streets, and a second police vehicle immediately arrived carrying Parole Agent Steven Nakamura and OPD officers Dave Martinez and Michael Mack.

Lucas and Robinson asked the officers why they'd been pulled over. They were met with silence. "You're pulling us over for being three black men in a car," Robinson said, repeating his accusation when Mayer asked if any of them were on court supervision.[36] Lucas identified himself as being on parole, but stated he had no drugs or weapons. Mayer ordered him out of the car, cuffed him, and patted him down. The search yielded nothing. Nakamura called Lucas's parole agent. Lucas, he learned, "was doing fine," but was homeless and sometimes slept in a hotel or a van.

Mayer then unbuckled Lucas's belt.

"Why are you doing this? Why are you pulling down my pants? I'm going to get off parole in thirty days," Lucas told the officer. He'd been on court supervision for three years and didn't intend to screw things up this close to the conclusion.[37]

"Not if I can help it," Mayer replied, asking Lucas if he had any "dope in your butt cheeks." The cop shook Lucas's boxer shorts, which slipped to the ground, exposing his butt and testicles to people walking and driving by on the busy street.

Again, no contraband.

"Disrespected, downgraded, humiliated. It was embarrassing. It was just a bad feeling to let all them people seeing you out there naked like that," Lucas testified later in court. While cuffed in the back seat of Mayer's patrol car, Lucas kept asking the cop why he'd stripped him in public and subjected him to such treatment. "He never gave me a reason why," Lucas recalled on the stand.[38]

Officer Mayer then turned to Bradshaw, who had also been taken out of the Cadillac. He ordered Thurston to take down Bradshaw's pants. Frightened of angering the cops and risking arrest, Bradshaw loosened his belt, dropped his pants to the ground, and shook his boxers out, still protesting. "And then the officers said, just go ahead and pull them all the way down. So I pulled them all the way down," Bradshaw recalled, describing how he slid his boxer shorts over his knees, leaving his genitals exposed to the morning sun and gawking onlookers. The officers had the young man stand in the street naked from the waist down as strangers passed by, including children walking to school. "I was terrorized. I was scared," Bradshaw said. "This is unlawful," he protested to the officers. "I don't know why you guys are doing this."[39]

"I'm not on probation. Why the fuck are you doing this to me?" Kirby demanded.[40] Like Lucas, Bradshaw had nothing on him. After having satisfied Mayer's curiosity, he pulled his pants back up. Bradshaw wasn't on parole, but he did have an outstanding warrant and was taken to North County Jail.[41]

Despite Lucas's parole agent indicating no problems with the young man, the task force cops drove him to his van, which was parked on West MacArthur Boulevard and Market Street. Mayer searched the van but turned up nothing. Still wanting to arrest Lucas, but without evidence of any crime, Mayer and Thurston had Nakamura check further possible addresses with

Lucas's parole agent. They drove across West Oakland to a house on Thirty-Fourth Street, where Mayer attempted to open the door using a key from Lucas's key chain. The resident opened the door and told the officer that Lucas didn't live there.

Two hours into this ordeal, Lucas was still cuffed and effectively under arrest, although there was no probable cause to detain him. Unperturbed, Mayer and Thurston then drove him to yet another address suggested by his parole agent, this time in Richmond. The address was the home of Lucas's estranged wife and her aunt. Without a warrant, the officers entered. No one was home. They flipped mattresses, pulled out all the drawers, and left the house in a state of disarray. The police didn't even leave a note that they had conducted a search, causing Lucas's wife to think she'd been burglarized. Inside the house, the Oakland cops and parole agent found a BB gun and used it to justify Lucas's arrest. In violation of the city policies that were supposed to be enforced by the NSA, Mayer didn't document much of the humiliating and unconstitutional episode, failing to fill out a stop data form, and not radioing in the movements around West Oakland and even to Richmond he took with his illegally detained prisoner.

Lucas's parole was revoked, and he returned to state prison for ten months. The ordeal evinced a tremendous sense of helplessness from the parolee, who'd been homeless and bouncing between relatives' couches, motel rooms, and his car, yet managing to keep in compliance with his terms of release until that morning.

When his lawsuit went to trial in 2010, Lucas maintained his composure for most of his testimony, but broke down sobbing while recounting how the pellet gun allegation sent him back to prison.[42] For someone who'd lived the street life and, by his own admission, dealt drugs in the 1990s, being violated for trying to live straight was crushing. Lucas was so deflated by his mistreatment that he didn't bother to file an Internal Affairs complaint with the department, first learning about the class action lawsuit through a 2007 *Oakland Tribune* article.[43]

At a civil trial years later, Kirby Bradshaw testified that the ordeal was the "craziest thing that I've ever been through in my entire life."

A couple of the cases against the Oakland Police Department for the illegal strip searches were tried before US District Court Judge Marilyn Patel. They served as tests for the roughly forty other similar cases in the queue. Patel dismissed one of them over credibility issues. But she believed Lucas and Bradshaw, ordering Officer Ingo Mayer to pay both men $100,000 in damages.[44] Based on the outcome, Oakland decided to settle the rest, rather than risk massive payouts after dozens of jury trials.

————

As in the warrants scandal, Oakland's cops seemed to be engaging in a pattern of racial profiling by routinely strip-searching narcotics suspects. The victims identified in Burris and Haddad & Sherwin's class action lawsuit were almost entirely Black, and they were frequently stopped for possession or sale of marijuana. As of 2010, two-thirds of all people stopped by Oakland police were African American, as were three-quarters of all people searched as a result of car stops.[45]

The department had an obvious racial profiling problem. Black Oaklanders knew it, and the degrading reality of such treatment just for having a criminal record only deepened mistrust in the Oakland police. Years after the Riders, cops were still stopping and violating Black men in pursuit of a never-ending War on Drugs.

"It's against the law to, you know, urinate on the street, so to be having your pants taken down by a law officer on the street, it was very humiliating," Bradshaw said. "I feel I was back in the Jim Crow days."[46]

————

The widespread falsification of warrants and illegal strip searches by OPD officers exposed deep problems in an unreformed police agency, but they didn't lead to sustained reporting by the media. Few outside the department, its court-appointed monitoring team, and civil rights attorneys connected the dots between the stalled-out NSA reforms and spiraling OPD scandals. It took an entirely different kind of scandal to peel back the layers of dysfunction at the Oakland Police Department for the broader public.

Chauncey Bailey was a middle-aged reporter who'd toiled in semi-obscurity for most of his career. A native son of Oakland who grew up in Hayward, Bailey had a lifelong love affair with journalism.[47] After a decade working as a reporter in Detroit, he returned to the Bay Area in 1992 for a job as the public affairs director for radio station KDIA, co-owned by Oakland mayor Elihu Harris and Assembly Speaker Willie Brown. Within a year, though, he left to work at the *Oakland Tribune*, then run by Robert and Nancy Maynard, who'd bought the Knowland family's onetime right-wing press organ in 1983, turning it into the first major newspaper owned and operated by African Americans.[48] But Bailey lost his *Tribune* job over a series of ethical lapses. First, he received a warning from editors for a puff piece about a small business owned by one of his romantic interests. Then, he threatened to write negative stories about the state Department of Motor Vehicles for not intervening in a payment dispute over a used car Chauncey sold to another man. He ended up at the *Oakland Post*, a small African American weekly newspaper.[49]

Even through his professional travails, Bailey's unwavering commitment to writing about the African American community meant his source base never deserted him. One topic that Bailey tracked obsessively was the fortunes of the Bay Area's Black Muslim community, in particular those of a local Nation of Islam splinter sect called Your Black Muslim Bakery, run by a renegade preacher named Yusuf Ali Bey.

Born Joseph Stephens, Bey grew up in North Oakland and began his career as a freewheeling, pleasure-seeking barber in the idyllic Southern California university town of Santa Barbara.[50] He radicalized there, and founded an NoI mosque and a bakery selling Elijah Muhammad's health-conscious foods, most notably bean pies.[51] In 1971 Bey relocated to Oakland. He eventually took over a brick building on San Pablo Avenue in North Oakland to run a large bakery and his religious sect, and adopted the name Yusuf Ali Bey. Bey's organization earned a reputation for employing any Black Oaklander in need of work, particularly recently released convicts. Over time, it purchased the houses abutting the Bakery's open backyard, forming a compound that housed many of Bey's workers and followers.

Yusuf Bey's congregation gained influence and generated business, but Bey had a secret. He was sexually exploiting his female followers, even raping underage girls.[52] Alameda County social workers would pass by, responding to anonymous complaints of horrendous mistreatment and abused children, but left empty-handed after cursory investigations.

A fervent polygamist, Bey kept several "wives," who lived in mortal fear of him. He fathered at least forty-two children and ordered women to exclude paternity from birth certificates in order to keep mothers and children eligible for state welfare aid as single mothers.[53] The fraud netted Bey tens of thousands of dollars in child welfare funds and Section 8 housing vouchers. Fear among his followers was buttressed with a gruesome reality: in 1986 a Bakery follower named Brother Usman was found murdered blocks from the compound after walking in on Yusuf Bey raping a young boy in a bathroom. His killing is still unsolved.[54]

In 1994 Bey ran for mayor, mounting an improbable challenge to incumbent Elihu Harris. He carried 5 percent of the vote after campaigning with the message that Oakland cops were a largely suburban department that treated Oakland as a "zoo." It rang true for many Oaklanders, and Bey might have done better had he not invited a virulent anti-Semite and racist to speak at a fund-raiser.[55] Nevertheless, Bey's run solidified his status as a force to be reckoned with in Oakland's Black community.[56] By 1998, Jerry Brown came to the Bakery during his mayoral campaign to give a speech.[57] When Joseph Samuels ran the department in the early 1990s, he frequently communicated with Yusuf Bey about improving police-community relations.

All the while, Your Black Muslim Bakery was essentially declared off-limits to the Oakland Police Department as local politicians and officials sought Yusuf Bey's favor.

"Joe Samuels was a very political animal, and he and other politicians were in bed with Mr. Bey and would do everything they could to garner his support," an OPD officer told *East Bay Express* reporter Chris Thompson years later. "No one ever reached down and said, 'Leave the Beys alone.' But when you work in an organization, you learn what the sacred cows are. The people you don't mess with. The Bey family was one of those." Thompson himself became a target after publishing stories critical of Bey's empire in 2002; a brick was thrown through the window of his newspaper's office, and the reporter skipped town for months to avoid threats.[58]

While covering Black Oakland, Chauncey Bailey would occasionally patronize the San Pablo storefront and run into Bey at the studios of the Black-owned TV station that was home to his public affairs program and Bey's show, *True Solutions*, on which the sect leader frequently railed against whites, Jews, and homosexuals.[59]

Bey's facade of respectability crumbled in June 2002, when a woman who'd left the Bakery recounted to Oakland police officers her rape at his hands when she was a minor. She'd borne three children while at the Bakery. Her eighteen-year-old daughter had also been raped by Yusuf Bey and borne his children. Jim Saleda of the OPD sex crimes unit investigated meticulously, obtaining search warrants for DNA from their children and Bey to establish parenthood. The birth certificates alone confirmed the women gave birth while underage—positive DNA tests would be grounds enough for criminal charges.

After legal wrangling, Bey submitted to DNA tests and turned himself in on September 20, 2002, on a single count of rape. When news of his charges broke, the floodgates opened. Saleda found himself inundated with more tips about rape, illegitimate children, and Bey's diagnoses of cancer and AIDS.[60] Bailey covered Yusuf Bey's criminal case for the *Tribune* along with his colleagues, angering Bakery followers who expected Bailey would pull punches.

After Bey's death, a bloody succession war consumed the Bakery: Waajid Aljawwaad, the caretaker Yusuf appointed as his immediate successor, disappeared in 2004, turning up months later in a shallow grave. Bey's twenty-one-year-old son, Antar, assumed control. One of Waajid's loyal assistants, a Bakery follower named John Muhammad Bey, who worked at the Bakery and ran security at a downtown hotel, avoided Antar Bey and stayed aloof. One morning, John Bey was ambushed as he left his home in the leafy hills enclave of Montclair, wounded in his legs by a hail of bullets. He survived, and fled Oakland. Antar would eventually fall victim to this cycle of violence, murdered by a nineteen-year-old drug dealer at a gas station in 2005. While the Oakland PD's investigation settled on the theory of a failed carjacking, in reality Antar's assassin, Alfonza Phillips, had been paid off by Antar's younger brother, Yusuf IV.[61]

Yusuf Bey IV, or "Fourth" as he was known within the organization, was a violent egomaniac who embraced street life, brandishing AK-47s, brawling at strip clubs, and leading a cadre of young foot soldiers. On Thanksgiving Eve 2005, Fourth led a group of suit-and-bow-tie-wearing Black Muslims on an anti-alcohol rampage against two North Oakland corner stores, smashing bottles, tearing apart the shelves, and pummeling the clerks at gunpoint. At the second store, Fourth's soldiers stole a 12-gauge Mossberg shotgun from a clerk they beat. The attacks put Your Black Muslim Bakery on the map again after closed-circuit TV (CCTV) video of the assaults aired on local television station KTVU.[62]

The dramatic images finally forced Oakland police to investigate the Bakery. The initial probe into the liquor store assaults was assigned to Sergeant Dominic Arotzarena, a popular figure within the department who would briefly run the Oakland Police Officers' Association. Unbeknownst to Arotzarena, his superiors assigned him a minder: Homicide sergeant Derwin Longmire, who'd first patronized the Bakery while training for bodybuilding competitions in the early 1990s. Longmire also investigated Antar Bey's murder and developed a close relationship with his and Fourth's mother. Arotzarena had no clue of the directive Longmire received from Deputy Police Chief Howard Jordan and Investigations Captain Jeff Loman. He took umbrage at Longmire calling him out of the blue to ask what details he could relay to Fourth's mother. Longmire's proximity to the Bakery made other Oakland cops uncomfortable: he'd taken to wearing a bow tie with his suit, a sartorial choice that made him look like a practicing Black Muslim.

Through his family's influence, Fourth was allowed by OPD commanders to cut a deal. He turned himself in and was charged in connection with the liquor store vandalism. However, no attempt was made to recover the shotgun stolen by his men, and OPD leaders wouldn't sign off on a search warrant to look for it in the Bakery.[63]

As Fourth dragged Your Black Muslim Bakery back into the spotlight, sales plummeted, unpaid taxes generated IRS notices, and the organization's books fell into disarray. In 2006 Fourth declared bankruptcy in a fraudulent application, shifting over a million dollars in assets to his mother's name to conceal the Bakery's wealth from the feds. Like his father, Fourth turned to fast money, employing fake identities to scam luxury cars, mortgages, and eventually flip twelve houses in Oakland's overheating real estate market.[64] In a poorly thought-out and ultimately unsuccessful scheme to keep the IRS off his back, Fourth met with Oakland mayor Ron Dellums and Congresswoman Barbara Lee, securing letters of support to the federal government, an astonishingly inept move for such experienced politicians.[65]

For his muscle, Fourth recruited violent ex-convicts. These new soldiers were put to use in the kidnap and torture of an Oakland cocaine dealer's girlfriend to secure money for the Bakery's debts, the murder of Alfonza Phillips's indigent uncle Odell Roberson in North Oakland as a lethal message for Phillips to stay silent about Antar Bey's killing, and the random execution of Michael Wills, a thirty-six-year-old white sous-chef in a schoolyard four blocks north of the Bakery.[66]

The crime spree would have been easily traceable to the Bakery. In the kidnapping case, officers recovered two cars and a cell phone that linked directly back to the Black Muslim congregation; the property where the woman was held and tortured before being rescued by a passing Oakland cop was one of the dozen houses flipped in Fourth's real estate scam.[67] Roberson and Wills were killed within a mile of each other by the same gun:

casings from the same SKS 7.62-caliber rifle littered both crime scenes.[68] But the OPD was still operating at a slow pace when it came to the Bakery.

Meanwhile, one of the Bakery's old guard had seen enough. Saleem Bey, a legal son-in-law of Yusuf Bey, went to the police about the fraud schemes: they turned him away, too inundated with an onslaught of gun violence to take a complex white-collar case. Desperate to jostle Fourth out of his position, Saleem turned to his last roll of the dice: the *Oakland Post*'s Chauncey Bailey.[69]

Saleem showed Bailey proof that Fourth was not the legitimate owner of the Bakery, and he tipped the reporter to criminal cases against Fourth in five Bay Area counties, including assault, car theft, and forgery. But word of Saleem's meeting with Bailey got back to Fourth, striking fear into the reporter and whistleblower.

On a parallel track, the Oakland police finally pieced together Fourth's pattern of lethal violence and were ready to raid the Bakery compound. The warrant application called for a search of the entire Bakery and mass arrests using more than two hundred officers from a dozen agencies. The last two weeks of July 2007 were consumed with preparation for what would be the biggest raid in OPD history.[70] On July 25 they began staking out the Bakery at night, with August 1 as the go date.

Unaware the police were closing in, Fourth seethed over the prospect of Bailey's exposé. Watching a VHS tape of Yusuf Bey's funeral late one night with his soldiers, Fourth paused the tape and pointed at a middle-aged Black man in a dark suit with glasses: "That's the motherfucker right there who killed my dad," he said, explaining that Bailey's articles hastened the Bakery founder's demise by cancer.[71]

As officers sorted out logistics for the raid, word came down that it would be delayed forty-eight hours. Two senior SWAT commanders, Deputy Chief David Kozicki and Captain Ed Tracey, were backpacking in Yosemite and wanted to be present for the operation.[72]

The consequences would be dramatic. Fourth summoned Devaughndre Broussard and Antoine Mackey, two of the San Francisco hardmen he'd recruited, and told them Bailey had to die. "We got to take him out before he write that story."

Early on the morning of August 2 Broussard and Mackey piled into a white minivan without license plates and waited for Bailey to catch the bus to work. The hit men almost missed their target: Bailey opted to walk along the shore of Lake Merritt. They tailed him along Fourteenth Street into downtown, where Mackey pulled the minivan over and Broussard slipped a ski mask over his face, jumped out, spotted his target, and broke into a run across the four-lane road. Broussard was armed with the Mossberg shotgun Fourth's men had stolen during the liquor store vandalism spree. He flicked off the safety and leveled it at the journalist. Bailey didn't notice him until the last second. The first blast caught him in the right shoulder, punching through his chest cavity. As Bailey fell into a bush lining the sidewalk, Broussard fired again, a load of buckshot that tore his victim's abdomen open above the belt buckle. Racking the shotgun a third time, Broussard then dropped the barrel toward the journalist's face and let a third round go, exploding the left side of Bailey's head.[73] Cops converged on the scene from all directions. One of them reached down to Bailey's bag, pulled out a copy of the *Oakland Post*, and laid it across the dead journalist's shattered skull.

Within hours, an OPD criminalist matched the strike marks left on the two shotgun shells left at the scene to spent cartridges left at a car shooting Fourth's men committed months before. The delayed raid on the Bakery went ahead under the microscope of the international media up in arms over the killing of one of their own, a rarity in the United States.[74] Shortly before five in the morning on August 3, two hundred cops poured into the Bakery on the heels of flash-bang grenades. Not a shot was fired: Fourth, Broussard, Mackey, and the other soldiers went without a fight, and Broussard even tossed the Mossberg shotgun out of a window at the feet of a cop down below.[75]

Fourth tried to pin Bailey's murder on Broussard, claiming the young San Franciscan acted on his own after learning about the forthcoming story on the Bakery's bankruptcy. Yet Broussard wouldn't go for it. For hours, he refused to confess. Sergeant Longmire went so far as to leave Broussard and Fourth unmonitored and alone in an interview room. During their conversation, Fourth cajoled Broussard into agreeing to confess to the murder, and to take sole responsibility.[76]

Even after Broussard was charged, Bailey's colleagues didn't accept the official explanation that the young, shiftless man acted alone. By that point, Yusuf Bey IV's desire to kill Bailey was well known: Saleem Bey told the *Oakland Tribune* on August 7 that he'd been Chauncey's source. "This thing should've been stopped well before it got to Chauncey," Saleem said.[77]

Even though investigators secretly recorded Fourth gleefully reenacting

Bailey's assassination to two followers in the Santa Rita Jail, District Attorney Tom Orloff wasn't interested in pursuing murder conspiracy charges against Bey IV: Broussard would suffice, since Fourth was already facing life without parole for kidnapping and torture.[78]

The Chauncey Bailey Project, led by journalists Bob Butler, Thomas Peele, and Mary Fricker, began an independent investigation of the *Oakland Post* editor's slaying. Their relentless digging would unearth evidence that key witnesses implicated Fourth in planning Bailey's killing, critical points that the OPD's overworked, slipshod homicide detectives didn't pursue for over a year.[79]

Roughly a year after the assassination, the Chauncey Bailey Project published the secret jailhouse video of Fourth gloating over the journalist's murder, causing an uproar and jarring the Alameda County district attorney into reopening the murder conspiracy investigation. Further disclosures revealed the OPD's missteps, including the alarming proximity of Sergeant Longmire to the Beys. Longmire, who had spoken over the phone several times with Fourth at Santa Rita Jail, came under renewed suspicion from both his department and the state Department of Justice, which opened its own review of the Bailey case at Mayor Dellums's request.[80]

———

As the negative headlines about the police's mishandling of the Bakery case piled up and the department reeled from the sprawling scandals involving warrants and strip searches, a ghost from the OPD's past was about to resurface and underscore just how much of a mockery the department had made of reform. Someone in the department, or extremely close to it, slipped an explosive bit of information to the Chauncey Bailey Project: documents outlining a hidden case of lethal police violence and a cover-up lasting almost a decade.

The cache of documents, hidden in a tree stump for the reporters to find, concerned the death of Jerry Amaro, the young man who died from a collapsed lung weeks after being beaten by cops during a drug sting in 2000.

During the year after his death, Amaro's family unsuccessfully pleaded with the OPD to investigate. Amaro had complained to his own mother that he'd been brutalized by police officers and attempted to sue the OPD in 2000, but the department successfully quashed its own criminal and IAD investigations into the case. The leaked documents showed that the

OPD knew all along Amaro's injuries were due to a police beating and the squad that ran the drug bust took steps to cover up the incident. Discipline handed down to the officers had been minimal. The department chose to move on from the killing.

The bombshell story hit the front page of the *Oakland Tribune* on January 22, 2009, under a banner headline: "Oakland Suspends Chief of Internal Affairs Amid FBI Probe."[81] Thomas Peele and Bob Butler wrote that Captain Ed Poulson had been removed from his post as commander of Internal Affairs. Tucker had put Poulson over IAD despite knowing about his interference with the Internal Affairs case years earlier.[82] The leaked documents included homicide investigator Gus Galindo's notes showing Poulson's squad omitted any mention of use of force. However, a source in the department told Peele and Butler that some of these officers had later changed their statements, admitting they'd punched and kicked Amaro and other suspects arrested during the drug sting.

The revelation of Amaro's killing and the subsequent cover-up had a seismic effect on the Oakland PD. Poulson was suspended almost immediately. Within five days, Chief Tucker resigned.

Armed with new evidence about Amaro's killing and the department's cover-up, Jim Chanin and John Burris sued on behalf of Amaro's family. During the discovery process, the sordid details of the botched sting and Amaro's awful death in a friend's basement would be made public.

Poulson was deposed in September. He repeatedly invoked the Fifth Amendment because of the ongoing FBI investigation. Other cops, including those who posed as dealers and the arrest team, told the attorneys they remembered little about what happened. But the documents spoke for themselves, as did the taped statements the officers gave to OPD Homicide and Internal Affairs back in 2000. And others arrested that day during the violent police operation spoke out, including Harry Kinner, who described how he and Amaro and others were treated. "They ran over, picked me up, body slammed me, and started choking me. . . . And the Black officer said, one of them said, 'You been fooled, you been tricked, you been bamboozled, you been hoodwinked,' and was laughing." Kinner recognized the mocking phrase; they were from a speech by Nation of Islam founder Louis Farrakhan.[83]

"The Amaro case is related to the warrant scandal cases of Oliver and Jackson because these cases also involve a widespread course of miscon-

duct which included providing false and intentionally misleading statements in sworn warrant affidavits and in police reports despite the fact
that the OPD was responsible for more closely supervising and monitoring
its officers' conduct as a result of the Riders Litigation," Burris and Chanin
wrote in a 2009 motion from the warrant case, linking the scandals to the
moribund NSA reforms.[84]

Although he was nearly a decade separated from the OPD, Keith Batt
was still closely watching the agency from his post in the Pleasanton Police
Department, hoping it would change.

"I was very tuned into it, for years I read the NSA reports when they
came out," Batt recalled in a 2022 interview. "What they were asking Oakland to do is what they should've been doing all along."

Warrantgate wasn't surprising to Batt. Karla Rush had been in his academy, and he knew about some of the other officers caught up in the scandal.
What had happened to Amaro—the brutality and unwillingness of officers
to be honest on their reports about tackling and abusing suspects for misdemeanor drug offenses—fit the pattern he'd experienced on the streets.

Batt felt "constantly disappointed" by the OPD's "repeated failings."

Poulson made a last-ditch effort to turn the tables on the department.
In October 2010 his defense attorney sent a 137-page "Analysis of the Jerry
Amaro Incident" to the OPD. The document, written by attorney Matthew Pavone, was originally intended as an analysis of statements made
by Poulson's colleagues during the original investigation in 2000 and more
recent depositions taken during the civil case, all of which would form a
foundation for Poulson's defense in case the US attorney decided to charge
him based on the FBI's findings. But Pavone claimed the analysis revealed
numerous misdeeds that "were not discovered, that were discovered and ignored, and that were not adequately addressed during the original Internal
Affairs investigation." Poulson's attorney essentially asked the OPD to open
a new Internal Affairs case, this time focusing on Poulson's colleagues for
allegedly lying to ruin him.

The Oakland PD initiated a new IA case in 2010. While the results
weren't what Poulson wanted to hear, they did shed new light on the department's failure to seek justice for Amaro.

Sergeant Brian Medeiros was assigned the case. After an intensive re-
evaluation of the record and fresh interviews with the cops involved in the
decade-old incident, Medeiros found that Chief Word had circumscribed

the original IA investigation so that Amaro's brutal beating would never be considered. Medeiros's interview of Anthony Rachal, who led Internal Affairs back in 2000, was particularly revealing.

"I asked Rachal why there wasn't an investigation into whether use of force used versus Amaro was within department policy. Rachal then said Poulson's discipline (ten days) had been pre-decided by Chief Word," Medeiros wrote in his final report. "Rachal said he understood a deal had been made with Chief Word and his chief of staff, Dave Walsh, who had a relationship with Poulson. Rachal said he became aware of these discussions during the investigation and that Rachal had become frustrated with this deal." According to Medeiros, another word the police chief used to describe how the investigation should go was "script."[85]

The parallels to the Riders case, where Word limited Internal Affairs Sergeant Jon Madarang's investigation to the events Keith Batt observed during his two weeks on the force, were obvious. Rather than hold Poulson accountable for the fatal reverse sting and attempting to convince his subordinates to lie about the incident, Chief Word meted out light discipline (against the wishes of Captain Ron Davis).

Walsh had played a role "in possibly influencing the discipline for Poulson," his friend and best man at his wedding. Chief Word was aware of the relationship between Poulson and Walsh, and should have intervened to keep his right-hand man out of the IAD case. By the time Medeiros wrote these words, Walsh was long gone, having moved in 2002 to Michigan to become a small-town police chief.

Medeiros's report also revealed that Sergeant Gus Galindo, the homicide investigator who worked the Amaro case, was never told that Holmgren, the rookie cop who participated in the fatal buy-bust, had changed his statement when he spoke to IA, telling them he'd felt officers hit Amaro several times while pinning him to the sidewalk. Had Galindo followed the IA investigation closely and included this in his report, or even reinterviewed Holmgren and the rest, the district attorney's decision not to pursue charges might have been different.

Among the other "numerous areas of concern" Medeiros flagged were that Galindo never made an attempt to interview other arrestees from that night; "these interviews could have shown a pattern of uses of force versus arrestees. This pattern of force may have been useful to [Deputy District Attorney] Quist in her review of criminal charges involving subject officers."

Although there was little doubt Poulson's squad was responsible for Amaro's death, Medeiros also found that Sergeant Mike Reilly's statements from 2000 and 2009 were filled with "major discrepancies," and that the OPD should never have allowed Reilly to communicate with the reverse sting team once the first investigation was launched.

Very little about the incident, from the buy-bust and violent tactics and cover-up, to the police's incompetent investigative methods, to the department's softball discipline, was appropriate.

Poulson would eventually be fired but win his job back thanks to the OPD's poor record on arbitration. He retired quietly in 2013 after spending years in low-profile administrative positions. After leaving, he took a security job with Ross, the clothing retailer, and launched several websites to try to rehabilitate his image.

The FBI's case never materialized into charges against Poulson. A Freedom of Information Act (FOIA) request we filed with the agency, and more than a thousand pages of case records, remain outstanding.

Chauncey Bailey's murder improbably led to the exposure of the Amaro cover-up. Another lasting effect of the journalist's killing was the end of the OPD's grace period with its court oversight. The festering flaws in several criminal and Internal Affairs investigations had cost Bailey his life. The press was now paying attention, and the public finally saw the deadly consequences of a department that remained hostile to external oversight and reform.

Devaughndre Broussard, Yusuf Bey IV, and several other Bakery followers would be convicted for their roles in Chauncey Bailey's murder. The San Pablo Avenue storefront was boarded up and sold off. Sergeant Longmire would be demoted but allowed to return to patrol, even though the California Department of Justice found that he intentionally compromised the Bailey murder investigation.[86] Over the years, Bailey's killing would fade into semiobscurity, still carrying tremendous significance for his family, friends, and colleagues in the Bay Area media, but leaving little impact on Oakland at large.

Perhaps the most important development to come out of the late-aughts shakeout of the Oakland Police Department was the de facto appointment of Ed Poulson's replacement at the head of IAD: his deputy, Lieutenant Sean Whent.

10

WHIPLASH

Hundreds of people filled the pews of South Hayward's Palma Ceia Baptist Church the morning of January 7, 2009, to say good-bye to twenty-two-year-old Oscar Grant III. He'd been shot in the back six days earlier by BART police officer Johannes Mehserle in Oakland's Fruitvale Station. Grant lay serenely in an open casket topped with red and white flowers. His youthful face bore no expression of pain, sadness, anger, or fear. But those attending his funeral, as well as the protesters who gathered that same day at Fruitvale Station, could not hide their sorrow, and their fury at the police and system they believed was failing them.

Reverend Ronald Coleman spoke of the love Grant's family had for their lost son and of Grant's reputation in the working-class South Hayward community fourteen miles south of Oakland. He was a loving son and hardworking father, a familiar figure behind the meat counter at the Farmer Joe's market in Oakland's Dimond district. He had persevered in life and had a bright future ahead of him. The reverend also acknowledged the boiling point the region was nearing because of the killing, which authorities still hadn't acknowledged as a murder.

"The world is watching," said Coleman, referring to the international media attention and calls for the swift arrest and prosecution of Mehserle. Grant's fatal shooting was the first to go truly viral on the internet, creating global awareness of a police killing that, while familiar now, was novel in 2009. "They wonder if we will start a fight or a civil commotion. We must respond with prudence," Coleman counseled. Many in the church nodded with approval, but the mood was different in the streets.

The first six days of 2009 were a whirlwind. At least four passengers riding the BART train that Grant and his friends had been forced off of by a squad of transit cops around two in the morning on New Year's Day recorded videos of the shooting. Although BART officers tried to confiscate at least one camera, they were unable to grab the others. In a world still straddling the dawn of the smartphone camera and social media eras, witnesses outraged by Grant's shooting turned to a traditional path for accountability: journalists.

Local news reporters at CBS 5 and KTVU obtained and aired separate videos of Grant's shooting. They were immediately picked up by national outlets and spread across the internet like wildfire.[1] It was impossible to escape the footage of BART police officer Anthony Pirone hitting Grant while he was on the ground, and Mehserle kneeling on the young man's back before standing and firing a single executionary shot into Grant's back. The bullet scar on the train platform tile remains to this day.

"All we want is justice. In the world today the police can kill anybody, shoot them, get away with it, and get paid," said one woman attending a downtown Oakland rally. Grant's slaying was already being compared to other grim mile markers in the movement against police violence, including the NYPD's killings of Sean Bell in 2006 and Amadou Diallo in 1999. "I've been beaten by the police myself," said the woman's brother. "And if you don't get big publicity like this, nothing will happen if you don't have money."[2]

Mehserle still hadn't been interviewed by BART Internal Affairs or the district attorney's investigators. Instead, he fled to Lake Tahoe's eastern shore in Nevada, hiding in a Zephyr Cove vacation home owned by family friends. The public couldn't fathom why he hadn't been arrested and interrogated, like any other homicide suspect. Nuanced questions about whether the DA's office had probable cause for an arrest warrant were thin excuses to those who'd seen the videos of Grant's death.

At the Fruitvale rally, protesters clogged the turnstiles as a line of transit cops closed the station with a rolling metal door. An organizer announced through a megaphone that Mehserle had just quit his job. The officer's attorney had passed the news on to BART, which had made January 7 its final deadline for his Internal Affairs interview. Mehserle's silence meant he faced summary termination for insubordination. Like many officers under scrutiny before him, Mehserle simply quit to escape the administrative penalty. The crowd briefly cheered news of his resignation. But the mood in front of the Fruitvale BART station remained furious.

The authorities' measured statements hinted that the formal investigation of Grant's killing was headed in a familiar direction, with the officer eventually being cleared. BART Police Chief Gary Gee had drawn calls to resign after claiming the shooting had no "nexus" to racial issues, and that it was "inconclusive" whether Grant was handcuffed after being shot. BART's board of directors were virtually silent.

District Attorney Tom Orloff, a by-the-book, publicity-shy prosecutor who worked in Alameda County his entire professional career, was careful in his public statements. Many people interpreted Orloff's caginess as reticence to treat Mehserle as a suspect. He'd handled lightning-rod cases before, including the unsuccessful murder prosecution of Huey Newton for killing teenage sex worker Kathleen Smith in 1974. And Orloff was no stranger to charging cops. He unsuccessfully pursued the four Riders in 2000. In 2005 his team successfully convicted Richard Valerga, an Oakland cop who sexually abused Asian women while on the job, and two narcotics cops who'd tried to solicit prostitutes during an Alameda County Sheriff's sting operation. He'd gone after a half dozen other cops for on-duty corruption. However, no police officer had ever been charged for an on-duty murder in California. Only a handful had ever been tried nationally. Charges against police for using force, including shooting people, were so rare at the time, experts interviewed by the media in the ensuing weeks could not recall any comparable cases.

Around the same time as Grant's funeral services on January 7, about a hundred Black community leaders gathered outside the downtown Oakland courthouse where Orloff's offices were located. Representatives of the city's biggest Black faith institutions like Allen Temple Baptist Church's Dr. J. Alfred Smith, Minister Keith Muhammad of the Nation of Islam, and young activists who organized the Fruitvale station rally voiced their frustrations with the glacial pace of the DA's investigation. Desley Brooks, an East Oakland council member who'd become a leading voice in the movement, said she was concerned about the "callousness" with which BART and the DA were treating the case. The group packed into the lobby of Orloff's ninth-floor office, demanding a meeting.

Bob Conner, the DA inspector who had doggedly pursued the Riders and was now a lieutenant, emerged from the prosecutor's suite and asked the group who was in charge. He received an answer that no one was leading the group: the entire coalition wanted to meet with the DA. After Conner ducked back into the office, the group chanted "enough is enough" until Orloff relented.

Standing akimbo in a rumpled tan suit and tie, Orloff told them in a measured tone, "I realize the importance of this to the community," and added that he was shocked by the footage.[3] The DA urged patience. Upon exiting the meeting, Minister Muhammad said they'd shared their desire that "the wheels of justice not turn so slowly," and their concern "that the community be informed more fully."[4]

Another source of ire for protesters was Oakland Mayor Ron Dellums. When elected in 2006, Dellums was viewed by many in the Black community as a reprieve from Jerry Brown's eight-year reign, during which the Riders ran roughshod over West Oakland, the OPD was placed under court oversight, reforms floundered, and communities of color were left behind as their superstar mayor courted real estate developers to remake downtown. Drafted by a Black/progressive coalition, at first blush, Dellums's victory promised a new radical era for city politics. As a congressman, he had played a small but key role in helping Nelson Mandela's African National Congress topple apartheid in South Africa and was a steady voice of conscience against state violence, from police brutality to nuclear weapons. Furthermore, he had impeccable pedigree: his uncle, C. L. Dellums, was an iconic labor activist with the Brotherhood of Sleeping Car Porters, the local NAACP chapter, and many other civil rights organizations.[5] But Ron Dellums's shy style of governing led to a perception that he was an absentee mayor. Oakland politics required more forceful personalities and a constant presence on the ground. When the Oscar Grant protests ignited, Dellums did not immediately step forward to lead in a time of grief.

At the Fruitvale Station rally on January 7, local radio journalist and activist Dave "Davey D" Cook shared a widely held opinion about Dellums. "So, you're the mayor of the city that's already seen its history drenched in the blood of police killings, from Bobby Hutton all the way up to Gary King, and now you can't even just speak to the people as a human being?"[6]

This was Oakland's prevailing mood: the authorities weren't acting with urgency to address a police murder caught on camera and broadcast to the entire world. While they dawdled, a "killer cop" fled the state. Later that afternoon, a breakaway march of hundreds left Fruitvale Station and headed west on International Boulevard toward downtown, a group of teenagers riding "scraper bikes" (tricked out to mimic the chrome-rimmed box-frame cars featured at sideshows) at the head of the crowd. Protesters took over the westbound traffic lanes. When they neared Oakland's Lake Merritt, BART police warned the OPD that the crowd was becoming unruly.

As darkness set in, the protesters converged on BART's Lake Merritt Station, where BART police were headquartered. Small groups peeled away to smash windows of cars and businesses, overturn trash cans, light small fires, and drag dumpsters into the streets. At Eighth and Madison Streets, hundreds surrounded an Oakland police car as the lone officer fled on foot. Young men jumped atop the patrol car and danced while their allies smashed its windows and lights, whooping in delight. The group rocked the Crown Victoria and dented its sides before rolling a flaming dumpster up against it. The image of young men of color furiously stomping on the cruiser's cracked windshield became one of the iconic photographs of the Oscar Grant movement, embodying righteous fury for some, and out-of-control urban youth for others.[7]

Oakland cops launched tear gas into the crowd and fiercely clubbed those who didn't retreat quickly enough. The marchers regrouped at Fourteenth and Broadway outside city hall as clusters of people continued to light small fires and destroy storefronts and cars. As word spread that a "riot" was taking place, reporters dashed to the scene to scribble notes about the chaos. Protesters lay down with their hands behind their backs before a line of riot cops, chanting, "We are all Oscar Grant." Three cars were lit ablaze and rows of shop windows, including the plate glass facade of a McDonald's on Fourteenth Street were shattered.

As the night dragged on, Oakland cops became more aggressive. Riot officers riding on an armored truck known as a BearCat fired less-lethal rounds from shotguns at the crowds, leaping off to club the slower protesters into submission. Tear gas wafted through the air. News helicopters circling above like vultures filmed scenes that harkened back to the 1992 Los Angeles Riots and 1960s urban rebellions, watching youngsters sprinting across streets to vandalize property while phalanxes of police herded crowds. These tropes were beamed into suburban homes just in time for the ten o'clock news. One clip briefly showed a group of officers beating a person with batons.

The televised spectacle of young people of color and "anarchists" rioting completely missed the political dynamic playing out on the ground. As the demonstrators left Fourteenth and Broadway under threat of arrest, they came upon Mayor Dellums and East Oakland councilman Larry Reid. Dellums and Reid tried to calm the crowd. The protesters pushed back, demanding to know why they should remain peaceful when the status quo included the unpunished killings of Black people by the police. Dellums waxed philosophical about nonviolence and his vision of a peaceful movement for justice, but these ideals rang hollow with many Oaklanders while officers were moving in with tear gas, flash-bangs, and nightsticks. Then Dellums told the crowd about a decision he'd just made earlier that day, as the city teetered on the edge of riots: "People have lost confidence in the investigation," he said. "A short while ago, I met with the police chief, and I directed them to insert the Oakland Police Department into this investigation and investigate this homicide as they would investigate any other."[8]

Some in the crowd harangued Dellums for showing up "too late," and the mayor and Reid walked back to city hall. "It's been seven days, and no charges have been filed! What's wrong with that?" one man shouted.

The next morning, the OPD announced the arrests of 120 people on charges of rioting, resisting arrest, vandalism, and assault on an officer. Mehserle was still free.

———

Oakland was on tenterhooks for the next week. Protesters continued to gather and march in Fruitvale and downtown, one group walking with a symbolic casket painted with Oscar Grant and Gary King Jr.'s names. Activists showed up to city council meetings to make systemic critiques, condemning the city for spending more than $230 million on policing—21 percent of the total budget—while the economy was in free fall following the 2008 financial crisis. "I don't see a whole lot of discussion happening among this group talking about what's going to be done to solve the poverty in the city of Oakland," a member of the Uhuru Movement, a Black radical organization based in Deep East Oakland, told the council on January 6. "What I do see is a lot of the money going toward the police."[9]

Unemployment was rapidly rising. Oakland faced a $108 million budget shortfall over the next two years, which would require layoffs and deep service cuts. The Great Recession began in December 2007, and Oakland, which, like many California cities, had been an epicenter of the subprime loans that banks handed out like candy in the early and mid-2000s, needed more funds to help its low-income residents weather the hard times. California was in no position to help. By the beginning of 2009, the state was staring down a $57 billion deficit, still crippled from the dot-com bust of the early 2000s and without any financial reserves.[10] Black and Latino borrowers in Oakland were hit especially hard by ballooning interest rates and job losses. They led to mass foreclosures, which were heavily concentrated in the flatlands areas of East and West Oakland.[11] There had always been a small homeless population in Oakland, but it began to grow, with large camps of tents and RVs expanding around the freeways and West Oakland's industrial areas, a direct result of housing's soaring cost.

Although Dellums ran as a progressive and was opposed by the Officers' Association, he had no intention of shrinking the police department. In a presentation at a city council meeting a week after the near riots of January 7, the mayor stated he intended to maintain its ranks at 803 officers, more than Brown had authorized as mayor. Oakland would need at least $10 million for three police academies. Dellums had already gone on a hiring spree, backed by the 2004 Measure Y parcel tax and state redevelopment funds, bringing the OPD up to 837 officers in 2008.[12] By November 2007, the imminent Great Recession forced Dellums to suspend the 166th police academy.[13]

Oakland's economic crisis would worsen, but in the first few weeks of January, its leaders were preoccupied with the ongoing civil unrest, which many feared could spiral out of control. The city never saw large-scale civil unrest like Watts in 1965. Oakland's peaceful reputation was memorialized in Johnson administration official Amory Bradford's *Oakland's Not for Burning*, a favorite target for radical critiques. Nor had Oakland erupted in 1992 following the acquittal of Rodney King's LAPD assailants, avoiding curfews imposed in Berkeley and San Francisco.[14]

Orloff announced on January 14 that Johannes Mehserle had been arrested in Douglas County, Nevada, on charges of murder. Oakland breathed a sigh of relief. An OPD Homicide report deemed the killing unnecessary and substantiated criminal charges. Mehserle waived extradition and was brought back to Alameda County, where he was booked into the Santa Rita Jail and placed in protective housing. Within weeks, decals began appearing on street signs, lampposts, water bottles, and refrigerators around the East Bay featuring a design of a jumpsuit-clad Mehserle behind bars. Two succinct words were at the bottom of a black-and-white sticker: "Riots Work."

The movement that rose up for Oscar Grant was, in retrospect, the genesis of what would eventually be named Black Lives Matter, a cause rooted simultaneously in the intricacies of local struggles around police violence and accountability but also connected through the web, where social media would create the conditions for viral death, instant outrage, and the decentering of traditional news media.

But before any of these changes could gel, another horrific shooting would rock Oakland and elicit a countermovement.

———

It was a calm, overcast Saturday afternoon on March 21, 2009, when Sergeant Mark Dunakin pulled over a maroon Buick Regal with chrome rims—a "scraper" in East Bay slang—on MacArthur Boulevard in Oakland's Eastmont district. Eastmont was far away from downtown, the scene of political turmoil after the murder of Oscar Grant three months earlier. Traffic was light, a few pedestrians were walking the street, and the air was cool and damp, hinting at afternoon rain. Dunakin radioed in the stop, dismounted his motorcycle, and walked toward the driver's-side window. In the Buick sat Lovelle Mixon, a twenty-six-year-old parolee who must have been thinking, as he heard the approaching thud of Dunakin's boots on the concrete, that he was about to be sent back to prison.

Born in San Francisco, Mixon grew up partly in Los Angeles, where he was arrested several times as a youth. After he moved to Oakland as an adult, where some of his family lived, Mixon caught cases for cocaine and marijuana possession, and car theft. In 2002 he was sentenced to Corcoran State Prison for carjacking. In 2008, a year after being paroled, he was sent back to prison for nine months for identity theft, forgery, possession of stolen property, and attempted grand theft.

Mixon was paroled again in November 2008. His family described him as an intelligent man with a troubled past who wanted to get his life together, get a job, and take on responsibilities. But he couldn't quit the streets. Police suspected Mixon of murdering an acquaintance, Ramon Stevens, with a bullet to the head outside an East Oakland church over an alleged $30 debt, but couldn't prove it. Police also believed he committed another shooting and had enough evidence to convince a judge to issue a warrant for his arrest. Mixon skipped a meeting with his parole agent, who his family described as a coldhearted bureaucrat opposed to giving men like Mixon any second chances.

He'd also developed into a sexual predator. On March 20 the OPD Crime Lab identified Mixon through a DNA sample as the suspect in the February 2009 rape of a twelve-year-old girl. Mixon snatched her off Seventy-Fourth Avenue early in the morning while she was on her way to Markham Elementary School, forced her inside an abandoned business, and ordered her to strip naked as he rubbed a black pistol over her body before raping her.[15] In the predawn hours of March 21 he accosted two young women setting up a taco cart on High Street and Foothill. Mixon pulled a handgun on the women, robbed them, and then forced the pair to walk four blocks to Forty-Fifth Avenue and San Leandro Street, where he raped them at gunpoint. The women immediately reported the assault to Oakland police, who took DNA samples that would later be matched to Mixon.[16]

His apologists would dispute the accounts of sexual assault, claiming that Oakland police manufactured the allegations to tarnish Mixon's character after the slayings of four police officers. No exculpatory evidence has been unearthed to date clearing Mixon of the sexual assaults connected to him via DNA evidence. One of Mixon's victims also identified him as her assailant in a photo lineup.[17]

By the time Dunakin pulled Mixon over for running a stop sign, the parolee had acquired a fake driver's license, a pistol, and an AK-47-type assault rifle that he stashed in his sister's apartment, where he stayed sometimes.

Dunakin, forty, an East Bay native who joined the OPD in 1991 after graduating from community college in Hayward, took Mixon's license and registration and walked back to his motorcycle. As he radioed the information in, Officer John Hege rolled up on a Harley-Davidson to provide cover. At forty-one, Hege had been in the department for ten years after leaving a career as a Hayward schoolteacher. A die-hard Oakland Raiders football fan who grew up in affluent, verdant Piedmont, Hege frequently worked overtime shifts, and umpired Little League baseball games in his spare time. His gregariousness made him one of the most liked officers in the department.

Mixon watched the two officers conferring in his rearview mirror. Perhaps he worried the women from the food cart had ID'd him. Perhaps he feared his parole had been revoked. Either way, the motorcycle cops were a threat to Mixon. He reached down, gripped the handle of his .40-caliber handgun, and made a fateful decision.

Dunakin's radio crackled: a dispatcher identified the name on the bogus license as a white man who, curiously enough, was on a terrorist watch list. This should have put Dunakin and Hege on guard, but it didn't. They walked to Mixon's car together on the driver's side, a violation of their training. Cover officers should approach on the passenger side. A witness in a nearby barbershop said Dunakin's and Hege's posture was slightly "raised up," like they were going to ask Mixon to get out of the car, but nothing else indicated they were approaching a man with an obviously fake ID who could be armed and had reason to flee.

Mixon's aim was clinical. He leaned out the window and squeezed the trigger. Two slugs tore into Dunakin's neck and severed his spine. Another round pierced Hege's neck and ricocheted through his head. They crumpled to the street, Dunakin's clipboard with Mixon's ID clattering on the pavement. After climbing out of the car's driver's-side window, Mixon stood over both officers and shot them again, execution-style. It didn't matter that both were wearing vests. The head shots were enough to kill both.

Several people in a salon, a barbershop, a pharmacy, and a few other businesses on the half-vacant strip saw portions of the shooting. So did a man in a parking lot and a woman driving by in a BMW. They watched in horror as Mixon gunned down the officers and ran around the corner of Seventy-Fourth Avenue while trying to shove the pistol into his waistband.

It was one of the deadliest days in the history of American law enforcement. Aside from the 9/11 Al Qaeda attacks, when seventy-two officers were killed, the 1995 Oklahoma City bombing that claimed eight officers' lives, and the 1993 Branch Davidian compound raid in Waco, Texas, when five officers died, nothing comparable had happened to law enforcement in the previous thirty-six years.

But further tragedy wasn't foreordained. In anguish over the loss of their fellow officers, the OPD commissioned a rare, brutally honest independent investigation that identified rampant failures in the manhunt and SWAT raid that left three more dead. Some of the errors were caused by shock and rage the department's commanders and rank and file felt, clouding their judgment with a thirst for vengeance. Several incident commanders badly mishandled the search and SWAT raid. Some went AWOL.

These deadly mistakes happened at exactly the same time the OPD was floundering in the wake of the Chauncey Bailey investigation's fallout, without a permanent police chief following Chief Tucker's January 28 resignation, and sliding further into noncompliance with the Negotiated Settlement Agreement.[18] In bitter disputes over discipline that would drag on for years afterward, some of the errors were shown to be the product of belt-tightening to cut back on supervisors and assign commanders extra duties to cope with a shrinking budget. The cutbacks created gaps similar to what allowed the Riders to run wild in 2000.

The bloody Mixon manhunt also gave Oakland and the country political whiplash. The national spotlight swung from the extrajudicial police slaying of Oscar Grant to the callous murder of four officers.

––––––––

It was a little after 1:10 p.m. when an officer sprinted through the Eastmont Substation yelling, "940-B, officer down," the department's code for "officer needs help." The same words went out over the OPD's radio with the location of Dunakin's and Hege's bodies.

At the Eastmont station, a lineup of a few dozen cops preparing for the swing shift heard the distress call. Officers scrambled into the parking lot and piled four to a vehicle. Dozens of other officers on patrol flipped their sirens and raced Code 3 from across the entire city. Alameda County sheriff's deputies, CHP, San Leandro cops, and others swarmed toward the intersection.

OPD officer Jason Mitchell was one of the first to arrive. He rolled Hege onto his back and began CPR. Officer Michael Cooper ran to Dunakin and gave him chest compressions while a witness to the shooting pressed a cloth against the neck wounds to try to stop the bleeding. A small crowd began to form as people came out of nearby businesses and homes. One witness yelled, "Catch him! He ran down Seventy-Fourth!" Within minutes, Mixon's description—Black male, early twenties, 150 pounds, five foot eight, wire-rimmed glasses, sweater with no hood—and direction of flight on Seventy-Fourth Avenue were broadcast.

Inside the Buick, Mixon had left a photo album containing his own picture as well as paperwork related to his parole. And as officers were relaying his California Department of Corrections number back to the substation, another strong lead came in that would confirm the killer's identity and location. Karla Rush, who was under investigation for her role in the search warrant scandal and would be fired within weeks, was off duty when news reached her of the shooting. She hopped on the phone with one of her confidential informants, an older man who was in the barbershop with a front-row view to the murders. He told Rush that he was standing on Seventy-Fourth and MacArthur trying to relay what he knew to cops on scene, but they "refused to listen." Frustrated and desperate to help, the man told Rush he didn't know the gunman's name, but he recognized him from the neighborhood, and saw where he fled.

Rush at first tried giving this information to OPD dispatch, but the person supervising the phones was dismissive. Instead, Rush relayed this information to one of the few people in the Oakland PD who could cut through the static: Lieutenant Ersie Joyner, the Homicide Division commander who still kept an extensive source network from his days as an undercover cop in his hometown.

After Rush connected them, Joyner had the informant meet him several blocks away from the chaotic crime scene, away from the eyes and ears of people in the neighborhood—including members of Mixon's family, who might retaliate against "snitches."

The informant, who had a decade-long track record of providing accurate intel, told Joyner he recognized the suspect's face. Other locals were surely familiar with the shooter, who sometimes stayed with relatives in Eastmont. Joyner had the informant make some calls and ask around. Within a few minutes, he had actionable information. Hege and Dunakin's killer was barricading himself in a ground-floor unit of a run-down beige apartment building at 2755 Seventy-Fourth Avenue, practically within sight of the bloodstained pavement where the two motorcycle cops breathed their last. Furthermore, a woman in a pink sweater seen in the crowd after the shooting was the suspect's "girlfriend." Per the informant, she knew where Mixon was hiding but was trying to throw off the police by feeding them misinformation.

When Lieutenant Drennon Lindsey, the citywide watch commander, arrived at the scene, the crowd of onlookers had grown to about a hundred people. Lindsey, a Black woman who grew up in Richmond, had been a middle school teacher in Deep East Oakland before joining the OPD in

1998. She was one of the few officers who, like Joyner, had deep ties to the community and was trusted outside the department. She didn't just view a crowd of Black onlookers as gawkers to be cordoned off from the crime scene: everyone present was a potential source of information. She was waved over by one witness, an older man, who discreetly told her that the woman in the pink shirt helped the suspect hide. Lindsey told Officer Steve Toribio to be on the lookout for this woman. A short time later, Toribio spotted her and took her into custody for questioning.

In the crowd, Lindsey also spotted an older woman who used to be a neighbor of hers in Richmond but now lived in a small bungalow house two buildings over from Mixon's hideout. As a child, Lindsey played with the woman's kids, and the woman sometimes watched after Lindsey while her own mother worked. The woman was terrified to speak to the police because members of Mixon's family were milling about the crowd. When she got a chance, she told Lindsey that she knew the killer was from Eastmont because she'd seen him parking his Buick in front of her house for the past couple weeks. She'd seen him with the woman who lived in the beige apartment building. The little old lady told Lindsey she thought Mixon had run down Seventy-Fourth and darted into the apartment, unless he'd broken into another house. But they should look in the apartment first.

As citywide watch commander, Lindsey was supposed to be in charge of the overall operation. In the first chaotic minutes, she calmed officers who were giving first aid to Dunakin and Hege and radioed for someone to establish a perimeter. Acting Lieutenant Blair Alexander, watch commander for Area 1, stepped up to the task. But when Lieutenant Chris Mufarreh arrived on scene, lines of authority began to blur. Mufarreh called Alexander to the Eastmont Substation, where he decided to set up an incident command post—a task he never completed, leading to the scattershot dissemination of information about the search for Mixon's whereabouts and civilian tips to the police.[19] Mufarreh told Alexander to continue handling the perimeter: he would personally oversee searches.

Mufarreh "tacitly took over incident command from Lieutenant Lindsey, which caused a lack of clarity regarding who was in charge of the incident," an arbitrator would later write about the chaotic line of command that day. Lindsey, however, accepted the division of labor and didn't try to reclaim control. By 1:39 p.m., Mufarreh had escalated the response to the OPD's highest level by issuing a SWAT team callout, another action he took unilaterally without notifying Lindsey.[20]

The emotional breakdowns of numerous officers made it difficult to impose order. "The guys were falling apart," Sergeant Jack Peterson, who was at the scene of the traffic stop shooting, later recalled. "[Officers] were all covered in blood and crying and shaking." Once the Seventy-Fourth Avenue address of Mixon's suspected hideout was put out over the radio, officers ran there. "At that point," said Peterson, "I was just kind of, in a fog, man. I didn't know what was going on."[21]

When Joyner asked over the radio for the incident commander to call him so he could relay the informant's intel that Mixon was in the apartment building, Mufarreh contacted him first, then Lindsey. Joyner agreed to meet them not far from the suspect's hideout. The informant told Joyner he wanted to come, so Joyner, sensitive to the code of the streets and the potentially lethal consequences for an Oaklander to speak with police, told him to get into the back of his car and lie down on the floor. However, the man was so upset about the killing of Dunakin, whom he personally knew, that he sat in the front seat while they traversed the neighborhood and crossed into the inner perimeter. "I don't give a fuck who sees me," he told Joyner as they drove.

Meeting with Mufarreh, Lindsey, and others, Joyner and the man once again insisted that Mixon was probably still inside the apartment. This was bolstered by the information provided by Lindsey's own informant. By 1:56 p.m., less than an hour after the shooting, Joyner got on the radio and broadcast a description of the building's layout. In recognition of the danger facing the cops, who were standing on the street just outside 2755 Seventy-Fourth Avenue, Mufarreh advised everyone to take cover while they waited on SWAT entry team members to arrive.

But Mufarreh would later tell investigators he wasn't convinced Mixon was hiding in the building. It seemed inconceivable to him that a cop killer would duck into a building just steps from the crime scene during a manhunt. Mixon's girlfriend, the woman in the pink sweater who'd been detained earlier by Officer Toribio, told officers that the suspect got into a "blue Jetta" and escaped the area. This red herring sowed doubt as to where the shooter was, precisely the sort of ruse Lindsey's informant had warned about.

The police had another tool at their disposal. Alameda County sheriff's deputies and an Emeryville police officer were nearby with tracking dogs that could pick up Mixon's scent from his abandoned Buick. One of the proponents of using tracking dogs was a young sergeant named Daniel Sakai, a UC Berkeley graduate and nine-year veteran who worked as a K-9 handler before becoming a leader on the OPD SWAT entry team. Sakai, Joyner, and others knew that if the dogs homed in on the apartment building, it likely meant Mixon was inside, and they could take all deliberate steps to force him out and make him surrender.

Mufarreh wasn't convinced of the danger, and no one took the information coming through Lindsey from her old neighbor into account. Lindsey would later tell investigators that she felt brushed off by the male commanders who'd usurped her authority as citywide watch commander.

The arrival of more brass further scrambled the command structure. Captain Ricardo Orozco showed up around two thirty in the afternoon, about the same time Mufarreh summoned the SWAT team to Seventy-Fourth Avenue. Orozco, Mufarreh, Lindsey, and others walked the scene, discussing the possibility Mixon might be in the building, and whether the dogs could trace the suspect's steps. Fifteen minutes later, while the SWAT team assembled nearby, Deputy Chief David Kozicki arrived. As the highest-ranking officer, Kozicki effectively took control of the situation. He called the entire group into a huddle in the street to discuss what they knew and what the next steps should be.

Kozicki was against using tracking dogs because he claimed that OPD hadn't done this before to locate an armed suspect.[22] He and other commanders on scene also opposed tossing gas into the apartment because it would require evacuating other residents in the building. Using a bullhorn or throw phone was also ruled out. They decided to send in an "ad hoc" entry team to "clear" the apartment. Although it included highly trained members of the SWAT team, this group wasn't the OPD's formal SWAT unit. It was hurriedly assembled from officers who had made their way to Seventy-Fourth Avenue with their equipment. And their instructions to "clear" the apartment were presented as a mission to confirm the suspect wasn't there, rather than a "kinetic entry" into a building with an armed, barricaded suspect like Mixon who'd already killed two police officers.

At three o'clock, Orozco and Mufarreh briefed the entry team, which consisted of Sergeant Sakai, Sergeant Patrick Gonzales, Sergeant Michael

Beaver, Sergeant Mike Reilly, Officer Michael Leite, Officer Anwan Jones, Officer Joe McGuinn, and Alameda County sheriff's deputy Derrick Pope. They weren't told about photos of Mixon that had just been printed out at Eastmont, nor that at least one photo was handed to Lindsey during the earlier commander's street huddle. They weren't informed of the apartment's layout. Sergeant Sakai also failed to tell his team that people had been seen earlier peering out of the apartment's windows. Most fatefully of all, the entry team wasn't told that Mixon might very well be inside.

Lieutenant Mufarreh, Captain Orozco, and Deputy Chief Kozicki were so cavalier in their preparations that an ambulance hadn't arrived on scene to treat anyone hurt in the encounter, a basic requirement for any SWAT team operation. As the "Code 33" went out over the radio to keep the air clear for the entry team, some nearby officers watched their colleagues file into the darkened doorway in surprise and dismay.

An officer pried open the apartment door, and Ervin Romans, a former Marine Corps drill sergeant who joined the Oakland Police Department in 1996, tossed a flash-bang grenade into the front room. The stun grenade exploded with ear-ringing force. Patrick Gonzales rushed in, followed by Romans. Instantly, they were under fire, but the officers couldn't tell from where. Gonzales felt a bullet rip through his shoulder. Romans was shot through the eye and dropped to the floor. Mike Leite rushed into the smoke-filled darkness and heard gunfire from the back room.

"I could see little powder clouds of white smoke coming off the walls, which I quickly realized was sheetrock exploding, and the white painted walls exploding," he would later tell investigators. "I quickly realized that rounds were coming in our direction through the wall."

Sergeant Mike Reilly screamed, "Where is it coming from? Where is he at?"

Mixon had the advantage, firing from a darkened rear bedroom through two narrow doorways into the front room at the heavily armed officers fumbling through the unfamiliar gloom. As Lieutenant Joyner feared, Mixon spotted the officers clustering around 2755 Seventy-Fourth Avenue from the apartment window and steeled himself for the assault, blocking out as much light as possible to the interior of the apartment and arming himself with a 7.62-millimeter SKS rifle capable of piercing body armor and ballistic helmets. Gonzales and Leite returned fire but couldn't tell if they hit Mixon, who pushed the door closed and ducked behind the wall for cover.

Reilly yelled, "Take the bedroom!" and Sakai ordered Leite to toss another flash-bang through a second door. As they advanced, Mixon's teenage cousin Reynette ran screaming from the bathroom past the officers, who somehow remained calm enough not to cut her down. As Reynette exited the apartment in terror, Sakai kicked the bedroom door open and stepped in, followed by Gonzales. Mixon was ready. Crouched in a closet behind and to the right of the door, he shot them from the side. One of Mixon's rounds caught Sakai in the head, fatally wounding him.

Gonzales tripped and fell into the center of the room, which was strewn with clothes and children's toys. He saw Mixon in the closet holding an AK-47-style rifle with the barrel pointed up, a bayonet affixed on the barrel. Gonzales, too, might have been killed, but a bullet struck Mixon's rifle magazine during the firefight and jammed his weapon. The wounded sergeant aimed center mass and let loose twenty-eight rifle rounds. Leite also opened up at Mixon. Deputy Pope was last into the room. He, too, pulled his rifle up against his chest and fired down through the door toward Mixon, who was now crumpled in the closet, his body mangled by dozens of gunshot wounds.

Leite told investigators later that he stood over Mixon, just after the shooting stopped, and put his boot on the cop killer's hand. "As I looked down at him, I observed his head kinda turn toward me and look directly up at me. His eyes, he started breathing—he started gasping for air." Mixon's hands clenched. "Fearing he was trying to grab the rifle and point it up at me as I stood over him, I began to fire downward at his direction, into his stomach and chest area." Leite "screamed and yelled" and pulled the rifle away from Mixon's corpse.[23]

Officers rushed to pull Romans from the front room into the street. Without an ambulance they had no choice but to put Romans in the back seat of a car. Officer Fred Shavies sped to Highland Hospital. Sakai's limp body was carried out of the apartment, placed in the armored BearCat, and rushed to Highland. Before the day was over Romans, Sakai, and Dunakin were pronounced dead. Hege was brain-dead and kept alive just long enough to donate his organs. Outside Highland Hospital, grieving cops chased away journalists. Fred Shavies, a former Fremont High football standout who played defensive line at the University of Washington, broke a KGO-TV reporter's camera and then shoved him down the street, enraged that the press dared to document their grief.[24]

———————

One week later, the Oakland police held a military-style funeral fit for a head of state, at a cost of $10 million. Thousands of officers—some from as far away as New York City, Boston, Minneapolis, Baltimore, plus a contingent of Canadian Mounties—filled the city's basketball arena to capacity. The bodies of the fallen four were driven in hearses escorted by one thousand motor-cycle officers and hundreds of police cruisers as Interstate 880, one of the area's major traffic arteries, was shut down. Squadrons of police helicopters conducted flyovers as the National Guard saluted with artillery. The show of law enforcement strength was a rebuke to the antipolice mood that had set-tled over the Bay Area since the murder of Oscar Grant two months earlier.

At least one of the deceased officers' families asked that Mayor Dellums not be allowed to speak during the ceremony. The year before, at the funeral of Lieutenant Derrick Norfleet, who committed suicide, Dellums mistak-enly referred to "Officer Fleetwood," incensing many within the OPD. Of-ficers also found it intolerable that Dellums hadn't rushed to the hospital or police headquarters after Dunakin and Hege were killed, or even after the botched raid, instead showing up later outside the police union's building.[25] Onstage behind the flag-draped caskets and two symbolically riderless po-lice motorcycles with empty boots set next to them, the mayor sat silently as OPD brass and other dignitaries eulogized the dead.

"Please know that these officers died doing what they absolutely loved: being Oakland police officers. Riding motors, kicking in doors, serving on SWAT," Captain Ed Tracey told the mourners. Also sitting silently onstage was Congresswoman and former Black Panther Barbara Lee, whose pres-ence went unacknowledged.

Instead, the OPD invited Governor Arnold Schwarzenegger and Sena-tors Dianne Feinstein and Barbara Boxer to honor the fallen. But it was former mayor Jerry Brown, now state attorney general, the top law enforce-ment official in California, who invoked the political meaning for the rank and file that day.

"We know it's a tough job," Brown said. "In Oakland, there are those who find fault with the police and criticize. And yet I can't think of any more honorable, exemplary profession than the men in blue who defend the people of this city."

As attorney general, Brown eschewed police reform. In response to the LAPD's Rampart scandal, and in the midst of the Oakland PD's Riders scandal that had been facilitated by Brown's actions as mayor, the state legislature passed a bill in 2000 empowering the AG to bring pattern-and-practice lawsuits against police agencies—just like the federal DOJ's power to seek a consent decree. However, the reform tool was rarely used.[26] Riverside police were forced into a brief reform agreement in 2001 by AG Bill Lockyer. No other department was subject to scrutiny until Brown's term from 2007 to 2011, but the former Oakland mayor only pursued one small department, the Maywood police, and only after a Latino member of the state assembly insisted because of rampant brutality and Keystone Kops incompetence.

"In a time of cynicism and opportunism, police stand forth as a profession, that as a group of men, show the way for the rest of us," Brown told the mourners, and the public, who could watch the ceremony live thanks to multiple TV stations. "And these four, as I look at the smiling faces in their pictures, snuffed out in the vitality of their life, what a loss." In the aftermath of the Mixon incident, Brown told reporters he thought it underscored the need to cut back on parole for prisoners and conduct more invasive surveillance of those granted release.[27] Brown used Mixon as the poster boy for his campaign to tighten terms of release for California prison inmates.

In a surprising turn of events that echoed Oakland's fractious politics in spring 2009, hundreds of mourners showed up to Lovelle Mixon's funeral. His family and friends, with help from the Uhuru Movement, organized a vigil and protest march days before the police funeral. "Lovelle Mixon's life, like that of thousands of young African men in the impoverished neighborhoods of Oakland, was over long before he was killed by police," the group wrote in a statement. "He faced a hopeless dead end of joblessness, poverty, and criminalization by a society that would rather lock up young African men than make college or jobs available to them."

Some cheered Mixon's deadly actions as a man who "shot back" at police, although he was clearly the aggressor. Others tried to frame the cop killings as justifiable "resistance" to the quotidian "police terrorism" in East Oakland. A few at the vigil, which ended up at the apartment where the shoot-out happened, held signs comparing Mixon to Jose Barlow Benavidez, the Chicano whose head was blown apart by OPD officer Michael Cogley in 1976. Others likened Mixon to Bobby Hutton, the young Panther slain while surrendering unarmed by the OPD after a gun battle in West Oakland. Someone taped a poster of Huey Newton to the wall of the apartment where the gun battle occurred. There was even a cynical attempt to compare Mixon with Oscar Grant, but the two had little in common.[28]

This didn't mean that the murder of four officers by an alienated man who turned to a life of crime had no relevance for police reform. The police department's catastrophic response to the killings of Dunakin and Hege was self-evident. Acting Chief Howard Jordan and city leaders commissioned a special board of inquiry to dispassionately dissect the department's mistakes.

The city selected James K. Stewart, a policing expert who began his career as an OPD patrol officer in 1966 and rose to the rank of commander of the Criminal Investigation Division in the late 1970s before serving in President Ronald Reagan's White House. Stewart, hardly a liberal police critic, went on to make a career of advising police agencies across the country, but doing so with tough-love honesty.

Stewart's final report, released in December 2009, pulled no punches. Deadly mistakes and policy violations were made at every stage, starting with the traffic stop. Dunakin and Hege improperly approached Mixon on the same side, casually, with their hands on their hips and standing next to each other. In the immediate aftermath of their murders, Lieutenants Drennon Lindsey, Chris Mufarreh, and Acting Lieutenant Blair Alexander "failed to coordinate their efforts and plans," resulting in a "poorly managed operation." The more than 115 police who responded lacked a leader. Lindsey failed to establish a command post, take charge, and give clear directions. Mufarreh "self-asserted overall command and inexplicably decentralized the command" of holding the perimeter, supervising the original crime scene, and searching for Mixon "into three separate and uncoordinated activities." It wasn't until ninety minutes had passed that a captain, Rick Orozco, first arrived on scene, and it would be longer until Deputy Chief Kozicki responded. Neither of them righted the sinking ship that was the manhunt.

Stewart reserved his harshest remarks for Mufarreh. The lieutenant's handling of the search for Mixon and raid on the apartment was "problematic from its inception" due to a failure to gather routine intelligence, including what several OPD officers were desperately trying to convey: Mixon was probably lying in wait inside 2755 Seventy-Fourth Avenue. Captain Orozco and Deputy Chief Kozicki should have quashed Mufarreh's dangerous plan to enter and "clear" the residence, but the senior leaders approved it after a rushed briefing that didn't even include all the members of the entry team. The team itself was an ad hoc assemblage that, although it was described by commanders as the department's "A-Team," was not the complete SWAT unit that drilled together for such situations. Sending the group of men into the building was a "clear violation of OPD policy."

Mufarreh "prematurely ordered the Entry Team to undertake a high-risk task from a position of extreme disadvantage," wrote Stewart. "The hasty approval of this plan by the senior commanders compounded this error." The raid also exemplified the department's ongoing failure to follow constitutional standards of policing; if it was unlikely that Mixon was in the apartment, then the police needed a warrant to enter and search it. But Mufarreh, Orozco, and the rest of the commanders on scene decided they didn't need a warrant under exigent circumstances, a rationale that only held up if they admitted there was good reason to believe Mixon was hiding there.

These unconstitutional practices were routine for the OPD, but typically resulted in abuses that harmed the public. On March 21 these familiar lapses led to the death of two more officers, the wounding of another, and the killing of a suspect. There could've been a fifth death that day: Reynette Mixon, Lovelle's teenage niece, was seriously burned by a flash-bang grenade that melted her pajama pants to her skin. It took extraordinary trigger discipline for the entry team not to fire on the sixteen-year-old girl.[29]

The board of inquiry report was intended as a clear-eyed look at the failures that led to four officers' deaths. Simultaneously, Internal Affairs examined the events of March 21, and came back with similar findings: all of the supervisors who responded to the first shooting were faulted for poor performance. IA concluded that Mufarreh's and Orozco's failures directly led to the deadly shoot-out inside the apartment, a situation that could have been avoided. In 2010 the department and City Administrator Dan Lindheim demoted Mufarreh and Orozco for "gross dereliction of duty." Kozicki, too, would have faced discipline, but he retired before the department's investigation finished, drawing a pension close to his $180,000 annual salary.

Mufarreh and Orozco didn't accept discipline. With the backing of the OPOA and the union's attorney, Mike Rains, they mounted a defense that criticized IAD for "second guessing" decisions made during an unprecedented tragedy. In an eighty-page letter, Rains cast aspersions on others, especially Lieutenant Lindsey. A private investigator working for Rains reinterviewed Lindsey's confidential informant and other witnesses and officers, claiming Lindsey didn't receive a tip showing Mixon was hiding in the apartment. Rains questioned why Lindsey didn't distribute photos of Mixon before the SWAT raid. Acting Chief Howard Jordan also came under fire in the letter, which alleged he was spotted on the phone in his car, implying he was far from the action and shirking responsibility. Rains also wrote that the OPD wasn't being "intellectually honest" because the department ignored the fact that Sergeant Sakai was the one participant in the ill-fated raid who both possessed the intel from Joyner's informant and knew people had been spotted looking out the windows.

Mufarreh and Orozco appealed their cases all the way to arbitration. In 2013—four years later, a delay mainly caused by arbitrator Paul Greenberg's slow pace of work[30]—the lieutenant and captain had their ranks reinstated with back pay. Greenberg ruled that the department couldn't scapegoat Orozco and Mufarreh while so many others went unpunished.

Rains's unrelenting investigation of the incident uncovered one other factor that pointed to the city's ongoing failure to take the NSA reforms seriously. In February 2009, a month before the carnage of March 21, the OPD had drastically changed its command structure. Deputy Chief Kozicki and Acting Chief Howard Jordan decided that due to budget cuts, one lieutenant would cover the entire city as its "watch commander." Captains Orozco, Rachal, and others sounded the alarm about this.

"We are setting our Lt's [lieutenants] for failure," Orozco wrote in an email. Rachal called it "bad policy."

The cutbacks essentially reduced the OPD's "span of control," a term that referred to the number of supervisors overseeing officers. During the Riders scandal, the West Oakland cops had been able to operate at times outside the supervision of their sergeants and lieutenants. To prevent misconduct (or tragedy), the NSA required a higher span of control so more supervisors could track their subordinates. Lieutenant Lindsey's competence was irrelevant: it was a new and controversial structure that thrust her into the role of leading the city's police force on March 21.

As Rains put it: "[B]ecause the department was attempting to cut economic corners, it had set into place an 'organization chart' for March 21, 2009, which resulted in well over 100 officers on March 21 being 'commanded' by Lt. Drennon Lindsey."[31]

———————

When the jury's verdict in the Mehserle trial was announced on July 8, 2010, hundreds gathered in anticipation at Fourteenth and Broadway. The case had been moved to Los Angeles after weeks of chaotic protests in early 2009, so residents were awaiting news from afar. A judge decided the street protests, media attention, and threat that Oakland would be smashed and burned by rioters could jeopardize a fair trial. The decision irked many Oaklanders, who felt the trial only happened because of strident protests, perhaps even the riots.

Throughout 2009 and 2010, the Oscar Grant case was inescapable in Oakland. Angry but nonviolent demonstrations sporadically took place downtown, and posters in remembrance of Grant appeared in the windows of stores and houses throughout the East Bay.[32] Student protests over fee hikes and austerity measures in California's public universities made common cause with the Oscar Grant movement, particularly after a violent attempt by University of California riot cops to break up the student occupation of Wheeler Hall on November 20 led to a day of street fighting. The student protesters had their own run-ins with OPD, when a March 4, 2010, protest traveled down Telegraph Avenue into downtown Oakland and onto the I-880 freeway. Dozens of demonstrators were clubbed into submission by Oakland officers and 157 people arrested on the overpass.[33]

Initially charged with second-degree murder, on July 8, 2010, the Los Angeles jury found Mehserle guilty of a lesser crime: involuntary manslaughter with a firearms enhancement. The three-week trial received national coverage and reignited passions over Grant's death. Mehserle faced up to four years in prison, with a maximum sentence of fifteen years because of a firearms enhancement. Grant's family and supporters were disappointed, but held out hope for a stiff sentence, perhaps six years. Outraged Oaklanders poured into downtown Oakland on the clear summer afternoon, filling the intersection of Broadway and Fourteenth Street under a giant homemade banner strung between stoplights that read "Oakland Says

Guilty." Some wore printed black-and-white masks of Oscar Grant's face, a ghostly remembrance of the young man. Encircled by a throng of supporters, Grant's grandfather, Oscar Julius Grant II, asked the protesters not to "tear up" the Bay Area and turn it into Watts, which never fully recovered from the 1965 riots. "I know the verdict was wrong, but let's not tear Oakland up," he told the crowd.[34]

Amped up by portable sound systems bumping rap tracks like Lil Boosie's "Fuck the Police" and Beeda Weeda's "We Ain't Listening," outraged demonstrators slapped and kicked police vehicles as they retreated from the edge of the intersection. Several hundred riot cops from as far away as Monterey County were in downtown Oakland that night. As the sun set, some protesters split off from the group and ransacked nearby stores, smashed windows, and rolled burning dumpsters toward police. Someone threw a Molotov cocktail at OPD headquarters, singeing the bushes outside. A Foot Locker near the intersection of Fourteenth and Broadway was looted, reporters were attacked, bottles were thrown at lines of riot cops, shots were fired, and the chaotic images fed a national conservative narrative about the Oscar Grant protests as an anarchic, violent antipolice movement rather than a true grassroots organization seeking justice for an unjustified killing. Police arrested seventy-eight people.

The night was a foreboding sign of what was to come.

Four months later, Judge Robert Perry of the Los Angeles County Superior Court handed down a two-year prison sentence to Mehserle, tossing out the jury's firearms sentencing enhancement.[35] Judge Perry claimed Mehserle had shown remorse about his actions, and the trial evidence wasn't strong enough to prove he'd intended to use his pistol rather than a Taser. With time served and good behavior reducing the sentence by 293 days, the former transit cop would ultimately serve eleven months in prison.

Outraged protesters gathered again at Fourteenth and Broadway. This time businesses anticipated vandalism and boarded up their storefronts. Local artists took advantage, painting murals of Grant and stenciling protest slogans on the blank plywood.

In a familiar pattern, the demonstration of several hundred faced off with police near city hall before hundreds marched into East Oakland, with a few individuals engaging in minor vandalism by breaking shop windows and throwing rocks. Oakland cops had been preparing for this moment since January 2009, when the fury of the demonstrators over

Grant's murder took them by surprise. The OPD assiduously developed intelligence on the Oscar Grant movement, sending undercover officers into organizing meetings, scouring the internet and nascent social media platforms, and recording street protests to identify key people. The Federal Bureau of Investigation was also involved: a police report from the arrest of Holly Noll, one of the January 7, 2009, arrestees charged with felony vandalism, shows the FBI were sending OPD information about the movements of a "black bloc" of anarchists. Throughout the Oscar Grant movement, law enforcement obsessed over the involvement of far-leftist militants, building off years of federal messaging that characterized vandalism and property-damage-focused underground groups like the Animal Liberation Front (ALF) and the Earth Liberation Front (ELF) as domestic terrorism threats.[36]

A student, teacher, and punk rocker from the Sonoma County farming center of Petaluma, Noll was living in a co-op house near Oakland's Greyhound bus station in 2009. When Grant's murder hit the news, she and her four housemates crammed shoulder to shoulder into a tiny room, crying in shock and disbelief. "I can't not do something about this. I have to go outside and yell about this somehow. We can't allow this to happen," she recalled saying more than a decade later.[37] Noll and her roommates went to the January 7 demonstration at the Fruitvale BART station. What began as a peaceful gathering turned into an angry march at dusk, and then everything went haywire. "All of a sudden we were flipping over cop cars, and there was tear gas in the air," Noll said. "There were shit-tons of helicopters, spotlights, big groups of marching cops everywhere, and that was the first time I'd experienced something that felt like legit war."

After two days of sustained protest, the cops finally caught up with Noll and her boyfriend, encircling them on a sidewalk on Alice Street, just west of Lake Merritt. Two cruisers boxed them in while they were walking to a protest. Noll was knocked to the ground by a cop, who kicked and beat her before throwing her in a paddy wagon. After cops found a screwdriver in her fanny pack—which Noll says she used to start her car—she was charged with several felonies and misdemeanors, including assault with a deadly weapon on a police officer.

In the course of her criminal case, Noll received voluminous discovery materials that made clear just how extensively she was being surveilled. There were several video recordings tracking Noll and her housemates at home and around downtown Oakland, both at protests and in everyday settings.[38] Noll realized her name had been flagged for special attention: a California Highway Patrol officer who pulled her over on the Bay Bridge for a moving violation told her that her driver's license and car registration were "on a list" and she was selected for secondary screening at airports. At a protest in San Francisco, she was pulled out of a street march by an SFPD riot cop and pushed against a wall. "You're Holly Noll? I know who you are," the cop said, then pushed her back toward the demonstration.[39]

Noll had a large group of hacktivist friends who often regaled her with tales of emerging surveillance techniques like facial recognition and networked CCTV cameras. "That sounded a little paranoid and a little crazy," Noll said. The police footage of her and her friends rocked Noll to her core. "Oh God, the dystopian future that I have been warned about is here, and apparently, I am the target? That's not good," she recalled thinking.[40]

Of the "Oakland Hundred," Noll's case was the last to be resolved. Only five defendants, including herself, had their cases pursued by the Alameda County district attorney, including radical Black journalist J. R. Valrey.

"We were all tokenized. I was the White College Anarchist," Noll said. After accepting a plea deal for five years' probation, Noll moved to Seattle, traumatized after eighteen months of dealing with the prospect of hard prison time and eager to get away from Bay Area cops who seemed to watch her every step.

Holly Noll's experiences were not isolated. The intense surveillance she was subjected to for participating in the January 2009 uprising was a harbinger of how Bay Area law enforcement would deal with large-scale protest movements in the months and years to come.

The preparations for the end of Mehserle's trial, labeled "Operation Verdict," was the culmination of a year and a half of steady intelligence gathering by the Oakland Police Department. The city would not be caught off guard again, especially with a high-profile court case under national scrutiny. With assistance from the FBI and other local cops, the OPD gathered intel on protesters. During the July 8, 2010, verdict protests, nearly three dozen agents from the US Secret Service, US Drug Enforcement Administration, US Department of Homeland Security, the California Bureau of Narcotics Enforcement, and the California Bureau of Intelligence monitored demonstrators from behind police lines and rooftops near Oakland City Hall. Others, like gang officer Michael Valle, dressed in plain clothes and mingled among the activists, feeding information back to Oakland's Emergency Operations Center.[41] Some of this information was used by the Alameda County district attorney to charge demonstrators arrested the year before with felony assault, arson, and other crimes.

While the OPD attempted to play the federal and state surveillance efforts off as merely additional eyes and ears, the extent of intelligence gathering on the Oscar Grant movement, from the first major protests through the end of Mehserle's trial, demonstrated a deep interest from law enforcement in suppressing the demonstrations. After the verdict protests, FBI agents Russell Romero and Kari McInturf obtained a complete list of all July 8 arrestees and met with OPD investigators later that month "to see if federal charges could be brought."[42] No arrests from the Oscar Grant movement ever went federal.

But on the night of Mehserle's sentencing, the OPD chose a different strategy, one more in line with the agency's century-long antipathy toward mass protests and left-wing social movements. Hundreds of officers clad in riot gear, including a crew of less-lethal-weapons-wielding "Tango Teams" riding in the armored BearCat, trailed the protest through downtown and around Lake Merritt. In the residential streets of Eastlake, they pounced, "kettling" the crowd on a small residential street by closing off both ends of the short block with riot cops. Trapped, the protesters were methodically arrested. The mass detention counted 150 people held in barren group cells, some for up to twenty-four hours. At a press conference that night, the OPD's new chief, Anthony Batts, signaled to the public that civil unrest would be crushed. "You have a right to voice your opinion and discontent. You do not have a right to tear this city up," he said.[43]

But the mass arrest sent exactly the opposite message. Rachel Lederman, a civil rights attorney who litigated a similar case almost twenty years before—when San Francisco police illegally arrested protesters en masse after the 1992 verdict for four of the officers who viciously beat Rodney King, ostensibly to quell a riot—sued the OPD and the Alameda County sheriff. It was undisputed that the police hadn't ordered the protesters to disperse before trapping and rounding them up.

Radio traffic between Deputy Chief Eric Breshears and Captain David Downing from the night of November 5, 2010, illustrated the department's plans for mass arrests, which the demonstrators would later claim was punitive and intended to deter future protests.

"The first opportunity you can, set up a surround-to-arrest," Breshears told Downing. "We'd like to employ that."[44]

No charges were ever filed, a sign the encirclement was about silencing a protest, not stopping a riot. According to Lederman, the mass arrest violated the OPD's own crowd control policy. While it wasn't originally part of the Negotiated Settlement Agreement's terms, the abuses of demonstrators' constitutional rights to assembly and free speech struck at the core of the reform program. Rather than take their chances before a jury, the city agreed to yet another settlement, including a payout of over a million dollars to those caught in the kettle, and more restrictive rules for when people could be arrested during a protest or other crowd control situation.

But this settlement and these new rules wouldn't be agreed upon until 2013. In the meantime, the OPD would leapfrog over its own wrongdoing, and its aggressive riot cops would play a leading role in sending the department to the brink of a takeover by Judge Thelton Henderson.

11

TURMOIL AND TEAR GAS

On February 18, 2010, John Russo, Oakland's longtime city attorney, stood stone-faced behind a podium emblazoned with the words "jus pro populo"—law in service of the people. Russo had overseen the Riders settlement, agreed to the OPD's court reforms, and shouldered the burden of defending the city in subsequent police scandals. Behind him stood Councilman Larry Reid, a staunch OPD supporter, as well as Chief Anthony Batts. Before a crowd of press gathered in city hall, Russo was about to make an announcement that, for once, wasn't about the latest accusations against the police department. Russo unveiled an OPD-led offensive on crime. The city attorney and police were pursuing an injunction against the North Side Oakland street gang. The Oakland PD would enforce the court order, which barred fifteen alleged gang members from gathering and imposed a curfew on them, among other restrictions.[1]

To make the public case for the injunction, Russo told a story about a grisly triple killing from the prior year. On May 16, 2009, four North Side Oakland gang members rode into West Berkeley armed with assault rifles and hunted down Charles Davis, a college student home on vacation. Davis's brother and cousin were alleged members of West Berkeley's Waterfront gang involved in lethal attacks on NSO members, a feud that dated back to 2003.[2] The four NSO gang members sprayed Davis with more than a dozen rounds. Attempting to escape the Berkeley police, who were in hot pursuit, the men sped through a red light.

"As they went through that intersection, they broadsided a car," said

Russo. The driver, Todd Perea, was killed instantly. His car careened onto the sidewalk, fatally striking Floyd Ross Jr., another innocent bystander. Two of the gang members, Stephon Anthony and Anthony Price, were arrested at the scene of the wreck. Samuel Flowers and Rafael Campbell escaped on foot and were arrested weeks later.

"North Side Oakland gang members have been the suspects in at least eleven murders," Russo said. "The North Side Oakland gang is also known for committing strong-arm robberies in a group, also known as 'rat pack' robberies. There have been at least two dozen of these in the last few years.

"They have terrorized our community, intimidated witnesses, and recruited children to their criminal enterprise," he told the media.

The injunction represented a profound change in Oakland. Civil injunctions, like most American antigang police tactics, were pioneered in Los Angeles and widespread throughout Southern California.[3] Oakland attempted a gang injunction in 1994 against the "B Street Boys," who controlled part of Deep East Oakland's lucrative drug trade, but a superior court judge rejected the request because it would interfere with constitutional rights to free movement and association. However, judges elsewhere in California upheld the court orders. By late 2010, more than sixty gang injunctions were in effect throughout California, as well as Utah, Minnesota, Florida, and Texas, with federal prosecutors training local DAs and cops on how to use them.[4]

Russo and the OPD were attempting to address the very real fears of Oaklanders by following the lead of San Francisco city attorney Dennis Herrera, who won four gang injunctions from 2006 through 2010, despite significant opposition and mixed evidence about their efficacy in reducing crime.[5] After a relatively less violent period in the early 2000s, Oakland's homicide rate spiked between 2005 and 2010, resulting in more than 670 murders in five years and thousands of firearms assaults and robberies. With the exception of 2009, more than one hundred people were murdered each year.[6] NSO was typical of Oakland "turf" gangs—a rough catchall tied to a specific neighborhood, encompassing several small, multigenerational sets that took over street drug dealing around 2001 following the murder of Dale Hodges, who controlled most of the local narcotics trade.[7]

Batts, who'd used injunctions when he ran the Long Beach Police Department, compared parts of Oakland to "a third world country." He promised the move would give the streets back to the "good citizens." This was the kind of work Batts, a relatively young and ambitious chief, had come to Oakland to do.

Following Tucker's exit, Dellums sought out a chief with a national profile as a crime fighter, but also someone who would prioritize OPD reforms. An outsider who could ruffle feathers in Oakland was another plus.[8] Dellums understood the NSA had stalled and believed Batts was committed to reform, but also aggressive enough to pull down the violent crime rate.

Whether Batts was ever actually committed to reforming the police department was an open question. Chanin and Burris met with the new chief early in his tenure to get acquainted and discuss the NSA. According to Chanin, Batts began the conversation by putting one hand high up in the air, and the other down low, as though he were measuring two different levels of public policy, and then said: "For too long constitutional rights have been up here," shaking his high hand, "while doing police work has been down here," waving his low hand. "I want to change that."[9] The injunctions were definitely high-handed police work. That fall, Russo and Batts pressed on with their antigang offense with a second injunction covering most of Fruitvale against forty-one alleged Norteños.

Reaction among activists was decidedly negative. Local groups already involved in the Oscar Grant movement, including Fruitvale activists (some of whom had grown up in the Norteño sets covered in the injunction), mounted a vociferous opposition campaign. They formed the "Stop the Injunctions Coalition" to fight Russo and the OPD in civil court, and the court of public opinion. UC Santa Cruz professor and former Black Panther Angela Davis even weighed in with an op-ed, claiming the injunctions targeted entire communities of color. Russo retorted with an op-ed of his own in the *Oakland Tribune*, noting the curfews and strict enforcement only targeted a few dozen named people.[10]

Several civil rights and criminal defense attorneys representing some of the alleged gang members fought the injunctions. The court battle dominated Oakland's public safety discourse for much of 2010 and 2011. But Superior Court Judge Robert Freedman was convinced by the city's evidence, which included details about the criminal records of the alleged gang members and hundreds of pages of statements by OPD officers about the defendants, including dozens of arrests for possessing firearms and other weapons, assaults and robberies, and narcotics.[11]

The coalition's attorneys appealed, arguing the injunction was an egregious civil rights abuse. However, a three-judge panel eventually rejected their petition, writing that the attorneys' arguments "can only be described as rants."[12]

However, while the city won in court, the injunctions would ultimately prove to be ineffective on the OPD's own terms. Most of the men named in the lawsuits would be arrested outside the "safety zones" they created and not for violating the terms of the court orders. The Norteño injunction particularly damaged the city's Ceasefire violence intervention program. Ceasefire was a carrot-and-stick initiative begun by Mayor Dellums in 2007. Gang-involved individuals were offered services to escape a cycle of violence, find employment, and seek mental health counseling and life coaching assistance. If they declined, the Oakland PD focused on them with laserlike intensity to send them to prison—if the streets didn't kill them first. The initial Norteño injunction was so sloppy, it listed a city violence prevention outreach worker as an alleged gang member.[13] Their inclusion and the wider distrust sowed by the injunction undermined the trust the city's nonpolice violence intervention workers needed in order to be effective. The injunctions were so detrimental that Oakland paused Ceasefire for half of 2011.

Public opposition also put the knife to a third gang injunction the city planned for Deep East Oakland, covering a violent drug crew called the Burnout Family. Its members were eventually arrested after federal prosecutors filed a conspiracy indictment the next year.[14] The court battles damaged John Russo's political standing in Oakland. He soon quit to take a job as Alameda's city manager.

For the police, still embroiled in fallout from the warrants and strip-searches scandals and revelations about the Amaro cover-up, the injunctions were a botched opportunity to reorient Oakland's public safety discourse toward the disturbing wave of gun violence. But while the anti-gang measures were an example of the OPD's desire to put scandal behind them, there wasn't equal enthusiasm to pursue reforms that could put the department on a stable course.

After seven years, the department's progress on fulfilling the fifty-two tasks in the Negotiated Settlement Agreement stalled. Although the original monitoring team's final report, filed with Judge Henderson in January 2010, concluded on an upbeat note—"We are confident that if the Department remains focused and committed to the goals of the NSA, it will be able to attain full compliance with the Negotiated Settlement Agreement and serve as a model for other agencies"—the bulk of the report made clear the brick wall obstructing further progress. Much had changed for the better: sergeants were no longer supervising fifteen or more patrol officers, having cut the number to an average of eight. Sergeants, lieutenants, and even some captains no longer worked months or even years before receiving necessary training. Reporting and investigating all serious uses of force, virtually nonexistent in the early 2000s, was now routine. And the public release of the report dissecting the police force's deadly mistakes during the Lovelle Mixon manhunt was a "sea-change event toward transparency" for an institution accustomed to burying its misdeeds and mistakes.

But "Oakland has not yet sufficiently achieved its goal of improving the Police Department's ability to protect the lives, rights, dignity, and property of the Oakland community," the monitoring team concluded. In their view, accountability was still absent: "OPD still has a difficult time sustaining misconduct. OPD now generally gathers and documents the appropriate evidence, but too often does not reach a finding consistent with that evidence." Too many cops still treated Oaklanders with contempt. A "lack of concern for the dignity and rights of individuals" was displayed too often during stops and searches, many of which were based on flimsy legal reasoning.

"At times it appears that supervisors, including some in [the Internal Affairs Division], do not recognize the level of inappropriateness of some officer's actions, whether an officer is describing in graphic terms to a young man how he will be raped in jail if he does not provide information the officer seeks, or simply loudly eating his lunch while on the telephone with a crime victim," the monitors observed, citing recent examples. "We have reviewed cases of officers leaving children on their front porch after having arrested their parents, or of leaving individuals by the side of the road late at night in high-crime areas of Oakland after towing their car."[15]

After seven years, Christy Lopez recalled, the monitoring team had lost its efficacy. "I realized that they were nowhere near done and I could spend the rest of my life as the monitor of the Oakland Police Department," Lopez said.[16]

As a result, Oakland officials and Chanin and Burris interviewed a new round of applicants for the job.

One team stood out. The OPOA and the OPD's brass preferred Robert Warshaw, a retired police chief of Rochester, New York: Warshaw and his colleagues would understand the Oakland police's work because they were cops. The retired chief had served as an associate director in the Clinton administration's drug policy office. His team included three other retired police chiefs who had served as monitors for the New Jersey State Police, Pittsburgh police, and Prince George's County police, all placed under federal consent decrees during the Clinton administration. Warshaw had also been selected recently to monitor the Detroit police, also under a consent decree since 2003.[17] In late 2009 Oakland officials, Chanin and Burris, and Judge Henderson agreed that Warshaw's team would take on the task of gauging the OPD's progress, or lack thereof.

Warshaw's first visit to Oakland, and his first report in the spring of 2010 to Judge Henderson, concluded on an "optimistic" assessment. The department was "well positioned to move past viewing the remaining tasks as 'imposed from outside.'" The new monitor urged the police department to internalize change rather than view reform as an outside mandate.

On paper, the OPD appeared to be moving in the right direction. Warshaw noted that of the remaining twenty-two incomplete tasks, the department was in "phase 1" compliance with all of them, meaning that it had drafted policies and knew what it had to do to check off these boxes. But only ten of these tasks had been implemented. None had proven sustainable without external oversight. Five tasks were simply not being put into practice, including matters like properly receiving Internal Affairs complaints, making sure IAD management was accountable, having officers report misconduct when they saw it, and making certain vehicle stops and detentions were lawful. The OPD hadn't yet demonstrated it could consistently and fairly discipline officers. The discipline system was still rife with subjectivity and bias favoring cops accused of wrongdoing, and supervisors over rank and file. Most important, the discipline didn't stick. Punishments and terminations, as in Warrantgate, were often reduced or overturned after arbitration.

It didn't take long before Warshaw made it clear he wasn't going to cut the Oakland PD slack simply because he was an ex-cop. The new monitor brought an even stricter perspective to the work, channeling his identity as a commander with zero tolerance for failure or excuses.

When Warshaw filed his second report in August, things still hadn't progressed. Rather, they had shifted. Although the department was able to show it now accepted all civilian complaints against officers, it had fallen out of compliance in a key area: the creation of a computerized early warning system that tracked officers' performance, including things like how often they used force, engaged in vehicle pursuits, or how many complaints were lodged against them. "The evidence of progress is limited," Warshaw sourly noted.

Concerned that the second extension of the NSA was nearing its halfway point and the OPD hadn't shown progress, Henderson ordered that the department name the personnel responsible for the remaining tasks. Up until then, the Oakland police vaguely identified teams or units within the department who were supposed to implement changes and show results. This led to a lack of accountability, according to Henderson. He wanted to know whom to admonish, or discipline, if results didn't materialize.

On September 16 the police department and city's representatives gathered with Chanin and Burris in Henderson's San Francisco courtroom. Henderson was one of the most respected federal judges on the West Coast and had overseen numerous institutional reform cases. He'd presided over public schools and hospitals, California's prison system, and several law enforcement agencies. At some point during their consent decrees, most of these entities managed to demonstrate they could operate in a manner that significantly reduced systemically racist outcomes and ensured a modicum of constitutional protections. Even if their internal cultures hadn't radically changed, they'd fulfilled the letter of their consent decrees. Oakland's police department, which was under a more comprehensive mandate than most public institutions, had become one of Judge Henderson's longest-running cases. It was nowhere near on-paper compliance, to say nothing of when and if the OPD would ever embrace the spirit of reform.

Henderson, a veteran civil rights activist and attorney before his appointment to the bench, understood that consent decrees took time, something that was lost on Oakland's leaders and police brass complaining about the interminable oversight seeming to be a never-ending process.[18]

But as the years dragged on, the option of placing the department under a receiver who could force changes became increasingly likely. Receivership was the nuclear option for judges in charge of stalled institutional reform cases. In Oakland, the reforms were coming undone. Almost a decade after court oversight began, it wasn't clear whether anyone in the OPD or the city was taking responsibility to turn things around.

"I sat right here and listened while then Chief Wayne Tucker told me that he believed the city would be in compliance by December 31, 2005. That was five years ago," Henderson recounted from the bench. "Like I said, similar circumstances, a relatively new chief, and a disappointing report from the now former monitors. Today we have a new chief, a new monitoring team, and the benefit of five years' time. . . . Yet, I'm unconvinced that the promise of change is any more real today than it was then."[19]

Batts, City Administrator Dan Lindheim, Deputy City Attorney Rocio Fierro, and other OPD officials listened as Henderson expounded on the department's resistance to change.

"I should not have to, and I do not want to have to police this department, but the actions of the department, or lack thereof may leave me with no other option," the judge warned. "Some leaders in the department have expressed concern that officers might stop policing to resist any further requirements that might be imposed. . . . If that were to ever to come to pass, I guarantee, I absolutely guarantee, that there would be consequences to pay in my courtroom."

Having excoriated Oakland's police and city leaders, Henderson gave the floor to Chanin, who quoted the late civil rights activist Fannie Lou Hamer to express his frustrations. "I'm sick and tired of being sick and tired," the lawyer said. Especially irksome was the city's decision to pay for the punitive damages some OPD officers were ordered to personally compensate victims of the strip searches and other abuses, like the 2004 choke hold used by Officer Michael Cardoza to detain Uganda Knapps. A nursing home worker, Knapps was trying to prevent a senile man from running into traffic when officers assumed he was assaulting the elderly man. Knapps was roughed up, arrested, and charged with an assault that never happened. Knapps sued the department and won a $200,000 verdict in 2009, including $30,000 in punitive damages to be paid by Cardoza and $20,000 against Francisco Rojas, another officer who lied about what happened in police reports and got Uganda fired from his job.[20] *How was Oakland setting an example and incentivizing constitutional policing if it was shelling out taxpayer money so that abusive officers didn't have to pay for their own transgressions?* wondered Chanin.

"In the Riders' case, no one above sergeant was disciplined in any way even though it was obvious that there was a systemic failure for which high ranking supervisors were responsible and should have been held account-able. In the Oliver case, again, no one above sergeant was disciplined in any way even though it was obvious that there was a systemic failure in the way officers were trained (or not trained) to write search warrants and use informants. In the Riders case, many of the officers who were initially disciplined later successfully argued that the lack of training and supervision caused the constitutional violations and that they should not be disciplined for the failure of their supervisors. The exact same arguments were employed in the Oliver case by the officers (none of them high ranking supervisors) who were subject to discipline.[21]

"I have come to the reluctant conclusion that, even though I like many individual members of this department, that the only way this will ever get done is for the court and for plaintiffs' counsel to exert the maximum amount of pressure on the department and make them clearly see consequences for this going on any longer," Chanin said.

The nearly eight years had been a dark comedy of stuttering progress, "and then two months later there's a backsliding of it," said Burris, who then put the city on notice that he and Chanin were considering receivership if real progress couldn't finally be made.

Before taking his seat to listen to what the city attorney or Chief Batts might say in their defense, Burris let his discontent be known by paraphrasing baseball legend Yogi Berra, as famous for his malapropisms as for his bat and glove: "I hope this isn't déjà vu all over again."

———————

The Great Recession's impact was like a second coming of Proposition 13. Oakland's finances were decimated at a moment of great need for housing, jobs, and basic food security, and coming at a time when greater police accountability was being called for. Revenues started to plummet in 2009 and the city council was forced to begin making cuts that would exceed $170 million over the next few years, about one-fifth of Oakland's budget. More than five hundred city staff positions were axed. It wasn't enough. The Dellums administration was forced to find further savings, so they asked employees to begin contributing an extra 10 percent of the cost of their health care and retirement benefits, a perk the city had provided up to that point.[22]

The Oakland Police Officers' Association rejected a version of the deal for their members. Officers would have been required to pay 9 percent of their pensions' cost, producing a savings of about $7.8 million for the city. In exchange, the Officers' Association wanted a guarantee that no officers would be laid off for three years. Dellums's team couldn't give this assurance. Following the housing market meltdown and collapse of once-mighty financial institutions like Merrill Lynch and Bear Stearns, small California cities were going bankrupt. All bets were off about a recovery.

Oakland unilaterally laid off 80 officers. City officials knew the layoffs would do more than cut the headcount from a high of 830 cops Dellums had built up to under 700, including attrition and cutbacks of police academies.[23] The biggest impact was actually *who* received pink slips: the newest officers were let go. Everyone from Chief Batts to Warshaw to Chanin and Burris agreed these younger officers represented a huge investment in the success of the NSA. They'd joined in the post-Riders era, been trained under revamped policies, and hopefully adopted some of the necessary cultural changes. Now they were sacrificed so that more senior officers could keep their gilded pensions. The manpower reduction had a more immediate collateral effect on the city's crime fighting strategies. Remaining cops were shifted to patrol, forcing the dissolution of the Targeted Enforcement Task Force, which pursued violent street gangs like the Acorn gang it broke up with federal assistance in 2008.[24]

Budget problems also kneecapped Oakland's violence prevention programs. In 2004, voters passed the Measure Y parcel tax. Most of the funds went to the police department but were tied to Dellums's community-policing strategy, which envisioned shifting officers from a patrol and enforcement mind-set toward community relations and problem-solving. Measure Y revenue also paid for violence interrupters and a slew of nonprofits that worked with the people most at risk of engaging in gun violence to turn their lives around. Operation Ceasefire, an initiative that included an OPD team to focus intensely on shooting suspects and crack down on those who refused counseling and job training, was also launched by Dellums in 2007. But funding constraints, the gang injunction conflict, and disorganization within the force hampered its effectiveness.

In August, Dellums surprised many by announcing he wouldn't seek a second term. The seventy-four-year-old former congressman had secured $80 million in federal stimulus funds to help bail out Oakland. Crime rates fell during his last three years in office. He'd grown the police force while also laying the foundations for alternative violence prevention programs.

But critiques that Dellums was absent during too many critical moments, that his legislative abilities didn't translate well into executive leadership, and revelations about his huge personal debts and unpaid taxes damaged his chances of winning reelection.[25]

Jean Quan, a council member and former school board member, summed up the views of many when she told a reporter Dellums was too much of a big-picture thinker to lead Oakland—a city where details mattered immensely and politicians had to show they could deliver services, not just moral lectures. "He did accomplish things during his term, like working to win the arbitration to get control of police scheduling," said Quan. "Big-picture stuff. But ask him to make a budget where he has to go through all the little details and mediate between community groups— that's just not his thing."[26]

Quan was one of ten candidates who leapt at the opportunity to become mayor, despite Oakland's financial ruin, stalled police reforms, 16 percent unemployment, and a tidal wave of foreclosures. The city was using "ranked-choice voting" for the first time, a system in which a candidate must win more than 50 percent of the overall vote to be declared the winner. After several rounds of ballots were tallied, Quan triumphed by a margin of roughly two thousand votes, besting former state senator Don Perata, despite the latter's endorsements from Jerry Brown and the OPOA.[27]

Quan thought Oakland needed more than a thousand officers, but as the author of Measure Y, she preferred community policing and nonpolice violence prevention programs. She believed the root economic causes of crime needed non–law enforcement solutions, a public safety philosophy that followed her predecessor, and also echoed the reformist ideals of past chiefs like Charles Gain, who sought to build a more diverse, less violent agency. Voters had sent a message that Jerry Brown's hard-line policies were a dead letter. Although the gang injunctions showed a willingness to try controversial tough-on-crime tactics, most Oaklanders still wanted to eliminate racial profiling, brutality, dishonesty, and build a police department with stronger links to the community.

Quan personified this complex political demand: she wrote Measure Y so that more cops would be hired alongside civilian violence prevention workers. These new officers were designated problem-solving community-policing officers, but because of how the OPD used them, they ended up being workhorses who assembled a large amount of the evidence used to draft the gang injunctions. They included officers such as Karla Rush, who'd written a prolific number of fraudulent warrants; Jack Kelly, one of the other officers terminated for writing false warrants, also contributed significantly to the gang injunctions through police reports he'd written while working on specialized task forces.[28] "Community policing" meant one thing to voters but another thing to the Oakland Police Department. Quan didn't oppose the injunctions, but never embraced them as an antiviolence strategy.

Like Dellums, Quan's views about the world were shaped in the 1960s. She was a UC Berkeley student radical and participated in sit-ins with the Third World Liberation Front to demand the creation of ethnic studies programs. She settled in Oakland and ran for school board and later city council, using the grassroots organizing skills she'd learned over the years.[29] While running for mayor, Quan marched with the Oscar Grant movement. During a rally after Mehserle's sentencing, she linked arms with other demonstrators and Councilman Rebecca Kaplan to shield people from a line of riot cops. The OPD responded by telling the media the two council members were under investigation, while OPOA-funded robocalls demonized Quan as the cause of police layoffs.[30] A few weeks after the election, police booted the mayor-elect's car outside city hall for unpaid parking tickets, a move that Quan's supporters viewed as the opening salvo in a low-level war between the mayor and her police department.

Paying old parking tickets was a distraction from Quan's real problems: Oakland's finances were in free fall. Despite stern warnings from Judge Henderson, Chanin, Burris, and reports from the monitor that the OPD was in crisis, the police department wasn't getting its act in order. Quan shared their view about its neglect of the NSA.[31]

Another fatal police shooting of an unarmed man would remind the city of the deadly consequences of an unreformed department. And this would only be a preview of the violence to come.

————

Three days after Johannes Mehserle's sentencing, Officers Omar Daza-Quiroz and Eriberto Perez-Angeles were driving through East Oakland when a woman flagged them down. Latoia Whitaker told them she'd been in a fight with her boyfriend, Derrick Jones. She claimed Jones choked her in his barbershop a block away on Bancroft Avenue and stole her phone, preventing her from dialing 911. The two officers drove to the barbershop and found Jones locking up. They began questioning him. After a minute or so Jones suddenly turned and ran.

Daza-Quiroz and Perez-Angeles gave chase. Perez-Angeles fired his Taser darts into Jones's back, but the shock did nothing, leading Daza-Quiroz to believe Jones "was on crack." Jones wasn't high, but he was drunk enough to not be thinking clearly.[32]

As he ran, Jones darted behind parked cars and out of sight. Daza-Quiroz and Perez-Angeles would later claim that they heard a metallic object clatter to the ground, a noise that to them sounded like a gun.

The officers drew their guns and walked slowly down Trask Street, shining their flashlights into the narrow alleyway lined with parked cars and overgrown with weeds. After a brief search, they spotted Jones lying face-down near a vehicle and ordered him to get up with his hands raised. Jones leapt to his feet, ran to a fence, and started to climb, but as the officers screamed commands at him, he whirled around. According to Daza-Quiroz and Perez-Angeles, Jones suddenly "reached toward his front waistband or pocket area." The two cops opened fire at close range. Jones toppled to the ground, fatally wounded.

Once backup arrived, the police combed Trask Street and the route of the foot chase: no gun was recovered. The thirty-seven-year-old carried only a small scale and a vial of cannabis. He was pronounced dead at the scene.

On November 12, four days after the shooting, Jones's ex-wife, Lanelle, and father, Frank Jones Sr., led a rally outside the barbershop protesting their loved one's killing. They were joined by the family of Oscar Grant. Together, they marched down Bancroft Avenue to Fruitvale Station, demanding an investigation. A month later, they took their protest to a city council meeting, but most council members walked out of the chambers after Jones's family and supporters angrily demanded to be heard. Councilwoman Desley Brooks insisted that her colleagues listen to Jones's father, and the rest of the council shuffled back to their seats.

"I never would have thought something like this would have happened to my son, just murdered, shot down by the Oakland police, and I worked with the Oakland police!" said Frank Jones, who'd lived in Oakland since 1969 and worked for the city. He'd participated in meetings with the police to improve safety in East Oakland and felt betrayed.[33] Other family members questioned whether they'd ever be able to trust the OPD, referencing the "Night Riders" scandal of 2000.

Chief Batts tried to mollify community concerns by asking the FBI to investigate the shooting and publicly announcing their involvement. It's unclear if the feds did anything.[34] Instead, the review was left to Alameda County's criminal justice system. District Attorney Nancy O'Malley declined to charge Perez-Angeles and Daza-Quiroz, concluding in 2011—based on the OPD investigation—that the officers "actually and reasonably believed they were in imminent danger of great bodily injury or death." Both officers gave statements to the prosecutor's office that they "could not see or hear Mr. Jones" when they followed him into the narrow street and were "concerned that they might be ambushed."

The story Perez-Angeles and Daza-Quiroz initially told Internal Affairs was similar to what they told the district attorney.

"I got a little scared because I didn't see him," Perez-Angeles said a day after the shooting. "He disappeared and the first thing I was thinking is this dude is going to ambush us."

Daza-Quiroz told IAD that once they entered the alleyway, he felt exposed. "Now we're just sitting ducks and one of us can catch a round," he said. "I turned onto Trask, and I'm like, 'Okay. This guy is gone,' but I didn't hear any fences hit, so I was like, 'This guy is hiding here, and I don't want to get ambushed.'"[35]

This was true: they'd rushed headfirst into a situation where a felony assault suspect held the tactical advantage. For this reason, their actions violated both training and policy: officers were required to maintain a safe distance from suspects during foot pursuits, and to seek cover rather than advance into potentially unsafe areas—especially dark alleyways.

Call for backup.

Set a perimeter.

Don't be a hero.

What followed was a convoluted internal investigation manipulated to exonerate the officers.

Internal Affairs recommended discipline for both Daza-Quiroz and Perez-Angeles over poor tactics. The final determination noted that the officers had displayed the same lapses in another fatal shooting two years earlier.

Perez-Angeles and another officer, Jeffrey Camilosa, were partnered up to patrol Deep East Oakland in 2008 when they attempted to pull over a gold Lexus. The two officers thought they saw drugs tossed out the window. During the chase, the Lexus ran red lights and tore down narrow city streets at over fifty miles per hour before spinning out of control. Perez-Angeles rammed the Lexus with his police cruiser. Camilosa got out and shot at the two men in the Lexus while its driver, Vernon Dunbar, reversed to escape the gunfire.

Meanwhile, Daza-Quiroz arrived and parked perpendicularly to block the Lexus's path. As Dunbar revved the engine, Daza-Quiroz opened fire, joined by Perez-Angeles, who'd just run up on the scene with Camilosa. Wounded and trapped, Dunbar surrendered and was taken to a hospital and treated for gunshot wounds. His passenger, Leslie Allen, died from a bullet to the head. A loaded pistol was found in Allen's seat.

IAD investigator Danielle Bowman found "Daza-Quiroz and Perez-Angeles, who were on foot, clearly placed themselves in a location vulnerable to vehicular attack on the part of the suspect."

Allen's killing was preventable: Daza-Quiroz and Perez-Angeles chose to use cowboy tactics instead of taking cover. Daza-Quiroz in particular had a tendency to engage in high-risk encounters: as of 2013, he was the subject of seventy-four use-of-force complaints.[36] Howard Jordan, then Oakland's interim police chief, decided to suspend both officers for three days on Internal Affairs captain Sean Whent's recommendation. However, after a Skelly hearing, another captain recommended reducing discipline to written reprimands, a suggestion Jordan accepted.

The Derrick Jones investigation followed a similar track. Six months after the shooting, a panel of captains reviewed the Internal Affairs report. Initially, members of this Executive Force Review Board focused on tactical errors of the officers who "continued to chase Jones on foot after losing sight of him, as opposed to stopping and setting up a perimeter." The board's members were concerned that the officers had willingly walked into an ambush situation—just as they admitted to IA and the district attorney—thereby ensuring a deadly encounter. But Acting Captain Kevin Wiley, one of the three voting board members, ordered Internal Affairs to reinterview both officers. In their second interviews, Daza-Quiroz and Perez-Angeles walked back their previous statements.

"Did you believe you were going into an actual ambush and if so, why?" an IAD investigator asked the pair in follow-up interviews.

"No, I did not," answered Daza-Quiroz.

"No," said Perez-Angeles.

Based on these new claims, the EFRB members decided the officers should not be punished.

However, when this report was submitted to Chief Batts for a final disciplinary decision, senior commanders decided both needed to face some kind of consequences. "Not only did they foolishly risk their own lives, but their poor tactics created an exigency that resulted in the loss of life of an unarmed man," deputy chiefs Jeffrey Israel and Eric Breshears wrote in a memo endorsed by Batts.

But Batts, Israel, and Breshears's effort to have the officers suspended for one day was unsuccessful. Once again, a police union lawyer, Justin Buffington, undercut the department's discipline system. Buffington argued that the officers couldn't have violated the force's foot pursuit policy because the regulations didn't give specific guidance for multiple officers chasing a suspect. Rather, it was a "solo" foot pursuit policy.

In February 2014, more than three years after Jones's killing, the brief suspensions were rescinded.

Between 2007 and 2011, one in seven mortgages on homes in Oakland were in default. Half of these loans, accounting for tens of thousands of properties, were foreclosed.[37] Like much of California, Oakland was a hunting ground in the early and mid-2000s for lenders and banks selling subprime loans that would be sliced, diced, and repackaged as mortgage-backed securities, bought by investors the world over, from sovereign wealth funds to philanthropic foundations, all seeking eye-popping profits. The city's Black and Latino homeowners were targeted with some of the most volatile and cynically structured adjustable-rate mortgages, home equity lines of credit, and other byzantine financial products. Homegrown companies like Golden West Financial and World Savings Bank started in Oakland in the 1960s as a conservative savings and loan and metastasized into a subprime lending giant. Its loan portfolio melted down in the late 2000s. Global behemoths were also active in Oakland's housing market, generating toxic loans that would shred the city's housing stock and displace thousands of households to Contra Costa, Solano, and San Joaquin Counties.

The cycle of job losses, personal bankruptcies, loan defaults, foreclosures, and investment bank failures fed on itself like a snake eating its own tail. The unwillingness of law enforcement at all levels, especially federal and state prosecutors, to pursue the financial executives responsible for these epic white-collar crimes was a source of mass discontent.

In September 2011, protesters in New York City took over lower Manhattan's Zuccotti Park, pitching tents in the privately owned plaza and articulating a message that combined their opposition to the War on Terror with opprobrium toward bank bailouts and golden parachutes for criminal financiers. The call to "Occupy Wall Street" (rather than Iraq and Afghanistan) rapidly spread.

An encampment grew in San Francisco's financial district, home to mortgage behemoth Wells Fargo and a Federal Reserve branch. Decentralized and guided by an anarchistic approach to politics that encouraged a multiplicity of demands, tolerance for diverse ideologies, and a thirst for direct action, Occupy spread to smaller cities and towns that were not hubs of the financial system.

By fall 2011, Oakland was well into a cycle of raucous, occasionally violent "Anticut" street demonstrations organized by the anarchist collective Bay of Rage. The actions, which focused on Oakland's gentrification, library budget cuts, and a hunger strike in the Pelican Bay supermax prison over solitary confinement, piggybacked on the 2009 anti-austerity student movement and the Oscar Grant movement. This mixture of movements against economic injustice and police brutality coalesced in front of Oakland City Hall on an overcast October afternoon.

Several hundred activists in Oakland who'd been gathering publicly in a "general assembly," a mass democratic meeting popularized by Zuccotti Park's occupiers, chose October 10 as the day to kick off a local action. A flier encouraged "people of the East Bay and beyond" to gather in Frank H. Ogawa Plaza, the massive lawn and amphitheater outside city hall "in solidarity with Occupy Wall Street, Occupy San Francisco & Indigenous Resistance Day." That afternoon, hundreds packed the plaza amidst a light drizzle and listened to speakers amplified by a "human mic," a process whereby the audience repeated the words of the speaker. Anita de Asis Miralle, a respected activist also known as "Needa Bee," shouted above the throng that she was concerned about Oakland's mismanaged schools, and she hoped the mushrooming social movement would be diverse. One other cause she cared about would become central to the events over the next few weeks in Oakland and beyond.

"I'm tired of the pigs," Bee yelled, with the crowd of hundreds echoing her antipathy toward police. "I'm tired of them occupying Oakland and every other fucking hood." The assembly repeated her words in unison so that everyone downtown could hear. "And if we don't start coming together, they're going to keep on fucking with us."[38]

Dozens of tents popped up on the lawn around the city's Jack London Oak tree as politicians, police, and the downtown business community watched from afar with concern. Quan voiced vague support for Occupy's goals. Desley Brooks, the East Oakland council member who'd been a strong advocate for the Grant family and whose district was being ravaged by the foreclosure crisis, joined the protesters, pitching a tent of her own for the first night. Other electeds kept their distance. A sign set up on the edge of the lawn called for an end to the "war on youth," linking debt and austerity with the gang injunctions, immigration enforcement, and the most recent police-driven campaign in Oakland: curfews.

The injunctions were still being contested in the courts in late 2011 when council members Larry Reid and Ignacio De La Fuente introduced legislation after three-year-old Carlos Nava was killed on August 8 in the cross fire of an afternoon gang shooting as his mother pushed him in a scooter on International Boulevard.[39] Even though Nava's killers were adults and the shooting happened in broad daylight, Reid and De La Fuente argued that a youth curfew would cut crime rates. Chief Batts badly wanted the curfew—he'd used one in Long Beach—but it quickly became clear that a majority of the Oakland City Council and Mayor Quan weren't supportive. The day after the Occupy camp was set up, Batts quit. His deputy, Howard Jordan, stepped in as interim chief.

When it came to strategy and crime, the outgoing chief complained he had "limited control, but full accountability." Batts faulted Oakland's government for imposing an "overwhelming load of bureaucracy" on the department. He told a UC Berkeley journalism student that in his previous job, cops were seen as a tool. "The body politic in Long Beach was supportive and thought of the police department as a mechanism, a part of the city. In Oakland," Batts claimed, "the police department is seen as a necessary evil and the government spanks the police department because it's the bad child."[40]

Aside from reports about Batts's frequent absences from Oakland, there were also indications the chief was fed up with Judge Henderson's scrutiny and the monitoring team, which was zeroing in on the OPD's use-of-force policies and investigations. "Some of our standards in that consent decree are 95 percent standards—do you get 95 percent of your stories right?" Chief Batts asked a group of reporters at a city hall press conference after a withering status conference in September 2011. "Those are brain surgery-level standards."[41]

By the time he tendered his resignation in early October, Batts knew Warshaw's team was about to publish a report showing the reforms had "stagnated" under his leadership.[42]

The monitor highlighted the 2010 killing of Derrick Jones as a big reason the department was backsliding. He noted that Daza-Quiroz and Perez-Angeles supposedly received training after the 2008 shooting when they put themselves in the path of a vehicle driven by two armed men, unnecessarily forcing a lethal confrontation. However, in examining their tactics in the fatal pursuit of Jones, the department didn't ascertain why the two officers repeated their lethal errors in the Jones case. The disciplinary findings didn't "reflect the actual conduct" of the officers, and their "poor tactics" were identified but not analyzed with an eye to rectification.

The OPD still had twenty-two unfinished NSA tasks. Warshaw placed these failures squarely at the feet of OPD command, starting with Batts: "In almost all instances where compliance falls short, it is because responsibilities for supervision and review are not met."

The Oakland PD was not demonstrating that it could learn and change on its own, Warshaw wrote. "It is an illustration—indeed, almost a caricature—of the key issue seen throughout our reports and across the history of the Negotiated Settlement Agreement: the department's difficulty in recognizing a problem, engaging in a problem-solving process, and staying focused until the problem is resolved."

By day ten of the occupation of "Oscar Grant Plaza," the protesters were organizing daily events, including marches, workshops, hackathons, teach-ins, free meals, and free libraries—including one named for Raheim Brown, a young man killed by Oakland school police in January during an encounter in the Oakland Hills: police maintained Brown was in a stolen vehicle, struck an officer with a screwdriver, and the officers spotted a gun in the car's door pocket as they wrestled with him. They held concerts and hosted political speeches and daily general assemblies. The energy was still building.

On October 20 the city posted a notice at the camp stating that the conditions and occupants' behavior had "significantly deteriorated." Mayor Quan, under pressure from business leaders and at the urging of her interim police chief, Howard Jordan, decided to close the camp. However, the occupiers adopted a hard line against allowing cops near the camp, on several occasions hounding curious officers out of the plaza when they wandered within yards of the massed tents. The OPD's efforts to spy on Occupy Oakland—like they had spied on the Oscar Grant movement—were also thwarted: undercover officers Fred Shavies and Michael Valle were outed by activists as they attempted to mingle.[43] Closing the camp would not be easy.

On the afternoon of October 24, campers cut a cake and danced to Stevie Wonder's "Happy Birthday," celebrating two weeks of messy, chaotic, exuberant self-governance. But as the campers partied, members of the OPD and two hundred officers from fourteen agencies, including the California Highway Patrol, San Francisco Sheriff's Department, and the Berkeley police, massed at the Oracle Arena in East Oakland for a predawn raid. They came at four thirty the next morning and encircled the lawn. Word of the raid leaked hours earlier, giving the protesters time to erect makeshift barricades from dumpsters and debris. After taking a few glass bottles, OPD officers lobbed canisters of tear gas and flash-bang grenades into the plaza, ripped down the barriers, and arrested 105 occupiers. Dozens of tents and their belongings were strewn across the lawn. By 9:00 a.m., Occupy Oakland was no more. Chief Jordan and City Administrator Deanna Santana declared the operation a success. Mission Accomplished.

But as news of the raid spread, organizers hastily drafted calls to action and broadcast them over Twitter and Indybay.org, the local Independent Media Center hub that played a central role in leftist organizing like the 1999 World Trade Organization demonstrations in Seattle.

That afternoon, at least seven hundred Occupy supporters gathered at the Oakland Public Library six blocks from the plaza. While speakers denounced the raid and amped the crowd up, street medics gave instructions for flushing pepper spray and tear gas from eyes. Then they marched to the North County Jail behind police headquarters. Skirmishes broke out: paintballs, firecrackers, and bike locks were hurled at riot cops, who returned fire with flash-bangs and shotgun-fired beanbags. Undeterred, the march looped through downtown as the sun set, gaining numbers and returning to Fourteenth and Broadway, where the now-empty plaza sat behind a row of metal barriers.

In the crowd was Scott Olsen, a twenty-four-year-old Marine Corps veteran who'd moved to the Bay Area that summer. Olsen was relatively new to activism, having taken part in the state capitol occupation in his native Wisconsin the previous year when labor unions tried to save workers' collective bargaining rights. He hooked up with Iraq Veterans Against the War in Northern California and took part in Anonymous-led protests in support of WikiLeaks source Chelsea Manning.[44] When the Occupy San Francisco encampment appeared, Olsen joined and became a fixture outside the Federal Reserve, sleeping overnight and returning to his apartment only to shower. "It was easier than commuting in from Daly City," Olsen recalled ten years later.

At Fourteenth and Broadway, Olsen spotted a familiar face: navy veteran Joshua Shephard, another IVAW and Veterans for Peace activist. Shephard was wearing his dark blue dress uniform and carried a white and black Veterans for Peace flag. Olsen was similarly decked out in his marine camouflage blouse, a Veterans for Peace T-shirt under it, and a wide-brimmed boonie hat, to show veteran support for Occupy—and in the hope that military uniforms would deter cops from using violence.

The crowd was met by a line of Oakland officers, sheriff's deputies from Alameda County and San Francisco, and a contingent of Palo Alto cops, all clad in riot gear. They carried an array of tear gas, flash-bangs, and other chemical and impact weapons. The throng now numbered more than two thousand people. Angry chants of "Who do you serve, who do you protect!" rang out as some demonstrators removed rows of metal barriers, pressing right up against the police line. The occasional plastic water bottle was hurled at the riot cops.

At 6:40 p.m., after declaring an unlawful assembly, Captain Paul Figueroa, the Internal Affairs Division commander in charge of the department's ground force that day, instructed Sergeant Roland Holmgren to disperse the crowd. Within seconds, a group of OPD "Tango" officers pulled the pin on canisters of tear gas and flash-bangs, lobbing them into the crowd with deafening explosions. Huge clouds of choking chemicals tinged orange by the streetlights billowed through downtown, mixing with the acrid scent of gunpowder from "CS Skat" munitions (40-millimeter shells that spray rubber balls in a shotgun pattern) and lead-filled beanbags fired from shotguns.

Screaming and choking on gas, the crowd scattered. Some hurled still-smoking gas canisters back at the riot cops, only to be struck with Skat rounds or beanbags. Officer Todd Martin was the only Tango Team officer who turned his body camera on to document the onslaught. In the grainy footage, Captain Figueroa's voice crackles over the radio, ordering the use of tear gas. Martin pulls the pin on a "triple chaser" gas canister and hurls it over the barricade. Noxious fumes billow into the night air as protesters scatter. Martin rushes to the barricade and fires three less-lethal rounds from his shotgun, the empty casings clattering on the pavement.

Olsen and Shepard were standing less than ten feet from the barricades, staring down the riot cops. Suddenly Olsen dropped to the ground: he'd been hit at point-blank range in the head with an OPD "less lethal" shotgun round. As he lay stunned on his back, blood oozing from his nose, several demonstrators hurried forward to pick him up.

Rob Roche, a Tango cop who'd also been standing at the barricade nearest where Olsen was struck, pumping beanbags from his Remington into the crowd, lowered the barrel of his shotgun and lobbed a CS blast grenade toward the Good Samaritans. The bomblet—designed to emit a deafening flash and spew toxic gas into the air—bounced into the group near Olsen's prone body and exploded. Some ran, but several turned back again, bravely, to rescue the young veteran. No police officers stepped out from behind the barricades to help Olsen, who was in obvious medical distress. The callous act was caught on film.

Olsen was loaded into a private car and driven to Highland Hospital. He was unable to speak and couldn't get his fingers to punch in the code to unlock his phone and call his parents in Wisconsin. The birdshot-filled beanbag, which left a black mark the size of a quarter on his hat, had cracked Olsen's skull, fractured his vertebrae and left orbital bone, and caused bleeding in his brain, which was swelling dangerously. The experienced Highland Hospital surgeons, accustomed to operating on complex gunshot wounds, induced him into a coma to allow his brain to rest and listed him in critical condition. Olsen came out of two combat tours in Iraq unscathed. He now lay unconscious in Oakland's Level 1 trauma center, hovering between life and death for merely being at a protest.

"I wasn't in Iraq anymore. I thought I was safe," he said years later about his assault.[45]

During the course of the October 25 clashes, riot control munitions were used at least ninety-one times and sheriffs' deputies and police from other cities fired and hurled another twenty-one less-lethal munitions at protesters.[46] Despite soaking downtown in tear gas—a chemical weapon banned by the Geneva Convention—only five arrests were made. Few officers acknowledged the extreme level of violence they engaged in that night. In their after-action reports, Alameda County sheriffs' deputies on the skirmish line next to the OPD's Tango Teams copied the same boilerplate disavowals: "None of the suspects remained on scene for medical treatment and all of the suspects fled by running, which indicated they were not injured as a result of the deployment."[47]

The police riot vaulted Occupy Oakland to the top of the news cycle within hours. The Occupy movement's center of gravity shifted, establishing the Northern California protesters as a militant alternative to Zuccotti Park media darlings. Video from reporters and protesters on the ground, as well as news choppers, documenting the hours of clashes, tear gas, and Olsen's brutal injury shocked viewers around the world.

"What the fuck happened in Oakland?" comedian Jon Stewart yelled in horror during a *Daily Show* segment recapping the mayhem. "Seems a little heavy-handed don't you think? Unless—was one of the protesters Godzilla?"[48]

Rather than break Occupy Oakland, the raid invigorated it: the camp was resurrected on the evening of October 26 without police opposition. On November 2 hundreds of thousands responded to Occupy Oakland's call for a General Strike, with a day of action ending in a gigantic march to shut down the Port of Oakland followed by a fiery nighttime confrontation between police and a fringe group fronted by a UC Davis political theorist attempting an ill-fated takeover of a vacant office. OPD unleashed with less-lethal munitions again and arrested dozens.[49]

Outrage coalesced on the severe injury inflicted on Olsen, whose stunned, bleeding face and inability to speak as he was carried to safety was broadcast all over the world. October 25 and November 2 turned Occupy Oakland into a police accountability movement. The police department began looking into the circumstances of Olsen's wounding within hours: homicide investigators Eric Milina and Phong Tran were dispatched to Highland Hospital late in the evening on October 25. Milina tried to question Olsen about his injuries at his bedside, but the young veteran was incapable of speech.[50]

Despite the national attention on the Oakland Police Department's brutality, no state or federal law enforcement leader intervened. Two FBI agents interviewed Olsen in March 2012, but the Justice Department determined there wasn't sufficient evidence to show that his civil rights had been violated after a two-month "assessment."[51] California attorney general Kamala Harris, who began her career as an Alameda County prosecutor before moving to San Francisco and launching a political career, spoke with Chief Jordan about the Occupy protests but declined his request for assistance to investigate what would swell to more than 1,200 complaints.[52]

It was left to the alt-weekly *East Bay Express* to find out who the riot cops were who assaulted Olsen. Through a combination of video analysis and public records sleuthing, the newspaper identified Robert Roche as the cop who threw the stun grenade into the group aiding Olsen. Through similar methods, the paper identified Frank Uu as the officer who bludgeoned Kayvan Sabeghi, another veteran who served as an Army Ranger in Iraq and Afghanistan, into submission on November 2, rupturing his spleen.[53] Both were longtime members of the OPD's SWAT team, with extensive use-of-force records. In addition to three fatal police shootings, Roche racked up complaints over the years for excessive force, racism, theft, and illegal searches.[54] His role in the Olsen shooting was noteworthy given that Roche, like Olsen, was a Marine Corps veteran, serving as a sniper before his discharge when he joined the Oakland Housing Authority's police force, then transferring to the OPD gang unit. Uu, a firearms instructor who joined the department in the 1990s, was among the cops who'd assaulted antiwar protesters and longshore workers at the Port of Oakland in 2003. Several of the officers on the Tango Teams that gassed and beat Occupy protesters played the same roles at the port protest.

The 2003 police riot on the Oakland waterfront was like a dress rehearsal for the carnage at Occupy. George W. Bush's administration had just invaded Iraq, and Bay Area radicals decided they'd blockade the port and prevent war matériel from moving. This was a potent tactic for a small group of dedicated activists. The 1934 West Coast waterfront strike—in which the San Francisco police, and to a lesser extent Oakland's law enforcement, carried out the bidding of shipping firms by attacking labor—instilled an indelible distrust in law enforcement in the longshore workers. Anytime there was a protest near the ports, longshore workers stood back and waited for word from their union about whether it would be safe to work the ships.

The Oakland police had received an incendiary warning from the California Anti-Terrorism Information Center, one of the many post-9/11 intelligence "fusion centers" established to fight the domestic "War on Terror." The inaccurate bulletin claimed the blockaders were violent anarchists bent on destruction. Howard Jordan, then a lieutenant, also received specious information from one of the shipping lines being picketed and San Francisco police. Jordan and other OPD commanders, including Ed Poulson, also a lieutenant in 2003, and Captain Rodney Yee, decided this was a potential act of terrorism.

The Oakland PD also operated under this paranoid mentality: Sergeant Derwin Longmire, then working in the intelligence unit, circulated emails the week before the demonstration echoing SFPD's experience with "black bloc" anarchists intent on property destruction in antiwar demonstrations the previous month. He anticipated this contingent would be present at the April 7 port demonstration.[55] Longmire also circulated information about a call by a "former leader" of the Earth Liberation Front for property destruction as part of the protest movement and reminded his colleagues the FBI classified ELF as a terrorist group. "This information was not directed toward any particular demonstration, but we should be aware of this mind-set for our upcoming masses," Longmire warned in an April 4 email alert.[56]

On April 7, protesters started arriving at the port gates before dawn. Officers rushed to Middle Harbor Road, where they continued to exaggerate the threat posed by protesters. Had the OPD thoroughly prepared, they would have learned the activists planned a peaceful direct action. Officers opened fire on the protesters with wooden dowels loaded in shotguns, rubber bullets, and gas, and then charged in with batons. Some of the longshore workers were struck and beaten. Motorcycle cops used the department's "BUMP" tactic by riding their eight-hundred-pound Harley-Davidsons into groups of protesters.

When the line of motorcycles approached one protester, an officer shouted, "Hey you! You better go home, or I'm going to fuck you up! I'm going to ride this motorcycle over your body and up your ass, up your ass-hole! You would like that? Wouldn't you?"[57]

The next day, Chanin and Burris read about the police riot in disbelief. The ink on the signatures enacting the Negotiated Settlement Agreement was barely dry, but the department had already violated the civil rights of dozens of people. The two lawyers teamed up with Michael Haddad to represent the protesters and International Longshore Workers Union Local 10 who sued, forcing another costly settlement agreement from the city in which the OPD agreed to create and abide by a crowd control policy. The new regulations were meant to prevent officers from maiming protesters and disallowing group punishment for the illegal acts of a few.

Had the civil rights lawyers not taken up the port cases, nothing would have happened. Although the Oakland police were forced to conduct several Internal Affairs cases based on complaints about officers' brutality, the department didn't punish anyone. In the case of the motorcycle cop who threatened to ride his bike up a protester's "asshole," the OPD failed to turn over photographs of the officers deployed on motorcycles during the protest to the CPRB investigator pursuing the case until March 2004, just a few weeks before the one-year deadline when discipline would become impossible due to the Police Officer's Bill of Rights. And the photos were a dump—forty-eight pictures spread across seven pages. When the protester made an ID, the officer in question denied the allegation, and his fellow officers maintained the blue wall of silence.

One of the "subject matter experts" that Internal Affairs investigators relied on to justify the use of munitions and other violence against protesters at the port, Gary Tolleson, also led one of the Tango Teams that fired into the crowd and struck people with batons.[58] Predictably, Tolleson exonerated his squad.

Still, the department couldn't ignore its own gross mishandling of the protest. Internally, a board of review found the inaccurate intel from SFPD and the shipping companies "painted a very negative picture of the demonstration." Longmire's intelligence bulletins had an effect: in interviews with CPRB investigators, Captain Rodney Yee said he and other commanders had a "concern about terrorism at [the] Port."[59] The board pointed to the need for an updated "crowd control" policy to protect protesters' First Amendment rights, even if it required OPD officers to "stand down" when confronting nonviolent protesters.[60]

––––––––

At the Occupy protests, many of the same cops who'd participated in the 2003 port police riot were on the front lines again. Frank Uu was a member of the Tango Team run by Sergeant Patrick Gonzales, who killed Gary King in 2007, and was wounded in the 2009 Mixon shoot-out. Christopher Saunders, who'd also been at the 2003 port protest, was on another Tango Team. And Sergeant Roland Holmgren—who'd been part of Ed Poulsen's drug squad that kicked Jerry Amaro to death in 2000 and also present at the port in 2003—led another Tango Team that included Roche, as well as Michael Leite, who had been in the lethal 2009 shoot-out with Lovelle Mixon alongside Gonzales. Eriberto Perez-Angeles, who'd killed Derrick Jones a year earlier, was also on the front lines during the Occupy protests. The number of violent shootings and misconduct incidents involving the Tango Team members was almost too difficult to track.[61]

The OPD's attempt to investigate the misdeeds of these officers during the Occupy protests suffered from many of the problems the Negotiated Settlement Agreement supposedly fixed. The thousand-plus complaints overwhelmed Internal Affairs, and glaring conflicts of interest undermined integrity from the start. The most serious conflict involved IAD commander Captain Paul Figueroa, who had been the operations commander on the ground on the night of October 25. The police department's baffling decision to place Figueroa in the position of deciding whether he and officers under his command were guilty of misconduct meant that many investigations couldn't be fairly conducted.

To deal with these conflicts of interest, in December the city hired former Baltimore and San Jose police chief Thomas Frazier to review the force's planning, tactics, and uses of force during clashes with Occupy Oakland. Frazier's scathing report, released in June 2012, found deep structural deficiencies in department management, an unwillingness to learn from the Negotiated Settlement Agreement reforms, ongoing failure to fix the Internal Affairs process, and a department with "dangerous and outmoded" crowd control tactics.

Frazier also found the blue wall of silence was still fully in effect. Tango Team officers prepared an "unacceptable number" of incomplete use-of-force reports and gave specious accounts of their actions on October 25. He found it preposterous that not a single officer on the streets that night reported seeing Olsen shot. "We walked that intersection," Frazier said about his investigation in a court deposition not long after. "So, we had a very good idea where the skirmish line was, where the officers were, where Olsen fell, and to say that no one saw him is not believable."[62]

Line officers told Frazier that there were no repercussions for dangerous behavior, and that they observed "tacit approval of misconduct by supervisors and commanders, so the behavior continues."

The Quan administration didn't take the criticism well. Before the report was publicly released, City Administrator Deanna Santana repeatedly asked for a copy of the report in "Word" formatting so she could redact the most damaging findings, including information about Scott Olsen's shooting. Santana also asked Frazier to split the report so that its most serious findings could be made confidential and concealed from the public. Frazier refused: it was important for his team to stay in their "ethical comfort zone."[63] At the press conference announcing the Frazier report's release, city officials clipped a press release to the front that claimed most of its seventy-five recommendations were completed. Frazier told reporters he'd never seen that chart before. "We have no way of knowing how accurate it is," he said.[64]

By May 2012, an outside law firm had been hired on a six-figure contract to investigate the Olsen incident. The OPD pulled officers from across the department into Internal Affairs to investigate 1,127 misconduct complaints.

Under the watchful leadership of Sean Whent, now an acting captain in charge of Internal Affairs following Figueroa's removal, IAD investigators scoured video and interviewed dozens of officers and civilian witnesses regarding dozens of misconduct and brutality allegations. And the outside attorney who took over the Olsen investigation pored over the half-complete casework, piecing together new leads. In September, their findings reached Whent's desk: Rob Roche, the acting sergeant and Tango Team member already identified by the *East Bay Express* as the cop who'd tossed the grenade at Olsen's rescuers, violated department policy with that dangerous use of force. He'd also lied to IAD during an interview. Furthermore, the outside investigator determined that Roche was the cop who shot Scott Olsen in the head with the beanbag. Joshua Shephard, the navy veteran and activist who'd been standing next to the former marine, identified him by his handlebar mustache and recalled how Roche fired at eye level toward another demonstrator. Roche, the independent investigation concluded, was "by far the least credible" of the Tango Team cops: his recounting of October 25 was embellished and easily contradicted by several witnesses and video footage.[65]

The final findings, released in October 2012, called for an unprecedented amount of discipline: two officers, including Roche, were terminated, and forty-two others punished for their conduct during Occupy. Officers had made false arrests, engaged in excessive force, lied in their reports and to investigators, and failed to activate their body cameras.[66]

The Oakland Police Department was not a "learning organization" that absorbed its mistakes. It was undermined by high levels of command turnover, staffing cuts, and a lack of long-term planning that left it conducting triage for scandal after scandal.

Even before Occupy thrust Oakland's brutal policing and intransigence into the national spotlight, monitor Robert Warshaw had been hammering the agency for two years about its use-of-force reporting and the Internal Affairs process. And for more than a year, John Burris and Jim Chanin warned the city they were considering asking Judge Henderson to place the department in receivership. "The past year has exhausted our patience," Burris told the *East Bay Express* in January 2012. "The question is: Has Judge Henderson exhausted his?"[67]

In October, the civil rights attorneys pulled the trigger, filing a voluminous motion asking Judge Henderson to take over the Oakland Police Department.

Such a radical step had never been attempted before with a law enforcement agency under a consent decree. More than a decade after the Riders scandal, and nine years after the reform program was signed by the city, Chanin and Burris saw no other viable path.

Something would have to give.

12

THE LEAST POPULAR MAN IN THE OPD

Jim Chanin was flying back to Oakland in early 2012 following a trip to Michigan, where he'd been invited to meet with Detroit Police Department leaders about their consent decree. Detroit's reforms were initiated by the US Justice Department after an investigation in 2000 uncovered problems similar to Oakland.[1] As he gazed down at Midwestern farmlands, Chanin recalled a conversation with a Detroit police captain. Chanin and Robert Warshaw, who also had the job of monitoring the DPD, were meeting with police brass to go over recent use-of-force figures. Out of curiosity, Chanin asked the captain how many times in her decades-long career she'd pulled her gun and pointed it at a suspect. The captain's expression indicated she felt it was an unusual question. Only a handful of times, she replied.

As Chanin learned that day, Detroit cops drew their guns far less than Oakland cops. Some Oakland officers held suspects at gunpoint several times a month. Many drew their guns hundreds of times throughout their careers. When he compared Detroit's and Oakland's stats later on, Chanin found that in 2011, OPD officers aimed their guns at people more than 3,600 times. During the same year, Detroit cops pointed their guns at people 80 times—a ratio of forty-five to one.

Detroit may not have completely fixed its police department, but it had made some progress during the same period the Oakland Police Department was making a mockery of reform. The firearms-pointing data was just one example. How could it be that in Detroit, a rust belt metropolis with a violent crime rate exceeding Oakland's (no small feat), that officers were astonishingly less likely to threaten suspects with deadly force?[2]

The question, and other things Chanin learned on the trip, caused him to rethink the path he and Burris had taken in Oakland. When he got back, the two civil rights lawyers had a searching conversation about the OPD's failures. Twelve years before, they'd rolled the dice and sued to place the agency under court oversight, thinking that would be a faster route to reform than their frequent and costly civil rights lawsuits against the city. This was another pivotal moment.

It was time to make the case that Oakland should be stripped of control over its police force.

The receivership motion Chanin and Burris filed before Judge Henderson in October 2012 was gargantuan. Along with the formal request and legal argument, they submitted eighty-eight supporting exhibits buttressing their view that Oakland could not be trusted to change itself. Court transcripts, news articles, monitor's reports, internal communications, and expert declarations were woven together in an exhaustive narrative, laying out both the thirty-thousand-foot perspective and ground-level mechanics of a nine-year failure.

The OPD's problems were "stunning."[3] Despite a massive influx of new police officers trained under the new policies, and millions of taxpayer dollars spent on the monitoring team, Oakland cops were still failing to write adequate reports and run an effective Internal Affairs Division that didn't put its thumb on the scale in favor of fellow officers. The department still couldn't track and correct practices that led to racial profiling and brutality, nor had it shown great interest in doing so. Systems that could be used to identify problem officers early on and rectify their behavior—a practice implemented by Charles Gain in the 1970s but discarded by his successor George Hart amidst budget constraints and internal resistance—were still not in use.

Three mayors, three city administrators, and four police chiefs made "repeated empty promises" to change the force, Burris and Chanin wrote. What's more, the city's current leadership under Mayor Jean Quan and City Administrator Deanna Santana was more interested in fighting a battle of public perception over the state of the Negotiated Settlement

Agreement and the conduct of Oakland cops rather than tackle the myriad problems head-on.

"High-ranking city and OPD officials have elevated 'political cover' and petty personality conflicts above fostering the leadership and commitment necessary to ensure that the reforms mandated by the NSA and AMOU are finally implemented," the attorneys wrote. As a result, Oaklanders kept suffering civil rights violations at the hands of the police. Adding insult to injury, they footed the bill for settlements and punitive damages. Bad cops stayed on the force, and its culture remained largely unchanged from the days of the Riders.

"Given the abysmal record of OPD misconduct from the time the NSA began, there can be little doubt that future extensions [of the NSA] will result in more constitutional violations, at great cost to Oakland taxpayers, and cause injuries, and even death, to innocent human beings, including members of the OPD," Chanin and Burris remarked.

Occupy Oakland was the straw that broke the camel's back. In Chanin and Burris's view, it was a "real world test for the integrity of all the reforms OPD claimed to have instituted and woven into the department's fabric," and Oakland "failed miserably."

The criticism raining down on the police wasn't entirely external. The few within the department who had the unenviable job of scrutinizing policy and procedure also recognized their organization's failings. Its Office of the Inspector General, established as part of the NSA reforms, issued a scathing report in August 2012, revealing a complete breakdown in the department's use-of-force reporting system.[4] They showed how OPD training manuals didn't instruct officers on how to complete use-of-force reports. They described how investigators still parroted subject officers' accounts of shootings or violent arrests. Investigations were often delayed without justification and completed in a rushed manner that made accountability less likely. Even sergeants and captains who were on scene during arrests still failed to document whether they witnessed other officers use force on someone.

Sean Whent, who by this time had been elevated to the rank of deputy chief, summed up one reason for these failures when he spoke with Frazier's team investigating the Occupy fiasco. "This organization values popularity over integrity," Whent said.[5] This truth applied across units and ranks. IAD investigators and command staff were reluctant to sustain a complaint against an officer because it would tarnish their reputation. Whent stated: "I do not have faith in the IA or CID process."[6] In their reports, officers studiously avoided any mention of witnessing another officer use force against an arrestee, cognizant that any discrepancy between their account and that of the officer who delivered a blow or fired a shot might result in an investigation. It was as if they had all been trained by Chuck Mabanag or Frank Vazquez.

Frazier alluded to this culture of silence in his report. In Scott Olsen's case, it may have gone beyond a cultural default of blindness to active misconduct. Frazier noted that "opportunities for group reporting existed and may have occurred" among Tango Team cops interviewed by IAD about Olsen's injuries. If any of the Tango Team members colluded to get their stories straight before writing reports or giving statements, it would amount to a blatant cover-up.

Yet another investigation was launched, this one by another outside law firm, but it couldn't be proven that the Tango cops had coordinated their statements. However, the investigation did uncover that Sergeant Rachael Van Sloten, a criminal investigator assigned to the Olsen case, improperly showed a video of Olsen's wounding to one of the suspect officers while he was in the process of writing his report. That officer, Todd Martin, claimed he didn't alter his report after seeing the footage, so Van Sloten was cleared of compromising a criminal investigation. Instead, she was disciplined for a lesser violation.[7]

Van Sloten was a close friend of Rob Roche, the officer fired by Sean Whent for tossing a flash-bang grenade on a wounded Scott Olsen and then lying to IAD investigators. When Roche was rehired in 2014 after prevailing in arbitration, Van Sloten changed her Facebook profile picture to a photo collage titled "Well Deserved Victory." The collage included a picture of Saint Patrick, an Irish Catholic saint, with an image of Roche's face superimposed over Patrick's, and Patrick's name replaced with "Rob." The collage also included a photo of police officers, including some of Roche's Tango Team buddies, having a celebratory drink at the Warehouse, a longtime cop bar near Jack London Square.[8]

To make another point in their receivership motion, Burris and Chanin listed some of these cases—the shooting of Mack Woodfox, the humiliating strip searches, the fraudulent warrants, the brutal 2003 attack on antiwar protesters and port workers. "The mounting human misery and monetary toll resulting from the lack of compliance with the NSA reforms by the city and OPD" couldn't be sustained, they wrote.

Like his predecessors, Robert Warshaw's monitoring team found severe deficiencies with how the agency investigated police shootings. Its criminal and administrative investigations didn't articulate justifications for the use of lethal force, were rife with conflicts of interest, failed to use the "preponderance of evidence" standard to justify conclusions, and weren't conducted in a timely manner. By and large, Warshaw wrote, the decision was made at the outset to clear Oakland cops of bad shootings, and then cherry-pick facts to support that conclusion.[9]

Between 2002 and 2011, the city had paid more than $46 million to settle police misconduct claims, far outstripping similar costs in larger cities like San Jose and San Francisco.[10] Court monitoring wasn't cheap, either: more than $8 million of Oakland taxpayer money went toward the monitoring teams and outside consultants from 2003 through late 2012.

The civil rights attorneys revealed new examples of the city police force's hostility to modernization in their receivership motion.

Jan Gilbrecht, a private investigator for defense attorneys, attended a "Citizen's Police Academy" in early 2012 to get a behind-the-scenes view of the force.[11] Her academy attended a lecture by Sergeant Randy Pope, who trained recruits in the uses of force. Pope told them that prior to the Riders scandal and the court reform agreement, they were a "blue collar" police force that got a little "hands on" with suspects. The NSA, Pope said, was a signal the city wanted "a white-collar kind of force," but by restricting the use of fists and nightsticks, lethal force increased.

"It's more physical use-of-force complaints but more live bad guys on the one hand, versus the NSA and more police shootings on the other," Pope framed things. "What do you choose?"

The Oakland PD averaged almost ten police shootings a year, several of which—Gary King, Andrew Moppin-Buckskin, Mack Woodfox, and Derrick Jones—drew intense scrutiny from investigators and outraged Oakland residents. The police department's rash of fatal shootings, Sergeant Pope believed, was directly connected to court reforms preventing cops from beating suspects into submission.

"If I were you and I cared about police shootings, I'd let the mayor and city council know about how the NSA is tying the OPD's hands," Pope said.[12]

Like the threatening graffiti that menaced Keith Batt and Scott Hewison, contemptuous anti-reform messages littered OPD headquarters. A modified World War II–era poster of an aviator in a heroic pose hung on a bulletin board in the basement firing range at OPD headquarters—the same range where a scene from the *Dirty Harry* sequel *Magnum Force* was filmed in 1973—with the caption: "You shut the fuck up. We'll protect America. Keep out of our fucking way, liberal pussies."[13] Officers justified their violence against the Oscar Grant and Occupy movements by claiming that "anarchists," both real and imagined, were instigating protests and had to be dealt with violently.

Those who offered a more nuanced view of these demonstrations and the need to respect First Amendment rights were dismissed as clueless liberals. A printout of an article about NSA's extension featured a defaced photo of Judge Henderson with exaggerated lips and bulging eyes. Elsewhere in the building, someone scribbled on a photograph of Mayor Quan to give her dragon wings, fangs, horns, and the caption: "You thought Ron Dellums was a good mayor . . . you'll love Jean Quan." The racist caricatures of a veteran Black judge and Oakland's first Asian American mayor were visual shorthand for the bigotry and contempt tolerated within the ranks.[14]

According to Burris and Chanin, all of this amounted to evidence of "bad faith" within the agency toward reform, necessitating a takeover of the department. As another example, they pointed to City Administrator Santana's efforts to alter the Frazier report. But in the weeks when the attorneys on both sides were filing briefs and exhibits for the receivership motion, Santana and Jordan made a play to undercut the monitor, suggesting Warshaw was abusing his power for profit and pleasure. The administrator and police chief showed up outside the judge's office one day and presented a letter containing allegations of misconduct: Warshaw had made sexually suggestive comments to Santana, suggesting they walk arm in arm on the street, and calling a meeting a "date." To Jordan and other staff members, Warshaw allegedly threatened that it was "nut cutting time," and called them "virgins" and "pussies." The allegations were soon leaked to the *San Francisco Chronicle*.

Henderson quietly investigated the claims. The supposed hand-holding happened after a rainstorm inundated streets: Warshaw offered his arm to Santana as they walked to a meeting because she was teetering in heels. The blunt language used during confidential meetings between the monitor and city leaders was mutual: people on all sides used words like "fucked" to describe failures and backstabbing within the city bureaucracy, and "balls" to refer to the courage city staff needed to make unpopular decisions. In the end, the claims backfired on Santana and Jordan and were viewed as further attempts to undermine court oversight.[15]

Oakland's city attorney, Barbara Parker, who'd taken over after John Russo quit in 2011, led the city's last-ditch legal effort to avoid being stripped of its police force. Her attorneys, and other city officials, argued there was still good faith on the part of the city and that the ship could be turned around.

But the city's case was further damaged from a surprising corner. The Oakland Police Officers' Association astonishingly took a position in line with that of Burris and Chanin. The OPOA's longtime attorney Michael Rains—whose firm represented nearly every Oakland cop punished over the term of the NSA—placed blame for the Oakland Police Department's interminable reform saga on the city's elected officials. Starting with former mayor Jerry Brown and Police Chief Richard Word, Oakland set its cops up to fail by ordering them to reduce crime by whatever means necessary, then abandoning them when their skull-cracking and law-bending methods were exposed.

Just as Rains had argued in court in the early 2000s when he defended Mabanag, Hornung, Siapno, and Vazquez, his brief characterized the Riders scandal as the result of Brown and Word's decision to adopt "zero tolerance" drug enforcement through "Project SANE." They'd been warned against absolutist strategies, including by Bill Bratton back in 1999 when they invited the policing guru to Oakland to consult with them. "Zero tolerance as a crime reduction strategy leads to intolerance and oppressiveness," Bratton advised, decrying the term as a media buzzword that, in practice, stripped police officers of situational discretion. "This is a term that should be used only when cops are found to be corrupt, use brutality, or take drugs."[16]

According to Rains, Brown and Word rejected this advice. When Keith Batt blew the whistle, "those who were uniquely responsible for the 'leadership decision' engaged in 'political cover' and were nowhere to be found." Rather than examine the behavior of OPD officers accused of beatings, false arrest, and other abuses as part of the Riders case, city management allowed four officers to become "scapegoats," shielding its supervisors and the OPD's command structure from repercussions.[17] In the OPOA's view, many of the subsequent scandals, including Warrantgate and Occupy, were due to "training discrepancies," not individual misconduct and intentional brutality. Oakland's political leaders wanted crime reductions but weren't willing to properly invest in their police force.

The OPOA also desperately wanted to keep a lid on the sorts of misconduct allegations against individual cops that were spilling out into the public through both independent reporting and Warshaw's and Frazier's reviews of the Occupy crackdown.[18]

Henderson had a lot to think about. If he stripped Oakland of control over its police and handed the reins to a special master, that person could potentially rebuild the police department from the ground up. But they would have to be the right person. Even with the perfect candidate, it would be an extremely costly and time-consuming prospect that would require Henderson—now seventy-nine years old, using a wheelchair because of health problems, and contemplating retirement—to take on the organizational minutiae he'd sought to avoid all along. Even if they succeeded, there was no guarantee the reforms would stick. Change imposed from without was unlikely to be sustainable in the long run. The cultural problems Burris and Chanin mapped out were deep-rooted. And the lack of political will and leadership among the city's elected officials was a constant throughout the reform saga.

In the end, Henderson didn't have to issue a ruling. Rather than seeking a takeover of OPD, Chanin and Burris relented and struck a new agreement with the city to have the court appoint a "compliance director." This person would be like a receiver-lite, with some expansive powers like the ability to veto policy changes proposed by the OPD or impose regulations of their own design. They would have final say over discipline, including the ability to override the police chief. And they would even have the power to fire the chief.[19] Oakland also agreed to something that city officials might not have at first fully grasped: the new agreement permitted this overseer to "review, investigate, and take corrective action regarding OPD policies, procedures, and practices that are related to the objectives of the NSA . . . even if such policies, procedures, or practices do not fall squarely within any specific NSA task."[20]

This expanded the NSA's scope beyond the original fifty-two tasks. In order to truly change the department, Henderson realized the monitor and compliance director could no longer focus narrowly on the NSA's technical fixes. They had to study the Oakland PD's problems like racial profiling during stops and rampant uses of force, and if necessary, propose entirely new solutions that would lead to cultural overhaul.

Thomas Frazier, who impressed Burris and Chanin, as well as Warshaw, with his integrity during the Occupy investigations, was appointed compliance director in March and began work at a city-paid salary of $270,000. Frazier made clear he answered only to Judge Henderson and intended to wield his sweeping powers to finish the job begun a decade earlier.

Day-to-day police operations, however, remained in the hands of Chief Jordan, whose challenges mounted by the day.

––––––––––

With the fallout of Occupy as backdrop, 2012 was becoming a nadir for Oakland. After a peak of 148 murders in 2006, gun violence and homicides declined for several years. By 2010, the city saw 95 killings, the first time the death toll dropped below 100 in five years.[21] But the double whammy of a crippling national recession and foreclosure crisis hit Oakland hard, putting up to 16 percent of working adults out of a job.[22] The OPD's head count dwindled to 635 officers by 2012 as a result of the 2010 layoffs stemming from the OPOA's refusal to renegotiate pensions and hiring freezes. Veteran officers retired on pensions bolstered by overtime, or were poached by neighboring police agencies like San Francisco, San Jose, or Vallejo.[23]

As the Oakland Police Department scrambled to fill patrol vacancies, the city's violence spiked again. In 2011, 710 people were struck by gunfire and 131 were killed in 2012, a per capita rate almost seven times the national average. It was Oakland's second-highest murder total since its early 1990s apogee.[24] The majority of the gunplay involved members of Oakland's myriad "turfs," a local term for street gang: in 2010 and 2011 combined, 709 out of the 1,315 shootings in Oakland were the results of gang disputes.[25]

By 2012, most of the city's lethal violence could be traced to beef between two umbrella gangs, Case Gang and ENT. These two groups bridged the traditional geographic boundaries of Oakland's gangs, transcending the literal meaning of "turf" by drawing members from across the city and far beyond. Their rivalries were something that had never been seen before.

Prior to the late 2000s, groups from Seminary City in the East Oakland flatlands and Ghost Town in West Oakland would not be associated with each other. Now they clicked up under the banner of Money Team, or ENT. The name was fluid, just like the group, but invoked bitter blood feuds and ride-or-die mentalities. Originally the group—about twelve core members at any given time—used the name Money Team, but when seventeen-year-old Edward Hampton and eighteen-year-old Nario Jackson were murdered by rivals in November 2010, their initials were combined to create the name "EN Team" by their friends and relatives. The next year, another influential member, Martin Flenaugh, was killed by OPD officer Richard McNeely as Flenaugh fled the scene of a shooting armed with two handguns. The gang's name remained "ENT," with T now standing for "Taliban," Flenaugh's nickname.[26] In time, ENT would also adopt "Stubby"—Ed Hampton's alias—as its calling card.

Money Team specialized in residential burglaries and home invasion robberies, targeting Asian immigrants known to keep large amounts of cash and valuables at home. They ranged as far as the South Bay, achieving infamy with the November 2012 murder of Raveesh Kumra, a millionaire venture capitalist, at his home in the exclusive community of Monte Sereno.[27]

Case Gang was the creation of a network of friends who inherited a legacy of violence from brothers Joe and Demarcus Ralls and their relatives and friends from the West Oakland Acorn housing projects and East Oakland's Brookfield Village. The Ralls brothers operated a robbery crew that called themselves the "Nut Cases" to emphasize the craziness of their actions.[28] They would act out scenes from the hyperviolent video game *Grand Theft Auto III* while "hitting licks" in the early 2000s, committing five murders before police caught up in 2003 and sent them to prison for manslaughter, murder, and other crimes.[29] Their mantle was taken up by the youngsters who had grown up around them and adopted the name "Baby Case." In time, they became "Case Gang." By the late 2000s, groups from the 1990s in Deep East Oakland, North Oakland, and the foothills around Mills College clicked up with Case.

Though the alliances may have changed, old rivalries retained their potency. The ENT and Case Gang feuds expanded in 2011 and 2012 as both crews picked up new members and built intimidating arsenals from the illegal guns pouring into Oakland. Smugglers trafficked heavy-caliber rifles, 9-millimeter and .40-caliber pistols, and high-capacity magazines into the

Bay Area from neighboring states with looser gun laws like Arizona and Nevada.[30] By the mid-aughts, the typical gun seized during traffic stops, search warrants, or arrests of robbery and murder suspects was a pistol or rifle with a thirty-round clip or a fifty-round drum. Shooting scenes were regularly dotted with dozens of bright yellow markers identifying spent bullet casings. Improvements in modern trauma surgery and emergency medicine helped save gunshot-wound victims who might have died in the the 1980s and 1990s. But the firepower in Oakland kept pace with these medical advancements, keeping body counts high.[31]

One weekend in January 2013, there were fifteen separate shootings and four murders, two of which were committed with an AR-15 rifle equipped with a hundred-round-capacity double-drum magazine.[32] Police attributed all four killings to the ENT–Case Gang feud. The gunplay spanned the entire city, with retaliatory drive-by shootings taking place in Deep East Oakland, Funktown, Ghost Town, and Glenview.[33]

Oakland's evolving gang wars threw the OPD off-balance: the department had spent decades building institutional knowledge about how to identify, track, and dismantle geographically based drug crews and turf gangs. Case and ENT didn't hold specific territory and made their money through robberies, credit fraud, pimping, and other means more difficult to track. The complex networks of interpersonal relationships, alliances, and feuds also redefined Oakland's street politics, and pushed police completely out of their comfort zone. For several months, the department struggled to adjust to the changing landscape—including the extensive use of YouTube and Instagram by gang members—and get the jump on the increasingly unpredictable violence.[34]

As Oakland's Black and brown neighborhoods bore the brunt of rising gun violence, its whiter, wealthier enclaves in the hills and flatlands bordering the college town of Berkeley experienced their own flavor of lawlessness. Robberies surged from 4,174 in 2012 to 4,845 in 2013. In September 2013 a former McClymonds High School football standout and two accomplices held up two dozen commuters waiting in line for morning carpools near Highway 24 in the affluent Rockridge neighborhood.[35] The carpool stickups and broad-daylight rip-offs in North Oakland's safer, gentrifying streets put additional pressure on local politicians.

"The frustration, impatience, and fear throughout Rockridge has gone way up," said North Oakland councilman Dan Kalb. He called for more police and license plate scanning cameras to track suspects. Burglaries also skyrocketed, with 12,841 logged in 2012, up from 8,819 in 2011. The adage that native Oaklanders never leave anything of value in a parked car rang true, as window glass littered city streets as a result of twenty auto burglaries per day on average.[36]

The Oakland Police Department was running on empty. The city had only 612 police officers even though most public safety experts believed it needed roughly 1,200 to adequately patrol Oakland and staff investigative units. In desperation, the OPD asked the California Highway Patrol and Alameda County Sheriff's Office for help patrolling the city. The senseless murder of eight-year-old Alaysha Carradine in July 2013 during a sleepover was a low point: Carradine was killed by Darnell Williams Jr., a member of Berkeley's Waterfront gang who was hell-bent on revenge for the killing of his friend Jermaine Davis Jr. just hours before in West Berkeley. Williams unloaded thirteen rounds into the apartment as Carradine's friend opened the door in the mistaken belief that the baby mother of his friend's killer lived there. Carradine's killing was the latest casualty in the decade-long feud between North Oakland and West Berkeley gangs that left more than a dozen people dead.[37]

OPD homicide investigators were saddled with thirty-five to forty cases each, an unmanageable load that resulted in basic mistakes such as the loss of critical evidence and an overreliance on notoriously error-prone eye-witness testimony, as well as confessions, which were rare. The crime lab was backlogged with several years' worth of evidence, paralyzing its ability to analyze everything from blood spatter to ballistics to rape kits.[38] By fall 2013, that backlog had nearly doubled to 650 cases. The OPD crime lab committed its resources to analyzing seized narcotics rather than ballistics, DNA, and clothing from murder scenes: a civil grand jury report found un-tested evidence from 330 unsolved Oakland murders.[39] The department's clearance rate for murders, which reached 54 percent as recently as 2007, plummeted below 34 percent from 2010 through 2012.[40]

Decisions in Washington, DC, also did harm. Budget cuts to the Bureau of Alcohol Tobacco and Firearms axed an ATF contractor assigned to trace firearms seized by Oakland cops, making it much more difficult to link guns to multiple shootings or uncover trafficking rings.[41]

Chief Jordan was already facing the worst scenario possible for a law en-forcement leader: spiking crime was stoking political pressure on Quan and the city council to act, and they looked to the Oakland police for answers. But Jordan's position was undermined by city hall's determination to dig in against the external oversight Judge Henderson had put in place. Compliance Director Thomas Frazier reopened a number of Internal Affairs cases from Occupy Oakland, but City Administrator Santana was taking steps to shield officers from discipline. The Citizens' Police Review Board faulted Sergeant Patrick Gonzales for failing to supervise Frank Uu on November 2, 2011, when Uu lacerated Kayvan Sabeghi's spleen with baton strikes.[42] Santana decided to reject the Citizens' Police Review Board's recommended punishment.

This and other obstructionist moves drew stern warnings from Henderson. "The City is attempting to limit unilaterally the scope of the Compliance Director's authority," the judge wrote in an April 2013 order. "The Court issues this order—which should be unnecessary—to clarify that its orders mean what they say." Frazier and Warshaw told Henderson they'd been obstructed while attempting to obtain information from the city and involve themselves in areas of OPD operations previously beyond the scope of the NSA. "The Compliance Director's powers are broad, and the City shall immediately cease its misguided efforts to constrict the Court's orders," Henderson warned in an order. "Any City officials or personnel, without exception, who fail to do so will be subject to show cause hearings before this Court as to why sanctions should not be imposed against them."[43]

By early May 2013, Frazier had enough. In addition to Santana's obstruction, Jordan wasn't making progress on the NSA. Frazier told Judge Henderson, Robert Warshaw, and Quan he no longer trusted the chief, and would fire Jordan unless they took action. Jordan got wind of his ouster and decided to resign instead, citing a medical condition as his reason for stepping down.[44]

Quan hurriedly appointed Anthony Toribio, Jordan's assistant chief, to lead. Toribio lasted just two days before quitting as well, knowing that he wasn't Frazier's or Warshaw's choice to run the department. That distinction belonged to someone who played a key role in every successful instance of internal accountability, from Warrantgate to the Chauncey Bailey case to Occupy: Sean Whent.[45]

———

Although he grew up in suburban Pleasanton, Whent frequently visited his grandparents in Oakland's San Antonio neighborhood in the 1980s and made a habit of listening to OPD radio traffic over a police scanner.[46] While a student at Cal State Hayward and working part-time at a local Jack in the Box, he joined the OPD cadet program, and in 1996 graduated from the police academy and married his childhood sweetheart. For the next seven years, Whent proved himself a capable beat cop, even winning the department's highest honor, the Medal of Valor, after he pulled a woman from a burning car at an East Oakland sideshow in 2003.

His transfer in 2005 to Internal Affairs was not something he wanted, but Whent had the requisite mindset. He pressed officers with hard questions in interviews when he suspected them of wrongdoing, but also went to bat for cops he felt were innocent. To outsiders like Frazier and Warshaw, Whent had integrity. For many OPD insiders, the new chief was a rat who climbed the ranks by backstabbing hardworking officers.

At thirty-eight, Whent was young for a police chief. Despite seventeen years on the force, he didn't have an extensive network of loyal colleagues he could call on. But while some officers continued to resent him, Whent quickly proved himself a capable leader.

Whent knew Oakland had one tool at its disposal that could help drill down on violent crime: the carrot-and-stick Ceasefire program first implemented by Mayor Ron Dellums in the late 2000s. During Chief Batts's term, Ceasefire languished as Oakland's gang injunctions undermined its credibility. With the assistance of state grants, Chief Jordan rebooted this violence intervention program under Captain Ersie Joyner, hosting a "call-in" at an East Oakland church that brought in twenty young men the police believed were either directly involved in or adjacent to gun violence.[47] Most of the men attending the October 2012 call-ins were associated with either Case Gang or Money Team. Many would be caught up in a series of local-federal sweeps and several dozen arrests in the spring and summer of 2013 as law enforcement amassed voluminous documentation of serial robberies and lethal cycles of retaliatory shootings.[48]

Chief Jordan's role in restarting Ceasefire would be overshadowed by Oakland's deteriorating court oversight and other problems, but Whent continued with the program's reboot. Making a gambit to deemphasize property crimes investigations, Whent let Captain Joyner handpick many of the thirty-five cops for his Ceasefire team and ensured ample funding.[49]

Instead of playing catch-up with fluid street politics like the South Berkeley–North Oakland vendetta that led to Alaysha Carradine's killing, Joyner's unit and Reygan Harmon, a civilian coordinator, proactively identified the groups and individuals causing the violence. Operating off Yale University sociologist Andrew Papachristos's theory that gun violence traveled along social networks, and that most bloodshed was caused by a small number of people, they used intel to put names to shooters and trace retaliatory links between homicides.[50]

With the California Partnership for Safe Communities, a nonprofit that helped design violence reduction strategies, the Ceasefire team analyzed eighteen months of murders and shootings, spanning the hyperviolent period from January 2012 through June 2013. They identified fifty-three gangs, eighteen of which were associated with up to 84 percent of the 171 murders over this period.[51] As opposed to a widespread belief that gun violence was largely perpetrated by juveniles and connected to the drug trade, the Ceasefire analysis pinpointed the Case Gang and Money Team feud—a gang war involving mostly adults—as the primary cause of the city's rising murder rate. From 2012, when twenty people participated in a group call-in and six people were spoken to individually, 2013 saw a marked increase: sixty-three people participated in group call-ins, while fourteen received "custom" notifications that they were on authorities' radar.[52]

Some heeded the call to change their lives and exit the violent street life. Others wouldn't, or couldn't, and were either gunned down or arrested. In March 2013 an IRS-led investigation resulted in the indictment of seventeen Case Gang members, stacking fraud and identity theft allegations on top of gun violence and prostitution-related charges and sending many to federal prison.[53] In August the Oakland PD arrested thirteen key ENT members, including Shawn Hampton, whose slain brother Ed was the "E" in "Eddie Nario Taliban." They were charged in a conspiracy indictment over allegations of kidnapping, "street terrorism," robbery, and home invasion.[54]

Homicides declined by 27 percent from 2012 to 2013, and then by 17 percent in 2014. Nonfatal shootings also dropped precipitously.[55]

Whent reorganized the patrol division into five geographic areas with a captain leading each and using tailor-made strategies to address problems unique to their sector. In North Oakland, Crime Reduction Teams hit robbery crews targeting pedestrians for their phones, while in the West and East Oakland flatlands, captains emphasized quick responses to shootings. Property crime rates began a slow descent.

In December, while still serving in an interim capacity as Oakland conducted a national search for a permanent police chief, Whent was driving through Fruitvale in an unmarked SUV when he came upon one of his officers holding a carjacking suspect at gunpoint. A man suddenly ran from the stopped car. Whent and two other officers gave chase. When the suspect jumped a fence into a backyard, the interim chief and patrol officers had a chance to model a relatively new policy—instead of rushing into the yard in pursuit, they set up a perimeter and waited for backup. The man emerged one street over, where Whent and several officers arrested him. Police later found a discarded gun along the man's path of flight.[56] The episode demonstrated that Whent's will to implement the NSA was matched by his desire to see the OPD regain its footing as an effective crime fighting force.

But not everything was going smoothly. Amidst a rush to hire new officers in 2013 and 2014, questions would be raised about the quality of recruits. And the department would find itself caught up in a major public controversy over surveillance at the same time whistleblowers were exposing disturbing federal spy programs.

It started with a security project to harden the Port of Oakland against terrorism and organized crime. In 2009 the Obama administration granted Oakland $10.9 million to install a network of security cameras and sensors to secure cargo facilities in West Oakland and the Oakland International Airport.[57]

By early 2013, the project was labeled the Orwellian "Domain Awareness Center." Police and port officials planned to build it out in phases, starting at the port and then expanding to surveillance cameras on city streets, in public housing, and schools, and drawing from license plate readers, motion detectors, gunshot detectors, social media feeds, and other data sources from across Oakland. All of this would be pulled into a unified "situational awareness" center where police could watch the city in real time.[58] Controversial technologies such as facial recognition weren't included initially, but Oakland's IT staff assured the city council that biometrics could be added with a simple software update.[59] The DAC's proponents marketed it as a significant addition to a police officer's tool kit, citing former NYPD commissioner and policing consultant Bill Bratton's recommendation that Oakland leverage the port's grant funding for citywide surveillance.[60]

The public was unaware of the DAC until a July 2013 meeting where, after a few questions about its costs and capabilities, a city council committee approved the project by consensus.

"Very exciting. I assume none of these cameras go into people's living rooms or anything like that?" Councilman Dan Kalb asked city staff, seemingly unaware of how technologies like license plate readers and cameras could undermine privacy rights.

Renee Domingo, a fire department official overseeing the DAC, assured the council members no cameras would be pointed inside homes.

"All right, sounds good to me," said Kalb.[61]

Oakland's decision to be Northern California's first city to build a mass surveillance center couldn't have come at a worse time. Former National Security Agency contractor Edward Snowden's monumental leaks had been dominating headlines since early May 2013, and the American public was just beginning to understand the disturbing truth about the post-9/11 surveillance state. When news of the DAC broke, it triggered an uproar from Oscar Grant movement activists, Occupy Oakland organizers, and the Bay Area's burgeoning privacy community, led by the Electronic Frontier Foundation and the ACLU's robust Northern California chapter.[62]

Police departments in New York City, Chicago, and Los Angeles had already built similar systems, with the NYPD's "Ring of Steel" the most prominent example.[63] But Oaklanders were still intensely distrustful of the police, with fresh memories of how law enforcement agencies surveilled the Oscar Grant movement and Occupy.

DAC opponents coalesced around the ad hoc Oakland Privacy group to hold street protests and pack city council hearings, imploring city officials to cancel, or at least limit, the project's scope. These pleas initially fell on deaf ears: the council voted six to one in November to push ahead despite a raucous, packed hearing that dragged on into the early hours of the morning and turned so contentious Oakland cops were ordered by Council President Larry Reid to clear the chambers.[64]

In December, however, an *Express* cover story revealed that the surveillance center, which was already in the process of being built at a nondescript downtown firehouse, had already been used to track several political protests, including local demonstrations over the murder of Trayvon Martin in Florida.[65]

Linda Lye, a staff attorney at the ACLU of Northern California, told the *Express*: "The fact that the focus so far has been on political protests, rather than the violent crime that's impacting Oakland residents, is troubling, and telling about how the city plans to use the DAC. Information is about control."[66]

By spring 2014, national reporters were parachuting in to cover the controversy. At a standing-room-only hearing where protesters harangued the council and one man read passages from French theorist Michel Foucault's *Discipline & Punish: The Birth of the Prison*, the city council voted five to four, with Mayor Quan casting the tie-breaking vote, to limit the DAC to the Port of Oakland and the airport.

Although it concerned the powers of the police, the eight-months-long surveillance controversy hardly registered with those who were involved with the OPD's NSA reforms. Chanin and Burris were worried about the surveillance system, but it had no immediate impact on the department's court oversight. However, the controversy did leave a lasting mark. Oakland created a civilian Privacy Advisory Commission responsible for investigating how surveillance technologies the police and other city departments hoped to acquire impacted civil liberties and advising the city council on future decisions. Dozens of cities, counties, and towns seeking oversight over law enforcement surveillance practices took notice.[67] It also foreshadowed the institutionalization of greater civilian oversight of the police in Oakland, changes that could hold the OPD in check beyond the NSA.

Whent wasn't greatly impressed with surveillance tools. He prioritized the technologies that were proving invaluable to the NSA reforms. Whent's ascension marked the first time since the inception of court oversight that the city had a top cop who put reform efforts above all else. Throughout his tenure in Internal Affairs, Whent witnessed and personally investigated dozens of officers for false arrests, falsifying warrants, cover-ups, perjury, and brutality. Now firmly ensconced on the eighth floor of OPD Headquarters, with court monitor Robert Warshaw buttressing his authority, Whent dove headfirst into the task of overhauling the organization.

Like the Ceasefire strategy, many of his initiatives weren't novel. They were a bricolage of existing programs that previous chiefs hadn't fully implemented. In 2010 Anthony Batts introduced 350 body-worn video cameras to collect evidence for misconduct allegations and criminal cases. A handful of Oakland cops were spotted wearing the rectangular devices during the July 2010 Oscar Grant verdict protests, making the department one of the earliest adopters of a now-ubiquitous policing technology.[68]

OPD policy required the cameras to be activated while officers made walking stops and arrests, or during protests. But the reality was different. During the crackdown on Occupy, several cops were caught with their body cameras off while making arrests. Whent sent a signal that policies mattered. Dozens of officers were reprimanded and one was fired for failing to turn on their cameras. Not long after, the practice became so ingrained that 95 percent of patrol cops were activating their recording devices during use-of-force incidents.[69]

Police behavior during protests changed under Whent. When angry, chaotic demonstrations erupted in 2013 following the acquittal of George Zimmerman for murdering seventeen-year-old Trayvon Martin, and the following autumn during the first national cycle of Black Lives Matter protests, the OPD acted with unusual restraint, particularly during freeway takeovers and vandalism in downtown Berkeley and Oakland. While Berkeley police and California Highway Patrol fired less-lethals into crowds and clubbed protesters, Oakland cops held back, moving in to make arrests only when they could target someone who clearly broke the law.[70]

Internal Affairs complaints, which rose to an all-time peak of 1,200 in 2012, plummeted under Whent. For the first three months of 2016, 255 complaints were filed against the OPD, as opposed to 538 during the first quarter of 2012.[71]

A longtime requirement of the court reforms, the collection of racial data on the people stopped, questioned, and searched by Oakland police was finally implemented, and OPD contracted with Professor Jennifer Eberhardt of Stanford University to study it and suggest changes. The results were groundbreaking: tens of thousands of stops from 2013 through 2014, involving more than five hundred officers, were analyzed. During this period, officers stopped more than 16,800 Black people and approximately 3,600 white people, searching one-third of the former group and only 10 percent of the latter. Despite being less than 30 percent of Oakland's population at the time, Black motorists and pedestrians accounted for 60 percent of all police encounters.[72] Moreover, the data showed Oakland cops were more confrontational, less polite, and less impartial toward Black drivers as opposed to whites, Latinos, or Asians.[73] That approach significantly increased the likelihood of resistance to the officer's commands and a negative interaction between cop and civilian.

"The stats are so off the charts," Alameda County Public Defender Brendon Woods remarked when the data was made public in early 2015. "There is a continual cycle where African Americans are stopped, they may or may not be charged, and a continual debtors' prison that results from bail, bond, traffic citations—it goes on and on."

Whent and his command staff began developing a new training regimen to deal with "implicit bias," the pervasive, unconscious racism that constantly steers interactions between police and Black people in negative directions.[74] Developed in conjunction with the California Department of Justice, this training was the first of its kind, attracting nationwide attention.

In December 2013 Compliance Director Frazier wrote to Judge Henderson that "notable progress across a broad range of complex issues and projects continues at an acceptable pace. A number of these projects and issues are extremely close to completion."[75]

The reforms were suddenly on track. In April 2014 Warshaw, who had by then taken on the role of compliance director, notified the court that "there are reasons for cautious optimism that the department can both comply and reform." Its ranks were growing, and citizen complaints were down even as arrests increased, a sign that Oakland cops could respect people's rights and change their internal culture without leading to a de-policing backlash.[76]

In May 2014 Mayor Quan ratified Whent's leadership by appointing him police chief. No longer a weak interim placeholder, Whent pledged to double down on his success. Warshaw's report, one month later, sounded the most positive note since the NSA had been signed more than a decade before: "The Department is currently in compliance with the highest number of Tasks in the eleven-year history of the NSA," the monitor observed. "We are optimistic that the Department can soon cross the finish line into full compliance."[77]

In just a year, the Oakland PD went from utter failure to a national leader in policing reforms. Politico ran a story titled "How a Dirty Police Department Gets Clean," detailing its rapid progress. Whent allowed filmmaker Peter Nicks, who'd won widespread acclaim for a 2012 documentary on Oakland's Highland Hospital's emergency room, to embed with officers for a full-length movie about the daily work of beat cops and the high-level efforts to finally fulfill the letter and spirit of the Negotiated Settlement Agreement.[78]

The accolades and long-overdue progress were part of a changing narrative for Oakland. Investment money was pouring into the Bay Area, driven by Silicon Valley's second tech boom and the intense concentration of talent in the region.[79] San Francisco's skyrocketing home prices pushed younger, hipper city residents to the sunnier, more affordable climes of the East Bay. Oakland also had a distinct countercultural cachet thanks to social movements cross-pollinating with the city's cutting-edge arts community. This attracted a different sort of resident: the squatter, the fellow traveler, the movement tourist seeking to catch some of the vapors of the Oscar Grant uprising and Occupy. While this greatly contributed to Oakland's vibrant cultural milieu, it also bridged a crucial gap in the squatters-punks-artists-yuppies conveyor belt of gentrification.

But the city's nascent economic boom wouldn't help Jean Quan. She had isolated herself from her progressive base with the violent crackdown on Occupy and public battles with Judge Henderson over the OPD's stalled reforms. At the same time, Oakland's murder spike and robbery surge—albeit receding—prompted a law-and-order backlash among voters.

Hills district councilwoman Libby Schaaf—who started in politics as an aide to Councilman Ignacio De La Fuente and Mayor Jerry Brown—secured support from moderate and conservative voters in Oakland's affluent hills and segments of the more diverse flatlands. Her campaign emphasized public safety by rebuilding the police ranks from 694 back to at least 800 through a hiring spree.[80] She also outflanked Quan and Kaplan with her early endorsement of a citywide $12.25 minimum wage and strengthened renter protections.[81] In November 2014 Schaaf won handily, and voters approved Measure Z, a ten-year, $277 million parcel and parking tax to bankroll both the OPD and the non–law enforcement components of Ceasefire.[82]

Schaaf indicated that she would retain Whent as her chief; not that she had much say in the matter, given the confidence the department's monitor had expressed in him. Just like Jerry Brown fourteen years earlier, Schaaf vowed to cut crime, this time by 80 percent, a number she would never come close to reaching.[83] And just like Brown, Schaaf's inauguration was protested by those who feared her public safety plan would give police license to abuse. Schaaf walked a fine line, expressing support for the Black Lives Matter movement, but promising to invest more in the police. Her political position depended entirely on the police department's progress with the court-mandated reforms.

Schaaf pointedly spent her entire first day on the job with OPD officers. Showing up at the Police Administration Building at six thirty in the morning and staying for all three shifts through midnight, she toured each floor of the PAB, meeting with officers before their patrol shifts and answering their questions behind closed doors.

However, for all the progress under Whent, there were still explosive problems beneath the surface that would soon boil over.

13

"TELL ME YOU WERE AN ADULT"

For decades, Oakland residents struggled against their police force. The city's activists built a movement that gained national attention after the killing of Oscar Grant by a transit cop and laid the ground for the campaign against Oakland's gang injunctions and Occupy Oakland. The Oscar Grant movement was arguably the genesis of Black Lives Matter, which took the United States by storm after the police killings of Tamir Rice, Eric Garner, Michael Brown, Philando Castille, Freddie Gray, and others. But from May 2013 through February 2015, no Oakland cop fired his or her weapon in the line of duty, a remarkable and sudden change for a department that historically held a reputation of being one of the deadliest in America. While the rest of the country was suddenly reckoning with seemingly daily episodes of lethal police brutality, Oakland was unusually calm. Not a single person died at the hands of an OPD officer in 2014.

What had changed were policies and training reinforced by Chief Sean Whent's resolve to punish officers who crossed clear lines meant to prevent the loss of life. Crime decreased as well, undercutting one of the rank-and-file complaints that court reforms hampered the force's ability to police the city. The OPD's homicide clearance rate—the percent of murder cases it was more or less solving and forwarding to the DA for prosecution—also rose, from about 29 percent in 2011 to 55 percent in 2015.[1]

Even though Oakland didn't have a corollary to Mike Brown or Eric Garner, protesters still hit the streets in solidarity marches. Following the Ferguson grand jury decision, demonstrators took over freeways in Oakland and Berkeley. There were sporadic incidents of vandalism, including the torching of auto dealerships near downtown. Whent's OPD mostly avoided using force or mass arrests.

"It's always a delicate balance between overreacting and underreacting," said Whent at a November city council meeting. He gently resisted political pressure from some of Oakland's elected officials for a more forceful crackdown on the Ferguson solidarity demonstrations. "We have seen the problems in the past of police overreacting, which I think leads to not only additional police violence protests, but also in some cases, significant lawsuits and payouts by the city."[2]

However, a string of police shootings in 2015 seemed like they might disrupt the department's incipient progress. The most controversial was of Demouria Hogg, who was shot and killed by an officer as he was waking up in his car, which was parked on a freeway off-ramp near Oakland's scenic Lake Merritt as the bustling Saturday farmer's market got under way. A pistol lay on his BMW's passenger seat. The vehicle had evaded police the night before in San Francisco following a burglary, and Hogg had been a fugitive for two months over a parole violation. Hogg's family and activists organized protests, but the killing did not lead to sustained demonstrations.

Two months later, in August, rape suspect Antonio Clements ambushed OPD officers with an assault weapon, wounding Sergeant Abdullah Dadgar before Dadgar returned fire and killed him. Nine days later, robbery suspect Nathaniel Wilks fled in a high-speed vehicle chase, crashed his car, and was shot by multiple officers while on foot with a gun in his hand. Before the month was over, Yonas Alehegne, an Ethiopian man with mental health problems who'd been accused of stalking a woman and assaulting another, charged officer Jennifer Farrell with a bicycle chain and lacerated her forehead, sending a stream of blood down her face before she fatally shot him.[3]

Finally, a sergeant and a squad of rookies preparing to tow several motorcycles involved in a November sideshow spotted Richard Perkins walking by a gas station with a pistol in his hand. The officers gunned him down; only after Perkins was dead did they realize his weapon was a BB gun.

The spree of police shootings was concerning. Local activist groups tried to rile up the public with demonstrations accusing the department of murder, but none of the killings undermined the narrative that Oakland had a progressive police department worth emulating, a stark contrast to just a few years prior. Oakland's mayor and police chief now spoke of ending the NSA within a year, a goal that Chanin and Burris agreed seemed feasible at last.

For his chief of staff, Whent recruited Holly Joshi, by now a rising star in the child exploitation unit who specialized in investigating the sex trafficking of minors in the city. Joshi was a skilled undercover officer and investigator whom Whent enlisted for nine months to work on the Occupy Oakland use-of-force complaints back in 2012.[4] She'd briefly served as a public information officer under Chief Batts.

When Whent made his initial offer, Joshi was reticent. Her unit reported directly to the chief, worked closely with federal and state prosecutors with an unusual degree of independence, and even influenced legislation in Sacramento. "Whent comes and he's, like, 'You know that I've built my entire career tearing cops' heads off. Everyone in this entire police department hates me, and I don't care. I know what you're about, and you don't care that people don't like you, either. You're here to change the police department.'"

Joshi's father was the respected lieutenant Rick Hart. Her grandfather was a pastor, and she had deep respect in the city's Black community. Whent knew he needed support from outside the department to bring about true change. "We need to become an example of what modern law enforcement is," Whent told her. Joshi was sold.

In 2015 Whent was invited to Washington, DC, by former OPD captain Ron Davis, now in charge of the DOJ Community Oriented Policy Services Office. The chief was to share his city's experience with implicit bias training, as part of President Obama's "Task Force on Twenty First Century Policing."[5] Among the things Oakland could teach other police departments was how to use body cameras to increase transparency and improve interactions with the public.[6] Its new policies could be adopted by other departments to reduce uses of force. Oakland's methods of building community trust were recommended for places like Ferguson. Mayor Libby Schaaf and a contingent of clergy and community leaders who worked the nonpolice side of Oakland's violence reduction programs accompanied Whent. And his insights on handling mass demonstrations were incorporated into the final report of the president's task force—a complete reversal for an agency that had almost been taken over four years earlier for abusing protesters.[7]

Positive reviews also kept coming from the most important quarter: Robert Warshaw. Over the summer and fall of 2015, Warshaw wrote that the Oakland PD "should be recognized as a strong leader in the field for its collection and use of data," and that the department's Office of Inspector General, the unit Whent led before becoming chief, was an internal force for reform, a development that "paves the way for sustainability," and the eventual end of the NSA.

However, the foundations of Oakland's success proved to be flimsy. At a nondescript apartment building in the East Oakland Hills, a single gunshot would set in motion a chain of events that brought the house of cards crashing down.

———

Brendan O'Brien's parents were worried. Nobody had seen the tall, dark-haired thirty-year-old Oakland cop in five days. He'd missed a training session and hadn't contacted anyone or gone out. So, on September 25, 2015, his mother, Rosemary, called one of Brendan's neighbors, another police officer, and asked her to knock on his door.

The neighbor found the door on the bottom floor of a boxy midcentury fourplex on Greenridge Drive unlocked. Concerned, she told Rosemary she'd better come look for herself. The building—located in the hills across the 580 freeway via a bridge named in honor of the four officers murdered by Lovelle Mixon—was owned by Eric Karsseboom, a longtime Oakland narcotics cop and liaison to federal law enforcement agencies. Karsseboom was also one of the young officers in 2000 who took part in the disastrous buy-bust that killed Jerry Amaro. Now a senior cop, Karsseboom rented the four units out to younger officers who wanted a cheap, secluded location with quick freeway access, but with distance from the neighborhoods they policed.

O'Brien's mother found her son seated on the couch, motionless, with a self-inflicted gunshot wound through the roof of his mouth. In his right hand, O'Brien clutched his pistol. His laptop computer and iPad were on the coffee table, and his cell phone lay on the couch. Two empty Guinness cans were discarded in the sink, and there were several empty prescription bottles for antidepressants and PTSD medication in the apartment.

Also on the coffee table was a typewritten suicide note signed by O'Brien.

"My name is Brendan Michael O'Brien," he began the letter. "I have tried to lead a good life, although sometimes I have not always made the right decisions."

O'Brien grew up in a big Irish family in San Francisco's Crocker-Amazon in the 1990s when it was still a mostly working-class neighborhood. He attended local Catholic schools, graduating from Archbishop Riordan in 2003. One of his passions was announcing at sports events. He didn't excel academically or stand out in other ways. After high school, he worked part-time at a Costco while taking classes at local community colleges, but O'Brien "got restless. He started searching for something. What he found was the US Marine Corps. In 2009 he enlisted."[8]

After the marines, O'Brien joined the OPD, graduating as part of the 166th Academy in 2013, the second police academy after a four-year hiatus caused by budget cuts. O'Brien's class was part of Mayor Quan's attempt to quickly bolster the department's threadbare ranks.[9]

O'Brien was assigned to a patrol beat in East Oakland. "I have a rewarding career, albeit a tough one," he told Riordan's alumni magazine, *Future*, in 2015.[10] One of the most difficult parts of his job involved responding to shootings. With less than a year on, O'Brien was first to respond to the New Year's Eve killing of a thirteen-year-old boy, Lee Weathersby. O'Brien cradled the child's head and pressed a cloth against a bullet wound in a futile effort to save the boy's life.[11]

The most traumatic things haunting O'Brien involved his personal relationships. "There are a lot of reasons why my life doesn't need to continue," he wrote in his suicide note. "I've been ostracized by much of my family and friends."

The "catalyst," O'Brien explained, was "Celeste Guap," a girl whose real name he claimed not to know. In his note, O'Brien admitted that he knew her mother, who worked a civilian job at the department. For months, O'Brien and Guap exchanged intimate text messages. Guap, a sex-trafficked teenager who'd gone "renegade" at times by breaking away from the men exploiting her, told O'Brien he saved her from a violent pimp on the streets by driving by at the right moment in a patrol car. O'Brien wrote in his note that he did not recall the incident and insisted that he'd only met her in person once, but did not elaborate. He claimed to have no real relationship to Celeste Guap, but he also alleged that she was "making threats" to expose him for sexually exploiting her when she was still only seventeen years old.

That much was true, and it was an act that Guap, whose real name was Jasmine Abuslin, would regret.

Abuslin and her mother, OPD dispatcher Monica Cedillo, were on a vacation in Puerto Rico in mid-September, belatedly celebrating Abuslin's eighteen birthday from the month before. While walking home from a bar late one night, Abuslin got lost. Drunk, with her phone battery running low, she tried calling and texting O'Brien. He didn't pick up. According to Abuslin, she'd met O'Brien many times in Oakland over the prior year, always in vehicles, and they'd shared intimate moments. She was seventeen at the time. However, the way she understood it, O'Brien was her lover and protector.

"I associated him with saving me, because that's how we met," Abuslin said in a 2016 interview. But Abuslin was angered by the fact that her "protector" wasn't answering his phone. He appeared to be trying to cut her off.

She "cussed him out" in a voicemail. Later that night, she started replying to messages from Leroy Johnson, the sergeant in charge of the Communications Division and close friends with her mother. Johnson had messaged her earlier through Facebook asking how she was doing.

"I slept with hella your officers as a teen," she wrote. "Most are rooks." Abuslin started naming names, including O'Brien and an OPD captain, as well as four other officers who'd preyed on her.

"Tell me you were an adult," Johnson wrote back, to which Abuslin replied, "I'd be lying."

"I would never say anything, but it is just sick to me," Johnson told her. "Just because you had a woman['s] body, you were a child."[12]

Later, feeling spurned by a man who she thought loved her, Abuslin texted screenshots of her confiding in Johnson to O'Brien. A few days later, O'Brien was found dead.

In his suicide letter, O'Brien portrayed himself as an innocent victim of a scheming teenager. "I have absolutely done nothing to scorn her. I have no idea why she is doing this to me.

"When you're a suicidal cop, you just can't tell anyone how you're feeling," O'Brien wrote. He believed that if he sought counseling, he'd be put on a psychiatric hold and short-circuit his career. Policing seemed to be the only thing keeping him alive.

O'Brien somehow thought he could exonerate himself, so he wrote down the passwords to his phone, computer, and iPad. Because he understood the chain of events that would unfold once he pulled the trigger, O'Brien wrote:

"To OPD homicide, if you do interview Celeste regarding my death, know that everything she tells you will be a lie."

O'Brien's suicide had the opposite effect. Much of what Abuslin would go on to tell investigators (and the media) was the truth. Soon numerous police officers, not just in Oakland, would be outed as sexual predators and liars. O'Brien's death would result in a half-hearted investigation. It was a neglectful (if not outright malicious) cover-up, the unearthing of a previous homicide case in which O'Brien himself was the suspect, and revelations that exposed a deep culture of misogyny within the force. By the end of the investigation, Oakland's narrative of reform would be shattered.

———

When Jasmine Abuslin was eight years old, her parents divorced. In divorce proceedings in Alameda County, Monica Cedillo called her marriage with Jasmine's father, Henry Abuslin, "bad from the beginning" because of constant "emotional, physical, and verbal abuse," which began when Jasmine was still a baby. Both parents drank heavily, but, on his binges, Henry's mood would darken. He'd accuse Monica of infidelity and become abusive. The divorce was Monica's first attempt to "make a clean break." Only three months passed when, in August 2005, she allowed her ex-husband to move back into her home, a small apartment in El Cerrito underneath the unit her parents lived in.[13]

The next three years were rocky. Henry's drinking intensified, prompting violent, jealousy-fueled fights Jasmine witnessed. One time, Monica came home from work and noticed Henry was drunk. She had Jasmine go to her room, and the divorced couple argued in their bedroom. Then Henry attacked Monica. "He had me on the bed, he choked me, he told me he was never going to let me be with anybody else," she said during a court hearing seeking a restraining order years later.

Henry allegedly began to threaten Monica's life, claiming he would kill her parents and harm Jasmine. The attacks became more frequent. Monica began looking for a way to make a break again. It was around this time that Jasmine's life could have changed in a big way.

John Hege met Monica in 2003, during a visit to OPD's dispatch center by the East Oakland shoreline. A member of the Motorcycle Squad, Hege was gregarious and loved showing appreciation for dispatchers, who juggled Oakland's often chaotic radio traffic over long, stressful shifts. Around 2007, their friendship grew into a romantic relationship. On Valentine's Day that year, Hege sent Monica flowers and chocolates, and the two talked about starting a life together. Jasmine liked Hege and started to feel that the officer would help them.

Henry found out about the relationship. One day he showed Monica that he'd found Hege's home address online. Monica told Hege about the unsettling implicit message from her ex-husband. She recalled the incident in court testimony years later: "I was worried that one day he might just get drunk and be stupid enough to go and confront Hege at his house." According to Monica, Hege didn't back down. "I don't think he knows what he is dealing with, let him go to my doorstep, and we will see what happens," she recalled Hege saying.

Monica obtained several restraining orders against Henry, but he continued to drive by her home, and text and call her. When Monica's relationship with Hege became more serious, she said that something in her ex-husband "snapped."

By the spring of 2009, Monica was convinced that she needed to leave Henry and move in with Hege for her and her daughter's sake. But Hege was gunned down by Lovelle Mixon during the March 21 East Oakland traffic stop that spiraled into tragedy.

Henry continued stalking his ex-wife and daughter until December 2010, when he sent a series of threatening text messages to Monica at work. She handed her phone over to OPD investigators, and Henry was convicted of making criminal threats, resulting in a day in jail, five years' probation, and an order that he stay away from Monica if he hoped to see his daughter someday.

With Henry mostly out of their lives, Jasmine and her mother lived in a house twelve miles north of Oakland in Richmond, the refinery town with its own sordid history of police misconduct and street violence.[14] By this time, Jasmine was in her early teens, and struggling in school. Although highly intelligent—for several years, she was the best student in her English courses—Jasmine often skipped classes and sometimes was disciplined by school administrators and Richmond police officers who worked with the department's Youth Services Division. She started developing unhealthy relationships with men and using drugs. "I noticed men checking me out at age eight," she said in a 2021 interview. "And at first, I was embarrassed about it." She sometimes walked around with her arms crossed on her chest, to hide her body from male gazes. By fifteen, she was being exploited for sex by men on the streets of Richmond and Oakland. However, Brendan O'Brien was not the first man, or even the first police officer, to sexually exploit Jasmine Abuslin.

She was twelve years old when the first man propositioned her for sex on the street near her home. He was sitting in a car near a children's playground. Jasmine was walking home late one night when the man noticed her and asked for sex. "For me it was almost like a lightbulb moment: I could get what I wanted from these dudes," she said. Those things included money and a sense of worth.

"How can I say this: the feeling of sex, the feeling of being intimate with somebody was robbed from me," Jasmine said. "So, for me, sex is very commercial."[15]

According to Abuslin, her mother had been flirting with an OPD officer in 2011. One day Monica introduced the man to Jasmine, and he offered to teach the girl how to drive a car in two years when she turned sixteen. By her fifteenth birthday, Jasmine and the cop had been exchanging private Facebook messages for some time. He picked her up one day from her friend's house across from a middle school in the small town of Albany— between Richmond and Oakland—and drove her to the Berkeley Marina, where he committed statutory rape against her.

"I thought we were in love," said Abuslin in a recent interview, describing how she felt about it at the time. In hindsight, she understood the cop "groomed" her; making her feel that he wanted her to become a part of his life, manipulating her for his own pleasure. (We have identified the ex-officer and have information showing that the Oakland Police Department is aware of his identity and the allegations against him, but no criminal case has ever been filed and the city has never taken steps to reveal his role in the sex exploitation scandal.)[16]

She was at her home one day when a relative sexually assaulted her. In a panic, Abuslin made a video call from her cell phone to the Oakland cop who'd groomed her. He picked up and watched as the girl was assaulted.[17]

"Then he ghosted me," said Abuslin, recalling the traumatic episode. The police officer cut all ties after witnessing the attack. The crimes were horrifyingly layered: the cop who had molested and raped Abuslin witnessed another man assault her. He then failed to report the heinous crime, in all likelihood because it would have exposed him as one of the teen's exploiters, cost him his job, and resulted in statutory rape charges.

When she turned seventeen, Abuslin's self-harming behavior escalated. She developed social media accounts with names like "YourDadTakesMeShopping" and "ShadyBizness," through which she would message men to see who would flirt with her. Many asked for nude photos and sexted. A few requested to meet up. These included cops from Oakland, but also officers from Richmond, San Francisco, Alameda County, Contra Costa County, and other agencies. O'Brien was one of those who exploited her when she was still seventeen. Another accused officer was Giovanni LoVerde, who graduated from the 170th police academy in October 2014 and allegedly met up with Abuslin for sex near Lake Merritt in mid-2015.[18]

But most of the police officers who trafficked Jasmine did so after she turned eighteen. Many of them took steps to ensure that the young sex worker had reached the bare minimum age to avoid a statutory rape charge lest their lecherous behavior become known to more honest colleagues.

One of them was Terryl Smith, a squat, balding thirty-year-old who commuted to Oakland from Sacramento. Smith sometimes slept on a mattress in his truck in the OPOA's parking lot between shifts. Smith and Abuslin messaged each other through Facebook in September, after O'Brien killed himself. They talked sex. Smith sent her screenshots of sex worker ads he'd found online, asking how much she charged. Maybe nothing, replied Abuslin, because he was a cop. On the day before O'Brien's funeral, which was attended by many OPD officers, Smith asked if they could meet. Late that night, the officer picked Abuslin up from her mother's home in Richmond and drove her to a secluded park in the hills, where they had sex. After this first meeting, they linked up consistently at two in the morning, on Sundays, when Smith's shift ended.

Another cop who took advantage of Abuslin was James Ta'ai. Like Smith and O'Brien, Ta'ai was a rookie. The twenty-five-year-old had graduated along with Smith from the 168th Academy in 2014. He also knew Brendan O'Brien. O'Brien often took overtime hours to work as part of Ta'ai's East Oakland dogwatch shift. Ta'ai would later deny ever talking with O'Brien about the girl known as "Celeste Guap," but he acknowledged that he was friends with both O'Brien and the girl on Facebook, and that he and O'Brien traded text messages. Ta'ai claimed it was only "work stuff."[19] He also met up in person with Abuslin around the time of O'Brien's funeral, taking the teenager to Wildcat Canyon, where he pleasured himself.

In OPD locker rooms, a handful of cops started trading stories about "Celeste Guap," bragging about their exploits, or showing pornographic photos she'd sent them. Had the department taken O'Brien's suicide seriously and investigated his disturbing note, this might have been stopped. Instead, numerous other police officers in Oakland and beyond would soon contact Abuslin to sexually exploit her, allegedly committing crimes like attempted rape, misusing sensitive police databases, sharing police intelligence with a sex worker, and other transgressions.

———

Chief Whent called Mayor Schaaf the night O'Brien killed himself to deliver the news about another officer suicide—previously, two officers killed themselves in the span of two months in 2013.[20] The next morning, Whent called Warshaw for the same reason, but the chief didn't mention the suicide note to either the mayor or the court-appointed monitor.

Five days after O'Brien's body was discovered, homicide investigators Bradley Baker and Jason Anderson brought Abuslin to headquarters. Over the next two hours, Baker and Anderson struggled to obtain information. During the interview—which was watched from another room by Lieutenant Roland Holmgren, now leading the Homicide Unit—the teenager was afraid and evasive, changing the subject frequently. She initially denied anything that might have been construed as a crime by any officers, and worried aloud if she could be jailed for what had happened.

Without naming names, Abuslin started asking questions—obviously non-hypotheticals—like whether Giovanni LoVerde, the officer who she said exploited her for oral sex near Lake Merritt, could be prosecuted for indecent exposure. And she cried while telling the story about when the first officer who victimized her when she was fifteen watched her being assaulted by her relative over a live video call. As she spoke, the scandal's true scope began unfolding.

But Baker and Anderson were unable to build trust with Abuslin. At times, the two detectives made comments that cast her as a liar and aggressor, putting her on the defensive. They told Abuslin that O'Brien's suicide note said she would lie about everything, and that the dead officer blamed her. Upon hearing this, Abuslin became even less willing to confide in the investigators.

When the meandering interview came to the subject of her other exploiters, Abuslin said she'd had sex with several other officers besides O'Brien, but only after she'd turned eighteen. For this to be true, the detectives observed, she would have to have slept with them over the past several weeks. Abuslin, after all, had only been eighteen for a month and five days. It was true, though: she'd had sex with several cops just a few days before the interview.

Baker and Anderson pressed again for names, but Abuslin refused to "snitch." She had no interest in seeing officers disciplined or charged. She had no desire to inform, a mirror image of the police's own code of silence. Also, the way the teenager viewed it at the time, while she'd felt betrayed by a few officers, and while she'd sent some of them warnings that she would expose them to Internal Affairs or their spouses, these policemen were still her friends, lovers, and protectors. After everything she'd been through, Abuslin still felt a sense of loyalty to them.

The detectives tried a new tack. They told her again she'd been the "catalyst" for O'Brien's suicide, and that she needed to name other officers in order to prevent more suicides. This strategy backfired grievously. Abuslin picked up her phone and began deleting text messages with at least six officers. The detectives watched as she destroyed crucial evidence of crimes and misconduct.

What Baker and Anderson failed to do—a failure the entire OPD organization was about to make—was to understand that while Abuslin was legally considered an adult when they interviewed her in the wake of O'Brien's suicide, the story she was telling—albeit in an evasive way—was that of a child who'd been sexually preyed upon, abused, and exposed to hard drugs like heroin from a young age. Her family's history of domestic violence conditioned Jasmine to view police officers as saviors.

"When my parents would fight, when the cops would show up, that's when things would be okay," Abuslin said in a recent interview.

She'd become extremely vulnerable and allowed police officers to exploit her in what she viewed as "relationships," starting when she was legally underage and continuing past her eighteenth birthday. She was also trafficked on the streets of Richmond and Oakland as a girl, sometimes working on her own, and sometimes under the exploitative coercion of older men. This trafficking continued past her eighteenth birthday. Jasmine's inner turmoil drove her toward increasingly self-destructive behavior.[21]

Instead of building on their first interview with a follow-up, or trying to obtain other evidence and interrogate officers identified as potential suspects, the Homicide Unit closed their case in under a week. Holmgren told his supervisor, Captain Kirk Coleman, that they hadn't obtained evidence showing criminal conduct by any officer. He suggested the Special Victims Unit take the case because of its complexity and nature.

SVU did not get involved. The criminal investigation was shut within the week without interviewing any other potential witnesses or suspects, without reviewing social media, without seeking a single search warrant, and without any discussions with the district attorney.

––––––––––

Days later, the case landed on Internal Affairs Sergeant Mildred Oliver's desk.[22] Oliver, a twenty-two-year OPD veteran who ran the nonprofit Police Activities League for youth and taught criminal justice courses at Merritt College, read Homicide's file, watched the video of Abuslin's statement, and reviewed the contents of O'Brien's cell phone. She called Abuslin on October 30. When the teenager declined to meet in person, Oliver acquiesced and interviewed her by phone. Oliver began by asking Abuslin how long she'd been a "working girl" and then launched into questions about her mother. Abuslin clammed up, concerned she or her mother could be charged with a crime.

When Oliver asked about the messages Abuslin had sent to Sergeant Johnson about "sleeping with" O'Brien and others when she was underage, the answer the teenager gave was clear.

"Did you tell him you had sex with O'Brien when you were under eighteen?" Oliver asked.

"Yeah," Abuslin replied.

"Okay, did you actually have sex with O'Brien when you were under eighteen?"

"Yeah."

But when Oliver asked about other officers still on the force, Abuslin denied everything. She said they hadn't had sex after she turned eighteen. She was still trying to protect some of the officers.

"I saw in some of the messages you sent," said Oliver. "You like officers because they make you feel safe."

"They save people," said Abuslin.

"They save people," Oliver agreed. "And they've saved you. I understand that."

"Brendan saved me."

Oliver's tone wavered between patronizing, motherly, frustrated, and dismissive. She called Abuslin "sweetie pie" in between assertions that Jasmine didn't "realize how serious this is," but also that her job as Internal Affairs investigator was only to try to clarify if officers had slept with Abuslin after she turned eighteen so she could "save some people's jobs."[23]

As the interview went on, Oliver should have realized that not only had something improper happened a few months before, but officers were currently engaging in untoward behavior with Abuslin.

"When you told Sergeant Johnson that you were sleeping with 'hella your officers,' was that true?" asked Oliver.

"Yeah," said Abuslin, "'cause that's not even the whole list. There's like five others I haven't even listed." She added she'd had sex with an OPD officer the night before.

In a moment of concern, Oliver told Abuslin she deserved better "than being a working girl. You don't have to go after men like this," she said. "There's so much more in life." Oliver offered to meet with Abuslin and help her. But she never did.

In November, Oliver and another IAD investigator interviewed Sergeant Johnson, Officer Ta'ai, and others.[24] Ta'ai lied and denied ever having sex with Abuslin. In his short interview, he claimed to have only "flirted" with the girl in texts.

Johnson was truthful. He told Oliver that in early 2015—well before O'Brien's suicide—he'd seen a Facebook post by another OPD employee telling people in the department not to friend "Celeste Guap" on Facebook or otherwise communicate with her. He thought the message was uncalled for because Abuslin was just a seventeen-year-old girl and the daughter of a department employee, so he reached out to Abuslin, asking her, "What's going on?"[25]

According to Johnson, Abuslin "opened up," telling him about the "relationship" she'd been in with the first OPD officer, the one before O'Brien who'd exploited her when she was a minor. She'd started befriending other Oakland cops to try to get through to the man, but other officers helped him avoid the underage girl.

She later told Johnson that she'd slept with ten other officers, including

O'Brien. He claimed he didn't believe her. He thought Abuslin was friending officers on Facebook and then, as he described it, "she turns around and says that she was sleeping with them as an attention-getter." That's why he didn't report it.

In an interview, Abuslin said part of the reason she started contacting so many OPD cops on Facebook in 2015 was to "get back at" the first officer who she thought she'd been in a "relationship" with, who then cut her off after witnessing her be assaulted.

In February, Oliver filed a draft report with her lieutenant, Trevelyon Jones. She recommended that Johnson be disciplined for failing to report allegations a minor was being sexually trafficked by police officers. But Oliver downgraded the other officers from subjects of the investigation to witnesses.

Lieutenant Jones noted that Internal Affairs should probably reverse that decision and treat the officers as suspects. There were plenty of signs they'd lied to IA, and there was more to it. A cop was dead. Another cop had sent a lewd photo to the girl. And a third admitted in an interview to knowing Abuslin was an "escort," another term for sex worker. But Jones was also "thinking about how that could affect the department" if the investigation were continued.[26]

It was well understood in both Homicide and Internal Affairs that Chief Whent and his command team didn't consider the Celeste Guap case a priority. It was a closed criminal case that had stalled out in Internal Affairs. But while the Oakland PD neglected the case, the crimes and misconduct of its officers started to multiply.

Late one night in February 2016 Jasmine Abuslin was stranded at the West Oakland BART station. She saw a patrol car and approached it, striking up a conversation with the tall, blond cop in the driver's seat. He called a cab for her to get to Richmond. Her phone buzzed a few hours later with the message "We just met." The text was from the officer who said his name was "BJ." She called him "Superman."

A week later, Abuslin invited "Superman" to visit her at a hotel near the Oakland Airport, where a San Francisco security guard she'd recently met named Daniel Troy Knight had paid for her half-week hotel stay in hopes he split her profits. "Superman" showed up, sexually used Abuslin, then took her phone from the couch and carefully deleted his text message thread with her. But they were soon texting again. The officer, whose real name was Brian Bunton, was another rookie. He'd been on the force less than a year, but feigned street smarts and acted like he knew the department's inner workings. One night, Bunton told Abuslin to stay off International Boulevard because he thought the police department was running a prostitution sting. Bunton also offered Abuslin advice, telling her to move from the avenues in the Twenties up into the Forties on International Boulevard to get more customers. She should also "show more skin" in her Facebook ads, comments that a judge would later say amounted to pimping.[27]

That same month, Officer Terryl Smith picked up Abuslin again and drove her to Wildcat Canyon Park. They crawled into the back of his truck, where he proceeded to demand anal sex. She refused, but he forcefully spun her around and attempted to rape her.[28] This was only the latest thing Smith had done to hurt her. He'd also looked her, her father, and a friend up in a confidential police database and shared some of the information, bragging about the power he had. She responded later by telling Smith she would let his wife know about his infidelity. Upon hearing this, Smith threatened suicide.

A former OPD captain who worked for the Alameda County District Attorney's Office flirted with her online, making sexual comments and suggesting they meet up for dinner. Another retired captain met her in a Richmond hotel and paid for sex.

OPD Officer Warit Uttapa began sexting with Abuslin in December 2015. In January they allegedly met up and Uttapa used her for oral sex. Afterward, Abuslin noticed her phone was missing. She thought Uttapa had stolen it to either erase information or communicate with other officers in her contacts.[29]

Other officers from across the Bay Area were also starting to prey on the eighteen-year-old. In Richmond, where Abuslin still lived with her mother, the local cops were just as predatory as their counterparts in Oakland.

Terrance Jackson, a Richmond cop who knew Abuslin when she was a student at De Anza High School where he worked as the school resource officer, friended her on social media and began sending lewd comments. Jackson drove to Abuslin's home one day when her mother was at work and fondled his eighteen-year-old former student, according to the Richmond Police Department's investigation.

Richmond police officer Jerrod Tong received oral sex twice from the teenager in full knowledge that she was a sex worker. Lieutenant Felix Tan, a twenty-year RPD veteran who served as Richmond's media liaison, sexted with Abuslin, as did Sergeant Mike Rood. And another sergeant, Armando Moreno, who first met her in a part of the city known for the sex trade, acknowledged her at-risk status by handing her a card meant to help trafficking victims, then sexually exploited her.

Andre Hill, a Richmond Police Department lieutenant who ran the high school safety program, exchanged hundreds of explicit text messages with the teen after friending her on Facebook in November 2015. Four months later, Hill also visited Abuslin's house for oral sex.

As she had done many times, Abuslin confided in Hill about the traumatic things she'd faced in life. She'd been kidnapped before, had an unplanned pregnancy, been placed into psychiatric holds, and used drugs, including heroin and cocaine. As an administrative investigation would later conclude, he "knew that Abuslin was an eighteen-year-old girl with a background of traumatic incidents and an at-risk youth who Hill was charged to protect." Yet Hill ignored his duty to report her self-harm. He didn't seek out assistance or attempt to prevent others from exploiting the vulnerable youngster.

Instead, Hill asked her for ID to prove she was eighteen before receiving oral sex from her, to protect himself against criminal liability.[30]

———

Had the OPD vigorously investigated the sex crimes case resulting from O'Brien's suicide note, much of what became known as the "Oakland police sex scandal" might have never happened.

But around the same time, questions about another earlier investigation, also involving O'Brien, were beginning to surface. There were rumors within the force that O'Brien killed his wife.

On June 16, 2014—well before he met Abuslin and more than a year before his suicide—O'Brien called OPD dispatch at 9:52 p.m. to report that his wife, Irma Huerta-Lopez, had shot herself in the head in the same apartment on Greenridge Drive.

When the first officers arrived, O'Brien stood on the rear patio outside the kitchen wearing shorts, slippers, and a T-shirt, smoking a cigarette.[31] One of the first cops on scene, Brandon Perry, observed that O'Brien had a "distant stare in his eyes." O'Brien said he and Huerta-Lopez argued earlier that evening. She suspected he was having an affair. O'Brien claimed he drove alone to a Shell gas station near the Oakland Zoo to buy cigarettes. When he returned, he found Irma's body. The pack of cigarettes lay on the dining room table alongside the receipt.

The austere apartment was furnished with a simple kitchen table, chairs, and an Ikea-style couch across the living room from a flat-screen television. A Bowflex exercise machine sat in a front room that was empty aside from stacks of O'Brien's police training manuals, bills, and other miscellany.

In the bedroom, twenty-nine-year-old Huerta-Lopez lay supine on the bed wearing white shorts and a sleeveless blue shirt, with a single gunshot wound on the right side of her head next to the top of the ear. Blood covered her face, arms, and torso, soaking into her clothing and the bedclothes.[32] An empty bottle of prescription pills lay on the bedside table. On the floor next to her foot was a black .45-caliber pistol with one empty casing four inches from the gun, a personal firearm of O'Brien's. A second casing lay on the beige carpet four feet away. There was a bullet hole in the wall opposite the bedroom door. The angle of her wound indicated that Huerta-Lopez had been shot on the right side of her head, at a five-degree downward angle with a ten-degree tilt pointing at her forehead to the left. The fatal shot was so close there were powder burns on her skin. The bullet exited her skull, punched through the wall, and was recovered by officers outside. The other round went through the floor and was later found in a crawl space.

There were signs in the apartment that O'Brien and Huerta-Lopez's two-month-old marriage was falling apart. Her wedding ring lay on a paper towel on the living room coffee table, and O'Brien's wedding band was on the bedroom dresser. In Huerta-Lopez's car, parked across the street, police found a large amount of clothing in the trunk. The couple's marriage certificate lay on the dining room table. However, there were no signs of a struggle: no bruises, scratches, or torn clothing on either O'Brien's or Huerta-Lopez's bodies. There was no knocked-over furniture or marks on the wall other than the bullet hole in the bedroom.

But there were more live pistol rounds and firearms in the apartment than there was artwork on the walls. Ammunition was loose and also loaded into magazines that investigators found scattered about several rooms, including a box of .40-caliber bullets on the bedroom dresser. In the closet, they came across additional .45-caliber ammo. They located two Glock pistol magazines under the coffee table in the living room. And in the pockets of a pair of black tactical pants on the living room floor, they recovered another twenty-five rounds.

Later, when they searched O'Brien's Mazda, they found a .40-caliber Glock Model 23 handgun with a loaded magazine and a live round in the chamber. Under the driver's seat, they also found a live .40-caliber round. Unlike the homes of many police officers and responsible gun owners, there was no gun safe.

As evidence technicians scoured the ground-floor apartment, taking photographs, marking evidence, and dusting for fingerprints, Homicide Lieutenant Roland Holmgren took charge of the scene along with Sergeant Caesar Basa, an "old school" Oakland cop who worked a dogwatch patrol shift in the early 2000s, when the Riders patrolled West Oakland. The other investigator, Sergeant Mike Gantt, arrived a half hour later and notified the district attorney's office of Huerta-Lopez's death, O'Brien's involvement, and the possibility of a murder investigation.

Basa wrote a warrant application to search the apartment, O'Brien and Huerta-Lopez's cars, their phones, and other electronic devices. "Suspects in a crime such as domestic violence will often attempt to conceal his/her involvement in the crime from police by misdirection of evidence or misrepresentation of the victim's involvement," Basa wrote in his affidavit. "A homicide scene could be staged as a suicide to conceal the actual crime."[33]

O'Brien was driven downtown to police headquarters and taken to a small room with graffiti-scarred cork walls known as "the box." This windowless room was where cops interviewed suspects and witnesses. Very seldom would an officer walk into the box on the sharp end of an interview.

When he sat down across from O'Brien at 5:19 a.m., Sergeant Gantt already had his suspicions: in twenty-seven years as an Oakland cop—five in Homicide—he'd never seen a suicide victim fire two shots. The first shell landed by Huerta-Lopez's foot, rather than by her side. The second shell casing's location, by the entryway to the bedroom door, over four feet away from Huerta-Lopez's body, also bothered Gantt: *If the gun had been fired from a similar location, the casings would be grouped closer together. And how did she fire two shots? Did she fire the first into the floor before killing herself?*

Despite authoring the search warrant for the Greenridge Drive apartment, replete with language about a possibly staged suicide, Basa was less suspicious. According to Gantt, Basa told him, "Don't be close minded," and that he thought Huerta-Lopez killed herself.[34]

As Gantt would tell it later, Basa kept asking softball questions. When Gantt's turn came, he focused on the young officer's dispute with his wife. O'Brien said they'd been arguing because Huerta-Lopez thought he'd been unfaithful. He left the apartment to buy cigarettes. O'Brien was reportedly not a smoker. No ashtrays, cigarette butts, or any other sign of smoking were found in the apartment aside from the pack he bought that night— a pack with a receipt and video footage from the gas station the OPD would later recover that perfectly established his alibi.

Gantt, who had a reputation as one of the best interviewers in Oakland's Homicide Unit, frequently securing confessions from murder suspects during exhausting, hours-long sessions, figured O'Brien could have killed Huerta-Lopez with a shot to the temple, then traveled to the gas station and back to create the alibi. But as Gantt would later claim, when he told O'Brien he didn't believe his version of events, he felt a jolt to his shin. Basa was kicking him under the table. "Let's take a break," Basa said, and the two homicide cops stepped into the hall.

"What are you doing? You're treating him like a suspect, a criminal, like a dude off the street!" Basa allegedly said outside the box, where O'Brien couldn't hear.[35]

"Basa, I think the guy killed his wife," Gantt replied, adding that O'Brien was acting like a suspect and that his story was thin.[36]

"He's a cop, you need to ease up," Gantt remembers Basa saying.

"You ask him what you want, and I'll ask him what I want," Gantt replied. "I don't care if he's a cop, he's a suspect. If he killed his wife, he's a criminal."

According to Gantt's version of events, as he walked to the restroom, he saw Basa enter Homicide Lieutenant John Lois's office and close the door. Five minutes later, Basa walked out, avoiding eye contact with Gantt.[37] Lois caught Gantt's eye, motioned him in, and asked him to shut the door. He was being replaced on the O'Brien case by Randy Brandwood, a former gang investigator who joined Homicide six months prior.[38]

When Basa and Brandwood concluded the interview that morning, they advised O'Brien he was free to leave. Over the next few days, OPD and Alameda County DA investigators would interview relatives and friends of Huerta-Lopez and analyze forensic evidence. Within four days, chemical tests of swabs taken from both Huerta-Lopez's and O'Brien's hands tested positive for gunshot residue, proof that O'Brien fired a gun some time before Huerta-Lopez's death.

Unfortunately, other tests were incomplete: an independent pathologist told the *East Bay Times* that although blood spatter on Huerta-Lopez's hands indicated she may have shot herself, police investigators erred in not requesting further analysis.[39]

O'Brien was never summoned for a second interview. The investigation into Huerta-Lopez's death was closed out as a suicide, and O'Brien returned to patrol in East Oakland.

But Gantt was hardly the only person to assert that O'Brien may have killed his wife. Huerta-Lopez's family didn't believe the official narrative of suicide.

"Why were there two shots if she killed herself?" her sister, Paulina Huerta, asked in a May 2016 interview. "He killed her." The sister also said the police had briefly interviewed her and other family members but ignored their pleas to keep the case open. "Nobody's listening," she said.

But others in the department also had suspicions that the case was hurriedly closed. They reached out to Desley Brooks, the longtime city council member who'd been critical of the police over the years.

Huerta-Lopez's suicide also presented a red flag to Sean Whent's chief aide, Holly Joshi. She'd begun noticing changes in Whent's demeanor over the year and a half since he took the top job: more deference to the OPOA, concerns about how line cops perceived his decisions. While he had been highly respectful toward Oakland's Black community during his ascent within the department, some of Whent's remarks to Joshi (herself half Black) were jarring. "My plan for Black men in Oakland is to put them all on a bus to Antioch," Whent joked to her one day in his office.[40]

But the investigation into Huerta-Lopez's death was the final straw. "Mike Gantt came up to my office and said, 'What is wrong with your boss?' I said, 'What're you talking about?' Mike said, 'They're taking me off of this case because they don't want me to ask the questions, because I think this white boy killed his wife.' Gantt asked if Joshi could get Whent to put him back on the case and keep O'Brien suspended. When Joshi made the request to her boss, Sean laughed it off. "From the perspective of the outside officers, Mike Gantt was known as the best interviewer in Homicide—he'd bring everything in on a plate, he got confessions, he was a smooth talker," Joshi recalled.

Gantt also cut corners—he had a girlfriend transcribe interviews, a policy violation that landed him in hot water during the Machiavellian recriminations within the OPD after the sexual exploitation scandal broke. Gantt wouldn't tell the public his story about being taken off the Huerta-Lopez case until November 2016, after the department placed him under investigation for mishandling the audio tapes by giving his girlfriend access. But Whent's refusal to listen to Joshi and reassign Gantt to Huerta-Lopez's death was another red flag.[41] She noticed Whent adopt an oppositional, even obstructionist attitude toward monitor Robert Warshaw and push hard to end court oversight. Joshi resigned in the summer of 2015 to work in the nonprofit sector and pursue graduate degrees.[42]

By the time O'Brien's suicide uncovered sex trafficking crimes in the department and beyond, the OPD's mishandling of the investigations was brought to the attention of Robert Warshaw by officials like Brooks and others with sources inside the OPD. The independent monitor was astonished by the allegations spelled out in O'Brien's note and reinforced by the police's initial—and flawed—examination. Seeing it all for what it really was—a miscarriage of justice—Warshaw went to Judge Thelton Henderson.

On March 23, 2016, Henderson issued a cryptic order: he'd been briefed "on irregularities and potential violations of the Negotiated Settlement Agreement." He ordered Warshaw to take over the Internal Affairs case. Chief Whent was suddenly cut out of the chain of command. John Lois, who'd been elevated to deputy chief, was ordered to reopen the case with a new team of investigators untainted by previous decisions, aggressively pursue all leads, and report directly to Warshaw.

Judge Henderson's resolve to have Warshaw seize control of the Celeste Guap case might have seemed unusual at first glance, but, given the Oakland Police Department's history of sexual misconduct, it was warranted that the NSA would be leveraged to investigate the case.

The Negotiated Settlement Agreement was forged in the aftermath of the Riders scandal to address the force's systematic mistreatment of Black people. All the subsequent violations causing the court to take notice or intervene—the strip-search cases, officer-involved shootings in the mid-2000s, Warrantgate, and Occupy—had a common thread with the

Riders case. At their core, they concerned police violations of civil rights—especially Black people—through brutal and dishonest means.

The Celeste Guap case was different in that it involved sexual misconduct. But OPD history was littered with examples of police officers abusing women. Like many other law enforcement agencies, misogyny ran deep within Oakland's police culture. The NSA hadn't been designed to address this, but the Celeste Guap scandal forced a reckoning.

Oakland cops had a complicated relationship with the sex trade. In the department's early years, many officers ran protection rackets for brothels and turned a blind eye to the oldest profession. Although the OPD's vice corruption was largely cleaned up in the 1950s and 1960s, the agency continued to ignore prostitution and pimping, which thrived on the streets and in nightclubs like Telegraph Avenue's Lamp Post. Sex work didn't top the list of police priorities in Oakland: gun violence, robberies, burglaries, and the burgeoning street drug trade took precedence in the minds of most residents and cops up until the late 1990s. In 1990, a *San Francisco Examiner* investigation revealed that the Oakland PD closed roughly a quarter of rape claims as "unfounded," oftentimes declining to interview the victim.[43] "Word spread through the streets that cases are dropped for no apparent reason," said Marcia Blackstock, the executive director of a local rape counseling center. "Candidly, we blew it," admitted Chief Hart.

In the 2000s Alameda County law enforcement began reframing the sex trade in a way that viewed sex workers as victims. But just because law enforcement leaders called it "human trafficking" didn't mean that male-dominated police forces still didn't abuse their power over the predominantly female victims of the sex trade. Holly Joshi developed a national reputation working as an investigator on sex trafficking cases (particularly minors) in Oakland along with the Alameda County district attorney and the FBI. However, when she began that assignment, her fellow officers had a far more callous view. "They were still running around calling these twelve-year-olds 'whores,' " Joshi recalled. Sex workers would often pass on rumors that certain officers sought sexual favors both off and on duty.[44]

During the first Riders trial in 2002, a small-scale sex trafficking scandal involving OPD officers came to light. Narcotics officers Eric Richholt and Mark Neely Jr. were arrested at a San Leandro beauty salon after offering $160 to several women for oral sex. The women were actually undercover Alameda County sheriff's deputies.[45]

There were signs the vice cops were up to far worse. When police searched Richholt and Neely's car, they found cash, ziplock bags of cocaine in the center console, heroin and marijuana, and firearms, including a shotgun Neely and Richholt allegedly seized from an East Oakland house earlier in the day in a warrantless search. Both officers falsely represented themselves as FBI agents during the incident.[46] Though Alameda sheriffs made the arrest, OPD Internal Affairs showed up and took possession of Richholt and Neely's car. Both officers resigned rather than face interviews and punishment.

In February 2003 Neely and Richholt pleaded guilty to one count of agreeing to engage in prostitution, receiving one day in jail and three years of probation. Their case file was destroyed in 2015, erasing much of the public record of their actions.[47]

Around the same time, another Oakland cop serially molested immigrant Asian women during traffic stops. Richard Valerga was part of an East Oakland squad supervised by Sean Whent, then a patrol sergeant. Whent thought Valerga was "lazy," and had heard a credible story that the portly middle-aged officer had once fallen asleep in his squad car with a suspect cuffed in the back seat. "Just really egregious, really poor performance," Whent said in a deposition about his officer. Whent made Valerga partner up with a hardworking cop to keep him busy, but at a certain point in 2005 Valerga broke away again on his own.[48]

Without a partner and unsupervised, Valerga began preying on Asian women. He pulled dozens of women over, often with no justification, made them sit in his patrol car against their will while he took photos of them, ordered them to show their breasts, groped them, and made some women kiss and caress him. The IAD case dead-ended when Valerga refused to be interviewed and quit. There was no effort to track down other possible victims. In November 2005 the disgraced ex-cop pleaded guilty to four misdemeanors, part of a plea deal drafted by Deputy DA Mark McCannon, who agreed that he would not actively seek any other victims.[49] Valerga was sentenced to 180 days in jail and three years of probation.

Valerga's conduct was so egregious that investigators in his own department thought he should be punished to the full extent of the law. Sergeant James Rullamas, who helped investigate Valerga's sexual misconduct, said in a 2007 court deposition that Valerga received "lenient" treatment.

"My opinion was, and still is, is that Valerga should have gone to prison," Rullamas said during the deposition.[50]

Other Oakland cops had substantial ties with organized crime figures who ran the massage parlors and nightclubs where the higher end of the sex trade was conducted. In 2012 TV station KTVU filmed Oakland Police Sergeant Warren Young and Officer Barry Ko making repeated visits to a Chinatown karaoke bar that doubled as a brothel.[51] Sergeant Young's conduct would surface years later during a labyrinthine federal case against leading underworld figures in San Francisco's Chinatown.

In 2013 Oakland resident and Triad member Wing Wo Ma was indicted on murder charges for killing a married couple in Mendocino County. While Ma's trial and related prosecutions (including that of telegenic San Francisco Triad leader Raymond "Shrimp Boy" Chow) were under way, in 2018 the feds indicted and flipped Harry Hu, the OPD's longtime expert on Asian gangs who'd worked as a DA inspector after retiring in 2007. Hu regularly took bribes from Ma and kept him out of trouble with law enforcement while also using him as an informant. In 2002 Hu wrote a letter to an immigration judge that helped Ma avoid deportation on pimping charges in Marin County.

When Hu turned state's evidence, he implicated Warren Young. Both Hu and Young had accepted free trips to Las Vegas, hotel rooms, and the "company of hostesses" from the Triad.[52]

———————

In May 2016 news broke that the department was investigating several officers who'd raped a minor, and that it was all tied to a cop's suicide. The code of silence crumbled as people inside and close to the OPD began leaking to the press. Over the next few weeks, the lurid saga surfaced in a torrent of media reports. O'Brien was identified, and his wife's suspicious death exposed. The sprawling scope of the sex crimes allegations across several departments dominated newspaper headlines and news broadcasts, prompting questions about why OPD administrators had done so little to investigate the case the prior year. Details of Jasmine's exploitation sparked angry protests outside OPD headquarters. One young man driving by leaned out the window and screamed, "They abuse kids!"[53]

All of this piled on top of other black eyes for the police, including high-profile incidents of young officers committing assaults, drunk driving, and other crimes and misconduct unrelated to the sex trafficking case. One caper involved rookie officer Cullen Faeth and his sergeant, Joe Turner, who got drunk at a Montclair bar and then violently barged their way into a home where they thought an OPD party was under way. It was the wrong house. Faeth ended up tackling a female probation officer who was wearing only a bathrobe, and wrestling her husband in an alcohol-induced frenzy. Another young officer, Matthew Santos, pulled a gun on a painter in his apartment building while off duty. The spree of misbehavior prompted Whent to ask the organization's inspector general to conduct an audit to see "if there were things we missed in the backgrounds or things that [OPD's] early intervention system should have caught."[54]

Nothing—not the Riders scandal, the Mixon raid, Occupy, or even seminal events such as OPD's lethal war with the Panthers—proved as explosive and damaging to the Oakland Police Department as the Celeste Guap sex scandal.

Behind the scenes, Lieutenant Alan Yu of the IAD ran the revived investigation. New interviews with Abuslin, treating her this time as a victim, and patiently working to build trust and obtain data from her cell phone, plus new interviews with subject officers resulted in the identification of twelve Oakland cops who exploited her or failed to report signs of the abuse. In May, Terryl Smith and James Ta'ai—the two officers whom there was the most evidence against—resigned rather than face certain termination.

As the scandal mushroomed, Warshaw's confidence in Whent disintegrated. The department's secrecy was inexcusable in the monitor's eyes, and Whent's characteristic punctiliousness had been replaced with an unusual urgency to close both the Internal Affairs and criminal probes. According to Abuslin, she also communicated over Facebook with Whent's wife, Julie, telling her about her relationships with OPD officers.[55] The department also tried to bury the case so that Mayor Schaaf and her city administrator, Sabrina Landreth, didn't know about it until May 2016.

In the face of almost certain termination, Whent resigned June 9 in a late-night email to City Administrator Landreth and Mayor Schaaf.

"Over the last three years, we have made significant progress at reducing crime," the outgoing chief wrote. "Additionally, we have also made vast progress at reforming the Department."

Whent cited a 40 percent decline in homicides and shootings over his tenure and a "significant decrease in complaints against officers," as two data points defining his leadership. "While we are not always perfect, our officers work very hard and risk everything in service of our community."[56]

The following week, the OPD was humiliated as the interim chief appointed by Schaaf the day after Whent's departure, former captain Benson Fairow, resigned abruptly after rumors circulated about his own alleged sexual misconduct from years past. The next chief, Paul Figueroa, resigned and took a voluntary demotion to captain in order to avoid the hot seat.

Similar to what happened during the explosive Chauncey Bailey murder case, the sex scandal caused an opening of the floodgates holding back OPD secrets. Years of internal feuds, rivalries, bad blood, and papered-over problems such as the influx of subpar recruits during the force's 2013 hiring spree spilled out into the public. The OPD and Schaaf's administration attempted to circle the wagons, opening leak investigations to ferret out reporters' sources, and even shutting out the documentary film crew they'd brought in for a laudatory account about police "reforms."[57]

With no one seemingly willing to take the job, Landreth stepped in to become interim chief in addition to city administrator.

The chaotic case flared again in August after Abuslin was sent to a Florida drug rehab center by the Richmond Police Department and Contra Costa district attorney. She left the facility and was arrested for allegedly assaulting a guard. The realization that an agency where several high-ranking officers had abused the girl was responsible for sending her—the percipient witness—out of state during an active criminal investigation against dozens of Bay Area cops caused an uproar. Local civil rights attorney Pamela Price and others demanded that California attorney general Kamala Harris or the US attorney for Northern California step in. But neither the feds nor California's top law enforcement official intervened—for Harris, a repeat of her 2012 refusal to help Oakland investigate hundreds of brutality allegations during Occupy.

A month later, Oakland announced its IAD case was finished. Twelve officers would be disciplined, including four terminations. District Attorney Nancy O'Malley announced around the same time her decision to prosecute officers from other agencies who'd also abused Abuslin, including Contra Costa sheriff's deputy Ricardo Perez for engaging in oral copulation with a minor and a lewd act in a public place, and Livermore police officer Dan Black for lewd acts and prostitution.

Five Oakland cops also faced criminal charges, including Giovanni LoVerde for oral copulation with a minor, Terryl Smith and Warit Uttapa for wrongful use of a sensitive police database, Brian Bunton for obstruction of justice and prostitution, and Leroy Johnson for failing to report Abuslin's original statement to him the year before that police had abused her. District Attorney inspector Ricardo Orozco, who served for twenty-eight years as an Oakland cop, also allegedly attempted to solicit Jasmine. After his name appeared in the *East Bay Express*, O'Malley swiftly fired him.[58] Orozco's last OPD assignment was commanding an East Oakland patrol sector that, according to a 2014 OPD report on sex trafficking, had the "highest concentration of younger prostitutes 'working the streets' along with online dates at motels." Orozco had led a letter-writing campaign to shame "johns" who solicited sex workers in Oakland. The criminal cases against Giovanni LoVerde, Warit Utappa, and Justin Bunton were all dismissed by the Alameda County district attorney. Orozco was never charged. Both Terryl Smith and Leroy Johnson plead guilty to their charges, with Smith receiving a deal that kept a criminal conviction off his record, while Johnson was placed on three years' probation.

For the Oakland PD, the lessons of the Celeste Guap case emerged a year later when Edward Swanson filed his report with Judge Henderson. Swanson, who clerked for Henderson and went on to become a top defense attorney, was a trusted and brilliant mind that Henderson drew on over the years to investigate complex problems.

Swanson and his colleague Audrey Barron wrote in their report that the initial investigations into the sexual exploitation scandal were "seriously deficient" and remained so even after more potentially criminal conduct surfaced. "If not for the court's intervention, we have no confidence that correct discipline would have ever been imposed, criminal charges filed, or departmental shortcomings examined."[59]

They excoriated the police's treatment of Abuslin as a nonvictim. "She was a challenging witness in many of the early interviews," they wrote. "But she was a young woman who was alleged to have had repeated sexual contact with law enforcement officers—officers who took advantage of her age and vulnerability. Given the allegation that she had been sexually exploited by OPD officers, OPD owed her at least the same patience, concern, and investigative attention that they afford other victims."

Because Abuslin was a sex worker, initiated contact with many of the officers who exploited her, and used drugs, the police department treated her as unworthy of justice. "Put simply, CID and IAD wrote off this victim," the attorneys explained.

The mind-set that Abuslin wasn't important enough to warrant a vigor-ous investigation was signaled from the top of the department. Swanson and Barron found that "Chief Whent sent an unmistakable signal that this case was not a priority" and "did nothing to ensure the allegations were being investigated appropriately.[60]

"Had OPD conducted a rigorous investigation on its own, the depart-ment could have demonstrated its ability to police itself without the court's supervision," they concluded. "Instead, OPD damaged its reputation by fail-ing to timely report the allegations to the appropriate authorities, by doing such a poor job of investigating the allegations, and by requiring Court in-tervention to correct course."

Abuslin made it back to California with the help of Pamela Price, but the teenager's life was now a nonstop media circus. Horrified by a kind of attention she never wanted, and asked by the DA to testify at the trials of seven police officers, she attempted to assist the prosecution at first, but found herself vomiting on the stand and seeking solitude. From every side now—law enforcement, the media, attorneys hoping to represent her civil lawsuits, and avaricious charlatan men wanting to become her Hollywood "agent"—Jasmine Abuslin was used again and again for every purpose ex-cept one she could determine for herself.

14

BACKSLIDING

Libby Schaaf was almost certainly going to pick a woman—and an outsider—to run the Oakland Police Department after 2016's catastrophic summer. The sexual exploitation scandal's most obvious lesson was that Oakland needed to root out what Schaaf called a "toxic macho culture" among its cops. As the mayor framed it, the city needed a chief who could run a police department, not a "frat house."[1] The scandal made it impossible to promote any of the current OPD deputy chiefs or captains (including the handful of women in these jobs) to run the department. All the command staff were essentially complicit in the neglect and mishandling of the Celeste Guap case. Others had skeletons in their closet that disgruntled colleagues were willing to divulge to the press should they be elevated.

The rapid exit of Sean Whent, Ben Fairow, and Paul Figueroa from the top job within a week in June 2016 showed just how much of a poisoned chalice the post had become. Accordingly, Oakland hired a recruiting firm to scour the nation in search of the right candidate. In early 2017 Schaaf announced she had found just the person to take command of OPD at arguably its lowest point in history.

Anne Kirkpatrick was a complete outsider. The Memphis native began her career in 1982 as a patrol officer in her hometown before moving to Redmond, Washington, where as a sergeant, she defied police culture and gender stereotypes by joining the tactical team and becoming an assistant commander for the state's law enforcement academy. In the Pacific Northwest, her career took off. Kirkpatrick earned a law degree and served as chief for the towns of Ellensburg and Federal Way before rising to the top job in Spokane.

But Kirkpatrick long had her eye on becoming a big-city chief. She'd been a finalist for the Seattle job in 2010, and she reached another shortlist for the job in Phoenix in 2012.[2] In 2016 she applied for the post of Chicago police superintendent. Her application indicated a willingness not just to go big, but to also rise to one of the biggest challenges confronting the policing profession.

At the time, Chicago mayor Rahm Emanuel had just fired his hand-picked chief, Garry McCarthy. An ex-NYPD believer in aggressive tactics like stop-and-frisk, McCarthy was axed in the wake of the release of the Laquan McDonald video and widespread anger that city leaders had tried to keep the explosive footage secret. The video showed officer Jason Van Dyke firing sixteen times at the seventeen-year-old McDonald, who was spinning around and walking away from police. McDonald's murder was Chicago's Oscar Grant moment.

Although the Windy City didn't erupt in Baltimore-style riots after the McDonald video was released, it would see widespread protests and a significant rise in shootings and homicides over the coming years as police-community relations disintegrated.[3]

Anyone who wanted to run the Chicago Police Department had to be a believer in reform. A mayor's task force was already advocating for measures like implicit bias trainings to reduce racial profiling, a civilian body to investigate police misconduct instead of Internal Affairs, body cameras for all officers, and other policies opposed by the local police union. The feds were also intervening, which resulted in a consent decree in 2019.

In true Chicago style, Emanuel picked a department veteran, Eddie Johnson, to run the CPD. But Johnson turned around and recruited Kirkpatrick to join his command staff. She would lead the Bureau of Professional Standards, which was in charge of making sure the post–Laquan McDonald reforms were implemented.

Kirkpatrick was there barely six months before packing her bags for Oakland. Although not a big city, Oakland has always been a big stage in the policing world, presenting all the same kinds of challenges as Los Angeles or New York. Oakland and Chicago had similarities: since the 1960s, the Chicago police waged campaigns of wanton violence against Black residents and political dissidents, starting with the department's televised riot at the 1968 Democratic National Convention—comparable to the draft protest crackdowns in Oakland the year before.[4] In the 1970s and 1980s, a CPD squad known as the "Midnight Crew," led by Detective Commander Jon Burge, terrorized the South Side, kidnapping and torturing more than a hundred Black people.[5] In the early 2000s Chicago cops such as Ronald Watts engaged in Riders-like behavior by planting drugs on numerous suspects, sending some to prison.[6] At her swearing-in ceremony on February 27, 2017, Kirkpatrick said she came to Oakland for the "opportunity" it presented.[7]

"I want to be a part of the team that makes the Oakland Police Department one of the most respected police departments in the nation," she told press and city officials crowded into a conference room. "I have already been a leader of reform, but I want to be a leader of an agency that wants to be transformed. Oakland meets that profile."

Kirkpatrick styled herself as more than a technocrat who would implement new policies and push the needle on various metrics. "I am more interested in transformation," she told reporters. "It's transformation I have a real heart for. Reform is part of transformation."[8]

Despite her flowery language, it became apparent that Kirkpatrick didn't understand the Oakland PD was under an external mandate for change, and its internal culture—laid bare for the country to see by the sexual exploitation scandal—was remarkably intransigent. During her first press conference, Kirkpatrick told local reporters she was not yet intimately familiar with Oakland's court-ordered reforms and hadn't read the Negotiated Settlement Agreement. The admission raised eyebrows: like her predecessors, Kirkpatrick would have to answer to Judge Thelton Henderson and the independent monitor Robert Warshaw while being watchdogged by Chanin and Burris. If she couldn't make progress on the NSA's fifty-two tasks, she wouldn't last. And if Kirkpatrick hadn't even *read* the NSA, she likely hadn't arrived in Oakland with a reform strategy in mind.

"She doesn't have a lot of experience in making reforms," Burris said upon Kirkpatrick's hiring, questioning whether Oakland could've found a police executive who'd successfully navigated a consent decree.[9]

Kirkpatrick did show an understanding of what was working in Oakland on the crime fighting front. Like Whent and Jordan, she gave the Ceasefire Unit leeway, funding, and personnel, reinforcing the department's focus on violent crime. Murders dipped by 9 percent and shootings by 16 percent her first year on the job.

Her policing philosophy was in line with how Whent had reorganized and trained the department. Kirkpatrick felt that "intelligence-led" stops—disallowing pretextual stops and requiring officers to have an articulable reason someone was directly connected to a crime before searching them—struck the best balance between catching shooters and avoiding the kinds of Terry stops that led to bitter feelings in the community. She approved changing the department's stop-and-search policies so that officers would be less likely to engage in pretextual stops in order to ask Black and Latino people whether they were on probation or parole. Although street cops swear by the effectiveness of probation and parole searches—a person "on paper" must truthfully reveal this when an officer asks, and officers may warrantlessly search those who are "on paper"—the question has always been a source of resentment.[10] Many activists say it reinforces an unwillingness among many to ever cooperate with the police.

Kirkpatrick also pledged to ensure the police discipline system was proactive. She was "unafraid" to impose discipline when officers crossed the line, she said. Why believe her? Kirkpatrick pointed to her most recent job in Chicago leading reform efforts, but said her time in charge of the Spokane police showed she was willing to fire bad cops.

Her first big move as chief proved highly controversial. In May, she announced her first set of promotions. That list included Roland Holmgren, rising from lieutenant to captain, and John Lois, who would become an assistant chief. Kirkpatrick also decided to move Kirk Coleman from his post as the captain running the Criminal Investigation Division over to the Internal Affairs Division. Jason Anderson, the homicide investigator who, along with Bradley Baker, conducted the first calamitous interview with Abuslin and blamed her for O'Brien's death, was also slated to receive a Silver Star Medal for courageous action.[11]

The meaning of these promotions and awards wasn't immediately clear. At that juncture, many details and scads of records from the sexual exploitation scandal were still not public. But when Edward Swanson and Audrey Barron's report on the police's mishandling of the Celeste Guap case became public the next month, Holmgren, Anderson, Lois, and Coleman's roles were revealed, leading many to question whether these officers should be in positions that allowed them to run much of the department.

On a cloudless Friday morning in July, protesters holding signs reading "Chief and Mayor promote 'good ole boys,'" "fire rapists," and "prosecution not promotion" stood at the entrance to Oakland's Ascension Greek Orthodox Cathedral in the hills, where the OPD was holding the promotion ceremony. The event, open to the public in previous years, had been turned into a private gathering for officers, their families, and city officials. Members of the press were corralled far from the auditorium entrance, where it was difficult to take photos of attendees and impossible to interview anyone. Previously, reporters and photographers were given free access to promoted officers either in the auditorium at the Police Administrative Building or the Scottish Rite Center by Lake Merritt. The change of venue to a hard-to-reach location, and the exclusion of the press, was interpreted by many as the OPD's closing itself off from unwanted attention. Officers arrived in small groups, strutting to the reception in their dress uniforms. Kirkpatrick shook hands with street cops and police union leaders in the parking lot. During the ceremony, Schaaf told the department that she knew what it was like to be under scrutiny, but that she supported them.[12]

"She's not interested in ending the good old boys' network," protester and attorney James Burch said about Kirkpatrick outside the church. "She's interested in business as usual, and that's what they're doing here, and it's been given the co-sign by Libby Schaaf."[13]

"They seem to be resisting change," said Gwen Hardy, a longtime member of PUEBLO who'd been involved in police accountability efforts in Oakland since the 1980s. Hardy and other members of the Coalition for Police Accountability had met with Kirkpatrick shortly after she was hired. The new chief swore she wasn't afraid to discipline officers. "But why promote them?" Hardy wondered about the brass who'd covered up the sexual exploitation scandal.

The reason for the promotions has remained something of a mystery ever since. Holding to his long-standing practice, Warshaw refused to speak to the press about the sex exploitation scandal and the promotions. The closest anyone got to a straight answer was days before the ceremony when Kirkpatrick, Schaaf, and other high-ranking city officials appeared before Judge Henderson for a status conference about the Negotiated Settlement Agreement. In court, Chanin and Burris questioned the wisdom of rewarding commanders who helped bury the sex trafficking case in 2015 before Henderson got wind of the matter. "I was under the illusion that the sex scandal was largely confined to the officers who committed unlawful acts and Chief Whent," Chanin told the court. Following the hearing, Burris told reporters that if commanders didn't take responsibility, "it will send a bad message, and young officers will not have confidence in the leadership."

But outside the courthouse, following the hearing, Kirkpatrick told reporters she'd consulted with Warshaw about the promotions and that the monitor blessed them prior to the promotion list's release on May 2. She called her commanders "men of honor" and rebuffed further questions.[14]

Judge Henderson ordered no sanctions of any kind for the sex scandal, or the promotions. Instead, he showed a willingness to give the new chief—Oakland's ninth since court oversight began in 2003—the benefit of the doubt. But that chance depended on Kirkpatrick immediately implementing the Swanson report's recommendations and pushing ahead with the NSA. Henderson made his feelings clear: he'd given Oakland too many second chances over the previous fourteen years.

In 2015 the Oakland police appeared to be on their way to completing the NSA, said Henderson, until they severely mishandled the now well-publicized allegations of officers' sexual misconduct.

"It's crystal clear to me that those allegations would not have been appropriately investigated were it not for the court's intervention, nor would the need for any procedural or structural changes have been identified but for the court's intervention," the judge said.[15]

Would Kirkpatrick be the chief who could finish the NSA and address the structural changes identified by Swanson and Barron in their dissection of the Celeste Guap case? Would she remake the OPD into a "learning organization" that drove its own progressive path without relying on external oversight?

Perhaps. But either way, Henderson let it be known that he wouldn't be the judge to see the department across the finish line. Sitting in court that day was Judge William Orrick III, who would take over the case in August when Henderson retired. Oakland's inability to reform its police force was so severe, the case had outlasted one of America's most legendary legal minds with decades of experience overseeing complex consent decrees.

In his final formal remarks about the case, Henderson described briefly some of the main obstacles between Kirkpatrick and success. "We're still talking about the way Internal Affairs investigations are conducted, and the city is still having issues with its risk management system," he said, referring to the police force's broken accountability process nearly fifteen years after court intervention began.

Kirkpatrick's message to the court was simple. She'd already met with Swanson, Warshaw, Chanin, and Burris, convened her leadership team, and ordered implementation of the fixes that would make a repeat of the sex trafficking scandal less likely. Kirkpatrick told Henderson she took the job knowing full well it would be a monumental challenge. If she failed, she invited the court and others to hold her fully accountable.

"What does it mean to be accountable?" Kirkpatrick said in her closing statement to the outgoing judge with the mayor and press seated behind her. "It means that I will answer to my decisions and my actions, and where there is a failing, I will own it."

———

In addition to the mayor, city administrator, judge, and independent monitor, Kirkpatrick had one other boss to whom she would be accountable. As city leaders and even Judge Henderson started talking in late 2015 about the light at the end of the NSA tunnel, Rashidah Grinage and other members of the Coalition for Police Accountability, the group that had grown out of PUEBLO, put their heads together and crafted what they felt would be a permanent means of external oversight strong enough to prevent another Riders-type scandal: a powerful, independent police commission.

Shortly before the sex trafficking scandal erupted in mid-2016, the Coalition for Police Accountability allied with Dan Kalb, a progressive councilman and policy wonk representing North Oakland, and Noel Gallo, a centrist councilman from Fruitvale with an unpredictably radical streak, to push through the police commission plan.

Coalition leader Rashidah Grinage had long thought that a police commission was necessary. After the death of her son, husband, and OPD officer William Grijalva in the early 1990s, Grinage's quest to find out what happened constantly ran up against departmental secrecy. The successful PUEBLO campaigns she was a part of to strengthen Oakland's Civilians' Police Review Board in the mid-1990s pulled back the curtain on police misconduct for a brief moment, but police unions, including the OPOA, fought oversight boards up and down the state and won favorable court rulings by the mid-2000s that killed what modicum of transparency existed. And up until 2016, Oakland's mayors and city council refused to create something more potent than the CPRB, which could only investigate complaints of misconduct and recommend discipline to the city administrator—all in secret.

Kalb and Gallo agreed to shepherd the creation of the new commission, one that in Kalb's words would have "real teeth." It would be made up of Oakland residents, none of whom could be current or retired police officers. Commissioners would be selected by an independent panel of people appointed mostly by the council members—not the mayor.

Kalb said Oakland's commission would borrow the best ideas other cities had devised to clean up their police forces. One idea borrowed from Los Angeles's post–Rodney King reforms was to create an inspector general who would work under the commission's guidance as the OPD's permanent watchdog. They would have the power to audit the department and recommend policy changes to the city council for ratification.

Kalb and Gallo's community-driven plan also called for abolishing the Citizens' Police Review Board and creating an investigative arm of the new police commission called the Community Police Review Agency. Pronounced "Sip-Rah," the CPRA would have more staff and power than the previous CPRB and would be required to investigate use-of-force complaints, in-custody deaths, racial profiling or any other kind of discrimination, and all complaints regarding the department's treatment of protesters. The new entity would also have latitude to investigate other kinds of complaints, if it chose to do so. In these ways, the design of the commission and CPRA seemed to incorporate lessons learned from past scandals, from Occupy and the Port riot to the spate of officer-involved shootings in the mid-2000s, to the killing of Amaro, Warrantgate, and beyond.

Crucially, the new commission removed the city administrator from police misconduct decisions. The final say on punishing a rule-breaking officer had always been the administrator's to make, subject of course to arbitration if the officer and police union wanted to appeal a case. Over the decades, this structure preserved mayoral control over the police department and insulated it from accountability-minded council members. The new police commission would create a more complex discipline system, but one that was less favorable for officers. The commission's CPRA team would investigate the same misconduct complaints as the OPD's Internal

Affairs team, and if CPRA and IAD concurred, then that finding would be final and imposed by the police chief. But where the commission's investigators disagreed with the OPD's, the case would head to a panel of three police commissioners who would have final say.

Other powers of the new commission were game changers. For example, the commissioners would be able to fire the police chief on their own, without consent of the mayor or city administrator, if they identified specific causes warranting termination. This meant that the chief now worked for the commission as much as they did at the behest of the mayor.

But this strong civilian oversight commission almost didn't come to pass. In May 2016, before the full horrifying scope of the sex trafficking scandal emerged, three council members elected with the OPOA's financial backing offered a defanged alternative. Larry Reid, Annie Campbell Washington, and Abel Guillen called for the creation of a weaker police commission and "independent monitor" to oversee the force. The mayor would have much more authority selecting the monitor and commissioners and the commission's powers would be limited: it would not, for example, have the power to fire the chief.[16] The sex trafficking scandal's revelations torpedoed this milder version of the police commission. No council member wanted to be cast in the role as an apologist for a department rife with apparent sex offenders.

That November, voters resoundingly approved the Kalb-Gallo strong police commission ballot measure by a vote of 83 percent in favor.

––––––––

Kirkpatrick didn't have to immediately contend with the police commission. It wasn't until December 2017, almost a year into her tenure, when the commission finally met for the first time. Its inaugural year was a clumsy comedy of errors as the short-staffed commission struggled to hire employees and train its members. The commission was also hamstrung by infighting, confusion over its authority, city council delays passing other legislation it needed to move ahead, and clashes with City Administrator Sabrina Landreth over its authority.[17]

But broader forces at work were shifting the terrain of policing. The conversations in Oakland after Oscar Grant's death and the Occupy crackdown had been elevated by 2014 onto the national stage by Black Lives Matter. California's new Democratic supermajority in Sacramento advanced a sweeping legislative agenda to shift the Golden State away from its hard-edged criminal justice system. Starting in 2015, state lawmakers such as Shirley Weber, a Black assemblywoman born to Arkansas sharecroppers and representing an overpoliced, majority-Black area of San Diego, authored a bill that explicitly outlawed racial profiling by law enforcement and created a state board to collect and analyze police stop data and complaints from all California law enforcement agencies. Signed into law in October, it laid the foundation for research that would unequivocally prove racial profiling was a widespread problem in the state.

Weber and other lawmakers hoping to push the envelope weren't seeing the kinds of pro-police opposition that devastated the careers of politicians in prior years. In 2007 and 2008 State Senator Gloria Romero introduced a bill attempting to open up police misconduct hearings after the *Copley Press* ruling. She described the reaction of police unions as "like wolves coming at you," and said, "You're basically like meat thrown to the lions." By 2015, the police unions, although still potent, were on their heels.

In early 2016 Attorney General Kamala Harris opened civil rights investigations into the Kern County Sheriff's Office and Bakersfield Police Department following reports showing the two agencies had killed more people per capita than any others in the country.[18] It was the first time the state DOJ had used this power since Jerry Brown's foray into police reform seven years earlier, when the department sued the Maywood Police Department.

Years of activism and reporting on CalGang, the state's sprawling, secretive gang database containing the names of more than two hundred thousand Californians—90 percent of them Black or Latino—led to bills establishing procedures for getting notified and removed, and regular audits.[19] Over time, CalGang's use declined under scrutiny from the legislature and scandals about false inclusions by promotion-seeking LAPD gang cops.[20] Court decisions would also spell an end to gang injunctions as judges took a more critical view of how they violated people's civil rights.[21]

In 2017, state lawmakers approved a bill requiring police to allow the public to view footage of critical incidents, including police shootings, after forty-five days, with few exceptions.

Then, in 2018, twenty-two-year-old Stephon Clark was shot and killed in the backyard of his grandmother's Sacramento home. The shooting in California's capital rekindled the legislature's willingness to take on police reform. A bill introduced in the State Senate the month before, SB 1421, broke through the logjam of police lobbying and was signed into law later that year. Written by State Senator Nancy Skinner of Berkeley, SB 1421 required police departments to make public records of police shootings, uses of force resulting in great bodily injury, and cases where an officer lied or engaged in sexual misconduct.

The election of Donald Trump, and his anti-immigrant rhetoric, also galvanized California to push back on hard-line deportation policies begun under Barack Obama, whose administration deported more undocumented migrants than any other presidency before or since. Starting in 2014 the state legislature passed laws reversing the decades-long status quo in which local law enforcement worked hand in glove with immigration agents. The ability for sheriffs and police departments who ran jails to hold undocumented people on "detainers" so that Immigration and Customs Enforcement could pick them up for deportation was restricted. Eventually most forms of communication between local police and federal immigration agents would be outlawed.

With over a quarter of its population foreign-born, Oakland made a hard U-turn. It ditched a 2016 cooperation agreement between its police and ICE signed by Sean Whent on his last day in office, reaffirming its status as a "sanctuary" city in mid-2017. The changes were a long time coming. Although Oakland declared itself a "city of refuge" in 1986 with the intent of shielding immigrants from Haiti, South Africa, Guatemala, and El Salvador from deportation, its city jail was used to house undocumented detainees until it was closed in the mid-2000s.[22] Oakland's new policy under Trump was to protect all immigrants, not just those from war-torn regions.

In August 2017 Kirkpatrick put her foot on this third rail by ordering several officers to close off a West Oakland street to help ICE agents raid a family's home and arrest two men. The OPD issued a statement afterward claiming ICE was pursuing suspects who were "sex trafficking juveniles." Kirkpatrick said later that her department hadn't violated Oakland's sanctuary policies because the officers were assisting in a criminal "human trafficking" case, and she claimed one person had been charged with a "crime."

In truth, the case had nothing to do with underage sex trafficking, and no one had been charged with a crime. Instead, one of the detained men was charged with a civil violation for being unlawfully present in the United States. He was sent before an immigration judge for possible deportation.

The uproar was instantaneous. Kirkpatrick and the OPD assisted ICE at exactly the same time the city's civilian leaders ordered an end to those kinds of operations. Still, the chief was unrepentant, making false statements about the ICE operation and insisting that her officers did nothing wrong.[23]

Then in January 2018 an internal OPD audit showed that the department had wrongfully denied U visas to about one in six applicants during Kirkpatrick's first year on the job. Intended to help people recover from crimes and participate in prosecutions to make communities safer, the U visa program gave undocumented people a path to legal status if they assisted the police in an investigation. There had been a sudden uptick in denials by the OPD. The department's inspector general studied the problem, identifying a systemic failure to process applications.

The finding might have been a positive had the Oakland PD discovered the problem entirely on its own, but the Alameda County Public Defender's Office first flagged the issue.[24] At a time when Oakland's residents very vocally pushed back against Trump's hard-line immigration policies, the police chief's actions ran counter to the city's electorate.

———————

As bumpy as Kirkpatrick's first year on the job was, at least the NSA appeared to be on track. When she was sworn in in February, the chief promised to transform OPD culture. She established a "Department Culture Working Group" in which senior officers met regularly with her for "facilitated discussions to provide input and guidance to the Chief on issues related to communication, effective supervision and the consistency of discipline through the ranks," and "the tenets and values of Procedural Justice within the workplace."[25] Chanin and Burris were impressed by this, writing to Judge Orrick in a report: "We see significant recognition that what is involved here is more than checking off unfinished tasks and going back to business as usual. It is instead the complete cultural transformation of the Oakland Police Department into an organization that has the trust and support of the community and whose members are proud to be part of a dynamic and responsive law enforcement agency."[26]

But checking the boxes remained necessary, too. Three of the fifty-two tasks in the agreement still needed to be completed.

One of them required the department to show that it could properly accept and investigate Internal Affairs complaints. This was the task Warshaw

and Henderson found the OPD out of compliance with the year before because of the way officers treated Jasmine Abuslin, and because of command
staff's willingness to bury the sex exploitation case.

The second unfinished task required the department to show it could
apply discipline consistently and fairly to all officers, without fear or favor.
Sean Whent had made great progress in this area, but the situation was
beyond his control. By 2014, Warshaw recommended that Henderson
also find this task out of compliance. The reason had to do with cops like
Rob Roche. Although OPD brass had recommended terminating Roche
for throwing the flash-bang grenade into the group of people aiding Scott
Olsen during the Occupy protests in 2011, the officer, with help from the
Oakland Police Officers' Association, fought the decision. In 2014 an arbitrator reinstated him.

Part of the failure to fire Roche or hand down a ten-day suspension for
an act of obvious brutality was a result of the thin cases assembled by IAD
sergeants through lazy and uncritical interviews or lack of follow-through
to document evidence and confront officers on inconsistencies. Another
shortcoming was the OPD's Skelly officers. In some cases, these supervisors
softened discipline before handing the decision off to the chief. But many
cases were also wrecked by deputy city attorneys who went into arbitration
hearings unprepared, or because the city administrator chose leniency in
order to maintain morale at the police department. Whent hadn't cleaned
up IAD or straightened out the Skelly process, and the city attorney's office
was only beginning to finally get serious with its police misconduct case-
loads (after being publicly raked over the coals by Judge Henderson) by the
time Kirkpatrick arrived.

The final unfinished task Kirkpatrick inherited was arguably the most
complex. Task 34 involved the creation of a system to track vehicle stops,
searches, field investigations, and detentions—the meat-and-potatoes work
of being a patrol officer—and then process this data so commanders could
identify and intervene with problem officers.

Warshaw wrote in his monthly reports through the end of 2017 that the
department was making slow but steady progress with Task 34. The department was successfully working with technology vendors and a team of
researchers from Stanford University led by Professor Jennifer Eberhardt to
collect and analyze huge quantities of stop data. Soon the OPD's "PRIME"
system, a custom-built software suite that could flag risky behavior by of-

ficers by crunching reports about vehicle pursuits, handcuffing, gun and Taser use, dog bites, complaints, and much more, would be operational. PRIME would supply the raw material for the department's weekly risk management meetings in which commanders would review high-level statistics and drill down on specific squads and officers, probing for answers to anomalous data points, questioning sergeants about recent activities, all geared toward preventing the next Riders scandal and constantly improving policing performance. PRIME was the latest iteration of the OPD's attempts to digitize officer behavior and identify reckless, dangerous, or illegal behavior before grievous consequences ensued. Almost a half century after Chief Charles Gain and his successor, George Hart, pioneered a computerized tracking system for officer conduct, by crunching the data with punch cards rather than twenty-first-century microchips, Oakland was just getting level with where the police department was in the analog age.

Led by Eberhardt's team, the department participated in stop data studies and became one of the first agencies in the nation to openly acknowledge the glaring racial disparities in police work. As of 2017, Black people made up 57 percent of all stops by Oakland cops, even though they accounted for just about a quarter of the city's population. When the percentage of stops yielding the discovery of a crime was analyzed, the injustice of this disparate treatment became obvious. Although one in four Black people stopped by OPD officers were searched, only 10 percent possessed a gun, drugs, or other contraband. White people were found with firearms and narcotics 15 percent of the time, and Latinos at a rate of 25 percent. The obvious conclusion was that Oakland cops were stopping too many Black people for no good reason.

If Kirkpatrick could keep the department moving forward, it might emerge from the consent decree in a couple years. In her first year, the work appeared to be on track, and the chief's policy pronouncements around shifting toward an intelligence-led strategy seemed in line with these changes.

But it soon became apparent that the momentum was inherited. Toward the end of her first year, Warshaw began warning that even with respect to the NSA tasks where the OPD had been performing well, like stop data collection and analysis, "the road forward with this project has not been easy and it is likely that at least some additional, potentially serious, potholes lay ahead."[27]

And there was another side to Kirkpatrick that would lead to her undoing. For those demanding greater police accountability, the new chief lacked the one trait that had made Sean Whent successful up until the sex trafficking scandal: the will to discipline officers, even if it meant falling out of favor with his department.

It was a little after six in the evening on March 11, 2018, when OPD Officer Josef Phillips crept onto the front porch of an abandoned house on Fortieth Street, not far from a busy BART station in heavily gentrified North Oakland. Phillips peered around the corner and spotted a young man. He was lying awkwardly on his side, wearing a backpack, and clutching a small gray pistol in his right hand. Following procedure, Phillips called for backup, relaying that the man appeared to be passed out drunk. Then he retreated to the street and took cover behind his car.

Soon other cops arrived, including Sergeant Francisco Negrete. A Coast Guard veteran of fifteen years, Negrete joined the Oakland PD in 2008 during the Dellums-era hiring spree that built the department to a record high of 837 officers.[28] He worked a port security assignment before becoming a member of the SWAT "Entry Team," and eventually the leader of a Crime Reduction Team. He had a clean discipline record and dealt previously with armed suspects. Several of his squad arrived shortly after, and Negrete took over the immediate tactical job of watching the unconscious man and devising a plan to disarm and arrest him.

As other officers blocked off both ends of the street and set a perimeter, Negrete had Officer Craig Tanaka drive the armored BearCat vehicle to the scene. Behind a patrol car at first, and then shielded by the BearCat's thick layer of bulletproof steel, Negrete huddled with CRT officers William Berger, Brandon Hraiz, and others. The sergeant's plan was that he would give orders to the unconscious man to wake up and surrender. If he didn't immediately comply, another sergeant would shoot the man with a bean-bag round, and Phillips would tase him into submission so they could rush him and cuff him. Hraiz and Berger would provide "lethal cover" with their rifles. If the man raised the gun to shoot, they would kill him.

This flawed plan wouldn't pan out. Shortly after Tanaka arrived with the BearCat, the man began stirring. Hraiz climbed into the BearCat's turret to use the steel-plated perch as a shooting platform. Berger took a position near Negrete, and the sergeant grabbed his own rifle, training it on the semiconscious man. Tanaka leapt out of the BearCat's driver's seat, took cover behind the armored car, and pointed his rifle at the figure, who was now groggily shrugging his shoulders and head, coming out of either an altered state or awaking after being attacked by someone.

"Don't move! Get your hands up!" one officer shouted contradictorily.

The man's body moved ever so slightly again, and another officer yelled, "Get your hand off that gun, young man!"

"That gun moves, bag him," Berger told Phillips, who was wielding a less-lethal shotgun. The waking man gave no indication he knew where he was or that he was surrounded by a virtual police firing squad.

About forty-five seconds after his first disoriented motions, as the officers screamed commands at him, the sleeper pushed himself unsteadily up onto his elbows. Negrete, Berger, Hraiz, and Tanaka unleashed a barrage of deadly rifle fire. Phillips also fired a beanbag at the same time. No one was armed with a Taser.

"Goddammit," one of the officers blurted as rifle smoke wafted past.

The officers were taken away from the scene and ordered not to speak with each other before their interviews with Homicide and IAD.

In the meantime, other officers searched the dead man's body and bag. In the backpack, they found over $100,000 in cash, a large amount of cocaine, and a computer. The OPD soon learned his name: Joshua Pawlik.

Pawlik had lived for years on the streets of San Francisco, one of countless lost souls drawn to the city's accepting counterculture. He'd been offered a healing future by its harm-reduction nonprofits, but also sucked into San Francisco's addictive underworld of street drugs. His only prior run-ins with the law included a couple arrests for drug possession and a protest he organized a few years before after San Francisco cops were accused of beating up homeless youth they caught camping in Golden Gate Park.

Originally from Virginia, the thirty-one-year-old suffered from mental illness. From an early age, he self-medicated with Adderall, a habit that grew into heroin and other drugs in his late teens. His working-class family couldn't afford drug treatment programs, and Pawlik's life spiraled downward for a number of years as his psychological issues intensified into a diagnosed form of schizoaffective disorder. Seeking a fresh start, Pawlik moved to New Mexico, then finally San Francisco. On the West Coast, he made new friends, got treatment, and briefly found housing and a semblance of health, but then fell back into cycles of addiction and homelessness. In the spring of 2018 he went north to work on a marijuana farm. When Pawlik reappeared in the Bay Area, he took a room in a West MacArthur Boulevard hotel in Oakland, one of several low-budget establishments on the strip known for prostitution, drug use, and manufacture.[29] No one knew how he came upon a small fortune in cash and a large amount of drugs, or why he was carrying a pistol.

The exact circumstances leading up to Pawlik's appearance in the Fortieth Street alleyway would never be determined.

TV news aired reports about the shooting the night it happened, but coverage of the case quickly disappeared. Activists declined to take up Pawlik's cause even though the circumstances resembled the 2015 killing of Demouria Hogg and was part of a pattern of police shootings in the Bay Area going back at least as far as the 2000 fatal shooting of Maurice Esters, who was also armed with a gun while asleep, awakened at gunpoint by officers, and killed when he panicked and tried to drive away.

But Pawlik's killing and the police mishandling of the internal investigation, and especially Kirkpatrick's disciplinary decisions, would come roaring back, calling into question the chief's commitment to accountability and true cultural transformation.

There was a telling antecedent to the Pawlik case in Kirkpatrick's past. In 2006 Otto Zehm, a developmentally disabled thirty-six-year-old janitor, walked into a Spokane, Washington, convenience store to buy a snack. He'd just been misidentified as a theft suspect when Officer Karl Thompson spotted him.[30] Thompson charged into the store and caught Zehm in an aisle, where he flailed away with his baton until Zehm fell to the floor. Zehm tried in vain to shield his head from the painful blows raining down. Beaten and bloodied, seven officers crowded around Zehm and tasered and hog-tied him on his stomach, then attached a plastic "non-rebreather" mask to Zehm's face without connecting it to an oxygen supply, effectively cutting off his airflow. Zehm, who had done nothing wrong and was never given a chance to comply before Thompson's assault, managed to utter plaintive and poignant last words: "All I wanted was a Snickers bar."[31] Two days later, he was declared brain-dead in a local hospital, his death formally declared a homicide.[32]

In initial public statements, the Spokane Police Department claimed Zehm was combative, refused orders to drop a plastic bottle of soda, and "lunged" at Thompson. In May, Spokane PD investigators determined its officers didn't commit any crime in Zehm's death, relying partly on Thompson's claims that Zehm attacked him, and that he never struck Zehm in the head.

But after viewing the convenience store video, Zehm's family demanded the police retract the statements blaming him. By July, the pressure campaign forced the local prosecutor to release surveillance footage that showed no "lunge" by Zehm and further undermined the official narrative: another angle showed the only time Zehm used the soda bottle was as a defensive shield while on his back, to block Officer Thompson's baton. The deadly police attack, the department's wagon-circling, and outrageous revelations once video of the killing was made public—all of it played out like a formula. Spokane residents were incensed.

Zehm's death took place six months before Kirkpatrick assumed charge of the Spokane Police Department in September 2006. By October, the FBI informed the new police chief they were investigating Thompson. By March of the next year, as the feds were deep into their case, Kirkpatrick declared her "unequivocal support" for Thompson.

A mentor to many other Spokane officers and extremely popular with the police union, Thompson had actually been on track to become chief before he killed Zehm. Kirkpatrick got the job partly because she pledged to clean up SPD, but she now sided with an officer who'd become the local poster child for police brutality. "I have determined that Officer Karl Thompson acted consistent with the law," Kirkpatrick said.

A federal grand jury indicted Thompson in June 2009 for using excessive force and lying to investigators. He was convicted later that year and sentenced to federal prison. When he was handcuffed and led away by the US Marshals, four dozen Spokane cops present in the courtroom stood in unison and saluted Thompson.[33]

Kirkpatrick had no choice but to admit the killing was wrong, but the immediate reforms instituted were of dubious value. She had her officers trained to identify people undergoing "excited delirium," a pseudoscientific condition that isn't recognized by the medical community but has long been used by police to explain in-custody deaths in a manner that blames the deceased.[34]

Although Kirkpatrick sided with the reactionary Spokane Police Guild and Officer Thompson throughout most of the Zehm case, she eventually tried to restore order by punishing other officers for a spree of violence, drunkenness, and other allegations that further outraged the city of two hundred thousand. But these efforts would run up against the litigious power of the police officers' union and cost the chief dearly.

Having come to Spokane as a fearless reformer of an extremely dysfunctional small-city police force—she famously told officers, "You lie, you die," to impress on them her strict standards—Kirkpatrick's record after seven years wasn't good.[35] She'd failed to oust some of the more troublesome officers and gotten herself and the city sued in the process. And she'd sided with Karl Thompson, whose on-video beating of a vulnerable man did the most damage to police-community relations.

As OPD investigators were reviewing the Pawlik shooting, other serious problems unrelated to the case began to emerge.

The same month Pawlik was killed, OPD inspector general Angelica Mendoza noticed something strange in a key dataset. Mendoza was an Oakland native unpopular with some officers because she followed Sean Whent's best example, acting as a thorn in the side of the department and pushing harder than most for accountability. Her team noticed that during the last week in March 2018, not a single officer reported using force against anyone stopped or arrested. The remarkable week without an officer drawing a gun, striking someone, or using a hold or a Taser seemed at first to be part of a positive trend. Officers were resorting to violence less often. Use-of-force levels had been gliding downward for several years, as reported through the department's PRIME system, and this metric was touted as a measure of progress to both the court monitor and public. But Mendoza decided an audit was in order.

On its face, the data told one story: in 2013, OPD officers reported using force a total of 835 times. This included drawing and firing their guns, spraying someone with pepper spray, or shocking them with a Taser, as well as baton and flashlight strikes, hand strikes, leg sweeps, holds, and hair and body grabs. Force even included drawing and pointing a gun at someone. The last category was the most frequent kind of force used by Oakland cops, and one of the most problematic. Too often, they held someone at gunpoint without good reason. Judge Henderson and War-shaw had repeatedly criticized the police for instances of excessive force in 2011 and 2012, at times pointing to specific instances, including unneces-sary gun pointing.

The OPD promised changes, and by 2014 reported force levels dropped by 27 percent to 611 incidents. This trend continued, and by 2017 there were only 309 instances of force even though arrest numbers remained high. Drawing and pointing guns at people dropped the most: from 2013 to 2017, officers reported 83 percent fewer instances of putting someone's body in their sights. Oakland cops seemed to be learning one of the lessons that helped drive reform in Detroit years earlier.[36]

The inspector general's audit showed otherwise. By examining body camera video and comparing it to officers' written reports, they found that cops were still drawing their guns very frequently but weren't report-ing it as a low-level use of force because they believed they were hold-ing their weapons in a "low-ready" position that didn't require filling out paperwork. According to OPD regulations, "low-ready" meant holding a gun with the barrel pointed down toward the ground, not anywhere over a person's body or extremities. But officers interpreted the term differ-ently; they considered pointing their gun at a person's legs, crotch, and sometimes stomach as a "low-ready" position. The flawed rollout of use-of-force policies and definitions for "low-ready" in recent years had either led to mass confusion and underreporting of gun pointing, or purposeful attempts by some officers and squads to underreport. Most important, the experience in the community hadn't changed; officers still frequently and unnecessarily ordered people under threat of being shot to comply with their orders. While the stats claimed progress, the word on the street was "same old."

Warshaw registered his concerns immediately and dove deeper into the data. By September the monitor's team found multiple instances where of-ficers drew and pointed guns directly at people, used other kinds of force—including strikes, pepper spray and Tasers, and holds—and reported none of this to their supervisors. More troubling, wrote Warshaw, was that "su-pervisors approved these reports even though there were no accompanying force reports," indicating "a significant supervisory failure."[37]

Judge William Orrick held a conference in his courtroom in November 2018 to discuss these troubling findings with Kirkpatrick, other city officials, as well as Chanin and Burris. This was his second public hearing since taking over from Henderson. Still new to his role in Oakland's oversight, Orrick continued to show deference to the city's leaders, recognizing first the positives: the police department had implemented most of the Swanson report's guidance, PRIME was on track to be completed soon, and stops of Black people were still declining as the OPD's ongoing work with Stanford continued.[38]

But the judge hadn't summoned the city to his courtroom for good news.

"I have a nagging question," said Orrick, "that the defendants are checking boxes on compliance that will prove ephemeral over time. One way to assure the change is real is to assure that assessments are honest and are not manipulated for any purpose."[39]

Orrick told Kirkpatrick and the rest of the city's leadership that the underreporting of use of force and the city's slowness to discover this and take corrective action had shaken his confidence. He used a legal metaphor he thought might resonate with the various attorneys in the room, and possibly even Kirkpatrick with her law degree.

"You know the jury instruction on credibility," he said in his typical firm but measured tone. "When you think you have not been told the truth in one thing, you can assume that you're not being told the truth on many things."

Oakland police officers reported bad data for years about gun pointing: Were they also misreporting other uses of force to hide instances of brutality or other misconduct? Were data for other NSA tasks being manipulated, massaged, or misreported to show compliance where there wasn't any?

Orrick made it clear that the department's progress hadn't just ground to a halt: it was backsliding.

"My concerns are not assuaged by anything that's been said," he told Kirkpatrick and the rest of the city's team before announcing he was reactivating two of the NSA tasks that had previously been considered complete and not in need of constant review: Tasks 24 and 25, which required officers to accurately report when they used force, and for the department's supervisors to competently investigate these incidents. He also reactivated Task 31, which outlined the proper ways that police brass should investigate officer-involved shootings.

"What's happened over the last few months has made me less optimistic than I would like to be," Orrick said before walking out of the courtroom, leaving Kirkpatrick and city staff stunned by the massive setback they'd just handed themselves.

————

The Executive Force Review Board's report about Joshua Pawlik's shooting landed on Chief Kirkpatrick's desk in January. The board's voting members, Deputy Chief LeRonne Armstrong and Captains Christopher Bolton and Nishant Joshi, spent three days set up in a conference room hearing presentations from Internal Affairs, Homicide, and several sergeants and lieutenants with expertise in firearms, armored vehicles, and tactics. They dissected a key piece of evidence: footage of Pawlik waking up to be shot. Sergeant Herbert Webber had placed his body camera atop the BearCat just before the shooting, creating an unflinching video of the incident. Several versions of the video were enhanced by forensic analysts who presented their interpretations of the footage to the board, including whether Pawlik's hand holding the gun ever really rose up toward the officers.[40]

When they were done, Armstrong, Bolton, and Joshi voted unanimously to endorse the use of deadly force. They believed Pawlik raised his firearm and therefore presented a potentially lethal threat.

But the officers' actions weren't entirely justified. The review board determined that Lieutenant Alan Yu, the highest-ranking officer on scene, failed to properly supervise by letting Sergeant Negrete run with a poorly thought-out plan. Yu was therefore culpable of Class 2 misconduct, a level that could result in a suspension or demotion. Officer Tanaka had also improperly armed himself with a rifle without telling his supervisors, a low-level rules violation.

Sergeant Negrete had done much worse. Two of the EFRB members, Armstrong and Joshi, felt that Negrete's decision to pick up his rifle while also assuming the role of talker and handcuffer instead of focusing on supervising others was a "grossly derelict" form of misconduct. Negrete set up a situation through poor planning that was bound to end in gunfire, then did worse by not following his own plan and "got sucked into the threat himself, losing supervisory control."[41] The Class 1 level of misconduct he'd committed, according to the board, could result in his termination if accepted by the chief.

Kirkpatrick didn't accept these findings.

Tanaka's "self-deployment" of his rifle was acceptable, she decided, because of the "heightened threat of Pawlik." And while the board made a correct decision to suggest punishment for Yu's failure to supervise, she wrote that Negrete wasn't grossly derelict in his duty to manage the arrest team.

"Despite his failures," Kirkpatrick wrote in her final report, "his conduct viewed as a whole does not demonstrate gross misconduct carried out with carelessness and reckless disregard for the safety of others." She decided Negrete should only be sustained for the same lesser form of misconduct as Yu, resulting in a suspension or demotion at most.[42]

The Oakland Police Commission's CPRA investigators might have come to a different conclusion had they carried out their own investigation. Instead, the police commission and its investigators were still mired in dysfunction. CPRA inexplicably waited until four months after the shooting before opening a case, doing so only because of public pressure and requests from the commission. The CPRA didn't begin its cursory "full investigation" until the following January, and this involved only reviewing the OPD's homicide report and video footage. Only one person was interviewed by CPRA (the agency never identified who this was) because its investigator determined that too much time had elapsed for accurate recall of the incident. Over a year after the shooting, CPRA filed its final report, siding with the police.

The watchdog agency's handling of the matter surprised not only police accountability activists, but also members of the police commission who had assumed their investigators would be hard at work given the case was one of the OPD's few fatal uses of force in recent years. But the commissioners had already made their displeasure with the agency's overall work known by firing its executive director months earlier and chastising its staff in public meetings for not conducting a truly independent review of the Pawlik shooting and other incidents.

A little over a week after Kirkpatrick signed off on her disciplinary findings, Robert Warshaw weighed in with a terse four-page report of his own, condemning the department's review and the chief's decision to soften discipline for the officers. Whereas the Oakland PD dwelled on minutiae such as whether Pawlik's arm rose off the ground with the pistol, Warshaw stepped back and viewed the situation in its context. Pawlik was found unconscious, armed, but in no way an immediate danger to anyone besides himself. There was no evidence he'd harmed anyone, and signs indicated he was impaired by alcohol and other drugs, perhaps even experiencing a medical emergency. (A toxicology report showed Pawlik had cocaine, fentanyl, morphine, and several psychiatric medications in his system.) Negrete, Yu, and the rest of the officers had more than forty minutes to plan their approach to disarm him. Warshaw was incredulous at the officers' claims that Pawlik was a deadly threat, necessitating that they unleash on him with four assault rifles from behind an armored vehicle.

"Mr. Pawlik roused to consciousness, and the video shows his actions to be consistent with someone who was waking up and attempting to orient himself," the monitor's report read. "He was moving minimally. He was a live human being—and any reasonable officer should not have expected him to remain perfectly still. His movements, as seen on the video, do not coincide with the movements to which the officers claim they reacted."

Despite all the tools at their disposal, the police decided to kill Pawlik rather than shield themselves and communicate. "Officers did not use the armored vehicle as cover," Warshaw observed. "They utilized it as a shooting platform."

Warshaw's decision to override Kirkpatrick was unusual, but within his authority. He felt the case "begs for consideration of the totality of circumstances," which showed a vulnerable unconscious man waking up to a firing squad, without any conceivable chance of surviving.

Warshaw ordered the OPD to fire Negrete, Berger, Hraiz, Tanaka, and Phillips.

Although the officers received notices that they were being terminated, the chief refused to accept Warshaw's findings. Within the OPD, she was applauded by rank-and-file cops who'd chafed at Warshaw's authority for nearly a decade. It was the first time Warshaw overruled the chief of police on a disciplinary decision since assuming his role in 2012. The older core of officers who'd been there for more than a decade, some as far back as the late 1990s, cheered the new chief's defiance of the monitor, as did some of the younger officers who were part of that police culture.

To the public, the chief communicated that the situation was simple: reasonable minds could disagree in this particular case. Her Internal Affairs investigators and the EFRB had reached the same conclusions as the police commission's investigator, all of them supporting her view. She also pointed out that the district attorney had ruled the officers weren't criminally liable for the shooting, which she felt supported her position, even though the DA's investigation was carried out under completely different standards. Kirkpatrick's play was risky: per Judge Thelton Henderson's 2013 decision, the court monitor had final say on discipline. By rejecting Warshaw's order to fire the four officers who'd killed Pawlik, Kirkpatrick directly challenged both Henderson's ruling and Warshaw's authority, a decision that the monitor called "disappointing and myopic."[43] Their working relationship was rapidly disintegrating.

Outside the OPD and the still dysfunctional CPRA agency, many Oakland residents felt that the shooting was an egregious abuse of power that showed a lack of concern for the sanctity of life, and that the chief had failed to send a necessary signal to her officers at a key moment.

Members of the Coalition for Police Accountability gathered on city hall's steps to denounce Kirkpatrick and call for her ouster. They cited the promotions, the ICE raid and false statements, the backsliding on NSA reforms, and the Pawlik shooting—which in their view should have been avoided had the department learned any lessons in the wake of the Demouria Hogg shooting—as a string of unacceptable developments.

"This chief was brought here under the assumption of keeping the department accountable," John Jones III, an Oakland resident who sat on the committee that helped pick members of the inaugural police commission, said at the rally. "But there have been a number of missteps along the way, including the bungled investigation of Pawlik's murder."[44]

According to the protesters, other things were unraveling. They cited a letter that the Oakland Black Officers Association sent to Kirkpatrick, Mayor Schaaf, and City Administrator Landreth, alleging that Black police recruits as well as officers were still being discriminated against, targeted with biased Internal Affairs investigations, and blocked from assignments they deserved. The fifty-year-old association had tried raising these concerns with Kirkpatrick, but the group's leadership claimed they were virtually ignored by the chief.

"The Chief's inaction and unwillingness to address disparate treatment in the hiring and retention of officers is egregious and hurts our members and the public at large," the group's executive board wrote. "It undermines the Department's ability to address one of the Community's top issues— secure candidates reflective of our community. And it fosters inequity throughout the Department and our subsequent treatment of the community. We cannot continue with this lack of leadership and ask that our concerns be addressed in a timely and transparent fashion."

In March Warshaw found the Oakland Police Department out of compliance with Task 30, which spelled out the requirements for Executive Force Review Boards. Orrick accepted the decision, another major setback for the OPD's compliance with the NSA. While Chanin and Burris viewed it as the reasonable thing to do also, both attorneys were now starting to worry that they, too, might have to retire someday before completion of the case they'd initiated.

By this point, bad news was cascading: the monitor warned the department that it was in danger of falling out of compliance with Task 26 because its Force Review Boards, used to analyze nonfatal incidents, were not delivering necessary policy recommendations that could reduce violent encounters. By December, the OPD would be found in noncompliance, a grievous regression. Warshaw cited a particular case: officers had made contact with a mentally ill man armed with a large stick. Cops on scene were successfully de-escalating the situation and establishing rapport with the distressed man when another cop rushed in without warning and fired beanbag rounds at the person. "It is clear from the several body-worn camera (BWC) videos that at the time of the discharge, the subject was not an immediate threat to anyone, including the officers on scene, all of whom appeared relaxed and almost nonchalant," Warshaw wrote in a report to Orrick. Members of the Force Review Board examining the incident noted the officer's actions seemed unnecessarily violent, and no one was capably supervising the scene. Still, they voted to exonerate the officer of misconduct.[45]

Still more bad news came in May, when the OPD fell out of compliance with Tasks 24 and 25 due to use-of-force misreporting. And in July, the department fell out of compliance with Task 2. IAD investigators were failing to complete cases within mandatory time frames, which imperiled the integrity of the discipline process because of the one-year statute of limitations on discipline.

In August, Orrick called the city into his courtroom again. For this pivotal meeting, Mayor Schaaf showed up alongside City Attorney Barbara Parker and City Administrator Sabrina Landreth. With Oakland's top leaders all present, Orrick made clear he wasn't yet ready to rule that the city had regressed.[46] Chanin and Burris weren't so forgiving. The two civil rights attorneys excoriated Kirkpatrick's leadership and lamented the loss of progress on several key NSA tasks.

Orrick recognized, however, that the city was in danger unless its leaders stepped up and claimed responsibility. "I'm not interested in PR justifications or press release status reports," he told Kirkpatrick, Schaaf, and the rest. "I'm looking for progress."

Orrick knew that behind the scenes, Kirkpatrick and other city officials, not just within the police department, were already criticizing Warshaw, laying the narrative that it was the monitor's subjective judgments that were the cause of recent problems, not the OPD's actual misdeeds. More pointedly, current and former officers were lining up to criticize Warshaw, claiming that his views on the OPD's backsliding were influenced by the hefty paychecks he collected from the city. Clashes with city officials and Department of Justice attorneys in Detroit, where Warshaw also served as court monitor over that city's police reforms, were cited as supporting evidence, and even ex–NYPD commissioner Bill Bratton took shots via Twitter at Judge Orrick and Warshaw over the latter's alleged profiteering.[47]

Orrick made it clear he would have none of this in his courtroom: across sixteen years, the monitoring team exposed egregious scandals and reined in the OPD at crucial junctures, and it was trying to do this again. "I have complete faith in them and their ability, and they are the eyes and the ears of the court," he said of Warshaw's team.

Toward the end of the hearing, one of the police union's longtime attorneys, Rockne Lucia, told Orrick that Oakland no longer had the overarching problems that necessitated court oversight. "We see a lack of reporting, maybe a lack of oversight," he said about some recent failures, chalking them up to bureaucratic problems and nothing more. "But we don't see evidence of unconstitutional policing in the bigger picture."

When it came to Kirkpatrick to sum up the department's state, she defiantly claimed the monitor was wrong. Chanin and Burris were wrong. The activists calling for her ouster were out of touch with reality. She was achieving her goals.

"Facts out of context will never lead to the truth," she lectured Orrick. "So I'm going to put some of our facts into context to show progress and not regression."

Statistically, only a tiny number of police contacts resulted in use of force or a complaint, Kirkpatrick explained, less than-one half of one percent. "That does not sound like an agency that is in deep backslide."

She had fired fourteen officers while leading the OPD and issued thousands of hours of suspensions for rules violations. There hadn't been an officer-involved shooting in over a year, and the drunk driving incidents that were common for a few years had stopped.

"So, Your Honor, OPD is on the move," she said. "We are progressive. We are not regressive."

It was a presentation Orrick could appreciate, balancing the clear and obvious failures during the chief's twenty months on the job with some good work. But Orrick wanted a little more soul-searching from the police commander. "Before you go, Chief, what do you think is your biggest challenge?" he asked.

Kirkpatrick thought about it for a moment and answered: "The narrative."

An astonished look came over the judge's face for a split second before Orrick frowned and asked her if she meant to say communication.

"No, sir, the narrative that we are not moving forward," explained Kirkpatrick.

"That's what you think your biggest challenge is?"

"I think that's a challenge," the chief replied. "I think there are other— I think that's the challenge. I think that we do indeed have culture shift. I think we have failed in explaining the proofs."

————

Members of the Oakland Police Commission had been meeting in closed session for several hours when they emerged on the evening of February 20, 2020, and filed into the city council chambers to disclose a decision they'd just made. Normally sleepy affairs covered with minimal substance—if at all—by local media, on this night TV cameras were rolling and reporters with the major regional newspapers were in attendance.

Regina Jackson, the commission's chairperson and a longtime resident of Oakland who ran a youth development center, got straight to business. "The Oakland Police Commission voted unanimously to join Mayor Schaaf in terminating the chief of police, without cause," she announced.[48]

The "narrative" shift that the OPD's first female chief attempted to make in Judge Orrick's chambers six months prior had backfired. The commissioners were alarmed by Kirkpatrick's brazen rejection of the court monitor's authority—and their own.

A few people in the audience applauded. Rashidah Grinage was the only member of the public to step to the microphone to comment. She said that while the commission chose to exercise its power to fire the chief in concert with the mayor, which did not require them to state their reasons, the Coalition for Police Accountability had already spelled out many of the possible causes.

"Thank you very much. It's taken a year, but we know about the arc of justice," said Grinage.

Jackson alluded to the rationale for Kirkpatrick's firing at a press conference after the vote: "the Oakland Police Department's failure to increase compliance with the court-ordered reforms" was the primary cause.

The reasons for Kirkpatrick's firing were spelled out much more clearly in internal commission records revealed over a year later. The commissioners had been evaluating Kirkpatrick's performance as chief for several months, as they were required to do under the city charter.[49] They determined that backsliding on the NSA had gone too far, too fast. Coupled with Kirkpatrick's other missteps, particularly her insubordination to the federal court's direction in the Pawlik case and her inattention to discrimination in hiring issues raised by Black officers, the commissioners felt the chief had lost the confidence of the community. She wasn't the person who could take the OPD to the NSA's finish line. But political considerations prevented the commission from transparently stating these reasons at the time.

On February 17—three days before the media spectacle of Kirkpatrick's termination—the commissioners unanimously voted in a closed-session meeting that they would fire her for cause, if necessary. They wanted to give Mayor Schaaf a chance to save face. After all, Kirkpatrick was Schaaf's handpicked leader. Were the commission to fire Kirkpatrick for cause, they'd have to publicly list all of the chief's failures, which would reflect poorly on the mayor. However, if Schaaf were to join them in firing the chief, her termination could be without cause. Kirkpatrick's litany of failures could go unstated in the official record, as could Schaaf's role in hiring and standing by someone who became an obstacle to reform.[50]

The mood among rank-and-file officers was mutinous. Though the court's power over the department had been codified almost eight years earlier, and the police commission's power to fire the chief was enshrined in the city charter, Kirkpatrick's termination made the authority of the NSA and the civilian commission over Oakland's cops tangible in a way they'd never felt. Back in the early 1980s, after Oakland first established its Citizens' Police Review Board, OPD officers scorned its authority, rarely showing up for hearings and trusting they'd be insulated from civilian oversight by Internal Affairs and the city manager, where the real power to discipline officers remained. Before this, the police officers' union rebelled against Chief Charles Gain's progressive policies with a vote of no confidence, pressuring him to leave Oakland. And they'd used aggressive lawsuits to attack their critics, most famously by suing Marlon Brando and the NAACP during protests over the killing of Melvin Black in 1979.

After 2003, when the Riders case was settled and the NSA started, the Oakland PD thought it could wait out court oversight. The strategy failed, and subsequent scandals chastened the police officers' union. Although OPOA continued to voice its displeasure with city leaders during budget season and contract talks, the union became less aggressive. But by 2020, OPOA decided to follow the outgoing chief in attacking the legitimacy of external oversight. The union took advantage of the ambiguity of Kirkpatrick's no-cause firing and the general public's ignorance of the OPD's deteriorating performance by orchestrating an emotional good-bye ceremony for the chief.[51]

In the bright winter sunshine on February 25, Kirkpatrick arrived at the union's headquarters a block away from the Police Administration Building. Wearing civilian garb, she was greeted by a line of more than a hundred Oakland cops and civilian employees, both in and out of uniform. The ex-chief hugged dozens of them and tearfully told TV news cameras "these officers are the best of the best and haven't deserved the criticism they've gotten."

After Kirkpatrick spoke of her own leadership qualities, OPOA president Barry Donelan denounced the firing as "political mayhem."

Inside OPOA headquarters, the former chief made remarks to a group of assembled officers and signed off to the entire department over the patrol broadcast frequency.

Kirkpatrick also issued a warning to Oakland, telling the public she intended to ask the Trump administration's Department of Justice to investigate the police oversight system with an eye toward removing Warshaw from his role. "I will be asking the Department of Justice to come in and open an inquiry into this whole reform process. Because something is wrong," she said.[52]

At Kirkpatrick's side throughout the day was Sam Singer, a Bay Area crisis management consultant who frequently worked for police unions, oil companies, and disgraced politicians seeking to change the narrative. Sure enough, the former chief filed a claim against the city for wrongful termination and appeared with former police chief Howard Jordan at a press conference to denounce the NSA and monitor. Appearing with them, surprisingly, was Noel Gallo, the council member who helped create the police commission but now aligned with the OPOA and the former chiefs. Gallo sent a letter to Judge Orrick a week after Kirkpatrick's firing asking that the court's oversight of the OPD be brought to an end.

"This is the longest agreement of its kind including Federal Consent Decrees in the history of the United States!" the council member wrote, adding that Oakland had been forced to spend $28 million to "satisfy the Court's requirements." Echoing Kirkpatrick and OPOA, Gallo claimed that the "tasks have been changing," making it harder and harder for the department to comply. "If it takes seventeen years to get out of a Federal Consent Decree or reform a Police Agency, and waste taxpayers millions of dollars, there is something definitely wrong with the oversight."

Gallo did not acknowledge the OPD's objective backsliding on reforms, including failures to report use of force and blowing deadlines on Internal Affairs cases, or the department's sex trafficking scandal, but he demanded the city be given the power to "manage its own future."

In August, Kirkpatrick filed a lawsuit in federal court, alleging she'd been fired because she was a whistleblower. She accused members of the police commission of seeking favors from the department, and when they were rebuffed, of retaliating, ultimately by having her fired. In concert with the police union's goal of ridding Oakland of court oversight, Kirkpatrick's attorneys attempted to subpoena Warshaw's records, part of a fishing expedition for anything that could be used to damage his credibility.[53]

OPOA carried on with its own frontal assault against federal court oversight. The union's attorneys filed lawsuits on behalf of the officers who killed Pawlik, asking a state judge to nullify the city's decision to fire them. The police union's argument was essentially that Warshaw did not have the authority to impose discipline on the officers. Kirkpatrick's decisions were the only ones that counted.[54] Ultimately, the five officers would win their jobs back after an attorney hired by the city to conduct a fact-finding hearing sided with them, and a judge upheld this decision.

None of these legal, political, or public relations gambits could alter the harsh reality: Oakland's police department still lagged behind modern standards for constitutional policing. Certainly, the OPD had made incredible progress in some areas. It had arguably become one of the most professional and transparent police agencies in America and was pushing the envelope with its work using stop data to reduce racial disparities, setting an example for other law enforcement agencies. But confronted with the prospect that civilians would ultimately have the power to determine its future, the department snapped.

For the seventeenth year running, the police department still hadn't made a clean break with what it was when the Riders roamed the streets of West Oakland.

CONCLUSION

Following Anne Kirkpatrick's ouster, and eleven months during which former San Mateo police chief Susan Manheimer served as interim OPD chief, the Oakland Police Commission and Mayor Libby Schaaf selected LeRonne Armstrong as the next police chief. An African American who was born and raised in West Oakland, Armstrong had unique leadership credentials. His older brother was murdered in a 1985 shooting at Oakland Technical High School, a tragedy that influenced Armstrong's desire to become a police officer. He joined the OPD in 1999 and trained alongside some of the officers implicated in the Riders scandal. Armstrong was steeped in the department's recalcitrant culture in the early 2000s. But he became an active member of the Oakland Black Officers Association, a loyal opposition group that raised concerns about racism within the department. Twenty years later as chief, Armstrong showed a willingness to work with the police commission and bring the OPD into the post–George Floyd era.

Unlike prior chiefs, he acknowledged when the department was wrong. Armstrong's most stunning admission came one year after the protests and civil unrest of 2020. He apologized for making false statements that justified police use of tear gas against a youth-led march. There hadn't been anyone at the June 1 protest preparing to lob Molotov cocktails at police. Recognizing the department's failure, and his own complicity, he announced thirty-three officers would be disciplined for the attack. It was swifter accountability than the department's handling of the Occupy police riot nearly a decade

before, and it was far removed from the complete lack of accountability following the 2003 port crackdown.

Armstrong also didn't have to wait long for a scandal to surface. In
late 2020 an Instagram account run by one of the officers fired for killing Joshua Pawlik found an audience among Oakland cops, who shared
the page's memes. Based on the account's content—pro–law enforcement jokes and the ample use of cop jargon—it should have been obvious it was run by an officer. Oakland cops "liked" and commented on the
"@crimereductionteam" page's harmful messages, including deeply racist
memes involving Black men raping white girls, and posts advocating insubordination and brutality. As happened so many times over the years, the
department's supervisors failed to see the Instagram page for what it was.
They did not open an investigation and shut it down. OPD leaders did not
swiftly identify officers who appeared to share its values and fire or suspend
them. The department's nonresponse was worse than the violation itself.

Once again, it was left to a single person within the department, this
time an anonymous whistleblower, to tip off the media. When Jim Chanin
and monitor Robert Warshaw finally became aware, they were the ones who
had to force the department, through an order from Judge Orrick, to take
action. Following an outside investigation, nine officers were disciplined.

Up to that point, the Oakland Police Department appeared to have gotten back on track to reach compliance with the NSA. The Instagram scandal was a serious setback. Reflecting on the investigator's report, most of
which will remain secret in perpetuity, Judge Orrick remarked in January
2022 that the scandal showed a "cultural rot" still deep in the department's
soul.

But Armstrong showed the same kind of resolve that had worked so
well for Sean Whent early in his tenure as chief, and by mid-2022 the
department had recovered entirely from the backsliding Kirkpatrick presided over. One by one, the department checked off the boxes of the seven
remaining reforms. In May, Orrick issued an order finding the OPD had
"achieved substantial compliance" with the NSA. "The path here has led
to tangible improvements in policing in Oakland and to the promise that
a culture that understands and supports constitutional policing is taking
root," he wrote.

If it could sustain this for one year—without any new egregious scandal and cover-up arising, and without backsliding again—then by early

2023, the OPD might finally regain full control over itself with the end of federal court oversight.

––––––––––

The roughly two decades of court oversight have been anything but linear. A half dozen police chiefs have come and gone. The reform program has outlasted four mayors, two judges, and two monitoring teams. For the first five years, the OPD ignored the NSA, leading to the cop riot at the port in 2003, Warrantgate, strip searches, the dysfunctions that culminated in Lovelle Mixon's killing spree and Chauncey Bailey's murder, the rash of deadly but preventable shootings in the mid-2000s, and Occupy Oakland. Even after the department started checking off the NSA's boxes, the Celeste Guap case erupted, systemic underreporting use of force was revealed, and Joshua Pawlik's shooting exposed reversals of progress.

None of this is to say that the OPD is the same department it was during the Riders years. The reforms that began in 2003 with the Negotiated Settlement Agreement have profoundly changed the Oakland police, and the city, for the better.

Today OPD officers are involved in far fewer deadly use-of-force incidents. Oakland was once the leading department in Northern California for police shootings. During the first twelve years of reforms after the Riders scandal, when the agency petulantly ignored the NSA, its officers shot fifteen people on average each year. Many of these shootings were deadly, and some of the deceased, like Gary King and Derrick Jones, were unarmed. Following the receivership motion and near takeover of the department in 2012, and Sean Whent's no-nonsense term as chief, the OPD finally put in place new policies, including rules that discouraged risky solo foot chases and backyard searches, and new accountability standards ensuring bad shootings would result in discipline. Altogether, these efforts caused police shootings to plummet to two per year from 2013 to 2020. To put it in terms of human life, police in Oakland are now shooting about thirteen fewer people annually because of NSA reforms.[1]

Oakland police officers' everyday behavior also changed dramatically over the past twenty years. Oakland cops were once known for abusive, explicit language, frequently using the n-word, and after racial slurs were banned, deploying euphemisms like "turd." In recent years, most officers have adopted a patient and respectful demeanor on patrol. Monitor's reports that include audits of police body camera footage rarely flag instances in which officers curse or show impatience or anger.

This behavior reflects more than just shallow proceduralism. Use of force other than firearms has plummeted. The days in which officers could, with impunity, choke a suspect (like Frank Vazquez and Matt Hornung), or pummel a person with a flashlight or baton (like Chuck Mabanag or Jude Siapno), are long gone. Police brutality complaints are less common nowadays, and many are resolved by Internal Affairs and the police commission's investigators through examination of body camera video that unambiguously exonerates officers. Audits by the department's inspector general and the independent monitor rarely identify unjustified uses of force.

Few departments in the nation have ever pulled back the curtain as far as Oakland has on their own stop data, revealing details about who they're pulling over, citing, arresting, and using force against. The OPD's unparalleled transparency on this front initially led to criticism that the department was stopping too many Black residents without good reason. However, following research and interventions, Oakland cops have been able to steadily dial back their most problematic enforcement activities that result in the greatest racial disparities. As a result, Oakland is one of the only law enforcement agencies in America that could actually show (before the George Floyd protests) that it took action to reduce racial profiling.

While the Oakland PD undertook these reforms, its officers showed that they could still effectively fight violent crime. The city's Ceasefire program, while it received attention at the highest levels from the mayor and police chief, played a key role in intervening in the social networks where feuds created the majority of gun violence afflicting the city. And patrol cops continued to make numerous felony arrests for robbery, assault, homicide, and rape. The department's hardworking officers never attempted to punish the city's residents with a de-policing backlash, as has happened in other cities, when subjected to intense external criticism.

———

It is possible to reform the police. That's one lesson Oakland can offer the rest of the nation.

What has worked in Oakland is outside intervention. Indeed, Oakland's consent decree is not only the longest-running court-ordered police reform effort in America, it is also one of the most sweeping in scope, especially since 2012, when the city agreed to allow a federal judge and monitor to have oversight of all aspects of the department that might advance constitutional policing—not just the fifty-two tasks defined in the NSA. And because it was initiated by plaintiffs and civil rights attorneys, Oakland's consent decree was insulated from the political winds in Washington, DC, and allowed to stay its course during times when the Justice Department might have packed up and left.

Without the involvement of Judges Henderson and Orrick, the two monitoring teams, and above all, the tireless work of John Burris and Jim Chanin, the Oakland Police Department would not have been able to reduce police shootings, or track and reduce racial profiling on a systemic scale. The OPD would not have placed heavy restrictions on the uses of crowd control munitions, or created a better version of Charles Gain's computerized early intervention system to identify problematic officers.

But consent decrees are not a panacea. Their biggest flaw is that they come to an end. While in effect, they create transparency and accountability, but after, there's a danger a department will revert to its old self. This is especially the case in cities where reforms are narrowly pursued only within the police department, where no thought is given to the broader changes in a city's institutions that might be necessary to sustain change. For the first decade of Oakland's consent decree, city leaders paid virtually no attention to the question of what kinds of new structures or watchdog agencies would be needed after the NSA was completed.

Other police departments "reformed" through consent decrees suffer from this problem.

It didn't take long until the Los Angeles Police Department, whose reform agreement formally concluded in 2013, was shown once again to be conducting widespread racial profiling. Its officers were caught falsifying huge numbers of records in gang database files, actions that permanently harmed the lives of thousands of Latinos and Black people. And the department's violent paramilitary reputation, forged by men like former chiefs William Parker and Darryl Gates, hasn't changed all that much, as illustrated by recent instances of officers manhandling protesters, and LAPD's disturbing number of police shootings.[2]

In 2009 the Southern California ACLU chapter opposed ending the LAPD's consent decree, warning that the department's own statistics still showed an egregious pattern of racial profiling and unjustified stops.[3] LAPD chief Bill Bratton claimed the Los Angeles Police Commission and inspector general were up to the job of catching and halting further abuses.[4] More than a decade later, it is evident that those two entities have not proved up to the task.

In New York City, a similar pattern is emerging with the NYPD's abusive, discriminatory stop-and-frisk practices that a federal judge ruled unconstitutional in 2013. Like in Oakland, a consent decree resulted from a massive class action brought by victims of police abuse, involving a court-appointed monitor responsible for gauging NYPD's progress in rectifying its training and patrol strategies. The original judge in the case has since retired, the monitor has died, and the NYPD as of 2019 was failing to document almost 40 percent of all stops.[5]

Oakland may be on a different trajectory. The police commission established in the wake of the 2016 sex exploitation scandal is said to be one of, if not the most powerful, police oversight boards in the nation. Its decision to fire Anne Kirkpatrick for backsliding on the NSA and refusing to punish the officers who killed Joshua Pawlik sent a powerful message. The city's Privacy Advisory Commission has also proven itself to be a formidable opponent of the secrecy and spying Oakland police have engaged in. Whether these branches of city government can fully institutionalize themselves and take on the accountability role played for twenty years by the federal court-appointed monitor remains to be seen.

But the obvious lesson is that external monitoring and accountability have worked to advance positive changes in policing in Oakland. And they are permanently needed because the police are, as former chief George Hart defined them, a "negative institution." Law enforcement is the repressive, coercive power of the state embodied in an armed officer. They are made to deal with societal problems when they reach a crisis point. The police have to respond to the symptoms of an unequal society and the alienation and suffering it produces. If they are allowed to do so—or encouraged, as they so often are—police will frequently subject a society's poor and racially oppressed to violence, surveillance, and harassment, all in the name of maintaining social order.

———

It's become a truism to say the police cannot police themselves. The reason external accountability structures are necessary is because police culture is insular and secretive. Those who work inside law enforcement for accountability, be they Internal Affairs investigators or inspectors general, are often shunned by the rank and file. Whistleblowers remain a crucial source of accountability, but they pay the highest price.

It was in direct reaction to the abuses perpetuated by the Riders that twenty-three-year-old Keith Batt courageously listened to his conscience and reported the crimes he'd been forced to take part in. It wasn't an easy decision: he was a promising young officer who'd already forged an identity as a lawman through his college education and six months in Oakland's rigorous police academy. Speaking up against abuses by fellow cops can be a dangerous proposition: in the 1970s New York police officer Frank Serpico uncovered systemic graft within the nation's largest police force. In exchange, he was ostracized and left for dead by fellow officers when he was shot in the face during a suspicious narcotics raid.[6] Keith knew the Riders were capable of extreme violence and retribution and still chose to take action.

Without whistleblowers, many of the most egregious abuses of police power in history would have never been exposed.

Reflecting on his role more than twenty years later, Batt said in an interview that he has never regretted coming forward. But he was surprised to find, over the years, that it was he who was scapegoated and expelled from the brotherhood of policing, not the Riders. To this day, Batt said he worries about his family's safety—after all, Frank Vazquez remains a fugitive. Batt wonders why there aren't more police like him, officers willing to speak up when something is wrong.

The answer has everything to do with police culture, which elevates loyalty to the badge over everything else, even when that means staying silent about wrongdoing by other officers. Thus, while whistleblowers have played indispensable roles exposing police corruption, the act of whistleblowing also has its limits. Few officers are brave enough to put their jobs, reputations, and lives on the line. Those who do pay dearly. And speaking up can only reveal problems; it's only the first step toward change.

But altogether, whistleblowers, civil rights attorneys, courts and monitors, and especially regular people banding together in protest movements can successfully reform policing. Long before reimagining policing became a topic of public discussion, or "defunding the police" became a boogeyman on Fox News, countless Oakland residents agitated and organized to change policing in their city.

Oakland's story shows that accountability isn't something that can ever be fully and finally achieved. It was only through continuous protest and obsessive scrutiny of the police department that Oaklanders were able to bring about progress. In the 1950s, Black Oaklanders and their allies in the civil liberties and labor movements realized they needed to fight tooth and nail to hold abusive cops accountable. They battled police violence and corruption in courts, in the media, in city hall, and in the streets. Their work, mostly unsuccessful, was carried forward by the radical movements of the 1960s and 1970s, and a new generation of civil rights lawyers and politicians who fought to dismantle violence and racism in the ranks. Change came in cycles. In the 1980s the nation turned away from police reform and embraced the War on Drugs. The tide changed again starting in the 1990s, and by the 2000s, Oakland was again a nexus of organizing, litigation, and new policies to reform policing. The city's story is far from over. Its residents will continue pushing hard against their police department to demand transparency and accountability. And if history is any guide, OPD will take two steps forward, and one step back.

Whether policing in Oakland will ever get to a point where most people can agree that it has been fundamentally transformed—no longer anything like the institution the Riders thrived in, no longer the force that terrorized Black Oakland after World War II and well into the 2000s—depends very much on whether there are broader societal shifts. So long as Oakland and the rest of America is riven by extreme racial and class inequalities and the power of the federal government is not brought to repair the economies of destitute cities and rural areas, and deal with the intergenerational trauma that leads to despair and hopelessness, then it's very likely the police will continue serving more or less the same function they have for well over a half century: containing and repressing the symptoms of broader social problems through violence.

Small reforms that save lives and prevent some egregious abuses of power are possible. However, Oakland has shown that this only happens through the utmost exertion by civil society. Relentless outside oversight and pressure, by activists, civil rights attorneys, elected officials with the guts to stand up, defense attorneys, the press, and whistleblowers was the only way these kinds of reforms came about. And after more than two decades of court oversight and a much longer string of protests, lawsuits, and civic reforms, the OPD still has incredible problems. Long after the NSA is completed, and well into the tenure of the city's new police commission, scandals will surely emerge, revealing once again the limits of reform. It's possible that a complete transformation of the institution and culture of American policing might not be possible.

Even in cases where reforms have been achieved, like Oakland, the danger of backsliding is ever present. Lurking beneath the surface of a reformed department, deep in its culture, are tendencies that constantly threaten to boil over in the form of violence and corruption. Oakland's ultimate lesson then is about vigilance.

Whenever the public, press, and watchdogs let up and allow the police to "police themselves," the violent, racist, and reactionary law enforcement culture that developed behind the thin blue line reemerges. In the absence of this consistent external pressure and transparency, the sun sets on a city and a dogwatch mentality will overtake any police department. In this darkness, the Riders come out.

ACKNOWLEDGMENTS

This book is the result of more than two and a half combined decades of reporting on the Oakland Police Department. Significant portions were pieced together from interviews, documents, recordings, news clippings, and voluminous other materials gathered along the way, but a fundamental shift in California's laws regarding the confidentiality of police records in 2019 allowed us to obtain tens of thousands of pages of previously confidential files from the city of Oakland about police shootings and a multitude of scandals and secrets. However, the intransigence of the city attorney and the Oakland Police Department in refusing to comply with state law meant that we had to resort to the courts to pry these records loose. Sam Ferguson, our attorney, took on our case pro bono and won a monumental victory in Alameda County Superior Court in 2020 that helped set precedent for public access to law enforcement records. Much of the chapters on the 2000s and the 2010s would not be possible in their current state without the documents and dozens of video and audio recordings Sam was able to force the city to turn over.

Our editor at Atria Books, Amar Deol, understood our vision for *Riders* from our first conversation. He was a steady hand during two years of intensive writing in the midst of a global pandemic. David Patterson, our agent, helped mold a sprawling jumble of chapters into a tight, coherent proposal that served as a reliable structure for the final draft. Thanks also to Elizabeth Hitti, Phillip Bashe, and the entire team at Atria and Simon & Schuster, and to John Pelosi for his astute legal read.

We are grateful to our past editors who encouraged us and helped focus our reporting over the years. Lowell Bergman, Ali's graduate school advisor at the UC Berkeley Graduate School of Journalism expertly guided Ali's 2011 investigation into shootings by OPD officers, which was underwritten, edited, and published by Esther Kaplan at the Nation Institute's Investigative Fund. While he was editor of the *East Bay Express*, Robert Gammon schooled us both in journalism and allowed us to pursue investigations into all corners of Oakland City Hall. Kathleen Richards and Nick Miller, also of the *East Bay Express*, Rina Palta at KALW Public Media, Ethan Brown at the *Appeal*, and Tasneem Raja and Jacob Simas at the *Oaklandside* also edited our coverage of OPD at various points in the last twelve years.

The Whiting Foundation and the Robert B. Silvers Foundation provided crucial grants to fund the research and writing process. We are honored and deeply grateful for their trust and support.

Among the dozens of people we interviewed, two of them were able to provide us with caches of essential records that, unfortunately, haven't been preserved elsewhere. Jim Chanin allowed us to read nonconfidential files from crucial civil rights cases, and Keith Batt gave us access to thousands of pages of transcripts and briefs from the Riders' criminal trials—records that were unfortunately shredded by the Alameda Superior Court in 2015. We'd also like to thank all of the sources who spoke to us, on the record and off, through the years, during both our coverage of Oakland and for this book. You know who you are, and we are eternally grateful for your candor.

Journalism is a group endeavor whereby individual reporters build on the work of their colleagues. There are many scribes on whom this book depends. We won't name but a tiny fraction of them here, but our reliance on their dogged investigations and beat coverage is evident in the endnotes. In particular, we'd like to thank our colleagues who at various times have focused their attention on the OPD or the broader problems of policing or public safety and have shared their insights with us: Thomas Peele, David DeBolt, Lance Williams, Carla Marinucci, Scott Morris, Brian Krans, Lois Beckett, and Rob Gunnison.

Ali would like to thank his mother, Zeynep Çelik, for her irreplaceable research assistance, unfailing wit, love, and encouragement, and his father, Perry Winston, who was taken from us too soon in 2015. This book owes Perry a special debt for his sharp-eyed criticism and enthusiastic support for my writing and reporting, encouraging me to follow in the steps of the journalists like our neighbor Bob Liff, whose shoe-leather reporting I read in the pages of *Newsday* my father would bring home every night. Adam Bloch was an invaluable reader of early chapters. Corey Scher and Stewart Emmington-Jones provided logistical and emotional support in the field and off the clock, both in the East Bay and New York City. Jeff Wozniak helped me thread the needle of the California courts and particulars of the street, in between film screenings. Rick Atkinson gave a master course in archival research, historiography, and method during a summer fellowship long ago, lessons that stayed with me to the present day. Thank you to Taya Kitman and the Type Media Center for kindly providing space and support during the writing process. Big ups to Tillary, Linda, Gilman, Underhill (RIP), 108th & Columbus, Cadman Plaza, and all the other pitches that let me blow off steam. In Oakland, Jose and Mary for their kindness, John for recounting Oakland's history and pressing me to keep the bigger picture in mind, and Evelyn for her steadfast love, support, and most of all, patience.

Darwin would like to thank his parents, Margaret Bond and Frank Graham. Mom and Dad, you never failed to support my endeavors, including my decision to make a risky career change years ago to pursue investigative journalism. And Angie Crone saw this project take shape from its earliest stages. Her love and patience and especially her encouragement to celebrate small milestones along the way made the writing process possible—and a joy.

NOTES

PROLOGUE

1. Elizabeth Hinton, *America on Fire: The Untold History of Police Violence* (New York: W. W. Norton, 2021).
2. Jeffrey Jones, "In US, Black Confidence in Police Recovers from 2020 Low," Gallup online, last modified August 14, 2021, https://news.gallup.com/poll /352304/black-confidence-police-recovers-2020-low.aspx.

1: DOGWATCH, GHOST TOWN

1. Oakland Police Department Internal Affairs case summary for Clarence Mabanag. None of the thirty-one complaints against Mabanag was sustained.
2. "Croakland" was slang used by some Oakland cops in reference to the city's high murder rate. Over the years, OPD officers have found other comedic ways to deal with the violence. One T-shirt popular with police in the 1990s had the West Oakland zip code 94607 surrounded by bullet holes, while another showed a Welcome to Oakland street sign with the population number falling as murders chipped away at the city's Black population.
3. Oakland Police Department Internal Affairs Report 00-137.
4. Janice Stevenson told police investigators in an interview on September 7, 2000, that she had secured the dog; otherwise, it would have escaped.
5. Charges were later dropped against the man. The incident was described in the OPD's Internal Affairs investigation as Incident No. 7.
6. Notes of Alameda County district attorney Inspector Bob Conner from the first jury trial of the Oakland Riders.
7. Delphine Allen, preliminary hearing testimony, June 4, 2001.
8. Danielle Keller, preliminary hearing testimony, June 4, 2001.

9. Henry K. Lee, "Whistleblower Cop Threatened, DA Says," *San Francisco Chronicle*, November 3, 2004.

10. Notes of Alameda County district attorney Inspector Bob Conner from the first jury trial of the Oakland Riders.

11. Oakland would pay a $195,00 settlement to the shooting victim, Ke'van Pope, in 2003. The OPD terminated Officer Lee for Pope's shooting in 2001, but his firing was overturned in arbitration two years later. Henry K. Lee, "Oakland Council Likely to Settle with Man Shot by Cop," *San Francisco Chronicle*, June 11, 2003, and "Oakland Cop Fired in Incidents," *San Francisco Chronicle*, May 15, 2001.

12. Keith Batt, interviewed by the authors, January 21, 2022.

13. Keith Batt, interviewed by the Oakland Police Department Internal Affairs Division, July 5, 2022; taped statements obtained from the Alameda County District Attorney's Office by the authors via the California Public Records Act.

14. Oakland Police Department Internal Affairs Report 00-137.

15. Kristofer Jenny testimony, second Riders trial, January 5, 2005.

16. Ibid.

17. Ibid.

18. Batt, authors interview, January 22, 2022.

19. Ibid., January 22, 2022.

20. Batt, Internal Affairs statement, July 5, 2000, 23.

21. Ibid.

22. Keith Batt, Internal Affairs statement, July 5, 2000, 18.

23. Many of the criminal case files for the Riders' two trials were destroyed by the Alameda County Superior Court between 2010 and 2015.

2: NOBODY WILL LISTEN TO JERRY AMARO

1. Associated Press, "Oakland Sets Record for Homicides," *Los Angeles Times*, December 25, 1991, A47.

2. Jerry Brown's critics later morphed the nickname Governor Moonbeam to stand for his eccentricities, some seemingly New Age–inspired.

3. Rick DelVecchio, "Potluck in Oakland: The Many Sides of Jerry Brown Surface at His Live-Work Space Near Jack London Square," *San Francisco Chronicle*, April 20, 1997, 1.

4. The term "ecopolis" was a conscious reference to *Ecotopia: The Notes and Reports of William Weston*, the 1975 utopian novel by Ernest Callenbach, which took place in a near future where the West Coast had seceded from the United States and practiced sustainable, communal forms of living.

5. Pamela Drake, interviewed by the authors, August 28, 2018.

6. Edmund Gerald Brown Jr., "Jerry Brown: A Life in California Politics," conducted by Scott Shafer, Martin Meeker, and Todd Holmes in 2019, Oral History Center, Bancroft Library, University of California, Berkeley, 2020.

7. Ibid.

8. "Crime strategy retreat," Jack London Waterfront Inn, March 1, 1999, docu-

ment included as exhibit A in "Declaration of Michael Rains in response to plaintiffs' motion for appointment of receiver," Delphine Allen et al. v. City of Oakland, case no. 3:00-cv-04599-TEH.

9. Peter Waldman, "Jerry Brown's Turnaround," *Santa Cruz (CA) Sentinel*, August 11, 1999.

10. Heather MacDonald, "Jerry Brown's No-Nonsense New Age Oakland," *City Journal*, Autumn 1999, available at https://www.city-journal.org/html/jerry-brown%E2%80%99s-no-nonsense-new-age-oakland-12032.html; Marc Cooper, "Mayor Jerry Brown, Take II," *Nation*, February 28, 2002.

11. Joan Walsh, "Jerry Brown Reinvents Himself as Mayor Macho," *San Francisco Examiner*, September 6, 1999.

12. Zachary Coile, "Oakland Eyes No-Frills Budget," *San Francisco Examiner*, April 23, 1999.

13. Jim Herron Zamora, "Mayor to Restructure Oakland Police Force," *San Francisco Examiner*, March 26, 1999.

14. Kathleen Sullivan and Vicki Haddock, "Brown Speaks to Oakland," *San Francisco Examiner*, January 5, 1999.

15. Zamora, "Mayor to Restructure Oakland Police Force."

16. Marcel Patterson, deposition, 53, October 30, 2009; Edward Poulson statement notes, April 25, 2000.

17. Edward Poulson statement notes, April 25, 2000.

18. Geraldine Montoya v. City of Oakland, California northern district, 9th Circuit of Appeals, D.C. No,. 3:09-cv-01019-WHA, opinion, July 28, 2011.

19. Roland Holmgren, deposition, 132, October 15, 2009.

20. Exhibit 9, OPD Report of Internal Investigation, file no. 00-0063.

21. Holmgren, deposition, 117–19, October 15, 2009.

22. Timothy Murphy, deposition, 24, September 17, 2009.

23. Former Oakland police officer present at scene, interviewed by the authors, May 6, 2021.

24. Murphy, deposition, 36, September 17, 2009.

25. Oakland Police Department, Report of Internal Investigation, file no. 00-063.

26. Murphy, deposition, 60, September 17, 2009.

27. Khalid Muhammad, deposition, 24, December 11, 2009.

28. Follow-Up Investigation Report, Oakland Police Department RD 00-36750, April 21, 2000, 4.

29. Ibid.

30. Report of Roger A. Clark, *Regarding: The Estate of Jerry A. Amaro III v. The City of Oakland et al.*, USD.C. case no. C09-01019 WHA, January 10, 2010.

31. Ibid.; Muhammad, deposition, 23–24, December 11, 2009.

32. Geraldine Montoya v. City of Oakland, 9th Circuit of Appeals, D.C. No,. 3:09-cv-01019-WHA, opinion, July 28, 2011.

33. Declaration of Louis Montoya, June 4, 2009.

34. Clark, *Regarding: The Estate of Jerry A. Amaro III v. The City of Oakland et al.*, 10–11.

35. Ibid.
36. Gus Galindo, deposition, 78–80, October 20, 2009.
37. Gus Galindo, Follow-up Investigation Report, April 21, 2000, RD 00-36750.
38. Holmgren, deposition, 114, 122, October 19, 2009.
39. Galindo, deposition, 36–38, 43–53, October 20, 2009.
40. Michael Yoell, deposition, 75–77, October 16, 2009; Clark, *Regarding: The Estate of Jerry A. Amaro III v. The City of Oakland et al.*, 21.
41. Yoell, depostion, 22–23.
42. Paul Berlin, deposition, 79, November 19, 2009.
43. Yoell, deposition, 75–77, October 16, 2009; Clark, *Regarding: The Estate of Jerry A. Amaro III v. The City of Oakland et al.*, 12.
44. Clark, *Regarding: The Estate of Jerry A. Amaro III v. The City of Oakland et al.*
45. Oakland Police Department, Report of Internal Investigation, file no. 00-063.
46. Patterson, deposition, 42–43, November 11, 2009.
47. Ibid., 48.
48. Ibid., 52; Report of Internal Investigation, file no. 00-063, 16.
49. In the OPD, lieutenants who wish to advance to the rank of captain take an exam. If they score high enough, they are promoted to a higher level of authority—high enough to dish out favors such as plum assignments or to punish lower-ranking officers who crossed them.
50. Oakland Police Department, Report of Internal Investigation, file no. 00-063, 16
51. Clark, *Regarding: The Estate of Jerry A. Amaro III v. The City of Oakland et al.*, 13.
52. Yoell, deposition, 33–34, October 16, 2009.
53. Oakland Police Department, Report of Internal Investigation, file no. 00-063, 14.
54. Theresa Batts, deposition, 44, September 22, 2009.
55. Ibid., 53.
56. Ron Davis, deposition, 55–56, November 9, 2009.
57. Oakland Police Department, Report of Internal Investigation, file no. 00-063, 14.
58. Anthony Keith Rachal, deposition, 21–22, 70–71, December 7, 2009.
59. Anonymous letter to Oakland Police Department, Internal Affairs, Attn Lieutenant Rachel [*sic*].
60. Oakland Police Department, Report of Internal Investigation, file no. 00-063, 28.
61. Ron Davis to Richard Word, confidential memo, re: Disciplinary Recommendation: no. 00-063 (Lieutenant E. Poulson), July 23, 2000, 4.
62. Ibid., 5.
63. Davis, deposition, 88, November 9, 2009.
64. Ibid., 58, 90, October 13, 2009.
65. Ibid., 67–68; Davis to Word, confidential memo, July 23, 2000, 5.
66. Ibid.
67. Richard Word, deposition, 65–68; Yoell, deposition, 51, October 27, 2009.

68. Yoell, deposition, 49–50, October 16, 2009.

69. Rick Hart, interviewed by the authors, November 11, 2019.

70. Scott Hoey-Custock v. City of Oakland et al., Alameda County Superior Court, no. 804630-3, Complaint for Damages, 2.

71. Ibid., 4.

72. Scott Hoey-Custock, deposition, vol. 1, 144, November 14, 2000; testimony of Ronald Riveira, February 5, 2001.

73. Scott Hoey-Custock v. City of Oakland et al., 5.

74. Testimony of Ronald Riveira, February 5, 2001.

75. Keith Batt, interviewed by the authors, January 21, 2022.

76. Hoey-Custock v. City of Oakland, testimony of Patrick Haw, February 8, 2001.

77. Ibid., 9532.

78. Ibid., 9623.

79. Ibid., 9627.

80. Testimony of Kris Jenny, January 4, 2005, 9600, 9672–73.

3: "REAL GANGSTER GUNSLINGERS"

1. By January 2001, sixty cases had been tossed out and three hundred arrests made by the four officers who were under review. Henry K. Lee, "Oakland Fires Last of 'Riders'—One of Four Cops Facing Charges," *San Francisco Chronicle* online, February 14, 2001, https://www.sfgate.com/bayarea/article/Oakland-Fires-Last-of-Riders-One-of-4-cops-2952349.php.

2. David Hollister, interviewed by the authors, November 12, 2019.

3. FBI files obtained by the authors via the Freedom of Information Act.

4. Hollister, authors interview, November 12, 2019; FBI files for Vazquez obtained via the FOIA.

5. "Rampart Scandal Timeline," in "LAPD. Blues," *Frontline*, PBS, May 15, 2001, https://www.pbs.org/wgbh/pages/frontline/shows/lapd/scandal/cron.html.

6. Jim Newton, Scott Glover, and Matt Lait, "US Prepared to Sue to Force LAPD Reforms," *Los Angeles Times*, May 6, 2000.

7. *US Department of Justice: Information on Employment Litigation, Housing and Civil Enforcement, Voting, and Special Litigation Sections' Enforcement Efforts from Fiscal Years 2001 through 2007* (Washington, DC: US Government Accountability Office, October 2009), 87, https://www.gao.gov/assets/gao-10-75.pdf.

8. Mark Arax, "8 Prison Guards Are Acquitted in Corcoran Battles," *Los Angeles Times* online, June 10, 2000, https://www.latimes.com/archives/la-xpm-2000-jun-10-mn-39555-story.html.

9. Janine DeFao, "Oakland Snubs Ex-officers: Civil Rights Suits Charge Misconduct," *San Francisco Chronicle*, July 12, 2001.

10. Ibid.

11. PORAC reportedly paid $2 million to defend the three Riders. Glenn Chapman, "Prosecutor Gives Up 'Riders' Case," *Oakland Tribune*, June 3, 2005.

12. Jabaree Highsmith testimony, Preliminary Examination, vol. 3A, May 31, 2001.
13. Oakland city manager Robert Bobb to Sergeant Jerry Hayter, January 9, 2001.
14. Keith Batt, interviewed by the authors, January 21, 2022.
15. Ibid.
16. Alex Conroy, preliminary hearing testimony, July 11, 2001, 2590–98.
17. David Hollister closing argument, Preliminary Examination, vol. 17, July 12, 2001.
18. Jim Herron Zamora, "In 'Riders' Trial, Witness Says He 'Misspoke': Former Cop Had Contradicted Testimony of Whistleblower," *San Francisco Chronicle* online, January 1, 2003, https://www.sfgate.com/bayarea/article/In-Riders-trial-witness-says-he-misspoke-2718178.php.
19. Jim Herron Zamora, "'Riders' Case Goes to Jury: Oakland Cops' Trial Is Longest in County History," *San Francisco Chronicle* online, May 30, 2003, https://www.sfgate.com/bayarea/article/Riders-case-goes-to-jury-Oakland-cops-trial-2644879.php.
20. Batt, authors interview, January 21, 2022.
21. Kim Curtis, Associated Press, "Defense Lawyer Strikes at Witness' Credibility in Oakland Police Trial," *Desert Sun* (Palm Springs, CA), May 23, 2003, A23.
22. Malcolm Miller testimony, Preliminary Examination, vol. 16, July 11, 2001, 2495.
23. Batt testimony, June 7, 2001, 1059–65. Vallimont denied that he wrote these words on the ball.
24. Ibid., 1060.
25. Bob Conner trial notes, "Follow-up on Batt's Testimony."
26. Alameda County District Attorney Inspector's Report, case no. SOU 00-106. Prepared by Inspector Bob Conner.
27. Ibid.
28. Internal Affairs statement of Steve Hewison, September 14, 2000, 4.
29. Bob Conner trial notes, "Follow-up on Batt's Testimony."
30. Shumarr Doernners, interviewed by Ali Winston, September 9, 2021.
31. Hewison testimony, Preliminary Examination, vol. 15, July 10, 2001.
32. Bruce Vallimont testimony, Preliminary Examination, vol. 16, July 11, 2001, 2504.
33. Keith Batt, deposition, 127, December 20, 2005.
34. "Riders v. City of Oakland et al.," Sergeant Jon Madarang, interviewed by Sergeant Maverick Grier, March 27, 2002, file in possession of authors.
35. Herbert Sample, "Accused Cop Denies Beating Claim," *Sacramento (CA) Bee*, April 10, 2003, 4A.
36. Testimony of Richard Word, May 1, 2003, 2.
37. Daily Police Bulletin, Oakland, California, Richard L. Word—Chief of Police, November 17, 2000, 2.
38. Richard Word, 6.
39. A program similar to SANE had been tried out earlier in OPD's history, in a small area of East Oakland near an elementary school. Ibid., 17–20.

40. Ibid.
41. Ibid., 21–22.
42. Ibid., 45.
43. Internal Oakland Police Department bulletin, "News from the Chief of Police—Oakland Police Department," September 8, 1999.
44. Ibid., 32.
45. Ibid., 38.
46. Lee Romney, John Glionna, and Carol Pogash, "3 Former Oakland Officers Acquitted of Some Charges," *Los Angeles Times*, October 1, 2003.
47. Doernners, author interview, September 9, 2021.

4: ONE HUNDRED NINETEEN BLACK MEN V. THE CITY OF OAKLAND

1. Jim Chanin, interviewed by Darwin BondGraham, August 20, 2019.
2. John Burris, interviewed by Darwin BondGraham, September 16, 2019.
3. "Family Seeks Charges in Fatal Shooting by Cop," *San Francisco Chronicle* online, June 27, 1997, https://www.sfgate.com/news/article/EAST-BAY-Family -Seeks-Charges-In-Fatal-Shooting-2820263.php.
4. Hollister, authors interview, November 12, 2019; John Russo, interviewed by Darwin BondGraham, August 8, 2019. Russo was Oakland's first elected city attorney. Voters created the position by approving a charter amendment via Measure X in 2000. Previously, the city attorney was appointed by Oakland's mayor and city council.
5. Chanin, author interview, August 28, 2019. According to Chanin, attorneys were unable to sue on her behalf, and she became one of many Riders victims who were never compensated.
6. The land known as People's Park had once been a block full of homes and apartments occupied mostly by students. But in 1968 the university purchased the property and demolished the buildings, with plans to develop. When a year passed, and the lot still sat vacant, a cadre of mostly youthful volunteers—Berkeley undergrads and grad students, local hippies, enthusiastic neighbors—began cleaning up the eyesore and transforming it into a park. They planted flowers, trees, and bushes, laid down sod, installed a swing set for kids to enjoy, and even constructed an amphitheater. It was a park built by the people. People's Park. See Tom Dalzell, *The Battle for People's Park, Berkeley 1969* (Berkeley, CA: Heyday Books, 2019).
7. Chanin, author interview, August 20, 2019.
8. *The Misuse of Police Authority in Chicago* (Chicago: Blue Ribbon Panel, 1972), https://chicagopatf.org/wp-content/uploads/2016/01/metcalfe-report-1972 .pdf. This report was based on four days of hearings chaired by Illinois representative Ralph H. Metcalfe in June and July 1972.
9. Don Martinez, "Oakland Lawyer Carries on 60s Crusade," *San Francisco Examiner*, May 2, 1988, 15.
10. Amy Linn, Andrew Ross, and Scott Winokur's five-part newspaper series on the Richmond Police Department's racial strife, including the story of the

"Cowboys" gang of mostly white officers, remains one of the best and only in-depth examinations of the Contra Costa County city's strife-ridden era of policing in the 1970s and early 1980s. Among other things, the reporters published a controversial photo of more than a dozen white RPD officers posing as Confederate soldiers for a reenactment photo that featured a Confederate battle flag flying above them. See Amy Linn, Andrew Ross, and Scott Winokur, "With the Authority of Law: Police Violence in Richmond," *San Francisco Examiner*, June 19–23, 1983.

11. *Report of the Independent Commission of the Los Angeles Police Department*, ix–xi. "The top 5% of the officers (ranked by number of reports) accounted for 20% of all reports."

12. C. A. Novak, *The Years of Controversy: The Los Angeles Police Commission, 1991–1993* (Washington, DC: Police Foundation, 1995).

13. Radley Balko, *Rise of the Warrior Cop: The Militarization of America's Police Forces* (New York: PublicAffairs, 2013).

14. United States of America v. Pittsburgh Police Bureau, CIVIL NO. 97-0354, April 16, 1997, https://www.justice.gov/crt/united-states-district-court-western-district-pennsylvania.

15. Sheryl Gay Stolberg, "'It Did Not Stick': The First Federal Effort to Curb Police Abuse," *New York Times*, April 9, 2017, A12.

16. *US Department of Justice: Information on Employment Litigation . . . 2001 through 2007*, 87.

17. "Special Litigation Cases and Matters," US Department of Justice online, accessed March 24, 2022, https://www.justice.gov/crt/special-litigation-section-cases-and-matters/download#police.

18. *The Civil Rights Division's Pattern and Practice Police Reform Work: 1994–Present*, (Washington, DC: Civil Rights Division, US Department of Justice, January 2017), 42–48, https://www.justice.gov/crt/file/922421/download; Erick Trickey, "The Obama-Era Police Reform Biden Can't Wait to Restart," *Politico* online, last modified June 29, 2020, https://www.politico.com/news/magazine/2020/06/29/obama-police-reform-341685.

19. Russo, author interview, August 8, 2019.

20. Kim Curtis, "City to Settle 'Rogue' Cops Lawsuits for $11 Million," *Los Angeles Times*, February 20, 2003.

21. Jeffrey Schwartz, interviewed by Ali Winston, November 17, 2020.

22. City of Oakland Office of the City Attorney, "City of Oakland Settles 'Riders' Civil Rights Suits," press release, February 19, 2003, available at https://www.oaklandcityattorney.org/PDFS/Riders/Riders%20final%20settlement.pdf.

23. Madrid v. Gomez, 889 F. Supp. 1146 (N.D. Cal. 1995), available at Justia, https://law.justia.com/cases/federal/district-courts/FSupp/889/1146/1904317/.

24. Rachel Burgess, Kelli Evans, Charles Gruber, and Christy Lopez, *Combined Fourth and Fifth Report of the Independent Monitor*, Delphine Allen et. al v. City of Oakland, December 2004.

25. Terence Monmaney, "Rampart-like Scandal Rocks Oakland Justice System, Politics," *Los Angeles Times*, December 11, 2000, A3.

26. "Goldenrods" was a term used within the OPD to refer to the yellow carbon copy of a police report that new officers were supposed to submit to their supervisors at the end of a shift. Holly Joshi, interviewed by Ali Winston, January 1, 2021.

27. Eric Bailey, "Brown Is Under Fire for Surge in Oakland Killings," *Los Angeles Times*, May 12, 2006.

28. Martin Reynolds, "End 'No-Snitch' Culture for Sake of the Community," *Oakland Tribune*, January 27, 2008.

5: THE ORIGINS OF WEST COAST COP CULTURE

1. "An Anomaly of the Law," *San Francisco Examiner*, April 20, 1890, 4; W. R. Andrus, "Annual Message," *Oakland Tribune*, February 4, 1879, 4.

2. Michael Dennis Griffith, "Law Enforcement and Urban Growth: Oakland, California 1850–1910" (PhD dissertation in philosophy, University of California, Berkeley, 1981).

3. "Jury Will Probe Petty Police Graft," *San Francisco Call* 100, no. 171, November 18, 1906, 32.

4. "Eighty-Six Caught in One Raid: Chinese Gamblers Hold Overflow Meeting at City Jail," *Oakland Tribune*, August 23, 1908, 1.

5. "Hanley Leaves Police Force Under Cloud," *San Francisco Call* 105, no. 118, March 28, 1909, 28.

6. "Heney Tells Large Audience Oakland Graft Is Honeycombed," *Sacramento (CA) Bee*, November 21, 1914, 2.

7. "'I Paid Cash to Cockrell,' Says Gee," *San Francisco Call* 106, no. 19, July 30, 1919.

8. "Grand Jury Fails to Indict," *Oakland Tribune*, March 27, 1917, 1.

9. Liam O'Donohue, "The Sinister, Evil KKK in Oakland Once Ruled City Hall," *East Bay Express* (Oakland) online, last modified February 21, 2017, https://eastbayexpress.com/the-sinister-evil-kkk-in-oakland-once-ruled-city-hall-2-1/.

10. "500 Initiated into Klan During Night Ceremony," *Oakland Tribune*, July 5, 1924, 13.

11. "KKK Warns Oakland of Moral Crusade," *San Francisco Call* 111, no. 89, April 19, 1922, 1.

12. "Officials to Unite Against Ku Klux Klan" and "Klan List Shows Many Oakland Police, Report," *San Francisco Call* 111, no. 108, May 11, 1922, 13; "Oakland KKK on Police Force to Be Ousted," *San Francisco Call* 111, no. 107, May 10, 1922.

13. Peter J. Boyer, "Bad Cops," *New Yorker*, May 13, 2001.

14. "Police Ban on Klan at Long Beach," *Los Angeles Times*, April 27, 1922, 7.

15. "Membership in Klan No Crime, Asserts Decoto," *Oakland Tribune*, May 18, 1922, 3.

16. "US Joins in Cleanup of Emeryville," *Oakland Tribune*, May 3, 1928, 1.

17. "Petty Graft Included in Police Probe," *Oakland Tribune*, October 22, 1931,

1, and "$3,000,000 Graft Laid to 150 Policemen in Oakland Department," *Oakland Tribune*, October 21, 1931, 1.

18. "Warren Refuses to Name Protection Collector, 'Ask Becker,' He Says," *Oakland Tribune*, October 24, 1927, 1.

19. The most comprehensive history of the police alliance with business groups to repress labor movements is Frank Donner, *Protectors of Privilege: Red Squads and Police Repression in Urban America* (Berkeley: University of California Press, 1990), but the documentation of the police department's one-sided and sustained assault on labor is extensive and includes Bud Schultz, *The Price of Dissent: Testimonies to Political Repression in America* (Berkeley: University of California Press, 2001), and Eldridge Foster Dowell, *A History of Criminal Syndicalism Legislation in the United States* (Baltimore: Johns Hopkins Press, 1939).

20. The Dutch sabot shoe had been a symbol of worker power since the fourteenth century, when European workers were said to have thrown their clogs into textile machinery in protest.

21. "Outlaw I.W.W. When M'Hugo Is Sentenced," *Oakland Tribune*, December 13, 1919, 1.

22. The links between the American Legion and the OPD were strong and grew with time. In 1932, Oakland officers established their own police officers and firefighters section within the Legion. By the 1950s there was a joint OPD–American Legion motorcycle drill team. "Police and Firemen Form State Club Within Legion," *Oakland Tribune*, August 16, 1932, 17.

23. "Police Failed Help I.W.W. Is Complaint," *San Francisco Examiner*, November 13, 1919, 2.

24. "Red Meetings Prohibited by Law in Oakland," *Oakland Tribune*, November 15, 1919, 2.

25. "Local Police Take Part in General Raid," *Oakland Tribune*, January 3, 1920, 1.

26. "10 Injured, 4 Jailed as Police Club Oakland Communists," *San Francisco Examiner*, May 2, 1930, 3.

27. "Eastbay Communists Raided, Bomb Found Near Cannery," *San Francisco Examiner*, July 17, 1934, 3.

28. Ed Cray, *Chief Justice: A Biography of Earl Warren* (New York: Simon & Schuster, 1997).

29. "Oakland Moves to Ban Open Air Red Rallies," *San Francisco Examiner*, July 16, 1941, 13.

30. Seth Rosenfeld, *Subversives: The FBI's War on Student Radicals, and Reagan's Rise to Power* (New York: Farrar, Straus and Giroux, 2012), 33.

31. Alexander Charns, *Cloak and Gavel: FBI Wiretaps, Bugs, Informers, and the Supreme Court* (Urbana: University of Illinois Press, 1992), 48.

32. Nick Petris, a longtime member of the California State Assembly and State Senate, recalled that West Oakland in the 1930s was "a marvelous mixture of people. We had every nationality that we knew of in that neighborhood. We had Chinese. We had Mexican, Portuguese, Greek, Italian, Yugoslav. Our immediate neighbor was a black family." Robert O. Self, *American Babylon: Race*

and the Struggle for Postwar Oakland (Princeton, NJ: Princeton University Press, 2003), 41.

33. Ibid., 50–51.

34. Jessica Mitford, *A Fine Old Conflict* (London: M. Joseph, 1977).

35. "New Oakland Group Maps Drive on Police Brutality," *California Eagle* (Los Angeles), July 10, 1947, 4.

36. "Brutality Exposes 'Red Plot,' Cry Oakland Police," *California Eagle* (Los Angeles), June 19, 1947, 20.

37. "Record of Spokesman in Council Row Revealed," *Oakland Tribune*, June 12, 1947, 1. DA Hoyt was appointed to a superior court judge seat later the same year by Earl Warren, then in his second term as California's governor.

38. "Daily Knave," *Oakland Tribune*, February 22, 1949, 19.

39. "Council-Labor Split Bared at Rally Here," *Oakland Tribune*, February 14, 1949, 1.

40. "Civil Rights in Oakland: State Will Check on Charge of Police Discrimination," *San Francisco Chronicle*, December 29, 1949.

41. Self, *American Babylon*, 78.

42. Robert B. Powers, interviewed by Amelia R. Fry, 1969, for Earl Warren Oral History Project, "Law Enforcement, Race Relations: 1930–1960," 55; transcript available at Online Archives of California, University of California, https://oac.cdlib.org/view?docId=kt0q2n97fc&&doc.view=entire_text.

43. Powers had a remarkable about-face when it came to race. In 1969 he admitted that he was a "bigoted racist" while running the Bakersfield Police Department, where his cops forcefully suppressed the local Black population. His attitudes changed notably while working in the California Attorney General's Office under Robert Walker Kenny. Both Powers's and Kenny's attitudes toward civil rights and race repeatedly incurred the ire of FBI director J. Edgar Hoover and his subordinates for initiatives such as pathbreaking race relations training for police in Richmond, California. Powers, "Law Enforcement, Race Relations," 58.

44. Mitford, *Fine Old Conflict*.

45. Gwynne Peirson, "An Introductory Study of Institutional Racism in Law Enforcement" (dissertation, University of California, Berkeley, 1978), 116–17.

46. "Prober Nabs Hostile Cop," *Daily People's World* (San Francisco), January 4, 1950; "Report Claims Oakland Cops Beat Negro," *San Francisco Chronicle*, December 31, 1949.

47. Emerson Street, "Nightstick Justice in Oakland," *New Republic*, February 20, 1950, 15–16; Thomas Peele, *Killing the Messenger: A Story of Radical Faith, Racism's Backlash, and the Assassination of a Journalist* (New York: Crown, 2012), 127.

48. Ibid.

49. Robert de Roos, "Oakland Police Inquiry Hears Brutality Charges," *San Francisco Chronicle*, January 6, 1950.

50. Robert de Roos, "Oakland Police Inquiry: Witnesses Charge Brutality, Racial Discrimination," *San Francisco Chronicle*, January 5, 1950.

51. Mitford, *Fine Old Conflict*.

52. de Roos, "Oakland Police Inquiry: Witnesses Charge Brutality, Racial Discrimination."

53. "Many changes initiated by the department were done to disguise racist practices, rather than to deal with them openly so they could be eliminated. Such alterations often tend to treat the symptom of the underlying problem rather than the problem itself, thereby eradicating the symptoms and making the cure (the solution) more difficult." Gwynne Peirson, *Police Operations* (Chicago: Nelson-Hall Publishing, 1976), 100.

54. Ibid., 105–9.

55. Ibid., 113.

56. Ibid., 122.

57. Ibid., 18.

58. Self, *American Babylon*, 68.

59. Donna Jean Murch, *Living for the City: Migration, Education, and the Rise of the Black Panther Party in Oakland, California* (Chapel Hill: University of North Carolina Press, 2010), 97.

6: NOTHING WILL GET DONE UNTIL OAKLAND BURNS TO THE GROUND

1. Murch, *Living for the City*, 38–39.

2. "School Pupil Shift Plan Told," *Oakland Tribune*, April 6, 1966, 5.

3. "Schools Hit by Dial In Protesters," *Oakland Tribune*, April 16, 1964, 1.

4. Robyn C. Spencer, *The Revolution Has Come: Black Power, Gender, and the Black Panther Party in Oakland* (Durham, NC: Duke University Press, 2016), 23–24.

5. "Racial: Negro Youths Run Wild in Oakland," *Los Angeles Times*, October 23, 1966, 91; John A. Haymond, "The Navy Called Them 'Mutineers.' But Were They Really Scapegoats?" *Navy Times*, February 12, 2019.

6. "Police Clamp Lid on Trouble Spots," *Oakland Tribune*, October 20, 1966, 4.

7. Huey P. Newton, with J. Herman Blake, *Revolutionary Suicide* (New York: Penguin Classics, 1973), 71–121; Charles E. Cobb Jr., *This Nonviolent Stuff'll Get You Killed: How Guns Made the Civil Rights Movement Possible* (Durham, NC: Duke University Press, 2015).

8. The Community Alert Patrol's chief spokesman was Ron Karenga, the founder of United Slaves, whose organization would later engage in lethal clashes with the BPP's Los Angeles chapter. The CAP program was a federally funded antiviolence program that employed current and former gang members to conduct civilian oversight of police activities on the street, an early form of what is now known commonly as "cop-watching." Mike Davis and Jon Wiener, *Set the Night on Fire: L.A. in the Sixties* (Brooklyn, NY: Verso, 2020), 268–327.

9. Julia Lovell, *Maoism: A Global History* (New York: Knopf, 2019), 279–80.

10. Joshua Bloom and Waldo E. Martin Jr., *Black Against Empire: The History and Politics of the Black Panther Party* (Berkeley: University of California Press, 2013), 72.

11. In time, the term was adopted by Oakland cops as an ironic form of self-identification. Some veteran officers got tattoos of cartoon pigs dressed as cops to commemorate their OPD service, while a photograph of a pig wearing a police cap in the passenger seat of a squad car was circulated within the department for a caption contest. The winner: "Gee, Sarge, so I guess I passed probation?" George Paul Csicsery, "Thursdays at the Clambucket," Salon, last modified October 19, 1998, https://web.archive.org/web/19990202081323 /https://www.salon1999.com/it/feature/1998/10/19feature.html. In the 1980s the Oakland police and fire departments sponsored a "Pigs vs. Pyro" charity football game between officers and firefighters, and the OPD players adopted the "Thunderhog" as their mascot.

12. Rick Perlstein, *Nixonland: The Rise of a President and the Fracturing of America* (New York: Scribner, 2008), 187–89.

13. Self, *American Babylon*, 65.

14. Howard Rilea, for example, was one of three remaining white residents on his West Oakland block by the mid-1960s. A retired railroad brakeman and staunch conservative, his views were out of touch with his district's residents, but citywide majorities of white middle-class homeowners repeatedly elected him, while Black candidates gained the majority of the Black vote but were defeated. Darwin BondGraham, "District Elections: The Surprising History Explaining How We Vote in Oakland," The Oaklandside, last modified September 29, 2020, https://oaklandside.org/2020/09/29/district-elections-the -surprising-history-explaining-how-we-vote-in-oakland/.

15. "Clausen Wins Council Seat by 3577 Votes," *Oakland Tribune*, March 15, 1950, 1.

16. Peele, *Killing the Messenger*, 128.

17. Self, *American Babylon*, 27, 90; Davis and Wiener, *Set the Night on Fire*, 44–45.

18. Davis and Wiener, *Set the Night on Fire*, 45; Liam O'Donoghue, "It Was Like a Carnival: The Betrayal of Oakland's General Strike," *East Bay Yesterday* (podcast), December 29, 2020, https://eastbayyesterday.com/episodes/it -was-like-a-carnival/; Gayle B. Montgomery and James W. Johnson, in collaboration with Paul G. Manolis, *One Step from the White House: The Rise and Fall of Senator William F. Knowland* (Berkeley: University of California Press, 1998). On the international front, William Knowland was even more of a hawk. He was jokingly called the "senator from Formosa" for his almost obsessive focus on supporting Chiang Kai-shek's dreams of retaking China and destroying international Communism.

19. Self, *American Babylon*, 64; Gray Brechin, The Living New Deal online, https://livingnewdeal.org/.

20. Self, *American Babylon*, 70–74.

21. In 1963, Houlihan, a Republican, criticized President John F. Kennedy as not doing enough to help Black people. "The Irish people in the United States, particularly those prominent in politics, have a grave responsibility to see that Negroes achieve their rights," he told a crowd during a visit to Ireland in

1963. "Houlihan in Ireland Criticizes Kennedy," *Oakland Tribune*, June 18, 1963, 2.

22. "Mayor Challenges Race Leader Claims," *Oakland Tribune*, October 30, 1963, 8.

23. Davis and Wiener, *Set the Night on Fire*, 84–85.

24. Gene Ayres, "Mayor Asks Suburban Bias Study," *Oakland Tribune*, January 6, 1966, 21.

25. Floyd Hunter, "Kill and Forget," *Campus CORE-lator* online, Spring 1965, https://oac.cdlib.org/view?docId=kt8q2nb2zn&brand=oac4&doc.view= entire_text.

26. Mike Davis, *City of Quartz: Excavating the Future in Los Angeles* (New York: Verso, 1990), 126.

27. Amory Bradford, *Oakland's Not for Burning* (New York: D. McKay, 1968).

28. Warren Hinckle, "Metropoly: The Story of Oakland, California," *Ramparts*, February 1966, available at http://www.cwmorse.org/metropoly-the-story-of -oakland-california/.

29. Gene Ayres, "Council Forum on Minorities," *Oakland Tribune*, September 1, 1965, 1.

30. Davis and Wiener, *Set the Night on Fire*, 373.

31. *Violence in the City—An End or a Beginning? A Report* (Los Angeles: Governor's Commission on the Los Angeles Riots, December 1965), 7.

32. Rosenfeld, *Subversives*, 393–400.

33. Norman Melnick, "Poverty Fighters Focus on Police Review Board," *San Francisco Examiner*, August 23, 1966, 1.

34. "Coakley Hits Police Review Board," *Oakland Tribune*, October 29, 1966, 3.

35. Robert L. Allen, *The Port Chicago Mutiny: The Story of the Largest Mass Mutiny Trial in US History* (San Francisco: Heyday Books, 2011).

36. "E. Bay DA Says Reds Spur Riots," *San Francisco Examiner*, October 27, 1966, 6.

37. In his personal life, Frank Coakley was accused of racism: His family sold its prestigious Calmar Avenue home in Oakland's Lakeshore neighborhood after a Black family moved onto the block. His brother, Tom Coakley, a judge and candidate for state attorney general in 1962, wrote racially restrictive covenants to cover other family properties. Jessica Mitford, *Decca: The Letters of Jessica Mitford*, ed. Peter Y. Sussman (New York: Alfred A. Knopf, 2006).

38. Bloom and Martin, *Black Against Empire*, 38.

39. Ibid.

40. Bob Distefano, "'Action Jackson'—From Con to Counselor," *Oakland Tribune*, March 21, 1970, 1.

41. "Panel Favors Police Review," *Oakland Tribune*, February 24, 1966, 23E.

42. "Playing Political Games Won't End Oakland's War on Poverty," editorial, *Oakland Tribune*, March 31, 1970, 16.

43. Bob Distefano, "Oakland War on Poverty Agency Doomed; Months Required for Successor," *Oakland Tribune*, April 13, 1971, 1.

44. Elizabeth Hinton, *From the War on Poverty to the War on Crime: The Making of Mass Incarceration in America* (Cambridge, MA: Harvard University Press, 2016), 134–79.
45. Ward Churchill and Jim Vander Wall, *The COINTELPRO Papers: Documents from the FBI's Secret Wars Against Dissent in the United States* (Cambridge, MA: South End Press, 1990), 129, 363.
46. "Oakland Officer Explains Demonstration Control," *Salinas Californian*, June 17, 1965, 12; "Reagan Study Group Recommends Establishment of Fifth 'Super-Agency' for Public Safety Units," *Sacramento (CA) Bee*, June 1, 1973, B-3.
47. Hugh Pearson, *The Shadow of the Panther: Huey Newton and the Price of Black Power in America* (Reading, MA: Addison-Wesley, 1994), 291.
48. Bloom and Martin, *Black Against Empire*, 99–100; Newton with Blake, *Revolutionary Suicide*, 184–87.
49. Murch, *Living for the City*, 148–49; Newton with Blake, *Revolutionary Suicide*, 184–87.
50. Newton with Blake, *Revolutionary Suicide*, 186.
51. Kate Coleman and Paul Avery, "The Party's Over," *New Times*, July 10, 1978, 25.
52. Spencer, *Revolution Has Come*, 57.
53. Ibid., 188–89.
54. Bloom and Martin, *Black Against Empire*, 100.
55. Murch, *Living for the City*, 162–63.
56. Eldridge Cleaver, interviewed by Henry Louis Gates Jr., "The Two Nations of Black America," *Frontline*, PBS, February 10, 1998. "So we saw it coming while the police were acting, so we decided to get down first. So we started the fight. There were fourteen of us. We went down into the area of Oakland where the violence was the worst, a few blocks away from where Huey Newton had killed that cop, so we dealt with them when they came upon us. We were well armed, and we had a shootout that lasted an hour and a half."
57. Richard Jensen, interviewed for Washington University Libraries, Film and Media Archive, Henry Hampton Collection, May 23, 1989, transcript available at http://digital.wustl.edu/e/eii/eiiweb/jen5427.0853.078richardjensen .html.
58. Bloom and Martin, *Black Against Empire*, 117–20.
59. "Newton Predicting His Acquittal," *San Francisco Examiner*, September 14, 1979, 38.
60. "Police Chief Charles Gain on Bobby Hutton's Shooting," KTVU News, 2:42, April 25, 1968, available at Bay Area Television Archive online, J. Paul Leonard Library, San Francisco State University, https://diva.sfsu.edu/collections /sfbatv/bundles/223881?fbclid=IwAR1iIjPqwJFP-JbDwSZhEM4e-SitZT 2PQA8Zf8DHX0KUQ30cBYKrijIPR8o.
61. A Los Angeles judge tossed out the police union's lawsuit against Brando after deciding the actor hadn't made defamatory remarks. Reuters, "Brando Free in Libel Suit," May 6, 1969. A panel of appeals court judges similarly dismissed the lawsuit against Caen.

62. "Gywnne Peirson, WW II Flier, Criminologist at Howard, Dies," *Washington Post*, May 17, 1991.

63. Bloom and Martin, *Black Against Empire*, 425n18; Peirson, *Police Operations*, 169–71.

64. Eugene Jennings, deposition, 4–5, April 10, 1968.

65. Peirson, *Police Operations*, 169–71.

66. Jennings, deposition, April 10, 1968.

67. Peirson's and Jennings's statements were never transcribed by the DA's office, even though audio recordings were taken. "This fact meant that the only evidence the district attorney presented to the jury was that which backed up the police department's official version of the killing," Peirson wrote years later.

68. Peirson, *Police Operations*, 183–84.

69. Ibid.

70. "OPD Officers Attack Black Panther Party Headquarters," KTVU News, 8:50, September 1968, available at Bay Area Television Archive online, J. Paul Leonard Library, San Francisco State University, https://diva.sfsu.edu/collections/sfbatv/bundles/223883.

71. "Police Fire on Black Panther Headquarters," KPFA Radio, 54:41, September 10, 1968, available at American Archive of Public Broadcasting online, https://americanarchive.org/catalog/cpb-aacip_28-n58cf9jn53.

72. Peirson, *Police Operations*, 176.

73. Ibid., 63–64.

74. Ibid., 10.

75. Ibid., 22.

76. Ibid., 113.

77. Ibid., 77–78.

78. Davis and Wiener, *Set the Night on Fire*, 111. "One of the society's chief constituencies was the LAPD, where under the benign eye of Chief [William] Parker, officers openly wore [Barry] Goldwater badges and distributed anti-Communist tracts such as *None Dare Call It Treason*, a favorite among Birchers, from station houses."

79. Peirson, "An Introductory Study of Institutional Racism in Law Enforcement," 111–12.

80. Kevin Fagan and Henry K. Lee, "1970 Killing Still Haunts Berkeley—Officer's Unsolved Slaying Divides City," *San Francisco Chronicle*, August 14, 2005; Peele, *Killing the Messenger*, 146, 389, endnote 146.

81. Associated Press, "Group Reports Downing Helicopter," *New York Times*, October 11, 1973, 23.

82. United Press International, "Sniper Aims at Police," *Desert Sun* (Palm Springs, CA), October 6, 1973, A3.

83. Michael Taylor, "Forgotten Footnote: Before Hearst, SLA Killed Education," *San Francisco Chronicle*, November 14, 2002.

84. Rosenfeld, *Subversives*, 279–80.

85. Ibid., 274.

86. Ibid., 280–81; Hunter S. Thompson, *Hell's Angels: A Strange and Terrible Saga* (New York: Ballantine Books, 2003), 237. "The Angels enjoyed these visits; they were much happier talking with cops than they were with reporters or even sympathetic strangers. . . . Despite the outlaws' growing notoriety, the Oakland police never put the kind of death-rattle heat on them that the other chapters were getting."

87. Rosenfeld, *Subversives*, 281–82.

88. Ibid.

89. Thompson, *Hell's Angels*, 244–46.

90. Ibid.

91. "Center Remains Open—Order Restored," *San Francisco Examiner*, October 1967, 1.

92. Associated Press, "Reagan, Finch Praise Lawmen," *San Francisco Examiner*, October 17, 1967, 6.

93. Daryl E. Lembke, "Oakland's Chief Defends Action as Most Practical," *Los Angeles Times*, October 18, 1967, 3.

94. San Francisco–Oakland Newspaper Guild to the Committee on Criminal Procedure, California State Assembly, Sacramento, December 5, 1967.

95. Peirson, *Police Operations*, 132.

96. Ibid., 146.

97. "Board Gets Report on Oakland," *Oakland Tribune*, May 26, 1966, 16.

98. Fran Dauth, "Charlie Gain and the Cops," *Oakland Tribune*, March 28, 1976, 1.

99. Jerome H. Skolnick, *The New Blue Line: Police Innovation in Six American Cities* (New York: Free Press, 1986), 150.

100. John Hall, "Two Chiefs Split on Idea of Anti-police Conspiracy," *San Bernardino County (CA) Sun*, October 10, 1970.

101. "Burglary Suspect Is Killed," *Oakland Tribune*, February 6, 1968, 1; Peirson, "An Introductory Study of Institutional Racism in Law Enforcement," 168–69.

102. James J. Fyfe, ed., *Readings on Police Use of Deadly Force* (Washington, DC: Police Foundation, 1982); Evan Golder, "Stop or I'll Shoot," *San Francisco Examiner California Living Sunday* magazine, March 7, 1976, 4.

103. Skolnick, *New Blue Line*, 150.

104. Wallace Turner, "Ex-Police Chief Speaks in Pride of Coast Career," *New York Times*, December 24, 1979, D5.

105. Larry Murphy, *Blackjack and Jive-Five* (Bloomington, IN: AuthorHouse, 2002), 55.

106. Ibid., 55.

107. Peirson, *Police Operations*, 186–87.

108. "The Making of an Oakland Cop," *Montage*, directed by Dominic Bonavolonta, written and produced by Johnny Barnes Selvin, aired 1980 on KTVU, available at Bay Area Television Archive online, J. Paul Leonard Library, San Francisco State University, https://diva.sfsu.edu/collections/sfbatv/bundles/229259.

109. "The People and the Police: Oakland," *Assignment Four*, written, directed,

and produced by Ira Eisenberg, aired 1974 on KRON-TV, available at Bay Area Television Archive online, J. Paul Leonard Library, San Francisco State University, https://diva.sfsu.edu/collections/sfbatv/bundles/210744.

110. Ibid. Sadly, the computers and accompanying data analytics program would fall by the wayside in the late 1970s as tax referendums and the outflow of businesses from Oakland to neighboring suburbs and farther afield whittled down local revenues.

111. Brenda Payton, "Hart Keeps Head Above the Contention," *San Francisco Examiner*, October 9, 1979, F1.

112. Barbara Lee, interviewed by the authors, September 4, 2020.

113. Don Martinez, "Oakland Vote Focuses on Crime," *San Francisco Examiner*, May 15, 1977, 4A.

7: SMALL WARS

1. Although many of the original OPD records regarding the Melvin Black case no longer exist, one of the jurors of the civil lawsuit brought by Black's mother against the city wrote a detailed account of the case: William Glackin, "Jury Duty Proves Tough, Instructive Experience," *Sacramento (CA) Bee*, October 21, 1984, B1.

2. Lloyd Boles and Harry Harris, "Report on Youth's Death: Mixed Reaction from Law," *Oakland Tribune*, September 15, 1979, 1.

3. Fahizah Alim, "Jury Awards $693,000 to Mother of Youth Slain by Police," *Sacramento (CA) Bee*, October 16, 1984, B4.

4. Raul Ramirez and Sue Soennichsen, "Council Approves Citizens Review Panel," *Oakland Tribune*, January 10, 1980, A10.

5. Del Lane, "Panel Briefed on Handling of Complaints about Police," *Oakland Tribune*, October 4, 1979, B11.

6. Lloyd Boles, "Task Force to Decide How to Handle Complaints on Police, City Workers," *Oakland Tribune*, October 23, 1979, B1.

7. Oliver Jones and Bob Foster, "Should Oakland Have a Police Review Board," *Oakland Tribune*, December 10, 1979, A13.

8. Raul Ramirez and Soennichean, "Council Approves Citizen Review Panel," *Oakland Tribune*, January 10, 1980, 1.

9. Pearson, *Shadow of the Panther*, 335; Flores A. Forbes, *Will You Die with Me? My Life and the Black Panther Party* (New York: Washington Square Press, 2007).

10. Spencer, *Revolution Has Come*, 160–63; Pearson, *Shadow of the Panther*, 235–38.

11. Pearson, *Shadow of the Panther*, 270–74; Spencer, *Revolution Has Come*, 161.

12. Coleman and Avery, "Party's Over," 30–31.

13. Lance Williams, "Panthers' Fall Didn't Faze Huey," *San Francisco Examiner*, July 27, 1987, 1.

14. Pearson, *Shadow of the Panther*, 273. Quote is from an anonymous interview with a former BPP member from 1992.

15. "Oakland Attack: College Teacher Beaten in Class," *San Francisco Chronicle*, November 16, 1972; "Panther Charge Now Is Murder," *San Francisco*

Chronicle, March 1, 1973; "Shooting in Oakland—2 Arrests," *San Francisco Chronicle,* April 27, 1973; Pearson, *Shadow of the Panther,* 273; Coleman and Avery, "Party's Over," 36. The Brass Rail restaurant was "regarded in the surrounding community as a headquarters at the time for cocaine dealers."

16. Coleman and Avery, "Party's Over," 41–43.

17. Ibid., 44–46. The financial irregularities eventually brought down the Panthers' school program, with Oakland mayor Lionel Wilson resigning from its board and the city council voting unanimously to end Oakland's contract with the Education Opportunities Corporation.

18. "City of Oakland, Alameda County, 1970–1980 Census," Metropolitan Transportation Commission (MTC) and Association of Bay Area Governments (ABAG) online, accessed June 14, 2022, http://www.bayareacensus.ca.gov /cities/Oakland70.htm.

19. Alfred McCoy, *The Politics of Heroin in Southeast Asia* (New York: Harper & Row, 1972), 394–96.

20. Sam Quinones, *Dreamland: The True Tale of America's Opiate Epidemic* (New York: Bloomsbury, 2015).

21. "Largest Heroin Bust in US Is Reported," *Los Angeles Times,* June 21, 1991, A3.

22. Carla Marinucci and Lance Williams, "Dealers Use Modern Business Techniques," *San Francisco Examiner,* November 27, 1984, 5.

23. "The Making of an Oakland Cop," KTVU online, https://diva.sfsu.edu /collections/sfbatv/bundles/229259.

24. Pearson, *Shadow of the Panther,* 4–5; Carla Marinucci and Lance Williams, "A Small War in Oakland," *San Francisco Examiner,* November 25, 1984, 1.

25. Carla Marinucci and Lance Williams, "The Ghetto's Drug Hero Tempts Youth," *San Francisco Examiner,* November 27, 1984, A4. Marinucci and Williams, "Dealers Use Modern Business Techniques," 5.

26. Coleman and Avery, "Party's Over," 36, 38, 41.

27. Marinucci and Williams, "Small War in Oakland," 1.

28. Ibid.

29. Thaai Walker, "Drug Kingpin's Sentencing Ends Bloody Era in Oakland: Decades of Turf Wars Over as Citizens Reclaim Their City," *San Francisco Chronicle,* February 16, 1999.

30. Marinucci and Williams.

31. Funktown USA forged extensive ties with the Black Guerilla Family, an African American prison gang of former radicals that remains today a significant force in national prison politics. Pearson, *Shadow of the Panther,* 307.

32. USA v. Brown et al., 3:81-cr-00054-WWS-2, February 5, 1981; P.B., former Oakland PD Narcotics and Homicide investigator, interviewed by the authors, December 15, 2021; Harry Harris, "Two Oakland Vice Cops Arrested on Drug Charge," *Oakland Tribune,* February 6, 1981, 1. A Berkeley police officer and an Alameda sheriff's deputy were also arrested in 1981 for trafficking in cocaine.

33. Lance Williams, "Minister Recalls Crack's Early Days," *San Francisco Examiner,* February 28, 1988, 10.

34. Gary Webb, *Dark Alliance: The CIA, the Contras, and the Crack Cocaine Explosion* (New York: Seven Stories Press, 1998), 169–171; *The CIA-Contra-Crack Cocaine Controversy: A Review of the Justice Department's Investigations and Prosecutions* (Washington, DC: US Department of Justice Office of the Inspector General, December 1, 1997), available at https://oig.justice.gov/reports/cia-contra-crack-cocaine-controversy-review-justice-departments-investigations-and.

35. United Press International online, "Felix Mitchell, an Alleged Small-time Heroin Dealer Who Rose . . . ," December 16, 1981, https://www.upi.com/Archives/1981/12/16/Felix-Mitchell-an-alleged-small-time-heroin-dealer-who-rose/3089377326800/.

36. Oakland's Castlemont Corridor was defined by Sixty-Sixth Avenue to the north, MacArthur Boulevard to the east, the San Leandro border to the south, and Hegenberger Road to the west. Lance Williams, "Mother's Crack Use Unraveled Her Life," *San Francisco Examiner*, February 7, 1990, 1.

37. Lance Williams, "How FBI Operation Broke Up Oakland Drug Ring," *San Francisco Examiner*, February 8, 1990, 10.

38. David DeBolt, "Oakland Crack King Gets Clemency from Obama," *Oakland Tribune*, September 1, 2016.

39. United Press International, "Reputed Oakland Drug Kingpin Charged After Cocaine Lab Raid," *Los Angeles Times*, December 11, 1988, 52.

40. Lance Williams, "Bloodshed in Oakland Traced to 3-Year Feud," *San Francisco Examiner*, February 9, 1992, 1.

41. John Silvester, "Of Outlaw Gangs, Strong Cops and Long Memories," *Age* (Australia) online, last modified July 28, 2012, https://www.theage.com.au/national/victoria/of-outlaw-gangs-strong-cops-and-long-memories-20120727-22zkv.html.

42. In 1972, during Barger's trial for the murder of a Texas meth and coke dealer, the biker told an Alameda County jury that his gang had cut deals with the OPD, including one scheme in which the bikers bought up illegal weapons on the city's streets and handed them over to the police, thus preventing bombs, bazookas, and machine guns from falling into the hands of leftist "terrorists." Michael Taylor, "Hell's Angels Run Out of Time: When the Law Embraced the Devil," *Los Angeles Times*, May 10, 1980.

43. Barger himself reputedly claimed to have murdered between eight and ten people, but he was never convicted for any killing. Cynthia Gorney, "The Case Against Harley's Angeles," *Washington Post*, October 26, 1979.

44. Hart, authors interview, November 11, 2019.

45. Penn/Stump v. City of Oakland; Skolnick, *New Blue Line*, 149; Peirson, *Police Operations*, 110. However, only 13 percent of all Oakland cops actually lived in the city, a constant to the present day.

46. Skolnick, *New Blue Line*, 151.

47. Ibid., 158.

48. Former OPD officers Rick Hart; Vic Bullock, interviewed by the authors, November 20, 2020; and Ersie Joyner, interviewed by the authors, July 23, 2020.

49. Skolnick, *New Blue Line*, 178.

50. Kate Coleman, "The Roots of Ed Meese: Reagan's Polemical Attorney General Has Prompted a Major Constitutional Debate, Surprising Those Who Knew Him in His Pragmatic Early Days, in the Quiet Hills of Oakland and During the Turbulent '60's," *Los Angeles Times Magazine*, May 4, 1986.

51. Associated Press, "Study Says Ounce of Interdiction Worth Kilo of Arrests," October 19, 1987; Sampson O. Annan, Brian Forst, and Craig Uchida, *Modern Policing and the Control of Illegal Drugs: Testing New Strategies in Two American Cities* (Washington, DC: US Department of Justice, Office of Justice Programs, National Institute of Justice online, May 1992), available at https://www.oip.gov/pdffiles1/nij/133785.pdf.

52. SDU II's area of operations stretched from the San Leandro border to Lake Merritt. SDU III covered the downtown, West Oakland, and as far north as the Berkeley and Emeryville borders.

53. Skolnick, *New Blue Line*, 172–74.

54. Ibid., 161.

55. Marilyn Johnson, *Street Justice: A History of Police Violence in New York City* (Boston: Beacon Press, 2004).

56. Terry McDermott, "Behind the Bunker Mentality," *Los Angeles Times*, June 11, 2000.

57. Davis, *City of Quartz*, 268.

58. Boyer, "Bad Cops"; David Kocienewski, "Success of Elite Police Unit Exacts a Toll on the Streets," *New York Times*, February 15, 1999. Hollywood has mythologized both SCU and CRASH in a number of feature films, including but not limited to *We Own the Night* (2007), *Rampart* (2011), and, most famously, *Training Day* (2001).

59. Albert J. Reiss Jr., *Policing a City's Central District: The Oakland Story* (Washington, DC: US Department of Justice, National Institute of Justice, March 1985), 4, 9, available at https://babel.hathitrust.org/cgi/pt?id=mdp.39015028421546&view=1up&seq=3.

60. Skolnick, *New Blue Line*, 174.

61. Ibid., 175; Chanin, author interview, August 28, 2019.

62. Skolnick, *New Blue Line*, 174–75.

63. Peter Fimrite, "Cop Brutality Called Routine in Flatlands," *San Francisco Chronicle*, August 8, 1991.

64. Skolnick, *New Blue Line*, 178.

65. Pearson, *Shadow of the Panther*, 283–84.

66. Ibid., 307–10.

67. Ibid., 319–21.

68. Ibid., 318.

69. Ibid., 328.

70. Robert Stanley Oden, *From Blacks to Brown and Beyond: The Struggle for Progressive Politics in Oakland, California, 1966–2017* (San Diego: Cognella Academic, 2018); J. Phillip Thompson III, *Double Trouble: Black Mayors,*

Black Communities, and the Call for Deeper Democracy (New York: Oxford University Press, 2005).

71. Liam O'Donoghue, "A Home Burned Every 11 Seconds: A Tragedy That Could Happen Again," *East Bay Yesterday* (podcast, episode 67), October 8, 2020, https://eastbayyesterday.com/episodes/a-home-burned-every-11-seconds/.

72. Dan Morain, "Oakland's True Believers See Greatness in Its Future," *Los Angeles Times*, January 7, 1991, 1.

73. Michael Taylor, Pearl Stewart, and Clarence Johnson, "Cocaine, Murder in East Oakland," *San Francisco Chronicle*, December 27, 1990.

74. Times Wire Services, "Oakland Mayor's Son Tied to Alleged Drug Ring," *Los Angeles Times*, December 15, 1988, 38.

75. Donald Sutton and Ralph F. Baker, *Oakland Crack Task Force: A Portrait of Community Mobilization* (Washington, DC: US Department of Education, June 1990), 2.

76. Peter Fimrite, "Oakland Police Close Down Reputed Drug House," *San Francisco Chronicle*, May 19, 1992.

77. Peter Fimrite, "Oakland Homeless People Sue Police over Rights," *San Francisco Chronicle*, July 8, 1992.

78. Michael Taylor, "What Oakland's Top Cop Would Do," *San Francisco Chronicle*, April 3, 1992.

79. Susanne Espinosa Solis and Henry K. Lee, "Sniper Kills Policeman on I-580," *San Francisco Chronicle*, January 11, 1999.

80. Peter Fimrite, "New Top Cop Named in Oakland: First Black Named Permanent Police Chief," *San Francisco Chronicle*, June 30, 1993.

81. Robert Nichelini and his son, Michael, would continue to be central figures in the OPD's old boy network: both served as presidents of Le Societe de Camaraderie, a professional law enforcement organization founded in 1940 by members of the Oakland PD. (The *Le* instead of *La* is intentional.)

82. Charles Hardy, "New Methods Sought with Next Oakland Police Chief," *San Francisco Examiner*, December 3, 1992, 8.

83. Rick DelVecchio, "Oakland Cops to Disband One Drug-Fighting Unit: Officers Freed to Patrol Neighborhoods." *San Francisco Chronicle*, January 7, 1994.

84. Rick DelVecchio, "Police Overtime Cuts Have Other Costs—Oakland Officers Feel Stretched to the Limit," *San Francisco Chronicle*, February 7, 1994.

85. Press Democrat Newspaper Services, "Veteran Policeman Slain Covering High-Crime Oakland Beat Alone," June 23, 1994.

86. Rick DelVecchio, "Oakland to Alter Style of Policing—Chief Pushes Community Ties," *San Francisco Chronicle*, October 12, 1994.

87. Rick DelVecchio, "Homicides Hit 12-Year Low in Oakland," *San Francisco Chronicle*, December 24, 1996.

88. Erin McCormick, "Number of State Prisoners Soared in '90s: One in 33 Blacks Was Behind Bars in April Last Year," *San Francisco Chronicle*, August 9, 2001.

89. "Incarceration Trends: Alameda County, CA," Vera Institute of Justice online,

last modified March 24, 2022, http://trends.vera.org/rates/alameda-county-ca?incarcerationData=all.

90. Hart, authors interview.

91. Ibid.

92. Ruth Wilson Gilmore, *Golden Gulag: Prisons, Surplus, Crisis, and Opposition in Globalizing California* (Berkeley: University of California Press, 2007), 7–11.

8: DEADLY CONSEQUENCES

1. Ali Winston, "Deadly Secrets: How a California Court Decision Has Shielded Brutal Oakland Police Officers from Accountability," Type Investigations, last modified August 16, 2011, https://www.typeinvestigations.org/investigation/2011/08/16/deadly-secrets/.

2. Oakland Police Department, Internal Affairs Division Investigative Report, UOF Report 07-0692, April 15, 2008.

3. Patrick Gonzales, interviewed by the authors, September 20, 2007; OPD Internal Affairs Investigative Report—Memorandum to Executive Force Review Board, April 15, 2008: "Sergeant Gonzales' intention was to detain King in order to identify him, and turn this information over to Sergeant Green for photo lineups at a later time."

4. Winston, "Deadly Secrets."

5. Gonzales, authors interview, September 20, 2007.

6. OPD IAD case no. 07-074085, 10.

7. [Redacted, King friend number one], interviewed by OPD Internal Affairs, January 17, 2008.

8. Patrick Gonzales, interviewed by OPD Internal Affairs, September 20, 2007, 32–33.

9. OPD Internal Affairs Division Investigative Report—Memorandum to Executive Force Review Board, April 15, 2008, 11.

10. Oakland Police Department Crime Report RD no. 07-074085 (Coglio, Richard #8630).

11. Oakland Police Sergeant Cesar Basa, RD no. 07-074085.

12. OPD Internal Affairs Division Investigative Report no. 07-0692.

13. Henry K. Lee, "Driver Shot Dead by Gunman Who Asked for a Ride," *San Francisco Chronicle*, August 21, 2007.

14. "The People, Plaintiff and Respondent v. Kevin Duarte, Defendant and Appellant," *People v. Duarte*, A134634 (Cal. Ct. App. Sep. 30, 2013).

15. Gonzales, interviewed by Internal Affairs, March 13, 2008.

16. People v. Eric Lee Perry, case no. 161564, Alameda County Superior Court.

17. Supervisory Special Agent Susan K. Sivok to Oakland Police Chief Wayne Tucker, January 10, 2008.

18. District Attorney's Report on the Fatal Shooting of Gary King, Alameda County District Attorney's Office, April 17, 2013.

19. Rashidah Grinage, interviewed by Darwin BondGraham, May 7, 2019.

20. Investigator D. Quinlan, Report of Investigation, Andre Dante Piazza, CPRB case no. 00-13, Hearing Date 01/25/01, January 2, 2001, available at https://www.scribd.com/doc/62335094/Andre-Piazza-Complaint-Pt-1?secret _password=1459cky91sqvzng5t7b4.

21. In 1974 the California Supreme Court granted defendants access to police employment files under certain circumstances. Subsequently, police departments started shredding records, until, in 1977, police associations and unions won the Peace Officers Bill of Rights, which, along with key sections of California's penal code, exempted all personnel-related information from laws allowing residents to access public records. In response, jurisdictions around the state created independent review boards to investigate complaints of police misconduct. These boards became the primary vehicle for communities to hold both individual officers and departments accountable for their interactions with residents.

22. Use of Force Series, *San Francisco Chronicle*, http://bapd.org/links/0602-sf -chronicle-series-on-police-use-of-force.html.

23. Winston, "Deadly Secrets."

24. Oakland Police Department Crime Report no. 07-100225, December 31, 2007.

25. Executive Force Review Board Report: Jessica Borello and Hector Jimenez, July 25, 2008.

26. Ibid., 18.

27. While the stop was highly pretextual, the hunch was accurate. Andrew Moppin-Buckskin had several gang-related tattoos under his loose black sweatshirt identifying him as a member of the Norteños, a Northern California Latino street gang with a decades-long history of violence, drug trafficking, and lethal rivalries in East Oakland. Oakland Police Department Crime Report no. 07-100225 (Rhoden, C).

28. Recorded statements of Jessica Borello, Hector Jimenez, and Barry Hoffman, January 1, 2008.

29. Jimenez Internal Affairs interview, 25.

30. Moppin-Buckskin EFRB report, 17.

31. Ibid., 12.

32. Bay Area News Group, "Judge Rules in Oakland's Favor in Police Shooting," *Oakland Tribune*, January 15, 2010.

33. The OPD's record-keeping regarding officer-involved shootings was extremely poor prior to its entering into the Negotiated Settlement Agreement in 2003. It would take several more years before the department instituted a more professional system of tracking these incidents.

34. Thomas Peele, "Oakland Police: Too Quick to Fire?," *Contra Costa (CA) Times*, May 1, 2013; Winston, "Deadly Secrets."

35. *Report of the Independent Commission of the Los Angeles Police Department*, ix–xi. "The top 5% of the officers (ranked by number of reports) accounted for 20% of all reports."

36. Christy Lopez, interviewed by the authors, September 10, 2019.

37. *Combined Fourth and Fifth Quarterly Reports of the Independent Monitor,* Delphine Allen et al. v. City of Oakland et al., 3:00-cv-04599-WHO, p. viii-x.

38. Transcript of Hearing, February 14, 2005, Delphine Allen et al. v. City of Oakland et al., 3:00-cv-04599-WHO.

39. Order by Judge Henderson requiring Report on Uninvestigated Citizen Complaints, Delphine Allen et al. v. City of Oakland et al., 3:00-cv-04599-WHO, May 31, 2005.

40. *Sixth Report of the Independent Monitor*, Delphine Allen et al. v. City of Oakland et al., 3:00-cv-04599-WHO, xi–xiii.

41. *Eighth Status Report of the Independent Monitor,* Delphine Allen et al., v. City of Oakland et al., May 30, 2006.

42. Ibid.

43. Independent monitoring team, "Oakland Police Department—Officer Involved Shootings—Review July 2003 through November 2005," no date, document obtained through Public Records Act request.

44. Ali Winston, "Why Oakland Can't Fire Bad Cops," *East Bay Express* (Oakland), September 17, 2014.

45. By the end of the aughts, the OPD would have thirty-four officers assigned to the Internal Affairs Division, and nine in the Homicide Unit. Bob Butler, Mary Fricker, and Thomas Peele, "Rank-and-File Begin to Question Bailey Probe," *Contra Costa (CA) Times*, December 30, 2008.

46. Harry Harris, "Oakland 'Street Cop' Recognized by His Peers Statewide," *Oakland Tribune*, March 8, 2006.

47. Kely Wilkins v. City of Oakland; Justin Berton, "Friendly Fire," *East Bay Express* (Oakland), May 25, 2005.

48. Randy Wingate made his views known in a June 6, 2020, Facebook post, writing: "My best friend Willie Wilkins was killed by overzealous rookies who should be in jail. If it was me standing in East Oakland pointing a gun at a suspect with a badge around my neck and a radio in hand, I wouldn't have been shot. I get it and acknowledge bias exists. The officers that killed my best friend walk free today."

49. Throughout the controversy, Scarrott and Koponen stayed on at the OPD for several more years. In 2004 Koponen was involved in another shooting after a "subject made a furtive movement." Kely Wilkins v. City of Oakland, "Plaintiffs' Response in Opposition to Defendants' Motion for Bifurcation of Trial," filed January 1, 2006.

50. Woodfox Skelly documents, 16 [May 21, 2021, production with lifted redactions]; Use of Force Incidents, Hector Jimenez, 8744.

51. OPD Use of Force Report, 08F-0506, April 7, 2008.

52. OPD Use of Force Report, 08F-0508, April 2, 2008.

53. Hector Jimenez CIR Index Log; Hector Jimenez, 8744, All IAD Cases Report.

54. Hector Jimenez, Annual Performance Appraisal, June 26, 2008, 6.

55. Ibid., 2.

56. Hector Jimenez, Quarterly Performance Appraisal, December 29, 2007.

57. Joel Aylworth, interviewed by Internal Affairs, July 25, 2008, 3–4; Hector Jimenez, interviewed by Internal Affairs, July 25, 2008, 3–4; Henry K. Lee, "Oakland Sees Second Cop-Involved Killing," *San Francisco Chronicle*, July 26, 2008.

58. Aylworth, IA interview, 3–4; Jimenez, IA interview, 3–4; Lee, "Oakland Sees Second Cop-Involved Killing."

59. Aylworth, IA interview, 10–11.

60. Ibid., 12; Jimenez, IA interview, 12–14.

61. Memorandum to Executive Force Review Board—Use of Force Report (08-0817), December 12, 2008, 8; Henry K. Lee, "Oakland Likely to Be Sued over Killing by Cop," *San Francisco Chronicle*, July 28, 2008.

62. Follow-up Investigation Report, Oakland Police Department RD no. 08-054357 (T. Jones), 2.

63. Woodfox Skelly documents 1–4.

64. Ibid., 3–4.

65. Ibid., 4.

66. Alameda County District Attorney's Report.

67. Oakland Police Department Crime Report RD no. 08-054357 (B. Christiansen).

68. Ibid., 27–29.

69. Follow-up Investigation Report, Oakland Police Department RD no. 08-054357 (T. Jones), 5.

70. Lee, "Oakland Likely to Be Sued."

71. Aylworth, IA interview, 38–39.

72. Ibid., 36.

73. Jimenez, IA interview, 20–21.

74. Ibid., 23–24.

75. Aylworth, IA interview, 28.

76. Jimenez, IA interview, 28.

77. Ibid., 44–45.

78. Memorandum—Disciplinary Recommendation—H. Jimenez (8744) IAD case no. 08-8017, February 11, 2009.

79. Sean Maher, "Oakland Police to Reinstate Officer Fired for Shooting Unarmed Man," *Oakland Tribune*, March 6, 2011.

80. Winston, "Why Oakland Can't Fire Bad Cops."

81. Lopez, authors interview.

82. *Combined Fourth and Fifth Quarterly Report*, Independent Monitoring Team, April 16, 2004, to October 15, 2004, Delphine Allen et al. v. City of Oakland, case no. 3:00-cv-04599-TEH.

83. T.S., former OPD officer, interviewed by the authors, on background, May 6, 2021.

84. Ibid.

85. "Charges of Cronyism Inside Oakland PD," ABC7 online, last modified July 29, 2008, https://abc7news.com/archive/6294775/. Scott Valladon never

graduated from recruit training and later sued Oakland for leaking his medical information to the press.

86. C.B., former Oakland police officer, interviewed by the authors, on background, May 6, 2021. By the early 2010s, approximately 90 percent of the OPD was from outside the city. Darwin BondGraham and Ali Winston, "The High Cost of Outsourcing Police," *East Bay Express* (Oakland), August 8, 2012.

87. C.B., authors interview, May 6, 2021.

88. Holly Joshi, interviewed by the authors, August 17, 2020.

89. Ibid., January 1, 2021.

90. Internal Affairs cleared Gutierrez of stealing cash but substantiated the accusation of falsifying reports. He was fired in 2002. However, a labor arbitrator overturned that decision, and Gutierrez was reinstated in a desk job the following year. The officer's street skills were sufficient for him to continue to instruct new undercover officers in the art of finding, developing, and maintaining informants. He retired on a full pension. Henry K. Lee, "Cop of the Year Accused of Misconduct: Oakland Narcotics Officer Faces Allegations of Taking Money," *San Francisco Chronicle*, November 30, 2001, and "Oakland Hires Back Fired Officer," *San Francisco Chronicle*, October 23, 2003.

91. Lopez, authors interview.

92. *First Quarterly Report of the Independent Monitor,* Delphine Allen et al. v. City of Oakland et al., December 22, 2003, viii.

93. *Second Quarterly Report of the Independent Monitor,* Delphine Allen et al. v. City of Oakland et al., case no. 3:00-cv-04599-WHO, vii–viii.

94. The law reads: "[N]o punitive action, nor denial of promotion on grounds other than merit, shall be undertaken for any act, omission, or other allegation of misconduct if the investigation of the allegation is not completed within one year of the public agency's discovery by a person authorized to initiate an investigation of the allegation of an act, omission, or other misconduct."

95. Harry Harris, "Oakland PD Swears in Chief, Promotes Officers," *Oakland Tribune*, September 17, 2005.

96. Henry K. Lee, "Riders Scandal Still Haunts Police Department: Oversight Extended to Give Agency Time to Make Changes," *San Francisco Chronicle*, March 20, 2007.

97. Chip Johnson, "Oakland Police Chief Wants Latitude to Deploy Civilians on Force," *San Francisco Chronicle*, October 22, 2007.

98. Rachel Burgess, Kelli Evans, Charles Gruber, Christy Lopez, Robin Busch-Wheaton, and Aubrie Nuño-Pelayo, *Twelfth Status Report of the Independent Monitor* and *Fourteenth Status Report of the Independent Monitor*, Delphine Allen v. Oakland, January 13, 2010.

9: "I FEEL I WAS BACK IN THE JIM CROW DAYS"

1. Harry Harris and Angela Woodall, "Suspected Acorn Gang Members Snared in Raid," *Oakland Tribune*, June 17, 2008.

2. Joshi, author interviews, August 17, 2020, January 1, 2021.

3. City of Oakland, Officer Karla Rush Skelly Hearing (prepared by Ed Kreins), IAD report no. 07-1071, 10.

4. Oliver et al. v. City of Oakland, case no. 3:08-cv-04984-TEH, second amended complaint.

5. Paul Rosynsky, "Illegal Ammunition Case Dismissed," *Oakland Tribune*, October 6, 2008.

6. Oliver et al. v. City of Oakland, case no. 3:08-cv-04984-TEH, second amended complaint; People of the State of California v. John Franko, no. 527964B, preliminary hearing, June 6, 2007; People of the State of California v. David Lamont Brown, no. 531223, preliminary hearing, July 24, 2007.

7. People of the State of California v. David Lamont Brown, no. 531223, preliminary hearing, July 24, 2007, 13–14.

8. City of Oakland, Officer Karla Rush Skelly Hearing (prepared by Ed Kreins), IAD report no. 07-1071.

9. OPD IAD Report no. 08-0986.

10. Sean Whent, deposition, Oliver et al. v. City of Oakland, case no. 3:08-cv-04984-TEH, August 18, 2011.

11. Ibid., 9–10.

12. City of Oakland, Officer Karla Rush Skelly Hearing (prepared by Ed Kreins), IAD report no. 07-1071, 12–13.

13. Ibid.

14. Oliver et al. v. City of Oakland, case no. 3:08-cv-04984-TEH, Joint Further Case Management Conference Statement, March 8, 2010, 12.

15. Oakland Police Department Crime Report no. 08-007277, January 29, 2008.

16. Oakland Police Department Internal Affairs Division Memo, "Review Attached Skelly Binder for Karla Rush (08-0333)," March 16, 2009.

17. Oakland Police Department Internal Affairs Division, Report of Internal Investigation, file no. 08-0333, 17.

18. Ibid.

19. Ibid., 13–14.

20. Oliver et al. v. City of Oakland, case no. 3:08-cv-04984-TEH, Joint Further Case Management Conference Statement, March 8, 2010, 11–12.

21. Harry Harris and Paul T. Rosynsky, "Oakland Police Department Fires Four Officers in Search Warrant Scandal," *Oakland Tribune*, April 24, 2009.

22. "Oakland Marijuana Enforcement a Low Priority, Measure Z (November 2004)," Ballotpedia, accessed September 5, 2021, https://ballotpedia.org/Oakland_Marijuana_Enforcement_a_Low_Priority,_Measure_Z_(November_2004).

23. Oliver et al. v. City of Oakland, case no. 3:08-cv-04984-TEH, Joint Further Case Management Conference Statement, March 8, 2010, 15–17.

24. Michael L. Rains, "'Reign of Terror' Terminations of Two Oakland Police Sergeants Overturned—The Continuing Saga of the Aftermath of the Riders Case," Police Officers Research Association of California (PORAC) Legal Defense Fund online, last modified September 1, 2006, https://poracldf.org/news/detail/166.

25. City of Oakland, Officer Karla Rush Skelly Hearing (prepared by Ed Kreins), IAD report no. 07-1071, 3–4.

26. Rush would lose a wrongful termination lawsuit. Karla M. Rush v. City of Oakland, case no. A134024; underlying case is Alameda County Superior Court no. RG 09477417, filed April 16, 2013.

27. Ibid., 13.

28. Wayne Tucker, deposition, Karla Rush vs. City of Oakland, case no. RG 09477417, April 20, 2011, 29.

29. *Eleventh Report of the Independent Monitor, August 1, 2007, to April 30, 2008*, 7–8.

30. *Tenth Report of the Independent Monitor, December 1 to July 31, 2007*, 8–9.

31. Sergeant Joseph Carranza, "Performance review of Department General Order O-4," February 23, 2009.

32. Oliver et al. v. City of Oakland, case no. 3:08-cv-04984-TEH.

33. John Smith et al. v. City of Oakland et al., case no. 3:07-cv-06298-SI, Complaint for Damages, December 12, 2007.

34. Ibid., Notice and Administrative Motion to Determine Whether Cases Should Be Related, March 4, 2008.

35. Ibid., Complaint for Damages, December 12, 2007, 6–8.

36. Ibid., Reporter's Transcript of Proceedings, March 9, 2010, 61–62.

37. Ibid., Findings of Fact and Conclusions of Law, Judge Marilyn Hall Patel, August 4, 2011.

38. Ibid., Reporter's Transcript of Proceedings, March 10, 2010, 405.

39. Ibid., 512–13.

40. Ibid., Complaint for Damages, December 12, 2007; Reporter's Transcript of Proceedings, March 10, 2010, 402.

41. Ibid., 11–12.

42. Ibid., 444–45.

43. Ibid., 452–54.

44. Ibid., Findings of Fact and Conclusions of Law, August 4, 2011.

45. Ibid., 21–22.

46. Ibid., Reporter's Transcript of Proceedings, March 10, 2010, 529.

47. Peele, *Killing the Messenger*, 137–47.

48. Frank Sotomayor, "The First 30 Years of MIJE: Making Newsrooms Look Like America," Robert C. Maynard Institute for Journalism Education online, accessed September 17, 2021, https://mije.org/about-us/.

49. Peele, *Killing the Messenger*, 261–65.

50. Ibid., 109–11.

51. Elijah Muhammad's dietary advice has long been one of the NoI's ways of making inroads in the African American community, eschewing the unhealthy, processed food, starch, and cholesterol-heavy diet of twentieth-century American culture for whole grains, fresh vegetables, fish, and intermittent fasting.

52. Peele, *Killing the Messenger*, 159–63.

53. Ibid., 169–70.

54. Ibid., 165–66.

55. George Raine, "Muslim Stirs Anger in Oakland," *San Francisco Examiner*, May 14, 1994, A7.

56. "They have no concern for us. . . . We're like, 'Go down to the zoo and work eight hours,'" Bey said. "They're out of touch. They're not serving us any longer. They're slave masters and overseers." Craig Staats, "Bey Calls for Basic Changes," *Oakland Tribune*, June 6, 1994, A-1.

57. Matthai Kuruvila, Kevin Fagan, and Jaxon Van Derbeken, "Muslim Bakery Head Wielded Political Clout," *San Francisco Chronicle* online, January 27, 2008, https://www.sfgate.com/bayarea/article/Muslim-Bakery-head-wielded-political-clout-3231015.php.

58. Chris Thompson, "The Sinister Side of Yusuf Bey's Empire," *East Bay Express* (Oakland), November 13, 2002; "The Killing of a Journalist," *East Bay Express* (Oakland), August 8, 2007; "How Oakland Officials Kept Bey Empire Going," *East Bay Express* (Oakland), November 20, 2002.

59. Thompson, "How Oakland Officials Kept Bey Empire Going."

60. Peele, *Killing the Messenger*, 192–98.

61. Ibid., 201–16. On Phillips's agreement with Antar Bey, Peele writes: "The author is informed here by a person with direct knowledge of the circumstances regarding Phillips's motive in shooting Antar Bey. Yusuf Bey IV's involvement in Antar Bey's murder is also atriculate in Alfonza Phillips's appeal of his murder conviction (in *People v. Phillips*), although Phillips, in this appeal, continued to deny shooting Antar Bey. The appeal was denied."

62. Ibid., 216–22.

63. Ibid.

64. Ibid., 227–28.

65. Ibid., 247–49.

66. Ibid., 254–55. Wills's shooting, per Peele's reporting, had uncomfortable echoes of the 1970s Death Angels murders: in the days before the murder and immediately preceding Wills's shooting, Yusuf Bey IV had been lecturing triggerman Antoine Mackey on Black Muslim lore, including the Zebra murders that targeted white people.

67. Ibid., 237.

68. Ibid., 256–57.

69. Ibid., 267.

70. Ibid., 273–79.

71. Ibid., 281.

72. Bob Butler and Thomas Peele, "Delayed Raid Likely Cost Chauncey Bailey His Life," *Oakland Tribune*, December 16, 2008. For almost a year and a half, Oakland Police would deny that the Bakery raid was delayed by the SWAT commanders' backpacking trip, until the Chauncey Bailey Project made it public.

73. Peele, *Killing the Messenger*, 280–95.

74. In a sensational case three decades before Bailey's murder, an investigative

journalist named Don Bolles was killed in a car bombing in June 1976 outside a Phoenix hotel as a result of his reporting in the *Arizona Republic* on organized crime involvement in the gambling industry. However, the murders of five Vietnamese American reporters as part of a terror campaign by South Vietnamese anti-Communist revanchists from 1981 to 1990 have long gone ignored. A. C. Thompson, "Terror in Little Saigon," ProPublica in partnership with *Frontline*, last modified November 15, 2015, https://www.propublica .org/article/terror-in-little-saigon-vietnam-american-journalists-murdered.

75. Peele, *Killing the Messenger*, 301–3.
76. Ibid., 304–10.
77. Ibid., 323.
78. Ibid., 316–19.
79. Ibid., 326–27.
80. Ibid., 342–43.
81. Bob Butler and Thomas Peele, "Oakland Suspends Chief of Internal Affairs Amid FBI Probe," *Oakland Tribune*, January 22, 2009.
82. Matt Artz, "Jordan Quit as Oakland Police Chief After Learning of Likely Ouster," *Oakland Tribune*, May 10, 2013.
83. Harry Franklin Kinner, deposition, The Estate of Jerry Amaro III et al. v. City of Oakland, 3:09-cv-01019-WHA, 16, September 18, 2009.
84. Administrative motion re relate cases, Oliver et al. v. City of Oakland, 5, case no. 3:08-cv-04914-TEH.
85. Oakland Police Department, Internal Affairs Division Report of Investigation, file no. DLI 10-1491, assigned investigator Brian Medeiros.
86. Thomas Peele, "Longmire Returning to Duty After OPD Declined to Discipline Officer," *Oakland Tribune*, October 21, 2009.

10: WHIPLASH

1. Jon Djokovic, "Criticism Mounts as Home Videos Show BART Cop Shooting, Killing Unarmed Rider," California Beat, last modified January 4, 2009, https://www.californiabeat.org/criticism-mounts-as-home-videos-show -bart-cop-shooting-killing-unarmed-rider/.
2. The nonprofit Youth Radio videoed the Oscar Grant protests the week after the shooting. "Oscar Grant Protest Part 2," YouTube, 3:04, YR Media, https:// www.youtube.com/watch?v=ZS-RMmA-pKI.
3. "Justice 4 Oscar Grant (A Look Back), Part 3: The DA Speaks with 100 Black Leaders," YouTube, 8:33, mrdaveyd, https://www.youtube.com/watch?v=bi U2Eza9p50.
4. "Oscar Grant—Funeral Resignation Riot," YouTube, 8:53, Haaziq4News, https://www.youtube.com/watch?v=Jay0LdOyv-0.
5. https://oaklandlibrary.org/blogs/library-community/cl-dellums-oakland -civil-rights-hero.
6. "Davey D Rants on Mayor Ron Dellums After Oakland Oscar Grant Murder, Riots, for Not Talking to the Media," YouTube, 3:11, Zennie 62 Oakland News

Now Daily Commentary Live, https://www.youtube.com/watch?v=aWZa2 Vioae0.

7. "Angry Citizens Confront Oakland Police over Murder of Oscar Grant," You-Tube, 3:17, herbnotbombs, https://www.youtube.com/watch?v=8DzqfE-LDzM.

8. Dellums was widely quoted in newspaper articles the next day, and his full comments were recorded by journalist Davey D. See "Oakland Rebels Mayor Ron Dellums Gets Confronted," YouTube, 9:58, mrdaveyd, https://www.you tube.com/watch?v=CUC_ZVbI4sM&t=5s.

9. Oakland City Council meetings of January 6, 2009, and January 20, 2009.

10. Mac Taylor, *The Great Recession and California's Recovery* (Sacramento: California Legislative Analyst's Office, December 2018), 3–11, https://lao.ca.gov /reports/2018/3910/recession-recovery-121318.pdf.

11. Steve King, "Foreclosures in Oakland, 2007 Through 2011," Urban Strategies Council online, last modified April 18, 2012, https://urbanstrategies.org /foreclosures-in-oakland-2007-2011/.

12. This is a modern high for the OPD; the department wouldn't approach similar staffing levels for almost a decade. Cecily Burt, "Oakland Redevelopment Funds to Go to Hiring Cops," *Oakland Tribune*, July 17, 2007; Kelly Rayburn, "Oakland City Council Approves Mayor's Request to Beef Up Police Force," *Oakland Tribune*, March 5, 2008.

13. Kelly Rayburn, "No Money to Train Police Recruits, Dellums Says," *Oakland Tribune*, November 21, 2008.

14. In both the 1960s and the 1990s, local politicians and community figures in Oakland worked exhaustively to head off civil disorder and riots in reaction to highly publicized instances of police brutality against Black Americans. Bradford's book painstakingly documents federal antipoverty programs, community outreach, and Great Society programs undertaken in Oakland to siphon off anger following the 1965 Watts rebellion. See Bradford, *Oakland's Not for Burning*; William Drummond, "Oakland Didn't Riot with Help of Black Leaders," National Public Radio, May 27, 1992.

15. Officer Herbert Webber, "Case Notes, Event #09-009012," February 9, 2009.

16. OPD investigator Herbert Webber also ran both assault victims' IDs through databases to look for warrants and criminal histories. He wrote in his report: "Even though both victims were saying they were running a legitimate business, I ran their phone numbers to see if there was any prostitution activity." After finding them innocent of sex work, he wrote, "it appeared that both victims might be illegal aliens." Herbert Webber, "Case Notes, Event #09-020412," March 23, 2009.

17. Herbert Webber, "Case Notes, Event #09-009012," February 9, 2009; Jill Tucker, "Community Wasn't Told of Oakland Girl's Rape," *San Francisco Chronicle*, March 26, 2009; Jaxon Van Derbeken, "Cop-Killer Raped Two on Day of Attack, Police Say," *San Francisco Chronicle*, May 5, 2009.

18. Christopher Heredia and Henry K. Lee, "Oakland Police Chief to Resign," *San Francisco Chronicle*, January 28, 2009.

19. Independent Board of Inquiry into the Oakland Police Department, March 21, 2009, Incident, 2, 6.

20. Ibid., 6.

21. Jack Peterson, interviewed by IAD, quoted in Mike Rains, "Pre-disciplinary Response, Oakland Police Captain Ricardo Orozco and Lieutenant Chris Mufarreh," March 16, 2010.

22. Deputy Chief David Kozicki was wrong. On May 19, 2007, the OPD used a K-9 unit to locate one of two suspects involved in the nonfatal shooting of Officer Kevin McDonald. Kozicki himself was one of the commanders who authorized a plan to use Sergeant Daniel Sakai's K-9 to find Jeremiah Dye underneath a house in East Oakland. When Dye was spotted by officers and wouldn't surrender, Sakai released his dog, which bit Dye and caused him to curl up in a fetal position. He was then shot fatally by Officer Rob Roche, who thought that Dye was reaching for a weapon. Paul Greenberg, Arbitration Between Oakland Police Officers' Association, Ricardo Orozco, and Christopher Mufarreh and City of Oakland, May 16, 2013, 74–76.

23. Mike Leite, interviewed by OPD Internal Affairs, March 24, 2009.

24. The actions of Shavies, Chief of Staff Richard Vierra, and several other cops led to Oakland's paying $175,000 to settle a civil claim brought by the cameraman, Douglas Laughlin. His mistreatment prompted Laughlin to retire early from KGO-TV. Henry K. Lee, "Oakland to Pay $175,000 to Manhandled TV Cameraman," San Francisco Chronicle, June 8, 2011.

25. Tammerlin Drummond, "Ron Dellums Didn't Speak at Oakland Police Funeral for Fear He Would Botch Names," Oakland Tribune, April 3, 2009.

26. Assembly Bill 2484.

27. Andrew Blankstein and Maria LaGanga, "Oakland Police Shootings Stoke Criticism of Parole Oversight," Los Angeles Times, March 24, 2009.

28. "While some see moral equivalence, there was a difference between Grant and Mixon: the latter was able to foresee his impending death and fight back, so as to not meet Grant's fate of catching a bullet in the back." Raider Nation Collective, "Lovelle Mixon, Police, and the Politics of Race/Rape," San Francisco Bay Area Independent Media Center (Indybay), last modified April 13, 2009, https://www.indybay.org/newsitems/2009/04/13/18588525.php.

29. Winston, "Deadly Secrets."

30. Mike Rains, "Demotions of Oakland P.D.'s Rick Orozco and Chris Mufarreh Overturned: Part 2," Police Officers Research Association of California (PORAC) Legal Defense Fund online, last modified December 9, 2013, https://poracldf.org/news/detail/428.

31. Rains, "Pre-disciplinary Response, Oakland Police Captain Ricardo Orozco and Lieutenant Chris Mufarreh."

32. For some businesses, the tributes to Grant were defensive—a means of avoiding the sort of vandalism that erupted in early 2009. For others, they were a way to remember a young man whose life was snatched away from him, and the posters remain up to this day.

33. It was at this protest, tellingly, that an Occupy Everything sign was first spotted. "Oakland: Protesters Arrested, Traffic Flowing Again on Interstate 880," *Mercury News* (San Jose, CA), March 4, 2010; Jake Schoneker, "Student Perspective: On March 4 During the Freeway Takeover, Some Reporters Got the Story. Four of Them Got Arrested," Oakland North, last modified March 12, 2010, https://oaklandnorth.net/2010/03/12/student-perspective-on-march -4-during-the-freeway-takeover-some-reporters-got-the-story-four-of -them-got-arrested/.

34. "Protesters Take to Oakland Streets After Mehserle Verdict Announced," YouTube, 5:26, thedailycal, https://www.youtube.com/watch?v=Ju—8zhIuuI.

35. Paul T. Rosynsky, "Ex-BART Cop Mehserle Sentenced to Two Years in Oscar Grant III Shooting," *Oakland Tribune*, November 5, 2010.

36. Will Potter, *Green Is the New Red: An Insider's Account of a Social Movement Under Siege* (San Francisco: City Lights Books, 2011), 25.

37. Holly Noll, interviewed by the authors, September 28, 2021.

38. Ibid.

39. Ibid., September 29, 2021.

40. Ibid.

41. Ali Winston, "Police Files Reveal Federal Interest in Oscar Grant Protests, 'Anarchists,'" The Informant, KALW News, last modified December 15, 2010, https://web.archive.org/web/20110507213317/http://informant.kalwnews .org/2010/12/police-documents-reveal-federal-interest-in-oscar-grant-pro tests-anarchists/.

42. Ibid.

43. Carl Nasman, "Mehserle Protests End with Limited Damage, Lots of Arrests," Oakland North, last modified November 5, 2010, https://oaklandnorth.net /2010/11/05/mehserle-protests-end-with-limited-damage-lots-of-arrests/.

44. Henry K. Lee, "Oakland, Alameda County to Pay Protesters $1 Million," *San Francisco Chronicle*, June 13, 2013.

11: TURMOIL AND TEAR GAS

1. "Oakland Gang Injunction," YouTube, 9:57, video, OaklandRusso, https:// www.youtube.com/watch?v=kQlvl3dpewc.

2. Declaration of John Cunnie, People of the State of California v. North Side Oakland, February 12, 2010. Joseph Carroll Jr., a documented Waterfront gang member and Charles Davis's cousin, would be charged, convicted, and sentenced to life without parole for Nguyen Ngo's murder in 2017, as well as the April 13, 2011, murder of Andrew Henderson. In July 2007 Carroll was wounded in a shooting at Martin Luther King Jr. Way and Fifty-Ninth Street that killed Kikhiesha Brooks. Angela Ruggiero, "Oakland: Man Charged in 2009 North Oakland Cold Case," *East Bay Times* (Walnut Creek, CA), December 18, 2017.

3. The first gang injunction dates from 1987's civil order against the Playboy Gangster Crips in the Mid-Wilshire section of Los Angeles. By the early

2010s, there were dozens of gang injunctions in California. See Ana Muñiz, *Police, Power, and the Production of Racial Boundaries* (New Brunswick, NJ: Rutgers University Press, 2015), 33–37.

4. "Webinar: Civil Gang Injunctions," Bureau of Justice Assistance, November 10, 2010; Ali Winston, "The Bay Area's Gang Injunctions Explained," KALW News online, last modified October 13, 2010, https://web.archive.org /web/20110123201515/https://kalwnews.org/audio/2011/01/20/are-san -franciscos-gang-injunctions-working_800405.html; John Russo and Anthony Batts, *Joint Informational Report from the Oakland City Attorney's Office and the Oakland Police Department on the City's Civil Injunction Cases Against the North Side Oakland Gang and the Norteños Gang* (Oakland: City Attorney's Office and the Oakland Police Department, February 11, 2010).

5. Ali Winston, "Are San Francisco's Gang Injunctions Working?," KALW News, January 20, 2011; City of Oakland Scope of Services/Retention Agreement #663125, Re: Area 3 Gang et al., June 7, 2010.

6. Oakland police annual crime reports.

7. Declaration of John Cunnie, 40.

8. According to City Administrator Dan Lindheim, toward the end of his second term, Jerry Brown was attempting to push out Tucker, but "we did not allow that to happen, even though the mayor was not yet sworn in. And the main reason was because Chief Tucker was seen symbolically as committed to the NSA, and we didn't want to give a symbolic message that the new administration was not so committed." See transcript of Proceedings, Delphine Allen et al. v. City of Oakland et al., case no. 3:00-cv-04599-TEH, September 16, 2010.

9. Chanin, authors interview, July 20, 2021. Anthony Batts did not respond to our attempts to contact him for an interview.

10. Angela Davis, "Oakland Residents Must Stop the Gang Injunctions," *Oakland Tribune*, March 3, 2011; John Russo, "Davis Wrong About Facts of Gang Injunctions," *Oakland Tribune*, March 11, 2011.

11. "Declaration of Oakland percipient witness police officers in support of injunctive relief, 'gang injunctions,' and other relief," filed November 16, 2010, case no. RG10541141, Alameda County Superior Court.

12. The appeals court derisively cited one passage from the civil rights lawyers' brief to make the point that they'd done a poor job arguing against injunctions. The attorneys had railed that the superior court judge's approval of the injunctions was based on "a mythology, framed around . . . a deep, singular instinct for repression, broadly shared within the system . . . which is itself, surely, firmly tethered to the never-flagging, ravenous, flesh-eating demands of the prison-industrial complex"—a passage that veered too far from the law into ideological terrain. The People ex rel. John A. Russo as City Attorney v. Abel Manzo et al., cases A133873 and A135242.

13. "Several people who called in during 2010 ended up on the Fruitvale injunction—as well as a former gang member who did street outreach for Measure Y, raising questions as to whether the two programs conflict with

each other." Ali Winston, "Oakland's Other Gang Program," *East Bay Express* (Oakland), October 5, 2011.

14. Ali Winston, "Records Show Legal Costs for Third Gang Injunction in Oakland," April 25, 2011, informant.kalwnews.org, https://web.archive.org/web /20130913101343/http://informant.kalwnews.org/2011/04/records-show -legal-costs-for-third-gang-injunction-in-oakland/; United States v. Marcel Alley et al., Cr12-00495, June 21, 2012; United States. v. Jamal Shaw et al., Cr-12-0485CW, June 21, 2012.

15. IMT, *Fourteenth Status Report of the Independent Monitor*, in Delphine Allen et al. v. City of Oakland, January 13, 2010

16. Lopez, authors interview, September 10, 2019.

17. George Hunter and Christine Ferretti, "Federal Oversight Forced Reforms upon Detroit's Violent Police Force," *Detroit News*, June 9, 2020.

18. The *Gautreaux v. Chicago Housing Authority* case, a lawsuit that resulted in a consent decree, lasted from 1966 to 2018 before it was settled. On the longevity of federal consent decree cases, especially in schools, see David Zaring, "National Rulemaking Through Trial Courts: The Big Case and Institutional Reform," *UCLA Law Review* 51 (2003–2004): 1015–78, available at https://www.uclalawreview.org/wp-content/uploads/2019/09/35_51UCLA LRev10152003-2004.pdf.

19. Transcript of Proceedings, Delphine Allen et al. v. City of Oakland et al., case no 3:00-cv-04599-TEH, September 16, 2010.

20. Uganda Knapps v. City of Oakland, Findings of Fact and Conclusions of Law, case no. 05-2935 MEJ.

21. Joint Status Conference Statement re Nonmonetary Settlement Issues, in Delphine Allen v. City of Oakland, case no. 3:00-cv-04599, September 16, 2010.

22. City of Oakland, "FY 2011-13 Proposed Policy Budget," April 29, 2011.

23. The city hit a low point of 613 officers in 2013. Antoné Hicks, *Monthly Police Staffing Report*, Oakland City Council Public Safety Committee, August 15, 2018.

24. Scott H. Bransford, "'Number 77': A KALW News Special Report on Desiree Davis, Oakland's 77th murder victim of 2009," KALW News, September 7, 9, 2010, https://soundcloud.com/kalw/feature-desireept2_me_9.

25. Robert Gammon, "Dellums Fails to Pay at Least $239,000 in Taxes," *East Bay Express* (Oakland), November 2, 2009.

26. Angela Hill and Kristin Bender, "Oakland Mayor Ron Dellums Won't Seek Second Term," *East Bay Times* (Walnut Creek, CA), August 4, 2010.

27. Alameda County Registrar of Voters, ranked-choice voting results report for November 2, 2010, General Election, accessed at https://www.acvote.org /election-information/archived-elections.

28. Terry Bowman, "Grievant's post arbitration brief," in the matter of the appeal of termination of Officer John (Jack) Kelly, 25.

29. Shoshana Walter, "Occupy Protests Test the Mayor of Oakland," *New York Times*, October 29, 2011.

30. Phil Matier and Andrew Ross, "Oakland Cops Probing 2 Councilwomen at Protest," *San Francisco Chronicle*, July 14, 2010.

31. Jean Quan, deposition, September, 25, 2012.

32. Oakland Police Department, Internal Affairs Division interview of Omar Daza-Quiroz, November 9, 2010, 40.

33. Derrick Jones Sr., statement at the Oakland City Council meeting, December 7, 2010.

34. To this day, no report on Derrick Jones's shooting has ever been made public by the FBI. Ali Winston and Darwin BondGraham, "Police in Oakland and Across California Are Failing to Comply with Records Requests," The Oaklandside, last modified May 5, 2021, https://oaklandside.org/2021/05/05/police-in-oakland-and-across-ca-are-failing-to-comply-with-records-requests/.

35. Daza-Quiroz, IA interview, November 9, 2010, 78.

36. Ali Winston, "Cops' Violent Past to Be Kept from Jury," *East Bay Express* (Oakland), March 20, 2013.

37. "Final Foreclosures 2007–2011," Open Oakland, accessed September 10, 2021, http://data.openoakland.org/dataset/final-foreclosures-2007-2011.

38. Dave Id (David Morse), "Occupy Oakland Kicks Off Hella Strong on Day One, Speakers & Wall Street Call" (audio, 1:02:00), San Francisco Bay Area Independent Media Center (Indybay), last modified October 11, 2011, https://www.indybay.org/newsitems/2011/10/11/18693176.php.

39. Laura Anthony, "Two Men Convicted of Murder for Death of 3-Year-Old Carlos Nava" ABC7 News online, last modified June 23, 2014, https://abc7news.com/two-men-convicted-carlos-nava-murder-oakland/134591/.

40. Tasion Kwamilele, "Anthony Batts, the Exit Interview: 'In Oakland, the Police Department Is Seen as a Necessary Evil,'" Oakland North, last modified November 7, 2011, https://oaklandnorth.net/2011/11/07/anthony-batts-the-exit-interview-in-oakland-the-police-department-is-seen-as-a-necessary-evil/.

41. Ali Winston, "Oakland Still Digging Itself out of 8-Year Police Corruption Scandal," The Informant, KALW News, last modified September 22, 2011, https://web.archive.org/web/20111019071028/http://informant.kalwnews.org/2011/09/oakland-still-digging-itself-out-of-eight-year-old-police-corruption-scandal/).

42. Warshaw described the lack of progress as "highly disappointing." Robert Warshaw, *Seventh Quarterly Report of the Independent Monitor for the Oakland Police Department* (Dover, NH: Office of the Independent Monitor, October 20, 2011), https://www.cand.uscourts.gov/filelibrary/1094/2011-10%20monitoring%20report.pdf; Ali Winston, "Could Oakland Police Go into Federal Receivership?," The Informant, KALW News, last modified January 19, 2011, https://web.archive.org/web/20111007203125/http://informant.kalwnews.org/2011/01/could-oakland-police-go-into-federal-receivership/.

43. The previous year, Michael Valle also went undercover in marches during the Oscar Grant protest movement. "Copwatch@Occupy Oakland: Beware of

Police Infiltrators and Provocateurs," YouTube, 1:40, Jacob Crawford, https://www.youtube.com/watch?v=VrvMzqopHH0.

44. Scott Olsen, interviewed by the authors, October 7, 2021.

45. Ali Winston, "OPD Promoted Cops Involved in Scott Olsen Case," *East Bay Express* (Oakland), March 26, 2014.

46. Sergeant James Rullamas, Follow-up Investigation Report, RD no. 11-052352, March 16, 2012; Oakland Police Department Crime Report, RD no. 11-052352, October 25, 2011.

47. Sheriff's deputies Victor Fox, Keith Gilkerson, and James McGrail used this exact sentence in their reports, and several other deputies used a similarly worded version. Alameda County Sheriff's Office Criminal Incident Report, Supplemental Reports, case no. 11-017257, October 10, 2011.

48. Robin Wilkey, "Jon Stewart Targets Oakland Police on 'The Daily Show,'" HuffPost, last modified December 6, 2017, https://www.huffpost.com/entry/jon-stewart-occupy-oakland_n_1035550.

49. Matthew Artz, "Oakland Officers Disciplined in Nameplate Flap During Occupy Protests," *Oakland Tribune*, January 11, 2012.

50. Oakland Police Department Report of Investigation Internal Affairs, no. 11-1135 (prepared by Nikki Hall of Renne Sloan Holtzman Sakai LLP, September 12, 2012).

51. Documents show that the FBI took no further steps beyond interviewing Olsen and reading publicly available media reports. No interview of any Oakland Police Department officer or percipient witness was ever attempted. Federal Bureau of Investigation file no. SF 282-0-ASSESS-A, 3/22/2012.

52. Howard Jordan to Anthony Toribio and Sean Whent, email re "Use of Force," February 23, 2012.

53. Ali Winston, "Cop Identified in Kayvan Sabeghi Beating?," *East Bay Express* (Oakland), April 12, 2012.

54. Ali Winston, "Cop Identified in Scott Olsen Incident?," *East Bay Express* (Oakland), February 22, 2012; Oakland Police Department Internal Affairs Division, Robert Roche #8580 Critical Incident Report Index Log.

55. Derwin Longmire to Benson Fairow, Charles Gibson, Cyril Vierra, Eric Breshears, Franklin Lowe, Jeffrey Israel, Ken Whitman, Kenneth W. Parris, Kevin Wiley, Paul Berlin, Rod Yee, Roderick Golphin, William Dorsey, and Zeddie Williams, email re "Monday the 7th," April 1, 2003.

56. Derwin Longmire to Benson Fairow, Charles Gibson, Cyril Vierra, Eric Breshears, Franklin Lowe, Jeffrey Israel, Ken Whitman, Kenneth W. Parris, Kevin Wiley, Paul Berlin, Rod Yee, Roderick Golphin, William Dorsey, and Zeddie Williams, email re "Alert," April 4, 2003. Active since the mid-1990s, Earth Liberation Front's apparent claims of vandalizing military recruitment vehicles and calls for direct actions to resist the invasion of Iraq in March 2003 increased the FBI's level of interest in the group. It would result in Operation Backfire, a major investigation that ensnared eighteen ELF members and other activists through 2010. Federal Bureau of Investigation Terrorism Enterprise Investigation records, Operation Foxfire/Operation Backfire (re-

trieved via MuckRock at https://www.muckrock.com/news/archives/2013/apr/29/fbi-file-details-earth-liberation-fronts-eco-terro/).

57. Oakland Citizens' Police Review Board Administrative Closure Report, case no. 03-131, May 13, 2004.

58. Benson Fairow to Richard Word, memo re "IAD Investigation of the 7 Apr 03, Port Cases," April 23, 2003. The city, in an attempt to have one of the brutality lawsuits dismissed, identified Gary Tolleson as the leader of the Blue Tango Team. "Defendants' Motion for Summary Judgment, or, in the Alternative, Summary Adjudication Against Individual Plaintiffs," in Sri Louise Coles et al. v. City of Oakland, case no. C-03-2961-TEH, November 3, 2005.

59. Major Incident Review Board case notes, May 22, 2003.

60. OPD, "Port of Oakland Port Protest of April 7, 2003, Board of Review Recommendations," October 2003, 3.

61. Ali Winston, "OPD Used Violent Cops Against Occupy," *East Bay Express* (Oakland), December 21, 2011.

62. Thomas Frazier, deposition, vol. 1, 125–27, August 23, 2012.

63. This wasn't the first time Santana tried to dilute findings critical of law enforcement: while working for the San Jose Police Department, she was publicly lambasted by independent police auditor Barbara Attard for diluting a report that Attard's office had authored about the SJPD's misclassifying IAD complaints. Ali Winston, "Deanna Santana Tried to Alter Damning Report," *East Bay Express* (Oakland), September 19, 2012. See also Frazier, deposition, vol. 1, August 23, 2012.

64. Winston, "Deanna Santana Tried to Alter Damning Report."

65. Oakland Police Department Report of Investigation Internal Affairs, no. 11-1135.

66. City of Oakland, "Report on Status of Investigations into Occupy Oakland–Demonstrations Released," press release, October 12, 2012, http://www2.oaklandnet.com/oakca1/groups/ceda/documents/pressrelease/oak038087.pdf.

67. Ali Winston, "Will OPD End Up in Receivership?," October 12, 2012, *East Bay Express* (Oakland), January 25, 2012.

12: THE LEAST POPULAR MAN IN THE OPD

1. From 1995 through 2000, forty people died at the hands of Detroit police officers, prompting the mayor to request a federal pattern-and-practice review that resulted in a full consent decree in 2003. George Hunter and Christine Feretti, "Federal Oversight Forced Reforms upon Detroit's Violent Police Department," *Detroit News*, June 6, 2020.

2. Delphine Allen et al. v. City of Oakland, case no. 3:00-cv-04599-TEH, Plaintiffs' Notice and Motion for Appointment of a Receiver, October 4, 2012, 39; Chanin, authors interview.

3. Delphine Allen et al. v. City of Oakland, case no. 3:00-cv-04599-TEH, Plaintiffs' Notice and Motion for Appointment of a Receiver, October 4, 2012.

4. "Audit of Use of Force Reporting and Investigation," Oakland Police Department Office of the Inspector General, August 14, 2012.

5. Independent investigation of Occupy Oakland response, October 25, 2011, Frazier Group, June 14, 2012.

6. Darwin BondGraham and Ali Winston, "Damning Report of OPD," *East Bay Express* (Oakland), June 20, 2012.

7. Complaint Investigation Report, Oakland Police Department, case no. 12-0281.

8. Winston, "Why Oakland Can't Fire Bad Cops."

9. Exhibit 56: Monitor's Redacted OIS Report, Delphine Allen et al. v. City of Oakland, case no. 3:00-cv-04599-TEH, October 4, 2012, 12–13.

10. "Oakland Paying Out Extraordinary Police Abuse Settlements: A Review of California Public Records Act," KTVU News online, last modified November 14, 2011.

11. Delphine Allen et al. v. City of Oakland, case no. 3:00-cv-04599-TEH, exhibit 38: OPD Postings re: Mayor and Judge Thelton E. Henderson, October 4, 2012.

12. Ibid., exhibit 39: Declaration of Jan Gilbrecht, October 4, 2012. Pope was also an elected council member in Oakley, a small Contra Costa County city where many OPD and other law enforcement officers live. In 2019 he and another council member attempted to block the city from officially recognizing LGBTQ Pride Month. See East County Today, "Pope, Hardcastle Attempt to Table Oakley LGBT Proclamation," last modified May 29, 2019, https://eastcountytoday.net/pope-hardcastle-attempt-to-table-oakley-lgbt-procla mation/.

13. BondGraham and Winston, "High Cost of Outsourcing Police."

14. Delphine Allen et al. v. City of Oakland, case no. 3:00-cv-04599-TEH, exhibit 38: OPD Postings re: Mayor and Judge Henderson, October 4, 2012. The flattening of the Left by OPD officers, equating those who participated in the civil rights movement or anti–Vietnam War movement with extremists, is evident in the cottage industry of crime fiction that former OPD officers have written. For example, John Taylor, a thirty-one-year OPD veteran officer who retired in 2002, wrote in his recent novel about Oakland cops, *OIS: Officer Involved Shooting*, that "the recent Occupy and Black Lives Matter protests joined the formation of the Black Panther Party, in the 1960s, and the Symbionese Liberation Army, in the 1970s, to cement Oakland's reputation as a hotbed for radicalism."

15. Howard Jordan, deposition, vol. 1 and vol. 2, August 9, 2012, and September 6, 2012; Deanna Santana, deposition, August 29, 2012.

16. "Crime strategy retreat," Jack London Waterfront Inn, March 1, 1999.

17. Response by Oakland Police Officers' Association to Plaintiffs' Notice of Motion for the Appointment of a Receiver, Delphine Allen et al. v. City of Oakland, case no. 3:00-cv-04599-TEH, November 8, 2012.

18. Ibid.

19. Dan Levine, "Judge Puts Off Court Takeover of Oakland Police Force, for

Now," Reuters online, last modified December 12, 2012, https://www.reuters.com/news/picture/judge-puts-off-court-takeover-of-oakland-idUSBRE8BB1T320121212.

20. Order Re: Compliance Director, United States District Court for the Northern District of California, case no. C00-4599-TEH, December 12, 2012.

21. Oakland Police Department, Homicide Section Monthly Statistical Report, December 2010.

22. Oakland-Berkeley-Hayward Unemployment Statistics, 2009–2021.

23. The influx of former Oakland cops to Vallejo in particular would coincide with the VPD's notoriety as the Bay Area's most lethal police department. See Shane Bauer, "How a Deadly Police Force Ruled a City," *New Yorker*, November 23, 2020.

24. Anthony Braga et al., *Oakland Ceasefire Evaluation: Final Report to the City of Oakland*, May 2019, 1, 11, available at https://cao-94612.s3.amazonaws.com/documents/Oakland-Ceasefire-Evaluation-Final-Report-May-2019.pdf.

25. Ibid., 3.

26. Much of the story of the founding of Money Team/ENT was told by Oakland Gang Unit Officer Daniel Bruce and Oakland Gang Unit Supervisor Frederick Shavies in the trials of several gang members and summarized in their appeals. See People v. Javier Ruben Rodriguez Garcia, Court of Appeal, State of California, case no. H043870; People v. Deangelo Joseph Austin, Court of Appeal, State of California, case no. H044073; and People v. Jereme Jermaine Brown, Court of Appeal, State of California, case no. H045689.

27. Demian Bulwa and Henry K. Lee, "Probe: Prostitute Fed Gang Info on Home," *San Francisco Chronicle*, June 26, 2013.

28. The Nut Cases' story is told in case filings in Demarcus Ralls v. Anthony Hedgpeth, US District Court, District of Northern California, case no. C-10-4732-CRB.

29. Jim Herron Zamora, "'Nut Cases' Gunman Gets 23 Years: Joe Ralls Killed Man, Boy at 2002 Holiday Party," *San Francisco Chronicle*, May 11, 2007; former Oakland gang cop, interviewed by the authors, November 5, 2021.

30. Darwin BondGraham, "The Gunrunner and the Peacemakers," *East Bay Express* (Oakland), January 27, 2016.

31. Ali Winston, "High-Capacity Magazines Flood Oakland," *East Bay Express* (Oakland), January 16, 2013.

32. Katie Nelson and Erin Ivie, "Oakland Gun Violence Continues Through Weekend," *Oakland Tribune*, January 14, 2013; Ali Winston, "Same High-Capacity Magazine Linked to Two Oakland Murders," *East Bay Express* (Oakland), January 18, 2013.

33. Winston, "High-Capacity Magazines."

34. Former Oakland gang cop, authors interview.

35. "Casual Carpoolers Robbed at Gunpoint in Oakland," ABC7 News online, last modified September 24, 2013, https://abc7news.com/archive/9259260.

36. "Oakland Police Department End of Year Crime Report—Citywide, 01 Jan.–31 Dec. 2013," City of Oakland online, last modified November 13, 2020,

https://cityofoakland2.app.box.com/s/0ol2ik52d1atan2sl5hovon3hs1szn04
/file/741365008183.

37. Emilie Raguso, "Years On, Alaysha Carradine Killing Is Still Haunting,"
Berkeleyside, last modified March 31, 2016, https://www.berkeleyside.org
/2016/03/31/years-on-alaysha-carradine-killing-is-still-haunting.

38. Ali Winston, "Getting Away with Murder," *East Bay Express* (Oakland), November 14, 2012.

39. Ali Winston, "Oakland Police Have Prioritized Drug Crimes over Homicides," *East Bay Express* (Oakland), October 30, 2013.

40. *Oakland Police Department Homicide Section Monthly Statistical Reports,*
December 2010–December 2012.

41. Darwin BondGraham and Ali Winston, "Who's Profiting from Oakland's
Gun Violence?," *East Bay Express* (Oakland), February 20, 2013.

42. Ali Winston, "Frazier to Re-Examine Police Misconduct," *East Bay Express*
(Oakland), May 8, 2013.

43. Order of Clarification re: Scope of Compliance Directors' Authority, United
States District Court for the Northern District of California, case no. C00-
4599-TEH, April 10, 2013.

44. Artz, "Jordan Quit as Oakland Police Chief."

45. "But while Jordan is a good guy and was a good cop, he was too much of an
insider to be a successful chief. During his 25-year career, he rose through
the ranks by forging close relationships with many people inside OPD, and
as a result, was unable—and perhaps unwilling—to effectively deal with the
department's two major failings: its inability to cope with police misconduct
and its failure to solve crimes, thereby making Oakland's crime problems
worse." Robert Gammon, "Howard Jordan Was Never the Right Choice," *East
Bay Express* (Oakland), May 15, 2013.

46. Matthew Artz, "Oakland's New Interim Police Chief, Sean Whent, Still Looking to Win Over Officers," *Oakland Tribune,* May 14, 2013.

47. Mihir Zaveri, "Ceasefire Starts as Members of Violent Groups Sit Down with
Those Urging Different Path," Oakland North, last modified October 26,
2012, https://oaklandnorth.net/2012/10/26/ceasefire-starts-as-members-of
-violent-groups-sit-down-with-those-urging-different-path/.

48. Samantha Masunaga, "OPD Leads Massive Arrest Sweep Against East Oakland's 'Case Gang,'" Oakland North, last modified March 8, 2013, https://
oaklandnorth.net/2013/03/08/opd-leads-massive-arrest-sweep-against-east
-oaklands-case-gang/; "Oakland: Reputed Gang Leader Gets 8 Years for Conspiracy Conviction," Bay City News, September 17, 2014.

49. Lori Preuitt and Kris Sanchez, "Suffer These Crimes in Oakland? Don't Call
the Cops," NBC Bay Area online, last modified July 13, 2010, https://www
.nbcbayarea.com/news/local/suffer-these-crimes-in-oakland-dont-call-the
-cops/2095121/.

50. Andrew V. Papachristos and David S. Kirk, "Neighborhood Effects on Street
Gang Behavior," in *Studying Youth Gangs,* ed. James F. Short Jr. and Lorine A.
Hughes (Lanham, MD: AltaMira Press, 2006), 63–84.

51. Braga et al., *Oakland Ceasefire Evaluation*, 16.

52. Ibid., 30.

53. Samantha Masunaga, "In Oakland, the IRS Criminal Investigation Division Solves Crimes by Following the Money," Oakland North, last modified March 22, 2013, https://oaklandnorth.net/2013/03/22/in-oakland-the-irs-criminal-investigation-division-solves-crimes-by-following-the-money/; Masunaga, "Oakland Leads Massive Arrest Sweep."

54. Harry Harris, "Authorities Release Names of Suspected Bay Area Gang Members Arrested," *Mercury News* (San Jose, CA), August 27, 2013.

55. Darwin BondGraham, "He Spent His Career Putting Gangs in Jail. A Radical Idea Changed Everything," *Guardian* (US edition) online, last modified June 4, 2019, https://www.theguardian.com/us-news/2019/jun/03/ersie-joyner-interview-oakland-police-ceasefire-gun-violence-prevention.

56. Henry K. Lee, "Oakland Police Chief Helps Chase Down Carjack Suspect," *San Francisco Chronicle*, December 25, 2013.

57. Ali Winston, "Oakland Surveillance Center Progresses Amid Debate on Privacy, Data Collection," Center for Investigative Reporting, July 18, 2013, available on NBC Bay Area online, https://www.nbcbayarea.com/news/local/oakland-surveillance-center-progresses-amid-debate-on-privacy-data-collection/1918876/. Regarding the Science Applications International Corporation's history of fraud involving a major defense contractor now known as Leidos, see Donald L. Barlett and James B. Steele, "Washington's $8 Billion Shadow," *Vanity Fair* online, last modified February 6, 2007, https://www.vanityfair.com/news/2007/03/spyagency200703.

58. "DAC Technical Requirements," San Francisco Bay Area Independent Media Center (Indybay), accessed November 7, 2021, https://www.indybay.org/uploads/2013/07/27/domainawarenesscentertechrequirements.png.

59. Statement of Ahsan Baig during Oakland City Council Public Safety Committee meeting, July 9, 2013, https://oakland.granicus.com/player/clip/1315?view_id=2&redirect=true.

60. *District-Based Investigations in Oakland: Rapid and Effective Response to Robberies, Burglaries, and Shootings* (Bratton Group, May 2013).

61. Oakland City Council Public Safety Committee meeting, July 9, 2013, video available at City of Oakland online, https://oakland.granicus.com/player/clip/1315?view_id=2&redirect=true.

62. The relationships between Bay Area law enforcement and federal agencies were a hot-button topic in the early 2010s: both San Francisco and Oakland police battled activists' repeated efforts to sever ties with the local Joint Terrorism Task Force, the main point of contact between police and the post-9/11 federal counterterrorism apparatus that generated tremendous amounts of fear and suspicion in Middle Eastern and Muslim communities. Oakland would eventually cut ties with the JTTF in the fall of 2020. Ali Winston, "Oakland Police Tight-lipped on Role in Joint Terrorism Task Force," The Informant, KALW News, last modified May 17, 2011, https://web.archive.org/web/20110522094442/https://informant.kalwnews

.org/2011/05/oakland-police-tight-lipped-on-role-in-joint-terrorism-task-force/.

63. Noah Schactman, "NYC Plans a High Tech Defense: Let's Hope It Works," *Wired,* April 21, 2008.

64. Jake Nicol, "Domain Awareness Center Moves Forward Despite Vocal Opposition," Oakland North, last modified November 20, 2013, https://oaklandnorth.net/2013/11/20/domain-awareness-center-moves-forward-despite-vocal-opposition/.

65. "While the emails reveal a great deal about the DAC, they are also notable for what they do *not* talk about. Among the hundreds of messages sent and received by Oakland staffers and the city's contractor team responsible for building the DAC, there is no mention of robberies, shootings, or the 138 homicides that took place during the period of time covered by the records. City staffers do not discuss any studies pertaining to the use of surveillance cameras in combating crime, nor do they discuss how the Domain Awareness System could help OPD with its long-standing problems with solving violent crimes. In more than 3,000 pages of emails, the words *murder, homicide, assault, robbery*, and *theft* are never mentioned." Darwin BondGraham and Ali Winston, "The Real Purpose of the Domain Awareness Center," *East Bay Express* (Oakland), December 18, 2013.

66. Darwin BondGraham and Ali Winston, "The Real Purpose of the Domain Awareness Center," *East Bay Express* (Oakland), December 18, 2013.

67. Brian Wheeler, "Police Surveillance: The US City That Beat Big Brother," BBC News online, last modified September 29, 2016, https://www.bbc.com/news/magazine-37411250#:~:text=Surveillance%20of%20ordinary%20citizens%20and,with%20the%20East%20Bay%20Express; Ali Winston, "Oakland Police to Outfit Patrol Officers with Video Cameras," The Informant, KALW News, last modified September 9, 2010, https://web.archive.org/web/20101018004321/http://informant.kalwnews.org/2010/09/oakland-police-to-outfit-patrol-officers-with-video-cameras; Ali Winston, "Lapel Cameras Are Now Part of Oakland Police's Uniform," The Informant, KALW News, last modified March 29, 2011, https://web.archive.org/web/20110504081717/http://informant.kalwnews.org/2011/03/lapel-cameras-are-now-part-of-oakland-polices-uniform.

68. Ali Winston, "Oakland City Council Rolls Back Domain Awareness Center," *East Bay Express* (Oakland), March 5, 2014.

69. Cyrus Farivar, "Oakland Cops Disciplined 24 Times for Failing to Turn On Body-Worn Cameras," Ars Technica, last modified December 15, 2014, https://arstechnica.com/tech-policy/2014/12/oakland-cops-disciplined-24-times-for-failing-to-turn-on-body-worn-cameras/; Vicky Nguyen, Liza Meak, and Mark Villareal, "Newly Released Data Shows Oakland Police Turn On Body Cameras 95 Percent of the Time," NBC Bay Area online, last modified May 20, 2017, https://www.nbcbayarea.com/news/local/newly-released-data-shows-oakland-police-turn-on-body-cameras-95-of-the-time/135413/.

70. Erin Baldassari, "Undercover Cop Disguised as Black Bloc Pulls Gun on Protest in Oakland Which Started in Berkeley," *Bay City News*, December 11, 2014; Evan Sernoffsky, "Berkeley, Police Sued over Black Lives Matter Protest," *San Francisco Chronicle,* November 23, 2015; Ali Winston, "CHP and Berkeley Police Target Protesters and Journalists with Questionable Force," *East Bay Express* (Oakland), December 11, 2014.

71. Ali Winston, "Oakland Finally Gets a Handle on Violent Crime," *Oakland* online, last modified May 31, 2016, https://web.archive.org/web/2016061214 3410/https://www.oaklandmagazine.com/Oakland-Finally-Gets-a-Handle -on-Violent-Crime/.

72. Darwin BondGraham and Ali Winston, "OPD Still Appears to Be Targeting Blacks," *East Bay Express* (Oakland), February 4, 2015.

73. Jennifer L. Eberhardt, *Biased: Uncovering the Hidden Prejudice That Shapes What We See, Think, and Do* (New York: Viking, 2019), 103–6; Jennifer L. Eberhardt and Rebecca C. Hetey, *Data for Change: A Statistical Analysis of Police Stops, Searches, Handcuffings, and Arrests in Oakland, Calif., 2013–2014* (Stanford, CA: Stanford University, June 16, 2016), available at https://stacks.stanford.edu/file/druid:by412gh2838/Data%20for%20Change%20 %28June%2023%29.pdf.

74. Darwin BondGraham, "Oakland Police Co-Developing a Statewide Racial Bias Training for Cops," *East Bay Express* (Oakland), April 17, 2015.

75. Thomas Frazier, *Oakland Police Department Monthly Progress Report*, December 1, 2013.

76. Robert Warshaw, *First Progress Report of the Compliance Director for the Oakland Police Department*, April 18, 2014, available at US District Court Northern District of California online, https://www.cand.uscourts.gov/filelibrary /1413/First%20Progress%20Report.pdf.

77. Robert Warshaw, *Second Progress Report of the Compliance Director for the Oakland Police Department*, June 16, 2014, available at US District Court Northern District of California online, https://www.cand.uscourts.gov/file library/1448/Second%20Progress%20Report.pdf.

78. Scott Johnson, "How a Dirty Police Department Gets Clean," *Politico*, March/April 2015; *The Force* (documentary), directed by Peter Nicks (Kino Lorber, 2017).

79. Richard Walker, *Pictures of a Gone City: Tech and the Dark Side of Prosperity in the San Francisco Bay Area* (Oakland: PM Press, 2018).

80. Will Kane, "Oakland Council Members Demand Action on Policing," *San Francisco Chronicle*, May 27, 2014.

81. Matt O'Brien, "Oakland Mayoral Election: Libby Schaaf's Political Savvy Behind Election Surge," *Oakland Tribune*, October 25, 2014.

82. Cy Musiker, "Schaaf Claims Victory in Oakland's Mayoral Race, Quan and Kaplan Concede," *KQED* online, last modified November 5, 2014, https:// www.kqed.org/news/10346513/oakland-voters-head-to-the-polls-to-elect -next-mayor.

83. Matthew Artz, "Libby Schaaf Sworn in as Oakland Mayor," *East Bay Times*

(Walnut Creek, CA), January 5, 2015; KPIX 5 News online, "Oakland Mayor-elect Libby Schaaf Envisions 80% Reduction in Crime: 'I Plan to Make It Happen,'" last modified November 13, 2014, https://sanfrancisco.cbslocal .com/2014/11/13/oakland-mayor-elect-libby-schaaf-promises-to-be-tough -on-crime-public-safety-police/.

13: "TELL ME YOU WERE AN ADULT"

1. Statistics provided by Oakland Police Department via Public Records Act request.
2. Sean Whent, Oakland City Council Public Safety Committee meeting, December 2, 2014, Oakland City Hall.
3. Farrell was one of the officers who Deputy District Attorney David Hollister proved lied in court to discredit Keith Batt during the Riders trial.
4. Joshi, author interview, January 1, 2021.
5. Rachel Swan, "Oakland Police Department Sets Good Example, Obama Official Says," *San Francisco Chronicle*, September 3, 2015.
6. At the time, body cameras were touted by the Obama administration and the private sector as a technocratic "fix" for police misconduct and accountability. But there was skepticism from some activists, academics, and journalists who focused on the privacy implications for citizens of turning each police officer into a sentient CCTV camera, on the market dominance of Taser/ Axon, a notoriously law enforcement–friendly firm, and questions over whether such a tool would actually change police behavior on the street.
7. "PERF Members Testify Before President's Task Force on 21st Century Policing," *Subject to Debate: A Newsletter of the Police Executive News Forum* 29, no. 2 (2015): March–May 2015, 1, available at https://www.policeforum.org /assets/docs/Subject_to_Debate/Debate2015/debate_2015_marmay.pdf.
8. The O'Brien family sought privacy and declined our requests for interviews during and after the 2016 sex exploitation scandal. The bits and pieces of Brendan O'Brien's biography presented here have been gleaned from public records, police reports, and the eulogy written by O'Brien's mother, Rosemary, which was posted briefly on her cousin's blog, *Through Irish Eyes*, last modified October 8, 2015, https://web.archive.org/web/20160516135050/http: //irisheyesshannon.blogspot.com/2015/10/our-beloved-brendan-obrien .html.
9. Darwin BondGraham and Ali Winston, "Oakland Police Underage Sex Scandal Involves Cop Who Possibly Killed His Wife," *East Bay Express* (Oakland), May 16, 2016.
10. Victoria Terheyden, "Civil Leaders and '03 Crusaders: The Riordan Brotherhood in Public Service," *Future*, Fall 2015, 8, available at http://docplayer .net/99148788-For-alumni-and-friends-of-archbishop-riordan-high-school -fall-2015-future.html.
11. Lee Weathersby's murder remains unsolved. The boy's mother, Dinyal New,

circulated on Facebook photos of O'Brien caring for her son in his final moments.

12. This Facebook Messenger exchange was mentioned in official reports, including that of the department's IAD and an independent investigation undertaken by an attorney reporting to Judge Thelton Henderson, but the authors obtained screenshots of the full exchange from Abuslin.

13. Monica Cedillo told the story of her troubled marriage to Henry Abuslin during several court hearings in 2010 in People v. Henry Abuslin, case no. 163162, March 18, 2010.

14. "The Cowboys and the Guardians," *60 Minutes*, CBS-TV, 1984.

15. Jasmine Abuslin, interviewed by Darwin BondGraham, December 10, 2021.

16. The city of Oakland has refused to hand over information about the officer, whose identity is protected under state laws that continue to permit high levels of secrecy for police personnel records.

17. As with the Oakland police officers who sexually exploited Jasmine Abuslin when she was fifteen, we cannot reveal the name of the relative who molested her because the accusations have never been verified in a public police report or court record.

18. People of the State of California v. Giovanni LoVerde, case no. 16-CR-007399, Alameda County Superior Court. Charges were dismissed against LoVerde after Abuslin declined to participate further in the prosecution of the officers who exploited her.

19. James Ta'ai, interviewed by the Oakland Police Department Internal Affairs Division, transcript, November 12, 2015.

20. Matthew Artz, "Suicides by Two Oakland Police Officers Prompt Calls for Change," *Oakland Tribune*, September 23, 2013.

21. Abuslin, author interview, December 10, 2021. Abuslin's traumatic life history is also described in bits and pieces in the dozens of Internal Affairs investigations carried out by Oakland, Richmond, and other police agencies in 2016, including in the Richmond case of Detective Erik Oliver, who was disciplined for sexting with the teenager. According to the report, Abuslin told Oliver "she did drugs and worked 23rd Street [a commercial street in Richmond] as a prostitute. Abuslin explained to Detective Oliver that she had been doing drugs since she was 12 years old, and that her father introduced her to 'brown'—referring to heroin. She told Detective Oliver the reason why she liked police officers was because her father used to beat her mother, and police officers were the only people her father respected. She said she felt safe because when the police showed up, the violence stopped." See Richmond Police Department Internal Affairs Personnel Complaint, case no. 2016-014-8.

22. The reason the OPD's criminal investigation preceded the Internal Affairs case is because of California employment law. Facts and evidence gathered as part of an IAD case, including officers' statements, cannot be shared with criminal investigators and prosecutors as easily as internal affairs investigators can access criminal information.

23. Audio recording of Internal Affairs statement of Jasmine Abuslin conducted by Sergeant Mildred Oliver on October 30, 2015.

24. The OPD refused to disclose the records of other police officers' IAD interviews because its investigations failed to "sustain" these officers for sexual misconduct. Under California law, when an IAD investigation fails to prove that an officer engaged in sexual misconduct, the case file, including interview records, stays secret.

25. Oakland Police Department Internal Affairs Division transcript of interview with Leroy Johnson, November 23, 2015.

26. Lieutenant Trevelyon Jones's comments were described by investigators Edward Swanson and Audrey Barron, whom Judge Thelton Henderson would appoint later to dissect the Oakland PD's miscarriage of justice in the Celeste Guap case. The department failed to produce documents with Jones's notes in response to our Public Records Act lawsuit.

27. "He's actually, in a way, pimping," said Alameda County Superior Court judge Thomas C. Rogers (a former Alameda County prosecutor) at Bunton's preliminary hearing in a Hayward courtroom on May 18, 2017. "He's assisting her like a pimp would." Darwin BondGraham and Ali Winston, "Badge of Dishonor: Top Oakland Police Department Officials Looked Away as East Bay Cops Sexually Exploited and Trafficked a Teenager," *East Bay Express* (Oakland), June 15, 2016, and "Judge Rips Ex-Oakland Cop: 'He's Actually, in a Way, Pimping,'" *East Bay Express* (Oakland), May 18, 2017.

28. Oakland Police Department investigators determined that Smith's attempts to sodomize the eighteen-year-old Abuslin "were not consensual" and referred the case to the Contra Costa district attorney for prosecution. However, the DA declined to press charges against Smith. See Oakland Police Department Internal Affairs case no. 15-0771 and OPD Crime Report no. 16-022375.

29. Oakland Police Department Internal Affairs case no. 15-0771.

30. Tentative ruling in Andre Hill v. City of Richmond, case no. MSN18-1677, Contra Costa County Superior Court, October 16, 2019.

31. Oakland Police Department Crime Report no. 14-030065, June 16, 2014.

32. Memorandum—Case File 2014-01779, Alameda County Sheriff's Office, Coroner's Bureau, June 17, 2014.

33. Superior Court of Alameda Search Warrant, June 17, 2014, signed by Sergeant Caesar Basa, Oakland Police Department.

34. James M. Gantt v. City of Oakland et al., Complaint for Damages and Injunctive Relief, Alameda County Superior Court, no. RG17850153, February 21, 2017.

35. Ibid.

36. Ali Winston and Darwin BondGraham, "Did an Oakland Cop Kill His Wife?," *East Bay Express* (Oakland), November 8, 2016.

37. Caesar Basa passed away in December 2021 after contracting Covid-19; therefore we were unable to get his account of what happened in the interview room and the hallway outside with Brendan O'Brien and Mike Gantt.

38. For the accounts of what took place among Gantt, Basa, and Lois, we rely

on Mike Gantt's 2017 press conference and documents from his wrongful termination lawsuit. O'Brien's interview with Homicide and the attached case notes have never been disclosed. In addition, neither Deputy DA Matthew Beltramo nor Inspector Tom Milner from the Alameda County District Attorney's Office took notes while monitoring O'Brien's statement to Gantt and Basa. Gantt's version of events doesn't exactly line up with what's in evidence and police reports, however.

39. Matthias Gafni and David DeBolt, "Oakland Police Sex Scandal: New Revelations in Death of Officer and Wife," *East Bay Times* (Walnut Creek, CA), August 6, 2016.

40. Joshi, author interview, January 1, 2021.

41. Darwin BondGraham and Ali Winston, "Veteran Oakland Homicide Investigator Mishandled Evidence in Ongoing Murder Case," *East Bay Express* (Oakland), June 17, 2016.

42. Joshi, author interview, January 1, 2021.

43. Jane Gross, "203 Rape Cases Reopened as Oakland Police Chief Admits Mistakes," *New York Times,* September 20, 1990, A14.

44. Joshi, author interview, January 1, 2021.

45. Sergeant Ray Kelly, interviewed by the authors, September 9, 2019.

46. Henry K. Lee, "Brothel Case Cops' Handling of Drugs, Cash Investigated," *San Francisco Chronicle*, April 4, 2003.

47. Darwin BondGraham and Ali Winston, "California Court Destroys Files in Historic Police Corruption Case," The Appeal, October 30, 2019.

48. Whent, deposition 16, July 23, 2007.

49. Mark McCannon has been an Alameda County Superior Court judge since 2013. James Rullamas, deposition 27, July 25, 2007.

50. Ali Winston and Darwin BondGraham, "California Court Destroys Files in Historic Police Corruption Case," The Appeal, last modified October 30, 2019, https://theappeal.org/california-court-destroys-police-corruption-cases/.

51. Matthew Artz, "Oakland Police Investigating Officers' Visits to a Bar Residents Suspect of Being a Brothel," *Oakland Tribune,* October 29, 2012.

52. George Kelly and Nate Gartrell, "Disgraced Oakland Cop Ties Second Officer to Chinatown Crime Figure," *East Bay Times* (Walnut Creek, CA), December 1, 2019; United States Sentencing Memorandum, United States v. Harry Hu, 3:18-cr-00495-CRB, District of Northern California, August 12, 2020; Nate Gartrell, "Ex-Oakland Cop Gets 30 Days in Federal Prison for Taking Bribes," *East Bay Times* (Walnut Creek, CA), August 19, 2020.

53. Ali Winston, observation of the protest outside OPD headquarters, June 19, 2016.

54. Sean Whent to City Auditor Brenda Roberts, May 17, 2016; letter obtained via Public Records Act request.

55. Darwin BondGraham and Ali Winston, "The Real Reason Why Oakland's Police Chief Was Fired," *East Bay Express* (Oakland), June 10, 2016.

56. Sean Whent to Sabrina Landreth and Libby Schaaf, email, June 9, 2016. Obtained by authors via Public Records Act request.

57. Darwin BondGraham and Ali Winston, "#LibbyLeaks: Oakland Mayor Launches Investigation Against City and Police Whistleblowers," *East Bay Express* (Oakland), June 22, 2016.

58. "Alameda County DA Inspector Fired over Police Sex Scandal," KTVU News online, last modified July 8, 2016, https://www.ktvu.com/news/alameda -county-da-inspector-fired-over-police-sex-scandal; BondGraham and Winston, "Badge of Dishonor."

59. Ed Swanson and Audrey Barron, *Court-Appointed Investigator's Report on the City of Oakland's Response to Allegations of Officer Sexual Misconduct*, Delphine Allen v. City of Oakland (San Francisco: Swanson & McNamara LLC, June 21, 2017), 2, available at https://cao-94612.s3.amazonaws.com/docu ments/Court-Appointed-Investigators-Report-on-Citys-Response-to-Alle gations-of-Officer-Sexual-Misconduct-June-2017_2020-10-30-000710.pdf.

60. Ibid., 3.

14: BACKSLIDING

1. At a June 17, 2016, press conference, Libby Schaaf said, "As the mayor of Oakland, I'm here to run a police department, not a frat house."

2. Another finalist for Seattle was former OPD captain Ron Davis.

3. David Graham, "The Firing of Chicago Police Chief Garry McCarthy," *Atlantic* online, last modified December 1, 2015, https://www.theatlantic.com /national/archive/2015/12/garry-mccarthy-fired-chicago/418203/.

4. The behavior of the police at the Chicago and Oakland protests was not that much different. The horrific events that took place on the streets of Chicago during the 1968 Democratic National Convention, in what can only be called a police riot, marked by deliberate excessive force against antiwar protestors, went down in history as a notorious instance of police violence. The image of the city and its police department would be tainted for some time to come because much of the country, as well as the world, saw the cops' ferocity on live TV. In the chanted words of the protestors: "The whole world is watching."

5. John Conroy, "House of Screams," *Chicago Reader*, January 25, 1990; Chicago Police Torture Archive, https://chicagopolicetorturearchive.com/; Flint Taylor, *The Torture Machine: Racism and Police Violence in Chicago* (Chicago: Haymarket Books, 2020).

6. Ronald Watts and a former partner, Kallatt Mohammed, were each convicted and sentenced to twenty-two months in prison in 2013. At least eighty-seven people convicted of drug crimes based on Watts's and Mohammed's casework have been exonerated by the Cook County State's Attorney's Office. Jon Schuppe, "Dozens Who Say They Were Framed by Corrupt Chicago Drug Squad Demand Exoneration," NBC News online, last modified July 20, 2021, https://www.nbcnews.com/news/us-news/dozens-who-say-they-were -framed-corrupt-chicago-drug-squad-n1274255. [[Multiple sources, including the 8-17-2012 *Chicago Tribune* online, https://www.chicagotribune.com

/news/breaking/chi-chicago-police-officer-admits-taking-drug-money-in
-fbi-sting-20120817-story.html.]]

7. Passed over by Schaaf was OPD Deputy Chief Danielle Outlaw, a Black
woman with even more ambition than Kirkpatrick. Outlaw left in 2017 to
lead the Portland Police Bureau in Oregon. In 2019 she was appointed head
of the Philadelphia Police Department.

8. Katie Mettler, "Introducing Anne Kirkpatrick, Just Hired to Fix Oakland's
'Frat House' Police Department," *Washington Post*, January 5, 2017.

9. Bay City News, "Reform-Minded Leader Chosen as New Oakland Police
Chief," Patch.com, Piedmont, CA, January 4, 2017, https://patch.com/cali
fornia/piedmont/reform-minded-leader-chosen-new-oakland-police-chief.

10. Kirkpatrick's initial suggestion was to give officers more flexibility and not require them to ask people they've stopped whether they're on probation or parole. Some reform activists, including formerly incarcerated people, pushed
the OPD to actually prohibit officers from asking about probation or parole
status unless they had probable cause to believe someone was engaged in
criminal activity. See Darwin BondGraham, "Oakland Police Consider Less
Intrusive Search Policy," *East Bay Express* (Oakland), September 11, 2018.

11. The OPD's Silver Star Medal is awarded to officers and civilian employees for
"courageous actions when the circumstances do not fall within the provisions
qualifying for the Medal of Valor," the department's highest award. Oakland
Police Department, Departmental General Order B-1, "Awards, Departmental Bars, Service Commendations, Departmental Awards Medal, Departmental Retirement Certificates, Service Bars," November 30, 1998.

12. Several city employees and officials who attended the ceremony spoke with
us on the condition of anonymity. Darwin BondGraham and Ali Winston,
"Oakland Police Hold Secret Ceremony Honoring Several Officers Accused
of Mishandling Celeste Guap Sex-Crimes Investigation," *East Bay Express*
(Oakland), July 14, 2017.

13. "Group Protests Outside OPD Officer Promotion Ceremony," YouTube,
1:14, KPIX CBS SF Bay Area, https://www.youtube.com/watch?v=n1DQIuIE
9ys&ab_channel=KPIXCBSSFBayArea.

14. Darwin BondGraham and Ali Winston, "Oakland Police Chief Doubles
Down on Promoting the Cops Who Covered Up the Celeste Guap Case,"
East Bay Express (Oakland), July 10, 2017.

15. Transcript of Proceedings in Delphine Allen v. City of Oakland, case
no. C-00-04599, July 10, 2017, San Francisco.

16. The OPOA spent more than $18,000 supporting Annie Campbell Washing-
ton's 2014 city council campaign, including paying for more than ten thousand
robocalls featuring endorsements from police officers and Kamala Harris.
The union and Campbell Washington were later fined by a state watchdog
agency because the calls failed to disclose the source of funding. See Darwin
BondGraham, "Oakland Councilmember Annie Campbell Washington and
Police and Fire Unions Fined for Illegal Robocalls," *East Bay Express* (Oak-

land), September 17, 2017; Darwin BondGraham, "Oakland Police Commission Battle Heating Up," *East Bay Express* (Oakland), March 23, 2016.

17. Darwin BondGraham, "Oakland's Lost Year of Police Accountability," *East Bay Express* (Oakland), January 9, 2019.

18. Jon Swaine, Oliver Laughland, and Mae Ryan, "The County: The Story of America's Deadliest Police," *Guardian* (US edition) online, last modified December 1, 2015, https://www.theguardian.com/us-news/2015/dec/01/the-county-kern-county-deadliest-police-killings.

19. Ali Winston, "You May Be in California's Gang Database and Not Even Know It," Reveal, last modified March 23, 2016, https://revealnews.org/article/you-may-be-in-californias-gang-database-and-not-even-know-it/; Kim McGill and Ana Muiz, *Tracked and Trapped: Youth of Color, Gang Databases, and Gang Injunctions* (Los Angeles: Youth Justice Coalition RealSearch Action Research Center, December 2012), https://www.youth4justice.org/wp-content/uploads/2012/12/TrackedandTrapped.pdf.

20. Mark Puente and Richard Winton, "Officers Falsely Portrayed People as Gang Members, Falsified Records, LAPD Says," *Los Angeles Times*, January 6, 2020.

21. Order Granting Plaintiff Peter Arellano's Motion for Preliminary Injunction, Youth Justice Coalition et al. v. City of Los Angeles et al., United States District Court Central District of California, case no. 2:16-cv-07932-VAP-RAO.

22. Administrative instruction, "City of Refuge Implementation," City of Oakland, October 31, 1986. The American Bar Association criticized the OPD's treatment of immigrant detainees in a 2003 report following an inspection of the jail. See American Bar Association Delegation to Oakland City Jail, memo regarding "Report on Observations During a General Tour of the Oakland City Jail, California," September 19, 2003.

23. Darwin BondGraham and Ali Winston, "Oakland Police Chief Made False Statements About ICE Raid," *East Bay Express* (Oakland), October 11, 2017.

24. David DeBolt, "Oakland Police Wrongly Denied Visas to Crime Victims, Chief Says," *East Bay Times* (Walnut Creek, CA), January 25, 2018.

25. Barbara Parker, Libby Schaaf, Sabrina Landreth, and Anne Kirkpatrick, "Delphine Allen v. City of Oakland et al., Progress Report No. 11," May 24, 2018.

26. James Chanin and John Burris, "Joint Case Management Conference Statement," in Delphine Allen v. City of Oakland, case no. 3:00-cv-04599-WHO, May 24, 2018.

27. Robert Warshaw, *Forty-Fifth Report of the Independent Monitor for the Oakland Police Department*, August 15, 2017, available at City of Oakland online, http://www2.oaklandnet.com/oakca1/groups/police/documents/webcontent/oak066604.pdf.

28. City of Oakland online, "Mayor Dellums and Oakland Police Department Reach Goal of 803 Officers," press release, last modified November 14, 2008, http://www2.oaklandnet.com/oakca1/groups/mayor/documents/pressrelease/dowd005265.pdf.

29. Darwin BondGraham, "Disappeared in Death: Homeless and Mentally Ill,

Joshua Pawlik Was Unconscious Right Before Four Oakland Police Officers Killed Him in March. His Family and Friends Are Seeking Answers," *East Bay Express* (Oakland), August 8, 2018.

30. "Otto Zehm Case Timeline," *Spokesman-Review* online (Spokane, WA), November 2, 2011, https://www.spokesman.com/stories/2011/nov/02/otto -zehm-case-timeline/.

31. "Zehm's Last Words Revealed in Court," YouTube, 2:57, 4 News Now, https:// www.youtube.com/watch?v=vrIhwjbXQaI&ab_channel=4NewsNow.

32. The local medical examiner classified Zehm's death as a homicide and listed as the cause of death "excited delirium," Taser use, baton strikes, and other uses of force not involving a gun; Amy Cannata, "Zehm Death Fallout," *Spokesman-Review* online (Spokane, WA), March 20, 2007, https://www .spokesman.com/stories/2007/mar/20/zehm-death-fallout/.

33. Thomas Clouse, "Karl Thompson Taken into Custody: Verner, Kirkpatrick Apologize for Salute," *Spokesman-Review* online (Spokane, WA), November 4, 2011, https://www.spokesman.com/stories/2011/nov/04/cit_thomp son_detention/.

34. The pseudoscience concept was offered up by Derek Chauvin's attorneys during their opening statement in Chauvin's trial for murdering George Floyd. In 2021 the American Medical Association (AMA) issued a public statement opposing the diagnosis of "excited delirium."

35. Karen Dorn Steele, "Suspended Cop's Lawyer Accuses Chief of Misconduct," *Spokesman-Review* online (Spokane, WA), May 23, 2008, https:// www.spokesman.com/stories/2008/may/23/suspended-cops-lawyer-accuses -chief-of-misconduct/.

36. Oakland Police Department Office of the Inspector General, *3rd Quarterly Progress Report, July–September 2018* (Oakland: OPD OIG, 2018), available at City of Oakland online, http://www2.oaklandnet.com/oakca1/groups/po lice/documents/agenda/oak072028.pdf.

37. Robert Warshaw, *Fifty-Sixth Report of the Independent Monitor for the Oakland Police Department,* September 13, 2018, available at US District Court Northern District of California online, https://www.cand.uscourts.gov/wp -content/uploads/cases-of-interest/allen-v-city-of-oakland/Monitors-Fifty -Sixth-Report-September-2018.pdf.

38. Orrick wasn't entirely unfamiliar with law enforcement reform efforts. His father, William Orrick Jr., who'd preceded him in the same role as a US District Court judge, handled one of the Bay Area's most significant cases when he oversaw reform of San Francisco's notoriously dangerous jails from the late 1970s through the early 1990s.

39. Transcript of proceedings in Delphine Allen et al. v. City of Oakland, case no. C-00-04599, November 27, 2018, San Francisco.

40. Records of the OPD's Executive Force Review Board obtained through a Public Records Act request.

41. Executive Force Review Board, Use of Force No. 18F-0067, November 28–29, 2018, and January 8, 2019.

42. Chief Anne Kirkpatrick's addendum to Executive Force Review Board Report, Use of Force No. 18F-0067.

43. Thomas Peele and Sukey Lewis, "Oakland Police Monitor and Police Commission Call for Firing of Five Officers," *East Bay Times* (Walnut Creek, CA), July 18, 2019.

44. KTVU, "Protesters Call for Ouster of Oakland Police Chief," first aired March 22, 2019.

45. Robert Warshaw, *Sixty-Fifth Report of the Independent Monitor for the Oakland Police Department*, December 19, 2019, available at City of Oakland online, http://www2.oaklandnet.com/oakca1/groups/police/documents/report /oak072657.pdf.

46. Transcript of proceedings, Delphine Allen et al. v. City of Oakland, case no. C-00-04599, August 21, 2019, San Francisco.

47. Bill Bratton (@CommissBratton), "The 2 to be criticized for the consent decree/monitoring failure in Oakland are Judge Orrick & his hand-picked monitor, Robert Warshaw, whose wallet was fattened by Oakland taxpayer dollars in 1 of the country's longest, least successful monitoring efforts," Twitter, August 27, 2019, 4:44 p.m., https://twitter.com/CommissBratton/status /1166451558453784576.

48. David DeBolt and Annie Sciacca, "Oakland Police Chief Anne Kirkpatrick Ousted by Commission," *East Bay Times* (Walnut Creek, CA), February 20, 2020.

49. The commission first sent Kirkpatrick a letter in September 2019 notifying her that it was considering terminating her. See deposition of Mike Nisperos in Anne Kirkpatrick v. City of Oakland, case no. 3:20-cv-05843, conducted remotely, August 31, 2021.

50. Deposition of Regina Jackson in Anne Kirkpatrick v. City of Oakland, case no. 3:20-cv-05843, conducted remotely, August 31, 2021.

51. Emails between Sam Singer and Kirkpatrick obtained by the authors through a Public Records Act request showed that in the weeks following Kirkpatrick's firing, her attorneys and Singer sent "Privileged and Confidential" communications to the police union's attorney, Rockne Lucia, and former police chief Howard Jordan.

52. "Officers Give Emotional Farewell to Fired Oakland Police Chief," KPIX 5 News online, last modified February 25, 2020, https://sanfrancisco.cbslocal .com/2020/02/25/oakland-police-chief-anne-kirkpatrick-farewell-200-offi cers/.

53. Subpoena to Robert Warshaw in Anne Kirkpatrick v. City of Oakland, case no. 3:20-cv-05834.

54. The union's argument was legally more complex, of course. According to its attorneys, the officers could not have been fired because under the city charter, when the police chief and the CPRA agency reach the same finding in a misconduct case, that decision stands. Kirkpatrick decided not to fire any of the officers who killed Pawlik, and her disciplinary recommendations were mirrored by those of CPRA investigators. However, Warshaw's intervention

and decision to fire the officers superseded the chief's decision. This created a conflict between the chief's official decision and the CPRA's, which led to the Police Commission's forming a "discipline committee." This committee sided with Warshaw and fired the officers. The OPOA never had a chance to convince a state judge of its arguments; the city asked Orrick to take over the case in federal court, which he agreed to. Orrick explained that in 2012, the city agreed to let the compliance director, Warshaw, override its police chief's decisions. The supremacy of federal law meant that no state court judge could reverse this. The US Court of Appeals for the Ninth Circuit agreed with Orrick, putting to rest the question of Warshaw's authority in 2021. See Francisco Negrete et al. v. City of Oakland et al., US Ninth Circuit Court of Appeals, case no. 20-16244.

CONCLUSION

1. Officer-involved shooting data obtained by the authors via California Public Records Act requests and by reviewing the OPD's annual reports. Since 2012, Oakland has been outstripped by the smaller Vallejo Police Department, where a number of former OPD officers went to work, including former deputy chief Bob Nichelini and his son, Michael.
2. Joel Rubin, "Federal Judge Lifts LAPD Consent Decree," *Los Angeles Times*, May 16, 2013; Ben Poston and Leila Miller, "Division Scrutinized for Allegedly Falsifying Interview Cards Issued the Most in LAPD," *Los Angeles Times*, May 26, 2020; "Report by Independent Counsel, Gerald Chaleff, of the Police Department Response to Protests in May/June 2020," Sharon Tso, Chief Legislative Analyst, City of Los Angeles, Council File no. 20-0729, March 10, 2021.
3. Joel Rubin, "Judge Ends Oversight of L.A. Police," *Los Angeles Times*, July 18, 2009.
4. Solomon Moore, "Monitor Cites Reform, Though Incomplete, by Los Angeles Police," *New York Times*, June 15, 2009.
5. Greg Smith, "With NYPD Stop and Frisk Case at Crossroads, Civil Rights Groups Demand Monitoring Reforms," The City, last modified February 7, 2022, https://www.thecity.nyc/2022/2/7/22920620/nypd-stop-frisk-case-crossroads.
6. Frank Serpico, "The Police Are Still Out of Control—I Should Know," *Politico* online, last modified October 23, 2014, https://www.politico.com/magazine/story/2014/10/the-police-are-still-out-of-control-112160/.

PHOTO CREDITS

1. Photo courtesy of Keith Batt
2. Files obtained by Ali Winston and Darwin BondGraham via Public Records Act request
3. Image obtained by Ali Winston and Darwin BondGraham via FOIA request
4. Photo courtesy of Ray Chavez, *Oakland Tribune* via Bay Area News Group
5. Photo courtesy of Darwin BondGraham and Ali Winston
6. Photo courtesy of Getty Images
7. Photo courtesy of Ali Winston
8. Photo courtesy of *Oakland Tribune*
9. Photo by Bettmann Archive. Courtesy of Getty Images
10. Photo courtesy of Getty Images
11. Photo courtesy of Getty Images
12. Photo courtesy of *Oakland Tribune*
13. Photo courtesy of Ali Winston
14. Photo from OPD, obtained via Public Records Act request
15. Photo courtesy of *San Francisco Chronicle*
16. Photo from OPD, obtained via Public Records Act request
17. Photo courtesy of Ali Winston
18. Photo courtesy of Ali Winston
19. Photo courtesy of Ali Winston
20. Photo courtesy of Ali Winston

21. Photo courtesy of Darwin BondGraham
22. Photo by Michael Macor in the *San Francisco Chronicle* courtesy of Getty Images
23. Photo courtesy of Jasmine Abuslin
24. Photo courtesy of Darwin BondGraham

INDEX

ABOUT THE AUTHORS

Darwin BondGraham was an investigative reporter for the *East Bay Express* and part of the team that created the *Oaklandside*. BondGraham's work has also appeared in the *Guardian,* ProPublica, and other leading national and local outlets. He holds a doctorate in sociology from the University of California, Santa Barbara, and was the corecipient of the George Polk Award for local reporting in 2017. Follow him on Twitter @DarwinBondGraha.

Ali Winston is an independent reporter covering criminal justice, privacy, and extremism. He has written for outlets such as the *New York Times, Rolling Stone,* and ProPublica, and contributed to documentaries for BBC's *Panorama* and PBS's *Frontline.* His work has been recognized with numerous awards, including the George Polk Award for local reporting in 2017 and an Alfred I. duPont-Columbia University Award in 2020. Winston is a graduate of the University of Chicago and the University of California, Berkeley. Follow him on Twitter @AWinston.